The Reading Curriculum

The *Reading Development* course team in the Faculty of Educational Studies at The Open University.

John Merritt (course team chairman)
Sheila Dale
Alan Davies
Judith Fage
Patricia Farrington
Nicholas Farnes
Donald Holms
Richard Hooper
Elizabeth Hunter
Ronald Johnson
Martin Lawn
Amelia Melnik
Edward Milner
David Moseley
Donald Moyle
William Prescott
Geoffrey Roberts
Lee Taylor

The Reading Curriculum

Readings edited by Amelia Melnik and
John Merritt for the Reading Development
Course Team at The Open University

University of London Press Limited in
association with
The Open University Press

ISBN 0 340 16781 5 Paper
ISBN 0 340 16780 7 Boards

University of London Press Ltd
St Paul's House, Warwick Lane, London EC4P 4AH

Printed in Great Britain by Hazell Watson & Viney Ltd,
Aylesbury, Bucks

Editors' acknowledgements

The editors would like to thank Pat Farrington for her editorial work and Lee Taylor, Sandy Patrick and Carol Hall for their unfailing help in the preparation of this Reader. They would also like to make an acknowledgement to the staff of the Institute of Education Library, University of London, and to the staff of The Open University Library.

Publishers' acknowledgements

The editors and publishers are grateful to the following for permission to reproduce copyright material:

1:1 Copyright © 1969 Penguin Books; 1:2 Reprinted with permission of Sidney J. Rauch and the International Reading Association; 1:3 Reprinted with permission of Olive S. Niles and the International Reading Association; 1:4 Reprinted with permission of Alvin Kravitz and the International Reading Association; 1:5 Reprinted with permission of Morton Botel and the International Reading Association; 1:6 Reprinted with permission of Leo Fay and the International Reading Association; 1:7 Reproduced with the permission of the Controller of Her Majesty's Stationery Office; 1:8 Dr Elizabeth Goodacre and the National Foundation for Educational Research in England and Wales; 1:9 Ouida M. Wright and the *McGill Journal of Education*; 1:10 *Reading* and Margaret Laybourn; 1:11 School Library Association and J. S. Nicholson; 1:12 Cassell & Co. Ltd.; 2:1 Routledge & Kegan Paul Ltd.; 2:2 Routledge & Kegan Paul Ltd.; 2:3 Copyright © 1967 by the National Council of Teachers of English. Reprinted by permission of the publisher and Constance M. McCullough; 2:4 Cassell & Co. Ltd.; 2:5 Copyright © 1970 by Russell G. Stauffer. By permission of Harper & Row, Publishers, Inc.; 2:6 *Reading* and D. G. Mitchell; 2:7 University of London Press, Vera Southgate and G. R. Roberts; 2:8 United Kingdom Reading Association and Ward Lock Educational. A paper presented at the Sixth Annual Conference of the United Conference Reading Association, Nottingham, July 1960; and later published in Gardner, K. (1970) *Reading Skills: Theory and Practice*. Some of the ideas mentioned in the paper had been mentioned previously in a paper entitled 'Structuring reading materials for beginning reading', presented at the Second World Congress on Reading, Copenhagen, August 1968, and later published in Staiger, R. C. and Anderson, O. (eds) (1969) *Reading: A Human Right and a Human Problem*; 2:9 *Reading* and John Downing; 2:10 School

Contents

General introduction

Two companion volumes *Reading: Today and Tomorrow* and *The Reading Curriculum* have been especially prepared for the post-experience course, *Reading Development*, offered by The Open University through its Faculty of Educational Studies. The theme of this course is the development of reading competence throughout the school years with special emphasis on the middle years of schooling. The purpose of the course is to provide a better understanding of the nature of the reading process, an appreciation of the importance of reading in education and society, and an understanding of how competence in reading may be developed in every curriculum area.

Taken together, these volumes are designed to provide 1) a broad overview of the field of reading; 2) a variety of views on the nature of the reading process; and 3) the multiplicity of factors involved in reading development. These objectives underlie each component of a course which includes correspondence texts, radio and television programmes, and a wide range of student activities and exercises. In its entirety, the course attempts to synthesize and extend current provision and practice in the teaching of reading.

Because these readers have been compiled to provide students with suitable background material for a broadly-based course on the teaching of reading, they should provide a valuable source for students undergoing initial training, as well as for other interested teachers and reading specialists.

Unlike other long-established studies in education, the field of reading is relatively new. At present, it is the centre of controversies stemming from its diverse and disparate parentage—a variety of specialists who examine its nature and dimensions from their own basepoints. For this reason, the first volume addresses itself to an examination of the various facets which comprise our present understanding of reading, studies the scope of reading, and some of the major problems in the field of reading. Problems for the reading curriculum which are introduced in the first reader are now taken up in this volume which presents a broad survey of what is to be taught, how reading competence may be developed, and how the teacher can evaluate reading proficiency and the reading curriculum.

In the past, curriculum reform has been studied in various ways: 1) intensive study of its social and historical foundations; 2) theoretical analysis of curriculum objectives, design and evaluation; 3) interdisciplinary analysis by teams which have included philosophers, historians, sociologists, and educational technologists. By and large, these theoretical explorations into the nature of curriculum problems have resulted in increasing the distance between educationists and classroom practitioners who have become more and more suspicious of philosophical abstractions and essays which, though logically sound, are remote from the immediate responsibilities and concerns of the classroom teacher. According to Barnes:

> All the efforts . . . to develop new curricula may be abortive if curriculum development is taken to exclude examination of the part played by teachers in the curriculum, which is after all not a thing but an activity. It is too dangerous therefore to relegate the teacher's part to a subordinate and secondary topic called 'method'; how the teacher behaves must affect how and what the pupils learn.[1]

For this reason, studies of the nature of classroom interactions have recently become a significant basis for curriculum reform. Exciting discoveries have been made from analysis of recorded transcriptions of teacher–pupil dialogue which reveal the effect of language on the quality of teaching and learning experiences. *Language, the Learner and the School* is one example of studies which promise to have far-reaching consequences in educationists' continued efforts to improve curriculum design.

Most of these studies, however, have been primarily concerned with the nature of thinking, talking, and learning in the classroom. Scant attention has been given to the role and influence of such interaction in relation to reading behaviour as it contributes to and affects the quality of classroom dialogue and other learning experiences. If the reading competence of teachers and/or pupils is limited, then the quality of instructional discussion will be similarly limited. The questions and responses of both teachers and pupils may be significantly improved by increasing their levels of reading comprehension of printed sources from which significant educational interactions flow. This, of course, is a two-way process; the improved quality of teacher–pupil interaction feeds back to bring about improved reading comprehension.

It is against this background of current curriculum study that this volume, *The Reading Curriculum*, has been prepared. Its contents and organization have been based on the following assumptions:

1   Reading is a tangible manifestation of talking, learning, and thinking.

1   Barnes, Douglas (1969, rev. edn 1971) 'Language in the Secondary Classroom' in Barnes, Douglas, Britton, James, Rosen, Harold, and the L.A.T.E. *Language, the Learner and the School* Harmondsworth, Middlesex: Penguin Education, 11.

Therefore, continuous development of reading competence can result in improved talking, learning, and thinking.

2   Reading unifies the related language arts of writing, listening, and speaking. What is written is read and what is read is discussed. Therefore, reading integrates and affects the nature and quality of oral and written language.

3   Reading permeates the curriculum and is a major source of knowledge in every subject field. Therefore, instruction in reading should be an integral part of every reading experience in every subject.

With these assumptions in mind, it is the intention of this volume to increase the reader's awareness and knowledge of the scope, content, and process of reading instruction and its influence on the quality of talking, thinking, and learning in the classroom.

In Part 1, *What is the place of reading in the curriculum?*, we present a broad overview of procedural policies, content areas, instructional media, and various patterns of organization which affect the total school reading programme.

Part 2, *How is reading competence developed?*, examines various approaches to the teaching of reading and the content of reading instruction with the aim of helping teachers to establish their own orientation and criteria for developing reading competence.

In Part 3, *What is diagnostic teaching?*, an effort is made to acquaint the reader with diagnostic teaching principles and procedures which fuse diagnosis and instruction into a single ongoing process to ensure relevant reading guidance for all pupils in the regular classroom situation. This is the point at which all the theoretical ideas about reading must be merged to ensure useful teacher–pupil interaction.

Part 4, *How is reading assessed?*, concludes our survey of the reading curriculum with an examination of various procedures and instruments designed to assess the readability of printed materials, individual levels of reading development, effectiveness of reading programmes, and characteristics of effective teaching of reading.

As in *Reading: Today and Tomorrow* the editors have had to draw heavily on American sources to supplement English material. It is to be hoped that it will not be too long before we have reached a stage at which this will become a matter of choice and, not, as at present, a necessity.

A note on the structure of the U.S. education system

To provide some background to the American material in the reader, the following diagram has been included to show the grade levels and equivalent ages and the general structure of the system.

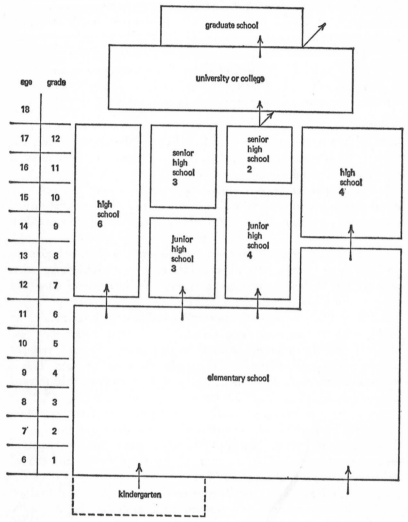

Typical school structures in the United States[1] (Oblique arrows show movement into employment)

1 Reprinted from Unit 3, *Other People's Curricula* by Nigel Grant, which forms part of The Open University course, *The Curriculum: Context, Design and Development* (E283).

NOTE   High school students in Grades 9 to 12 are commonly referred to as *freshman, sophomores, juniors* and *seniors*. These terms are also used for undergraduate students in a four-year college.

Part 1 What is the place of reading in the curriculum?

Introduction to Part One:
What is the place of reading in the curriculum?

A reading policy which states the goals and plans for the development of reading competence in the schools—does such a document exist? If reading is indeed 'The First R', then by now it seems reasonable to expect to find a reading policy which establishes the basic framework and guidelines to ensure provision for the development of reading competence by all pupils.

Our own search for such a document proved fruitless. We have therefore drawn upon a document by the London Association for the Teaching of English, 'A language policy across the curriculum' (1:1) as a useful statement to initiate our survey of the reading curriculum as broadly outlined in this volume. By substituting 'reading' for 'language', a significant portion of this policy statement is equally pertinent to reading throughout the curriculum. If books '. . . provide an inexhaustible supply of material by means of which pupils can teach themselves' (1:1, p. 16), then a reading policy is imperative to ensure that pupils' reading abilities are developed to that purpose. (Many of the language competencies as outlined in the L.A.T.E. policy will contribute largely towards the development of reading competencies.)

Rauch's (1:2) brief description of a total school reading programme indicates the breadth of provision required to achieve such a level of attainment and implies some of the focal points which need to be considered in developing a reading policy, which includes realistic and effective in-service education. If the teaching of reading is to cross the curriculum, how has the subject of reading been treated in content areas?

Niles' juxtaposed excerpts (1:3) from a variety of school texts graphically illustrate the varied demands made on the reading skills of the pupil. Teachers often forget 'that Student X has to shift gears in his reading again and again as he moves during the day from one subject area to another' (p. 29). More specific examples of reading instruction in social studies, maths and science provided by Kravitz (1:4), Botel (1:5) and Fay (1:6) suggest various types of instruction to improve reading skills in the content areas, which can be adapted or extended by the classroom teacher.

Instructional media are an essential part of the curriculum. What kinds of books are provided and how are they used? Information about the quantity and quality of books in one division of an English county is provided in a survey (1:7) which reports some disturbing evidence on the kinds and use of books in the curriculum:

> It would be difficult to fault the initial procedures adopted to arouse in children a burning desire to read. It was in the next step that differences crept in and were later magnified. This stage was that exemplified by the set reading scheme, often there was only one, followed by supplementary readers. That final stage was all too often paralleled by the traditional use of text books, an approach that assumes that each child's development and interest follow the pattern set by the authors of the series. It was significant that many children knew the number of the book they were reading, few the title. (p. 68).

By far the most widely used instructional tools for reading development in the primary school are published reading schemes. Goodacre's study (1:8) of their use and Wright's position paper (1:9) suggest that criticisms levelled against reading schemes may partly be directed toward their misuses, the main one being total dependence on one scheme. Laybourn's analysis (1:10) of a wide range of non-book materials and their uses reminds us that exclusive use of reading schemes for reading instruction does not prepare children for their reading needs in adult life:

> ... the overwhelming importance of five categories of information: forms, instruction notices and regulations, directions and diagrams, letters, advertisements. Legal necessity, safety, and the acquisition of property are all closely linked to the effective management of these social literacy problems. (p. 89).

Nicholson (1:11) describes the organization of access to books, and the quiet and comfortable reading environment in one new (and fortunate) middle school. Nila Banton Smith (1:12) suggests a number of ways of organizing groups for reading, including using competent readers as pupil-teachers, or 'secretaries' in group study activities. It is clear that an effective reading curriculum requires diverse and flexible organizational patterns.

In Part One we have attempted to provide the reader with some of the components of a reading curriculum which are extended in the subsequent parts of this volume. Together they provide a basic framework for the kinds of questions and problems to which a reading policy must address itself.

1:1 A language policy across the curriculum

London Association for the Teaching of English

Language and the teacher

Language permeates school life. Boys and girls in their attempts to master the school curriculum and in the process of growing up have to call upon their language resources. Moreover they are expected to increase these resources by making the language encountered in their school learning a living part of their thinking and communicating. We take the view that we have chosen a most promising moment to put before *all teachers* a document which will open discussion on the educational implications of these obvious facts. We think it is a promising moment because teachers of all subjects and in all kinds of schools are becoming aware that language is inextricably bound up with all the learning that goes on in school. They are becoming acquainted with the research on the relationship between language and thought, with theories on the acquisition of language and with work on the nature of language itself, for these ideas are finding their way into the most important educational debates of our day. Innovations in the curriculum and the discussions which surround them have helped to focus attention on language. We believe that many teachers are now prepared to go far beyond the older view that language was someone else's business, or, perhaps, that they were the guardians of linguistic properties. They are now prepared to consider what needs to be done to improve our procedures in schools in such a way that language becomes a facilitating force in learning rather than a barrier bristling with formidable difficulties.

London Association for the Teaching of English (1969, rev. edn 1971) 'A language policy across the curriculum', in Barnes, Douglas, Britton, James, Rosen, Harold, and the L.A.T.E., *Language, the Learner and the School*, Penguin Education, 160–8 (rev. edn.).

For all the dissemination of new ideas relatively little has been done to work out in detail just what needs to be modified or changed in our day-to-day practices in order to achieve solid advances. We still have ahead of us that crucial and demanding phase of realizing in classroom practice the theories which seem so promising. Therefore we want to move discussion to this stage.

We would like to see more teachers of all kinds and of all specialisms talking together about language, their pupils' and their own in all its variety. We would like them to join us in studying how changing situations change the productivity and potentiality of talk. We would like them to join us in considering the differences between speech and writing and what it means to the young writer to compose in words his own observations, conclusions and attitudes. We would like them to observe with us the effects of giving scope to the full expression of the personal view in all new learning. We would like them to consider critically with us what we offer pupils to read in school books and to decide how pupils can best make sense of the printed word. We want to go beyond wringing our hands at the low level of literacy, at shrinking from contemporary speech manners, at frustration in the face of inarticulacy and reticence. We want instead to evolve a realistic programme that could be implemented by any school which was convinced that a change was necessary and possible.

Language and the pupil

In children's encounters with the curriculum there is a confrontation between their comfortably acquired mother-tongue and the varieties of language which have grown up around institutionalized areas of learning. In many of these areas special demands are made on their thinking—they are expected to reason, speculate, plan, consider theories, make their own generalizations and hypotheses. These are in many respects language activities, that is, language is the means by which they are carried out, the means, therefore, by which children do much of their learning. The effort to formulate in the pupil's own words the appearance of something, or to draw conclusions from an experiment, or to express the significance of an historical document is an essential part of the learning process, for he will be using language to give meaning to his experience. But there are formal mature ways of expressing these things which have arisen in a different context, are designed to meet different expectations and are directed at more or less public audiences. The school pupil is remote from such a situation and its attendant language needs. His healthiest need is to make sense in his own terms of what he is learning. It will take many years of development before his situation begins to approach that of the scientist, historian, technologist, etc. This stage is likely to be reached towards the end of his secondary schooling.

Mature language is highly differentiated, modified to meet many differing and complex functions. Some of these functions require from the mature adult that he inhibit all those features of language which are the expression of personal and inter-personal feeling in the interests of dispassionate objectivity and undistracted communication. Since these are very sophisticated achievements we cannot expect to find them in school pupils. If such writing is to develop at all it must grow out of the confident use of personal expressive language and the thoughtful, conscious consideration of the new language the teacher has to offer.

Talking

The speaking voice precedes the writing pen and the reading eye in the life-history of every normal child. Given the opportunity and a favouring environment he can use it to do more things than he can do with the written word. Through improvised talk he can shape his ideas, modify them by listening to others, question, plan, express doubt, difficulty and confusion, experiment with new language and feel free to be tentative and incomplete. It is through talk that he comes nearer to others and with them establishes a social unit in which learning can occur and in which he can shape for public use his private and personal view. Thus we think that school learning should be so organized that pupils may use to the full their language repertoire and also add to it. From our discussion and exchanges of experience we would make these suggestions.

1 Many school activities should be carried out by small groups which can use their talk to move towards understanding by means which are not present in the normal teacher-directed classroom.

2 Though much of this talk may seem uneconomic, tentative and inexplicit, it is often the only way in which genuine exploration can occur. Teachers can frequently help forward discussion at the crucial moment, but probably we need less intervention and more patience.

3 We need to find ways of helping pupils without putting words in their mouths. We could perhaps be less concerned to elicit from them verbatim

repetitions of time-honoured formulations than to ensure that pupils engage in a struggle to formulate for themselves their present understanding. Discussion is an essential part of that process.

4 Teachers should encourage pupils to consider the language of the subject in ways which are appropriate to their development. Time spent in considering why reports, observations, theories, etc., are expressed in one way rather than another should be an essential part of intellectual development. We all need to learn more about the language of our subjects.

5 Room should be found for speculation and fantasy.

6 As teachers we might free ourselves much more from situations which confine our own language to the most formal exposition and most limiting kinds of questions. Talk with small groups and individuals gives the teacher greater linguistic scope and makes it possible for him to influence the pupils' language more profoundly. We need to experiment more with questioning so that it leads to fuller and more adventurous responses.

We acknowledge that more talk by pupils creates its own problems and that not all talk is productive. We need to identify these problems and find ways of overcoming them.

Writing

The written language has the advantages of permanence, completeness and elaboration. It gives the writer the time and scope to examine his own language and fashion it more precisely to his purposes. Yet young writers are frequently at a loss when confronted with a typical school assignment or they are reduced to summaries and paraphrases from textbooks and notes. Some of their difficulties are an inevitable part of the transition from the spontaneous spoken word to the new and complex conventions of the written word. Other difficulties arise from special features of the school situation. Much they are asked to write is broadly speaking informative; yet no genuine informative act is taking place, i.e. no one is being informed. The tasks frequently seem to lack a clear function, nor do they seem to leave room for the expression of the writer's own ideas and his way of seeing things. All too rarely in school writing assignments is the writer expressing something he wants to say to others.

It is probably in the written work of pupils that the most stereotyped and uniform language is to be found. We do not believe that most teachers *prefer* it to be like this. How could it be changed?

1 By written work arising as a logical need from the learning in hand—the need to record, to report, to propose solutions, to weigh possibilities, to sort out ideas, etc. The ideal to aim at is the genuine need to communicate something to somebody. An exchange in talk beforehand is likely to help pupils discover this communicative need.

2 By greater tolerance for the pupil's own expression of his observations, ideas and conclusions, and the positive encouragement of very varied responses including personal imaginative ones.

3 By discussing with pupils the formalities and conventions of particular kinds of documents (e.g. laboratory records, notes, etc.) and allowing them to devise their own.

4 By avoiding stereotyped conventions irrespective of the function of the writing and by encouraging appropriateness of response. The impersonality of certain kinds of prose is appropriate only for certain purposes.

5 By encouraging self-initiated work and providing generous choices or at least the possibility of modifying the set task.

6 By attempting to develop a genuine sense of audience not only through a genuine message from pupil to teacher but also by widening the audience to other pupils in the class and school and people outside the school.

7 By breaking the bonds of the school 'exercise' designed to be completed in a standard homework stint or school period and written in a standard exercise book. More sustained efforts can be made with books, pamphlets, displays, etc., and may be the result of a successful collaboration.

It follows from these suggestions that written work asks for the teacher's attention and interest more than (perhaps, instead of) his marks. If prior and exclusive attention is given to spelling, punctuation and correctness (in its narrowest sense) then all too easily the writer feels that the message itself and his effort to communicate it are of less importance. If his writing is made more public then he is more likely to develop the incentive to become his own editor and to set himself higher standards of presentation.

Many hours are spent by pupils *copying* notes but many pupils never learn how to *make* them. This would not only be for many an investment in their educational future but would be for all part of the process of learning. They would be engaged in abstracting and verbalizing the essence of what they had learnt. Moreover, note-making could be their living experience of how writing needs to change as its function changes, for notes will be different in kind as the writer's purposes change. The co-operative composition of notes under the teacher's guidance; a set of notes made by pupils for each other's use; the study of extracts from the note-books of scientists and writers; these could all help to build up a notion of the varied

criteria for the selection and presentation of material. The dictation or copying of notes then may seem to be a quick and efficient method for accurate
learning but in the long run actually omits a vital process in teaching.

Reading

The books made readily accessible by teachers not only provide an inexhaustible supply of material by means of which pupils can teach themselves
and supplement what has been taught, they also represent the chief means
by which they can learn the varied adult forms of discourse and when they
should be used. The standard textbook supplied to every member of a class
can scarcely fulfil such ambitious requirements even if it is well-written.
Frequently it is not. Many textbooks seem to be addressed to the teacher
rather than the pupil and their language shows little awareness of the kinds
of linguistic difficulty confronting the pupils they purport to address.

The excellent work already done by teachers and librarians has pointed
the way to the following suggestions.

1   Pupils should have access to all types of reading material relevant to the
topic they are studying, reference books, newspapers, periodicals, cuttings,
documents, stories, biographies.

2   They should have the opportunity to observe the varied emphases, com-
mitments, attitudes and presentation of different writers.

3   Textbooks should not be treated as sacred sources of irrefutable data
but rather as one of many sources of handy reference. For the study of some
topics the school textbook may well be dispensed with.

4   For children who have difficulty with reading, material should be taped
and the tape made available with the text. Pupils might make some of these
tapes.

5   There should be time for reading in class not only for specific assignments but also for reading of a more exploratory kind.

6   The teacher should read aloud material which is compelling and provocative.

The teacher

The teacher's role in schools is changing and much of what we have proposed is in line with this change. The more teachers work *alongside* their

pupils the more likely it is that our suggestions will make sense. The more they foster the initiative of their pupils the more likely it is that their pupils will develop a confidence in their own use of language. The less they attempt to verbalize ideas for their pupils the less stereotyped will their pupils' language be.

How could the policy be implemented?

1 Teachers in schools, teachers' centres, etc., should pool their observations of language in use in school (including, of course, their own). They should examine in detail specific problems, e.g. teachers' and pupils' questions, the language of textbooks. Teachers with different specialisms should compare their problems, e.g. Is note-making in history different from note-making in chemistry?

2 Subject associations should devote conference time and meetings to language problems, e.g. The metaphors of biology.

3 Wherever possible teachers should attempt to make themselves familiar with relevant recent studies and researchers on the nature of language, how it works and how it is acquired.

4 Small-scale investigations should be made by teachers to furnish documents, tape and videotape for their discussion, e.g. the use of language on a field-trip including the preparation and follow-up.

5 Arising from discussion and investigation it should be possible for some schools to put into operation a language policy which would act as a guide to *all* their teachers. Such a policy would, of course, be developed and modified in the light of the experience gathered from its formulation and application and would, therefore, be shaped to meet the needs of specific schools.

As a step towards implementing the last suggestion we put forward this document. It is not, we would emphasize, a blue-print but a starting-point. We would be disappointed if it were taken over lock, stock and barrel.

1 : 2   Reading in the total school curriculum

Sidney J. Rauch

For many years, it has been commonplace for reading specialists to list as one of the basic principles of reading instruction the following credo: *There is no one best program or method for teaching reading. Each program must, of necessity, be different, depending upon such significant factors as the individual pupil's abilities and needs, the strength and weaknesses of the teachers, the purposes and objectives of the administrative and supervisory personnel, the materials available, and the interests and pressures of the community.* In his evaluation of the twenty-seven first grade reading studies sponsored by the U.S. Office of Education in 1964–65, Russell Stauffer (1966) summarized his reactions as follows:

> I have become acutely aware of one tidy generalization—there is no one method of teaching reading. Regardless of the criterion used, there is no one method and this is so in spite of the tragic consequences of internal dynamism that some so-called methods have sought to advance—tragically, eccentrically, and captivatingly, . . . no approach has overcome individual differences or eliminated reading disability.

The more one reads about various types of reading programs and observes and evaluates programs in action, the more one becomes convinced that the ultimate success of any program is dominated by three factors: 1) the amount of time specifically devoted to the teaching of reading, with special emphasis upon the direct and systematic teaching of skills; 2) the moral and material support given to reading instruction by the administrators and supervisors responsible for the program; and 3) the awareness of content area teachers that they have a responsibility to extend and refine the reading skills of their students. However, this third factor does not

---

RAUCH, SIDNEY J. (1968) 'Reading in the total school curriculum', in Figurel, J Allen (ed.), *Forging Ahead in Reading*, Newark, Delaware: The International Reading Association, 212–17.

imply or suggest that content area teachers are reading teachers, per se, or remedial reading specialists.

To involve the total faculty in the improvement of reading, the following three conditions must exist: 1) genuine interest and support of a school-wide reading program by the administrative and supervisory staff; 2) concentration on the classroom teacher's immediate and specific problems; and 3) realistic and effective in-service education.

Support of the administrative and supervisory staff

What does the administrator need to consider in initiating or extending a total reading program? Nila Banton Smith (1966) has offered the following suggestions. (Though these suggestions are in reply to administrators who wish to start reading programs in the secondary school, they appear to apply equally well to the elementary level.)

1 The administrator should have some background in reading gained through attending meetings and conferences dealing with secondary reading, and as a result of his own reading of recent books and articles on this subject.

2 The administrator should be enthusiastic about starting a reading program and confident of its success. He should take leadership in providing interest-stimulating activities such as those suggested in the appendix to *Corrective Reading in the High School Classroom* (Perspectives in Reading, No. 6, International Reading Association).

3 The administrator should make budgetary provisions for purchasing extra reading materials.

4 The administrator should schedule time for teaching reading except in schools where team-teaching is being used. In such schools, teams of teachers schedule the time with the approval of the administrator.

5 Support of the entire staff should be enlisted.

6 Support of the students and their parents should be obtained.

7 The undertaking should be a cooperative one in which all members of the faculty participate in planning the program from the beginning.

8 While the plan is cooperative, the responsibility for developing the program should be given to one person: the reading specialist, principal, curriculum director, classroom teacher, or someone else who is interested and competent.

9 The person to whom the above responsibility is given *must* be trained in reading.

10   When ready to start the program, care should be taken to make sure that each person involved knows what his responsibility is.

11   The administrator must be ready to accept small beginnings. A well-rounded reading program takes time to develop. The administrator needs to keep enthusiasm at a high ebb, but he often will find it necessary to temper enthusiasm with patience.

It must be emphasized that the chief school administrator (i.e., the principal) sets the tone for the reading program. His interest and concern in better reading permeate the entire program. His sensitivity to the needs of his staff and realistic appraisal of the total school–community environment lead to the enthusiastic cooperation of all concerned. Above all, he provides the leadership necessary for the total involvement of the faculty. According to Ruth Strang, 'The aim of the administrator is to provide the experiences every pupil needs to improve in reading.' A list of 'do's' and 'don'ts' for the administrator is supplied by Dr Strang on pages 77–78 of *The Improvement of Reading* (1961).

Attacking immediate, specific classroom problems

The following question was asked of elementary teachers taking graduate courses in the teaching of reading at Hofstra University during the spring term, 1967: 'What aspects of the teaching of reading concern you most?' The five major areas in order of importance were grouping, seat work activities,[1] classroom diagnosis, teaching of phonics, and helping the slow learner.

The same question was asked of secondary teachers. Their responses in order of importance were critical interpretation, working with problem readers in the classroom, vocabulary improvement, improving reading in the content areas, and grouping.

Implicit in the above informal survey is the fact that the administration must be aware of these immediate needs and be ready with solutions for these problems. Classroom teachers will not respond to vague generalities. They want answers to problems they meet in the classroom every day.

It has been the writer's experience that content area teachers can contribute most to the improvement of reading by emphasizing the study skills. Basically, the study skills are those reading skills in which the primary aim is to obtain information. In a very helpful New York City

1   *Editorial footnote*: Practice exercises done by individual pupils following a group session in reading instruction.

Curriculum Bulletin (1959), these skills are referred to as 'reading for information, study, and research'. Of all the reading areas improvement in the study skills seems to relate most directly to improvement of class work, resulting in higher grades. Thus, both the student and teacher can see benefits almost immediately. These skills may be categorized as follows:

Skills of locating information

Using parts of the book (author's organization of materials, preface, introduction, table of contents, index, glossary, etc.)
Use of dictionary skills
Use of encyclopedias, almanacs, atlases and other references
Reading maps, charts, graphs, diagrams, etc.
Use of library techniques

Skills of evaluating information

Reading with a critical attitude
Using several sources to evaluate materials
Judging author's competency
Distinguishing between fact and opinion
Learning propaganda techniques
Evaluating relevancy of information to topic being studied

Skills of organizing information

Note-taking
Classifying facts and ideas
Arranging ideas in sequence
Knowing outline format
Knowing how to outline
Techniques of summarizing

Skills of retaining information

Use of Survey Q3R—See Spache (1963) pp. 345–346, for a good summary and evaluation of his study technique [2]
Systematic study v. cramming
The need for rereading
Note-making vs. note-taking as a memory aid

[2] *Editorial footnote*: For a description of Survey Q3R, see Kravitz, Alvin, 'Teaching the essential reading skills in social studies', 1 : 4, pp. 45–48.

Adjusting rate to purpose and to the difficulty of the reading selection

There is no such thing as rate in isolation. It must always be considered as *rate of comprehension*.

A good reader must have at least four basic rates of reading:

1 Skimming (skipping with judgment)
2 Rapid reading (timed-reading exercises—no skipping of material)
3 Intensive reading (the art and necessity of rereading)
4 Recreational reading rate.

In teaching the study skills, five basic principles should be kept in mind.

1 Instruction in the study skills should begin at that grade level in which the student begins to read extensively in the content areas. . . .
2 Instruction in the study skills should be spread through several grades rather than concentrated at one grade level. The teacher should think of the study skills as a 'spiral curriculum' in which each major skill is re-emphasized at each grade level, using more difficult material and proceeding at a faster rate.
3 It should be noted that each major study skill has levels of difficulty. The teacher should begin with the most obvious level of the skill and work toward the most difficult. For example, there is a world of difference between skimming a selection to find a name or date and skimming a chapter to get some idea of the author's pattern or organization.
4 Factual material, rather than narrative or story-type, is more conducive to effective instruction in the study skills. Such factual materials should have a minimum of word recognition problems for the student. The teacher's purpose is to teach a study skill, not to be bogged down in word recognition problems. Avoid materials that are at a student's 'frustration level'.
5 Though special materials and exercises may be used to teach the study skills, application should be made to the content areas. For example, teaching Survey Q3R is practically valueless unless application is made to a content area textbook.

Another effective way of involving the total faculty in a reading program is to make them aware of the major skills of reading instruction and to show that these skills are involved in practically all the subject areas. A very helpful guide to reading skills in the subject areas, including specific developmental lesson plans pertaining to many of these skills, can be found in the New York City Board of Education publication, *Reading in the Subject Areas, Grades 7-8-9* (1964). This curriculum bulletin lists the skills as indicated on the chart below.

READING SKILLS	Language Arts	Social Studies	Science	Math.	Industrial Arts
Word recognition					
1. recognize basic sight words	x				
2. use phonetic analysis	x				
3. use structural analysis	x				
4. use contextual clues for word meaning	x	x	x	x	x
5. use dictionary to check meaning	x	x	x	x	x
Comprehension					
1. understand word and sentence meaning	x	x	x	x	x
2. find main idea and related details	x	x	x	x	x
3. organize and classify facts	x	x	x	x	x
4. perceive sequence of ideas	x	x	x	x	x
5. draw inferences and conclusions	x	x	x	x	
6. understand problems	x	x	x	x	x
7. form judgments	x	x	x	x	
8. predict outcomes	x		x	x	
9. read critically—distinguishing fact from opinion	x	x	x		
10. read for appreciation	x				
11. understand relationships	x	x	x	x	x
12. follow directions	x	x	x	x	x
Work study					
1. understand parts of a book	x	x	x	x	
2. understand the index of a text	x	x	x	x	
3. use of the dictionary	x	x	x	x	
4. use of the encyclopedia	x	x	x		
5. understand library techniques	x	x	x		
6. interpret maps	x	x	x	x	
7. understand charts	x	x	x	x	x
8. interpret graphs	x	x	x	x	
9. understand diagrams	x	x	x	x	x
10. adjust reading rate-skimming	x	x	x	x	x
11. select and evaluate information	x	x	x	x	x
12. use techniques of retention and recall	x	x	x	x	x

(The 'x' under each subject area indicates that the reading skill is relevant to that particular subject.)

Realistic and effective in-service education

A group of reading specialists enrolled in the writer's course in the 'Supervision of Reading Instruction' offered at Hofstra University during the fall semester, 1966, prepared a statement of basic principles for in-service education in reading. All involved were actively engaged in organizing and participating directly in their school's in-service programs. The IRA publication, *Conducting In-Service Programs in Reading* (1965), was a helpful reference in the preparation of these principles:

1 In-service education must be responsive to the needs of the school or district. These needs could be established through
a surveys, including studies of the community;
b questionnaires to ascertain teacher needs;
c classroom observations by principals and reading specialists; and
d requests by teachers.
2 In-service education must have the whole-hearted support of the administration. The administration must indicate in every way possible that reading instruction has been given top priority
a in terms of participation of administrators in workshops, special courses, conferences;
b in terms of personnel made available to contribute to the reading program; and
c in terms of financial support.
3 In-service training should stress the *practical aspects* of the teaching of reading. For example:
a preparation of informal tests and other materials for particular grade levels;
b specific grouping procedures; and
c special activities and materials for the slow learner.
4 In-service training should stress complete involvement of those participating:
a participants should help in establishing the goals of courses or workshops;
b participants should help in planning the content as well; and
c groups should be small.
5 In-service training should include demonstrations, observations, pre-conferences, and post-conferences as integral parts of all in-service courses:
a reading specialists must have the skills and experience for successful demonstration lessons; and
b observations of master teachers should not be limited to one session. (Some activities need to be observed for several consecutive sessions.)
6 Evaluation should be an ongoing concern in all in-service training through

a evaluation of courses, workshops and conferences, etc. by supervisors and teachers; and

b yearly testing of pupils.

7 In-service training should, for obvious reasons, be conducted during released time, rather than after school hours. Time must be provided not only for courses but also for visitations and conferences.

8 New teachers will be hired with the understanding that their in-service training will be an important part of their responsibilities. This training will be provided according to school and personal needs.

9 In-service training, especially for new teachers, should be defined not only in terms of workshops, courses, and institutes but also in terms of contacts with principals and reading specialists. More and better supervision by those who are well versed in the problems of teaching reading is the *sine qua non* for any program aimed at the improvement of reading instruction.

10 In-service training should have as its final goal the improvement of instruction in *all areas* of reading.

11 There must be a greater awareness of the fact that individual differences exist among teachers as well as they do among children.

To supplement the preceding matter Robinson and Rauch (1965) have offered the following suggestions:

1 An in-service program that threatens the security of staff members cannot succeed. The consultant must be sensitive and realistic in his demands upon the teaching staff. Programs that require too much of the teacher's 'free' time are likely to breed resentment and failure. At the same time, participants in the in-service program should have the opportunity to share in both the planning and the evaluating of the program.

2 Programs that try to accomplish too much in too short a time will not have lasting results. It is better to concentrate on one grade level or one subject area at a time rather than attempt to reorganize the entire system-wide program in one year. A successful program in a limited area will mean much more in the long run than questionable progress on a broad scale.

3 The active support of teachers who are reputed to be extremely capable instructors and who are respected by other teachers greatly helps the reading consultant in organizing and conducting the in-service program.

4 In-service reading programs that involve persons who teach in a subject area must reflect the goals and objectives of that area. To help ensure fuller cooperation from content area teachers, the consultant should use the

materials of their subject to demonstrate the application of specific reading skills.

To summarize; the chances for involvement of the total school faculty in a reading program will be determined to the extent that the following conditions are met: 1) teachers must recognize the need for such an effort; 2) realistic goals must be set; 3) the necessary teaching materials must be available; 4) in-service instruction must be down-to-earth and directed towards immediate classroom problems; and 5) school leaders must be sincerely and actively devoted to the cause of reading improvement on a school-wide basis.

References

STAUFFER, RUSSELL (1966) 'Some Tidy Generalizations', *The Reading Teacher*, 20, 4.

SMITH, NILA BANTON (1966) 'Questions Administrators Ask About Reading in Secondary Schools', in Robinson, H. Alan and Rauch, Sidney J. (eds) *Corrective Reading in the High School Classroom*, Perspectives in Reading no. 6, Newark, Delaware: International Reading Association, 124.

STRANG, RUTH (1961) *The Improvement of Reading* New York: McGraw-Hill, 77–8.

Reading Grades 7–8–9: A Teacher's Guide to Curriculum Planning (1959) Curriculum Bulletin no. 11, 1957–58 Series, Board of Education of the City of New York.

SPACHE, GEORGE D. (1963) *Toward Better Reading* Champaign, Illinois: Garrard Press, 345–6.

Reading in the Subject Areas, Grades 7–8–9 (1964) Curriculum Bulletin no. 6, 1963–64 Series, Board of Education of the City of New York, 2.

AARON, IRA E., CALLAWAY, BRYON, and OLSON, ARTHUR V. (1965) *Conducting In-Service Programs in Reading* Newark, Delaware: International Reading Association.

ROBINSON, H. ALAN, and RAUCH, SIDNEY J. (1965) *Guiding the Reading Program: A Reading Consultant's Handbook* Chicago: Science Research Associates, 47–8.

1:3   Reading skills common to the content areas

Olive S. Niles

It is the first period in the morning. In his social studies cláss Student X is reading several pages from his history book, containing paragraphs such as the following:

> Even more dangerous than the continuing crisis over Berlin was that of the Soviet arms build-up in Cuba. On this rich island, just ninety miles from Florida, a flamboyant young revolutionist, Fidel Castro, had overthrown the reactionary dictatorship of Fulgencio Batista in 1959. At first Castro's government appeared to promise democracy and progress, but it became more and more dictatorial and leftist. Thousands of Cubans fled to the United States as Castro abolished civil liberties and nationalized much property, including that owned by citizens of the United States. American leaders began to take drastic economic action against Castro's Cuba by cutting off loans and restricting trade. More and more Castro turned to the Soviet Union and China, while he and his followers shouted against 'Yankee imperialism'.

> (Boyd C. Shafer *et al, United States History for High School* Laidlaw, 1966, 663.)

Fifty minutes later, Student X may be reading this paragraph from a biology text:

> Since euglenas possess some characteristics of plants and some of animals, they have been claimed by both botanists and zoologists. Because of one of their methods of locomotion, they are often placed in the protist phylum *Mastogophora* (mass-ti-GAH-fuh-ruh), although some biologists put them in a phylum of their own. The organism swims by means of a flagellum attached

NILES, OLIVE S. (1969) 'Reading skills common to the content areas', in Robinson, H. Alan and Thomas, Ellen Lamar (eds) *Fusing Reading Skills and Content* Newark, Delaware: International Reading Association, 1–16.

to the anterior end. The flagellum—nearly as long as the one-celled body—
rotates, thus pulling the organism rapidly through the water.

(James H. Otto and Albert Towle, *Modern Biology* Holt, Rinehart and
Winston, 1969, 257.)

In English class, a little later, we might find Student X interpreting
this poem:

REFUGEE IN NEW ENGLAND

Across the snow the water-color blue
shadows of woods ran out to meet the wall
crannied with whiteness and the thin boy, new
to alien winters, watched his shadow fall
beside a pine's, and saw himself grow tall
in the wide sunlight where the rime-frost flew.

In this American woods there was no sound
save when a green bough slipped its load to earth.

Strange peace was here. Even the dog's bark, bound
hillward from the farmhouse, held a dearth
of urgency. The bright air flung its worth
upward: 'Oh, there you are!'—a friendly sound.
The young boy wept, his cheek against cold ground.

(Frances Frost, 'Refugee in New England', in G. H. Clarke, ed. *The New
Treasury of War Poetry* Houghton Mifflin, 1943.)

In his math class, Student X may read this problem:

An airmail parcel may weigh from 8 ounces up to 70 pounds, but the sum of
the length and girth may be no more than 100 inches. What are the dimensions (length, width, height) of the longest acceptable airmail parcel, in the
shape of a rectangular solid, that is twice as long as it is wide and that is two
inches higher than it is wide?

(Mary P. Dolciani *et al, Modern School Mathematics, Algebra 1* Houghton
Mifflin, 1967, 125.)

We might continue to follow Student X to other classes, perhaps
industrial arts,[1] music, a foreign language, or some business subject.
Everywhere he goes, all day long, day after day, much of his success
depends on his ability to read material similar to the samples cited.
Secondary teachers know this fact well; but, because they are all specialists,
usually in just one subject area, they often forget the concomitant fact

1 *Editorial footnote*: Boys' crafts, such as woodwork and metalwork.

that Student X has to shift gears in his reading again and again as he moves during the day from one subject area to another. Admittedly, it is unfair to take brief excerpts out of context as samples. Discount, if you will, fifty percent of the difficulty that would seem inherent in these samples. Of course, it is a great deal easier to read them if you have read and understood what preceded them, but it is still apparent that Student X is confronted with a situation which challenges a good reader and is perhaps downright impossible for a poor reader.

We can make the situation somewhat less threatening if, as a group of teachers, we can see the elements which are common to the study of all these kinds of materials and if we can help Student X to understand that there are important similarities as well as differences between a method of study appropriate, for example, to reading the poem and a corresponding method of study appropriate to solving the algebra problem.

In order to analyse the common elements present in reading, even of materials as diverse as those represented in the samples, I have taken two approaches to the task. The first of these involves analysis of the act of reading itself; the second, analysis of basic skills and abilities needed to handle any and all types of reading material.

The act of reading

Definitions presented by various authorities range from a simple equating of reading with the decoding process to definitions which are extremely broad and include skills which probably have more to do with thinking in general than with reacting to print alone. These various definitions are not necessarily contradictory; they differ in scope rather than in meaning. For the purposes of this paper, I am using a broad definition which includes 1) recognition of, 2) reaction to, and 3) use of the meaning behind printed symbols. The broad definition is necessary in defining the role of reading in the content areas.

The reading act, according to this broad definition, may be subdivided into six large, interdependent parts: word recognition, association of meaning with individual printed symbols, literal comprehension, interpretation, evaluation, and assimilation. Each of these basic parts of the reading act is present in some degree in the reading required in any of the content areas. Differences lie in the ways in which the parts are used in handling differing materials and in the degree of importance each has in a given subject.

Word recognition

No reading in any subject can take place without word recognition. By this term we mean the ability to translate, orally or subvocally, the written symbol into a spoken symbol. Many secondary students have mastered this skill and most of them have a fair command of it. Except for the very poorest readers, the secondary teacher may assume a knowledge of the four kinds of clues the mature reader uses to identify words which are not a part of his instant recognition vocabulary: context clues, phonetic clues, structural clues, and—as a court of last resort—the dictionary with its diacritical markings. However, most secondary students need consistent review of the principles and procedures necessary for ease in word recognition because what has been learned in the elementary school about recognizing words has not yet become an automatic process. Problems with word recognition may occur in any subject field; they probably occur most often in science, where a concentration of new words with unknown pronunciations often appears. In the paragraph about euglenas there are five or six words which might give many students pause in their reading.

The polysyllabic words in the English language can all be classified in one of four groups as follows:

1 Words which are compounds—officeholder, carpetbagger, radioisotope.
2 Words which should be attacked by structure because they are English root words with affixes—hyperthyroidism, reforestation, suburbanization.
3 Words which must be attacked by dividing them into syllables—corollary, mutation, alliteration.
4 Words which are so irregular as to require the use of a dictionary (mostly proper names and foreign words)—habeas corpus, ichneumon, quaestor, Gounod.

Quick recognition, usually unconscious, of the pronunciation grouping to which a word belongs triggers, for the mature reader, the procedure he needs for quick, easy pronunciation.

Association of meaning with printed symbols

Association of meaning with the printed symbol is the second part of the act of reading. The student may pronounce *phylum* very readily if he is familiar with a few phonetic principles, but the word may be just a mouthful of sound. If the concept is not already there, the symbol is useless.

There is no essential difference between reading the usual verbal symbol (the word) and reading such nonverbal symbols as $<$ or H_2SO_4. The mathematical or scientific symbol often stands for a complex relationship, but it may be no more difficult to understand than such very abstract verbal symbols as *imperialism* or *irony*.

A major responsibility of all content teachers is to develop many new concepts with which printed symbols may be associated. This is a very different emphasis in vocabulary teaching from that of the elementary school and is one of the strongest reasons why the teaching of reading has to continue in the secondary school. The little child comes to school with many words in his aural-oral vocabulary and few, if any, in his reading vocabulary. During his elementary school days his energies are directed mainly toward learning to read words which are already in his aural-oral vocabulary. By the time he is in secondary school, he has probably succeeded in completing most of this task. The emphasis then shifts to developing new meanings. This is a natural and fruitful area in the teaching of reading for all content teachers since each time a new word is taught, a new concept has been taught. Hence, there is a total melding of the teaching of reading and the teaching of content—they are actually one and the same thing.

Some of the concepts behind the words used in content areas are highly generalized. A word like *approximation* is useful in mathematics, English, and social studies—in fact, a student may meet it almost anywhere. Other words have both generalized and highly technical meanings; an example is *rational*, which, in addition to its common meaning, has a very precise technical meaning in mathematics. Still others, like *parabola*, have technical meanings only, often specific to one particular area of study. Responsibility for teaching all three types of words as students encounter them must be shared among all teachers. It is a particularly important responsibility because accurate communication cannot take place unless the author and the reader have a common understanding of the concept behind each symbol. A very simple example is the word *girth* in the algebra problem cited earlier. Unless the student knows exactly what concept this word triggers, he cannot do the problem.

Literal comprehension

Literal comprehension is also clearly a part of the reading act and must be stressed in every content area. It involves some very important sub-skills, such as reading for central ideas and noting the way details are organized around these central ideas. Solving the algebra problem, for example, requires that the student knows how to express two of the unknowns in terms of the third unknown; that is, he must understand the relationships of the details stated in the problem.

Various patterns of organization of details produce different effects, though the facts themselves may be essentially the same. Thus, if facts are compared, we receive a meaning different from that which we would obtain if the same facts were merely related in chronological sequence. Students, therefore, must be taught not only to read for accurate literal understanding of individual facts but also to understand the particular relationship these facts may have to other facts in the material.

Consider this paragraph:

> Even in our successful declaration of the Monroe Doctrine we were not leaders. Only the agreement of Great Britain, whose interests it also served, made it enforceable. We went through the rest of the nineteenth century doubling our population every twenty years. We increased our industrial capacity and established unity at home. By 1900 we were a power, a nation consulted wherever diplomats convened. That is, we had exposed Spain as a has-been by defeating her handily at war; we had acquired new and distant interests in the form of Puerto Rico, the Philippines, and Queen Liliuokalani's romantic Hawaiian Islands. We now had the beads that go with being a dowager.

Whatever we may think of the author's choice of metaphor in the last sentence, the paragraph as a whole builds a picture of rapidly growing maturity and power, of a nation coming of age and proud.

Consider how quickly this impression is modified by the very next paragraph in the text:

> But we were still a little gangly in our new maturity; we tripped over our own feet entering the conference rooms. We were uncomfortable at the green felt tables of diplomacy. Conditioned by a long century of self-concern and a distrust of our own social competence we turned in on ourselves; we built up a spirit of diplomatic isolationism.

> (Robert Rienow, *American Government in Today's World* D. C. Heath, 1966, 511–512.)

Either paragraph by itself creates a picture of the relationship of the United States to other parts of the world at a certain point in history; but to understand what the author means, the student must recognize the relationship between the two paragraphs. Over and over again, competent reading requires a study of such relationships for accurate literal comprehension.

Exact, literal comprehension always seems very important to teachers of mathematics, science, and related areas. It may seem less important in a subject such as literature, but in my opinion it is not. Before a student can react imaginatively and critically to literature, he needs to be in full command of literal meaning. If he does not understand, for example, the full literal meaning of the phrase in the Frost poem 'crannied with whiteness', the opening image will be unclear—as will the second image if he fails to know literally how a boy can see 'himself grow tall'.

Interpretation

Interpretation takes the reader beyond the printed page by requiring that he put together ideas which the author has not overtly related to one another, and by requiring him to see the connections between what he is reading now and his past reading and life experience. As an outcome of this process, the reader is able to make inferences and draw conclusions— in other words, to learn things the author only said indirectly. This process is at work in the reading required in all subject areas, though with differing degrees of complexity. Some poetry, for example, depends so heavily upon the ability to interpret that, for the unsophisticated reader, it is nearly unintelligible. But the same process is involved in reading an algebra problem.

Consider what is required in this algebra problem:

> With a tail wind, a jet plane flew 2400 miles in 4 hours, but it required 6 hours for the return trip against the wind. Find the airspeed of the plane and the wind speed.
> (Mary P. Dolciani *et al*, *Modern School Mathematics, Algebra 1*, Houghton Mifflin, 1967, 250.)

There are unstated facts which are necessary to the solution of this problem: that distance is the product of time and rate; that the speed of a plane flying with the winds equals its own speed plus that of the wind; that, conversely, its speed flying against the wind is equal to its own speed minus the wind speed; that the solution of a problem like this requires two equations. All of this information has to be brought to the problem by the reader, either from previous experience with similar problems or from reasoning from the facts as given. This process is as much an act of interpretation as is drawing conclusions about the characters in a novel by piecing together various bits of information about their behaviour, their speech, or their appearance.

Evaluation

The evaluation aspect of the reading act—often called critical reading—requires that the reader depart from the printed page in another direction. He must make judgments rooted in what he has read, not in his personal feelings and prejudices. He must sort facts from opinions, ask whose opinions they are or what the sources of the facts are, and evaluate the logic of the reasoning represented in the material he has read. He must consider the relevancy, authenticity, and utility of factual material. He should see, for example, that the first half of the first sentence of the algebra problem presented at the beginning of this paper is irrelevant to the solution of the problem. The student who intelligently evaluates will also see immediately that the writer of the paragraph about Castro was using prejudicial words in describing him as a 'flamboyant young revolutionist' with a 'dictatorial' and 'leftist' government which encouraged 'shouting' against 'Yankee imperialism'. That this kind of language may be acceptable to many people in describing Castro could tend to blind the young reader to the fact that it is not straight reporting. He should be alerted to the situation and reminded that more than one major figure in history has been thus described by his contemporaries. He needs to learn to be intelligently wary in his reading, to know that many writers, deliberately or otherwise, reflect a specific point of view or are 'grinding an axe'. He must also realize that such axe grinding does not make writing bad; it only makes reading bad when it is unrecognized.

Critical reading or evaluation in literature is basically the same, though materials with which literature deals are usually non-factual. The reader must weigh and judge, always from a background of experience or earlier reading. Hence, he may evaluate the logic of a character's behavior by comparison with his own experiences or by his observation of characters in other novels. In another, more abstract sense, he may evaluate the way an author has written—the style rather than the content. Thus, the reader may judge the effectiveness of the caesura in the Frost poem: 'Strange peace was here. Even the dog's bark,' etc. He must also see that style often has a good deal to do with the way he feels about the content. If he doesn't recognize this fact, he may be 'taken in' by an interesting style to the extent of being uncritical of meaning.

Assimilation

Assimilation is the process through which the reader makes use of his reading. Every act of reading potentially affects not only every other act of reading but also the nonreading acts which a student will perform. The simplest, most direct way in which assimilation affects the student is in the growing confidence he acquires in the use of the skills. Gradually these skills become, through practice, so natural to him that he develops an automatic response, the goal of all skills teaching. When he needs to skim, he automatically does so. When he needs to read for complete recall, he does. He has truly assimilated the skills; they have become a part of him.

The content teacher in any area has much to do with skills assimilation. First of all, the student needs as much practice as he can get to hasten the development of the automatic response, practice of the kind which keeps him aware of the skills he is practising. If this activity is provided in every class all day long, the student will have full command of the process much sooner.

But assimilation is more than this. It is concerned also with concepts which are derived from reading. Assimilation of concepts is necessary for all in-depth, evaluative reading. The first material a person reads about any given subject, unless that subject is something very familiar to him in his personal life, will necessarily be read superficially, though the person may spend a good deal of time and effort in the reading. Thus, the paragraph about euglenas is all but meaningless unless the student has assimilated at least the information about one-celled plants and animals which precedes it in the text. No one can read in depth unless he has acquired ideas about the subject from much previous reading and/or experience; all reading is shallow until the reader has assimilated many related facts and ideas. This is why broad library reading is so necessary. It is also why the learnings from sources other than printed materials are important to the reading process.

In addition to assimilation of skills and concepts, the student assimilates attitudes derived from reading. Most educated people can name one or more books which have really changed their lives. The printed page is a powerful instrument. We too often assume that it is the English teacher's special responsibility to help students learn to use this instrument wisely in their struggle to grow mature morally and spiritually, as well as in- tellectually. The assumption that the English teacher has the breadth of background to introduce students to significant and powerful books of all kinds—books which can really change attitudes—is unfounded except, perhaps, in rare instances. In many cases, and with certain students, the science teacher, the physical education instructor, or any other member of the faculty outside of the English department could have far more success.

The skills

From a totally different viewpoint—that of the skills involved in the various parts of the reading act—the teacher may also recognize common elements which are inherent in the study of printed materials in any content area. Complete analysis of specific skills would be much too lengthy a process to be included within the scope of this paper. I shall, therefore, consider only three groups of related skills which are particularly important. These groups of skills cut across all subject areas:

1 Ability to survey material, set purposes for reading, and determine an appropriate technique for the reading of any given piece of material.
2 Ability to handle graphic and illustrative materials.
3 Ability to locate, comprehend, and combine information from a variety of library resources.

Surveying

Too many students plunge headlong into any and all types of material and find themselves immediately swamped and even drowning. A few preliminaries would prevent this problem. The preliminaries include the act of surveying the content (looking at graphic material contained therein, noting headings in a different type, and reading study questions prior to reading the text itself); deciding upon the specific purpose or purposes for the reading (hopefully established as a part of the assignment); and, after considering what has been learned by surveying and setting purposes, determining the kind and depth of reading and study necessary. Poor readers are often passive readers who expect, somehow, that all they need do is look at the page. They naïvely believe the author has done all the work. They tend to ramble through the material, expecting they will somehow remember what is there. The survey technique prevents this kind of reading. It is suitable for all kinds of study reading and provides a general framework within which the student may work purposefully and aggressively toward a known goal.

The survey technique is appropriate in the reading of mathematics, where the first quick reading (a survey of the problem) alerts the student to the kind of problem he must solve and gives him the mindset for a problem of this type. It is appropriate, also, in a literature assignment. Though we don't want the student to read the ending of a short story before he has read the story, we *do* want him to look at the illustrations, which should pique his interest and make him wonder about the characters and what they are doing; we *do* want him to read the study questions so that he will be alerted to problems of character or theme; and we *do* want him to discover during his survey whether this is an easy story about something familiar to him or a difficult one, set in some remote time or place, making it necessary to adjust reading speed and give attention to details.

Surveying prior to detailed study is particularly important in social studies because of the extreme concentration of detail; there are at least fifteen facts in the paragraph about Castro. Surveying prior to complete reading helps students focus on important points. It results in greater efficiency. It is a technique all content area students need to use with most assignments.

Reading of graphic materials

Study materials frequently make wide use of illustrative and graphic devices: pictures, charts, tables, maps, graphs, cartoons. We live in a picture age. Modern techniques of printing make it possible to use these devices in profusion. The materials involve a condensed type of language which expresses various kinds of relationships, often very complex ones. Some illustrations are particularly difficult to read; yet, once mastered, they may contribute more to understanding than the verbal symbols which they accompany. Since they are found in the study materials of practically every subject field, developing student skill in handling graphics is an important responsibility of all teachers.

Using many sources

Ability to locate, choose selectively, discard systematically, comprehend, and combine information from a variety of resources are complex skills important in every content area. Organized note-taking is a part of the process. Teaching these skills and seeing that they are used repeatedly are responsibilities which require the best energies of both media specialists and subject teachers. The day when single textbook teaching was adequate —if it ever was—has gone. We are moving so fast today that every content textbook is obsolete before it can be written, published, sold, and placed in the hands of students. Without the resources of the media center, students could never be up-to-date in their information. It becomes, therefore, a major responsibility to teach students how to find information they need (in whatever medium it best appears), to take notes from a variety of sources, and to combine this information in well-organized, meaningful ways to supplement what they may be learning from their texts. Library materials place a special premium on the evaluative and assimilative aspects of the reading process and they are often neither so clearly written nor so carefully organized as textbook materials. Greater reading skill is required to use them successfully. Using related media adds a new and very important dimension to the student's study, but it makes his task harder. Unless we all stand by to help, the student may drown in the mass of material at his disposal.

Concluding statement

In summary, then, all six parts of the reading act are common to every subject in which printed materials are used: word recognition, assigning of meaning to the printed symbol, literal comprehension, interpretation, evaluation, and assimilation.

Cutting across all six parts of the reading act are three very important generalized types of activities, each involving several subskills, which must be taught if students are to read intelligently for purposes of study: ability to survey, set purposes, and determine an appropriate technique for study; ability to handle graphic and illustrative materials; and ability to locate, comprehend, and combine information from a variety of media.

The degree of emphasis given to each of these aspects of reading in each content area depends particularly upon four factors. In the first place, the subject materials themselves control to a large extent the kind of emphasis needed. The expository language of science and mathematics tends to be terse and exact, allowing no fuzziness in its literal comprehension. Texts in these areas are also highly sequential, making the assimilative component of reading crucial. On the other hand, foreign language texts, at least for the first- and second-year courses, have some of the characteristics of basal readers[1] for primary grades. Vocabulary is severely controlled and comprehension is very simple. Students are busy learning to read words and to understand increasingly complex sentence patterns.

1 *Editorial footnote*: Basal readers, basic readers and basals are terms used interchangeably in the United States to identify published reading schemes.

Secondly, student readiness governs the emphasis on particular aspects of the reading act. This readiness is partly a product of the elementary school reading curriculum, including the amount of transfer which elementary teachers have succeeded in accomplishing between a basal reading program and the reading of content materials at that level. Too often, the elementary program is weak in developing strength in the reading of exposition, and we find students in secondary school for whom 'reading' means 'reading a story'. Readiness is also a product of the intelligence of the students, of their socio-economic background, and of their probable goals in future education.

In the third place, the degree of emphasis which is given to each of the common elements in the reading act depends upon the basic philosophy of the school as to its curriculum objectives. If the school is content-centered with emphasis on *what* students learn, the emphasis will tend to be on literal comprehension (including grasp of organization) and on recall of facts. If, on the other hand, the school is child-centered with a major concern for *how* students learn, the emphasis will tend to be on critical reading, the ability to collect and collate materials from many sources, a broadened taste, and more catholic interests in reading materials.

Finally, the kind of class activity which is most frequently used will have a good deal to do with determining the emphasis given to various aspects of reading in each content area. For example, individualized instruction or intra-class small-group work tends to emphasize the interpretive and evaluative processes and the ability to locate and combine ideas from many sources.

Basically, however, the job is the same in all content areas. To put it very briefly, it is the task of showing students how to get into a printed page, how to get what they want from it, and how to get out of it when any more time spent on it would be wasted. There probably isn't a reading specialist anywhere who really knows how to do this equally well in all content areas. Only the content specialist can accomplish the task with real understanding. This is one of the important reasons why the teaching of reading in the secondary school belongs in the content area classrooms.

References

CLELAND, DONALD L. (1965) 'A Construct of Comprehension', in Figurel, J. Allen (ed.) *Reading and Inquiry*, 1965 Proceedings, 10, Newark, Del.: International Reading Association, 59–64.

CLYMER, THEODORE (1968) 'What is Reading? : Some Current Concepts', in Robinson, Helen M. (ed.) *Innovation and Change in Reading Instruction,* The 67th Yearbook of the National Society for the Study of Education, part 2, Chicago: University of Chicago Press, 7–29.

FISHER, JOSEPH A. (1967) 'Improving Comprehension–Interpretation Skills', in Hafna, Lawrence E. (ed.) *Improving Reading in Secondary Schools,* New York: Macmillan, 117–27.

ROBINSON, H. ALAN (1964) 'Teaching Reading in the Content Areas: Some Basic Principles of Instruction', in Figurel, J. Allen (ed.) *Improvement of Reading Through Classroom Practice,* 1964 Proceedings, 9, Newark, Del.: International Reading Association, 35–6.

ROBINSON, HELEN M. (1966) 'The Major Aspects of Reading', in Robinson, H. Alan (ed.) *Reading: Seventy-Five Years of Progress,* Supplementary Educational Monographs, no. 96, Chicago: University of Chicago Press, 22–32.

SPACHE, GEORGE D. (1958) 'Types and Purposes of Reading in Various Curriculum Fields', *Reading Teacher,* 11, 158–64.

STRANG, RUTH (1961) 'Secondary School Reading as Thinking', *Reading Teacher,* 15, 155–61.

WHIPPLE, GERTRUDE (1964) 'Essential Types of Reading in the Content Fields', in Figurel, J. Allen (ed.) *Improvement of Reading Through Classroom Practice,* 1964 Proceedings, 9, Newark, Del.: International Reading Association, 31–3.

1:4   Teaching the essential reading skills in social studies

Alvin Kravitz

Within the past few years teachers have become aware of the need for teaching reading skills in the content areas. One of the major content areas, social studies, requires an approach somewhat different from other subject areas. Let us view the topic from four interrelated, yet different, angles.

Directed reading activity

Elementary and secondary teachers who are involved in teaching social studies have found increasing success in presenting their subject matter through the use of a directed reading activity.

Whipple (1960) states the format of present day social studies texts is similar to a reading book used for basal instruction. However, the reader's job is quite different. Children need guidance in selecting what to remember and then techniques in how to remember (*The Teaching of Reading*, 1963).

The New York State Curriculum Guides (1963, 1965) point out the advisability of a directed reading activity for basic instructional purposes. Spache (1963) indicates the superiority of guided reading in the teaching of social studies.

All too often students are forced to plunge into complex materials with little idea of what to look for or even why they are reading a particular text. The involved structure of social studies texts requires preparation and assistance for the student. Strang (1961) suggests that the teacher can guide the student through the use of prepared questions. Let us go a step further and prepare not only the questions for consideration during the lesson but the necessary matter prior to beginning any part of the lesson.

KRAVITZ, ALVIN (1967) 'Teaching the essential reading skills in social studies', in Figurel, J. Allen (ed.) *Forging Ahead in Reading* Newark, Delaware: International Reading Association, 223–8.

A plan for a directed reading activity in social studies is contained in *Five Steps To Reading Success* (1960):

Step one: readiness

Arousing pupil interest
Setting a purpose for the reading
Developing a background and a sense of continuity
Creating an awareness of the reading required

Step two: concept development

Discussing the vocabulary and concepts which need clarification
Explaining how context may give a term meaning
Studying pronunciation and spelling when appropriate

Step three: silent reading

Locating specific details
Finding the main idea and supporting details
Seeing a vivid picture through word concepts
Locating information by skimming
Determining accuracy of statements

Step four: discussion (oral or written)

Checking comprehension
Sharing different points of view

Step five: rereading (silent or oral)

Checking accuracy
Examining critically

Karlin (1964) discusses a directed reading activity with a slight modification. His five-step process includes:

1 Readiness—vocabulary and purpose
2 Silent reading—refer to question
3 Discussion—relating to silent reading
4 Rereading—for different purposes
5 Application—to the lesson

Gates (1960) suggested that we cultivate student interest in each content subject. He believed that social studies texts needed to be reformed because of the too difficult readability, the poor literary quality, and the lack of organization of school materials. Since it is extremely difficult for the classroom teacher to rewrite texts while teaching the students in the classroom, perhaps the next best thing would be to circumvent the problem through the use of a directed reading activity.

Vocabulary

Each subject area has its own vocabulary which is unique. Social studies certainly is no exception to the rule. It is vital for the teacher to develop the vocabulary of the specific lesson within its own context, or comprehension of the total subject will be much less than expected (Strang *et al.*, 1961). Smith (1963) indicates the child's ability to deal with the content area improves as training is given in the vocabulary of that subject. *Reading in Secondary Schools* (1965) shows the desirability of vocabulary development through the use of context meaning, word study, and the attainment of word attack skills as a means of improving overall comprehension.

Bamman (1961) points out that reading social studies is more difficult than reading narrative material to which the elementary student is accustomed. The vocabulary is not controlled; the student must organize a mass of unrelated facts; the ideas are very complex; and much previous knowledge must be brought forward to assist the student in developing concepts.

Vocabulary is a general term which covers various subdivisions. Bamman (1961) has made six headings to include the types of difficult word areas the student may meet in his social studies work.

1 *technical terms—*
would include words such as feudalism, vassal, primogeniture, guild, and crusade.
2 *multisyllabic words—*
formidable words are totalitarian, accountability, telecommunication, endowments, and philanthropic.
3 *abstract words—*
maturation would help the student to understand such words as liberty, justice, equality, democracy, and despotism.
4 *general terms—*
multiple meanings arise in the use of elevator since the student may not realize we speak of a grain elevator.

5   *mathematical terms—*
usually included in the use of time designations, area, population statistics, graphs, and charts.

6   *concepts—*
these words produce mental images which are really abstractions such as 'tolerance'. A student's view will broaden as he begins the study of human relations. What is tolerance to one child may be intolerance to another.

Jenkinson (1966) has an interesting approach to vocabulary development as she uses the term Functional Word Knowledge. She has divided the topic into three areas:

a   *function words—*
    this area includes small words that are often ignored. Some examples of structure words are as follows:
    i   cause and effect—
          because, since, so that
    ii   suggest condition—
          unless, if, although
    iii   indicate contrast—
          whereas, while
    iv   time relationships—
          as, before, when, after
    v   parallel ideas—
          however, therefore, hence

b   *shifts in word meaning—*
    the use of familiar words in unfamiliar context, i.e.

    i   cabinet — minister / clergy / furniture

    ii   iron curtain? cold war? tariff wall?

c   *classifying—*
    since learning often takes place through recognizing similarities and differences, it is essential to use this procedure.
    i   compare similarities and difference—
          declaration and proclamation
    ii   contrast differences—
          a kingdom and a democracy
    iii   paired qualities—
          kind and gentle
          humid and dank

No matter what procedure a teacher may wish to use for the introduction of vocabulary to any lesson it is vital that we understand the value of instruction in this area. If we wish to improve comprehension, we need to broaden our approach to include vocabulary development as a basic tool.

The SQ3R study formula

Students need to be taught how to study social studies as well as other subject areas. We often find elementary and secondary pupils who are so disorganized in their approach to the basic procedures that they do not know where or how to begin a study program. Robinson (1961) proved the effectiveness of his study formula in his examination of college students' study habits. As a result, we have the SQ3R study formula in use throughout the entire educational strata.

Preston (1960) suggests a modified approach for the elementary student beginning at the intermediate level. Strang (1961) indicates a more difficult process whereby students at the high school level ask themselves a general question which cuts across the author's organization. We would not expect the same thoroughness or ability from an elementary youngster as we anticipate from a high school student. Since the application of the study method is one of degree dependent upon the grade level of the student, it is worthwhile to consider the following approach as a means of reaching most children.

Here is a sample lesson for the development of the SQ3R Study Formula that may be used from the intermediate level right on to the high school student. The language has been simplified in order that almost any child who reads at the fourth level or above might be able to understand the directions. Naturally, the teacher would direct the beginning lessons in the use of the procedure, but the student could retain the directional sheet for further study and reference.

S—Survey
Q—Question
R—Read
R—Recite
R—Review

Step 1—Survey

Look through the whole assignment before you actually read to answer your questions. You should look for all of the following items before you begin to read.

a Boldface type

This is the heavy, dark, large print at the beginning of each chapter, section, and paragraph. Look at the name of the chapter and the section heading.

b Pictures with captions

The picture and its caption, which is the explanation of the picture, will help to tell about the material you will soon read.

c Charts

A chart will give you much information at a glance. When you read the chart before you read the story, you will have much information to help you understand the paragraphs.

d Drawings with captions

A drawing is considered the same as a picture when you survey the material before you read. Look at the drawing and its caption to help you understand the chapter or section.

e Maps and diagrams

A map or diagram will explain many paragraphs of written material if you look at it before you begin to read. A map or diagram may reduce half a page of writing into one small drawing.

f Summary

At the end of most chapters there is a summary. The summary tells very briefly about the information that is in the chapter. After you have read the summary, you will usually have a very good idea of the main topics in the chapter.

g Questions

The author has added questions to his chapter to direct your attention to some of the important ideas. Be sure to look at the questions before you read the selection. This step will help you to be ready for the new thoughts you are about to read.

Step 2—Question

Use the boldface type to make your question. If the heading of the section is 'Great Plains Soil', use these words to make the following questions:
What is Great Plains soil like?
Of what is Great Plains Soil made?
What must farmers consider when using Great Plains soil?

If there is no boldface type to help you make a question, use this question : What does the author expect me to learn about *this* topic from studying this selection?

a *Study guide*
    i Fold or rule a sheet of large-sized notebook paper lengthwise, down the middle.
   ii Write your questions on the left side of the page.
  iii Answer your questions on the right side of the page.
  iv When you write your answers use only key words to describe the ideas or facts you have decided are most important. *Do not write long answers.*
   v Be sure you have read the paragraph or section after your question and thought about it before you write the answer.

Step 3—Read

Read the paragraph or section to find the answer to your question. Do not stop to read every word carefully; concentrate on finding the main point. You cannot remember all the facts you find, so you must look for the important ones. There are usually *one or two main points* for each section.

Step 4—Recite

After you have finished the assignment, go back over the lesson immediately. Cover the right side of the paper where the answers are written, and ask yourself the questions on the left side of the page.

Answer the question orally. That means you must say the answers *out loud* so that you will know if you have made a mistake.

If you find you cannot answer the questions, look back at the key words which are your answers. Sometimes you will have to go back to the book to restudy the particular part which you did not understand or have forgotten.

Step 4 is very important. When you give yourself an immediate quiz on what you have studied, it is the best possible way to prevent forgetting.

Practice until you can recite the whole study guide without looking back to the key words. Then practice some more. This extra practice is what pays off.

Step 5—Review

About four weeks later, and also before every examination, go back to your questions and answers again and quiz yourself. Reread only those parts which you have forgotten.

If you have taken steps 1 (Survey), 2 (Question), 3 (Read), and 4 (Recite) faithfully, you will find that you do not have too much to restudy.

Study skills

Here is an area that encompasses all others previously discussed. In order for a student to apply himself to the full understanding of the material he has read in social studies, he must have basic knowledge of the study skills pertaining to his subject area.

Spache (1963) states most students only receive training in reading of a basal reading type which often concludes by the fourth or sixth grade. This has been the situation until quite recently. The influx of federal aid money has encouraged many school districts to begin advanced training and even developmental programs at the secondary level. The writer would certainly agree with Spache (1963) and Strang (1961) that advanced reading training should be provided by all teachers for effective reading in the content fields.

Smith (1963) has pointed out that study skills improve in a specific content area if they are pulled out and given special attention. She has indicated how teachers may help children if they are taught to recognize the major patterns found in elementary textbooks which deal with content areas. The necessary skills defined for social studies are indicated by Smith (1963): reading pictures; reading maps, globes, atlases; reading for cause and effect content; reading for comparison; reading for sequence; reading to locate dates with events; and reading critically to determine different viewpoints, facts mixed with opinion, and when propaganda is used.

Smith's (1949, 1963) basic grouping of skills common to all areas appears wide enough to include many authors in the field of reading study skills. Five major areas are listed for classification purposes: selection and evaluation, organization, location of information, following directions, and specialized skills.

Other authors have listed those skills necessary for learning social studies. Spache (1963) has three categories which include a) locating information, b) organizing information, and c) retaining and using information. Russell's (1961) emphasis for the social studies area is applied to the ability to locate information in reference books. Bamman's (1961) suggested skills fall into the general pattern of information skills. Robinson (1962) applied the major areas as established by Smith with a slight variation in the EDL Study Skills Library. Here the same concepts are involved, but they are classified under the headings of interpretation, evaluation, organization, and reference (locating information) with the theme of following directions throughout all the lessons. *A Teacher's Guide To Curriculum Planning* (Board of Education of the City of New York Curriculum Bulletin, 1957–8) has extensive listings of skills which should be covered by the teacher as instruction is given to students in the social studies curriculum.

Robinson's (1965) pilot study attempted to determine the reading skills fourth grade pupils actually used as they tried to solve problems in social studies. Although many study skills were put into practice properly, it is interesting to note those skills in which deficiencies existed or application was not made by the student. This small group of intermediate students did not make maximum use of retaining details, comparing information, grasping unstated main ideas, remembering relevant details, making inferences, or using the table of contents, headings or guides, pictorial aids, and the index. The author of the pilot study suggests the teacher should be aware of the student's reading skills, analyse the skills necessary to carry out an assignment, and teach those skills required to carry out the assignment.

Karlin (1964) has prepared a checklist of study skills based upon the classifications suggested by Smith (1949, 1963). It would be most helpful for the teacher to use this format in planning a program of instruction in study skills for the student.

Checklist of study skills (5)

1 Selection and evaluation
   Can the student do the following?
a recognize the significance of the content
b recognize important details
c identify unrelated details
d find the main idea of a paragraph
e find the main idea of larger selections

f locate topic sentences
g locate answers to specific questions
h develop independent purposes for reading
i realize the author's purpose
j determine the accuracy and relevancy of information

2 Organization
  Can the student do the following?
a take notes
b determine relationship between paragraphs
c follow time sequences
d outline single paragraphs
e outline sections of a chapter
f outline an entire chapter
g summarize single paragraphs
h summarize larger units of material

3 Location of information
  Can the student do the following?
a find information through a table of contents
b locate information through the index
c use a library card catalog to locate materials
d use the *Reader's Guide to Periodical Literature* to locate sources of information
e use an almanac to obtain data
f understand and use various appendices
g use glossaries
h use encyclopedias to locate information

4 Following directions
  Can the student do the following?
a see the relation between the purposes and the directions
b follow one-step directions
c follow steps in sequence

5 Specialized skills
  Can the student do the following?
a understand the significance of pictorial aids
b read and interpret graphs
c read and interpret tables
d read and interpret charts
e read and interpret maps

f read and interpret cartoons
g read and interpret diagrams
h read and interpret pictures

Conclusion

Many factors are involved in teaching essential reading skills in social studies. Teachers of this content area need to apply diverse methods and techniques in order that students may become more skilled as they read subject matter material. It would be useful to consider the overall approach which includes the directed reading activity, vocabulary development, a workable study formula, and applicable study skills for a worthwhile and effective program at the elementary and secondary level.

References

BAMMAN, HENRY A., HOGAN, URSULA and GREEN, CHARLES E. (1961) *Reading Instruction in the Secondary Schools* New York: David McKay, 135–54.

Five Steps to Reading Success In Science, Social Studies and Mathematics (1960) New York: Metropolitan School Study Council, Teachers' College, Columbia University, 8–9.

GATES, ARTHUR I. (1960) 'The Nature and Function of Reading in the Content Areas', in Figurel, J. Allen (ed.) *New Frontiers in Reading*, International Reading Association Conference Proceedings (Scholastic Magazines, New York) 5, 152.

JENKINSON, MARION D. (1966) 'Increasing Reading Power in Social Studies', in Robinson, H. Alan and Rauch, Sidney J. (eds.) *Corrective Reading in the High School Classroom,* Perspectives in Reading no. 6, Newark, Del.: International Reading Association, 75–87.

KARLIN, ROBERT (1964) *Teaching Reading in High School* New York: The Bobbs-Merrill Company, 140–1, 236.

PRESTON, RALPH C. (1960) 'Sequence in Reading in the Content Areas in Social Studies', in Robinson, Helen M. (ed.) *Sequential Development of Reading Abilities*, Supplementary Educational Monographs no. 90, Chicago: University of Chicago Press, 128.

Reading—Grades 7-8-9. A Teacher's Guide to Curriculum Planning (1957–58) Board of Education of the City of New York Curriculum Bulletin, series no. 11.

Reading in Secondary Schools (1965) The University of the State of New York, Albany, New York: The State Education Department, Bureau of Secondary Curriculum Development, 44–7.

ROBINSON, FRANCIS P. (1961) *Effective Study* New York: Harper and Row.

ROBINSON, H. ALAN, TAYLOR, STANFORD E. and FRACKENPOHL, HELEN (1962) *Teacher's Guide EDL Study Skills Library* Huntington, New York: Educational Developmental Laboratories, 4–5.

ROBINSON, H. ALAN (1965) 'Reading Skills Employed in Solving Social Studies Problems', *The Reading Teacher*, January 1965, 263–9.

RUSSELL, DAVID H. (1961) *Children Learn to Read* New York: Ginn and Co., 339.

SMITH, NILA BANTON (1949) 'The Development of Basic Reading Techniques', *A Report of the Fifth Annual Conference on Reading* University of Pittsburgh, 46–60.

SMITH, NILA BANTON (1963) *Reading Instruction for Today's Children* Englewood Cliffs, N.J.: Prentice-Hall, 312, 348–9.

SPACHE, GEORGE D. (1963) *Toward Better Reading* Champaign, Illinois: Garrard Publishing Company, 273–5, 334–7.

STRANG, RUTH, MCCULLOUGH, CONSTANCE M. and TRAXLER, ARTHUR E. (1961) *The Improvement of Reading* New York: McGraw-Hill, 142–56.

The Teaching of Reading (1963) The University of the State of New York, The State Education Department, Bureau of Elementary Curriculum Development, Albany, New York, 58–9.

WHIPPLE, GERTRUDE (1960) 'Sequence in Reading in the Content Areas', in Robinson, Helen M. (ed.) *Sequential Development of Reading Abilities*, Supplementary Educational Monographs no. 90, Chicago: University of Chicago Press.

1 : 5   The study skills in mathematics

Morton Botel

Over the past five years I have had the good fortune to work with a group of five mathematicians in the development of a program to improve the teaching and learning of mathematics for elementary school pupils.

Much of our attention has focused on approaches which improve the ability of pupils to study and to think.

The four major math study skills which we have identified and for which we have developed new or improved approaches are: 1) skill in relating mathematical statements to real world situations;   2) skill in dealing with open-ended problems;   3) skill in exploring and discovering patterns and in formulating the rule of formation;   and 4) skill in relating mathematical statements to physical models and representations.

In this paper only the first two problems will be explored. (Further development of these ideas can be found in *Math Workshop*, published by Encyclopedia Britannica Press, Chicago, Illinois.)

Skill in relating mathematical statements to real world situations

Over the years, 'story problems' or 'word problems' have been a source of vexation to many teachers of arithmetic, to many children—and to many parents. This activity, which properly seeks to relate the abstractions of mathematics to the world of events, often ends without a sense of accomplishment for anyone.

Such story or word problems are usually reserved for the end of a development, as a sort of test or exercise of the pupil's ability to "apply" an acquired knowledge of arithmetic.

BOTEL, MORTON (1965) 'The study skills in mathematics', in Figurel, J. Allen (ed.) *Reading and Inquiry* Newark, Delaware: International Reading Association, 88–92.

Headline stories

When we notice a pattern repeating itself in the limited world around us—the world we can manipulate—we often use an expression in the language of arithmetic that points to that pattern, such as: $2+3=5$.

At this point we ought to direct children's attention to an application of this idea to the wide world of fact and fancy that they live in.

'Suppose this is a headline:'

$$\boxed{2+3=5}$$

'Tell a story that might fit such a title or headline', the teacher urges.

'There are five children in our family, two boys and three girls.'

'Fine. Who has another story that would fit?' the teacher asks.

'I have three cookies out of the five I started with. I ate two of them.'

'It's the second of December and my birthday is on the fifth. My birthday is in three days.'

Each of these situations has within it the conditions we point to in the headline. Each of the story-tellers reveals that he is beginning to grasp the relationship between arithmetic and the real world.

The headline story is a handy device for eliciting such examples. Box in the mathematical expression and ask for fitting stories. Here are samples that are suitable at different levels of development:

$7-3=$	$19+\ =35$	$8+\ -22=10$
$\times 10=70$	$\frac{1}{2}\times 314=$	$4=15\div\ +1$

Thought starting devices

Pupils may begin with examples that are on the dull side, such as, 'There are 9 boys and 5 girls, or 14 altogether.' Or, if a child prefers the original question form, he might change the story to, 'There were 9 boys and some girls. There were 14 in all. How many were girls?' One way to help break children loose from parroting typical word problems is to write several beginning sentences or phrases on the board as 'thought starters'. For example:

$$9+5=14$$

a   'Harry and Jack captured some men from Mars . . .'
b   'Alice met the Mad Hatter . . .'
c   'When the Pilgrims landed . . .'
d   'Mary is very fond of . . .'
e   'The telephone rang . . .'

Here is another thought-starter device teachers have found helpful. The children are asked to fill in a chart with numbers in two columns and words in a third. Completed, the chart might look like this:

A	B	C
7	baseball game	(25)
(18)	a party	15
5	astronauts	6
125	(a trip)	9
60	setting a table	40

'Select one item out of each column and weave them together in a brief story. Then write an appropriate headline in the language of arithmetic.'
Here is a sample response:

$$25-18=7$$

'After we had gone 18 miles on the way to the lake, we stopped for lunch. Since our house is 25 miles from the lake, we had 7 miles to go.'

As children exercise their ability to *make up stories to fit headlines*, they begin to understand what goes on in the minds of others who make up *story problems*. The mysteries disappear. Once they can make up stories, children gain confidence that they can reverse the process. They begin to understand the relation between life situations and mathematical sentences. Teachers who have used this approach find pupils become enthusiastic about expressing a creativeness they never associated with arithmetic.

The reading problem

Very often, *word problems* present a difficulty because the child's reading ability is not yet sufficiently developed. He struggles with reading the words; he is unsure; he is puzzled. In such a state of mind, he is not prepared to extract a mathematical problem from a set of words that are already a *reading problem*. The method we have been developing lays bare the connection between a mathematical sentence expressed in symbols and a life situation expressed in words. A pupil need not read at all to gain confidence in this area. Then when he is confronted with a situation in which his first task is to decipher the written language, he is better equipped to find the cues he needs to translate the situation into a mathematical statement. He has tackled two very different problems—but he has tackled them one at a time.

Changing the conditions

Further interest in the problem can be created by posing such questions as: 'If we changed the story, how would we reflect the change in the headline? If we changed the headline, what changes would be required in the story?'

Emphasis on the total situation

Note that in this approach the usual emphasis has been taken away from 'the answer'. The situation turns on the *mathematical headline*, or statement, and pupils create their own applications. The answer-oriented approach no longer preoccupies the attention of children and we see clearly ourselves that it wasn't only the answer we wanted—it was the whole mathematical statement.

Skill in dealing with open-ended problems

In the past, word problems in arithmetic represented the total fare of problem solving experience. And we have already noted the staleness of the usual approach and have suggested ways of improving the connection between mathematical sentences and the real world.

We have further developed more interesting 'open-ended' or 'discovery' problems which primary grade pupils can tackle and which promote study skills and thinking ability. Many such activities follow under two headings: *a*) Short open-ended problems, *b*) Situations in which conditions can be investigated from many angles. In each of these situations, the answers are 'less than obvious' and require real thinking and planning. Each calls for a series of responses best recorded in a table of some sort so that patterns can be noted more easily.

Here are examples of these kinds of problems:

a   *Short open-ended problems*

    i   Dan had 6c. If he spent —c, then he has —c left. (Make a chart.)

   ii   There are 7 days in a week. (Pupils extend the story.)

  iii   Mary and Bill each had the same number of books. Draw a sketch to fit.

  iv   Harry had more blocks than John. Draw a sketch to fit.

   v   How many different combinations of coins amount to 18c?

  vi   Katie is 3 years older than Lou. If Katie is —, then Lou is —.

 vii   How many ways can you make 25c with an even number of coins? (An odd number?)

viii   In how many ways can we arrange 12 cans in columns and rows?

  ix   I have coins worth 50c in my pocket. What can you say?

   x   I gave the clerk a quarter. He gave me two coins as change. What can you say?

  xi   In how many ways can you make this sentence true using one odd and one even number: $- + - = 10$.

 xii   Make up a time-saver chart for the movie cashier. Admission prices are 35c for children, $1.25 for adults.

xiii   Mother had three bills, one each for $1.00, $5.00, and $10.00 and three coins, one each for 10c, 25c, and 50c. She gave Jill one of the bills and one of the coins. How many possible combinations could Jill get? How much is each combination worth?

b   *Situations in which conditions can be investigated from many angles*

A different kind of open-ended problem is initiated by a sale situation—one in which pencils cost 5c each and pads of paper cost 9c each. The notice that limits a customer to not more than 6 of each introduces an unusual aspect that multiplies the interesting questions that can be asked.

'If Bill spent 45c, can you be sure that he bought 5 pads of paper?'

'No', Sarah argues, 'he could have bought 9 pencils at 5c each. That's 45c.' But after a moment's thought about the problem Sarah realizes that such a purchase is a violation of the terms of the sale which state: 'Not more than 6 of any item to a customer.'

Such situations can be varied at will, and the conditions can be investigated:

SALE

Small	Large
Erasers	Erasers
2c	3c

Limit: 2 of each to a customer

The results of these conditions can eventually be revealed rather easily in the following chart:

Notice that each possible purchase is unique. Had the limit been '3 of each to a customer', the situation changes: a purchase of 6c might consist of 3 small erasers or 2 large ones.

		Small Erasers @ 2¢		
		0	1	2
	0	x	2c	4c
Large	1	3c	5c	7c
@ 3c	2	6c	8c	10c

What happens if the limit of '2 of each to a customer' applies only to small erasers? Now, 9 large erasers and 1 small eraser would cost 29c. How else could 29c be spent? (There is no other way.)

Next, put back the limit of '2 each' on large erasers and lift it on the small erasers. Now, 9 small erasers and 2 large erasers would cost 24c, but so would 12 small erasers and no large ones.

A more involved sale:

SALE

| Pencils | Erasers | Pencil Boxes |
| 5c | 4c | 25c |

Limit: 4 of each to a customer

These conditions are carefully selected, since the amount of any purchase will reveal the exact items included. For example:

32c: 4 pencils and 3 erasers
33c: 1 pencil box and 2 erasers
36c: 4 pencils and 4 erasers

This kind of problem can be adapted in most grades simply by varying the number and price of the items.

Some children might make up their own sale conditions and explore the results of setting various limits on the number of items a customer may purchase. They will find surprises in store for them.

1:6   Reading study skills: math and science

Leo Fay

As an introduction to this topic it would be well to remind ourselves of the meaning of study. A sixth grader turning to his dictionary would discover that study was 'one's own effort to learn by reading or thinking'. This definition suggests that the good student develops control not only of study techniques but also of himself. He must learn to use his time wisely, start a task without delay and complete it although the task may be very demanding. In the process of developing mastery of self through study, the student also gains insight into his own strength and weaknesses. However, while study involves these important personal aspects, the concern of this discussion is with more specific applications of the problems of reading study skills in the areas of math and science.

Reading study skills in mathematics

The job analysis technique used widely in business and industry can be applied profitably to the function of the reading study skills in these two curriculum areas. The two major tasks in mathematics for the young reader are to develop skills in computation and problem solving. Each task requires mastery of certain reading study techniques.

With regard to computation the child must learn to react to the numerals meaningfully, must recognize the symbols that indicate the process to be used, and must understand the form within which the problem is presented. The first two of these tasks are well mastered by most elementary children. The third task, unfortunately, is often the source of confusion or error. Simply changing a multiplication problem from the conventional two-by-two block model $\times \frac{23}{46}$ to a less conventional form such as 23 times 46 $=$ __

FAY, LEO (1965) 'Reading study skills: math and science', in Figurel, J. Allen (ed.) *Reading and Inquiry* Newark, Delaware: International Reading Association, 92–4.

results in a significant increase in the percentage of error among sixth grade pupils. Obviously, a reading study skill for this phase of mathematics is to be able to react intelligently to a computational problem regardless of its form.

It is in the problem-solving phase of mathematics, however, that the reading study skills have their major applications at both a general level of study procedure and a more specific level involving vocabulary, comprehension and interpretation skills.

At the general level the student may use an adaptation of the widely-taught SQ3R procedure. The problem should be read fairly rapidly as a preview to arrive at a general understanding of the problem. Following this reading the student should ask himself the question, 'What is the problem?' or 'What is the problem trying to find out?' In reaction to this question the student should be encouraged to restate the problem in his own words or, if possible, attempt to visualize the problem with a simple drawing. When the student is satisfied that he understands the problem, he should carefully reread it to identify the facts and their relationships. The outcome of this second reading should include determining the process or processes to be used in solving the problem. Once this has been established, the student is ready to proceed with his computation and checking. In summary, the reading study procedure in problem solving is to survey, question, read, question, compute, question (check).

This SQRQCQ procedure may be applied to the following problem:

> Dan and Wendie bought their mother a pair of earrings for her birthday. The earrings were on sale for $1.50 off the regular price. If Dan and Wendie each paid $2.25, what was the regular price for the earrings?
> S—The problem is read rapidly to determine its nature.
> Q— What is the problem? To determine the total presale price of the earrings.
> R—Reread for details and interrelationships—$1.50 off of the regular price; two children; each paid $2.25.
> Q—What process should be used? To find the cost, add the various amounts.
> C—Carry out the computation.
> Q—Is the answer correct? Check the computation against the problem facts and the basic arithmetic facts.

To apply this general study procedure successfully a twofold foundation is needed. The first is mathematical. The student must understand the number system and know the basic arithmetic facts. The second is a vocabulary foundation that provides the basis for quantitative reasoning and the clues for the use of mathematical processes. Some of these terms are simple labels (one, seven), others indicate processes (add, divide), still others quantitative relationships (ratio, diminish, average). Still other common terms serve as clue terms in verbal problems (how much more, less than, share equally, how much change). Symbols and abbreviations also add to the complexity of the vocabulary foundation.

Building upon the mathematical and language foundations, problem solving demands the application of a range of comprehension and critical reading skills. At the general comprehension level, the child needs to obtain the literal meaning of what he reads. In addition, specific comprehension skills such as reading to gain a general impression, to follow a sequence of events, to note detail and to follow directions have application in different problem-solving situations.

As he reads, the student must also exercise judgment in various ways. He must judge the relevance of particular facts in relation to the overall problem and the reasonableness of the answer. He must generalize a process from the details presented and at times visualize a problem situation from a group of facts.

Reading study skills in science

Developing the reading study skills in science parallels the outline in mathematics. A general study procedure makes it possible for the student to systematize his study and make efficient use of his time. Spache's variation of the SQ3R procedure is especially appropriate with science content. The steps Spache suggests are:

Preview—Rapid skimming of the total selection.

Question—In terms of the study purposes raise questions to guide the careful reading to follow.

Read—Read the selection keeping the questions in mind.

Summarize—Organize and summarize information gained.

Test—Check your summary against the selection.

As in mathematics, the successful application of a study procedure depends upon certain foundations and upon specific comprehension and study skills. The first foundation relates to science. The student must understand the objectivity of science and the scientific method built upon that objectivity. For example, the student needs to understand the scientist's procedure of defining a problem, developing a hypothesis for the solution of the problem and subjecting the hypothesis to rigorous testing. Biographies of scientists are useful for developing this understanding.

A second foundation is vocabulary where in addition to a vast and rapidly-growing technical vocabulary the child is faced with symbolic language and abbreviations. To be sure, he has encountered abbreviations before, but in science abbreviations often stand for far more than a shortened form of a word. For example, the symbol 'Fe' is more than the abbreviation for the word 'iron' if the child is to understand its use in a chemical formula. The symbol includes atomic weight, valence and the relationship of iron to other elements. The very size of science technical vocabulary has raised the issue as to whether science material for children should avoid using technical terms. This is neither desirable nor possible. One of the characteristics of science writing is clarity and preciseness which makes the use of technical terms essential. Part of the task of reading science content is to build a basic technical vocabulary.

Science content reading also demands specialized applications of various comprehension, interpretation and study skills. The reading of formulas, charts, and graphs is especially important. The young researcher will need to develop skills for locating information. He needs to know which source materials to use for reliable information and which key words are used for classifying scientific information. In no other area is the careful following of directions more critical than in science. Significant facts must be determined and factual material must be organized into larger, meaningful wholes as a basis for the inductive and deductive reasoning used in arriving at understandings and applying generalizations to new situations.

The above analysis leads to an obvious conclusion. To develop superior problem solvers in mathematics and science, the elementary teacher must guide children in applying reading study skills as well as teach the multiplication tables and conduct simple science experiments.

1:7   Half a million books

With the co-operation of the LEA concerned, a survey was undertaken in 1970 to assess the quantity and quality of books being used in the 96 primary schools of one division of an English county. The information on which the final document was based was obtained partly from answers to a questionnaire and partly from visits which were made by HMIs to each of the schools involved.

The overall book policy of a primary school is determined by decisions about the purpose of reading and the way books are to be used. Is it merely to receive information or to acquire a socially acceptable habit? Is it to promote language skills essential to the development of thought? Does it have a spiritual value enabling the imagination to expand and flower? Is there a therapeutic value in role playing which encourages even small children to identify themselves with the characters in simple stories?

Provision of books

The schools which co-operated in this survey contained 17,933 children and 567,373 books, a ratio of 32 books per child—a figure very close to the 30 books per child which was suggested as reasonable in discussion with teachers and librarians before the survey was launched. The distribution of these books, both between schools and between types of books, showed however a wide variation from the norm. The books were divided into three categories as shown in the table below:

TABLE I

All pupils		Books	Books per pupil
17,933	Library	178,966	17
	Readers	70,571	6
	Text books	192,033	18

'Half a million books' (1971) *Trends in Education*, 24, 28–34.

The number of text books was surprising and the average in that category conceals the provision of 52 text books per child in one school and over 30 in ten other schools. In contrast, two schools provided only two text books per child, supplementing these with work cards. Needless to say, both these schools made extensive use of their libraries.

When the children were divided between those in the junior schools or departments and those in infant schools or departments, the figures again hide the variation of provision between individual schools and between types of book.

TABLE 2

	Pupils	Books	Books per pupil
Juniors	10,627	441,570	41.5
Infants	7,306	125,803	17

In the infant schools and departments, the figure of 17 books per child is an average concealing a spread from 5 to 54. The overall figures for the different types of book seemed reasonably balanced but, again, concealed extraordinary local variations. However, if the number of children in this age range who could not read could be taken into account, the ratio would presumably be better for those who could. Also, in many infant schools, the reading of 'readers' was being abandoned in favour of the reading of books. Some book-corners were outstanding in both selection and presentation. The realization that very young readers appreciate a 'proper book' early on, rather than a succession of sets of little books, was also apparent in some schools. But in many the number of readers was somewhat depressing; it appears to be self-defeating to teach reading in the infant departments to enable children to read 'readers', whose quality in respect of such things as story line, development of character and vocabulary, is often inferior to that of the many good children's books now available.

Quality of books

If numbers were the only yardstick there would be little else to say than that a more equitable distribution of the total book stock available in the schools would be an acceptable solution. Such a simple criterion is clearly inadequate and ignores the question of what is the *right* book. One head suggested that the purpose of a junior school library should be to enable children 'to seek, search, select and record in a variety of ways'. If such a view is held, then the right book is an information book and this would help to explain the make-up of the total number of library books in these junior schools. Information books numbered 102,646, fiction 76,320. The pressures are all in favour of building up the non-fictional element, one contributing factor apparently being the inclination of schools, influenced by catalogues and advertisements, to acquire all the titles of series or sets. That the quality and suitability of the contents may vary from title to title is often hidden until too late, or, possibly, never noticed.

Excluding the provision made by the Schools Library Service of the County, most school collections of fiction presented a sorry sight. A rational and well-publicised procedure for writing-off obsolete and shabby stock would be advantageous. Many head teachers had not realised this was possible. Others retained old books in the belief that they might come in useful in the future. The acceptance of unwanted old books from friends, parents and children, to build up libraries appeared to have contributed to this dilapidated stock. There was little evidence that books acquired in this way were worth shelf-space.

In most schools the good examples of children's literature were dated. John Buchan, Arthur Ransome and A. A. Milne were to be seen on the shelves as they would have been in a good junior school collection 30 years ago. Some teachers showed little familiarity with contemporary children's literature. The general quality certainly seemed to improve when one teacher had been given the encouragement and opportunity to develop a special interest in books for children.

The Schools Library Service

A vast amount of help has been provided by this comparatively short-staffed service which has entirely merited the praise of both heads and teachers. A stock of some 300,000 books, of which 225,000 are on loan at any given time, is organized by four librarians and three assistants and the organization is geared to making their stock available to people who want to use it.

Three travelling collections are provided, enabling schools to borrow books at the rate of one-and-a-half volumes per child, for a six-month period. The vans are accompanied by a professional librarian who will give advice on selection. Advice is also freely available on housing and shelving as well as help with basic cataloguing.

A new-book supply service with a minimum of form-filling is used by some 50 schools. The books, provided from the largest selection of children's books in the county, have all been processed and all the fiction titles have been selected after reading and discussion.

These two important services help to supply a constant stream of new and exciting books. Some 90 per cent of the worthwhile fiction seen in the schools was on loan from the county, though this formed only about a quarter of the fiction stock.

In addition, the service provides study boxes of 20 to 30 titles on specific subjects. The list of topics has been compiled in direct response to requests from the teachers who can generally get a box within 14 days. There are 2,300 of these boxes though many of the more popular topics are duplicated. The contents of the boxes are revised as and when volumes become worn or new and relevant titles are published. Every effort is made to include fiction as well as straight information books.

The teachers are full of praise for this service which is nevertheless not without some questionable features. The most disturbing of these may be a tendency for the children's work to be determined by the choice of box rather than by their own interests or by what may arise from the current teaching/learning situation. There may also be a tendency to orientate work towards a known and successful box—and many schools re-order the same box at regular intervals. Where such repetition is felt desirable it would be better to obtain those books for their own collections. Furthermore, this system tends to blind teachers to their school's own resources. This was well illustrated by one class using a study box on 'Elizabethan England' when 15 of the 20 books in the box were on the school's shelves. Resources in this instance were being needlessly duplicated and the children were being denied a relevant opportunity of practice in using a library.

The visits of the vans also perform a vital function in that they are occasions for collecting out-of-date or worn books. The service expects a three-year turn-over of stock and if schools were to adopt the same criterion the half-million books of the title of this account would be decimated.

Administration

In many schools the availability of books was restricted not only when subject to conditions outside the control of the school, such as evening lettings. Ideally the books should be available for use at all times and children allowed to take them home, but where much use is being made of information books these may have to be returned to school each day.

Freedom of use requires organization of issue and return. Once introduced, the normal method of card and pocket can be operated by children. Only 11 schools date-stamped books on issue, yet this is a simple process which children can do themselves. If re-ordering and replacement of popular books and the discarding of unused books are to be efficient, some system of noting which books are borrowed is essential. Wear-and-tear, which most teachers mention as the sure sign of popularity, is by no means a foolproof guide. As one head remarked, 'It is exceedingly difficult to determine whether a book has been borrowed 30 times or been kicked around the cloakroom once'.

The desirability of one teacher being in charge of all the book resources of a school has already been mentioned. In seven schools this task was undertaken by a part-time teacher, with notable results. These teachers really knew the stock, its strengths, weaknesses and usage.

If the argument about central or dispersed collections were to be decided on the evidence assembled during these visits, the decision would seem to favour a centralized system. The best use of books in both infant and junior departments was observed in schools with a central provision. In the infant schools this prevented unnecessary duplication of 'readers' and in the junior departments enabled children, whose reading age varied far more than their chronological age to have a full selection of suitable books. Every teacher ought to be interested in children's books, but a centralized collection and buying policy can and does enable one teacher to develop special expertise. In this context it was noteworthy that the one school with a dispersed collection, but with the enthusiastic interest to compile a central catalogue, was engaged in strenuous efforts to create a central library provision. Books in the classroom should, of course, remain an essential feature of primary school work even when central provision is made.

Another essential feature of a good book policy, observed in a number of the schools, but unfortunately only a minority, was a conscious effort to promote books. Colourful book corners in reception classes, containing well-illustrated books attractively displayed, contrived to set a tone from the beginning. Book corners for older children, with books appropriate to the different age-groups and closely linked with their activities, interests and experience, were in evidence in some schools. Book displays in some central position confined to a given subject or a single author were to be seen in two schools and had stimulated great interest. The effect of these and other devices can only be achieved by an abundant supply of good quality reading material including paperbacks.

Use of books

'To me it is the most important thing we do' said one headmaster when discussing the use of books. Other opinions expressed were, 'Reading is for enjoyment' and 'Books are only worth reading if matched with comprehension cards'. The emphasis on enjoyment is surely well placed because once children enjoy reading they seem quickly able to develop the skill of obtaining information. When too much insistence is placed on the informational aspect, there may be no spur to read unless specific facts are required. There appeared to be general agreement with another head who said 'Children have got to read for fun first'.

It would be difficult to fault the initial procedures adopted to arouse in children a burning desire to read. It was in the next step that differences crept in and were later magnified. This stage was that exemplified by the set reading scheme, often there was only one, followed by supplementary readers. That final stage was all too often paralleled by the traditional use of text books, an approach that assumes that each child's development and interest follow the pattern set by the authors of the series. It was significant that many children knew the number of the book they were reading, few the title. A wide library provision, in a number of cases colour-matched to a reading scheme, enabled some fortunate infants to expand their reading horizontally as well as vertically.

The use of text books and work books noted in over half the junior schools visited, seemed to be inconsistent with modern primary school method. If they are being used as reference material or as reinforcement for previously identified weak points, criticism is disarmed. All too frequently they were being used as the lesson itself and this in unstreamed classes of wide abilities. In only seven schools of those visited were information books being used as they should be as sources of reference for a planned project. In all too many schools they were the project itself. Children were writing about 'Butterflies', aided by a single book entitled 'Butterflies'. Whether they copied or 'put into their own words' was immaterial. It is in this area that the use of books needs the most thought and planning. Another aspect that deserves consideration is the information value of story books. The apt book can give the feel of another age, another place or the point of view of a different race. The county library study boxes attempt to meet this by including relevant fiction with the factual material.

Above all, reading for enjoyment implies first and foremost that the teachers enjoy reading and know about children's books. A positive attitude can be set by the teacher who promotes better books, leading children on by sample or example and always making sure that books are available. It was a matter of concern that children in a number of schools which were following a weekly television programme on named books were unable to obtain those books at the relevant source—the school. There is no virtue in whetting appetites if good food is not readily available.

Purchase and replacement

Thirty-four of the schools visited spent more on library books than on text books, and of these 17 spent more than the average £1 per head on books from capitation allowances. The highest expenditure per head, excluding new or reorganized schools obtaining special grants, was £1.95 and all of this had been spent on text books. The lowest expenditure per head was 15p and all of this was also spent on text books.

So far as could be ascertained, no school had a regular policy of book replacements; worn-out stock might be replaced. A new set of 'readers', a new set of text books, could be ordered after considerable discussion. New mathematics and decimalization were hastening replacement in that subject. It was interesting to note that new schools with no sets of text books to replace were ordering very few. Work cards, a more economic way of providing set exercises, had been bought or made. Information books had replaced texts in all other subjects.

Planning for the future

The book resources are an area in which large or small schools ought to be able to establish equality. If, as was seen during this enquiry, text books are progressively to be replaced by information books and if, as it urged, reading for enjoyment is promoted, book collections should be more uniform in size. This would give the child reader a better selection whether he or she went to a small or a large school.

Thinking in terms of the actual numbers of books already in schools, that is 32 to a pupil, a first step towards redistribution might well be to set a maximum of 10 text books and 10 readers per child, and to aim at a library provision of 10 books per child. Progressively the number of text books and readers could be reduced to 3 or 4 per child and the number of library books increased. Once this stage had been reached school libraries would be running at the 10,000 mark for a middle school of 480 and expenditure would be fully committed to maintaining this, or a somewhat smaller collection in a serviceable and up-to-date condition. It is worth stressing that 10,000 books need 1,000 feet or 300 metres of shelving. Lest these figures appear too idealistic, four junior departments in this area, all with good libraries, are providing 160, 225, 267 and 327 children with 4,658, 3,013, 4,897 and 5,648 library books respectively.

First schools may well be much smaller. Some are planned to hold only 40 or 60 children. Here provision must be on a much more lavish scale per head than in the larger schools. There is an argument for a great concentration of the County Loan Service in those areas which are generally further removed from public libraries. It is at least arguable that no school should have a book stock of less than 2,000 volumes or the number of children multiplied by 30, whichever is the larger figure. New schools and smaller schools tend to suffer in this respect and here again County Loan and administrative action could be used to level out inequalities.

In first schools there appeared to be two main bodies of opinion about reading. The majority of teachers held that they must keep track of children's progress and that to do this they must ensure that their pupils completed a given scheme, plus supplementaries, before they were allowed to venture further. The minority view, lately reinforced by the development of *Breakthrough to Literacy*, argues that once children have reached a reasonable degree of fluency they should choose their own reading material from the school or class library. There is a half-way position which insists on children completing the scheme but allows them to have a library book and sometimes differentiates between periods of time available for class readers and for library books.

The movement appears to be towards the minority view and this will influence the growth of library provision. Apart from mathematics text books, there is a virtual disappearance of text books in the more modern infant schools and it is even possible that in time work cards will supply all the needs previously satisfied by text books.

In terms of numbers projected, first schools of 160 would have 4,800 books, roughly divided between the library and the reading schemes. In time and with good organization this might be split—3,200 in the library and 1,600 shared between text books and readers. That this too is not idealistic is shown by one or two sample figures from schools where the reading provision was good. One with 193 children had 4,781 books, 3,274 in the library. Another with 182 children had 4,222 books, 2,550 in the library and no text books. It is worth noting in passing that the standard of book provision in infant schools tended to be considerably better than that of the infant departments of all-through schools. Reading was a subject of relatively greater importance at this stage, and it appeared to have the greatest care, thought and provision.

Libraries of the size suggested above, and the word library is still being used to mean no more than a collection of books, will patently need some-one with time, enthusiasm and some degree of expertise to organize them. Teachers will need to be taught and helped to use them properly. Far too many books were being used as copying material disguised by terms such as 'topic' or 'project'.

Ideas suggested by teachers during the survey would combine to pro-duce the following developments in a school:

1 Each teacher would be reading at least one new children's book a month.
2 No book would go into the school library without a teacher having read it.
3 Schools would join library associations.
4 Books about children's books would be available in every staff room.

Regular interchange of book information between teachers should be possible within and between schools.

Once these ideas are common practice there would be better books in our schools and their use would be substantially improved.

1 : 8   Published reading schemes[1]

Elizabeth J. Goodacre

In a recent article in *Educational Research* (Southgate, 1968) on the factors to be studied when considering children's reading progress, the 'materials' category was sub-divided into basic reading schemes, library corner books, printed charts, cards and apparatus, home-made and hand-written materials. The present article considers in some detail one of these subdivisions, the published basic reading scheme.

Several questions can be asked about this particular type of reading material. What is a basic reading scheme, or in American terminology a 'basal reading series'? What is its aim and scope? Do publishers produce a range of schemes, or are schemes broadly similar in their approach? To what extent are they based on the findings of reading research?

One can then turn to the teachers for whom they are intended. The Plowden Report (1967), in discussing teaching children to read, stated: 'Instead of relying on one's reading scheme, many teachers use a range of

1   The writer carried out   1) a postal survey of 71 educational publishers producing books for the primary age range. Publishers were asked whether they produced reading materials or apparatus, and in certain cases where publishers produced a reading scheme, a follow-up letter was sent asking for further information about date of publication, type of approach, etc.;   2) a postal survey of primary teachers on the subject of teaching reading. Two samples were used—Sample A consisted of 27 infant-only schools in an industrial city structured to represent the distribution of schools in three social areas, suburban, upper and lower working class (96 per cent co-operation); Sample B was a one-in-three sample of infant-only and junior mixed and infant schools in one of the home counties (61 per cent co-operation). Heads and all their staff completed questionnaires in sample A; heads, reception class teachers and one other infant teacher in sample B. Completed questionnaires were returned by 350 teachers.

Acknowledgement

The writer would like gratefully to acknowledge the assistance she received from the Computer Centre at Enfield College of Technology. She is greatly in debt to the heads and their staff who so kindly assisted her with her survey during 1968.

GOODACRE, ELIZABETH J. (1969) 'Published reading schemes', *Educational Research*, **12**, *i*, 30–5.

schemes with different characteristics, selecting carefully for each child: some schemes emphasize sight reading, others phonics; some consist of short books, with a very slow build-up of vocabulary, and suit children who need quick success; other schemes help children who are able to advance rapidly and to discard primers.' Is this observation justified? Do teachers in this country use a single scheme or several? If they use several schemes, are the most popular schemes very different in approach? What is the function of the published reading scheme in most infant classrooms?

Studies such as those by Austin and Morrison (1963), Barton and Wilder (1964) and Chall (1967), provide useful information about trends in the use of reading schemes in the American setting. In this country there has been only limited research on this subject. However, reports by Morris (1959), and Goodacre (1967), and findings from two surveys carried out by the writer during the past year do provide answers to some of the questions posed.

The basic reading scheme

A 'total' reading programme

In her book *Learning to Read—The Great Debate*, Chall describes a basic reading scheme as an attempt by publishers to give teachers and pupils a 'total reading program' embodying a system of teaching reading (in the teachers' manuals), a collection of stories and selections for pupils to read (the readers), and exercises for additional practice (the workbooks). She describes in some detail the range and scope of a 'typical' scheme. A survey of British publishers showed a lack of consensus among publishers as to what constituted a reading scheme. For analysis purposes, the writer eventually defined a reading scheme as any series, scheme or programme which consisted of graded readers and *additional* material—either supplementary books, workbooks, apparatus, or a teacher's manual. (Series consisting solely of a set of graded readers, although termed a 'scheme' by publishers, were not included in the following analysis.)

Using this definition, it was found that 22 firms produced 34 schemes (1–4 schemes per firm). An analysis of the schemes showed that the number of readers in a scheme varied from three to twelve; 85 per cent of the schemes included supplementary or platform readers (often with the same controlled vocabulary as the main reader or basic book); twelve per cent had extension readers (books extending the scheme 'upwards', usually no control of vocabulary); 65 per cent had a manual (varying from 'notes for the teacher'—booklet size—to a detailed volume providing guidance to the teacher); 53 per cent teacher's apparatus, 53 per cent children's apparatus; 59 per cent workbook(s); twelve per cent picture dictionaries (usually based on vocabulary of the scheme); 32 per cent pre-readers; nine per cent tests (word recognition using words of scheme, not standardized). Taking Chall's definition of a scheme (readers, manual and workbooks), twelve schemes could be described as 'total reading programs' although only six of these corresponded to the 'typical' scheme described by Chall. (Two of the latter group were English adaptations of American schemes.)

After reviewing the popular basic reading schemes of the previous decade, Chall concluded that children using these books were taught by a sight or word method. The beginning book started the child off on learning to read words and throughout the rest of the scheme words were 'pre-taught'. The names and sounds of the letters were taught but they received comparatively less emphasis, the main aim being to build up a sight vocabulary of meaningful words which the pupil would eventually use to arrive inductively at generalizations and rules about phonics. That is, most schemes were characterized by an analytic rather than a synthetic approach. To provide 'interesting' reading matter, publishers and writers of the schemes more often than not used the commonest words in the language, which incidentally were often the most irregularly spelled words. Therefore by the time children reached the phonic stage in the scheme, they were more than likely to have acquired the idea that letter-sound correspondences were highly irregular and inconsistent.

Austin and Morrison (1963) reported that those who subscribed to the concept of the basic reading scheme believed that such schemes were a means of ensuring that all the reading skills were developed in sequence and that only through this type of programme could vocabulary control be assured. Chall's view, however, was that such schemes in practice were not total programmes in which all aspects of reading were introduced. It was her opinion that only scant attention was paid to the teaching of phonics and that what was taught was often not applied. (She uses phonics in the sense that children learn that printed symbols have speech equivalents.) 'Nor do the basals alert the child to apply the phonic elements previously taught to his reading of stories. Generally speaking, until third grade the phonics lessons seem almost an afterthought.' Further, although vocabulary may be controlled (i.e. the number of different words used is known), this does not mean that the number of different *letter-meanings* is controlled, as Diack (1960) has pointed out. Also, where phonic word lists are included and phonic 'rules' covered there appears to be little consensus as to the grading of generalizations and the level at which they are introduced. Even in a well-known attempt to maintain a consistent sound-symbol relationship such as i.t.a., the consistency is improved if 'high frequency' words are omitted (Birnie, 1968).

Criteria for selecting materials

Olsen (1968) has reported that he and his co-workers at Wayne State University have identified more than two hundred principles that could be used in selecting materials. They learned that a great many of the principles were seldom used as criteria either because they were *not widely known* (e.g. symbol–sound correspondence as distinct from formal, systematic phonic instruction; dialect differences; deliberate stimulation of children to read widely outside school hours) or *contradictory*. As an example of the latter, he cites the principle that reading materials should contain a carefully controlled vocabulary. Materials based on this idea present a limited number of words; the words are repeated many times to assist pupils to build a functional stock of sight words. To expect the content of such materials to have a high literary quality is therefore not feasible. The two principles are incompatible.

Barton and Wilder (1964) briefly examined the basic reading materials being used by the teachers in their study and came to the conclusion that they had remained substantially unchanged since the 1930's. In fact, with the possible exception of technical laboratory studies of contrast between print and background and illumination, reading research appeared to have had no effect on basic reading schemes for the past 30 years. Vocabulary loading continued to decrease, word repetitions were frequent, and almost all characters in the books were children. Chall also queried this emphasis on rigid vocabulary control, suggesting that this control was much stricter than any research evidence had justified.[2]

2 In this context it is interesting to consider the maximum number of repetitions for words in the Introductory Book of two schemes being used in infant classrooms in this country. Scheme A) published 1949–1967 used in 7 per cent of infant-only classrooms, 1968, maximum number of repetitions =23; Scheme B) published 1962 used in 42 per cent of infant-only classroom=37. Gates once estimated the number of repetitions per word that children of different degrees of brightness would need to obtain a basic reading vocabulary, e.g. children with IQ 120–129=20 repetitions; IQ 60–69=55. It should be noted that the maximum number of repetitions quoted above applies only to the Introductory Book; the same words would also be met in supplementary books, apparatus, etc.

A brief examination of the schemes being published in this country in 1968 indicated that a number of them follow the American pattern of the late fifties, being based on vocabulary control, use of 'meaningful' words, the introduction of phonics comparatively late in the scheme, emphasis on pictorial clues, and reading for meaning from the beginning. Chall comparing the 1956 and 1962 editions of the most popular conventional basic schemes detected that some changes had taken place. The 1962 edition of one of the schemes studied showed some loosening of vocabulary control, an earlier and heavier emphasis on sound–symbol relationships, and a reduction in the amount of non-reading follow-up activities. Changes are not noticeable in the conventional British schemes, nor with one exception, do recent new schemes seem to differ drastically from the conventional pattern. There seems to be a limited range of schemes available from which teachers can choose. Publishers seem to have concentrated upon basing their schemes on only one or perhaps two principles and, in some cases, to have carried these to excess as a means of ensuring success, e.g. control of vocabulary. They appear to be unacquainted with the less widely known or obscure principles of the type propounded by Olsen.

Teachers' use of published schemes

Austin and Morrison (1963) after carrying out their survey of the content and conduct of reading instruction in all school systems in the larger cities and counties in the United States concluded: 'Despite discordant views over its value, the basal reader is unquestionably the predominant tool of instruction in most of the school systems sampled. In fact, for many teachers it would be unthinkable and impossible to teach without them.' They reported that 64 per cent of their respondents indicated that they relied 'predominantly' or 'exclusively' on a *single* basal series, while 31 per cent indicated that a number of series were used. After surveying over 15,000 teachers at the primary level, Barton and Wilder (1964) concluded that reading instruction in almost all schools started from a similar basis, 98 per cent of teachers instructing beginners using basic schemes on 'all or most days of the year'. Writing three years later, Chall endorsed this view: 'for all practical purposes American reading instruction is basal-series reading instruction'.

Are the same trends apparent in this country? Are teachers dependent on a single scheme?

Dr Joyce Morris reported (1959) that Kent schools tended to use one main reading series supported by other readers, the most popular in 1954 being *Happy Venture, Janet and John* and *Beacon*. The NFER 'Teaching Beginners to Read' reports (Goodacre, 1967, 1968) included evidence based on the teachers' answers to written questionnaires which suggested that in the late fifties nearly all London infant schools (96 per cent) were using published reading schemes, and that four out of five said they used a single scheme.[3]

Despite the fact that the teachers in that survey stated that the main considerations dictating their choice of teaching methods were their pupils' individual needs and social background, two out of three schools were very dependent upon the same particular scheme—*Janet and John*. This is an English adaptation of an American scheme published and revised 1949–1967. It is characterized by strict vocabulary control and limited narrative development and the use of middle-class characters in a some-what vaguely defined social setting. The scheme has a detailed manual, workbooks, a range of supplementary material and apparatus using the same vocabulary limitations. In its scope it closely resembles the type of 'typical' scheme described by Chall. In regard to content and characters, it presents a world of round-faced, pink-cheeked children who live in nice houses and are well-behaved. Anger or sorrow, dirt or suffering rarely if ever obtrude into this world. As the introductory note to Book One says 'the subject matter . . . is always in good taste'. In present day Britain, a significant proportion of the population belong to minority groups (racial, national or religious) yet no mention is made of minority groups except as something exotic—strange creatures, who live a long way from this country.[4]

One of the aims of the survey of teachers carried out by the writer last year was to find out whether trends in the teaching of reading had altered since the NFER London inquiry. The 1968 survey findings suggested that most schools were using several schemes rather than a single scheme; e.g. *Mean number of schemes per school—*

---

3 In the NFER follow-up study, it was found that most of the schools selected for the intensive study were, in fact, using three or four schemes in the classroom despite their replying 'one scheme' in the initial survey questionnaire. It would probably be safe to say, however, that the majority of London infant teachers felt themselves to be highly dependent upon one scheme.

4 The writer is grateful to Mr I. Stewart for allowing her to see an unpublished study of his which deals with racial bias in infant school reading schemes (personal correspondence, May 1969).

Infant-only schools:
  London (1959)[5]=1·1 (N50); Home county (1968)=3·8 (N26); Midland city (1968)=3·2 (N26).
Different social areas:
  London (1959)[5] middle class=1·1 (N30); upper working class=1·3 (N29); lower working class=1·2 (N37).
  Midland city (1968) middle class=4·8 (N8); upper working class=2·6 (N9); lower working class=2·6 (N9).

Combining the figures from the infant-only Home County and Midland city schools (N52), the following schemes proved to be the most popular:[6] *Janet and John* published by Nisbet (1949–67)=81 per cent of schools (70 per cent); *Happy Venture* published by Oliver and Boyd (1939, 1958)=38 per cent (less than ten per cent); *Happy Trio* by Wheaton/Pergamon (1962)=37 per cent (not published)[7]; *Ladybird* by Wills and Hepworth= 37 per cent (not published)[8]; *Gay Way* published by Macmillan (1950– 1960)=33 per cent (less than ten per cent); *Beacon* published by Ginn (1922–1964)=31 per cent (less than ten per cent); *McKee* published by Nelson=31 per cent (less than ten per cent).

Analysing the teachers' answers, the writer's impression was that although infant schools were using *more* schemes, the schemes being chosen were similar in approach, i.e. emphasizing the principle of vocabulary control, or as Diack (1960) has called it, the principle of 'few-and-frequent' words. Schemes which were based on other principles tended to be used by few teachers, e.g. *Royal Road Readers*; *Colour Story Reading*; *Downing Scheme* (i.t.a.); *Sounds and Words*.

The teachers were asked about the criteria they used in judging when a child was ready for the 'next book' in the scheme. Analysing their answers it appeared that a sizeable group of teachers stressed the ability to read the book aloud fluently, and when children could not manage this it was their practice to give the child a book of 'similar difficulty' or the 'same level' from a different scheme. Now although schemes may be based on the same principle ('few-and-frequent' words) this does not guarantee that they have a large number of words in common. In practice, it seems to mean that these children are being asked to learn to recall without hesitation yet another different set of sight words. Further

5 Based on initial survey figures, not selected schools sample.
6 Other schemes were mentioned but were used in less than ten per cent of the schools; the percentage figures in brackets refer to the percentage of London infant schools using the schemes in 1959 initial survey data.
7–8 Not published at time of initial survey.

research seems to be urgently needed into means of assessing the level of difficulty of individual books in reading schemes and the extent to which popular schemes tend to have words or cognitive concepts in common.

Discussion

None of the British studies to which reference has been made dealt with the problem of how often schemes were used, and therefore to what extent teachers were dependent upon them. Certainly, it would seem justified to suggest that the published reading scheme plays an important part in the teaching of reading in this country. Why is this?

To the writer it seems possible that the published reading scheme fulfils three very definite functions at the present time, acting as a curriculum and means of assessment for the teacher, and a factor of stability in the classroom.

1 Curriculum

If there has been a shift in training college courses away from curriculum-centred views of education to predominantly child-centred views, then it is possible that college courses on teaching reading have focused more attention on children's development and educational psychology and less on the criteria of choice regarding methods and materials. In these circumstances teachers in the classroom may look to the published reading scheme (especially when it has a detailed manual) for guidance and may be using the scheme as a curriculum.

2 Assessing pupils' progress

In the Midland city infant-only schools in 1968, five out of 26 head teachers were using standardized reading tests. In the classroom though, the published scheme seemed to be the usual means of assessing pupils. Of the classroom teachers, 51 per cent kept children's cards or book marks on which they recorded the child's progress (i.e. book and page number); 86 per cent kept their own record book or card system recording progress in the scheme and/or notes on reading ability; 22 per cent recorded individual children's reading difficulties (on book card, or in teacher's record book); 11 per cent recorded child's knowledge of letter sounds; 12 per cent made a monthly or termly check on recorded progress; 6 per cent kept a wall chart or graph of children's progress in the books of the scheme. As can be seen from these figures the class teachers' record keeping would seem to be mainly in terms of pupils' progress through the readers of the scheme(s).

3   Factor of stability

Particularly in urban infant schools, where there is a certain degree of mobility among both teachers and pupils, the published reading scheme can act as a stabilizing force. Teachers may come and go, faces change from one day to the next, but those characters Janet and John remain familiar figures found, as they are, in practically every classroom in the British Isles.

Conclusion

To date we know very little about either the incidence or the relative importance of various types of reading materials. It is possible to think of the teaching of reading as a social system and then to consider the respective roles and functions of the various status groups in that system (e.g. the colleges and institutes of education, teachers' centres, LEA advisers, the educational publishers). What part do these various agencies play in the application of reading research to reading instruction?

The interaction of these various status groups and institutions determines 1) what research is done; 2) how it is interpreted by advisers and teachers; 3) how it is communicated in text books (for the teacher) and instructional materials (for the pupils); 4) how teachers act upon research findings in the classroom.

It has been reported that the educational publishers would like to improve their 'image'. One way this could be done would be for them actively to support a teachers' centre devoted solely to the study of materials used in teaching reading. Such a centre could act as a co-ordinator of classroom experiments related to 'readability' research, inquire into improving the methods of disseminating information on materials to the teaching profession, and generally act as a stimulator and facilitator in closing the communication gap which seems to exist at the moment between the producers (the educational publishers) and the users (teachers and advisers) of reading materials.

References

AUSTIN, M. C. and MORRISON, C. (1963) *The First R—The Harvard Report on Reading in the Elementary Schools* New York: Macmillan.

BARTON, A. H. and WILDER, D. E. (1964) 'Research and practice in the teaching of reading: a progress report', in Miles M. B. (ed.) *Innovation in Education* New York: Bureau of Publications, Teachers' College, Columbia University, 361–98.

BIRNIE, J. R. (1968) 'Inconsistencies in i.t.a. and t.o.—A further examination of four popular children's readers', *Reading, 2, iii*, 13–18.

CHALL, J. (1967) *Learning to Read—The Great Debate* New York: McGraw-Hill.

DIACK, H. (1960) *Reading and the Psychology of Perception* Nottingham: Peter Skinner Publishing Ltd.

GOODACRE, E. J. (1967) *Reading in Infant Classes* Slough: NFER.

GOODACRE, E. J. (1968) *Teachers and their Pupils' Home Background* Slough: NFER.

MORRIS, J. M. (1959) *Reading in the Primary School* Slough: NFER.

OLSEN, H. C. (1968) 'Criteria for selecting materials to teaching reading (elementary)', in Figurel, J. A. (ed.) *Forging Ahead in Reading* 12, Part I. Proceedings of the Twelfth Annual Convention, International Reading Association, 133–9.

SOUTHGATE, V. (1968) 'Formulae for beginning reading instruction', *Educ. Res.*, 11, i, 23–30.

1 : 9   Are basal readers obsolete ?[1]

Ouida M. Wright

Are basal readers obsolete? The confirmed individualist is likely to answer with a thunderous 'Yes!' The more conservative teacher, loyal to materials which have served him well, will respond with an equally resounding 'No!'. At times the critics and advocates of basal readers have taken such extreme positions as to leave themselves little opportunity for evaluating the readers objectively. Although the mounting tide of research in the English language arts has not yet revealed the one best way to teach reading—if indeed such a one may be found—it has emphatically demonstrated that children learn to read by several different methods and by using a wide variety of reading materials, among them basal readers.

There is no doubt that basal readers are the major materials used for teaching reading both in Canada and the United States. A survey of a nation-wide sample of 1,300 teachers in the United States conducted in 1961 by the Bureau of Applied Social Research of Columbia University showed that an estimated 'ninety-five to ninety-eight per cent of primary teachers and at least eighty per cent of intermediate grade teachers use basal readers every school day (Spache, 1964). Another survey of 6,000 teachers attending summer courses within a two hundred miles radius of Toronto, Ontario, carried out in 1964 by the Ontario Curriculum Institute, led to the conclusion that 'a large number of teachers used a basal reader approach, along or in some combination' (Ontario, 1965). It is likely that prevailing practice and response in other Canadian provinces would not differ markedly.

1 *Editorial footnote*: Basal readers, basic readers and basals are terms used interchangeably in the United States to identify published reading schemes.

WRIGHT, OUIDA M. (1967) 'Are basal readers obsolete?', *McGill Journal of Education*, 2, i, 61–5.

The case against basal readers

Criticisms of the traditional basals are both lexical and sociological. The vocabulary load of different series of basal readers varies so greatly that the difficulty level of any word cannot be arbitrarily fixed. Partly because of this, even the exponents of basal readers agree that no one series of basal readers can by itself provide appropriate reading experiences for all pupils in a given class. In addition, it is said that basal readers are socially unrealistic, represent only middle-class North American life, and may even set up barriers to children of deprived cultural and social backgrounds or of non-Caucasian origin who find it impossible to 'identify' with the central characters; that the mores they demonstrate are reminiscent of McGuffey or the New England Primer; that they tend to emasculate boys and set them at a disadvantage against the verbally more precocious girls because of the 'feminine' situations and values they illustrate.

The most damning criticisms, however, appear to be pedagogic: that the grouping procedures usually associated with basal readers as a means of providing for individual differences are psychologically unsound; that teachers frequently assign workbook material inappropriately, and in a conscientious effort to teach the pupils as effectively as possible—or out of inexperience or insecurity—accord the teachers' guidebook the veneration due to holy writ and fail to modify suggested procedures in terms of the needs of their particular class; that because of the conservatism of their language patterns the basals may actually retard rather than promote language development.

Now, it *is* true that some basal readers *are* out-of-date: they are in content and appearance unattractive to space-age children. There *is* no conclusive evidence that any given pattern of 'a sequential development of reading skills' contributes significantly to effective reading as we interpret the word today. Some teachers *do* plod unimaginatively through a series of basal readers following the guidebook slavishly in every dot and title. Some pupils *have* become discouraged because they have found themselves always in the 'slow' group. It *is* true that a major cause of high-school dropout is reading inefficiency. Therefore, since the chief means of teaching reading to date has been the basal readers and their accompanying procedures (chiefly the directed reading lesson and ability and achievement grouping) the major part of the blame for reading failure appears to rest inexorably on them.

The case for basal readers

On the other hand, basal readers are being constantly revised and improved. The language of beginning basals more closely approximates that of children's spoken language and, as the child's proficiency in reading develops, the contents of the readers include an increasing quantity of good literature rather than material specially written for teaching reading. Readers are becoming more attractive in appearance as typeface, photographic and other illustrative material are made appealing, colourful and varied. Numerous topics of current interest to children are now being included. Some readers provide aids for the teacher in the form of vocabulary and comprehension exercises which assist in individualizing instruction. Finally, publishers are preparing basals designed for particular achievement and interest levels rather than merely one text for each grade.

In addition to this, basal readers are being supplemented not only by other basals but by skill-building materials available on stencils, in pamphlets, boxes and kits of all kinds. More and more teachers are using trade-books as complementary, rather than supplementary, to the basal reader. The one-to-one relationship of individualized reading is being integrated with the grouping activities of the basal-reader programme. For research has not conclusively demonstrated that individualized reading, despite its advantages, is more effective for teaching reading than achievement grouping with the basal reader. Though the opportunity to read library books in classtime can no longer be allocated as a prize to the fast worker, and one library period per week is manifestly inadequate for stimulating a lasting interest in books in most children, the directed reading lesson still serves a valuable purpose in enabling the teacher to reinforce a skill by methodical emphasis.

The basal reader is particularly useful to the beginning teacher who needs guidelines for that overwhelming first year of teaching. It is helpful even for the experienced teacher who has little time to assemble for himself a major core of materials for a particular grade but can be provided with basic lessons under one cover for at least a section of his class. Perhaps the most conclusive arguments in favour of basal readers are that the majority of children exposed to them have learned to read and that in carefully controlled research studies they usually demonstrate undeniable strengths—as well as weaknesses—when evaluated with other tested materials.

The teacher's role

Having said this, one must examine other sources of inadequacy in the basal reader programme and the finger of research points unwaveringly at the teaching profession. Teachers must accept research findings that no one series of basals can form an adequate reading programme for all the children in a given grade. No longer should they assign one level of textbooks for a given grade in flagrant disregard for the wide ranges of reading achievement among the pupils of any one class. (Several copies of three or four different levels of basals in any one room cost no more than thirty-five of one level.) No longer should teachers expect all thirty-five children in a given grade to read at the same page at the same time. Nor are grouping procedures so infallible that they alone can solve the problem of catering to individual differences in reading development. Each teacher must be so skilled in the application of several approaches to the teaching of reading, so sensitive to the needs of the individual child, so flexible in his attitude to teaching that having accurately ascertained the reading level, strengths and weaknesses of each of his pupils, he can adopt procedures and select materials which will enable each child to progress at his own rate. The teacher must be ready and able to combine the teacher-initiated activities of a skill-building programme with those associated with pupil-selected material in a manner beneficial for each child.

In short, the effectiveness of basal readers—or for that matter any teaching tool—depends as much on its appropriateness for the specific learner as on the competence and training of the teacher to whom his instruction has been entrusted. Austin's report on the reading courses offered in teacher-training institutions in the United States indicated that:

> Almost every college requires elementary education students to enroll in basic reading instruction, although one-half of them include it as a part of a course in Language Arts. Among the latter group, 60 per cent devote between $4\frac{1}{2}$ and $11\frac{1}{4}$ hours to it; 30 per cent give it less time (Austin, 1961).

It is likely that conditions in Canada also leave room for improvement. At McGill's Faculty of Education most student teachers preparing for teaching receive thirty-six lecture hours of instruction in the teaching of reading, a time allotment barely adequate for treating the major aspects of the subject. Granted that these students after graduation will learn from experience and by attending local workshops or short summer courses, it is doubtful, whether they and most other teachers can, unaided, select from the vast supply of material available the most suitable collection for their classes. The prescribed basal readers provide systematic, welcome and necessary guidance and ensure that children will receive at least a minimum programme of reading instruction.

It is possible, of course, that too much emphasis is now being placed on discovering *what* materials are most effective rather than *how* children of various categories learn to read. When research is directed to the basic problem of how children learn, then materials take their proper and equally important place as aids to learning.

Possible future use of basals

What, then, of the future? The recent trend to multiple series of basals in any one classroom is likely to accelerate. These will be increasingly supplemented with other skill-building materials and trade books. Not only basal readers but also other reading materials will be used more flexibly to cater to individual rates of learning. For, what with programmed readers such as those being developed by Sullivan Associates in California (Buchanan, 1963) and the rising spate of 'good books for children', it is conceivable that the 'basal reader' may become a basic core of teaching aids which might include 'children's literature', structured materials, films, filmstrips, records and tapes supplemented with an ever-expanding library of illustrated books, encyclopedias and other reference works.

Because this mass of materials will be available, the teacher must actively participate in the selection of those which are likely to be appropriate for his class. It is equally evident that the individual teacher needs guidance in the wise selection of reading aids. Reading consultants have a place, but equally important, major supervisory bodies should indicate which of the existing materials and procedures are most effective for teaching specific skills to particular categories of children so that local authorities can more intelligently decide on specific texts for their own schools.

Finally the teaching profession must subject to the scrutiny of long-range, extensive, carefully-controlled research and supervised practice all approaches and materials for use in schools, constantly removing the obsolescent and prudently introducing the more useful. (Publishers, always sensitive to the temper of the market, are likely to cooperate with—and indeed have initiated—reasonable moves towards a better product.) At the same time provision must be made for the retraining of teachers as more successful approaches become available.

It seems quite clear that basal readers are not obsolete; only their misuses are.

References

AUSTIN, M. C. *et al* (1961) *The Torch Lighters* Cambridge, Mass.: Harvard Graduate School of Education, xiii.

BUCHANAN, C. D. (1963) *Programmed Prereading* San Francisco: McGraw-Hill.

Ontario Curriculum Institute (1965) *A First Look*, Report on the Survey of Current Practice in the Teaching of Reading in Ontario, 20.

SPACHE, G. D. (1964) *Reading in the Elementary School* Boston: Allyn and Bacon, 58.

1:10 Structuring a programme of graded exercises in social literacy for less-able pupils

Margaret Laybourn

In constructing a learning situation aimed at improving social literacy in less-able school children, it is essential initially to assess the areas of need. Next, examples of materials which impinge on these areas, and which are likely to be met with by the pupils in their lives as young workers, must be assembled.

In deciding which examples to select for the learning programme, the social background of the pupils must patently dictate the choice. The higher the social status and financial level, the more numerous the amount of forms, pamphlets, leaflets, catalogues, licences, application forms and so on which must be dealt with. Consequently, the demands upon the higher reading skills become more complex too. But among the children of the 'submerged tenth' who are so frequently found in Special Schools and Remedial Departments in under-privileged city areas, the needs tend to be much simpler, and teachers must beware of gearing the project too much towards a middle-class life pattern. Such occupations as motoring, holiday-making and home ownership, for instance, are not generally part of the lives of these children. Ironically, these are the very children who most need arming with social competence skills essential to their needs; and the problem of filling this gap in their education, in view of their poor reading attainment, constantly preoccupies teachers.

So, in order to cover as wide a range of requirements as possible, while allowing for the less sophisticated needs of the Special School pupil, it was thought advisable to make three different collections of documents by groups of children in three different educational establishments. One was a Special School for ESN girls, one a newly formed Comprehensive School with a small population of 'non-examination' pupils, and one a Technical College organising day-release courses for early school leavers. In all cases,

LAYBOURN, MARGARET (1971) 'Structuring a programme of graded exercises in social literacy for less-able pupils', *Reading*, 5, *iii*, 14–18.

the pupils were asked to bring to school examples of reading material which came into their homes, with which their parents had either to cope, or seek assistance in order to do so. Where the amount proved sparse, it was supplemented by the teacher's collection; but it is essential, as has already been mentioned, to match the material realistically to the pupils' future requirements.

The break-down of the areas of need was based on work by J. E. Merritt, from whose ideas the accompanying chart was developed.[1] Following this scheme the following modules were chosen as being meaningful and familiar to less-able pupils:

1 Home and family.
2 Leisure.
3 Work.
4 Consumer skills.
5 Community responsibility.

Next, ten documents were selected for each category, and they included such examples as National Health leaflets, vaccination certificates, frozen food instructions, advertisements for employment, canteen notices, job applications, library ticket applications, record-player instructions, radio/ TV savings cards, food bargain leaflets, postal code information, National Savings books, fire prevention in the home leaflets and so on.

An analysis of this material revealed the overwhelming importance of five categories of information: forms, instruction notices and regulations, directions and diagrams, letters, advertisements. Legal necessity, safety, and the acquisition of property are all closely linked to the effective management of these social literacy problems. Form-filling proved to be a particularly complex category, involving as it does licences, passports, H.P. and permits.

The pupils' kit which was assembled as the result of these analyses consisted of a five-part folder corresponding to the five areas of need, each section containing ten documents. These were graded in difficulty according to their complexity in the use of symbols, terms, information, instructions or calculations involving checking operations—the correct interpretation of which might ensure protection against legal action, fraud or wastage of time, energy or money. Attached to each document was a questionnaire aimed at testing the readers' ability to understand the text. Self-checking

---

1 *Editorial footnote*: An expansion of these ideas will be found in Unit 10, *A Framework for Curriculum Design*, by John Merritt, which forms part of The Open University course, *The Curriculum: Context, Design and Development* (E283).

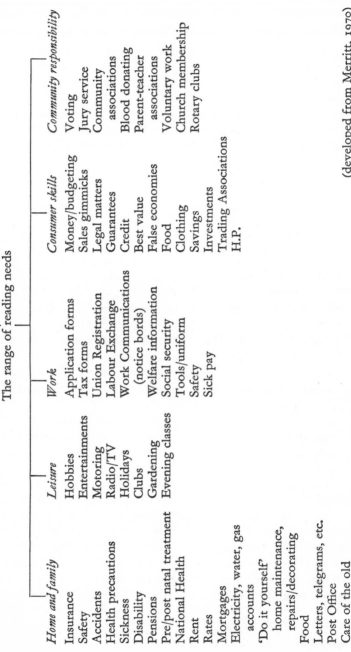

Human needs

Cooperant roles

The range of reading needs

Home and family	*Leisure*	*Work*	*Consumer skills*	*Community responsibility*
Insurance	Hobbies	Application forms	Money/budgeting	Voting
Safety	Entertainments	Tax forms	Sales gimmicks	Jury service
Accidents	Motoring	Union Registration	Legal matters	Community
Health precautions	Radio/TV	Labour Exchange	Guarantees	associations
Sickness	Holidays	Work Communications	Credit	Blood donating
Disability	Clubs	(notice bords)	Best value	Parent-teacher
Pensions	Gardening	Welfare information	False economies	associations
Pre/post natal treatment	Evening classes	Social security	Food	Voluntary work
National Health		Tools/uniform	Clothing	Church membership
Rent		Safety	Savings	Rotary clubs
Rates		Sick pay	Investments	
Mortgages			Trading Associations	
Electricity, water, gas			H.P.	
accounts				
'Do it yourself'				
home maintenance,				
repairs/decorating				
Food				
Letters, telegrams, etc.				
Post Office				
Care of the old				

(developed from Merritt, 1970)

answer lists were incorporated in the question cards, the students taking themselves through the course and recording their successful answers on prepared grids. Neither speed nor competition were involved, satisfaction being gained by an increasing score of correct answers as the result of improved reading, or, in the case of special difficulty, of consultation and discussion with the teacher.

Nevertheless, in spite of every effort to make the kits full and comprehensive enough to meet the needs of all pupils, initial use of the work cards in the actual classroom situation showed that the programme was still failing to benefit pupils of the lowest reading attainment. These pupils, while capable of some sight vocabulary as well as some primary phonic ability, seemed to require the isolation of certain skills essential to the acquisition of reference reading, and it became obvious that exercises were needed involving much finer grading.

A more detailed set of exercises, therefore, with the specific intention of teaching *one* skill at a time was devised, as follows: Using a catalogue, *Mothercare*, questions were composed involving the minimum of reading, but rather designed to direct the eye to items, numbers, prices and sizes in order to accelerate skimming and scanning, and to inculcate the ability to read an alphabetical index. The ultimate aim of the exercises was to equip the students with the ability to fill up an order form. The grading of the questions was as follows:

1 Turning to a specific page and extracting *one* fact.
2 Knowing name of item, turning to correct page through use of index and extraction of *one* fact.
3 Use of index to extract a second fact.
4 Differentiation between two facts and selection of appropriate one.
5 Differentiation between three facts, and selection of two items.
6 Relating two facts; e.g. knowing one fact, finding another.
7 Interpretation of the order form.
8 Filling in the form.

It was found that retarded adolescent girls whose reading ages were below 8.5 years (on the Schonell Graded Word Test) achieved considerable success on these exercises, and the next step must be to incorporate such card material into each area covered by the kits, so that the whole group will be participating. Whereas the poorest readers may never achieve the mechanical skills to be able to interpret the more difficult material, there will be a valuable spin-off from merely seeing the documents, and hearing their class-mates discuss them.

The author is well aware that in the theoretical exposition of what is basically a practical teaching device, it is not possible to include more than a cursory indication of the lists, analyses and exercises mentioned. The intention in writing this article was to give some assistance to those finding difficulty in bridging the gap between theory and practice in the teaching of reading to older backward pupils.

Reference

MERRITT, J. E. (1970) 'Priorities in curriculum design', *Durham and Newcastle Institutes of Education Journal*, 22, cx, 44–7.

1:11   Books in the middle school: their organization and use

J. S. Nicholson

When the Education Act of 1964 made possible the provision of a new type of school, outside the normal pattern of primary and secondary schools, catering for children in an age range extending below ten years six months to above twelve years of age, Bradford was selected as one of the first two authorities to be permitted to build such a school. It was arranged that the planning and designs should be undertaken by the Architects and Building Branch of the Department of Education and Science. The school, Delf Hill Middle School, caters for 420 children in the nine-to-thirteen age-range. The plan and its description are featured in DES Building Bulletin No. 35 (HMSO).

The working accommodation is in the form of four centres each serving as a base for one of the age groups of 105 children and providing, in addition to working areas, storage, cloak and toilet facilities. Additional to the centres there is a central studio, workshop and home economics area and spaces for music, physical education and dramatic work. An eighteen-booth language laboratory and a science room with ancillary heated greenhouse and animal house are incorporated into the working areas used by the older children. The whole accommodation is conceived as a range of spaces varying in size, character and equipment and it owes its shape to the efforts made by the architects to build into it the kind of flexibility teachers were trying to make for themselves. In brief, the school allows a far more variable and interesting relationship between the children and their teachers and this at both primary and secondary level is clearly the present trend. It is most certainly not a school designed for classes of

NICHOLSON, J. S. (1970) 'Books in the middle school: their organization and use', *The School Librarian*, 18, *iv*, 390–4.

children all doing the same thing at the same time or for the conventional class teaching situation.

In centres 1 and 2, 210 children can be based in a variety of groups. Of the three large rooms which are used as bases for registration and other welfare purposes in each centre, two, similar in shape and size, extend outwards into a large joint work bay. The third room is completely enclosed and like the conventional classroom. French, at this stage entirely oral, music and indeed any lesson where the noise is likely to be intrusive should be taken in it. A shared practical area joining centres 1 and 2 has provision for art, craft and other practical activities. It will be readily seen that the plan invites co-operative working by the three teachers in each of these year-group centres. Indeed, these two centres only appear on the school timetable when the children leave their area for physical education, music and some specialized forms of craft. Working within a given time-evaluation of the various subject areas of the curriculum, the entire planning of the work is undertaken on a co-operative basis by the three teachers concerned. It has therefore been possible to match, to some extent, their respective strengths and weaknesses especially in the preparation of the work to be done.

In centres 3 and 4, the other 210 children between the ages of eleven and thirteen are accommodated. There are three rooms to each centre, one in each being a large double-purpose room opening out into a practical area with round-the-wall benching, surfaced in both wood and metal, at which gas and electricity are laid on. As well as the language and science rooms already mentioned, the third room in each area is an enclosed one in which points for radio and television are provided. These rooms are much used for reading and written work. Whenever the children use a specialist room they will generally come under a specialist teacher and this means that a minimum of four or five teachers will be involved with each year group. This will vary according to the abilities available among the staff involved but the intention, always kept in mind, is to limit the amount of specialization to the minimum required for effective working. Streaming has no place, and because we work with each age group on a team-teaching basis we can adequately plan the individual attention needed by the children at all levels, particularly as this method of working enables us to vary the sizes of the teaching groups quite frequently.

The main centre for books in the school is the open-sided library and reference area attached to centres 3 and 4. While there is accommodation within the area for about eight children to work at tables and for a further eight on the window seats, the dining tables round two sides of the centre court and immediately adjacent to the library provide excellent accommodation where the children can work without distraction once they have selected the books they require.

The provision of quiet, carpeted and graciously furnished reading rooms in each area of the school is quite delightful, but the arrangement of the books, particularly on the walls of the main library, is not so satisfactory. The use of metal runners screwed to the walls and adjustable shelving of varying lengths certainly allows a pleasing design in the housing of the books but it leaves many of them out of reach of the children and it is very wasteful of wall space. This pattern of book storage may go well with a system of book use which is based on sets of textbooks and work books for the various subjects, supplemented by a collection of reference books and fiction bought from what remains when the sets have been acquired. The very nature of individual and group learning and the design of the school, inhibiting, as it does, class teaching, implies that sets of class books no longer have any purpose and that in their place a very wide variety of books will be in constant use. Book storage rooms, other than one to be used for book repair and maintenance, are not necessary, for every book in the school must be on view and available. We have too little money to spend on books out of sight and out of use. If the value of the many many thousands of books, some expensive and of recent publication, lying unused in the bookrooms of grammar and comprehensive schools throughout the country could be given to the infant and junior schools, it would go a long way towards bringing the number of books available for them to a more acceptable level.

Each year-group, in consultation with the librarian (who is herself the head of one of them), selects the books required and these are arranged to the best advantage in the respective areas. To retain flexibility, these books are not considered the sole property of any one group, and arrangements can be made through the librarian to replace or augment them when and as required. The individual provision to the children of an atlas and a dictionary was carefully considered and it was felt that much more was to be gained from having a number of both atlases and dictionaries of varying quality and difficulty available for reference and extended use where necessary, both in the main library and in the areas. The full range of dictionaries from *The Shorter Oxford* to the simplest dictionaries suitable for the few severely backward readers, as well as the range of specialist ones published by the Oxford Press and Penguin Books, are already available in the main library and to a more limited extent in the areas.

The collections in all of them will be completed as soon as money is available.

Centres 1 and 2 have their own quiet reading rooms carpeted and fitted with upholstered window seats, small tables and chairs. To prevent disturbance to the children using them, all books are housed outside the rooms. The children are very fond indeed of the rooms and there is some competition for their use. Because of this prestige value which has arisen we have quietly reserved a generous allotment of the time available in them for the remedial groups. Anything which gives these children confidence and pleasure is of very real value to their reading progress. Attached to the craft area is a reading alcove carpeted and furnished to the standard of those in the centres. Books relating to art, craft and home economics are kept here and they must not be taken into the working areas without the direct permission of the teacher in charge. Expensive books left about in practical areas are always at risk.

As well as the books permanently in the centres, regular provision has to be made for temporary additions of books upon particular topics when the changing patterns of work demand this. Where our own library cannot supply the books demanded, the Bradford Public Library has always very willingly supplied a box of books on loan. This is a voluntary arrangement between the children's librarian and individual head teachers, for there is no official scheme for loans between the education and library departments.

Once books are out in the centres they are lost to the main library. In certain circumstances books urgently required can be transferred between centres through the librarian and the heads of the centres concerned, but children are not permitted to wander into other areas looking for the book they want. It follows that, if this system is to be really successful, copies of all the books in the areas must also be in the main library. This means that at least 8,000 to 10,000 volumes will be necessary to provide a really adequate supply for the school. This, no doubt, sounds to be a very large number of books for a school of rather more than four hundred children but it must be remembered that, except for the few books used in the remedial work, this represents the total number of books in the school.

In addition to an initial requisition allowance of £4,650 from which more than £1,100 was spent on books, there was a separate library allowance of £1,500. Since then a further £1,200 and some purchases from the private funds of the school have enabled us to put together rather more than four thousand volumes. As all books are shelved in the library or in the centres and not carried about in children's bags or crowded into their desks, wear and tear is comparatively light and from further requisitions supplemented by the help of the parents it is hoped to bring the total to 8,000 within the next four years. Book allowances have to compete these days with the rising demands for sophisticated hardware and the expensive maintenance involved but books are surely still a first charge on the money available.

As many paperbacks as possible are bought each year for general reading and these are kept almost entirely in the working areas. The importance of a supply of good literature freely and immediately available more than justifies our continuing expenditure on the increasing number of first-rate books now obtainable in paperbacks.

Reading is no longer the only means of living in vicarious experience but only one of several, and while this does not diminish its importance it certainly modifies it. Our non-readers come to school today anxious to know more about information that has come their way from films, radio or television. Perhaps it is a side-effect of the examinations in English literature that has given the impression that the best prose is confined to prose fiction, but we now have to range well outside this field and include diaries, biographies, travel books and essays to fulfil the demands the children make upon us. We welcome any means that can help us to make the literary heritage come alive for our children and none more than the literary features for children of various ages in the BBC schools and other programmes. The high quality of the readings, the generous amount of material made available and, not least, the widening of our horizons, particularly in the field of modern literature, must be acknowledged with gratitude.

Stress is laid on reading to the children right through the age range and the flexibility of the groups and the organization of the working day allows this to be done at precisely the apposite moment. In our reading to the children the use of adult books, where these have a link with their own experience, is much encouraged and we add the books used successfully in this way to the library. The descriptions of the children going to and from school, as well as their lessons within it, in *Lark Rise to Candleford* have the originality, truth, simplicity and force which touch the experience of the children instantly, as do the descriptions of his schoolmaster father by J. B. Priestley in *Margin Released*. Similarly the early chapters of Emlyn Williams's autobiography *George* are very real to children. As these are the qualities by which we judge the work the children do for us, they are surely the qualities by which we should judge the books we read to them.

New forms of classroom organization as related to reading

Nila Banton Smith

Fresh viewpoints and new patterns

The newer psychologies, philosophies and continuing streams of scientific data concerning reading and child development combine to give us new outlooks and deeper insights into grouping practices.

New concepts of grouping embrace keen recognition of individual differences, not only in reading but also in other aspects of child development. They respect the fact that ability in reading varies widely in one classroom. Perhaps the outstanding characteristic of new grouping concepts, however, is that they recognize that children vary not only in reading ability but in intellectual capacity, rate of growth, motivational drive, experience, interests, social maturity, and social predilections. The most effective grouping plan gives consideration to all these factors. Reading is a part of total child growth and a classroom organized to respect and utilize all growth factors holds out more promise for each child's success than a classroom which uses only one factor as the basis of its organizational plan.

As an outgrowth of changed viewpoints concerning child development, several new grouping plans are being evolved. I will describe briefly a few of these plans with special applications to reading instruction.

Ever-changing, multiple-grouping plan

It is not easy for a school system to depart from the conventional grade organization. It often takes time for grouping to change to a totally new plan. In the meantime many teachers are making good headway in improving grouping arrangements within their own classrooms in which they

---

SMITH, NILA BANTON (1966) 'New forms of classroom organization as related to reading', in Downing, J. (ed.) *The First International Reading Symposium, Oxford 1964* London: Cassell, 264–268, 272–275, 276–280.

work. They start out with their usual three groups, then gradually change. The guiding assumption underlying the change is that their classroom organization must be flexible, moving, ever-changing. They do not have permanently set groups, but are continuously creating and disbanding groups for different purposes. There may be just one group at times that embraces all children in the classroom. At other times there may be groups of two or three, of nine or ten. No group remains permanent and fixed. Groups are ever-changing in personnel in accordance with varying individual needs and interests.

The teacher has a major role in this plan. At the beginning of the school year a group, usually consisting of twenty-five to thirty, is assigned to a certain teacher and a certain classroom where the children are to work together for a year. The assigning is done by an understanding administrator who takes into consideration the general needs of the group as a whole. It is the teacher, however, who through her daily living with these children, develops a sensitivity to the needs, interests, and potential growth possibilities of each one, individually. Only she can organize, disband, and reorganize groups daily, weekly, and monthly to insure the continuous, well-rounded growth of each child.

Working with the entire class. Occasionally, the entire class may become a reading group. All the children in the room may meet with the teacher while preparing and reading plans for an excursion; questions in connection with a center of interest, directions for making slides or a movie, and so on. There will also be sharing activities in which all the children will participate; for example, when they share the stories in books they are reading independently; when one child reads to the entire group something of interest that he has found; when one group enacts a dramatization of a story; when one group has done research reading and shares its findings with the entire class. In addition to motivating reading, such total-group situations develop a sense of togetherness, of social give and take, of being a worthy member of a larger whole.

Skill grouping. There may be one, two, or even more groups with whom the teacher works rather consistently in skill development, probably with basic readers. However, since skill groups are continuously formed as new skill needs are revealed, these groups will not always be intact. For example, maybe fifteen children need help in using the dictionary, and these children work with the teacher in a group while the rest of the children who don't need such help do something else. Perhaps five of the children in the entire class have difficulty in pronouncing words in which the sound of a is influenced by r. These children have one or more practice periods devoted to this need. Possibly ten minutes now and then will be devoted to one child alone to give him the special boost he needs to overcome his particular difficulty.

Skills are not neglected in this type of organization. As much and perhaps more attention is given to skill development than in the conventional three-group program. The difference is that skill development and practice take place with smaller groups in terms of their personal needs rather than being given to all children in larger, set groups whether or not they are in need of the particular skill elements being emphasized. The teacher must be very skill-conscious, however, and she must be sure that she is distributing her skill time to the best advantage.

Interest grouping.   At times reading groups are formed on the basis of mutuality of interests.

Tom, Mary, Susan and Guy, a group of children from Miss Gray's third-grade room, were strolling along together on their way to school on a bright sunny morning when Guy spied a 'shining stone'. Small particles in this rock glistened in the sunlight. The other children gathered around to examine the find. 'Did it have gold in it?' 'Maybe the glistening parts were diamonds.' Thus they speculated, and interest was still high at the opening of the morning session. The children wanted to identify the composition of the stone. Miss Gray said that they might sit in one corner of the room and work on their problem. Incidentally, it might be added that as the children worked with this problem they extended their interest to rocks in general.

Tom, who could read at sixth-grade level, procured two juvenile encyclopedias from the library. Mary, who was reading at eighth-grade level, brought back two adult encyclopedias from the library. Susan, who was at third-grade level, surrounded herself with all of the different science textbooks in the room. Guy, who read at first-grade level, couldn't read well enough to get anything out of any of the books mentioned above. However, because he had the same interest that the other three children were experiencing, Miss Gray obtained a trade book on rocks from the librarian for him. He couldn't read the information given in this book, but it contained attractive colored pictures, usually accompanied with simple captions, and Miss Gray helped him with these. Guy spent a long time 'studying' this book, after which he told Miss Gray what information he had gathered. She helped him to write his 'notes', which he read to the other three children and again when the group made a report to the class.

Reading in an interest group such as this is valuable as a learning situation because of the motivation involved. Meeting the needs of children in the group who are at different reading levels often taxes the time and resources of the teacher. Many, however, feel that it is worthwhile.

Social grouping. The above example illustrates grouping in terms of interest. There are also many occasions in which children may be grouped on the basis of social choice, those children being permitted to work together who want to be together or who want to work with a certain leader. This type of organization best lends itself to such activities as finding a suitable story to dramatize or pantomime, to use in a puppet show or mock radio or television program, or to tell or read during a story hour. It is also especially adapted to research reading in which a group decides to take charge of one aspect of a construction project, such as making the moat and drawbridge in a model of a feudal castle or preparing the miniature trees to be used in a diorama of a South American jungle.

As small groups are organized on the basis of self-selection of working companions, there may be two excellent readers and two poor readers in the same group. The good reader will probably read independently, but at the same time stand ready to give individualized help to the poor readers —and all will proceed happily because of group compatibility.

It takes a good teacher and an experienced teacher to do a highly successful job with the ever-changing, multiple-grouping plan described above. However, all teachers, new or experienced, can begin gradually to loosen up their classroom organization in some of the ways mentioned. As their skill develops they will find increasing opportunities to create, reorganize, and disband groups according to individual capacities, needs, interests, and social choices.

Teacher team teaching

In the interest of concrete illustration, one example of classroom organization under a teacher team-teaching plan will be presented. Bahner (1960) [1] describes a program carried out by a team composed of a female teacher having a third–fourth grade combination and a male teacher having a fourth–fifth grade combination.

The typical day for this team began with a fifteen or twenty-minute planning period during which each group discussed with its teacher the day's general plan and individual work. Reading groups then occupied the next hour and a half. Each teacher had from two to four groups (this varied as the need arose throughout the year) composed of children with similar reading achievement levels from both rooms regardless of their grade placement.

Next came a short break for the morning fruit juice, followed by the physical education period when the two classes combined. The teachers planned this period together. Then one assumed responsibility for the total group while the other took a break, collected materials, evaluated the work of pupils, or performed other needed tasks. After the physical education period, these sixty-five children remained together for a story period, music, or art. The teacher who had the preceding half-hour away from the class assumed full responsibility now, while the other teacher had an unscheduled period of approximately twenty minutes.

From this point until lunch, the sixty-five children were divided into four arithmetic groups on the basis of achievement—again without regard to their grade placement. Each teacher worked with two groups.

The program after lunch varied considerably. Often there was some type of project going on, with the two classes sometimes combined and sometimes working separately. Special interests and abilities of the two teachers often determined just how the two classes operated. For example, both classes worked together on an electricity unit with the man assuming the major responsibility for planning the lesson, gathering the materials, and doing the group instruction. The woman member of the team performed as an aide during this project, helping individuals and small groups. Later on, the teachers reversed their roles while undertaking a unit on space.

Usually social studies, science, music, and art were integrated during the afternoon period. Of course, individual work going on during reading groups was often based on the units or projects then in progress.

Raabe (1959) [2] evaluated an experiment in which four teachers worked as a team with 139 intermediate grade children as follows:

> We have found the team approach to organizing for reading instruction to be very rewarding. The teachers were enthusiastic, as were the children and their parents. According to standardized tests, learning was greatly facilitated. For example, the average gain in reading made during the first semester was eight months or nearly one full school year. During the entire year, the average gains were approximately two grades. It is interesting to note that the greatest gains were made by the most and least able groups, rather than by the average groups.

Pupil team grouping

Several schools are now using the plan of having children work together in groups or teams of two to seven, with a pupil leader as teacher. This

2 Reprinted by permission of the University of Chicago Press.

plan has been the subject of considerable experimentation by Durrell who recommends three or five pupils as being the best sizes for groups.

Durrell (1956) explains the way in which the pupil team organization may function as follows:

> ... At beginning grade level most of the superior readers have had considerable experience as teachers in 'playing school'. These teachers may replace the regular teacher in giving extra practice in many stages of reading readiness, such as letter matching and letter names. They may lead in various kinds of 'games' in word recognition and word analysis and may help in oral-reading practice.
>
> The teacher will need to observe the work of the pupil-teachers and provide counsel and assistance at points of difficulty, but most pupil-teachers will prove very helpful. Groups may be asked to choose a pupil-teacher. Generally it is better if all of the eligible pupil-teachers are given the opportunity to teach a group; so the 'available' list of pupil-teachers should be somewhat flexible. This small-group work should be 'extra practice' and should not replace the regular contact between teacher and pupil in small-group instruction.
>
> Pupil-teachers of superior reading ability may be used in intermediate grades if the teacher is skilled in making such work acceptable. They may serve as consultants to help a group of slower pupils with difficult words encountered in silent reading. When assigned materials are much too difficult for a very slow group, the pupil-teacher may present the lesson orally and explain unfamiliar words or passages. They may direct word-analysis practice or dictate spelling words to small groups. Or they may serve as 'secretaries' or recorders in group study activities.
>
> The pupil-teacher is more effective in following routine activities and providing skills practice. The development of meanings and concepts is better done by the classroom teacher, although some pupil-teachers will be highly effective in explaining particular meanings of words or sentences. Generally the pupil-teacher will need prepared materials, such as lists of questions, lists of words, charts, flash cards, and other devices selected by the teacher. When a child or group of children is aware of the need for extra instruction, and when that instruction is helpful in attaining higher achievement, a pupil-teacher is always acceptable. However, if the extra practice seems pointless or comes as a penalty, the pupil-teacher will have trouble. In no case do pupil-teachers replace a regular teacher. They only engage in supplementary activities.

McHugh (1959) made a study of reading results obtained in the use of this form of grouping with a fourth, fifth and sixth grade, respectively, for a year. In his particular situation, the plan showed superior results in the sixth grade but not in the fourth and fifth grades.

The plan has the advantage of allowing a maximum of pupil participation. The most frequently heard criticism is that having one pupil teach other pupils is not desirable from the social and psychological standpoint.

Individualized reading instruction

The type of organization called 'individualized reading instruction' is the most popular of all the new attempts to change from old grouping patterns. This is now being used more widely in the United States than any of the others. According to this plan, each child has a different book and progresses at his own rate.

This is not the Dalton method which was popular in Britain and America in the 1920s. This was based on a 'contract' or 'job' system by which individuals contracted to cover prepared lessons at their own individual rates. This form of individual instruction died out in the late twenties and we've heard no more of it since.

The new plan of individualized instruction in reading is quite different. Perhaps the briefest way to explain the psychology and philosophy back of this plan is to quote Willard Olson's (1952) synthesis of his studies in which he sums up the needs of children in three words: 'Seeking, self-selection, pacing.' To explain these words, I will add that children are supposed to be seeking certain satisfactions, that they should be allowed to select by themselves whatever meets these satisfactions and that they should be allowed to proceed at their own pace in meeting their satisfactions.

Based on this theory, individualized instruction in reading proceeds as follows:

The teacher assembles as many books as she can collect on different subjects and at different levels of ability. These are mostly tradebooks, but in some cases a few readers may be included, one of a kind. Each child goes to the collection and picks out a book that he wants to read. He then takes the book to his seat and keeps it until he finishes reading it. During an individual conference period the teacher sits in some particular spot in the room as each child comes and reads to her.

The length of the conference with each child varies from two to ten minutes. During this time the teacher checks the number of pages the child has read and perhaps chats with him briefly about what he has read. She may have him read parts of the story orally, ask him questions on these parts or other parts, check his word-recognition by asking him to pronounce certain words, give him help on some skill element he especially needs, or discuss and plan follow-up activities with him. Thus during the conference period the teacher checks, diagnoses, teaches, evaluates, and extends the pupil's interests and activities.

Skill groups are frequently formed to meet individual needs. If two or three or more children need help on the same skill, these children meet as a group with the teacher for development of and practice on the skill. This group is disbanded one by one as children master the skill, and new groups, possibly composed of some of these children and others, assemble to meet other skill needs.

Considerable research has been carried on in connection with this plan of classroom organization and teaching. All studies have shown that children read more books by the individualized plan, and it is reported that children taught the individualized method are more interested in reading.

In so far as actual reading achievement results are concerned, however, research is controversial. Some studies have shown that much better results are obtained through the use of individualized instruction than through the use of basal readers[3] in the usual three-group plan. Other studies have shown that the basic reader with the usual grouping arrangement is superior in getting reading results.

We need more carefully controlled experiments. Such variables should be described and controlled as the kind of basal reader program being measured, the kind of individualized program being measured, the experience of the teacher in using the particular method being measured, the amount of supervision that she receives, etc. We won't have truly conclusive evidence concerning the effectiveness of individualized instruction until better studies are made.

So far I have been talking mostly about grouping for reading at the elementary level, but now I should like to say something about high school. There are some reports of using the individualized approach during a free library period in classes who are retarded in reading at high school level. The individual students choose the book they want to read and read aloud to the teacher and have skill development during individual conference periods.

In some schools the entire class works on reading without being broken into groups but having differentiated assignments according to their ability.

Sometimes students are grouped according to achievement, one English teacher having all the poor readers at a certain grade level. Then there are 'special needs' groups—those needing speed are grouped together, those

3 *Editorial footnote*: Basal readers, basic readers and basals are terms used interchangeably in the United States to identify published reading schemes.

needing comprehension are grouped together, etc. We also find student team groups where two or three work together, and tutorial groups where one student helps the others. Some schools have a reading laboratory equipped with many different kinds of reading material and instruments. Students go to this laboratory and work by themselves, two or three times a week.

Finding time to teach reading with any kind of grouping is a problem in high schools. Several of our high schools are now finding a place in their schedule for separate reading courses. Other plans are to teach reading as a four-to-six week unit within an English course, to teach it during a free period or a study period. In other cases students are asked if they want help outside school hours and are taught in groups after school, on Saturdays or during summer vacations.

These, then, are some of the forms of classroom organization which we are using in teaching reading in the United States. The practice of teaching reading in high school is spreading rapidly but it is bringing many problems with it.

Literature dealing with research on grouping is voluminous, but results are conflicting. Research is still in the same state as that expressed by Cornell (1936) many years ago when, after reviewing the numerous studies on grouping, she said, 'A review of the objective results of grouping leaves one convinced that we have not yet attained any unequivocal experimental results that are capable of wide generalization.'

Perhaps the chief reason why research on grouping is so inconclusive is because the real bases for grouping are too varied, too deep, and too numerous, to lend themselves to one set pattern. Individual differences in ability, rate of progress, and emotional, social, and motivational factors are too personal and unpredictable to adjust themselves to any one 'formula' for organizing all children into the most productive working groups.

The wise teacher will try out different kinds of grouping with different classes of students and use the one or ones which work out the best for him or her and the students in a particular situation.

References

BAHNER, JOHN M. (1960) 'Grouping within a school', *Childhood Education*, 36, 8.

CORNELL, ETHEL L. (1936) *The Grouping of Pupils*, Thirty-Fifth Yearbook of the National Society for the Study of Education, Bloomington, Ill.: Public School Publishing Company, 290.

DURRELL, DONALD D. (1956) *Improving Reading Instruction* New York: Harcourt, Brace & World.

MCHUGH, WALTER J. (1959) 'Team learning in skill subjects in intermediate grades', *Journal of Education*, 142, 22–51.

OLSON, WILLARD C. (1952) 'Seeking, self-selection, and pacing in the use of books by children', *The Packet*, Spring 1952, Boston: D. C. Heath, 3–10.

RAABE, BILLY H. (1959) 'In Grades Four through Six', *Reading Instruction in Various Patterns of Grouping*, Supplemental Educational Monographs, no. 89.

Part 2 How is reading competence developed ?

Introduction to Part Two
How is reading competence developed ?

While whole volumes have been devoted to the development of reading competence, here we can only present a broad survey of some of its aspects: 1) the variety of methods and approaches through which reading instruction is provided; 2) the basis upon which the teacher may organize her own approach in fitting reading instruction to the needs of the individual pupil; and 3) some of the necessary reading skills which enable pupils to become fluent and thoughtful readers.

The different methods of teaching reading are summarized historically by Goodacre (2:1). Her review includes current research findings on each method: alphabet, phonic, word (sometimes called look-and-say), and sentence method (on which the language-experience approach is based). Goodacre (2:2) describes recent linguistic studies which have tried 'to evolve a technique of analysis of the *internal structure* of both spoken and written speech' (p. 129). These techniques of analysis are currently having a significant impact on the phonic and sentence methods of teaching reading. Although recognizing the contributions of linguisticians to the field of reading, Goodacre nevertheless cautions that 'it is up to educators to apply this knowledge' (p. 133). McCullough (2:3) then describes how reading teachers may apply linguistic knowledge to extend their approach to the teaching of reading. Her analysis of meaningful word units and structural thought patterns suggests the kind of curiosity through which reading competence is developed through discovery rather than routine memorization.

Several conclusions may be reached from this overview of reading methods: 1) each method has a distinct function; 2) the advantages of one method are the disadvantages of another; and 3) a combination of methods is necessary to ensure a balanced and comprehensive approach to the teaching of reading. Whichever combination of methods a teacher evolves will be influenced by her concept of reading and the relative weight she places upon the varied units in the printed media—its ortho-graphy (alphabet), its letter-sound relationships (phonics), its meaning-thought relationships as represented by words, sentences and larger struc-tures of thought patterns.

Whichever methods are used, there are only two sources of reading materials: 1) *published* reading schemes, textbooks, library books and other printed media; and 2) *unpublished* reading material created by pupils themselves. Use of the latter material is known as the language-experience approach to reading. According to Carrillo (2:4), this approach is the most flexible of all, applicable to both individuals and groups, useful in conjunction with any other type of printed material, and adaptable to any preferred conceptualization of teaching reading. This conclusion could also apply to published texts, except that experience-stories can be pro-duced immediately for a specific purpose and production is relatively inexpensive. Since experience-stories start with children's own language and experiences, they are also likely to be of most interest and relevance to them. But the use of this approach demands the utmost skill and knowledge on the part of the teacher who must be immediately prepared to teach the reading skills appropriate to the material obtained, as sug-gested by Stauffer (2:5) in his practical description of sources and ways of developing experience-stories. Experience-exchange, as presented by Mitchell (2:6), extends the purpose and use of pupils' written material.

Teachers' use of methods depends on the criteria they establish to guide their points of departure. The guide provided by Southgate and Roberts (2:7) is helpful in its comprehensive coverage of considerations which teachers must examine to determine their own position and ideology. To Southgate (2:8), the need for structure has a pervasive influence on the entire reading programme. Relevance is seen as the basic and continuing concern of the teacher of reading by Downing (2:9). To Buzzing (2:10), the intrinsic and extrinsic purposes of reading are the most important influences which underlie what and how pupils should be taught to read. How might the teacher integrate all three concerns into meaningful and systematic reading guidance for individual pupils?

To a large degree, the previous papers are concerned with the develop-ment of the comprehension aspects of the reading process. What is com-prehension? McCullough (2:11) views comprehension as a matter of 'relativity'—between language and life, word code and meaning, thought patterns and various units of composition, reader–author interaction, and teacher–pupil shared explorations as readers. Niles (2:12) examines com-prehension skills needed to uncover and retain these relationships and

Robinson (2:13) explores various levels of comprehension which lead to critical reading. Various concrete techniques to increase reading rate presented by Smith (2:14) are extended by Catterson's proposal (2:15) that only through an analysis of the conceptual structures of both fiction and non-fiction materials can a teacher understand and influence the development of reading comprehension. All papers refer to the crucial nature of questions in the teaching of reading process which is treated in more detail in Part 3, *Diagnostic teaching of reading.*

A broad reading vocabulary also contributes to reading comprehension. How children acquire and extend their knowledge of printed symbols depends on the teacher's knowledge of elements common to all words. If a 'word' is a printed symbol that has meaning and is an independent unit of speech, then all words have form, meaning, sound and structure. Reading skills designed to enable pupils to analyse these elements as they come across unfamiliar words are known by several terms which are used interchangeably: word perception skills, word analysis skills, word recognition skills and word attack skills, all of which include configuration clues, context clues, phonics and structural analysis. Gray's examination (2:16) of what is involved in word perception describes the integrated function and use of all word analysis skills needed for the development of a reading vocabulary.

Because the multiple meanings and varied connotations of words can significantly intrude to distort comprehension, even when the reader correctly recognizes and pronounces the word, Burns' analysis (2:17) of context clues and their development helps us to understand how

The logical barriers between vocabulary and comprehension, reading and grammar reading and writing, form and meaning, reading and thinking, language and life, will fall away. By crossing these rigid boundaries, the teacher and pupils together will see the miracle of the living language, a network of interactions which make comprehension possible. (McCullough 2:11, p. 227.)

2:1   Methods of teaching reading

Elizabeth J. Goodacre

The main methods of teaching reading are usually understood to be the alphabetic, the phonic, the 'whole-word' or 'look-and-say' and the sentence method. However, the growing emphasis upon the importance of individual differences has led to the discussion in the literature on method of two approaches—the 'language-experience' approach and 'individualized reading'. This chapter therefore concludes with a description of these two approaches and outlines some of the advantages and disadvantages of using such approaches.

The alphabetic method

By this method it is assumed that familiarity with the *form* and *names* of *letters* will help children to recognize and pronounce words. By constant repetition of the letter-names (e.g. 'dee-oe-gee'), this spelling out of words will enable the learner to become familiar not only with the form and name of individual letters but also become accustomed to meeting certain letter-strings or letter-clusters, the component parts of many words. Generally, the main emphasis was laid on the recognition of new words rather than the grasp of meaning. To this extent this method relies heavily on the conditioning aspect of the learning process.

The difficulty with isolating and discussing particular methods is that one never knows exactly how far such methods are successful in their ostensible aims and how far they may inadvertently be teaching other helpful sub-skills. Also, as Diack (1965) has pointed out, it is hard to tell

GOODACRE, ELIZABETH J. (1971) 'Methods of teaching reading', *Children and Learning to Read* London: Routledge & Kegan Paul, 25–43.

how far specific methods are differentiated one from another. It is not very far from teaching the *names* of the letters to teaching their *sounds*. As Diack notes 'of alphabetic and phonic methods it can indeed be said that "thin partitions do their bounds divide"'. Children make their own deductions and in the case of teaching the letter names, it is quite possible for the bright child to realize that there is a fairly close correspondence between the name of the letter and its sound for *some* of the letters. This can help them to realize that there is a code involved in learning to read and to pronounce initial letters which can be helpful for trying to read unfamiliar words.

Durrell (1968) has suggested that for all the consonants (the letters of the alphabet with the exception of the vowels *a, e, i, o, u*) letter-names, except for the letters *h, q, w* and *y*, contain their phonemes or sounds plus an extraneous vowel, and the names of the vowels are the 'long' sound *ae, ee, ie, oe, ue*. In the names of the 'long-e' letters; e.g. *b, c, d, g, p, t, v, z* (this last in American though not in English), the ·phoneme comes in front of the vowel in the letter-name—*b-ee, s-ee*, etc.; to say these letters the child uses exactly the same speech mechanisms as in giving the 'sounds'. The names of the 'short-e' letters, e.g. *f, l, m, n, s, x*—have a similar value, with the phoneme following the vowel in the name; e.g. *eh-l, eh-m*. The names *r, k,* and *y*, also contain their phonemes or letter-sounds. Durrell considers that the close association between name and sound in 22 of the 26 letters is a great help for word recognition and pronunciation. He cites work which showed that when the letter-name was known, the sound of the letter was easier to learn.

With these considerations in mind, it is interesting to note that in studies of children who learned to read before going to school, interest in and concern with letters was found to be positively associated with early success in reading (Durkin's studies, 1964, etc.). The American Government spent an enormous amount of money on a research programme called First Grade Reading Programmes which produced as the most important finding the fact that no one method was superior to any other and that the really important factor was the understanding and competence of the teacher. However, another interesting finding was that the best single predictor of success in the beginning stages of learning to read was a test of the letter-names (Bond and Dykstra, 1967). Indeed, work by Hillerich (1967) has suggested that knowledge of the letter-names at the beginning of schooling is a better predictor of later reading achievement than even the scores of a specially designed reading readiness test.

However, such findings should not be interpreted as indicating a causal relationship, or that it is therefore necessary that children must be taught the letter-names in order to read. In trying to discover how children learn to read, Muehl (1962) found that children who were taught letter-names experienced an initial handicap in identifying nonsense syllables because, in trying to identify the printed symbol, the child had to pass through an intermediate step of saying the letter-name before he arrived at the beginning sound of the word. Certainly, many teachers prefer not to teach the letter-names, or to postpone this until after the child has acquired an extensive sight vocabulary.

Porter and Popp (1967) prior to development of a teaching device called an alpha-board made many attempts to teach school beginners the letter-names. They used Lotto-type games, card sorting and spelling games, stories about the letters, and 'alphabet' songs. Their efforts were largely unsuccessful, but their comments are useful. Children could find a letter named by the researcher more easily at this stage than they could name the letters themselves. The researchers came to the conclusion that the popular 'alphabet song' can lead to very serious confusions and that the alphabetical sequence, particularly at the beginning of the alphabet, generated auditory and visual discrimination difficulties; e.g. *b* and *d*. They concluded that letter-names were really 'nonsense syllables' to most of these young children, but a useful concept was to teach the visible difference between *letters* and *words*. Certainly letters whose names are very similar should not be taught at the same time, as this is much too confusing for young children.

It has been suggested that the explanation for the high relationship between knowledge of letter-names and reading success is that a test of letter-names is really a very crude or naïve intelligence test. It measures such things as 1) the child's exposure to print; 2) the amount of attention he has received at home; 3) his ability to retain knowledge gained from these experiences with letters; 4) his ability to pay attention and look closely at letter forms. A recent review of the various readiness measures for predicting reading achievement has suggested that the child's ability to 'attend', to look closely and see differences, and his level of oral development and therefore use of language concepts are factors in reading readiness which need to be more closely investigated. Chall (1967) has also drawn attention to the importance of letter knowledge as a clue to the child's cognitive development.

> The alphabet is a code, an abstraction, perhaps the first that a child learns (and one that is valued because adults value it). Pointing to and naming a letter, or writing a letter, at an early age is quite different from pointing to or drawing

a picture of a cat, a truck, or a tree. The child who can identify or reproduce a letter engages in symbolic representation, to borrow a phrase from Jerome Bruner, while the child who is working with a picture of an actual object engages in iconic representation. When the child engages in symbolic representation, he is already practising a *higher form of intellectual behaviour* [my italics].

Work by Wheelock and Silvaroli (1967) suggests that young children can be trained to make instant responses of recognition to the capital letters. What is of interest though is that the training in letter recognition appeared to be of most benefit to the children who came from lower socio-economic homes. Matching letter-shapes, possibly even naming the letters (but not in alphabetic order) are means of helping the young child to pay attention to the letters, and this must be of help in observing differences in the *order* of letters in words and the use of letters as clues to beginning sounds of words. We know from the study of Marchbanks and Levin (1965) that specific letters formed the most salient cues in children's word identification. The 'standing out' quality of first and last letters seemed to be related to the fact that each is isolated on one side by white space, whereas middle letters are 'lost' in the word form. Thus, print and words themselves draw the child's attention to the importance of beginning and end letters, i.e. the positioning of letters as well as their shape.

It has been suggested that the alphabetic method is of limited usefulness for reading words and sentences, and it has been long held that it is a mechanical and difficult method, and that at its heyday it produced uninteresting reading material; e.g. *the cat sat on the mat*. However, we are now at the stage of considering *how* methods can be adapted to children's cognitive development. The teacher's ability to work out means of simplifying the learning task for each child, building on whatever information or knowledge the pupil already possesses, is an important factor.

We know that *some* children will, by the time of beginning school, be interested in letters and how they differ one from another (some boys can easily distinguish letter forms, even names, from experience with car number plates, or engine numbers). In talking about letters, they must be called something and probably at *this* stage their names are the most appropriate term. As Reid (1966) has pointed out children go through a process of differentiating symbols from pictures, numbers from letters, and letters from words. As she says, later they come to realize that there are different kinds of letters—capital and lower case, and different kinds of words (e.g. the confusing use of the term *name* for children's names, letter-names, etc.). However it seems fairly obvious that very young children need plenty of experience in playing with *letter-forms*, so as to become familiar with their shape and learn their correct orientation; e.g. which way round. Tracing round wooden letters, feeling cut-out letter forms in felt stuck on to paper or card; matching small case letters in in-set trays; matching capital letters—possibly matching capital and lower case letters; making familiar words on felt boards from cellograph letters, or plastigraph letters on plastigraph boards. Some teachers use a system whereby children act out letter-shapes so the memory of the shape is firmly implanted.

The phonic method

In this method, the *sounds* of letters are substituted for the letter-names.

Originally, the sounds of individual letters were taught but mainly in the last decade, linguists have pointed out that letter-sounds are never produced singly but in the context of words, and that usually the positioning of the letter determines its particular sound. If individual letters are sounded there is a tendency for *uh* to be added, so that one gets the distorted pronunciation *huh, ruh,* and *guh.* When the sounds of individual letters are 'blended' or synthesized, one gets the word *bat* sounding more like *barter*, which can be very confusing to some children.

Certain educationists have suggested a more suitable synthesis is achieved by beginning with a consonant-vowel combination (since consonants cannot be accurately sounded except with a vowel), such as *c-at* or *ca-t*. Durrell (1968) favours the former rather than the latter practice. He cites a study of the abilities of school beginners to read unfamiliar words in which it was found that even those children who were taught the *ca-t* approach could get from *cap* to *nap* with greater ease than from *man* to *map*. There are not all that number of three-letter words with medial short vowels in the ordinary child's vocabulary, but *at* is a fairly reliable generalization in comparison with *ca* which can say different things in *came, call, car, care, catch.* Durrell claims that in most of the 225 phonograms from which stem many of the words familiar to young children, the vowel is stable; relatively few change vowel sounds with the *initial* consonant, in the way that the *ant* phonogram changes in the word *want*. Then, of course, the same sound cluster can be spelled in different ways, e.g. the *air* sound more often than not being spelled *ear, are, air.* However, this may not be such a difficulty for children when they are *reading* since context can help to indicate the pronunciation if the word is already in the child's oral vocabulary.

Problems and controversies have, and still do, abound in the teaching of phonics. Probably the one that must be dealt with first is the difference in *approach* to the teaching of phonics, since many of the criticisms in the past levelled at phonics as a method, in practice, relate to the approach adopted by the teacher. One type of approach is to introduce children to pictures of an *a*pple, *e*lephant, *I*ndian, *o*strich (not bird!), and *u*mbrella, so that the children are familiar with the short vowel sounds through this use of key pictures. These key pictures carry a phonic clue which provides information about the beginning letter's sound and not its name. This is followed by more pictures of a *squirrel, monkey, fox, rabbit, goat, nest, bear, tiger, pig* and *dog*, to illustrate the more common sounds of the consonants *s, m, f, r, g, n, b, t, f* and *d*. Once the short vowel sounds and the sounds of these ten consonants are learned they are blended together, first into syllables (*su, so, si, se, sa*), then into words (*sun, sob, sit, set, sat*). These initial exercises are followed by reading matter of the following sort:

> Sam sat in the sun
> The sun is good for Sam (Hay and Wingo, 1948).

As can be seen the procedure tends to be a deductive one. That is, beginning with generalizations about the sounds of letters (which may or may not use *picture* clues of objects which may or may not be familiar to the individual child), these are then applied to the pronunciation of specific syllables and words. It tends to be a *synthetic* process in that it initially concentrates on parts of words which are later combined into whole words. As with the confusion between letter-names of similar sound or letters which are similar in form, it may be difficult for some children to differentiate between similar word parts and three-letter words, i.e. words of similar length.

Sometimes in this use of phonics, reading of interesting material is delayed until the pupils have achieved a high degree of mastery of the 'sounds' and are competent at word building. Critics of this way of teaching phonics instance the difficulties of combining letter-sounds into meaningful words by synthesizing, which may lead to awkward articulation and a slower rate of reading. Although the training or conditioning element in the approach can lead to the discovery of phonic generalizations, it is not yet clear how far these expectations can be substantiated in ordinary classroom reading materials, as distinct from the specially designed phonic readers; i.e. what degree of transfer operates.

Also, how valid are these phonic rules?

Clymer (1963) and Bailey (1967) found the two-vowel rule 'the first vowel says its name, the second is usually silent' sometimes stated as 'when two vowels go out walking, the first does all the talking', to be more often wrong than right. They found that others among these so-called 'rules' lack desirable dependability. Programming a computer to spell, some researchers devised 111 vowel rules and 92 consonant rules, but the computer only managed to spell correctly half the 17,000 words demanded of it.

Along with the development of 'sight' methods in the late nineteen-twenties in America went a 'new' method of teaching the letter-sounds called *intrinsic*, or *incidental* phonics. By this approach the pupil learned a small sight vocabulary of words (words recognized on sight), usually personally meaningful, and then began to compare these words for similarities and thus to extract from the experience valid phonic generalizations; e.g. when a child knows *my, mother, must* and *me*, or *baby, big* and *baker*, he is ready to make generalizations regarding the sounds of the consonants *m* and *b*. Then as more words become familiar, more generalizations can be made about the sounds associated with other letters or letter groupings. This particular way of progressing in phonics can be termed *inductive* or *analytic*, because specific words are used to discover a generalization regarding the sounds of letters, and whole words are analysed to identify and find recurring letters and their associated sounds. Teachers using this approach play the familiar games 'I Spy' and 'I Went Shopping' (I bought *butter, bananas* and *beef*); they encourage children to collect words beginning with the same sound; list the children's names under the same beginning sound; make displays of objects beginning with the same sound; have children sort and classify toys or small objects beginning with similar but different sounds; e.g. *v* and *f*, or *t* and *f*— difference between voiced and voiceless consonants, between two voiceless consonants. When a child making his own list of words beginning with the consonant *g* comes to the teacher with *ginger* and says it does not begin the same way as the previous word *game*, he has discovered for himself that certain letters have more than one sound, and he may be able to go on after this insight to discover that *c* has two sounds, but *y* has three, and the vowels have many. The last of these generalizations may not be quite the problem adults have considered it, because one researcher has demonstrated that one can get on quite well in reading when dashes are substituted for vowels!

McCullough (1968) writing on balanced programmes has stressed the importance of achieving a balance between teacher guidance and pupils not only discovering but also *using* generalizations about letters and their sounds.

The child who must do something with what he has learned learns it better because he knows he will have to use it, and he learns it better because he does use it. If the child who has discovered the sound represented by the letter *m* by means of the teacher's models, *milk* and *man*, then has to record his own induction with his own models (such as *mouse* and *match*, which he chooses), he will remember what he has learned better and will have a record from which to retrieve it if he forgets it.

Children can discover a lot of things for themselves about words and their sounds, as they experiment with a word's *head, body* and *tail*, rearranging and twisting them to suit their fancy. This follows on easily from such commercially produced games as 'Jumbled bodies' or 'Misfits'. *Pan* can be turned into *fan, fan* into *fat*, and *bill* into *bell*, or he can try to make new words out of old ones such as making *star* turn into *rats*, or by adding a letter make a *can* into a *cane*, but the effects are limited and usually this word play appeals most to the bright child who studies the structure, changes it and experiments with it in a trial-and-error way.

It should be noted that *phonics* is a method of applying what we know about the study of speech (phonetics) to the reading process and, as such, it involves bringing into play not only the auditory and visual senses, but the ability to combine these two sensory modes of thought. *Phonetics* on the other hand is concerned with classification, description and articulation of the *sounds of speech* and there is a means by which one symbol can represent one sound (International Phonetic Alphabet) but this is not the traditional alphabet. Pitman's i.t.a. or the Augmented Roman Alphabet endeavours to produce a symbol for each sound, and so ensure phoneme/grapheme correspondence; one symbol for each sound. It is useful to make this distinction between phonics and phonetics, as writers, particularly linguists such as Fries are conscious of the confusion in the literature on reading methods between the two terms.

The word method

The difficulty with categorizing methods and trying to describe them briefly is that one is tempted continually to describe them historically in order to place them in some sort of perspective and to cover the many criticisms or qualifications which can be made by the informed reader. Hunter Diack (1965) does this in a brilliant *tour de force*, and the reader unfamiliar with this historical survey of reading methods is recommended to read it for elaboration of the points being made in this chapter.

As reading research at various times concentrates on different aspects of the reading process, so different methods emphasize different factors in the process, and as a method becomes more acceptable one sees a hardening of its new and valuable 'insight' into the reading process, into rigid dogma which usually justifies teaching techniques as soulless and ill thought out as those the 'new' method was intended to change.

The word method or 'whole-word' or 'look-and-say' way of teaching reading stresses the word and not the letter-name or sound, and has been used as a means of trying to make the reading process more meaningful to children. At least this is the intention and in some ways the popularity or the revival of word methods has provided evidence of the realization by teachers and educationists that the *letter* methods can become boring and meaningless for children if taken to the extreme. In the word methods, it is thought that children's attention can be drawn to an element which is already familiar through the child's speech. Children will see the difference between words on the basis of length and the shape or configuration of the words, and then easily be able to recognize words using such clues. By using words familiar to the child, that is, in the child's own oral vocabulary, it would be possible to get away from the difficult-to-transfer learning situation of phonic word building and blending, and the spelling units of the alphabetic method. Thus children would be more highly motivated to read, and not bored by the 'delayed reading' element which can exist with the use of letter methods, e.g. the synthetic (building up) approach rather than analytic (analysing from known words).

It is useful to distinguish between 'whole-word' and 'look-and-say' methods. Using the former it is possible to associate picture and 'name', that is pictorial representation and the word which stands for it, so that the child is conditioned to accept that the image and the symbol of the word are related. Similarly, objects in the environment can be labelled. This is usually only possible for nouns, and difficulties of interpretation and language experience interfere when it comes to concrete or pictorial representation of verbs, adverbs, adjectives, etc. For this reason 'look-and-say' becomes a means by which the teacher or the adult can tell what the particular word says. As Flesch (1955), a bitter critic of the word method, has insisted, it is in certain circumstances a crude form of conditioning.

It goes straight back to Pavlov and his famous salivating dogs . . . It was not long before the conditioned reflex psychologists . . . found out that

Pavlov's discovery can be used to train a human being . . . Of course you can teach a child to read that way—nothing easier than that. You show him the word *chicken* seventeen times in succession, each time in connection with a picture of a chicken and an explanation by the teacher that this combination of letters means a chicken . . . Don't you see how degrading the whole process is? The child is never told *why* this heap of letters means 'chicken'.

Obviously this method provides little technique for deciphering unfamiliar words. In some classrooms one can see a line of children waiting to be told 'what the word says'. In large classes, the use of this method does produce particular difficulties. Children are encouraged to recognize words by their shape or pattern, but also to think what particular word would fit into the context. I remember reading with a small boy who stuck on a three-letter word beginning with *b*. The reading material was about a washing line of clothes with an appropriate illustration. Foolishly ignoring the picture 'clue' I said, 'Now you think what's on your Mum's line at home that begins with that letter.' A look of anticipated success passed across his face as he cried, 'Mum's bra'. The word in the text was *bib*.

Terms such as 'configuration', 'word-pattern', 'total form' and 'internal characteristics', tend to be used in books on this method rather than the word 'letters' and as Diack (1965) has pointed out 'the mental attitude of thinking about words as not being primarily composed of letters is reinforced'. Not looking closely enough at the letters in words can lead to individual letters being ignored and to guessing; e.g. *bra* for *bib*.

One would have supposed that not being confined by the restrictions of only using regularly phonic words (*mat, hop*, etc.), would lead to the production of more interesting *reading materials* firmly based on children's interests. However, if letter clues are underplayed, it does become difficult for the child to recognize easily the few hundred words necessary for the telling of an interesting story. For children to recognize even 'interest' words it is found necessary to *frequently repeat* them. Also if one has *fewer* words it is still easier. This has led to readers or primers with strict vocabulary control, which in practice tend to be few words frequently repeated. Beginning books in schemes have come to have less than twenty words, and Diack (1965) carrying the idea firmly to its logical conclusion has asked whether even these twenty words are necessary. 'From one point of view, no. The pictures tell what story there is and if reading is *at all stages* a matter of getting meaning from the printed page, then those twenty words are all of them unnecessary. So the wordless method had virtually arrived.'

Although there is insufficient space here to go into it in detail, the Gestalt theory of learning has been used as the theoretical basis for word methods, and basic ideas in this area of thinking are the importance of the *whole*, the innate organization of perception, and the insight or sudden understanding of personal experience. It was thought that young children could recognize the whole word *aeroplane* long before they knew its component letters—that there was a tendency for individuals to perceive 'in wholes'. To a large extent this type of thinking ignores the time element and the effects of previous learning. Indeed skilled readers and adults may part see a word then read it whole. The process or operation of the skill becomes so automatic it is difficult to reflect and realize how the skill has developed. The method has a certain element of imitation in it and to this extent, it can be simply the adult forgetting the difficulties of childhood saying, 'Do as I do, this is the way', and failing to provide the child with the real key to reading, means of visual and auditory analysis. Stressing reading for meaning is much more closely linked with the *performance* of the skill rather than its gradual growth and development.

Also, the emphasis in the word method upon the meaning and importance of word forms at the expense of the recognition of the importance of letters, illustrates my impression of the way in which reading research has concentrated on one factor of the reading process at a time. By noticing one aspect of the relationship, it has been difficult to keep in mind the rest of the situation, but if we pay attention to word form and ignore letter form, we play a game of black-and-white thinking. There need be no controversy between the word and phonic methods. Both are just different ways of looking at the reading process and trying to isolate one factor at a time for closer attention.

Sentence method

The sentence method is an extension of the word method in that it emphasizes the importance of comprehension but uses the sentence instead of the word as the unit of meaning, and tends to attach less importance to letter-names or sounds. Although it is difficult to define a sentence, the method tends to make use of reading material from the beginning which is characterized by a group of printed words that make sense, not single words. As with the word methods, context is used as an aid to recognizing unfamiliar words, reading material is based on children's interests and spoken vocabulary, although the actual speech patterns of children are not necessarily utilized. It is hoped that the use of continuous prose leads to children reading more fluently and rapidly. Again there is behind this idea an adult insight into the level of performance. Because children read aloud in a manner unlike their level of speech competency, it does not necessarily follow that they fail to understand what they read.

Recent research by the writer (1969) suggests that some teachers place considerable importance on the attribute of *fluency* as a criterion of children's reading progress. However, recent studies have shown that fluency may be characteristic of a higher level of reading attainment, which can only be acquired after passing through certain subsidiary stages, characterized by stumbling and by rereading; e.g. the work of MacKinnon (1959) and Clay (1966, 1969) already mentioned.

In learning to read, repetitions and stumbling are not so much serious errors as means by which the teacher can diagnose the particular child's stage of reading development, and for the child, the means of reinforcing correct responses. Word-by-word oral reading often in the past looked upon as a sign of poor oral expression—'barking at print'—may serve a very real function in the learning process.

Both word and sentence methods are important, emphasizing as they do the importance of obtaining meaning from what is read. But to the extent that they emphasize the function of the skill and the quality of its performance, they underrate the skill's complexity and the long and often slow process of acquiring it. Also, they ignore the importance of being able to use reading in a flexible manner; e.g. adapting the rate of reading to *what* is read.

Teachers often use both methods, sometimes starting with the word and proceeding to the sentence, sometimes in the reverse order. Flash cards and matching devices are often an important part of the procedure. The word 'flash' is usually applied to cards with a single word or sentence rapidly presented to children so they are discouraged from looking at the letters in words, or words in a sentence as an aid to recognition, but rather are encouraged to recognize 'at a single glance', a familiar word or a short easily understood and remembered phrase or sentence. Words or sentences may have distinct personal meaning for the children with whom the teacher uses this type of teaching apparatus. Teachers need to be aware of the way in which children are identifying and recognizing words; for instance, that they are not recognizing the card with *the* on it from the milk stain on the back of it rather than letter or word shape clues.

The use of matching devices may proceed through a series of development tasks, such as:

a)   matching two pictures of an object;
b)   observing the picture with its appropriate word label;
c)   matching separate word and picture cards;
d)   matching word and word—no pictorial clue, moving away from the
concrete level;
e)   then the stages *b—d* may be repeated using a sentence or group of
words in place of a single word label.

The 'language-experience' approach

Some teachers, of course, realize that individual children or groups of
children have different experiences and encourage them to share these
with the class as a whole. Sometimes the experience is initiated by the
teachers and children are led to talk about what they have been doing.
The teacher and children write these oral expressions on the blackboard
or in individual news books or class 'books'—often large sheets of stapled
paper. Illustrations to accompany the children's words or phrases are
added by the pupils. The children then read the material and become
familiar with the words or phrases. Sometimes the teacher duplicates the
sentences and phrases, and then these are matched starting with the whole
sentence or phrase and proceeding to the individual words in the original
'news' or story in order to develop 'sight' vocabulary.

In this approach the emphasis is placed on experience as a basis for
learning, and the reading materials are based on the child's own language.
A popular variation is the practice of teachers encouraging children to
draw pictures of their interests or 'News', the teacher then writing at the
child's dictation the appropriate caption. It is intended that during the
recording process the children will observe the relationship of speaking to
writing and reading. Discussion about the captions leads to pupils learning
about sound and symbol, the alphabet, repetition of words and symbols,
punctuation, sentence meaning. Later the child writes his own reading
material which the teacher may edit. At this stage he will need formalized
spelling instruction and vocabulary development; he may be encouraged
to make his own 'word file' or record new words in alphabetic order in a
word dictionary of his own compiling. Eventually he uses more formal
published materials.

Believers in this approach feel that one of the most important results is
the concept the pupil develops about himself and about reading. Two

American proponents (Lee and Allen, 1963) have outlined a sequence which they believe children follow as they learn by this approach:

1 What a child thinks about he can talk about
2 What he can talk about can be expressed in painting, writing, or some other form
3 Anything he writes can be read
4 He can read what he writes and what other people write
5 As he represents his speech sounds with symbols, he uses the same symbols (letters) over and over
6 Each letter in the alphabet stands for one or more sounds that he makes when he talks
7 Every word begins with a sound that he can write down
8 Most words have an ending sound
9 Many words have something in between
10 Some words are used over and over in our language and some words are not used very often
11 What he has to say and write is as important to him as what other people have written for him to read
12 Most of the words he uses are the same ones which are used by other people who write for him to read.

It should be noted that this approach includes at various stages emphasis upon sentences, words, letters and letter-sound correspondence. It proceeds from the egocentric stage of the child's cognitive development to growing interest in other people. To this extent, it is a balanced programme but it demands from the teacher some form of recording of individual children's vocabulary growth and diagnosis of their progress in phonic knowledge. It is not an easy approach to use in large classes. It has little in the way of training in visual and auditory ability built into it. It is very dependent upon children attaching importance to writing and reading as valid means of expression, in comparison say with painting, 'play' and other forms of free activity.

References

BAILEY, M. H. (1967) 'The utility of phonic generalizations in Grades One through Six', *Reading Teacher,* **20,** 413–18.
BOND, G. L. and DYKSTRA, R. (1967) *Report of the Coordinating Center for First Grade Reading Instruction Programs* Minneapolis: University of Minnesota.

CHALL, J. (1967) *Learning to Read—The Great Debate* New York: McGraw-Hill.

CLAY, M. M. (1966) 'Emergent reading behaviour', Unpublished doctoral dissertation, University of Auckland, New Zealand.

CLAY, M. M. (1969) 'Reading errors and self-correction behaviour', *Br. J. Educ. Psychol.*, **39**, i, 47-56.

CLYMER, T. (1963) 'The utility of phonic generalizations in the primary grades', *Reading Teacher*, **16**, 252-8.

DIACK, H. (1965) *In Spite of the Alphabet* London: Chatto & Windus.

DURKIN, D. (1964) 'Early readers—reflections after six years of research', *Reading Teacher*, **18**, 3-7.

DURRELL, D. (1968) 'Phonics problems in beginning reading', *Forging Ahead in Reading*, **12**, i, 12th Annual Convention, I.R.A., 19-25.

FLESCH, R. (1955) *Why Johnny Can't Read* New York: Harper & Row.

GOODACRE, E. J. (1969) 'Published reading schemes', *Educational Research*, **12**, i, 30-5.

HAY, J. and WINGO, C. E. (1948) *Reading with Phonics* New York: J. B. Lippincott.

HILLERICH, R. L. (1967) 'What's one way to teach beginning reading', in Moloney, R. (ed.) *Reading: Research to Reality* California Reading Association, 36-54.

LEE, D. M. and ALLEN, R. V. (1963) *Learning to Read Through Experience* New York: Appleton-Century-Crofts.

MACKINNON, A. R. (1959) *How Children Learn to Read* Toronto: Copp Clark Publishing Co.

MARCHBANKS, G. and LEVIN, H. (1965) 'Cues by which children recognise words', *Journal of Educational Psychology*, **106**, 57-61.

MCCULLOUGH, C. (1968) 'Balanced reading development' in *Innovation and Change in Reading Instruction*, 67th Yearbook, National Society for the Study of Education, **11**, 320-56.

MUEHL, S. (1962) 'The effects of letter-name knowledge on learning to read a word list in kindergarten children', *Journal of Educational Psychology* (Aug.), 181-6.

PORTER, D. and POPP, H. M. (1967) 'Narrative progress report on programmed reading research project (1)'. Unpublished duplicated paper: Harvard University.

REID, J. F. (1966) 'Learning to think about reading', *Educational Research*, **9**, i, 56-62.

WHEELOCK, W. H. and SILVAROLI, N. M. (1967) 'An investigation of visual discrimination training for beginning readers' *Journal of Typographic Research*, **1**, 147-56.

2 : 2   Linguistics and the teaching of reading

Elizabeth J. Goodacre

It has already been mentioned that linguists have been critical of teachers' methods of teaching children the sounds of the letters and sound-letter relations. Also, in discussing the sentence method, I sometimes used the phrase 'a group of words' because an accurate definition of a sentence as a unit of meaning is not always easy. For instance, some modern linguists use the term 'phonological unit' (a measure of sound waves), which despite the number of the so-called sentences in it, or the interminable run-on nature, seems to be synonymous with a sentence as a unit of meaning. A phonological unit ends when the speaker shows by falling intonation or silence that he has reached a terminal point. In other words, a sentence in written language is connected with the convention of the use of a capital letter, a verb and a full stop. In spoken speech the 'sentence' is something else again. Indeed, a great deal of the present work being done by linguists is concerned with the effort to evolve a technique of analysis of the *internal structure* of both spoken and written speech.

Linguists may be critical of the reading teacher's ideas on language, its structural form and the teaching of 'sounds', but to many teachers of reading it seems that linguists underrate the complexity of the reading process. Certainly, many linguists subscribe to the belief that speech is the primary language function and that writing or reading are secondary or are even derived from oral language.

Importance of speech and language development

It is not surprising therefore to find current in their writings the ideas that 1) simple 'ordinary' speech development is all that a child needs to be

GOODACRE, ELIZABETH J. (1971) 'Linguistics and the teaching of reading', *Children and Learning to Read* London: Routledge & Kegan Paul, 47–53.

ready for systematic reading instruction; 2) reading is very dependent upon auditory memories—being able to recall the sound patterns of speech; 3) comprehension or understanding of what he reads depends in the main upon the reader's ability to 'hear' or internally conjure up the sound of the written word in its normal inflection and to hear the combination of stress, tone and pitch of what is read to give it 'meaning'. At least one linguist has questioned these ideas by pointing out that children such as deaf-mutes can learn to read. The foreign-born, the bilingual and the hearing-impaired can learn to read and write, and these are all children whose auditory memories for spoken language are disadvantaged.

How far does speech coincide with written language? Does speech fulfil a superior function to reading? Harrell (1957) has produced evidence that the length of written stories does not correspond to oral compositions and that written stories tend to share more complicated sentences (as indicated by the index of subordinate clauses). Studies using a technique called 'transformational grammar' have indicated that oral compositions show significant differences from written language in structural elements at various age levels and therefore possibly different stages of children's cognitive development. (Spache, 1968, has described transformational grammar as a system of analysis 'which attempts to interpret the manipulation of syntactic units, as by expansion, reduction or re-arrangement of basic or kernel utterances or by the combining of several sentences into one'.) Marquardt (1964) has noted also a number of differences between reading aloud and conversation, including the even tempo used in reading, the relationship of pauses to grammatical structure in oral reading as contrasted with the unpredictability of such pauses in conversation, the lack of meaningfully filled silences in oral reading in comparison with the frequency of these (accompanied by shrugs, grimaces and gestures) in conversation, and the repetitive structurally incomplete nature of conversation, particularly the use of almost meaningless phrases and words ('you know') to ensure rapport with the listener or provide the speaker with thinking time.

Obviously some of the difficulties between linguists and reading teachers result from the linguists' ideas about 'ordinary' speech and the development of language. Reading the writings of some linguists one has the impression that they underrate the effects of environmental factors (e.g. social class differences in speech usage, institutional effects on early language development of children). The more recent studies of children's writing and speech seem to concentrate on the analysis of syntax (i.e. sentence construction and rules of grammar, etc.) and although this is valuable, one needs to know more about the effects upon language development of family relationships and parental personalities.

In this country, Bernstein and his colleagues have studied the relationship between language and social factors. Bernstein (1971) has suggested that if the social relationship is close (i.e. much is shared in the speakers' environment) then a *restricted language code* can operate (heavy dependence on gesture and facial expression, short 'sentences', few logical connections used because it is assumed the listener is familiar with the content of the conversation). When the relationship is not close, more has to be put into the 'messages' (sentences are longer, more clauses used) and the speaker uses an *elaborated code*. According to Bernstein, the middle-class child is exposed at home to *both codes* while the lower-class child's environment is that of the restricted code.

From work on readability measurement (Chall, 1958; Bormuth, 1964), it would seem that the restricted and elaborated codes of Bernstein are basically simpler or more complex forms of spoken language, and as applied to reading materials would be written language that is easier or harder to read. In this connection, the *cloze procedure* has provided us with information about how readers derive meaning of unknown words from the reading content. This technique involves the deletion of words from printed passages, the reader being expected to supply the exact word that has been left out. The deletions may be every fifth, tenth or whatever determined word, constituting what is termed a structural or 'any-word' deletion, or there may be selection of particular parts of speech (e.g. noun, verb)—a lexical deletion. The test may be given before or after reading the original text. Many of the studies using the technique use an 'every fifth word' deletion in a pre-cloze procedure, i.e. before reading the undeleted text. The cloze technique can serve not only to measure the reading difficulty of passages, but also as a measure in studies of learning, motivation and personality, and as a teaching device. It may be a valid means of studying the syntactic and semantic effects of context on language units and their basic differences.

Broadly speaking then, linguists have tended to minimize the differences between speech (restricted or elaborated) and reading (oral or silent) of reading materials (easier or harder to read).

Reading as 'decoding'

Three linguistic specialists, Bloomfield, Barnhart and Fries, have been taken fairly seriously in the last decade by those interested in the teaching of

reading. They believed that the process of learning to read could be simplified if linguists could identify the basic speech sounds in English, and
establish the relationships between these sounds and the letters that usually
represented them. In the reading schemes they designed, the most frequent
and most regular phoneme-grapheme correspondences were taught first.
They also considered the best way to teach these correspondences in words
carefully selected to permit the learner to discover for himself the relationship between letters and sounds. They disliked the isolation of sounds, and
the teaching of 'phonic rules'. They were opposed to the use of pictures
and to encouraging the learner to use context clues, since this might dis-
tract from the main task—paying close attention to the *letters*. Words used
in practice reading material for the beginner were chosen on the basis of
correspondence already taught, e.g. 'Nan had a fat cat' (Bloomfield); 'Dan
can pat the cat' (Fries). Thus gradually the most common spelling patterns
were mastered by reading orally words which contain these patterns. The
learner avoided the irregularities of English which might confuse him and
gained plenty of practice in applying the alphabetic principles or relating
spelling to spoken language.

Levin's experiments (1964–67) suggest that this type of programming of
one sound for one spelling pattern may have limitations (i.e. mastering
can, man, tan and then moving on to *cat, mat, rat*). Although Levin found
that it takes longer to learn two sounds for one letter (e.g. to learn that *g*
is pronounced as in *garage* and *giraffe*), than to learn one association at a
time, dual association learning has a greater transfer value (e.g. more useful
in a wider context). Thus systems that teach single associations may be
easier for beginners, but their transfer value for 'real' reading is limited,
since English spelling has not been reformed and more than one sound for
one letter or letter groupings occurs.

Further, more recent analyses of English words by linguists go considerably beyond the simpler correspondences put forward by Bloomfield (e.g.
Venezky and Weir, 1966). Work by Chomsky and Halle (1968) suggests
that there are more complex and powerful rules for the relations between
spoken and written words and that English spelling may indeed make
more sense than we have been led to believe by the purely descriptive
linguists, since it supplies the native speaker with considerable syntactic
and semantic information—'clues' and expectations in regard to both the
meaning of particular words and the meaning of the total phrase or paragraph. As Chall (1969) has suggested, when analysed on a deeper level,
retaining the 'silent' *g* in *sign* and silent *b* in *bomb* makes sense when we
come to the derivatives *signal* and *bombardier*. Also Chomsky believes

that written language has a life of its own—at a certain point it is not a direct representation of the spoken language, but a carrier of complex semantic and syntactic information.

Probably a 'decoding' type beginning programme may be useful but if children are kept on it too long—looking for graphic similarities—they are receiving insufficient practice in using syntactic and semantic cues, and therefore fail to develop flexibility in reading techniques. The danger is that children kept too long on a programme in which there is a consistent correspondence between letter and sound may become conditioned to this aspect of the reading situation, developing a 'mind set' for consistency which impedes progress.

Early training probably should emphasize building up a large bank of words and concepts, nouns and main verbs, so the child is able to deal with or process a *wide* variety of ideas. But at the same time, there should be ample exposure to varying structural patterns or writing styles to permit reactions to variations in sentences. Roberts (1969) has referred to the way in which the use of books of the rigidly controlled type tended to produce the same characteristics of language style in the written work of the children using them.

In case I appear to have been overcritical of the contribution of linguistics, let me hasten to add that linguistics has a great deal to offer the classroom teacher but I believe it is up to educators to apply this knowledge. Certainly some aspects which deserve consideration are the following.

Linguistics can provide the reading teacher with a fairly accurate description of the spoken language; techniques for language and reading research, e.g. cloze technique; new criteria for judging the readability of reading materials; new insights into children's language and how to describe more accurately the way children learn; and clues on how language conveys meaning.

References

BERNSTEIN, B. B. (1971) *Class, Codes and Control* London: Routledge & Kegan Paul.

BORMUTH, J. R. (1964) *Relationships between Selected Language Variables and Comprehension Ability and Difficulty*, U.S. Office of Education Cooperative Research Project no. 2082, Los Angeles: University of California.

CHALL, J. (1958) *Readability: An Appraisal of Research and Application* Bureau of Educational Research, Ohio State University.

CHALL, J. (1969) 'Research in linguistics and reading instruction: implications for further research and practice' in J. A. Figurel (ed.) *Reading and Realism* 13, *i*, Proceedings of the Thirteenth Annual Convention, International Reading Association, 560–71.

CHOMSKY, N. and HALLE, M. (1968) *Sound Patterns of English* New York: Harper & Row.

HARRELL, L. (1957) 'A comparison of the development of oral and written language in school-age children', *Monograph Society for Research in Child Development*, 22, *iii*, serial no. 66.

LEVIN, H. (1964–7) *Project Literacy Reports*, nos. 1–8, Ithaca, New York: Cornell University.

MARQUARDT, W. F. (1964) 'Language interference in reading', *Reading Teacher*, 18, 214–18.

ROBERTS, G. R. (1969) *Reading in Primary Schools* London: Routledge & Kegan Paul.

SPACHE, G. D. (1968) 'Contributions of allied fields to the teaching of reading' in *Innovation and Change in Reading*, 67th Yearbook, N.S.S.E., II, 237–90.

VENEZKY, R. L. and WEIR, R. H. (1966) *A Study of Selected Spelling to Sound Correspondence Patterns*, Cooperative Research Project, Stanford University.

2 : 3   Linguistics, psychology and the teaching of reading

Constance M. McCullough

I

With every contribution and every criticism from relevant disciplines, the teaching of reading has the opportunity to improve. All you have to do to realize this is to see what happens in classrooms in which there are poorly-informed teachers as compared with classrooms in which well-informed teachers continuously reassess their practices in the light of new information. Historically and hysterically, as these contributions and criticisms have come, we have tended to go overboard, doing too much of the new thing or applying it in ways and at times that are not best or even desirable for reading growth. Materials have appeared which stress the new, and completely ignore some very worthwhile elements in the total reading program. They are welcomed like manna from heaven. Sometimes I wonder which is worse—to be poorly-informed or to be caught in the hysteria of the new bit—though ordinarily I try not to say this aloud.

The thing we must learn as teachers is that there is no perfect contribution or perfect material; there is only a perfect teacher; and that perfect teacher is the one who evaluates each contribution to see what it can be and mean in an entire program which consists of much more than any one contribution.

As teachers we have been trained in the application of psychological principles to classroom procedures. We might be said to be amateur psychologists. Certainly we have had a great deal of help from psychologists in the teaching of reading. But most of us have had little training in the linguistic concepts which now clamor to be recognized. We have been flying on one wing. Somehow, now, in mid-air, we must assemble that

MCCULLOUGH, CONSTANCE M. (1967) 'Linguistics, psychology and the teaching of reading', *Elementary English*, April, 1967, 353–62.

other wing—of appropriate size and shape and timing to provide balance and efficient progress in flight.

It is interesting to note that when children have difficulty learning to read, we tend to blame material or method, and a critic comes along and says, "Do *more* of *this*." More phonics, for example. Actually, instead of doing more of what we have been doing, we should be exploring for the missing parts that we haven't known and haven't used. This is what Marianne Frostig (1961) did in developing her tests and materials for the identification and improvement of subskills in visual perception, and what Samuel Kirk (1961) did in developing his tests of psycho-linguistic abilities in young children. There are plenty of parts still missing in our knowledge of language. There is much still to explore. And I believe it will be only when the teacher of reading informs herself of the new findings in linguistics and psychology, and studies the possibilities of their congenial application, that a program superior to the ones currently used will emerge. It is in that belief that I present this paper.

II

At the recent Dallas meeting of the International Reading Association, I had the good fortune to hear a paper by Lee Deighton of Macmillan Company. Deighton is an editor and author who explores the problem of language and learning, and has made some very helpful contributions to vocabulary development.

In his paper he reminded his audience that, while the reading eye progresses in a series of pauses and movements, from left to right, in the case of English, it cannot during any one pause take in more than about an inch of print. On many occasions it may not view a whole word in any one pause. It may even see the back end of one word and the front end of another. The speed at which the eye performs in this manner is relatively limited, especially in unfamiliar material in which guesswork about the words the eye has skipped can be fatal to meaning.

The brain, meanwhile, is champing at the bit. It must assemble all of this garbage into something meaningful. While the eye trots earnestly along, the nerve impulses which process its findings may be going at as great a rate as 200 miles an hour. Various estimates have been given by various sources. For the nerve impulses it must be worse than wiping dishes for a meticulous washer. But the point that Deighton made is that the brain has a chance to do a thorough job of mulling over meanings, a chance to be right and wrong several times about the author's meaning. He speaks of it as a circular movement, though I am not sure that 'circular' exactly describes it and I suspect he is not either.

But with the example of an expression like 'the little white house', he shows that the ideas of 'little' and 'white' are modified when the eye comes to 'house', for a little house has not the littleness of a little dog, and the whiteness of white paint is not the same as the whiteness of feathers in a little white feather, or the whiteness of a stone in a little white stone. Therefore, Deighton believes that the mind holds in abeyance certain ideas as it explores the effect of other ideas upon them.

Let's see how Deighton's theory works on a sentence which I shall now read. My first word is *In*. I shall continue slowly to add words, and you as a listener try to determine what adjustments your thought has to make to grasp the meaning of this sentence: 'In . . . its . . . hose-like . . . gray . . . trunk, . . . the . . . little . . . figure . . . on . . . the . . . matchbox . . . carried . . . a . . . Republican . . . banner.'

The word *In* has several different meanings, such as that referring to time, place, manner, or state of being. *Its* suggests possession by an in-animate either in a previous sentence or in the current one. Linguists call *its* a noun determiner and expect a noun to follow it sooner or later. *Its* con-firms the fact that *In* is being used as the beginning of a phrase. *Hose-like* has an attributive form implying that a noun is soon to come, but is puzzling in meaning because there are several kinds of hose. *Gray* is another attributive form which still does not identify the hose. *Trunk* is a surprise, for the usual trunk into which one puts things is not shaped like a hose of any kind and is not ordinarily owned by an *it*.

My pause, which is here signaled by a comma, marks the end of the phrase, and gives hope for the coming of a noun. *The*, indeed, signals that coming. *Little*, another attributive word, is again a puzzler, this time because littleness is relative. *Figure* qualifies as a noun and as an inanimate; *its* must refer to *figure*. But *figure* has several meanings, too. Does a figure eight have something in a hose-like gray trunk? Or is the word *figure* used as a general term for a shape of some kind? If *hose-like gray trunk* has suggested *elephant* to the listener, the reference to a little figure is indeed baffling. The listener feels still worse when he hears that the little figure is *on the matchbox*, for now the size is whittled down to nothing like an elephant.

Carried follows the noun phrase in the expected position for the verb in a Noun-Verb-Noun type of basic sentence (NVN), and confirms this hunch with its *d* ending. But there are different meanings for *carry* too. The listener must settle for the idea that this *carry* is used in the sense of 'hold in a stationary position', for you can't go far on a matchbox. *A* denotes the coming of another noun. *Republican* is in either an adjective or noun position. The sentence could stop there. But *banner* proves that *Republican* is an adjective, and the listener does not have to imagine what kind of square a Republican would have to be to fit on a matchbox. *Republican* confirms the hunch that the figure is an elephant after all; the trunk belongs to the elephant. The *In* at the beginning of the sentence means the trunk was curled around. It is an embracing *In*. The listener must imagine what the banner may have on it, who might own such a thing, whether the little figure is a statue or a picture, upright or prostrate, attached or unattached, and so forth.

The listener who had had no experience with the Republican emblem would not get the meaning of this sentence at all. Or if, in listening, he did not catch the word *Republican*—if, in reading, he skipped over it—he would be mystified. The African listening to this and knowing the Republican emblem might still see in his mind an African elephant; an Indian, an Indian elephant.

Now, what did you smart people have to be able to do to get this message clearly? You had to listen carefully. It is said that we catch seventy-five per cent of the sounds we could hear, and that we then add the missing links by context or situation, to realize the intended words.

You had to note the similarity of my Indiana English pronunciation to that to which you were born or are accustomed. You had to invest these spoken symbols with the meanings your experience has given them. You had to group into meaningful English units—that is, words, phrases—the stream of sounds you heard. Intonation and pauses peculiar to the English sentence helped you. In reading, of course, you would have had to reinvest the *symbols for sound* with intonation and pauses.

Familiarity with the structure of the English sentence helped you. The little words, like *in* and *on* and *the*, were important clues, also. You had to know what they signaled and what they might mean if they were words of multiple meaning. You had to catch the signal for the past tense of the verb *carry*, in order to know the time of this observation. You had to know the function of a pronoun and be able to reason that *its* referred to *figure* and not to *matchbox* or *banner*.

If this sentence had carried an emotional intent, you would have had to be sensitive to that, also. As it was, if you are a Democrat, you simply had to restrain yourself.

III

The English language is literally laced with signals, or lacily littered with signals, however you like it. In a composition of ten sentences, it is quite possible that an *it* in the last sentence refers clear back to a noun in the first sentence. Phrases and synonyms echo one another from one sentence to another, the same meaning sometimes serving even different functions.

Our study of meaning, therefore, cannot be confined to one word or one phrase or one clause or one sentence or even one paragraph. The meaning and even the pronunciation of some words depend upon the purpose of the speaker or author. Some of the things which we have thought of as niceties —perhaps to be observed and taught, and perhaps not—such as the style or mood of the speaker or author—even deliberate ambiguities—cannot be optional if, as in many cases, clear reception of meaning cannot be gained without them.

What I have been saying is that all of these skills and knowledges, all of these dimensions of concepts, are the concern of teachers of reading. The readiness of the young child for reading, the readiness of the college student for a science text assignment, depend upon such preparation. And in passing I should like to observe that what Robert Lado (1957, 1964) has done for the understanding of the language needs of a Spanish-speaking child in learning English, what Claude Wise and others have done to compile the linguistic needs of children from still other backgrounds, must be put in a form readily useful to teachers. Houghton Mifflin's *Introducing English* for the reading readiness of Spanish-speaking children is a step in the right direction. But *is* it not possible to produce comparable material with suggestions and additions to accommodate the needs of children of other language groups as well?

IV

Meanwhile, back at the ranch, psychologists and educators have tried to extend their understanding of the reading process. You probably know of the work of Irving Lorge at Columbia University, who investigated certain vocabulary problems with Thorndike, and on his own developed a formula by which the difficulty of reading material could be roughly determined. His formula was one of several, such as the Flesch, the Dale-Chall, and the Spache, by which school systems and teachers can estimate the difficulty of textbooks and tradebooks before perpetrating them on youngsters.

Lorge was aware that elements were missing from the formula. Obviously conceptual difficulty was one. But he believed that organization of material was also a potent factor. From John Carroll, the well-known linguist at Harvard, he obtained some paragraphs from essays written for College Board Examinations. He selected passages of equal length and difficulty according to his formula. The vocabularies, the sentence length and complexity, the topic treated, were the same. The only apparent difference, as far as Lorge could tell, lay in organization and in clues to organization. He tested students on the meaning of these passages and found that they were better able to answer questions on passages well-organized *and* bearing clues to organization.

I read his unpublished paper on this experiment in, I believe, the fall of 1960, and it so aroused my interest that I have really never recovered from the fascination of this problem.

It led me back to the work of James McCallister (1936) at Chicago Teachers College, in which he identified nine different kinds of paragraph organization which students should learn to recognize to facilitate their reading of textbooks. I studied a set of textbooks in science for the elementary school and found two kinds of pattern throughout the series— one in which an illustration is followed by a statement of principle, and one in which the steps in an experiment are enumerated. In a tenth-grade chemistry text I identified twelve different patterns of paragraph organization.

The problem, as I saw it, was to make teachers aware of these patterns and of ways to teach them so that students would not read everything the same way and come out with the main idea every time—sometimes useful and sometimes not so useful. You know, we have hypnotized our students and ourselves for years by stopping with 'the main idea and a few significant details' instead of considering the author's trend of thought.

Of course, the flaw in my thinking at the time was that I hoped to find comparable patterns in every text, whereas the truth is that each author tends to have a habit pattern of his own. The teacher must be able to recognize the patterns the author habitually uses if she is to help students to recognize and use them. The problem is to find the units of thought, composing patterns.

Unaware of Bloom's (1956) now famous taxonomy or of Guilford's (1959) now famous cube of cognitive processes, I produced empirically from my observations of textbooks in science and social studies a schema of the cognitive ingredients which are expressed in such material. To distinguish it from the creations of other great geniuses throughout history, I entitled it 'McCullough's Excelsior'—referring, of course, to the analogy someone once made, likening the action of ideas in the brain to the dumping of a raw egg into a box of excelsior. A linguist will tell you that this schema may be true of English speakers and not of speakers of some other languages, and so as I describe it you must realize that I am a prisoner of my own language.

Here it is: The brain of a human being receives sensory impressions of objects and living organisms in patterns of events and situations, modified by his own thought-and-feeling predispositions and reactions. He becomes conscious of various relationships; whole-part, cause-effect, sequential, comparison-contrast, and coordinate-subordinate. From these he can develop certain products of the mind: theories, laws and principles, generalizations, definitions, classifications, and procedures. These, in turn, he can support with examples, elaboration, and application.

The order in which he does any of these things is individual.

This schema does not include processes, such as induction or deduction, because I was concerned about what was on a printed page, not about how it got there. Neither does it include such topics as evaluation or analogy, for they are special cases of existing categories.

When you think of *words*, in connection with this schema, you see many more possibilities for the development of concepts and vocabulary relationships than we have ever used before. Dictionary definitions begin to look extremely sick, by comparison—as indeed they must be if the book is not to weigh a ton.

You also begin to see that if reading is thinking, then we should be sure that a child cannot only *speak English* but think in the various ways in the English language before we expect him to *decipher the print* and think in it. And if the child is to keep fresh the various ways of thinking, then our daily activities should offer this variety over a period of time. For example, what happens to other thought patterns when some preschool and kindergarten programs emphasize the use of context clues? This is good, but what is being done about other elements?

And if, in word-analysis, we use a set of cards on which the child must analyze words and then put them under headings, such as 'toys' and 'food', what are we doing to balance this with experiences in which *he* must decide the heading under which certain words he selects might belong; and what are we doing to give him equal exercise that is not simply a classification experience? You begin to see that in giving the child fifteen minutes of this and ten minutes of that in the classroom all of these years, we have been making decisions without knowing it—decisions that distort his readiness to meet the thought challenges of the reading task.

As I tried to identify the types of thought in sentences within paragraphs, I discovered for myself some very important facts about language in habitat. Let me give you an example. Take the sentence, 'He ran'. This is a statement of fact. It does not reveal the situation in which 'he' is. Now add, 'As he looked back over his shoulder he could see that the bear was still after him'. This second sentence does a lot. It suggests why he ran and tells what he did next:

The bear ran after him.
He ran.
He looked over his shoulder.
The bear was still coming.

So 'He ran' is not only a statement of an event but also a statement of the effect of a cause.

If, instead, the sentences read, 'He ran. Each step was the biggest he could possibly take', the second sentence describes the way he ran, elaborating the first. The first sentence may be a summary or generalization of the series of descriptive sentences to follow.

If, instead, the sentences read, 'He ran. She skipped after him', you have two statements of event, one event following another, and providing a contrast. You don't know the human motivation for this—whether they were both going toward the candy store, whether she just liked him, or whether he had learned early to stay away from women.

The upshot of this is that, just as the linguists have discovered that the sound of a letter depends upon the situation of the letter in the word—'back, bake, bark, balk'—and as Deighton (1959) found that the meaning of a word is altered by its relationships with other words—'The bare branch could bear the bear no longer'—so I found for myself that the meaning of a sentence, the contribution of a sentence, the classification of a sentence, depends upon its surroundings. The student who reads sentences like a string of beads, each at its isolated face-value, is headed for trouble. The teacher who confines her help to only what she considers the new, hard words, is missing many of the serious problems that confront the student. The elements of language are not islands. They create a fabric whose very open spaces are significant.

V

Another fascinating observation you can make if you *study* language instead of just using it, is that a second sentence seems sometimes to put a spotlight on a word or phrase in the preceding sentence. In 'He ran. She skipped', the contrast of *he* and *she*, *run* and *skipped*, stresses both of these elements. But in 'He ran. Each step. . . .' 'Each step. . . .' features the *ran*. In some paragraphs you can follow the author's progress in stressing first one dimension, then another, as though you were watching fireflies on a summer night. Language also contains an echo effect:

August was a very *dry* month.
The *thirsty* cattle stood by the *empty troughs*.
Farmers looked for *clouds* in the *blazing* skies.
But *no rains* came.

Listening activities can sharpen a student's sensitivity to types of ideas. I have enjoyed considerable enlightenment from listening activities myself. There is a person who has always reduced me to utter silence. I realize now that she has an intimidating habit of sounding like God but with less wisdom. Her emphatic judgmental statements about everything render further comment unnecessary if not unwelcome. I have also followed conversations in which the same person tells the same story to a succession of different people. With one partner who attempts to placate him, comment by comment, he becomes disgusted at what he interprets as lack of sympathy. With another partner who adds fuel to his fire—'How outrageous! . . . Well, I never! . . . *etc.*'—he is more angry at the end than he was at first. Students can learn a good deal about *sources of ambiguity* in language by recording conversations in which remarks have been misunderstood and misinterpreted. They don't have to leave home to get ample evidence for analysis in class.

Hilda Taba (1966) in her effort to encourage the use of higher thought processes in class discussions, has charted the level of challenge of teacher questions and the quality of student comments, with some very insightful results. And Hayakawa (1941) has shown how the insertion of certain loaded words can trigger feelings and reactions.

VI

Now, how can we help students gain some mastery over the linguistic problems in reading? If you wish to prove to your students that there is no telling where an author will go from one sentence to the next, give them a sentence and ask each student to say or write what might sensibly come next. In spite of the unpredictability of an author's next step, students must form hunches about what the author will do. You can give them a typical opening sentence for a paragraph of classification or comparison or cause and effect or illustration of a principle or definition or description or interpretation, and ask them to say what may happen next and why they think so.

Students of limited English background are not ready for the many ways in which English can express a single thought. They need experience in listening and reading to find duplication of thought in different wording.

If you wish to prove to your students how dependent they are on signal words, word order, and word endings in unfamiliar material, you may be inspired by Lewis Carroll or C. C. Fries to give them a sentence like this: 'The lorks of the inksy anks glom sterb stonk by co-glickent gunding'. They'll never guess that the atoms of the common gases form diatomic molecules by co-valent bonding, but they will know something about the relationships of the words and the nature of the statement.

Carl LeFevre in his helpful book, *Linguistics and the Teaching of Reading* (1964), gives lists of signal words. What he does not tell you is the frequency with which they don't signal what you expect. For example, 'both . . . and' are coordinates in the sentence, 'He was both clever and wise'. But in the sentence, 'They were both clever and wise', 'both' may be referring to *they*, signaling backwards instead of forwards to 'clever and wise'. The language is full of untrustworthy characters. Take the word *since*: 'Since you left the company, much has happened.' Is the *since* causal, with the meaning that nothing could happen as long as a bottleneck like you was around, or is it temporal, indicating only the passage of time? And what about the word *by*, an innocent-looking word which we have often passed over as we dwelt upon the rare noun which followed? 'Come by ten o'clock. Come by train. Come, by the way. Come by the house. Come by sometime.' The dictionary lists ten uses of *by* as a preposition alone, and several more as an adverb. In unfamiliar material the student should be cautious—should hold in abeyance, as Deighton says, his decision about its meaning.

For years we have told students that the word *however* signals a change of direction, a reversal; but it doesn't always. In written material, the questions, 'However did you do it?' and 'However, did you do it?' show their different intent only by the presence of the comma. And in many sentences, *however* adds to or limits the preceding idea rather than controverting it. We have had students look up hard words in the dictionary. Sometimes we should have them look up the easy ones to see the many meanings that are well established, not to speak of those which may be gathered in time.

How can we tell when 'you were' is singular and when it is plural and when it is condition contrary to fact? How can we tell that a question in a textbook is a question even before we come to the mark at the end? How can we tell the passive voice is being used and the subject is not the actor? What are the signals for the remote past that help us sense flashbacks and time change?

If the author uses signals such as *first, next, finally, on the other hand, besides, another point, in summary,* his organization is easy to follow. That is, it is easy if the student recognizes the signals. But if an author just as well-organized does not give these helpful signals, the reader has to sense them. How can the student sense that a new point is being made, not just an addition to the old? How can he tell that a subordinate point is being made? How can he tell that now the author is telling all the negative things about a topic, having just told all the positive things? How can he tell the flavor of a generalization from a specific fact, a definition from a statement of function, a principle from an illustration? By ear training and by visual analysis, students must learn how to detect such differences: but if we ourselves do not know the points to be observed, we cannot teach students to follow the ideas of the author.

A characteristic of English is the use of pronouns or alternate words instead of repetition of the same word. What proof is there that the pronoun refers to *this* word and not to *that*? What tells the reader that two words are being used synonymously?

Some nouns like *reindeer* and *fish* have the same form for singular and plural. In what situations do these dual purposes create reading difficulty and a dependence upon signals?

VII

I do not have to tell you that this kind of learning can be done only by children who are well-acquainted with the English language. We should expand our idea of the disadvantaged to include all of us: children who do not speak English, children who do not recognize 'book English', children unready for the concepts in assigned texts, and teachers unready to help them decode the meanings they encounter.

The reading act requires the decoding of written symbols into the sounds which those symbols rather inaccurately represent. The decoding of written symbols into sounds gives the reader the original speech-symbol for an idea. The interaction of these ideas, appraised by a knowledge of the order of

English, the signals of relationship, and the possible meanings each word or phrase or clause may have in a variety of contexts, gives the reader what, from his experience, the author has meant to say. If the reader stops here, he will be fair game for any propagandist and will never produce ideas of his own. Now he must use his thought processes upon what he has observed and gathered, to develop products of his mind stimulated by this reading. The last step in the reading act is the use or expression of these ideas, these products, and the testing of them to see their validity.

In this paper I am concerned mainly with the second step, the decoding of meanings. But it is only one part of the total process. We should never magnify it to the exclusion of other important parts. Neither should we neglect it, either as teachers or as students of the language.

One wonderful contribution that this study of meaning can make is that it can vitalize some of the erstwhile deadly parts of the English program, those whitened bones set in orderly rows on the blackboard, defying utility and interest. Who hasn't hated the so-called irregular verbs: *drink, drank, drunk; see, saw, seen?* But Archibald Hill (1958) in his classification of verbs shows fifteen or more patterns in which verbs are found. One realizes that the so-called irregular verbs are friends in disguise, with built-in signals to tense, whereas a verb like *cut,* which we have always appreciated for its dependability, gives no clue. We can realize the 'signal' advantage to the child-who-*sounds* these endings or internal changes *correctly.*

The structural approach to English, used by many teachers with foreign students and the disadvantaged, is notoriously dull. Here is a who-dun-it I wrote in India, in structural English: 'This is a man. This is a robber. This is a knife. This is a murder. This is a jail.' I couldn't get a publisher. But if children can make discoveries about verbs, about structure, about the ways language works—in listening, speaking, reading, and writing activities—the language arts program will get a better Hooper rating.[1] Curiosity will supplant lethargy, and discovery will replace boredom and inefficiency in learning. Practice will have more meaning.

I believe that we are on the verge of a great awakening in the language arts. (Perhaps it is niggardly of me not to say 'RE-awakening'.) There are more reasons for thinking this than I have time to convey. If we inform ourselves about the nature of our language, if we are curious and interested ourselves, neither we nor our children will need the artificial stimulus of color on letters, or the evasive crutches by which we first teach a symbol for the symbol of a symbol, and then the symbol of a symbol that the

---

1   *Editorial footnote*: In Britain, the equivalent to the Hooper rating is the TAM rating—Television Audience Measurement.

symbol for the symbol stands for. While some linguists would have us start with the alphabet, others with 'Nan can fan Dan', and others with children's natural language, we should be good enough specialists in the teaching of reading to know that none of these alone is sufficient.

Let the linguist tell us about the language in his orderly way. Let the psychologist tell us how children learn. Let us then use this information to make a more suitable program for learning than either can conceive. Let us be curious about our own language so that the zeal created by our own efforts of discovery will electrify our classrooms. Let us have the restraint not to impose the fruits of our discoveries in dull little lists or artificial sentences upon children whose being cries to express itself. Rather, let us set the stage so that the discovery can be theirs and the learning confirmed by the intensity of their attention at the moment of insight.

Twenty-three years ago I reported the discoveries my college students had made about seven types of context clues to the meaning of unfamiliar words. *My* thinking stopped with theirs. I realize now that we were seeing only the top of the iceberg. Nine-tenths of the signals suggestive of meaning were hidden by our ignorance of other supportive linguistic clues. Those context clues are still valid. But think how much more you and I can do today to give our children power through insight.

References

BLOOM, B. S. *et al* (1956) *Taxonomy of Educational Objectives* New York: McKay.

DEIGHTON, LEE (1959) *Vocabulary development in the classroom* New York: Teachers' College Press, Columbia University.

FRIES, C. C. (1962) *Linguistics: The Study of Language* New York: Holt, Rinehart & Winston.

FRIES, C. C. (1962) *The Structure of English* New York: Harcourt, Brace & World.

FROSTIG, MARIANNE (1961) *Developmental Test of Visual Perception* Los Angeles: the author.

GUILFORD, JOY P. (1959) 'Three Faces of Intellect', *American Psychologist*, 14, 469–79.

HAYAKAWA, S. I. (1941) *Language in Action* New York: Harcourt, Brace & World.

HILL, ARCHIBALD A. (1958) *Introduction to Linguistic Structures* New York: Harcourt, Brace & World.

KIRK, SAMUEL A. and MCCARTHY, JAMES (1961) 'The Illinois Test of Psycho-linguistic ,Abilities: An approach to differential diagnosis', *American Journal of Mental Deficiency*, 56, 339–412.

LADO, ROBERT (1957) *Linguistics Across Cultures* Ann Arbor: University of Michigan Press.

LADO, ROBERT (1964) *Language Teaching: A Scientific Approach* New York: McGraw-Hill.

LEFEVRE, CARL (1964) *Linguistics and the Teaching of Reading* New York: McGraw-Hill.

MCCALLISTER, JAMES (1936) 'Reading ability of junior college freshmen', *Chicago School Journal*, 18, 79–82.

TABA, HILDA (1966) *Teaching Strategies and Cognitive Function in Elementary School Children*, U.S. Office of Education Cooperative Research Project, no. 2404, San Francisco: San Francisco State College.

2:4 The language-experience approach to the teaching of reading

Lawrence W. Carrillo

Introduction

One of the major difficulties with any *published* materials for the teaching of reading, whether printed in traditional orthography or in i.t.a., is the necessary assumption of common experiential background. That is, the important thing in the teaching of reading, from the first word, is the fact that the process is made meaningful to the children. If the words, sentences, concepts included are full of meaning for the children, if they have linguistic relevance, if they have been heard and spoken by the children prior to their printed presentation, learning to read will be relatively simple for most. If, on the other hand, the printed page represents a type of communication which is different, and if the situations found in the story are some which have never been experienced, learning to read is difficult.

A large number of studies, including my own dissertation (1957) have seemed to show that children from homes which provide a broad experiential background, especially in language-experience, have little difficulty in learning to read. Success in reading is more certainly guaranteed if you have the right parents, and they are economically fortunate enough to provide you with both experiences and conversation about the experiences. But let us examine this!

Such studies may only have proven that the materials with which we have been teaching reading are designed to fit *the particular experiences* of children from a particular kind of home background. Our school culture may be attuned to upper-middle-class values, language and concepts; children who do not have this background fail because *so much* is new

CARRILLO, LAWRENCE W. (1967) 'The language-experience approach to the teaching of reading', in Downing, J. and Brown, H. (eds) *The Second International Reading Symposium* London: Cassell, 197–205.

and different. Perhaps, for children from different environments, there was so little meaning in the educational task that it is rejected from the outset. Another fact which may add to the possibility of this interpretation has to do with intelligence testing, where there is also the assumption of commonality of experience. We now know that you can trust intelligence-test results only insofar as commonality of experience and conceptual background holds (if that far).

This problem is brought home with great force when you attempt to be an educator in a country different from your own. In Liberia, where I have spent this last year, neither British nor American materials 'fit' the children well enough to produce much meaning from the reading process. To see a teacher attempting to describe something included in a primary grade story which the children (and perhaps even the teacher) have never seen, is a very frustrating experience. It is worse because, even though you may have experienced this thing yourself, your own ability to communicate the concept will be as limited as the overlap between the two cultures. You must know the Liberian culture rather well in order to draw parallels for explanatory purposes. All this is true even though the official language in Liberia is English. Obviously, the answer is materials for the teaching of reading which fit the culture in which they are used. But in a small country, where only a small percentage of the population is literate, and without a great deal of money, the publication of suitable educational materials presents a nearly insurmountable problem.

There is a *partial* answer, however, in the language-experience approach. Recently, this way of teaching reading has become more widely known, to lay readers as well as educators, through Sylvia Ashton-Warner's book *Teacher* (1961). I find Peace Corps Volunteers using an adaptation of this approach deep in the bush, simply because this book and its inspirational account of a comparable situation (in New Zealand) has made such an impression on them. . . .

The language-experience approach

The language-experience approach may be basically outlined in only four steps, as follows:

1 *Experience.* The first essential is a first-hand group (or individual if the approach is applied in an individualized fashion) experience which contains sufficient inherent interest to produce a discussion. This may vary

from daily events, including descriptions of the weather, to describing and evaluating experiences occurring on a study trip.

2   *Awareness.* The teacher leads the children in a discussion of the experience, recording (usually on the chalkboard) phrases and sentences used by class members. Manuscript writing is used in primary grades and either manuscript or cursive in higher grades.

3   *Composition.* The class, with teacher guidance, decides on the sentences and the order of these sentences needed to tell their story. The teacher may then write this story on the chalkboard in the order decided upon, and the class reads the story.

4   *Permanence.* Depending upon the nature of the story, the teacher may decide to give the material greater permanence by transferring it to an oaktag chart[1] or large newsprint sheet. This step converts the class's effort to a large book form, and it may then be used again for review or reteaching at any later date. The several charts may be kept in order on a chart rack, hung in the room, or bound together in some way. These pages may be illustrated, preferably by children. It is possible to duplicate copies in a smaller size, so that each child has a 'book' of his own. This is particularly appropriate for more advanced pupils.

This basic method is applicable to both individuals and groups, and may be employed at any grade level. Most often it is used as a step in teaching beginning reading. The use of other media, such as the basal reader[2] or i.t.a., is easily possible in conjunction with the language-experience approach. In short, this is an extremely flexible approach, adaptable to any conceptualization of the teaching of reading which you may prefer. It may be used anywhere, even if the sand is your 'chalkboard'. And since it starts with the children themselves, it is almost guaranteed to fit them better than use of published material alone.

Advantages and disadvantages

As in any approach to a skill as complex and abstract as that of reading, there are both advantages and limitations to the language-experience method. Anyone who claims that any 'system' of teaching reading will be successful with all children and adults is doomed to disappointment. But

---

1   *Editorial footnote*: A sheet of light cardboard.
2   *Editorial footnote*: Basal readers, basic readers and basals are terms used interchangeably in the United States to identify published reading schemes.

let us see what the language-experience approach has to offer on the positive side.

1   The language, since it comes directly *from* the children, is the most meaningful possible language *to* the children. This applies not only to the vocabulary, but to the word order and degree of complexity within sentences. The teacher may use *his own* experience to exercise a few judicious choices in what finally appears in permanent chart form, but these changes must be applied very gradually.

2   The experiences, since they are recent and real to the children, provide intrinsic motivation, interest and vitality in the reading materials resulting from these experiences. Occasionally such materials may even be used with another class, depending upon the applicability of the material to the overlap in background experience between the two groups concerned.

3   Teaching of all the language arts is possible in a single, unified method. Oral communication, listening, handwriting, spelling, the mechanics of composition and grammar, creative writing and reading are taught together—without the artificial separation into subject-matter areas which tends to destroy them.

4   The basic concept of reading fostered by the method is both professionally sound and easily understood by children. The 'oneness' of all the communication skills becomes obvious; the association of the written form to the spoken form is made directly, both in sound and sense; and the process of reading becomes something children have already known in another form and, therefore, easier because it is less puzzling.

Limitations found in the use of the language-experience approach are likely to be:

1   The vocabulary can range widely, providing insufficient repetition for any word to ensure retention, or providing such a variety of words that the learning of many of them is unlikely.

2   The oral discussion and organization of the story may be dominated by a few individuals. Very careful and skilful teaching is required to attain the objective of total group-participation. This one problem is likely to be the reason why the method is not employed more. Teacher security is a key factor.

3   Chart stories, because of their size (to be seen clearly by the entire group, they must be large), have a tendency to be quite short, and may therefore be easily memorized. This may cause a serious misconception of the reading act on the part of the child in the beginning stages. This is often quite difficult to overcome later.

4   Since the approach depends upon a daily teacher-led activity, the teacher must be extremely conscious of the developmental sequence of the multiple skills with which he is working. Otherwise the learnings are more accidental than systematic, and the method is time-wasting.

5   The daily preparation of sufficient material takes a great deal of teacher time.

6   The method does not adapt easily to the practice of teaching several reading groups at their different levels in a single classroom.

Conclusion

The language-experience approach to the teaching of reading is enjoying a recent resurgence. An increasing concern over children with different environmental backgrounds and the effect of these different backgrounds on learning seems to be basic to this resurgence. The language-experience approach uses and incorporates environmental differences, rather than ignoring them, to produce materials which fit the group.

For many years in education, we have been saying 'We must start where the child is.' The language-experience approach is one way of doing just this.

But a caution is in order. No one method of teaching reading will, when used exclusively, do the complete job. A combination of methods will reach and teach more children than any single method.

Combining the language-experience approach with almost any other approach should produce more children who read with meaning, who understand what reading is, and who therefore enjoy their reading. Not only that, but it will make the very process of learning to read more enjoyable. Sufficient reason, in spite of difficulties, for at least occasional employment of the language-experience approach? I think so.

References

ASHTON-WARNER, SYLVIA (1961) *Teacher* New York: Simon & Schuster, 1961; London: Secker & Warburg, 1963.

CARRILLO, LAWRENCE W. (1957) 'The relation of certain environmental and developmental factors to reading ability in children', unpublished Ed.D. dissertation, Syracuse University.

2:5   Dictated experience stories

Russell Stauffer

Introduction

Most teachers of reading agree in the belief that there is no single method
of teaching reading to all pupils. Teachers who follow the Language Arts–
Experience Approach heartily endorse this educational axiom. They do
so, not in spite of their belief in the Language Arts–Experience Approach,
but because of it. The approach represents an integration of conditions, all
of which are rightly a part. Language arts encompasses the four facets of
language and is founded on the social-personal condition of purposeful
communication. Experience encompasses an individual's perceptual and
conceptual world, his interests, curiosities, and creativity, his culture, and
his capacity to adjust, learn, and use.

Other conditions, even though quite commonplace, warrant repeating
and re-establishing. *First* is the fact that among typical six-year-olds the
range of individual differences is at least five years. This means that, if reading instruction is to be paced even in part on ability grouping, the range
and frequency of pupil distribution has to be determined and considered.
Second, reading is not only to be thought of as a communication process
but is also to be taught that way. Meaning is the important thing—not saying words. Reading is a thinking and not a parroting process. *Third*, individualized reading procedures as well as group reading procedures are
to be used. *Fourth*, written materials must convey meaning in much the
same way as does the oral communication of six-year-olds. Stilted artificiality must be avoided and no excuse can be trumped up for its use. *Fifth*,
the vocabulary, concepts, and cognitive processes that children have developed for oral communication purposes must be utilized to the fullest

STAUFFER, RUSSELL (1970) 'Dictated experience stories', *The Language-
Experience Approach to the Teaching of Reading* New York: Harper &
Row, 19–58.

degree possible by linking written words as the stimulus to trigger the same concepts. *Sixth*, word-attack skills must be taught as a first-aid to meaning. Words must be introduced in a communication context so that, as the reader moves along, meaning clues to recognition may also be a first-order, functional source of help. Phonic elements must be taught in a pronunciation unit or in context, not in isolation. *Seventh*, pupil interests, experiences, and knowledge must be used as a basic source of funds and must be extended and refined. *Eighth*, reading skills must be taught and paced in such a way that individuals are able to assimilate and use them. *Ninth*, the rules of the psychology of learning must be observed. *Tenth*, the freedom and responsibilities of self-selection must be initiated from the beginning. *Eleventh*, a love of and appreciation for what reading can do for people must be fostered.

Getting started

Most children come to first grade eager to read. The few who can read want to show that they can. Others are eager to show that they want to try. An immediate or at least an early start should be made. The object of the start is to show pupils that reading is no more than talk written down.

A good way to accomplish this is by means of a pupil-dictated experience story. Arrange to have available in the room some item that will catch and hold interest. One teacher began in a unique way by using a white mouse; its uniqueness contributed to its value as an attention-getting device and a means of stimulating oral language. There are many other similar ideas that could be used: a puppy, chick, baby rabbit, turtle, or parrot, a novel toy, a well-illustrated book such as *Hop on Pop* (Seuss, 1963), or a story well told.

With the mouse, the teacher placed its cage in the center of a pupil-viewing-level table. The pupils gathered around and watched the mouse move about in its cage. They saw it stand up on its back legs with its front feet upon the side of the cage. They saw it eat from a food tin. Then the teacher took the mouse out of the cage and allowed it to walk along the top of the desk. She showed no concern about handling the mouse and her confidence and poise very much influenced the class.

As the pupils watched, they talked and exclaimed: 'Look, he's standing up!' 'He has pink eyes.' 'See how long his tail is!' When this comment was made, the teacher asked the class to say how long they thought the tail was. Estimates were given that ranged from six inches to four feet.

Regardless of the accuracy, the question had caused all to look again and examine with a different and specific purpose.

'What should we name him?' asked the teacher. This evoked a number of responses such as 'Whitey', 'Snow White', 'Pink Eyes'. Of the different names given, the class preferred 'Snow White'. The choice was made by a show of hands, which allowed all to participate, express an opinion, and operate in a democratic atmosphere. Group cohesion as *esprit de corps* was being developed.

The teacher put the mouse back into the cage, covered the cage, and set it aside, and then she gathered the class around an easel on which she had tacked a large piece of newsprint. (Newsprint is lined paper approximately two feet by three feet in size.) After printing the mouse's new name, 'Snow White', on the top line, she invited the class to tell about the mouse, indicating that she would print what they said, just as she had recorded the name.

Dick said: 'Snow White scratched around in his cage.' Jane added: 'Snow White has pink eyes.' Alice said: 'He stood up on his hind legs and looked at us.' And so on.

As each child offered an idea, the teacher recorded it, using appropriate printing and a heavy black crayon. Pupils noticed immediately that she could not write as fast as they talked. Even so, she wrote at a good pace and the waiting time was not long. After each idea had been recorded, she read it back to the group in general and to the pupil dictating in particular. Thus she proceeded, recording the ideas of six different pupils and completely filling the newsprint sheet. All this took but a few minutes; the pupils were fascinated by the performance and were eagerly attentive. The account when she finished read as follows:

Snow White
   Dick said, 'Snow White
   scratched around in his cage.'
   Jane said, 'Snow White has pink
   eyes.' Alice said, 'He stood up
   on his hind legs and looked at us.'
   Jerry said, 'His tail is two feet
   long.' Bill said, 'Snow White ran
   around on the table.' Nancy said,
   'Snow White is soft and furry.'

Now the teacher read the entire story to the class. As she read, she pointed quickly and briefly to each word. Then all the class read the story together. The teacher pointed to each word as they proceeded, saying each word and the pupils saying it with her. Even though the pointing and the repeating after by the pupils made for some arhythm, a surprisingly even paced performance resulted. The tone and intent of the teacher's voice helped bridge the slightly arhythmical gaps.

Next, she gave each pupil an $8\frac{1}{2} \times 11$-inch sheet of white paper and asked them to make a drawing of Snow White. While the children were drawing, she went about the room, printing the words *Snow White* at the top of each paper. She gave some a chance to show that they had already learned to copy her printing as they proceeded to label their paper by themselves.

Some of the things that resulted from the experience are:

1 Pupils saw that reading is no more than talk written down.

2 They saw that the teacher could read back all the story or just parts of it.

3 They followed the reading process from left to right.

4 They made return sweeps from the end of one line on the right to the beginning of the next line on the left.

5 They saw that different letters are made differently. Some were capitals. *Snow White* always started with capital letters.

6 They saw the use of punctuation in a meaningful language context.

7 They experienced the thrill of 'reading' as they read with the teacher.

8 Some of the pupils saw their names in writing and their ideas in writing.

9 They had displayed *curiosity* as they watched and examined the mouse and *creativity* as they told about their reactions.

10 They were stimulated to oral-language use as they reacted to seeing the mouse.

11 Ideas were shared in the dynamics of a class situation and in response to an immediate experience.

12 The teacher's questions had caused them to observe more carefully.

13 Each had opportunities to listen to others speak, to hear their ideas, and to discover how others reacted to the same circumstances.

14 Each had an opportunity to vote and express preference for a name for the mouse and to learn how to accept the decision of the majority.

15 Each had an opportunity to make his own drawing and thus show the attributes of the mouse that he was reacting to.

16 The name 'Snow White' written on each drawing gave pupils an opportunity to link two symbols for one referent: a printed name and a picture.

In addition, the teacher had had an excellent opportunity to discover some things about her class:

1 their curiosity about the mouse.
2 their concern or lack of concern about seeing the mouse out of the cage and on the table and their reluctance or readiness to touch the mouse.
3 their willingness to move about the table and among each other.
4 their oral-language usage and, particularly, their choice of words.
5 their attention span, persistence, and cooperativeness;
6 whether some could read (as the story was being read back by the class, some continued to read ahead correctly).
7 their ability to use crayons and to illustrate ideas (the illustrations were some index to maturity and were revealing in ways similar to the Good-enough-Harris Drawing, 1963).

For all concerned, this was a profitable experience. To be sure, the parents heard about the event. They also heard that reading had been done. 'I read a story about Snow White', said one girl to her mother. 'Oh', was the pleased reply, 'You read about Snow White and the seven dwarfs?' 'No, Mother, we read about a white mouse. We named him Snow White. See, here's his name on my picture. He's standing up looking at us.'

The next day, the teacher divided the class into three arbitrary groups. In each group were two of the children who had dictated lines for the Snow White story. Then she had each group take a turn sitting with her in the back of the room around the story of the previous day.

She started each group session by rereading the story to them. Then they all reread it together as she pointed to the words. Next she invited Jerry to stand by her and read the chart with her. She started by merely pointing to the name of the chart and Jerry immediately supplied 'Snow White'. Each time the name *Snow White* appeared in the story, Jerry hurried ahead and read the words. He also recognized his name. 'Reading' for Jerry had been a booming success.

Jane stood by the teacher next. Jane read the title, too, as Jerry had. But, each time the words *Snow White* appeared thereafter, Jane hesitated. All the teacher needed to do, though, was point in each instance to the same words in the title and Jane responded immediately. She also read her own name.

Others in the group were given opportunity to 'read', too. The teacher stayed alert to the interest of the group and the activities of the rest of the class. Some were looking at books that had been placed on the library table. Others were in the house corner, playing. Still others were drawing.

Some sat together; some preferred to work alone. The teacher was careful not to overplay the attention span and interest of the group sitting with her or of others in the class.

In the next group, Nancy did a fine reading job. She read '*Snow White*' each time it appeared. She read the name of each pupil and the word *said*: 'Dick said', 'Jane said', and so on. When they got to the sentence she had dictated, she read all of it: 'Nancy said, "Snow White is soft and furry." '

Dick took his turn and needed a little help with the story name. All the teacher did, though, was make an *s-s-s* sound, and Dick caught on. This help was needed each time. A pause on his name was sufficient to prompt him to remember that this was his contribution and therefore his name.

In the third group, Alice performed as Jerry had. Bill, however, astonished the group. He read almost the entire story, needing help only with *scratched* and *furry*. Now the teacher went a step further. She asked Bill to locate certain words. First, she said, 'Point to your name.' This he did quickly. Then she had him point to *Dick, Jane, Nancy, Jerry,* and *Alice* in that order. He found each name almost as quickly as he had located his own. Next, she asked Bill to count the number of times *Snow White* appeared in the story. He proceeded to count as he pointed, starting with the title, and gave the number five.

By this time the teacher had gathered the entire class around. Next, she had Bill locate the words *table* and *around*. Both appeared in his contribution, so she had felt reasonably confident about these two requests. Then she said, 'One of those two words appears at some other place in the story. Which one?' This was a challenging question. Bill had to compare words and make a decision. In a few seconds, though, he had located *around* in the second line.

Now the teacher tried one more thing. She saw that all this was holding the attention of the class and she realized that she was being given an ideal opportunity to make points about how interesting reading can be. She printed the word *table* on the chalkboard and asked Bill to read it. This he did instantly, even though it was in isolation. Then she wrote the number *two* on the board and he named it. Next, she wrote the word *pink*. He could not say the word but he apparently recognized its configuration or knew it iconically. On his own he walked to the chart and located the word. Then he announced that the word was 'pink'. How did he do this? The power of communication had taught him to recognize words not only by their configuration but also by their total language context.

Many things occurred during this second day with the 'Snow White' story that were very desirable, both for the pupils and for the teacher. For the pupils, the following observations are particularly relevant.

1   They had an opportunity to work in a group as well as work on their own or with some other classmate.

2   When they were not in the reading group, they had an opportunity to decide what they would do from a list of opportunities prescribed by the teacher.

3   They could do some 'book selecting' at the library table.

4   They could read. As is revealed by the performance of the six children who dictated, reading performance varied according to ability.

5   They could listen to others read.

6   Each pupil who had a chance to read also had a chance to succeed. Some read only the title but some, like Nancy, read six or more words.

7   The range of words read varied from Dick, who knew two words with a bit of hissing help from the teacher, to Bill, who knew thirty-five of the thirty-seven different words and who read fifty-four of the fifty-six running words.

8   Visual discrimination of words was accomplished early in the school year, *without* drawing shadow boxes, an extremely artificial crutch. The teacher did not have to frame any of the words with her hands, this, too, a weak sort of aid.

9   Visual-auditory discrimination occurred each time the pupils located a word the teacher had spoken and each time they read with her.

10   The sounds that letters represent were linked in a phonetic word attack. When the teacher helped Dick recall 'Snow White' by making the *s-s-s* sound, the attack linkage became more specific.

In many respects, the teacher was able to make an informal inventory of pupil readiness for reading. Each pupil's performance allowed her to make notes about their skills. For example, she learned that Bill could read many words; he had already indicated that he knew thirty-five words. This total is higher than what is found in the first two preprimers of most reader series. He knew words in isolation as well as in context. But above all, he knew how to use context clues and word meaning as an aid in word recognition. When Bill returned to the story and located and identified the word *pink*, he showed command of one of the most important skills in any word attack—the use of meaning clues or the power of comprehension.

Jerry, on the other hand, indicated that he recognized only three words: *Snow, White,* and *Jerry.* He knew *Snow White* each time it occurred, showing clearly that he had a visual image for the word. It also provided evidence that he linked the right auditory image with the right visual image.

It is to be noted again that the total performance of the class stands in sharp contrast not only to the result of the use of the content of pre-primers but also to the memoriter skills-in-isolation approach to word learning. This teacher did not give the class a list of words to take home, so distaste for reading was not reinforced at home as well as in school. Instead, she got their attention through an old psychology-of-learning trick: she used a *novel* experience, *different* and *vivid* and within their grasp. Then she allowed the pupils to react by letting them talk rather than by imposing her ideas. She arranged to have recontact or reinforcement of learning within twenty-four hours, when forgetting occurs at a rapid rate, both in logical and in rote learning. Each time a pupil read the story, others in the group had recontact with the words.

By the third day, this teacher had reproduced the 'Snow White' story on hectograph and had a copy available for each pupil, giving them an opportunity to pour over the story as much as they wished. This day, she moved about from individual to individual, and in private person-to-person sessions she read through the story with each pupil. This time each word that a pupil could read on his own was underlined by the teacher. Some had only the title underlined, whereas Bill had every word underlined. In addition, the teacher wrote the name of each pupil at the end of the story. In a few instances, pupils were able to write their own names.

On the classroom library table was the story of *Snow White and the Seven Dwarfs.* Pupils gained a great deal of scholarly pleasure from the fact that they could read the words *Snow White* in a book. In addition, the teacher had a booklet about a snowman, and some pupils discovered they could read the word *snow* there, too. Some could read the entire word *snowman.* One little girl had brought with her from home a copy of *Jack and Jill* magazine, in which, in a story with a winter setting, the word 'snow' appeared a number of times.

So these children were encouraged to make immediate transfer of their reading knowledge to different contexts—manuscript writing and print in books. Interestingly enough, they made the transfer without raising any questions about the differences in the printed form and the shape of letters with different type-face styles and in manuscript writing.

In addition, the teacher had found time to accomplish all the other pupil-getting-acquainted activities that are a part of the first days in school: recognizing names and name cards, locating seats and desks, closets and lavatories, meeting the teacher next door, the school nurse, the principal, and so on. She read orally to the children, told stories, had them listen to music, and soon had them settled into the business of school life.

Grouping as an aid to individualized instruction

Not all the time during the first weeks was devoted to getting acquainted, nor was all the time devoted to reading. The teacher did, however, continue with other experience stories which the pupils dictated in response to a shared and immediate firsthand experience. The school librarian stopped in one day and told a story to the class, and this story was used as a prop for other pupil-dictated stories. A group of eight-year-old children came in one day and performed a puppet show. This was an excellent source of stimulation for dictated stories.

By the end of the first three weeks, this teacher had acquired much understanding concerning the language facility, the interest and tastes, the intellectual maturity, and the social-personal poise of each pupil. Now, to differentiate reading instruction and pace the learning of each one as individually as possible, she organized the class into groups, thus permitting opportunity for enough individually-dictated stories to make them useful. Moving around the room from pupil to pupil was not as efficient for systematic help as working with small subgroups, so the teacher placed Bill and five others in Level IV group, Nancy and seven others in Level III group, Jerry and eleven others in Level II group, and Dick and five others in Level I group. In most instances the groups were otherwise formed spontaneously along interest lines.

In the Level IV group, Bill was advanced well beyond the others. He already had a sizable reading vocabulary and was having a grand time reading his way through the books in the library corner. The teacher, with her modified individualized reading approach, had made provision for Bill and the other budding Bills. He was keeping a record of the books he read and was sharing his enthusiasm and book knowledge with others in the room. He shared informally with his friends, and he discovered as well that he could share interests with other classmates. Two others in his 'dictating' group were catching on fast, learning words and reading.

Dick and the pupils in his group, on the other hand, seemed almost miles apart from Bill. Even so, they were doing just what Bill was doing. They were dictating stories, oftentimes about the same stimulus or experience areas as he did. This was especially true when the interest was one in which the whole class participated. They 'read' their stories on the two-voice (teacher-pupil) level. They read, and that was the important thing! They took books from the library shelf and 'read' them. Then, too, at times Bill would sit next to Dick in the library corner and, in a low whisper, read a story to him. Furthermore, at times Bill would help Dick with words when he was 'rereading' his old experience stories or reading a library book.

Everyone in the class knew that Bill was just about the best reader and that Dick was not. But they also knew that Dick was coming along. Dick knew this too. So did Dick's parents and so did Bill's parents. The climate that prevailed in the classroom was best measured by the rising enthusiasm, good will, and self-reliance.

Once the class had been organized into dictating groups, the teacher was able to sit with each group for pupil dictation on an average of twice a week. (The cycle will be enlarged upon later.) It seems timely to study how the teacher worked with groups IV and I.

Group IV, Bill's group, had six members. At the appointed time, they came to the dictating corner. The pupils sat in a semicircle facing the teacher in the center. This is how the group assembled and prepared for the *individual* story-dictating session.

In this instance, the source of interest was a turtle that one of the boys had brought to school. Earlier in the day, all the children in the class had gathered around to watch the turtle and to hear Bob tell how he had found it. The turtle was in a box that looked like a suit box. Grass and twigs and a small rock were in the box, as well as a pie tin containing water and stones to help anchor it. The group was gathered about this natural science exhibit, watching it and talking about it.

The teacher moved to the dictating table, a small table at pupil height, on which she had placed sheets of lined paper, approximately 11×15 inches in size, and a black crayon. A small screen provided some privacy by partially separating the table from the rest of the classroom. Then, one at a time, the pupils took turns sitting with the teacher and dictating. Bill dictated the following story:

The Walking Fort

    I called the turtle
    'The Walking Fort' because
    that is what he is. He

carries his fort on his back.
When he walks along, if he
sees some trouble, he pulls
in his neck and his feet.
Then he is safe in his fort.
I told my dad about the
walking fort and he said
the turtle was like an
army tank. But I like
'The Walking Fort' better.

After Bill had dictated the story, the teacher read it back to him to see if everything was in order. Bill said the story was correct as he had dictated it. Then the teacher gave the story to Bill, and he returned to his regular classroom seat to do what he chose with it. He could do a number of things. First, he reread the story. Bill was already so facile at learning new words that he was asked to underline only words he did *not* recognize or was not sure about. In this instance, he could read the entire story. He paused at the word *carries* but was able to recognize it when he read on and the sentence-meaning provided recognition closure. Even so, he lightly drew a line under *carries*.

This done, he turned to his vocabulary book, or new-word book, as he called it. Bill's mother had bought this alphabetized notebook for him, but he could have alphabetized it himself because he already knew the alphabet and could write the letters. Some that he was not too sure about he copied from the alphabet chart on his desk. In his book he entered only words 'new and interesting' to him. From this story he chose *turtle, fort, carries, trouble, neck, army, tank, better*.

While Bill was doing this, the five other members of the group were taking turns dictating. Edna dictated the following:

Race
I could run a
race with the turtle.
He has four feet but
he can't go fast. I
have only two feet
but I could win the
race.

The story was read back to Edna and then she went to her seat. Even though no one in the group was as advanced as Bill, they had progressed to the point where they too could underline only words they did not know or were not sure about. In this story, Edna underlined *could, can't,* and *only.* Then she started to draw a picture to accompany her story.

She had just started with her picture when the four others in the group had finished dictating their stories. Then the six reassembled with the teacher and took turns reading their stories to each other. One at a time they stood by the teacher and read the story aloud to the group. This allowed the teacher to follow the oral reading and to note which words were underlined so she could be ready to supply the unknown words if necessary. This helped the oral-reading performance and helped the listener hear and understand the story. Edna needed help with *could* and *only.* Rereading the story aloud led her to recognize the word *can't.* Somehow, the demands of oral reading, language rhythm, and the flow of ideas often serve recall this way.

When the group meeting ended, all returned to their seats. Bill continued with his vocabulary book. Edna and the others continued with their illustrations to accompany their stories.

At another time that day, the teacher sat with Dick's group of six. They, too, assembled around the turtle box and talked again about the turtle. Bob was in this group and he told again how the turtle came out of the water when his dad was fishing. With this group the teacher did more perceptual prodding as the pupils watched the turtle move about in the box. She made such comments as 'See how he pulls his head in' and 'See how he goes around the rock'. Then she set up the easel with newsprint thumbtacked to it and proceeded to record what the members of the group had to say. She used a group-story approach with these pupils because none seemed verbal enough or responsive enough to dictate a more detailed account on his own. The stimulation of one upon another helped elicit a story. The account recorded in this instance was as follows:

Bob's Turtle
    My dad saw the
    turtle when he fished.
    The turtle is little.
    The turtle can pull
    his head in. He has
    spots on his back.
        Bob
        Mae
        Gale
        Jimmy

The names on the end were those of the four pupils who gave sentences. The fact that not all the children in the group contributed was of little concern. Some days all added an idea; some days only a few did. Some days the group selected one member to tell the story for the group.

After the story was dictated, the teacher read it back to the group, pointing very briefly to each word as she proceeded. Then different pupils took turns standing by the easel and participating in a two-member (teacher and pupil) oral reading of the story. Bob was up first. He knew his own name and said 'turtle' when he read the title. When he came to the word *turtle* in the first sentence, he did not recognize it again. Instead of telling him the word immediately, the teacher pointed to the word in the title. He recognized it and made a discovery association—the two words were the same. The teacher's resourcefulness prevented the need to tell him the word. Bob knew the word *fished* when they got to it and he recognized *turtle* the next two times it occurred in the story.

Two more pupils read through the story with the teacher. Then they all returned to their seats to draw pictures to accompany their story. Bob drew a picture of his father fishing, Jimmy drew one to show the spots on the turtle's back, Dick drew a turtle on a rock, and so on. They knew that by the next day the teacher would have reproduced a copy of the story for each.

By the time the teacher was through reading the story with the group, Bill had read it silently at his seat and so had Edna. They had both been prompted by interest in reading and curiosity about what the others said. And, of course, Bill was interested in how Dick was doing.

The next day, Jerry's group of twelve met around the turtle box. At this early stage, this group occasionally dictated a group story, as Dick's group had. Whenever a story or account had been dictated as a result of a first-hand experience, however, individual stories were obtained.

Teachers sometimes voice concern about time, when so many individual stories are to be obtained. Such concern is not unfounded, but the best thing to do is to meet the situation and thereby discover that it can be carried through. Time need not be a factor. It was not in this case. Teachers working with comparable groups have been timid. In one instance, a demonstration in the Seaford, Delaware, Central Elementary School was observed by five first-grade teachers. Their presence added some pressure that might have interfered.

A group was assembled and the interest area was briefly discussed with the pupils. Thinking was stimulated and ideas were shared. Then, one at a time, the pupils sat down with the teacher and dictated. The stories averaged about three sentences in length. In this demonstration, done late in September of the school year, the pupils had already had some experience dictating stories and expressing their own ideas. Even so, they were not unusual, verbose, or creative. Each pupil had his own ideas, however, and voiced them in his own way.

After each child had dictated, he returned to his seat with his story and reread it silently. As he read, he underlined with a single black line each word he felt he *knew*. Guesses were not to be underlined—only words the pupils felt sure about.

When each child had dictated a story and the last one had had a few minutes to reread and mark his story, they all reassembled, and, one by one, they read aloud with the teacher as Dick's group had. The teacher clipped each child's story on the easel and pointed to each word as she proceeded, allowing for enough hesitation to encourage the child to say the word if he knew it or thought he did. Again, as with the Level I pupils, the language pattern and context of the story often helped the pupil recall words that he did not recognize on his own.

The time for the whole group was thirty-three minutes. Dictating and writing took twenty-three minutes; oral rereading and sharing took ten minutes. Even so, the whole procedure was unhurried.

Some typical stories are:

Mr Turtle
Mr Turtle walks on
four feet. He is very slow.

The Funny House
The turtle walks around
in his house. His house
has a hard roof. It's a
funny house.

Slow and Easy
I like a turtle. I
like to watch him crawl
around. He is slow and
easy.

Spotty
The turtle has spots
like my cat. I called
him Spotty. That's my
cat's name.

The Turtle
  When the turtle eats,
  he sticks his head out.
  His eyes are open.

The words underlined are the ones that the pupils felt they knew when they reread their stories silently at their seats. Underlining this way is a positive approach to word learning, because the emphasis is on what is known. Also, it calls for a facing up to the facts: One either knows or does not know, or one guesses. Underlining therefore requires a certain amount of intellectual honesty. The need to 'prove knowledge' occurs at the time of the oral reading. The teacher pauses a bit longer on each underlined word. If the word goes unrecognized, the teacher supplies the word and the underlining is marked: ⫻⫻⫻⫻

These pupils now prepared a picture of a turtle or a turtle scene. (Pictures of turtles may be available in magazines. If the magazines are expendable, the pictures may be cut out. Drawings by the pupils are to be preferred, however.)

Next Nancy's group, the Level III group, was assembled. All eight gathered around the turtle to watch and talk and share ideas. Then one by one they sat down with the teacher and dictated their accounts of their turtle observations and their ideas. Some were much like those dictated by members of Bill's group, insofar as length and originality were concerned. Others were more like the Level II accounts. Nancy dictated the following:

The Lonesome Turtle
  I believe the turtle
  is lonesome. He walks
  around so slow and looks
  so sad. Sometimes he
  looks out at us and
  then he pulls his head
  in again. I believe he
  is lonesome.

Nancy returned to her seat and underlined words she did *not* know or was not sure about. Nancy was a cautious person, more inclined to underestimate her knowledge than to overestimate it, as is reflected by the underlined words.

Nancy's reaction to the turtle also reflects her personal dispositions and motives (Allport, 1961). Her response to the turtle suggests strong regard for the welfare of others. The one little turtle in the big box being watched by so many people, poking his head out and pulling it in again, apparently aroused her flow of ideas. Nancy's general disposition found many stimuli that were functionally equivalent and that guided her to a form of behavior that was already being labeled as: 'That's Nancy for you.' This was not only Nancy's way of reacting to her environment but her way of meeting it.

It seems opportune here to repeat Ben Jonson's counsel in his statement: 'Speak, that I may see thee.' Dictated stories give pupils an opportunity to speak and show themselves. Similarly, they give teachers an opportunity to learn what the pupils' essential characteristics are, because dispositions are in continuous flow. As Gordon Allport (1961) has stated: 'Interests, ambitions, compulsions, phobias, general attitudes, inclinations, hobbies, values, tastes, predilections—all are personal dispositions (some only secondary) and are at the same time motives' (p. 373). Thus Rick, dictating the following story, revealed his personal dispositions.

The Explorer
> This turtle is an
> explorer. He goes
> around exploring. He
> came out of the water
> to explore. He explores
> our box.

In this section of the chapter, three ways of obtaining pupil-dictated experience stories have been described: whole class, group, and individual. The first few days and weeks of school are opportune moments for obtaining whole-class stories, and any number of teaching-learning effects can be accomplished by starting early.

Children interacting as members of a class have the opportunity to get acquainted with each other linguistically, socially, culturally, emotionally, physically, and intellectually. Each stimulus permits the children to move about, to listen and talk to one another, to show or acquire regard for the rights of others. The whole-class story becomes a possession of each pupil, even though only five or six may have contributed literally. Their language unfolds what is cognitively and linguistically latent in all, because it is brought into operation functionally and dynamically as first-hand experience.

Much the same can be said for smaller groups, although there are a number of important differences. Each time a different group is formed, whether spontaneously or by the teacher, different kinds of social-personal arrangements occur: understandings, habits, and practices relating to social choice and individual values and the reconciling of conflicting individual and group desires or interpretations all become powerful sources for promoting adjustment and emotional reinforcement. In our mobile society, such opportunities should help children adjust to changing functional organization related to learning and communication.

In both the class and the group, each individual may be stimulated to do his own thinking and reacting but, as a member of a group, he is susceptible and responsive to the language habits of others. He is one among many and subject to the polarization that occurs along different lines at different times. But adaptability to change, particularly the free exchange of ideas, is latent in the flexibility of the shifting group membership.

Individual stories yield the best return to an individual and are best for achieving the reading skills aimed at by the teacher. The shift from whole-class and group stories to individual dictation should be made as soon as possible. Many of the benefits associated with group circumstances will continue if procedures such as those just described are followed. The sharing of experiences and the oral interchange of ideas is particularly valuable.

Furthermore, the opportunity for each child to express his own ideas in his own way is most productive. He has the teacher's attention; his words are recorded; he is the author. At a later time, he can share his account of an experience with his classmates and he can share their accounts. The likelihood that he will recognize and remember words in his recorded accounts is greatly increased, because the words are of his choosing and represent his oral language-experience commitment.

Stimulus interest areas

Many people are familiar with the 'Acres of Diamonds' story told so often by Russell Conwell, founder of Temple University in Philadelphia. He told about the man who searched around the world for an acre of diamonds and was unsuccessful. He returned home and started cultivating his garden and there he found his acre of diamonds. This is a most fitting introduction to the question of interest stimuli or what the children shall dictate about. Every classroom, school building, and playground represents literally an acre of diamonds of ideas. If to this is added the experiences children bring with them to school, it becomes readily apparent that acres of 'interest' diamonds are available—personal, home, neighborhood and community, school, historical and cultural specialities, current and seasonal events, books and papers, TV and theater, and so on.

Personal

This is the world of 'I', 'me', 'my', and 'mine'. What I am and what is mine have been impressed on me by each of my years of experience. As I have grown I have walked, talked, laughed, cried, eaten, slept, played, worked, given, received, loved, hated. Now that I am six, I know who I am and what is mine. What I know may not be what you know or how you see me, but it is my summation. I am developing my style of life. I may not be a well-rounded person, but already many rough edges have been rounded. I have my likes and dislikes, my fears and anxieties, my feelings of adequacy, my attitudes and biases, and a will to live and be loved. The effects of my experiences have shaped my affections, my expectations, my needs. If you want, I will tell you about them. (What child does not want? Some may require special reassuring that 'you want', but that is all that is needed.) Already I have secret thoughts. I may reveal some and conceal others. But if you see me as a person—my hair and the way I wear it, my eyes, my nose, my smile, my walk, my talk, my friends—then I am more apt to be free and alert and willing to share my most precious possession— my self. The following stories dictated by children from either Seaford or Rehoboth, Delaware, are illustrative.

All About Me

I like to ride my bicycle.
There is a hole at home and I
like to play in it. I make
mud cakes. I play with my
dollbaby, and sometimes she
cries, and these are real
tears. She blows bubbles in
her bubble pipe. I play in
my house, too, with my books.
                    Debbie

Me

Me and my brother ride into
Seaford to play at the Seaford
school and my Dad drives my
little brother in and he plays on
the swings. Me and my

R.C.—10

brother, we go over there on
the trapeze to play. And on
the monkey bars. One night we
went over to the football field.
And tomorrow we are going up
home.

                    Michael

Myself
I have brown hair. I can
read some books. I am in the
first grade. I like to unfold
my picture. It is called a
snapshot. I like to build with
my Tinker Toys. I like to watch
television. I like to watch
Superman. I am six.

                    Jimmy

Me
You don't know who my girl-
friend is. Guess, Penny B. or
Beverly. It is Beverly. She
is pretty. She goes on my bus.
My brother's name is Tony and
so is Jeff's. My best boy
friend is Jay Clark and I got
some more. My hobby is sports
cars. Tony collects sports car
models.

                    Keith

No matter what the stimulus, a pupil has only his own experiences, first-
hand or indirect, to call upon when he is invited to respond. It is easier
for him to respond when he is asked to react to a direct experience. When
he is asked to project, though, what he says is the product of a process
that takes place in the pupil's mind. To a degree, each dictation has some
of the revealing qualities that Henry Murray (1943) sought when he used a
series of pictures to elicit from a subject data about himself. He suggested
that a person's perceptual reactions yield information about the ways he
looks at his world. He labeled the method the Thematic Apperception
Test (TAT): thematic refers to the themes dictated and apperception
describes the perceptual-interpretive use made of a stimulus.

In a way, each dictated story is a TAT. Each is revealing, and the alert teacher can become increasingly more sensitive to the psychodynamics displayed. It is generally said that a TAT can yield information about seven aspects of adjustment: 1) thought organization, 2) emotional organization, 3) needs, 4) the subject's view of the world, 5) interpersonal relationships, 6) the subject's conception of and attitude toward himself, and 7) the dynamics of development and illness (Holt, 1951).

This reference to the TAT and its use as a clinical test is not to suggest to teachers that they become amateur clinical interpreters. The stories and accounts children dictate are not TAT protocols. On the other hand, to a sensitive teacher the stories reflect the moods and traces of recent experiences, the psychodynamic features of a pupil's intellectual and emotional functioning. They can be revealing and helpful. Each dictation opportunity may provide a catharsis that may be quite helpful to a pupil and revealing to a perceptive teacher.

Home

Be it ever so humble, there is no place like home. Stories about home and the family are easy to obtain. It is a place dear to each one, and each in his way is ready to talk about some aspect of home. Home consists of mother, father, sister, brother, grandparents, uncles, aunts, cousins, pets, toys, bedrooms, bathrooms, living rooms, family rooms, kitchens, play-rooms, yards, sidewalks, elevators, garages. All these for some children, only a few for others. In almost every instance, be it ever so humble, pupils feel warmly about their homes. As stated earlier, the following stories were dictated by children from either Seaford or Rehoboth, Delaware, and are examples of the variety of topics children choose when dictating about home.

My Mother
   My mother is nice.
   She does nice things. She
   is pretty. She loves me.
                    Steven

My Father
   My father works in
   Oklahoma. My father loves me
   and I love him too. He buys
   me a lot of toys. He is nice.
                    Steven

My Baby Brother
> My little baby brother has a
> broken collar bone. When Tommy
> was little he used to cry a lot.
>   Scott

My Mother
> My mother cooks breakfast
> for me. Then she takes me to
> school. She brings me in a
> car.
>   John.

Neighborhood and community

Everyone lives somewhere. Everyone has neighbors and a neighborhood. The city child knows his block and can tell you when he is near his neighborhood. Suburbanite and village children can do the same. The child in the country knows his home area and can tell you about it.

Each interest and stimulus provokes its own feelings and responses, its own vocabulary. Each has its own horizon. Note how this is reflected in the following stories:

The Acme
> When my mother carried me to
> the Acme Market, I saw some toys
> and a tommy gun.
>   Frankie

Crickets
> I like to find crickets.
> One is five and one is six.
>   Ronald

We Go Hunting
> I like a BB gun that shoots
> BB's. That is my favorite thing.
> I like to shoot birds. I kill
> 'em with my BB gun. I go hunting
> with my daddy. My daddy has got a
> real rifle.
>   Conrad

Firemen
>   I like firemen. They put out
> fires. They wear strong hats, and
> they wear these hats so that nothing
> can hurt their heads.
>
>   Sam

Neighborhood and community resources are so numerous that ideas could supply an entire year's dictating program, ranging from the home to the zoo, the park, the theater, the courthouse, the mayor's office, churches, and the YMCA. It should be realized that some do not require field trips, and, for those that do, valuable time should not be lost or wasted by unwise planning or making trips too frequently.

Current and seasonal events

As all teachers know, the school year has a number of fixed events: Halloween, Thanksgiving, Christmas, Lincoln's Birthday, Valentine's Day, Washington's Birthday, Easter. Some schools have even more. For the teacher using the language-experience approach, these events are a boon rather than a liability. The interest stimulated by them can be used to advantage for communication.

In addition, current happenings are a constant and ready, as well as novel and variable, source of stories: ships to the moon, inauguration of a President, a bridge collapse, a hurricane, a snowstorm, a centennial, a fire, an accident, and so on. They command attention and turn up in discussions in school corridors and cloakrooms. The alert teacher brings the discussions into the classroom and takes full advantage of the intense motivation they provide.

The Easter Bunny
>   The Easter bunny's ears are long.
> He is gray. The Easter bunny has a
> little round tail. He gives all of
> us Easter eggs for Easter.
>
>   Pearl

Spring
>   In the spring we see flowers.
> There are pussy willows. We see
> daffodils. They are yellow. We have
> spring showers. Last night we had a

thunderstorm. I saw some lightning
in my window. We have seen a robin.
This is a sign of spring.

Arlene

School and curriculum

In 1963, when the directors of the twenty-seven studies concerned with different approaches to first-grade reading instruction met in Minneapolis, one of the variables they wished to stabilize and control was reading-instruction time. No decision could be reached at that summer meeting. When they met again, in December, it was thought urgent that reading-instruction time be defined. Still no agreement could be reached (Stauffer, 1966). A principal reason for this was that the language-experience people insisted that reading is a process and that a teacher can use any content as a source of reading material. In other words, all phases of the curriculum can provide material for reading instruction and require the use of reading skills.

Advocates of basic-reader programs,[1] phonic programs, linguistic programs, and the like limit reading instruction to a fixed time in the school day. In addition, their instructional materials consist primarily of the contrived plot and exercises provided in their basal reader collections, no two of which use the same stories or even the same themes. The vocabularies differ and words are taught in different sequences with different controls for word introduction. Word-attack skills are taught in varying order. Yet, the instructors all agreed on a specified time limit to the otherwise 'non-agreement' reading instruction—approximately ninety minutes.

The language-experience people, and to some degree the i.t.a. advocates, agreed that all parts of the curriculum provide materials and motivate interests that can be used for reading instruction. A look back at the wide variety of stories dictated by children provides much evidence to support this contention. In addition to the topics being widely varied, the vocabulary, syntax, grammar, and semantics clearly far exceed what is found in any basic-reader first-grade reading program.

Stories, dreams and wishes

The best school and cummunity with its many first-hand opportunities cannot provide all the resources that children are able to use to stimulate and

1 *Editorial footnote*: Basal readers, basic readers and basals are terms used interchangeably in the United States to identify published reading schemes.

express their ideas. Children are creative and love to improvise and, when encouraged to do so, they create with an eagerness and a zest that clearly suggests pleasure. Talking about dreams and wishes requires self-revelation—my dreams, my wishes. It suggests that someone else wants to know about them and will be interested enough to read about them or listen to them tell about themselves. Telling about 'my wishes' may cause many pupils to stop and think about themselves in a way they have not done before, and it may lead to better self-understanding. Books like *Is this You?* by Ruth Krauss (1955) may help a child see himself in a different way and enjoy the ridiculous as good fun.

Creating stories is a wonderful way to stretch life. Stories begin as all invention and make believe does, with an idea, frequently a once-upon-a-time idea. How the ideas interact with things, people, and processes depends upon each child's experience and ability to create and spin a yarn and, of course, upon the degree to which the teacher invites and encourages story writing. It also reflects the amount of reading to the children that the teacher does.

Record books

Each child in first grade can keep a record book in which to place all the dictating he does for the year. A standard $8\frac{1}{2} \times 10$-inch notebook will serve the purpose well. If the stories are typed, the typed copy can be taped or pasted into the book. If the dictation is recorded in manuscript by the teacher, it can be done directly in the notebook. Each story is dated, providing the pupil with a chronological record of his dictation. Throughout the year, a pupil can reread any or all entries. (As one boy said in February when he reread a story he had dictated in September, 'That's the way I talked when I was little.') Drawings for each story can be made on the pages facing the pasted-in dictation, a drawing on the left and a story on the right. Notebooks can be exchanged and classmates can read each other's stories. The notebook serves many purposes and is especially valuable as a learning-to-read aid.

The titles of the entries in one boy's book are illustrative of the variety of interests and themes that children derive:

How I Come to School	The Halloween Story
The Funny Man	The Trip to the Coal-Mining
Jane Jumps	Country
Helping at Home	Dandelions
My Weekend Story	Dick, My Brother

The Fireman's Big Truck

Help

Something Funny

The Lost Money

What I Want to Be

The Pilgrims

Santa Claus

When I Was Sick

What Animals Do in Winter

Teeny's Two Puppies

My Birthday

The Hands-Down Game

Going to the Reading

Conference

Note that some of the titles listed here are the same as those used earlier in this book. On occasion children select a common title for all to use and frequently reflect joint ventures, such as field trips.

This list represents only David's record of dictated stories. In addition, he had a long list of creative writings that he started in November and continued throughout the school year. Furthermore, not all his dictated accounts were placed in this notebook. Some were gathered in a science book, others in a health book.

In summary, it should be strikingly apparent that the abundance of stimuli with which to motivate dictation is limitless. Ideas and props are as extensive and numerous as experience and knowledge, not only of the immediate geographical area—home, community, and school—but also of the curriculum. Any teacher can tap this tremendous reservoir. In so doing, she gets the children to examine more carefully the world about them, to see new horizons, to view the past and the future, and to act upon it all intellectually.

A look at the vocabulary displayed in the stories in the preceding pages shows how wide-ranging it is. Nomenclature in them is used correctly, concepts are refined and attained, and intellectual growth is stimulated and accomplished. Above all, attitudes toward knowledge and communication are fostered, as is the spirit of inquiry. Knowledge comes first. Reading and books are viewed as one means of obtaining ideas. Reading is learned as it is taught, not as an end in itself, but as a means of obtaining information or entertainment.

Individual language and experience levels

Without a doubt, the chief use of language is to communicate meaning. Sounds have no intrinsic meaning of their own:

A stream of speech consists of a succession not only of units of sound, but also of units which convey meaning to the speakers of the language. How do we know they contain meaning, and how can we test for meaning? The only way we can test with absolute assurance is by collecting large quantities of specimens of continuous speech from a speaker of a given language (Hamp, 1967, p. 13).

The illustrations of children's dictation provided in this chapter are indicative of the stream of language children use to convey meanings. Morphemes (words), unlike phonemes (sound units), have meaning and catalogue the vast universe of experience. The stories here show the range of experience of children, the influence of instruction, and the use of language to tell others about experiences and ideas.

Furthermore, it should be noted that, by and large, the children communicated their ideas quite effectively. They learned to make themselves understood within the framework of the linguistic patterns pertaining in their society. If they lack adroitness in using the right expressions, this is a matter conditioned largely by opportunity to speak, by considerations of prestige within their social-cultural-linguistic environment, which now includes the classroom and the school, and by the taste, temper, and maturity of each pupil. To say that these children speak in nonstandard fashion is nonsense. Certainly they speak differently from the way they did when they were four years old; they change continuously and at varying rates in different groups. And such change will continue as fostered by the new opportunities provided by the school and if it is not stifled by a premature demand for 'correctness'. Finally, it is on the point of correctness that much confusion exists. Linguistically, what the children normally say is 'correct'. If one considers the forms that are admired and accepted by certain groups, though, then the language of the children does not really find favor. The conventions of society are inescapable and represent a form of correctness that is a good thing. But, at this stage of a child's communicating life, attention must be focused on communication so that the 'why' and 'when' of communication become soundly inculcated. Then language refinement, or how to conform to the best language patterns, becomes significant. Until then, children must manage to say practically everything they ever have a need to by learning to handle with ease the language that is their own.

If the language is a public language in which short simple sentences abound, few subordinate clauses used, sequence limited, adjectives and adverbs rigid and few in number, and reasons and conclusions confounded, then the rate of change will be slow and attempts to make for change will meet with resistance. If the language in the peer group in school approximates this kind of communication only, then change to a more formal language will be slow:

> To ask the pupil to use language differently, to qualify verbally his individual experience, to expand his vocabulary, to increase the length of his verbal planning function, to generalize, to be sensitive to the implications of number, to order a verbally presented arithmetic problem, these requests when made to a *public* language user are very different from when they are made to a *formal* language user. For the latter it is a situation of linguistic development whilst for the former it is one of linguistic change (Bernstein, 1967, p. 99).

The task of reading instruction appears to be to preserve for the children the force and dignity that their language possesses while making available to them the possibilities inherent in a linguistic form oriented toward higher conceptualization. Their cognitive and affective states must be channeled in such a way that disequilibrium does not result. Small classes, individual attention, frequent opportunity to think, speak, listen, opportunities to use language not only to label and enumerate but also to categorize objects, events, and people, along with many opportunities to internalize the role of the speaker as well as the listener are all required in the task.

This is what the use of the language-experience approach provides so abundantly. There are numerous opportunities for children to see, react, think, speak, be listened to, read, share, acquire increasingly more acceptable forms of language. This is what the stories reproduced here reflect so clearly. Notice again the quality of the sentences, the range and size of the vocabulary, the use of sequence, prepositional phrases, and personal pronouns, the use of divergent and convergent thinking, the use of logical qualifiers, and the processing of relevant data to reach acceptable conclusions.

Conclusion

The purpose of this chapter is to describe how teachers can use the dictated experience stories of children to initiate and maintain instruction in how to read. Most teachers are uncertain about how to get started in the beginning of the school year. To help them understand the how, when, and what of getting started, procedures were described in detail. Of special significance is the fact that, if on the first or second day of school instruction is initiated as described, all the children can go home feeling that they have read. Favorable attitudes toward reading will be fostered from the very beginning.

The use of a whole class as a base for obtaining dictation serves a useful purpose and is a means of getting started. But the best procedure is to obtain individually dictated accounts. Transition from whole-class stories to individual dictation can be made quite effectively through groups that reflect some arrangement by ability or that are randomly organized. Children can see how an interest or stimulus is dealt with in the whole class or in one story, when three or four groups result in three or four similar but different stories about the same theme, and in individual dictation resulting in perhaps thirty versions. Teachers will find that they can direct and obtain individual stories with greater ease if they operate out of group situations. As any teacher who tries the approach soon discovers, individual stories are most productive and have the best utility for instruction.

What to talk about or how to get children to talk has been described and illustrated with numerous children's stories. The big question is not what to use as a stimulus but how and what to select from among the innumerable possibilities. All living provides a ready source, with the curriculum and its many concepts as a structural fountainhead.

Certainly the language levels of children will vary from some command of a public language to good control of a formal language. Use of the children's language and acceptance of their level is the important guide line. Great care must be taken not to stifle their language by demanding 'correctness'. At this point in their language development, the purpose of language as communication is paramount. Of course, this is true throughout life, and at a later time the formalities of language will have to be taught, but not at this early stage.

Above all are the manner and degree to which the use of children's language and experience fosters a favorable attitude toward reading. Because they are learning to read much as they learned to talk, functionally, the children are forming intellectual and emotional dispositions that will result in reading habits. As Dewey said (1916, p. 57), 'the intellectual elements in a habit fix the relation of the habit to varied and elastic use, and hence to continued growth'. This is precisely what occurs—children acquire the reading habit and practise it constantly because they enjoy doing so. This is the aim of sound reading instruction.

References

ALLPORT, GORDON W. (1961) *Pattern and Growth in Personality* New York: Holt, Rinehart & Winston, 373.

BERNSTEIN, B. B. (1967) 'Social structure, language, and learning', in DeCecco, John P. (ed.) *The Psychology of Language, Thought and Instruction* New York: Holt, Rinehart & Winston, 99.

DEWEY, JOHN (1916) *Democracy and Education* New York: Macmillan, 57.

GOODENOUGH, FLORENCE L. and HARRIS, DALE B. (1963) *Goodenough-Harris Drawing Test* New York: Harcourt, Brace & World.

HAMP, ERIC P. (1967) 'Language in a few words: with notes on a rereading, 1966' in DeCecco, John P. (ed.) *The Psychology of Language, Thought, and Instruction* New York: Holt, Rinehart & Winston, 13.

HOLT, ROBERT R. (1951) 'The Thematic Apperception Test' in Anderson, Harold H. and Anderson, Gladys L. (eds) *An Introduction to Projective Techniques* Englewood Cliffs, N.J.: Prentice-Hall, 211.

JONSON, BEN 'Oratio Imago Animi' in Herford, C. H. and Simpson, P. (eds) *Ben Jonson* London: Oxford University Press, 1925-1952.

KRAUSS, RUTH (1955) *Is This You?* New York: William R. Scott.

MURRAY, HENRY (1943) *Thematic Apperception Test* Cambridge, Mass.: Harvard University Press.

SEUSS, DR (1963) *Hop on Pop* New York: Random House.

STAUFFER, RUSSELL G. (1966) 'The verdict: speculative controversy', *Reading Teacher,* **19,** *viii,* 563-4.

2:6   Experience-exchange in schools

D. G. Mitchell

The language-experience approach to reading has been most adequately defined by M. G. Cooper (1967) as 'the teaching of reading . . . based upon the real experiences of the learners'. Language-experience appears in the classroom in a variety of forms: news, diaries and accounts of visits. A thrilling development of this approach is for these experiences to be exchanged with other children.

Experience-exchange has been a feature of the educational scene for some time. Gagg has suggested that children in one school write to children in a school in another area; his book was first published in 1951. Cutforth (1956) also suggested that correspondence between schools can be undertaken. More recently, Merritt (1969) sees experience-exchange as a natural development of language experience. The Plowden Report refers to the linking of country and urban schools and arranging for exchange visits. Individual teachers have arranged for their classes to exchange written work, tape recordings and pictures. The *Teachers World* organised a tape exchange service in the autumn of 1960; unfortunately this was discontinued in the spring of 1967.

There has been no sound scientific basis for the experience-exchange approach up to the present time, but insightful teachers are enthusiastic; their aims may be summed up in a typical remark: 'the emphasis would be on children communicating with one another, using means in accordance with their abilities'. The general aim of this type of work is to motivate the children in their written work and to give them greater understanding of their own environment and that in which other children live. These are obviously excellent objectives.

Experience-exchange, if its value ever was in doubt, has recently received a boost which one hopes will see the establishment of an organisation

MITCHELL, D. G. (1969) 'Experience-exchange in schools', *Reading*, 3, *iii*, 17–21.

whose aim will be to exploit the many valuable aspects of this type of work. Ruddell (1965) has demonstrated that under certain conditions there is a relationship between similarity of oral and written language patterns and reading comprehension: a claim which linguists have made for some time. This lends support to experience-exchange because comprehension will be facilitated as the children concerned will be reading familiar language patterns. Loban (1963) stresses that flexibility within language patterns proves to be a measure of language proficiency, and that elementary pupils need many opportunities to grapple with their own thought in situations where they have someone with whom they wish to communicate successfully. One assumes that this desire will be satisfied by the child communicating successfully with his peers; certainly one cannot be said to be communicating successfully with the teacher, whose attitude generally is of a disciplinary nature in the shape of a red pencil. Because of this response, the teacher would appear to be the last person with whom the child should communicate, and what is even more important the child realises this and his communication becomes atrophied. He realises, however, that his peers desire to hear of his experiences and he reacts in a positive way. Loban (1963) in his conclusions states: 'It would be difficult not to conclude that instruction can yet do more than it has with oral language. Many pupils who lack skill in using speech will have difficulty in mastering written tradition. Competence in the spoken language appears to be a necessary base for competence in writing and reading.' These statements by Loban and Ruddell are fundamental to experience-exchange; certainly if language proficiency is to be improved by the means suggested by Loban; that is, by communicating with someone with whom the pupils wish to do so, then experience-exchange should become as fundamental a requirement of schools as pen and paper, and, where under-privileged children are concerned, the exchange of tape recordings is essential in order that they gain the required competence in the spoken language. This then is the theoretical basis for experience-exchange.

Experience-exchange can be practised in three situations:

1) in the classroom,
2) in the school,
3) between schools.

The attitude to adopt towards this work in the classroom is as follows. The written work done by the children should be seen by as many people as possible. This can be done in a number of ways, the most satisfactory being where each child does his written work inside a folded sheet of paper allowing a picture to be drawn on one side and the back to be decorated. This is then placed round the classroom for other children to read. The children can also compile a series of questions on their written work for the reader to answer.

Basically the approach to experience-exchange in the school setting is similar to the approach in the classroom, although the organisation is more complex. If reference is made to the description of the situation in the classroom, then the children's work should be seen by as many other children as possible, and it is in this area that the situation becomes complex. The work can be distributed throughout the school by the children writing directly on to a master sheet of a spirit duplicating machine and it is then a simple matter to provide copies for each class.

Experience-exchange can be utilised to reinforce the learning absorbed on a visit. The teacher may have taken photographs of such a visit; these can be arranged in a sequence, a tape-recorded commentary to accompany the series of slides made by the children, and then shown by two or three children to another class. Even a formal lesson, say on cocoa farming, can be enlivened by such an approach. The children can paint pictures of the various stages of harvesting and processing the beans. The pictures can be photographed on a sunny day and a tape-recorded commentary made to accompany the slides; these can be shown to other children. However, it is certainly not necessary to use as dramatic an approach as photography in presenting the pictures, as the originals can be presented in some other way.

Experience-exchange between schools causes problems of a different nature to those encountered in the school and class. The first problem to be overcome is that of contacting a teacher with similar wishes to one's own regarding experience-exchange. No well-known organisation exists whereby teachers can be put in touch so that this type of work can be commenced, but it is hoped that such an organisation will be formed in the near future for this purpose.

Liaison between the teachers concerned is of great value. This liaison becomes tenuous if the parties concerned live a great distance from each other, and particularly if they live in different countries. Experience-exchange can probably be more thoroughly exploited if schools are situated within the same region or county. The advantages of experience-exchange between schools within such areas are twofold. Liaison between the teachers is easier, and the children can visit the areas and perhaps spend a week or longer with their experience-exchange peers. There are practical problems associated with younger children taking part in such work whether at the class, school or inter-school level. One of these is that primary school children often have difficulty in reading the various styles of handwriting; the simple solution is for the children to print. An essential requirement of this type of work is a constant diet of experiences for the children. Help can be obtained from books concerned with environmental studies. Teachers are overworked and experience-exchange is arduous. It is essential, therefore, to have good organisation and first-class team work if this type of work is to be worthwhile. It must have the blessing of the headmaster and, what is more important, his active cooperation and involvement in the project.

The account so far has been concerned primarily with reading and writing. These two activities predominate in all subject areas, but nevertheless it is worthwhile outlining the other obvious areas in which experience-exchange work can be carried out.

Environmental studies is a fertile field for experience-exchange, indeed one wonders whether environmental studies should be carried out unless experience-exchange is going to be an integral part of the work, for surely communicating with someone about one's own environment is as essential to the work as male is to female.

In the Schools Council Bulletin Number 1, *Mathematics in the Primary School*, the suggestion is made that a simple method of finding out whether the children understand the computational processes which they have been given is for them to write a story embodying a given piece of computation. These stories should be treated in the way described for other written material; the answer should be omitted from the stories thus allowing the reader to work out the problem for himself. Mathematics is also involved in the exchange of the personal statistics of the children. Art and music are two other areas suitable for this type of work: the children can paint pictures of themselves and send them to other children. Songs which are peculiar to an area can be recorded and exchanged.

Language-experience and experience-exchange will have little impact upon educational practice unless teachers in training are given the opportunity of studying teaching methods intensively. Downing (1969) has stated the problem most succinctly when he implied that high standards of scholarship need to be applied to the study of important practical problems in the schools. Experience-exchange is worthy of such examination in colleges of education and in schools.

References

COOPER, M. G. (1967) 'The language-experience approach to reading', *Reading,* I, *ii,* 20–4.

CUTFORTH, J. A. (1956) *English in the Primary School* Oxford: Basil Blackwell.

DOWNING, J. (1969) 'Neglect of reading most serious defect in training', *Times Educational Supplement,* 28 March.

GAGG, J. C. (1951) *Common Sense in the Primary Schools* London: Evans Bros.

LOBAN, W. D. (1963) *The Language of Elementary School Children* NCTE Research Report no 1. Champaign, Illinois: National Council of Teachers of English.

MERRITT, J. E. (1969) 'Developing competence in reading comprehension', in Jenkinson, M. D. (ed.) *Reading Instruction: an International Forum,* Newark, Delaware: International Reading Association.

RUDDELL, R. B. (1965) 'The effect of oral and written patterns of language structure on reading comprehension *Reading Teacher,* 18, 270–5.

2:7 Criteria for assessing reading approaches

Vera Southgate and G. R. Roberts

Summary of points requiring consideration

A The teacher

1 What are the teacher's basic beliefs about children's acquisition of reading skill? Do these beliefs lean towards systematic teaching or towards incidental learning?

2 What is the teacher's preferred role? Does she see herself as a consultant and counsellor in the background or rather as a leader in the foreground, initiating instruction and learning?

3 What are the classroom procedures in which the teacher believes and which she prefers to adopt, for example:

a a formal or informal régime;

b children working in large groups, small groups or individually;

c an early or delayed beginning to reading;

d dependence on one reading scheme, use of a number of reading schemes or no scheme at all;

e pre-choice and organization of reading materials by the teacher or freedom of selection by the children;

f reading closely integrated with spoken and written language or not;

g reading tuition confined to definite periods of the timetable or integrated informally and incidentally throughout most of the activities of the day?

SOUTHGATE, VERA and ROBERTS, G. R. (1970) 'Criteria for assessing reading approaches', *Reading—Which Approach?* London: University of London Press, 91–7.

4 Which medium does the teacher support for beginning reading: t.o., a simplified spelling system such as i.t.a., or a coding system such as a colour code or system of diacritical marking?

5 Which main method does the teacher prefer for beginning reading: a look-and-say approach or a phonic approach?

B The situation

1 In what type of school or educational institution is the reading to take place: for example, an infant school, primary school, secondary school, special school, child guidance centre, remedial centre, evening institute or hospital?

2 In what sort of area is the building situated? Is it in a deprived area or a high socio-economic area? Is it industrial or rural?

3 What are the physical conditions in which the reading tuition is to be undertaken? Is the room small or large? Is it a confined space, is there opportunity to spread beyond one room or is it an open-plan school? Is there sufficient space to permit the adoption of the teacher's preferred procedures?

4 What sort of furniture and equipment are available?

5 How many children form the teaching unit?

C The children

What are the characteristics and needs, both as a group and as individuals, of the children with whom the approach will be used?

1 *The group*

a What is the size of the group?

b What is the composition of the group?

    i Is the group heterogeneous or homogeneous in terms of chronological age, reading age and range of intelligence?

    ii Does the group consist of both sexes?

    iii What is the general socio-economic and educational background of the children in the group?

2 *Individual children*

What are the individual needs of each child?

a What is his age, intelligence, interests and abilities in reading?

b Is his ability in oral language sufficiently developed to ensure the possibility of reading progress?

c Does he have a preferred method of working, such as in short, sharp bursts or for long, concentrated periods?

d Has he any physical or personality defects likely to handicap his progress in reading?

D   The reading materials

1   The author

a Has the author written a teacher's manual for the reading scheme or instructions for using the apparatus?

b What are the basic beliefs of the author and are they in line with those of the teacher?

c What is the role which the author assumes the teacher will adopt and what are the procedures he expects her to follow? Do these assumptions correspond with the teacher's preferences?

d What is the author's background of experience?

e What have other people to say concerning the author's ideas and how they work out in practice?

2   The medium and method employed

Are the medium in which the reading materials are printed and the methods which underlie their construction those of which the teacher approves?

3   Children for whom the materials are appropriate

a For exactly which children were the reading materials planned? The age, intelligence, linguistic competence, home background, interests and so on which the author had in mind are all important. Whether the materials were originally planned for retarded readers or for children making normal progress must also be considered.

b Do the children with whom the teacher is thinking of using the materials resemble, in most of the preceding respects, the children for whom the materials were planned?

c If the children in the proposed group differ greatly from those for whom the materials were designed, can the materials or ways of using them be satisfactorily adapted?

4   Optimum situations

a In which situations did the author contemplate the reading materials being used? The particular situation, the physical conditions and the educational 'climate' are relevant features of the situation.

b   Are these same conditions prevalent in the teacher's class or group?

c   If not, is it likely that the best use will be made of the reading materials in different situations?

5   *Scope of the materials*

a   Are the reading materials planned to form a complete reading scheme or intended as supplementary materials?

b   If the materials are supplementary, what are they intended to supplement?

c   If the materials are intended to represent a complete scheme, do they really achieve this?

d   What is the scope of the materials in terms of initial and final levels of difficulty, and the gradient of progression within these two levels?

6   *Structural and functional competence*

There are two related questions regarding competence.

a   Does an examination of the structure of the materials show that the author has devised them in a technically competent manner? Examples of questions relating to structural competence are as follows:

   i   What is the gradient of the introduction of new words or rules?

   ii   Is there adequate repetition of new words and rules?

   iii   Are there sufficient supplementary materials to encourage recognition of newly introduced words or to provide practice in the application of new rules?

   iv   Is the sentence structure and flow of the prose designed to further understanding?

b   Will the materials prove functionally effective; in other words, will they work? If they are used as suggested, with the appropriate children and in the expected situations, are the stated aims likely to be achieved?

7   *Production of the materials*

a   Is the size and format of the books appropriate? Consider the appearance of the paper, print and covers. Are the books and apparatus durable, easy for the child to handle, easy to pack away and display?

b   Are the illustrations attractive and appropriate? Do they fulfil a teaching function in relation to the text or are they solely decorative additions to the books?

8 *Excellence*

a Has the author displayed more than just competence, by devising something which is original, imaginative, absolutely appropriate, inspirational or of high literary merit?

b Has the author's special flair been supported by sensitive or exciting illustrations and high publishing standards, to produce reading materials of real merit or excellence?

9 *Cost*

a What is the actual cost of purchasing the complete scheme or set of materials?

b What will be the relative cost? This is a more important question than the actual cost and not easy to determine. Questions such as the following need to be considered:

   i   What is the scope of the scheme?

   ii What quantity of materials does it comprise?

   iii For how many children will it cater and for what length of time?

E *Apparatus*

The selection of reading apparatus poses special problems for the teacher. Many of the preceding points relating to reading materials apply equally well to the selection of apparatus as to books, but the following additional points merit consideration in respect of reading apparatus.

1 What is the precise purpose, in terms of learning to read, of the particular game or piece of apparatus? Is it intended as a tool for teaching, for reinforcing learning or for practising a newly acquired skill?

2 Will the reading progress of the child who is to use the apparatus or play the game actually be helped or will he merely be kept occupied?

3 Is the apparatus part of a complete scheme, a supplement to some other scheme or a discrete piece of apparatus? If it is not part of a complete scheme, will it prove a useful supplement to the teacher's reading programme?

4 Will it take the teacher a long time both to prepare the apparatus before it can be used and to store it away after use? Alternatively, are pieces clearly marked and containers provided so that children can be responsible for the distribution, collection and storage of the apparatus?

5 Are the pieces which make up the whole, attractive, appropriate in size and durable?

6 Are there clear instructions for the teacher's benefit, regarding how the apparatus should be used or the game played?

7 Are the rules which the children have to follow sufficiently simple and clear?

8 Is the apparatus self-checking?

2:8 The importance of structure in beginning reading

Vera Southgate

I Reading in progressive infant classes

In primary education in Britain today the most noticeable trend is towards what are usually termed 'progressive' schools or classes. The keynotes of such schools are fluidity and informality in the grouping of children and in time-tabling, freedom of movement, individual choice of activities and discovery methods of learning. In view of what follows in the remainder of this paper, I should like to stress from the outset that I approve of this development in primary education, with its emphasis on the child himself and how he may learn rather than on the teacher's instruction. Indeed, it would be difficult not to appreciate the opportunities which such schools provide for highly motivated and purposeful learning, for individual progress, for the development of independence, responsibility and attitudes of enquiry, for the encouragement of creativity and for social interaction.

On the other hand, I am seriously concerned by the fact that the movement towards child-centred learning in progressive schools is frequently accompanied by a decline in the belief of the importance of young children learning to read. The Plowden Report (Department of Education and Science, 1967), for example, very clearly reflects this attitude. In this 500-page report covering all aspects of primary education, only five pages deal specifically with reading, and of these only one page relates to 'Teaching Children to Read'. This is certainly a far cry from the time when the work of the primary school was centred on the 'Three Rs'. While one would not wish to advocate a return to such concentration on 'Three R' work, I fear that we are in danger of going too far in the opposite direc-

SOUTHGATE, VERA (1970) 'The importance of structure in beginning reading', in Gardner, K. (ed.) *Reading Skills: Theory and Practice* London: Ward Lock Educational, 37–52.

tion. I still consider that one of the main functions of primary education should be in the inculcation of literacy. Accordingly, we should guard against any tendency to believe that it is less important for young children to learn to read and write than it is for them to learn about mathematics and science or for them to have opportunities to express themselves, to create and to discover.

The current deprecation of the importance of learning to read is accompanied by a swing in emphasis from teaching to learning. 'Progressive' teachers try to avoid the use of the phrase 'teaching children to read', and to replace it with some such phrase as 'providing an environment in which children will be encouraged to learn to read'. A wide variety of books, which the teacher reads to the children and which they freely handle, reading apparatus, paper and pencils, all form important parts of this environment. These teachers believe that in such a situation children will soon want to learn to read and, with a little encouragement and guidance, will succeed in doing so.

Both the older approach to reading tuition, that of systematically planned instruction, and the newer theory of incidental learning contain inherent dangers. When teachers pin their faith on instruction, the grave danger is that they may assume that what has been taught has also been learned. One has only to observe either class or group reading instruction taking place, to realize the fallacy of this assumption. The proportion of pupil time devoted to features of the environment other than the teacher or the task, and likewise the proportion of the teacher's time devoted to attempts to focus children's attention on her instruction, increases rapidly as the lesson proceeds.

In contrast, when the emphasis is on learning, the main danger is that the teacher will assume that in a stimulating environment, with freedom to explore and experiment, all children will eventually want to learn to read, and will be able to do so without direct instruction. Brighter pupils or those from homes in which literacy is valued frequently do so. Yet I am certain that many other children will fail to learn to read in infant classes unless a good deal of guidance and instruction is undertaken by the teacher. There are some children who would be neither 'motivated' nor 'ready' by the time that they were eight or nine or ten, if someone did not do something about it. The situation is somewhat similar to that of children learning to eat green vegetables or salads; many would never do so unless adults encouraged them to try, and fed them with small initial doses.

Furthermore, I do not see why it should be assumed that it is bad for young children to do some directed work. On the contrary, children both want and enjoy a certain amount of direct teaching and systematic practice. It would be a pity if teachers were to reach the stage when they become almost ashamed of doing some teaching. Yet this situation is in sight. I have been in infant schools where teachers apologize when one finds them actually teaching a small group of children; they hasten to assure one that this is exceptional!

It is also interesting to note that many of the strongest supporters of the incidental learning theory are advisers, inspectors, lecturers or writers on infant education; in other words, those who do not have to cope with the aftermath, in junior classes and remedial groups, of children who have been left in infant classes to explore the reading environment. Such children have more often ignored or floundered in the reading environment than explored it purposefully.

Nevertheless, there is no doubt that the good teacher in the informal infant class does manage to ensure that each child makes progress in reading, according to his individual needs and abilities, in ways which might be described as 'incidental learning'. Close observation in such a class, however, would show the experienced teacher to be structuring the learning situation for the individual child, and particularly for the slower child. It would be seen that both individual diagnosis and planned learning were being carried out intuitively and functionally by this teacher, and that individual records of children's progress were being kept. Ensuring reading progress for all children in these conditions, however, is an extraordinarily difficult task, and younger, less experienced, or less able teachers are not always able to succeed.

II   The need for structure

I have three main reasons for believing in the need for structure in beginning reading tuition. In the first place, written English does not constitute a regular spelling system. If the written form of our language represented a one-to-one relationship between written symbol and spoken sound, we might have a reasonable basis for hoping that, by heuristic methods, children could be encouraged to discover these relationships and so form generalizations. But our spelling system actually prevents children from making generalizations. For example, the child who has just begun to form a mental concept of the letter *a* after meeting it in 'cat', 'man', and 'bag', will quickly have his theory demolished when he comes across words such as 'cake', father' or 'water'. Such a situation not only discourages the child from trying to discover things for himself, but makes it practically impossible for him to do so. Discovery methods in the fields of mathematics and science are more practical propositions, for here there are regular rules waiting to be discovered. Given sufficient opportunities and encouragement in the appropriate environment, which contains a wealth of carefully structured equipment, brighter children are able to explore these subjects by heuristic methods. Yet it should be noted, in passing, that certain teachers are already realizing that slower children make little progress in discovering for themselves even the unalterable laws of mathematics and science without a great deal of teacher guidance, as well as a certain amount of direct instruction.

Secondly, discovery methods of learning, to be effective, require certain basic skills of which reading is probably the most important, followed closely by the knowledge of how to use an index, simple dictionaries and reference books. While it is true that young children, even before they have started to read and write, can begin to discover, observe, experiment and compare, their progress is necessarily limited by lack of these skills. Thus heuristic methods of learning will be greatly facilitated, and can only be fully developed, when children are able to read and write.

Thirdly, the staffing position in our primary schools today presents a picture of constantly changing members of staff. The newly trained teacher is often in schools only two or three years before she is married and leaving to have a family. Older married women return to teaching when the youngest of their children have started school, which may be after absences of fifteen or more years. There is also a floating population of temporary teachers. The older, experienced infant teacher is frequently the exception rather than the rule. This pattern of changing staffs in primary schools seems likely to continue. It has already been suggested that the informal infant class is far from easy to handle, and that mastery of the printed and written forms of our language represents a difficult task. In these circumstances, continuity in reading tuition is unlikely to be achieved for individual children if learning to read is an informal, often haphazard, feature of the school environment. New members of staff will be greatly helped, and children's reading progress more easily ensured, within a planned reading programme based on a certain amount of structured reading materials.

It is not always realized that the meticulous planning of a framework for learning to read does not have to be accompanied by formalized instruction. Indeed, I should go so far as to say that the reverse is true. My observations and experience in infant classes have led me to conclude that the freer the atmosphere and the more informal the working procedures, the more imperative it becomes that the reading environment should be so structured as not only to encourage reading but also to forward its progress.

III   Structuring the reading environment

In the past ten years or so, in contrast to the growth of 'progressive' primary schools, there has been a noticeable movement towards structured reading materials and procedures. This trend can be seen in a re-emphasis on phonics; in an awareness of the contribution of linguistics to reading tuition; in the publication of equipment such as Sullivan's (1963) *Programmed Reading* and the *S.R.A. Reading Laboratories* (Parker, 1958); in the introduction of new media; and in the growing interest in teaching machines and programmes for reading tuition. Teachers in progressive primary schools have usually stood aside from this stream of thought. My contention is that progressive teachers, even more than relatively formal teachers, should give serious consideration to this movement towards structure. I am certain that if they would examine, adapt and incorporate into their progressive schools some of these forms of structuring, the reading and writing as well as other work in the school would benefit.

In this paper I shall limit myself to a discussion of only three of the many areas within the total reading environment which may be restructured in such a way as to facilitate the acquisition of beginning reading skills. The first relates to either regularizing the written code or drawing attention to the regularities within it which already exist. The second entails devising a master plan of reading tuition, with built-in diagnostic and recording devices. The third concerns the selection, organization and use of reading materials in a manner designed to further the master plan. I shall only touch on the first two points and devote the majority of my time in this lecture to presenting you with samples of reading materials to illustrate the third point.

1   Structuring the written code

Most practising teachers of beginning reading are well aware of those difficulties, caused by the irregularities of the English system of spelling, which children experience when they first try to read. Our efforts to ease this burden may turn in either of two directions. We can either carefully consider the new media for beginning reading which are advocated or we can concentrate on ways of emphasizing the regularities of the language.

One of the most noticeable innovations in beginning reading materials in recent years has been the introduction of a variety of regularized codes. We have had, among others, *i.t.a.* (Pitman, 1959), *Words in Colour* (Gattegno, 1962), *Diacritical Marking System* (Fry, 1967), *Colour Story Reading* (Jones, 1967) and *Reading by Rainbow* (Bleasdale, 1966). New media for beginning reading have been devised with the aim of regularizing, or at least simplifying, the code. The elimination of alternative pronunciations for the same printed symbol should not only simplify the process of learning to read for the child but should also make discovery methods of learning to read a more practical proposition. Yet progressive teachers who favour heuristic methods are often those who are most reluctant to experiment with new media. It would seem that they have assumed that any attempt to regularize the medium must necessarily be accompanied by a return to formal teaching procedures. Yet this need not be so.

The more regular the new medium, and the more reading materials which are available in it, the more feasible does the possibility of children learning to read by discovery methods become. With an absolutely regular medium and an abundance of reading materials, discovering how to read would fall into the same class as discovering about mathematics and science. While none of the new media mentioned fulfils both criteria, each may be found in different ways to have a certain value for heuristic methods. Reading materials printed in all three colour codes are limited in contrast to i.t.a. with its long list of published reading materials. From the point of regularity, *Words in Colour* is an absolutely regular code; i.t.a., as far as decoding is concerned, approaches regularity very closely; and the remaining two colour codes are better described as partial codes which will help children to pronounce many, but not all, irregular words.

Alternatively, teachers in progressive schools who do not want to employ a regularized medium for beginning reading should seriously consider the various current means of drawing attention to the regularities of our traditional spelling system. Certain of these approaches, for example, linguistic approaches to reading, do require formal teaching procedures of which such teachers would not approve. On the other hand, certain phonic approaches could fit in very well with the progressive infant teacher's aims regarding active participation and discovery by the children: for example, *Programmed Reading Kit* (Stott 1962) and *Fun With Phonics* (Reis 1962). Other approaches such as *Royal Road Readers* (Daniels and Diack, 1957), *Sounds and Words* (Southgate and Havenhand, 1959), *Step Up and Read* (Jones, 1965), *Six Phonic Workbooks* (Grassam, 1966) and *A Remedial Reading Method* (Moxon, 1962), while they do require the teacher to adopt the role of instructor for very short periods of time, also provide for plenty of active and individual learning by children.

Yet, progressive infant teachers have been inclined to ignore phonic approaches to reading equally as much as new media, probably because they associated them solely with rigid, formal teaching. Such teachers might do well to consider whether phonic schemes or colour codes, for example, *Words in Colour*, which depend to a certain extent on teacher instruction in the early stages, should be automatically eliminated on that count. It might then be concluded that their use would be more than justified if it led, as it inevitably would, to the child becoming independent earlier. The child whose attention has been drawn to the phonic regularities of our language has been provided with a structured framework which will encourage his interest in words and their spellings, help him to discover and learn the irregularities, and generally make him an independent reader much earlier than the child who is left to discover the regularities and irregularities himself. The child's mastery of reading skills, by enabling him to acquire information from books, will then place him in a much more favourable position for discovery methods of learning in all subjects.

Thus, I am suggesting that teachers in progressive infant schools, who have frequently been those most strongly opposed not only to reading approaches which emphasize the regularities of the code but also to attempts to regularize the code, should be the very ones to show the greatest interest in such developments.

2   A master plan for reading tuition

Efficient reading entails the mastery of many different sub-skills. This is unlikely to occur by chance, without adequate guidance and a certain amount of direct instruction. Accordingly, teachers need to have clear ideas of their aims and detailed plans of exactly what has to be learned and the order and progression of the small steps which will lead to the ultimate goal. In other words, unless a teacher has a master plan children's reading progress will be extremely patchy. Such a plan should include preparatory work before formal reading tuition commences, arrangements for the acquisition of a sight vocabulary of commonly-used words, the development of word attack skills, training in reading with understanding, and reading for different purposes and at different speeds. Arrangement for graded practice and for supplementary reading at progressively more difficult levels need including in this programme, along with some form of checking what has been learned and the keeping of meticulous records.

Unless a teacher knows exactly all the minute stages in learning which each child has actually mastered, how can she plan for the next stages?

British educationists are often rather scornful about the formal, detailed plans for reading instruction which exist in American, Canadian and most European schools. We might do better to look carefully at those meticulous plans of what needs to be learned and then, rather than set about *teaching* all of it, attempt so to structure the reading environment that children would be led to discover much of it for themselves.

Only a well-considered master plan, accompanied by accurate diagnosis and meticulous recording, can lead to structuring the learning situation for continuous individual progress. The more informal the classroom regime and the more individualized the reading programme, the more essential does this behind-the-scenes structure become.

3 Selecting and organizing the reading materials

A large proportion of British infant schools now contain extensive collections of miscellaneous books, many of them well produced and illustrated, which children are free to handle at any time. In such an environment, there is no doubt that for many children the motivation to learn to read is strong. Yet, if all or the majority of children are to learn to read, I suggest that this reading environment needs structuring in two ways. First, the selection of books, charts, apparatus and all reading equipment must be the result of a conscientious appraisal undertaken by the teacher in the light of a master plan for reading tuition. Secondly, planned procedures for the use of certain of the reading materials need establishing so that freedom of choice for the child can operate within a framework of graded stages.

The discussion which follows does not apply to those general books such as picture dictionaries, reference books and illustrated story books, which are usually available on display shelves and book corner units in infant classrooms, corridors and entrance halls. It concerns those books and pieces of equipment which have been produced to teach or provide practice in particular stages in learning to read.

Reading books and other reading equipment need to be examined in respect of both content and the required procedures. The content should be so planned as to facilitate child-learning, while procedures for mastering the content should necessitate the child being active, rather than requiring great efforts from the teacher in order to gain small returns from the children. It might be suggested that five minutes teacher-guidance and instruction and fifteen minutes pupil activity is a more appropriate proportion than if these figures are reversed.

The teacher who decides to begin reading with phonic training will find that most phonic reading schemes require quite a large amount of teacher-instruction in the initial stages, although in the later stages minimal teacher-guidance can lead to considerable amounts of learning in the form of pupil-directed activities. If, however, phonic training is introduced after the initial stages of a look-and-say approach, it is possible to find published apparatus, games, equipment and supplementary workbooks which provide active learning situations for children.

If reading begins with a look-and-say method, the first books the child handles should be such that the teacher does not have to put each word into his mouth, and repeat this procedure *ad nauseam* until he has learned the words by rote. If the teacher is to step down from this role of permanent prompter, illustrations, vocabulary control and sentence structure must all be planned to aid the child's independent learning. The illustrations in the books should be so simple, unambiguous and appropriate that the words printed on the page are those which will spring immediately to the child's mind. The structure underlying the build up of words from page to page should be such as to lead the child inevitably and successfully forward. A simple form of sentence structure, used repetitively, will be found more helpful than complicated and varied sentence structures. Many well-known look-and-say reading schemes, and popular supplementary series of books, are deficient in these respects.

Yet look-and-say books can be so structured, with simple words, phrases and stories, accompanied by illustrations which are aposite, that a child can 'read' his first books himself with very little teacher guidance. *What is Little* (Melser, 1960), one of the *Read it Yourself Books* is a good example of this, with the text on successive pages reading 'A baby is little', 'A doll is little', and so on. The same is true of *Martin's Toys* (Southgate, 1968), one of the *First Words* series, in which the text under succeeding illustrations reads 'Martin', 'Martin's ball', 'Martin's book' and so on. *This is the Way I Go* (Taylor and Ingleby, 1965) and *Methuen Caption Books* (Randell, 1966) are additional examples of simple introductory books, so constructed that children can read them with little help from the teacher.

At a slightly more advanced stage, many of the well-known traditional tales containing repetitive phrases, such as 'The Three Little Pigs' and 'The Little Red Hen and The Grain of Wheat', do help the child to read for himself. So too do books such as the *Reading with Rhythm* books (Taylor and Ingleby 1961), *Mouse Books* (Piers 1966) and *Stories for Me* (Ryder

1957) and *Springboard Readers* (Mail 1968). Most of these books also employ the helpful technique of presenting meaningful phrases as separate lines of print. They are all simple stories which by means of phrasing, rhythm and repetition are so designed that very little teacher guidance is required. The *Oxford Colour Readers* (Carver and Stowasser 1963) is a particularly good example of a reading scheme for older retarded pupils which is planned in such a way as to help the child to help himself.

The selection of equipment, supposedly designed to help children to read, requires particular caution, as it can frequently prove no more than a time-filler. One should consider exactly what the child will be learning by playing a game or using a piece of apparatus—whether the apparatus has been designed to guide the child towards a particular discovery, to reinforce his learning, or to provide him with practice in a newly acquired skill. Different clues and self-checking devices are required at different stages. For instance, if the child is being guided to recognize the initial sounds of words, by matching two pieces of card, one bearing the letter *e* and the other the picture of an egg, a simple clue, such as a background colour or a jig-saw shape, might help him to do so with little chance of failure. At the same time, the teacher needs to be aware that the child is likely to use the minimum clue necessary to achieve success. If he can match a red colour to a red colour or fit a sticking-out curve into an inward bending curve, he will not necessarily note that the printed symbol *e* relates to the initial sound of the word 'egg'. After some practice at this particular stage, his knowledge of initial letter-sounds could only be checked by removing extraneous clues from the front of the pieces of card, and replacing them by self-checking devices on the back.

This raises the important point of the distinction between clues and self-checking devices. Clues are clearly visible and help the child to make the correct moves. The clues themselves should be sufficiently simple for the child to understand them on his own; for example, indistinguishable colours, or similarly shaped jig-saw pieces which require the teacher's aid, defeat their own object. Clues cannot be considered as real self-checking devices, because they do not necessarily indicate to the teacher whether or not the child has mastered the reading skill which the apparatus was designed to help him to learn. Thus clues should be used solely in the preliminary stage of learning any skill. Real self-checking devices only come into effect *after* the child has completed the operation. They should indicate that the child has mastered the relevant skill *without* extraneous clues. A teacher would be wise to hesitate before purchasing or using reading games and apparatus which lack true self-checking devices, unless she can see ways in which such devices can be added. Otherwise, children will spend a few brief minutes carrying out the activity and long periods waiting for the teacher to check what they have done.

With all equipment and apparatus, as with books, the teacher needs to consider the ratio of her instruction time to the pupil's learning time. Apparatus and games which require lengthy or complicated instructions are rarely worthwhile, unless the technique being mastered is one which can be repeatedly utilized for other learning. The game of Bingo or Lotto, for instance, is well worth teaching as it can be played over and over again for practising different skills.

It should also be noted that many sets of apparatus for beginning reading, relating to both sight words and phonically regular words, concentrate almost exclusively on nouns. Yet, McNally and Murray (1962) who list 200 'key' words which account for 'half to three-quarters of the running words occurring in everyday reading matter', note that only 21 of these are nouns. Clearly children's early reading progress will be facilitated if the sight of these 200 key words evokes automatic responses from them. In fact, much of the time which children spend playing with ill-designed pieces of apparatus, relating to nouns they are unlikely to encounter in their reading books, could be much more profitably spent in activities designed to aid their instant recognition of the most common, and often irregular, words in our language. This need not be done by drilled instruction, although, as children are unlikely to discover how to read these irregular words for themselves, the teacher may at first need to take a leading role in group games to ensure superficial mastery of the words. Perfect mastery can then be accomplished by means of activities and games undertaken by groups of children or individual children without the teacher's help. McNally and Murray (1962) in *Key Words to Literacy* suggest a few games for learning 'key words'. Galt publish games entitled *Key Words Self-Teaching Cards* consisting mainly of nouns, and also *Basic Words Lotto* and *Key Words Lotto* containing a proportion of words other than nouns. Many practising teachers have also developed their own apparatus and games designed to aid children's mastery of these words. It is a pity that their ideas are not more publicized.

Yet the selection of appropriate reading materials is only part of the plan for structuring the reading environment towards individualized child-learning. My second suggestion was that the skilful pre-organization by the teacher of a considerable proportion of the available reading materials was necessary before children's free choice became operative. As far as reading games and apparatus are concerned, infant teachers usually accept that children should use them in a particular sequence, rather than in random order which would nullify their graded levels of difficulty. Yet, in certain infant classes this principle is not accepted for books.

I believe we need to develop a form of procedure half-way between that of children's unrestricted access to a miscellaneous collection of books, and complete reliance on a basic reading scheme under the teacher's direct control. Once motivation to learn to read is aroused, not only are small amounts of instruction valuable but graded practice is also necessary. This can best be arranged by ensuring that, at every stage, a child can be guided to choose books and equipment from a selection appropriate to his level of attainment. Both the miscellaneous collection and the graded collection of books are necessary. For the latter, the teacher needs to select certain simple books at different levels, which should be so arranged, on different shelves or marked with distinctive bindings, that every child can always know where to find something of interest which both he and his teacher realize he will be able to read with a fair degree of success.

Many of the books already mentioned can be selected to fulfil this purpose. So can the supplementary books of many look-and-say reading schemes, for example *McKee Platform Readers* (Castley *et al.* 1958–61), *Janet and John Supplementary Books* (O'Donnell and Munro 1951), and also the supplementary books of certain phonic approaches, for example *Gay Way Red Stories*, etc. (Boyce 1959), *Royal Road Miniatures, Royal Road First and Second Companion Books*, and *Sounds and Words Stories* (Southgate 1967). The child who has read the preceding basic book and is able to recognize the appropriate sight words or grasp the relevant phonic rules, as the case may be, can be left free to choose his own supplementary book and to read it by himself. The phonic supplementary books can also prove valuable for the child who has been reading a look-and-say scheme and whose teacher has introduced incidental phonic words, providing the child is given access to them at the appropriate stages. Both look-and-say and phonic supplementary books, wisely chosen and introduced as part of a plan of graded practice, provide perfect opportunities for individual choice within a structured framework. Yet how often one sees these very books being used in two opposing, and equally inappropriate, ways.

The 'progressive' teacher often places on display shelves simple supplementary books from many schemes for children's free choice. Then children, not fully prepared for them, pick up these books at random and, finding them too difficult, quickly discard them. We should realize that although supplementary books from different look-and-say reading schemes may look of equivalent simplicity this is not so. The overlap of words between one scheme and another is not nearly as great as one might imagine. In contrast, the more formal teacher often uses a different procedure. She insists on 'hearing' the child read all the supplementary books in a reading scheme. What a waste of opportunity for individual choice and private reading practice!

Neither of these extreme forms of procedure seems to me to be entirely successful. To have every step of reading tuition dominated by the teacher can crush the eagerness of the young child, deprive him of the pleasure of freedom of choice and sap his initiative. On the other hand, complete freedom for the child to try to read materials which the teacher knows to be too difficult for him is merely providing him with a frustrating situation. I believe that subtle arrangements made by the teacher, to ensure the child's inevitable success with the books he chooses to read or the reading games which he plays, would represent the most practical form of freedom likely to ensure individual learning. Accordingly, although the selection of reading books and equipment to form graded collections at different levels of difficulty is not an easy task, I am certain that it is important for us to devote more attention to it.

IV Summing up

There are many advantages to be gained when the emphasis in beginning reading is on pupil-learning rather than on teacher-instruction. Yet the creation of a school environment designed to promote motivated, individualized learning should not lead to the conclusion that all instruction should be taboo. In fact, I am certain that the ideas now being developed in our 'progressive' primary schools will soon become discredited if they are accompanied by an acceptance of the idea that it is no part of the role of a teacher to teach.

The freer the school environment, from the child's point of view, the more carefully should the teacher have structured it, particularly with regard to learning to read. There are three main reasons for this conclusion. First, English is not a regular language and therefore does not lend itself so easily to discovery methods of learning as do mathematics and science. Secondly, as heuristic methods of learning can only be fully developed when facility in reading and writing has been acquired, the creation of some structure in the process of learning to read and write becomes even more important in progressive schools. Thirdly, the position of changing staffs in primary schools strengthens the need for a certain amount of structure in reading tuition.

Three broad ways of structuring the reading environment have been suggested. First, systems of regularizing the written code or of drawing attention to the existing rules should be stringently examined rather than being discarded out of hand as inappropriate, particularly for progressive schools. Secondly, in both formal and informal schools, every teacher requires a master plan for reading tuition, the latter probably having even more need of it than the former. Thirdly, all reading materials should be selected in the light of how they will encourage children to help themselves. Procedures for the use of these reading materials should be so planned that children's freedom of choice will operate within a framework of graded stages.

References

BLEASDALE, E. and w. (1966) *Reading by Rainbow* Bolton: Moor Platt Press.
BOYCE, E. R. (1959) *Gay Way Red Stories* London: Macmillan.
CARVER, C. and STOWASSER, C. H (1963) *Oxford Colour Readers* London: Oxford University Press.
CASTLEY *et al* (1958–61) *McKee Platform Readers* London: Nelson.
Central Advisory Council for Education (England) (1967) *Children and their primary schools*: a report, 2 Vols. HMSO (Plowden Report 1967).
DANIELS, JOHN and DIACK, HUNTER (1957) *Royal Road Readers, Royal Road Miniatures, Royal Road First and Second Companion Books* London: Chatto and Windus.
FRY, E. (1967) 'Diacritical Marking System', in Downing J. and Brown, A. L. (eds) *The Second International Symposium* London: Cassell.
GATTEGNO, CALEB (1962) *Words in Colour* Reading: Educational Explorers.
GRASSAM, E. H. (1966) *Six Phonic Workbooks* London: Ginn.
JONES, J. K. (1967) *Colour Story Reading* London: Nelson.
JONES, W. R. (1965) *Step Up and Read* London: University of London Press.
MAIL, A. (1968) *Springboard Readers* London: Warne.
MCNALLY, J. and MURRAY, W. (1962) *Key Words to Literacy* London: The School Master Publishing Co.
MELSER, J. (1960) *What is Little* (Read It Yourself Books) London: Methuen.
MOXON, C. A. (1962) *A Remedial Reading Method* London: Methuen.
O'DONNELL, M. and MUNRO, R. (1951) *Janet and John Supplementary Books* Welwyn: Nisbet.
PARKER, D. H. (1958) *S.R.A. Reading Laboratories* Chicago: Science Research Associates.
PIERS, H. (1966) *Mouse Books* London: Methuen.

PITMAN, J. (1959) *The Ehrhardt Augmented (40-sound 42-character) Lower-case Roman Alphabet* London: Pitman.

RANDELL, B. (1966) *Methuen Caption Books* London: Methuen.

REIS, M. (1962) *Fun with Phonics* Cambridge: Cambridge Art Publishers.

RYDER, E. (1957) *Stories for Me* London: Macmillan.

SOUTHGATE, VERA and HAVENHAND, J. (1959) *Sounds and Words* London: University of London Press.

SOUTHGATE, VERA (1967) *Sounds and Words Stories* London: University of London Press.

SOUTHGATE, VERA (1968) *Martin's Toys (First Words Series)* London: Macmillan.

STOTT, D. H. (1962) *Programmed Reading Kit* Glasgow: Holmes.

SULLIVAN, M. W. (1963) *Programmed Reading* Maidenhead: McGraw-Hill.

TAYLOR, J. and INGLEBY, T. (1961) *Reading with Rhythm* London: Longman.

TAYLOR, J. and INGLEBY, T. (1965) *This is the Way I Go* London: Longman.

2:9   Relevance versus ritual in reading

John Downing

Intuitive teachers

There have always been great teachers who intuitively have understood the need to make reading vitally relevant to their pupils. Instinctively they have rejected abstract, artificial and mechanistic teaching methods which make reading and writing mere rituals which children must perform to satisfy the incomprehensible whims of the grown-ups. Sylvia Ashton-Warner (1963) is one such great teacher. She reveals that intuitive genius in her own description of her adventures in teaching Maori children in New Zealand. She says:

> First words must have an intense meaning.
> First words must be already part of the dynamic life.
> First books must be made of the stuff of the child himself, whatever and wherever the child.

One of her chief aims, which she shares with all teachers of school beginners, is to teach reading, but, although this is an important goal, the focus of Sylvia Ashton-Warner's attention is on the child's own characteristic and individual needs, particularly the psychological and motivational ones.

This same intuitive understanding that reading and writing activities need to be essentially relevant to individual children if they are not only to learn the associated skills, but also to become life-long readers by choice is shown by another great teacher, Sybil Marshall (1963). In the following quotation, she is writing about art education in the primary school, but she applies the same principle to all her teaching including reading and writing:

DOWNING, JOHN (1970) 'Relevance versus ritual in reading', *Reading*, 4, *ii*, 4–12.

Every teacher should, however, be able to understand the fundamental principle of the change: that before the new movement it was the adult conception of what art was that was applied to the child. . . . The new conception of child art simply takes into account that children are not solely adults in the making, but creatures in their own right, as tadpoles differ from mature frogs, or caterpillars from butterflies. They have their own set of emotions, abilities, and techniques. What is expected of them is child-like, not pre-adult work.

This does not mean playing down to children in their reading books, and Sybil Marshall is emphatic on this point:

> The ability to turn again to childhood and see the world truly through childish eyes is given to very few men, though among them we number some of the literary geniuses of our language. The absence of this ability, on the other hand, accounts for a good deal of nauseating whimsy found in story books for children and the illustrations that decorate them.

Indeed, such 'playing down' and 'whimsy' arise from the failure to recognise the essential point which is made by the work of such great teachers as Sybil Marshall and Sylvia Ashton-Warner. Children are not just miniature adults. It is the qualitative rather than the quantitative differences between the child's and the adult's view of the world which are stressed in this approach to education. Such differences are of great importance because what may be relevant to the teacher may seem a meaningless ritual to a child of six.

Research evidence

If the tough-minded educationist is getting ready to reject this approach as soft, permissive, or woolly, he should note that the change in this direction has a firm basis in learning efficiency. As Featherstone (1967) remarks, 'rote learning and memorising have been abandoned by good British primary schools, partly because they are dull, but more because they are poor ways to learn'. Blackie's (1967) authoritative description of the modern British primary school makes the same point. With 'the new type of teacher' in a modern primary school in Britain, he says, the children 'are wasting far less time and doing much more work than under the old system'.

One of the chief defects of traditional 'chalk and talk' methods of teaching is that they usually assume naïvely that children are merely miniature adults whose minds simply need to be 'filled up' with 'the facts' that the teacher knows. All she has to do is to tell them. Blackie puts it like this: 'The old type of teacher was all the time rather like an electric current. When he was switched on something happened. When he was switched off it stopped.' But the inadequacy of such a teaching approach ought to be clear from what research tells us about children's cognitive development.

Jean Piaget's (1959) theory of the development of thinking, which is supported by a wealth of evidence, does not address itself directly to the problem of learning to read and write. However, it certainly applies to the learning of such skills. At the conventional age for beginning reading, abstract ideas are least appropriate and the child's ego-centric view of his environment and his pre-school experiences are not likely to lead to a natural understanding of the purpose of written language, which is an artificial two-dimensional product of civilisation.

Direct research evidence which supports these hypotheses was obtained by Lev Vygotsky (1962) in his investigations designed to 'account for the tremendous lag between the schoolchild's oral and written language'. From his research results he drew only two conclusions:

1   Our studies show that it is the abstract quality of written language that is the main stumbling block.

2   [The child] has little motivation to learn writing when we begin to teach it. He feels no need for it and has only a vague idea of its usefulness.

Working quite independently in Scotland, Jessie Reid (1966) has arrived at similar conclusions. She intensively interviewed five-year-olds three times during their first year in an Edinburgh infants' school and found that for these beginners:

1   Reading is 'a mysterious activity, to which they come with only the vaguest of expectancies'. They showed a 'general lack of any specific expectancies of what reading was going to be like, of what the activity consisted in, of the purpose and the use of it'.

2   They had great difficulty in understanding abstract technical terms such as 'word', 'letter', 'number', 'sound'.

On the premise that the more effective teaching of reading cannot be achieved without a fuller understanding of how children think about the purpose and nature of reading, a new research project to discover more about children's cognitive development in reading has been started by the author of this present article. The first results have been given in an interim report (Downing, 1970).

Briefly, three research approaches have been employed with the following results:

1   Reid's interview method has been replicated and used with English

five-year-old beginners. The results were very similar to those obtained by Reid, and their analysis led to similar conclusions:

a Such young children have only a vague notion of the purpose of the written language and of what activities are actually involved in reading.

b They displayed a great deal of confusion over the use of abstract technical terms, such as 'word', 'number', 'letter', 'name', 'writing' and 'drawing'.

2 Certain concrete aids were added to the interview situation, for example, pictures of reading situations, books, toys with incidental written language on them. These stimulated motor and verbal responses from these five-year-olds showing that they were groping towards an understanding of the purpose of writing and the meaning of the technical concepts of language, although they were very much less able to use them accurately in verbalising about reading and writing.

3 Two experiments were conducted to discover how five-year-olds use the categories 'word' and 'sound' in thinking about language. None of these children used these categories in the way that a teacher might assume. The *most mature* children (a minority) thought that 'a word' could be anything from an actual single word to a phrase or even a sentence. Most children used the term 'word' even less rigorously. The concept 'sound' was still less well understood.

The research conducted thus far provides strong endorsement of hypotheses derived from Piaget's theory and confirms the conclusions of the earlier investigations by Vygotsky and Reid. In summary, the consensus of the research conclusions indicate that:

1 Young beginners have serious difficulty in understanding *the purpose* of written language.

2 They have only vague expectations as to how people read, and they are especially confused by the use of *abstract* linguistic terminology.

Practical implications

These fundamental problems brought into focus by the research are just the very learning needs which are ignored by rote teaching methods of the 'chalk and talk' variety. All too often, it is assumed that young children do know the purpose of the written form of language, and, all too often, terms like 'word' and 'sound' are talked *at* the child as if he must know their meaning instinctively.

Helping children to understand the *purpose* of literacy should be the basic initial and continuing concern of the teacher of reading. There are two chief reasons why this must be the chief aim:

1   It is a fundamental truth about reading and writing that their purpose is the communication of ideas. Therefore it is essential that we provide activities for children which will give them this correct orientation to the task.

2   Motivation for learning the skills of reading and writing depends on making these activities *relevant to the child for a lifetime*. Therefore, we must associate reading and writing behaviour from the beginning with their *intrinsic* rewards; that is, receiving worthwhile information through reading and satisfactorily expressing one's own ideas to others through writing.

These two reasons for giving first priority to an understanding of the purpose of reading and writing come together if we make the resolution that all our teaching work must reflect the real-life relevance of the written form of language to our pupils. The other aspect of this resolution is that we should reject materials or methods which may give children a false impression of the purpose and relevance of reading and writing. This is why Ruth Strang's (1968) criticism of Jeanne Chall's (1967) *Learning to Read—The Great Debate* is of such significance. One of Strang's four reasons for doubting the wisdom of the proposal 'to begin with the synthetic or code-emphasis method' is that it may 'give him [the child] the wrong initial concepts of reading'. The danger in such methods is that children may learn the falsehood that reading is making noises to letters or that writing is performing certain strokes of the pencil in a certain order and direction, instead of the truth that reading is interpreting another author's ideas and that writing is expressing a part of oneself to others.

It is such unintentional learnings as that suggested by Strang's warning which the teacher must continually guard against in selecting materials and methods for beginning reading. This is why teaching methods are important. Children do not learn always what the teacher thinks she is teaching. Therefore, it is important to consider the *concealed lessons* unintentionally taught by different methods. What may children be learning about the purpose and relevance of reading from such methods as those which require children to learn by rote such rules as, 'when two vowels go out walking the first one does the talking'? Many children in such methods must think that reading is some kind of mystic ritual.

Such 'chalk and talk' approaches are based on a fundamental misunderstanding of the way in which children develop concepts. Vygotsky's research led him to conclude:

> Direct teaching of concepts is impossible and fruitless. A teacher who tries to do this accomplishes nothing but empty verbalism, a parrot-like repetition of words by the child, simulating a knowledge of the corresponding concepts but actually covering up a vacuum.

But it may be much worse than Vygotsky says, for children may not learn simply nothing from such methods. A teacher who is working on the assumption that when she 'switches herself off' (to use Blackie's analogy) the children are automatically 'switched off' too, is making a grave error. Children are 'switched on' all the time and learning is continuous whether the teacher wants it or not. In old style teacher-centred methods children can learn wrong habits and ideas which may spoil their ability for later learning. For instance, they may become habitual school parrots, and they may learn that reading is a ritual, ceremonially performed in school, but without any relevance for the real world as they know it.

Herbert Kohl (1968) has suggested that:

> the school does not, and cannot, add anything to the language of the child at the level of linguistic structure. One may confuse the child by teaching *about* language. It may be that asking a child to give too close or too early an attention to 'rules' and individual skills, that asking a child to give attention to specific tasks in handling the spoken language, may interfere with his mastery of language, a mastery that usually develops quite naturally through exposure.

The same seems to be true of learning the written form of language and its relationship to spoken language. The basic misconception of the 'chalk and talk' approach derives from the failure to recognise the way in which concepts naturally develop. Piaget's research led him to conclude: 'A child is actually not conscious of concepts and definitions which he can nevertheless handle when thinking for himself' and that 'verbal forms evolve more slowly than actual understanding'. Thus, the natural order of development is from concrete experience through generalisation to concept attainment, and the latest ability to develop in this chain of stages is verbalisation about the concept.

This explains the suggestions which Reid (1966) makes as a result of her investigations. She proposes that there should be some 'fostering of the understanding of classification, order and regularity', and, although she recognises that successful progress seems 'to depend on whether or not a child had at his disposal the vocabulary which would help him to grasp the various schemata which even elementary discussion of language involves' she nevertheless explicitly warns against any naïve emphasis on labelling or naming, that is, the verbal aspect only of the basic concept. She states 'that the teaching of the letter-names is not being advocated as part of early teaching of reading' and points to her own previous research (Reid, 1958) which showed that the danger of confusion with the basic sounds is considerable.

A firm foundation in theory and research on children's cognitive development underpins Millie Almy's (1967) recommendation that:

> An environment that provides the children with many opportunities for varied sensory and motor experiences is essential. So, too, is the presence of people who talk *with* (not merely to or at) the child, people who read and write and who share these activities with children.

The best way for a non-reader to learn the true purpose of reading is to share in a purposeful reading activity with a reader. For example, the youngest beginners can bake cakes with their teacher while she looks up the instructions in a written recipe. A non-reader can work with a reader from a written assignment. Writing activities also provide vital experiences for learning the purpose of reading as well as writing. The chief value of Roach Van Allen's (1961) 'language-experience' approach probably lies in the opportunities it gives to children to learn by induction what it means to be an author, and thus that writing and reading are, in essence, purposeful and relevant modes of communication.

The Plowden (1967) report on primary education concludes:

> Books made by teacher and children about the doings of the class or of individuals in it figure prominently among the books which children enjoy. They help children to see meaning in reading and to appreciate the purpose of written records.

Sharing purposeful reading and writing experiences thus provides a sure foundation for learning their relevance for communication in everyday life. All through school such relevance needs to be maintained and reinforced. But, from the beginning, there is another important way in which reading must be made relevant to children.

The actual language used in learning to read, as Sylvia Ashton-Warner points out, must be relevant to young beginners. The research of Reid and of Downing indicates that young children do not perceive language in terms of abstract segments like 'word' or 'sound'. Their view of language is much more likely to be in terms of larger meaningful chunks of language such as phrases and sentences.

This provides a further reason for using methods and materials in which the content is focused on helping children to understand the communication purposes of the written form of language. Such approaches are bound to use sentences and phrases rather than isolated segments such as single words or letters, and this proves to be appropriate at the same time for the child's natural perception of human speech.

In summary, whether we are concerned with which alphabet to use (e.g., i.t.a. or t.o.), whether we are concerned with which reading scheme to obtain, whether we are concerned with which teaching methods to apply, the most important consideration in deciding between these choices seems to be—which of them will make reading and writing *more relevant* for the individual girls and boys in our care?

References

ALLEN, R. V. (1961) 'More ways than one', *Childhood Education,* 38, 108–11.

ALMY, M. C. (1967) 'Young children's thinking and the teaching of reading', in Frost, J. L. (ed.) *Issues and Innovations in the Teaching of Reading* Chicago: Scott, Foresman.

ASHTON-WARNER, S. (1963) *Teacher* London: Secker and Warburg.

BLACKIE, J. (1967) *Inside the Primary School* London: HMSO.

CHALL, J. (1967) *Learning to Read: The Great Debate* New York: McGraw-Hill.

DOWNING, J. (1970) 'Children's concepts of language in learning to read', *Educ. Res.,* 12, 106–12.

FEATHERSTONE, J. (1967) *The Primary School Revolution in Britain* (Pamphlet reprinting of three articles) Washington D.C.: The New Republic.

KOHL, H. (1968) 'Children and the language of the schools', *California Monthly,* June–July issue, 22–3.

MARSHALL, S. (1963) *An Experiment in Education* London: Cambridge University Press.

PAIGET, J. (1959) *The Language and Thought of the Child* (Revised edition) London: Routledge and Kegan Paul.

Central Advisory Council for Education (England) (1967) *Children and their Primary Schools* (Plowden Report) London: HMSO.

REID, J. F. (1958) 'A study of thirteen beginners in reading', *Acta Psychologica,* 14, 295–313.

REID, J. F. (1966) 'Learning to think about reading', *Educ. Res.,* 9, 56–62.

STRANG, R. (1968) 'Is it debate or is it confusion?' *Reading Teacher,* 21, 575–7.

VYGOTSKY, L. S. (1962) *Thought and Language* Cambridge, Mass.: MIT Press.

2:10   Influences on primary school children's reading

R. S. Buzzing

What is the child's reaction when first he is confronted with a book? He seems to pause, think and then reach out for it. If its impression upon him is now good, he wants to read it. What, however, is he in fact doing in that initial 'thinking' period? He seems to be deciding whether the book will offer him a source of enjoyment or be of some use to him. Such a confronting can be accidental—the casual picking up of a book lying about or on the bookshelf—or it can be deliberate, i.e. introduced by an adult, teacher, parent, librarian. There is sometimes a third motive for reading, namely, to master the skill. Very young children on learning a new sound or movement will repeat it endlessly until they have mastery over it. Similarly some children will exercise the reading skill just to gain mastery over this form of expression. These might be called the fundamental motives for reading, but we must not overlook the vital need to encourage children to develop from these earlier motives.

One such development is seen as books begin to be chosen because they offer an outlet. Sometimes the outlet is purely hedonistic, the story is amusing or exciting. This may be because it embodies something the child would simply love to do but cannot in fact do. The reading of books concerned with childish escapades may predominate for such reasons. This early interest will probably lead to a much closer identification with the heroes of books, especially those who meet with and overcome real difficulties. Children seeking such identification will prefer deeper books, e.g. those by Rosemary Sutcliff, Rhoda Power or Hans Baumann, where they identify themselves with 'historical' heroes. By the ages of ten and eleven such identification with heroes may well be taking place with members of the Kon-Tiki or Everest teams.

Sometimes too there is another outlet, a form of escapism. Younger

BUZZING, R. S. (1963) 'Influences on primary school children's reading', *The School Librarian*, 11, *vi*, 584–90.

children who are surrounded by a limiting, frustrating or unprepossessing environment often seek to escape into the world of fantasy by reading fairy tales and similar stories. Many good books are to be found in this range, especially in the O.U.P. and Dent collections. However, there are many children who live in much happier surroundings who welcome the world of fantasy and gentle make-believe. Developing children attracted to this type of material will begin to demand and appreciate stories by Alison Uttley and Patricia Lynch. Then many will progress to books like the 'Borrowers' series of Mary Norton, the 'Land of Narnia' adventures by C. S. Lewis, and *The Hobbit* and the 'Ring' cycle by J. R. R. Tolkien.

A second major development is that of reading to obtain information. Children of junior age are frequently collectors of many things, and books which encourage this collecting instinct are in considerable demand. This is true not only of books on stamps, coins and butterflies, but also of those on less common subjects such as brass rubbings and heraldry. The motivating force for the child here is his innate curiosity which demands to know the whys and wherefores of life. This kind of reading can be for enjoyment as much as for strictly utilitarian purposes. There are children who want to learn for learning's sake (the budding intellectuals?), and there are those who seek learning because it enables them more clearly to understand where they are going or how a thing works.

A third major impulse to read is that of filling up time. When a child is bored, perhaps because he cannot be active in bad weather, he may well turn to a book as an antidote to boredom. Sometimes, of course, the filling up of time by reading is an antidote to other forms of work. A child may wish to escape his share of the chores about the house or classroom, and so he picks up a book to read. At such times the apparent grip of a book upon the child's imagination and concentration is truly phenomenal!

In all that has been written so far it is suggested that the child is activated by internal motives or impulses. He has chosen to read for one or more of several reasons, but mainly because in himself he wants to read. It is now fitting to turn and see if there are any external factors which influence children to read. In seeking to establish these factors it is apparent that some of them have been mentioned already. In the first paragraph it was stated that children might be deliberately confronted with books. Here is an important external factor: teachers to a marked degree and parents to a lesser degree expect children to read. Children may very well then be expected to 'go through the motions' of reading because it is expected, the done thing. Perhaps it is time for the daily period of reading; perhaps the child is encouraged to read because somehow, quite mysteriously, it is hoped that this will improve his chances in the selection process. In this sense reading is not merely inflicted, it can correctly be called compulsory or even punitive. Such influences for reading might well be considered second-rate, and with justification, but they must not be ignored just because the motive is suspect.

Another external stimulus lies in the child's leisure pursuits. One who is enthusiastic about fishing will want to raid the library shelves to find a book on the subject. A second child may have an interest awakened in modelling and through this interest, which originated elsewhere, come to seek books on the subject. Both of these are examples of actual happenings —and there was a most reproachful look from the child whose search for a fishing book went unrewarded (this lack of provision has long since been remedied!). Here is the factor of utility re-emerging, for know-how will bring a greater efficiency—surely a very commendable and welcome impulse to improve. Even the much maligned mass media of newspapers, comics, radio and television do from time to time have the very beneficial side-effects of sending children scurrying for books. In my own experience, for example, television programmes on sport have helped juniors to realize their need to develop skills. Similarly, programmes on natural history have stimulated research into animal behaviour and geographical studies of other lands. The result of viewing has been a searching of the shelves next morning for the 'do-it-this-way' or other kind of information book. These influences have also resulted in children seeking further information simply as an intellectual exercise or again merely for the pleasure that searching affords. Often enough the casual reference to, say, the *Oxford Junior Encyclopaedia* for information on one topic has led to seemingly chance interest in another topic dealt with in the same volume. The provision of time for browsing is a matter demanding serious consideration and I shall return to it later.

Other external influences are far too frequently neglected and close attention might profitably be given to them. Children will often be influenced to read by hearing a good excerpt from a book. If the reading is lively, interesting and well delivered, many children will want to read the excerpt for themselves. This then leads to reading on in the book and even back in the book until the whole is read. In the past year I have been able in this way to stimulate first-year juniors by reading to them excerpts from *The Good Master* by Kate Seredy, *Jascha* by Franz Hutterer, and even *Prince Caspian* by C. S. Lewis. Similarly my own third-year class has been arrested by the ballads about Kon-Tiki and Everest by Ian Serraillier, and by excerpts from *Old Possum's Book of Practical Cats* by T. S. Eliot. Then propaganda pinned up in the library has also proved very useful; I refer in particular to the excellent O.U.P. series of posters on children's authors and children's artists.

Again a child may want to read a book after hearing one of his peers saying how much *he* enjoyed the book. This stimulus through recommendation is one which has borne much fruit in my experience. It must be remembered that children will frequently listen without prejudice to one of their own number and follow his advice where they would have reservations about an adult's opinions. We have a system in class whereby children fill in a form after reading a book. One question asks the child to state whether he would recommend the book to other children and for what reasons. (If he rejects the book he also says why he does not wish to recommend it.) As a result of the information thus acquired, children are from time to time asked to choose and read excerpts to the class. A girl dissolving into laughter as she read one of Pippi Longstocking's adventures drew demands for those books. A boy reading an excerpt from *Tom-Toms in Oworo* by René Guillot brought an as yet unsatiated demand for his books. By this means during the past year children have had their attention drawn to books by Cynthia Harnett, Rosemary Sutcliff, Geoffrey Trease, C. Day Lewis, Tove Jansson, Arthur Ransome, William Mayne, Monica Edwards, Ronald Welch—the list is not exhausted. Significantly, too, there has been a developing awareness that if one book by an author is enjoyed then other books by the same author may offer similar enjoyment.

Finally there is an outstandingly important influence upon the child and his attitude towards reading—and it is the one which seems to be forgotten far too readily—namely that of example. In the family circle and indeed in the school circle where all those present sit down to read, or naturally spend a significant portion of their spare time in reading, the child in turn is likely to follow the same pursuit. It is almost a reflex action on his part. Here it is the matter of atmosphere which is important, the reading being done without any sense of artificiality. Even as one would expect in the home that parents and children should be reading together, so with older juniors one might experiment in having the teacher and children reading their own books at the same time. There can still be reference to the teacher when necessary, or the teacher can still find opportunities to hear the children read. The primary child is so obviously sensitive to atmosphere and naturalness that it is essential to develop the conveyed impression that reading is a natural habit. It thus becomes worthwhile in its own right and so impressed upon the child's mind that it may well be the most important single factor of all in influencing him to read. Reading then becomes enjoyed for its own sake, as an outlet, pleasurable in itself and practical—in fact as a major key to the following of a fuller life.

All the foregoing, however, begs the question of where the child is to find the books. Of the utmost importance is the school's own collection of books. If each classroom library is well endowed with books of the best quality; and if attention is regularly drawn to the fact that these books are there—by using some of the methods suggested above, or by using others —then progress will be made. This progress will be further enhanced if alongside the regular reading times there are frequent opportunities for browsing during school and play times. It is imperative that there should also be a first-class central collection of books, both fiction and non-fiction, for borrowing purposes. The central collection should contain further examples of the work of authors represented in class libraries and also a wider range of authors and books than a class library can contain for reasons of space, expense and so on. A good central collection must also be regularly and imaginatively advertised.

In my experience close co-operation between school and city or county library branches brings enormous dividends. Our city children's librarian visits the school upon request or receives classes from the school at the library. There she talks to them, arousing curiosity, setting simple library projects. She has also helped me considerably by recommending authors and books which I had not met. Parents are advised that this co-operation exists, and they then are able to encourage children to visit the city library for reading during leisure and holiday times.

Parents, too, often fail to realize the interest which children have in establishing their own personal libraries at home. From the earliest reading days children can begin to set up their own collections. Many suitable books are obtainable at reasonable prices in these days of paperbacks, and the Puffin books are especially useful. Active and financial encouragement from parents is a potent aid in influencing children to read, but parents themselves often need to be stimulated and made aware of opportunities by teachers.

The purpose of this article is to call for a renewed and re-invigorated approach to the question of children and their reading, especially stressing the vitally inter-related influences of example and accessibility. Given these, we are some way on the road to success in encouraging children to read simply because they are interested in books and authors.

2:11   The sub-skills of comprehension

Constance M. McCullough

One of the most endearing stories of the Christmas season is that of the little juggler who, penniless, took refuge in a monastery. He alone, of all the people there, had nothing to offer the Virgin. There in the chapel he watched the monks as they offered their gifts. Then, to their horror, he stood before the statue of the Virgin and gave his only treasure, his skill at juggling. At the end of his juggling act he knelt, and the statue, moved by the quality of his mind and heart, reached out and touched him in blessing.

This story has something to say to the teacher of reading, who is, in many senses, a juggler, too. But this paper will confine itself to the juggling that creates in the child the ability to evoke the author's conception and intent, the juggling that impresses the child with the idea that reading is a search for understanding.

The metamorphosis of a teacher

The teacher can easily become confused by the many tasks a reading program presents, and the many trends in educational practice which beckon and beguile. He may be enticed away from attention to the heart of the reading program, which is the search for understanding and the evocation of the author's conception and intent. He begins to think that a different organization will solve all of his problems. Or he becomes

MCCULLOUGH, CONSTANCE M. (1972) 'The sub-skills of comprehension', in Southgate, Vera (ed.) *Literacy at all Levels*, United Kingdom Reading Association Conference, 1972, Manchester, London: Ward Lock Educational, 103–8.

convinced that a new material provides the entire answer. Yet, all the time, there is a job to be done, and there is insight to be brought to that job.

Over the years, perhaps, the teacher learns that *every* type of organization has shortcomings and *every* material has limitations for which the teacher must compensate. So, instead of being motivated solely by the prospect of a new organization or new material, he learns to be motivated also by increasing delight in the living act of reading, in the growing power of the child to engage in it, and in the discoveries both child and teacher make about language, thought, and reality. The teacher learns to put first things first.

Relativity in decoding

Perhaps the greatest lesson the teacher needs to convey to the child is the relativity which pervades both language and life. Even the decoding of a word is an opportunity to sell this principle. An exchange of two letters is the only difference between the word *quiet* and the word *quite*. A person reading g-o-i-n-g for the first time could choose to read it as a word of one syllable: (/g oi ng/). But the appearance of this word in a sentence like *I am going to school* leads the experienced English speaker to expect a progressive form of a verb.

The different spellings of h-e-i-r and a-i-r signal the reader to expect someone to open a window when the sentence is *The air is stuffy*, and to effect avoidance if *The heir is stuffy*.

When a word is spelled t-e-a-r, the reader must look to the context to determine whether it is a tear to be shed or a tear that shreds.

If the word is used as a verb instead of a noun, as in *Don't tear your shirt*, the reader learns to turn his thinking from the saltwater to the rip.

In these examples the reader is helped by attention to the order of letters within the word (*quiet, quite*), the variant spellings of the same sounds (*heir, air*), alternative ways of decoding the same form (*going, tear*), and the role of the word in the sentence (*going, tear*).

When the child misreads the word f-r-i-e-d as *friend*, relativity may come to his rescue. The context may suggest that the role of the word rules out a noun, as in:

He ———ed the shrimp in butter.

Or the case may be that the words associated with the word *fried* are not ordinarily associated with the idea of *friend,* as in :

He ate ——— shrimp.

One sometimes hates his friends but he seldom eats them.

In the sentence:

He liked ——— shrimp better than boiled.

the child who may tolerate the oddity of *friend* shrimp as a combination, may finally gag on the contrast between *friend* and *boiled.*

Notice that in this last example:

1   The child must be used to reading for meaning. If something doesn't make sense, he returns to it to see what is wrong.

2   The child must also be accustomed to signals to contrast:

liked———better than

3   He must furthermore be skilled in thinking about the contrasts in his experience, and in calling forth from his memory a contrastive idea to match the one which presents itself to him. 'Liked fried better than what?'

4   He must also know when something is missing from the author's structure, and supply it for himself:

He liked fried shrimp better than *he liked* boiled *shrimp.* It may be helpful to a reader to think of this arrangement of words:

He liked fried shrimp
better than (he liked) boiled (shrimp).

Relativity in word meaning

Just as these behaviors are necessary to the proper decoding of the word form, so are they necessary in the determination of word meaning. For example, teachers are familiar with exercises which require the reader to choose the proper meaning for a word of multiple meanings.

'Choose the meaning appropriate to *band* in the sentence'

The band played several marches.

1   Something which ties things together.

2   A group of musicians.

3   A range of wave lengths.

The reader must understand the meaning of the word *before* he can be sure of the meaning of the sentence; yet his conjecture as to the meaning of the sentence helps him converge upon the proper meaning for the word.

The child chooses an answer, and whether he is right or wrong, he has a reason for his choice which should be discussed. Here are some possibilities:

1 Did he know all the things that *band* could mean, or did he just pick a number?

2 Did he know how to decode the word form, or did he misread the word as, say, *hand*? Did he then flounder among the unsuitable choices?

3 Did he read *band* as *hand* and decide, regardless of the sense of the sentence, that a hand can tie things together?

4 Was the reader helped by the fact that the sentence states that something acted upon something else? Did he sense, even if not analytically, that a range of wave lengths doesn't play marches; that one might expect a sentence starting with a range of wave lengths to tell, rather, where it is or what it is, or what is done in relation to it? In other words, was the reader able to eliminate the third meaning because of his knowledge of several meanings of *band* and the sentence structures commonly expected in relation to those meanings?

Relativity in larger units of composition

Relativity in units of composition larger than a single sentence is more complicated. Take as an example the following sentences which might initiate a paragraph:

Mars is the fourth planet from the sun. It travels in an elliptical path through space around that small star.

Knowing the book or chapter from which these sentences are taken would help the reader with the meanings of some of the words. For instance, Mars is the name of a candy bar as well as a god of war and a planet in our solar system. If the book is on astronomy, the candy bar can be ruled out. The god of war is eliminated because he is not a planet.

In order to understand these sentences and their relationships to each other, the reader must know what a *planet* is and is not, what a *sun* is and is not, what is meant by *space* and *path*, what is meant by *elliptical*, and what is meant by *small* in relation to the concept of a *star*, e.g. a big house is smaller than a small star.

He must know that *the* sun is a particular sun.

He is in danger of misinterpreting the sentence unless he chooses a special meaning of *from* or realizes that the author has shortened a longer expression: *Mars is the planet which is fourth in order from the sun.*

If the reader knows that a planet cannot be a sun and a sun is a star, then he gathers that in the second sentence *it* refers to Mars rather than to the sun.

He knows that a path through space is not a path made of substance but is a course or direction.

The good reader knows that the first sentence tells what something is, and the second tells what it does. The form noun-linking verb-noun is a common form for a statement which names or classifies. *Fourth from the sun* describes the order or position of the concept, *Mars*. The second sentence tells where Mars travels, by what course it travels, and in what relationship that course is taken.

Relativity in expectation

How can the reader anticipate what the author is going to do next? He can expect something only if he can remember what the author has expressed and the order in which he has expressed it. If the author has told what something is and one thing that it does, what else might he say? If he sticks to his subject after two sentences dealing with Mars, what else might he say?

Here the reader's awareness of all the kinds of things which can be known about a concept helps him in his guesses. What other qualities, behaviors, does it have? What are the relationships between these qualities or behaviors and the rest of the world? What theories, principles, laws, generalizations, are possible or known in relation to the concept? What applications of these theories can be made? What illustrations can be offered as proof of their truth? What language is associated with the concept? The reader doesn't sit there thinking *all* of these things, but he does draw upon his knowledge of them in establishing his expectations.

Actually, so far, the author of the two sentences has presented only one main idea: that Mars is the fourth planet from the sun. The second sentence simply expands the meaning of *planet*. One expectation could be that the next sentence will continue to deal with the concept, *planet*. Another could be that it will add individual characteristics of Mars, such as its color, which make it easily distinguishable in the night sky.

If, however, the next sentence deals with the position of Venus, the paragraph can conceivably end with a statement that Earth has these two planets as its nearest traveling companions. In that case, the reader must adjust to the idea that the purpose of the paragraph was not to feature Mars but to place Earth within a system.

Where will the next paragraph go, and the next after that? The author is the architect; the reader, the student of that architecture and the anticipator of it. Divergent thinking about possible directions the author may take is a valuable experience for a group of children.

Relativity in the reading program

If one purpose of education is to make readers of children, current reading programs may be considered, in varying degrees and aspects, successful. Many children read, enjoy reading, and read widely. But if the purpose of education is to make the most of children's potential, if it is to make children better readers than their parents or their teachers, then the success of current programs is more in doubt.

The sub-skills of comprehension, about which little enough is known, must be explored by teachers and pupils alike, not only in reading emergencies on a casual basis, but directly in intensive individual and group study. As the teacher *himself* studies the demands that the written language makes upon the reader, he will have more to juggle in his development of sub-skills of comprehension. The logical barriers between vocabulary and comprehension, reading and grammar, reading and writing, form and meaning, reading and thinking, language and life, will fall away. By crossing these rigid boundaries, the teacher and pupils together will see the miracle of the living language, a network of interactions which make comprehension possible. Together they will evolve a realization of the dynamic quality in their own roles in relation to that print. Even from prereading years, the child should be trained to be more than an inchworm.

What has all of this to do with the Christmas story of the little juggler? Teaching is more than the fulfillment of rituals. It is more than going through the approved motions and expecting a miracle. The true teacher evokes the miracle through his own study and art and skill, and faith in the human potential. Because the teacher is filled with wonder and emotion as he witnesses the dynamics of language, thought, and reality, the child is similarly affected. And because *both* the teacher and the child are at work at the frontiers of understanding—neither of them an ultimate authority, but both reflectors in the presence of a phenomenal human invention, they develop and enjoy a mutually motivating and enlightening relationship.

2:12   Comprehension skills

Olive S. Niles

Middle-of-the-road reading teachers seem universally to agree that teaching students to read with comprehension is their major responsibility. Colleagues to the far right sometimes appear to leave the concept of comprehension out of their definition of reading. They talk as if they equated word pronunciation with reading. If this equation existed, phonics might indeed be the panacea for all ills. Colleagues on the far left, on the other hand, among them those who favor the more extreme forms of 'individualized reading', often exhibit surprising faith that ability to comprehend will appear somehow with a minimum of specific teaching of comprehension skills.

Lists of comprehension skills which appear in professional books on the teaching of reading often seem formidable to teachers, who wonder how they can teach all the comprehension skills and also the word recognition and word meaning skills, the locational skills, the oral reading skills, and perhaps others. The question arises: Is it really necessary to teach all these skills separately? Are they truly basic or are they, perhaps, at least one step removed from those abilities, probably much fewer in number, which are truly fundamental to the process of comprehension?

The number of skills to be taught could probably be reduced if teachers got closer to an understanding of what is essential. Also, the time and effort expended in teaching skills would have a greater effect upon the student's power to read. In the writer's opinion, there are three abilities which clearly differentiate between the reader who comprehends well and the one who does not.

The first of these abilities is the power to find and understand thought relationships: in single sentences, in paragraphs, and in selections of vary-

NILES, OLIVE S. (1963) 'Comprehension skills', *Reading Teacher*, **17**, Sept. 1963, 2–7.

ing lengths. Ideas are related to each other in many ways. Here is a simple example of the most common kind of thought relationship:

> During our visit to the museum, we saw the first Stars and Stripes ever carried in battle; after that we enjoyed a collection of old silverware, later wandered into the room filled with Indian relics, and finally found ourselves absorbed in a display of old wedding gowns.

The parts of this sentence, obviously, are related to each other chronologically. We follow the trip through the museum in the time order in which the rooms were visited.

Now examine the same sentence parts arranged in a different way:

> During our visit to the museum, we saw a collection of old silverware, an absorbing display of old-fashioned wedding gowns, a room filled with Indian relics, and the first Stars and Stripes ever carried in battle.

This sentence tells less than the preceding one. We know what the visitor saw, but we cannot follow him from room to room. The relationship present among the parts of this second sentence is a simple listing.

Here is another sentence:

> During our visit to the museum, we enjoyed seeing the first Stars and Stripes ever carried in battle and the absorbing display of old-fashioned wedding gowns much more than we did the room filled with Indian relics and the collection of old silverware.

Now the ideas have a comparison-contrast relationship. The things the author saw have fallen into two groups: two displays which he enjoyed, two others he liked much less. An important *additional* meaning has been added because the relationship of the parts of the sentence is different.

Once more, observe the same facts but in a fourth relationship:

> Because, on our visit to the museum, we had seen the first Stars and Stripes ever carried in battle, a room full of Indian relics, a display of old silverware, and a collection of old-fashioned wedding gowns, we were able to present a successful class program in which we compared relics of the past with their modern equivalents.

In this last sentence, we have a cause-effect relationship. The experiences of the museum visit have produced an effect: a successful class program.

These four kinds of thought relationship—time, simple listing, comparison-contrast, and cause-effect, plus others—occur in a great many combinations, some of them complex. The ability to observe and to use these relationships seems to be one of the basic comprehension skills.

The ability to set specific purposes in reading is a second important ability or skill. William G. Perry (1959) has reported a study done with fifteen hundred Harvard and Radcliffe freshmen to determine their habits of study when presented with a typical chapter in a history text. In presenting his results, Perry has this to say:

> We asked anyone who could do so to write a short statement about what the chapter was all about. The number who were able to tell us . . . was just one in a hundred-fifteen. As a demonstration of obedient purposelessness in the reading of 99 per cent of freshmen we found this impressive . . . after twelve years of reading homework assignments in school they had all settled into the habit of leaving the point of it all to someone else.

These same freshmen were able to do very well on a multiple-choice test based on the details of the material they had read.

If this purposelessness in study exists among students like those at Harvard, what must be the case with others less able? It might be argued that the moral of the tale is that teachers should give better assignments in which they *tell* students what to look for. But it would seem more important to suggest that by the time young people are freshmen at Harvard, it is high time they know how to set their own purposes. It is obvious that Perry questions whether the students he tested had any real comprehension at all. They could answer multiple-choice questions, but they failed to get, as he says, the 'point of it all'.

Suppose, for example, that a student is studying a chapter about life on the Southern plantations. The inefficient reader plods straight through the material, often with wandering attention because his goal is only to 'read the lesson'. Contrast the careful attention to detail, the search for visual imagery of the student who studies the same chapter in order to make a drawing of the plantation grounds. Contrast again the procedures of the student who wants to compare the way of life of the Southern plantation with that in colonial New England. Or, again, the method used by a student whose responsibility is to report on one very specific topic: the duties of the mistress of the plantation. This last student, if he is reading efficiently, will skim rapidly through the chapter until he comes to a paragraph which seems to have a bearing on his special topic, then settle down to read carefully for detail. The student who thus reads with purpose, and its corollary flexibility, has comprehension impossible to the student who merely 'reads'.

A third basic comprehension skill is the ability to make full use of previous learning in attacking new material. It is 'reading readiness' in an extended form.

Jokes sometimes make an adult realize how a child must feel when he has to read something for which he does not have the requisite readiness. The following is supposed to be a story told by Helen Taft Manning about her father. When Taft was recuperating from a spell of illness, he wired a friend of his recovery and remarked that he had just taken a long horseback ride. The friend wired in reply, 'How is the horse?'

Whether the reader sees anything funny at all in this story depends entirely upon whether he happens to remember from his previous reading or from pictures he may have seen that Taft was one of the heftiest of our presidents.

It is partly a matter of chance whether a reader happens to have a fact like this stored up in his head, but there is more to it than chance. Many students actually have the background information for full comprehension but fail to realize that they have it and to use it. Associational reading— the act of drawing upon all one has experienced and read to enrich what he is currently reading—is a skill which can be taught.

To summarize to this point: If an analysis is made of what lies at the foundation of comprehension, there seem to be at least three basic skills, 1) the ability to observe and use the varied relationships of ideas 2) the ability to read with adjustment to conscious purpose, and 3) the ability to make full use of the backlog of real and vicarious experience which almost every reader possesses. These basic skills are developed and strengthened in part by the kind of questioning which teachers use. Questions must be of the type which clarify thought relationships expressed in the material and which bring into focus meaningful associations with previous reading and experiences. 'Thought' questions can turn a superficial test of comprehension into a learning experience.

Suppose, for example, that students have read an account of the Olympic Games. It is obvious that the first and last in the following set of four questions will make pupils use their comprehension skills, while the second and third will merely test their ability to skim or, if the exercise is unaided recall, to remember a couple of facts:

1 Why do the Olympic Games today feature a marathon race?
2 Who suggested that a marathon be added to the Olympics?
3 What is the official distance of the modern marathon?
4 Does anyone know of a famous American marathon race? Can you tell about it?

The kind of question is important. So, also, is the timing of the questions. Most questions should precede reading rather than follow it. If students knew *before* they read about the Olympics that they were to look for the cause-effect relationship required in question 1 above and that they should be making the associations with previous knowledge called for in question 4, they would read the account with better comprehension because the questions would guide their reading. Questions asked *before* help students set purposes; questions asked *after* may do little but test.

A second kind of guidance which helps students learn basic comprehension skills involves the application of the directed-reading-lesson pattern of teaching to lessons in the curricular areas such as social studies, science, and literature. Teachers in elementary schools are very familiar with the directed reading lesson, which appears so often in the manuals of basal readers.[1] Applied to a lesson in one of the content areas, it starts with the development of background and purpose. The teacher builds readiness for the new lesson by introducing new vocabulary and concepts and by reviewing materials from previous lessons or from the students' experiences to show them how the new content connects with the old. He also helps them set purposes for study. After skimming through the pages of the lesson, looking at pictures, reading headings, reviewing what they already know about the subject, students are able to answer questions like these:

Is this a lesson we can read rapidly or must we study it carefully? Why?
What are some of the things we should try to find out in this lesson?
What questions can we anticipate *before* we read?
How can we use this new information?

It is during this first part of the directed lesson that students learn one of the basic skills: how to set purposes for reading.

The second step, silent reading and study, will be effective in proportion to the skill and thoroughness with which students are guided during the first step.

The third part of the lesson is the follow-up, usually some kind of questioning or testing. The type of questions and discussion the teacher uses determines how much students improve in their understanding of thought relationships and how much skill they acquire in making associations between what they are presently studying and the many other things they know—in fact, whether or not they get the 'point of it all'. Thus two more of the basic skills receive constant practice if the directed-reading-lesson pattern is used.

It is the writer's experience that some secondary teachers react nega-

1 *Editorial footnote*: Basal readers, basic readers and basals are terms used interchangeably in the United States to identify published reading schemes.

tively to this procedure. They may feel that it helps the student too much. He ought to be more on his own. The truth is that most students, even some very able ones, are not ready to study alone by the time they enter secondary school; we should be well content if they have acquired complete independence by the time they are ready for graduation. Skillful teachers know how to allow students to take more and more responsibility until one day, for most students not until some time late in senior high school, it is time to introduce SQ3R (Robinson, 1961). SQ3R is a grown-up directed reading lesson.[2] The steps are virtually the same, but now the student is on his own. That Robinson's well-known technique is not more successful and popular stems from the fact that they have been expected to learn and use it before they are ready.

Teachers need to know what materials are available with which to help students learn comprehension skills. Many reading texts and work-books have been written, some of them very useful, though, as has been implied earlier, the tendency has probably been to fragmentize the skills and perhaps to confuse both teachers and students by presenting too many *different* skills to teach and learn. Many of the exercises are tests of the application of the skills rather than devices for teaching them. Too often, they consist merely of passages to read followed by questions for students to answer. It is the unusual practice exercise which really shows the student how to see relationships, set purposes, and make associations.

Probably the very best materials for teaching comprehension skills are the regular textbooks in social studies, science, and literature. Because the student knows that the content of these books is important to him, he approaches them with a very different attitude from that with which he does a practice exercise in a work-book. He welcomes the teacher's help in seeing relationships and making associations which guide him in his task of understanding and remembering. Setting purposes for study makes sense to him. Every lesson in every textbook is a potential source for the best teaching of reading skills. Few secondary teachers seem to realize this. They are always searching for something different—something 'special'. Or, on the other hand, they make the assumption that the mere act of assigning reading in a textbook will insure growth in reading skill. Assigning is not synonymous with teaching. Only when the majority of teachers in secondary schools realize that purposeful teaching of reading skills is necessary in the everyday work of the content fields will the 'reading problem' be solved.

2 *Editorial footnote*: For a description of SQ3R, see Kravitz, Alvin, 'Teaching the essential reading skills in social studies', 1:4, pp. 45–8.

What role does library or 'individualized' reading have in this process of building comprehension skills? A very important one, but *not* the kind of role which most enthusiasts for 'individualized reading' seem to visualize. Every bit of reading which a person ever does is a potential source of background understanding for all the reading he will do in the future. 'Reading maketh a full man', said Francis Bacon, and he must have meant full of ideas, full of understandings, full of the background for rich comprehension. Any reader's experience can make this clear. He chooses a book or article on some subject with which he is familiar and reads easily with full and deep comprehension.

Contrast this experience with what happens when a reader undertakes to read a book in a field in which he has had no background of experience or previous reading. He can make no associations; he probably has no particular purpose except the very general one of getting some ideas about this new field; he misses many of the relationships which are obvious to the sophisticated reader in the field.

Here, then, is the reason why a broad program of individualized or library reading is essential to development of comprehension skills, not that it is likely, as some authorities have claimed, that most teachers will be able to do a good job of teaching the skills as a part of the individualized program itself. Rather, through the reading of many books, children acquire the understanding and the background which make the teaching of full comprehension skills possible.

If the skills described here are accepted as fundamental to good reading, teachers must make sure that students themselves understand and accept them. Practice of a skill without the student's understanding of what and why he is practising leads to success in only a hit-or-miss fashion. Strong motivation, so necessary in learning any skill, springs from two main sources: specific evidence of progress in learning the skill and proof of its practical application. The more teachers share their own purposes and understanding with their students, the more likelihood of success in their teaching.

References

PERRY, WILLIAM G. JR. (1959) 'Students' use and misuse of reading skills: a report to the faculty', *Harvard Educational Review*, 29, 3. See also Reader 1 (*Reading: Today and Tomorrow*, 2:8).

ROBINSON, FRANCIS P. (1961) *Effective Study* (rev. edn) New York: Harper & Row.

2:13   Developing critical reading

Helen M. Robinson

Critical reading is an ambiguous term, because each person who writes
about it uses, but doesn't always state, his own definition. Furthermore,
the process itself is variously described, ranging from simple choices
between two answers to a question to the highest levels of intellectual
criticism. Therefore, it is essential for me to preface my formal discussion of
developing critical reading by two considerations: first, 'What is critical
reading?' and second, 'How does it fit into the hierarchy of skills and
abilities which combine to characterize a mature reader?'

What is critical reading?

Most investigators and theorists agree that critical reading is an instance
of critical thinking. This close relationship was noted in 1924 by Lyman
who stated that 'The activities of reading, of thinking, and of studying
are considered as three aspects of the one process by which we learn to use
materials which we find in printed form . . . We *read* serious books to get
ideas; we *think* about them to see what these ideas mean; we *study* ideas
and their meaning, endeavoring to make them our permanent possessions
and to get ready to use them in problems of our own.'

If critical reading involves critical thinking, then a definition or description of the latter is essential. Therefore, Russell's (1956) description of
critical thinking is used in this paper. He believes that it is 'to exercise the
powers of judgement, conception, or inference; to reflect for the purpose of
reaching a conclusion'.

Gans (1940) defined critical reading comprehension as the ability to

ROBINSON, HELEN M. (1966) 'Developing critical reading', in Downing, J.
    (ed.) *The First International Reading Symposium* London: Cassell, 249–
    61.

select or reject reference materials in solving a problem. Her study involved pupils in the intermediate grades (ages nine to twelve).

A broader description was offered by De Boer (1946) who wrote that 'Critical reading involves the search for relevant materials, the evaluation of the data, the identification and comparison of sources, and the synthesis of findings. It involves the capacity for suspended judgement and the interpretation of the writer's motives. But chiefly it involves a sufficient background of knowledge to provide a sound basis for judgement. Critical reading implies the existence of appropriate criteria in the mind of the reader.' This description implies the necessity for background experience sufficient to develop criteria for judging the value or worth of materials used.

As one views the range of materials to be read, it is clear that some are designed to provide information or knowledge, others to influence the attitudes and opinions of the reader, and still others are for pleasure and/or appreciation. In order to cover this range of materials, a broad definition has been adopted for this paper. Thus, critical reading is conceived as the judgement of the veracity, validity or worth of the ideas read, based on sound criteria or standards developed through previous experience. *Veracity* might apply to a political statement in the newspaper, *validity* to the description of a scientific experiment, and *worth* to a value-judgement of the literary quality of a poem, short story or book. The judgement of each requires previous experience with the specific kinds of materials, or knowledge of the general area, which is organized as criteria or standards against which the ideas are projected and evaluated.

The role of critical reading

It is necessary to describe the attributes or aspects of reading as I view them in order to determine the role of critical reading. I should make it clear that many will disagree with this description, as I shall point out later.

Throughout his lifetime, Dr William S. Gray analysed the steps involved in reading, reviewed the research dealing with the psychology and teaching of reading, examined the studies designed to determine the component skills, abilities and attitudes essential to mature reading. From these data, he developed a conceptual framework for the total reading act (Gray, 1960). He outlined and described four major aspects of reading.

First, perception of words includes both the recognition and understanding of the meanings of each word used by the writer in the total context of the printed selection. Second, the good reader grasps the meaning of continuous discourse, including: 1) the literal meaning, or what the passage says; 2) the extended or fuller meaning, or what the passage implies or signifies beyond what was said. The third aspect of the reading act includes insightful reaction to the ideas and attitudes presented and to the manner in which they are expressed. This aspect includes making intellectual judgements and emotional responses. The fourth aspect of reading involves assimilation and is achieved by fusing the new ideas, understandings or feelings with those already acquired. Assimilation is conceived as creative thinking which results in new insights, fresh ideas, and new organizations or patterns of thought, and is described as 'an act of discovery'.

In the foregoing brief description, attention should be called to the fact that each aspect described requires higher levels of intellectual and emotional activity than the preceding one, and that each successive aspect requires competence in the preceding ones. However, they are not viewed as *steps* in the reading act because in the mature reader all may occur almost simultaneously, while each aspect reinforces all others.

Earlier I noted that there are differing views of the reading act. Some would limit their definition of reading to the first aspect—perceiving words —while others would include the second aspect which is comprehending the meaning of the continuous discourse. Even the inferential or non-literal aspects are indeed dependent on the so-called higher levels of mental processes. Consequently, some reading experts dichotomize the reading act into word-perception and thinking.

In recent years, scholars have attempted to analyse the processes of listening and viewing, pointing out the similarities of mental processes to those described as part of the reading act. Undoubtedly there is such a communality, and if reading, listening and viewing were taught in schools, it might be practical and expedient to concentrate on their unique attributes. But reading is taught more thoroughly and consistently, at least in the United States, and is the basis for most independent learning. Beyond the middle grades, students are expected to read extensively in order to secure information and to provide the raw material and process models to learn to think. Even in the modern world of radio and television, adults continue their self-education through reading. Hence it follows that the medium of reading offers an unusual opportunity to stimulate thinking and accounts for the extension of reading instruction beyond the aspect of the mastery of word-perception.

In the framework referred to earlier, Gray included critical reading in his third aspect—thoughtful reaction. He described critical reading as 'the evaluation of what is read in the light of sound criteria or standards', involving an inquiring attitude, wise selection of facts and relevant standards for making judgements, and rigorous checking on the validity of conclusions. Furthermore he included emotional responses, which may be related to value judgements and appreciation of literature.

The conceptual framework of the reading act has been supported by one empirical study of the reading of ninth-grade poetry (Letton, 1958). Additional research is needed to understand fully critical thinking and critical reading. However, as is true of all aspects of reading, teachers must proceed while the evidence is still accumulating.

Factors in critical reading

At this point, I am assuming that you agree that all of us should teach critical reading. If so, the first premise is that developing competence in word perception is not enough, although no reading can be done without it. The second requisite is full comprehension of what the author says (literal meaning) and of what he means by what he says (implied meanings).

Smith (1960) examined research and practice to determine the skills essential to comprehension. She included: understanding relevant details or facts, securing the main idea or central thought; the ability to follow directions; securing implied meanings and drawing inferences; understanding characterization and setting; ability to sense relationships of time, place, cause and effect, events and characters; anticipating outcomes; examining the author's purpose by identifying the tone, mood and intent of the selection; making comparisons and contrasts; and drawing conclusions or reaching generalizations. In our eclectic plans for teaching reading, each of these strands is considered from the beginning of learning to read because each places demands on the word-recognition program and, in turn, enhances it and gives it purpose. Research is not yet available to substantiate most of the sequences proposed, but it seems clear that the mature reader must rely on the foregoing skills to be a critical reader.

In addition, an inquiring attitude is essential. From the earliest experiences with reading, pupils can be taught to accept or question what they comprehend. Young children can determine whether a story could be true or if it was make-believe. Later children learn to identify propaganda, to note omissions of information, to determine the logical development of a presentation. But these aspects of reading are acquired only by an inquiring mind.

Furthermore, one cannot react to materials without a certain amount of information, knowledge of specific facts or established principles. For this reason, critical reading is dependent on what one usually considers a basic education. As pupils progress in school and acquire understandings and knowledge, standards or criteria against which that which is understood may be judged should become increasingly mature. As a result, secondary-school and college students continue to learn to read more and more critically in a specialized or given field of knowledge as they acquire increased familiarity with each field. But the inquiring attitude and the habit of evaluation should be so well established that they are used continuously.

Several attempts have been made to delineate, and name, levels of critical reading. De Boer (1946) suggests that the first level is determining the relevancy of materials to a question or topic. To determine relevancy, a reader must select and reject, must make judgements about many aspects of the content. The second level, according to Dr Boer, is an evaluation of the accuracy of 'so-called' facts or the determination of the reliability of sources of information. To explore accuracy and reliability, it may be necessary to read several sources, compare presentations, and examine the qualifications of the author. The third level is to appraise the validity of the author's conclusion. At this level, the relevancy, accuracy and validity of facts and arguments must be supplemented by a knowledge of what has been omitted or suppressed. Ability to follow the logic of an argument or knowledge of the bias of the author is helpful.

All of the foregoing skills, abilities and attitudes should be sufficiently well-developed to be applied automatically as the types of materials call for various combinations of them.

The willingness to apply evaluation and judgement may be enhanced or reduced by the reader's attitudes, feelings and beliefs. Attitude has very little effect, among eleventh-grade students, on obtaining the literal meaning according to McKillop's study (1952). However, when judgement, evaluation and prediction were required, attitude became highly significant.

Implications of Crossen's study (1946) of the effects of attitudes on critical reading are that 'Attention must be given to three important points: 1) the effect which preconceived and emotionally toned ideas may have on reading, especially the effect of prejudices of long standing; 2) a method of identifying the attitudes held by pupils; and 3) methods of taking attitudes into account in the selection, interpretation, and evaluation of materials.'

Attitude of the reader has been the subject of a large group of studies within the last five years. The significance of such research becomes apparent only as one thinks of efforts to 'brainwash' members of the armed services and civilians. Knowledge of how to help adults maintain a balance of judgement is essential.

Unfortunately, in too many of our schools children are taught that they must not question their texts. Their interpretation of the textual materials may vary markedly and in the direction of their biases. As McCaul (1944) has summed it up, 'He [man] is not purged of emotion, prejudice, and attitudes just because he has a book in his hands. When he reads he is as much a dupe of his attitudes as he is under any other circumstances.'

To become a critical reader requires competence in the basic skills and abilities in word-perception and comprehension, an inquiring attitude, a background of information about the topic, ability to weigh evidence while one suspends judgement, and understanding or control of one's basic attitudes.

Teaching critical reading

Pre-school children are capable of critical thinking, according to a study conducted by Smith (1932). While the level of criticism is simple, and the topics limited to those with which the children have had experience, they are prepared to exercise such criticism of the earliest materials that they read. They can begin to compare and contrast as soon as they are sufficiently mature to identify similarities and differences in ideas or events. McCullough (1957) asked of primary-grade pupils questions which required them to draw conclusions, pass judgements, and identify relationships. She found that they had no special difficulty in answering these questions.

Personal reading of many different books in the primary grades permits teachers to help pupils make critical responses. However, it is essential that the right kinds of questions be asked or most pupils will be satisfied to state that they like or dislike the story, book or article. Questions are needed which call for comparisons of similar books or characters; those which ask what a character from another story or book would have done in this situation; those which call for judgements as to what the pupil himself might have done under the circumstances and the like. Questions of increasing complexity lay the foundation for higher level critical reading.

At the middle-grade level, where children begin to read widely in many textbooks, magazines and newspapers, judgement of relevance and quality can continue. Gans (1940) demonstrated that at this level they can judge relevance and authenticity of materials when the relationships are close or fairly obvious, but not with materials remotely or tangentially related. The latter must await greater maturity. However, if children 'read widely they will surely encounter different reports of the same event and at that time they are ready for help in determining veracity, validity, and worth of the differing accounts by considering such questions as the author's biases and the recency of the publication.

Propaganda analysis is taught by many teachers to students in the early adolescent years. This is one of the few types of critical reading that has been analysed carefully enough for specific techniques to have been identified. The Institute of Propaganda Analysis (1937) report the following techniques: 1) 'bad names'; 2) 'glad names'; 3) 'transfer'; 4) 'the testimonial'; 5) 'plain folks'; 6) 'stacking the cards'; and 7) 'the bandwagon'.

A slightly different approach was used by Dale (1941) in his book about ways to read the newspaper. He points up the use of slanted words such as 'economical' which is favorable, 'frugal' which is slightly unfavorable and 'stingy', considered unfavorable, to describe the man in the sentence, 'The man saved two dollars a week'.

Second, he suggests that glittering generalities which are often used are meaningless unless closely related to the facts. 'Nothing ventured, nothing gained', for example, may or may not apply to the particular situation in which it has been used.

Third is endorsement by famous persons—doctors, lawyers, baseball players, or ordinary citizens.

Fourth is inferring relationships that, in fact, do not exist, and false reasoning. He explains them with these two examples: 'All locks have keys. I have a key. Therefore I am a lock.' A statement in which the error is less obvious is: 'All communists believe in revolution. Mr X believes in revolution. Therefore, Mr X is a communist.'

A fifth procedure is argument by diversion. For example, criticism of the Soviet treatment of some satellite people may be answered by reference to racial problems in the United States.

A sixth fallacy is assuming that because two things occurred simultaneously, one caused the other. This reasoning may be found in reading research. For example, children improve in reading from ages six to twelve.

Their feet grow larger so that they wear increasingly larger shoes. Therefore, the reading improvement is caused by the growing feet.

I should like to add one more, which is deliberately omitting information. Certainly those persons who write cigarette advertisements today are well aware of both the British and American reports on the harmful effects of cigarettes, yet this information is deliberately omitted.

Such approaches as those just suggested are useful to know only if they are applied. Eleven- to twelve-year-olds can learn to identify these devices and still be unable to resist propaganda, according to Nordelli's report (1957). Either the pupils were not sufficiently mature, or the devices were used for such a short time that they were largely exercises. Instruction over a long period of time may be needed to internalize or habitualize the skills and develop an inquiring attitude.

Important as it is to recognize propaganda devices, they are only a small segment of critical reading. Hence, teachers of all subjects in the upper grades and secondary schools need to be alert to the many opportunities to teach critical reading. Gainsburg (1961) pointed out that critical reading is essential to the appreciation of literature. Social studies offers many differences in interpretations of events, cause-and-effect relations, consequences of accumulated problems of people and the like. Thus, the social studies teacher has a unique opportunity and responsibility to help students read critically. Science is based upon logical reasoning, so that the reading of scientific materials, too, readily elicits critical responses.

The college student meets continuous demands for critical reading, yet finds little help from professors in developing the essential skills and attitudes for satisfactory performance. Even graduate students need direction in reading critically. In my own doctoral courses enrolling superior students, guidance is needed to teach them to read research critically. As on all levels, instruction involves development of standards for judging good research. The standards must then be applied by exposing students to research that has defective designs, that is inadequately executed, and ineffectively written. To provide contrast, excellent research is also interspersed. Discussion following independent critical effort highlights the skills required and permits one to determine individual weaknesses. Redesigning published reports offers practice in applying the competencies as they are developed.

The demands on adults to read critically are greater today than ever before. Many people spend their entire professional lives writing to influence others. Adults need to be aware of this situation and prepared to cope with it.

In order to develop critical readers in school, this aspect of reading should be taught continuously and each year higher levels should be attained. To do so, materials must be specifically provided and instruction should be direct. A single textbook, considered to be authoritative, is not conducive to critical reading. Differing versions of the same event, different points of view on a single occurrence, are essential.

Teachers must read critically before they can help their students do so. Hence, it seems logical to instruct teachers in training so that they can become increasingly effective with their students.

The kinds of questions asked are exceedingly important. Questions that require only *verbatim* reproduction of the ideas read deter critical reading. Instead, questions should elicit judgement of quality of writings, accuracy of statements, logic of arguments and the like. Students must be prepared to read slowly enough to weigh evidence, make comparisons, determine authenticity and judge values.

Teachers should plan to allot adequate time for instruction in critical reading. They cannot cover large quantities of materials if discussion is carried on in depth to obtain the critical responses of each student. Sharing reactions, diagnosing and correcting weaknesses and leading students to sound conclusions requires considerable time. However, the ultimate quality of students' reading should be sufficiently rewarding to justify the extra time spent in teaching critical reading.

Do students read critically?

In the United States, as elsewhere I suspect, there is a dichotomy between theory and practice. However, in a survey of reading practices, Austin *et al* (1961), reported there was general agreement among teachers that critical reading should be one of the goals of instruction. However, few teachers understood how to go about this type of instruction. Furthermore, only a small number of college teachers felt secure in guiding teachers-in-training towards accomplishing their goals in this area.

One study of high-school students, many of whom were having their terminal education, seems appropriate to report here. Rogers (1960) compared the performance of thirty high school seniors in an undirected situation with a simulated school assignment where questions about the selection were expected. She used paired articles from three issues of the *USSR* magazine. A descriptive rating scale permitted her to ascertain the level of critical responses made by her subjects. She reached the following conclusions:

1 'There tended to be a focus on "remembering facts" to the exclusion, in many instances, of evaluative thinking about what was read.' For example, students were asked to tell what they thought about an article but responded with the content of the article.

2 'There was little awareness of the need for evaluative response.' This behavior was exhibited especially when direct questions were not asked. The students showed no curiosity about the purpose of the magazine, or its publisher, but accepted its slanted content fully.

3 'The subjects demonstrated question-answering skills rather than reading skills.' The subjects attempted evaluation of the selections, with varying degrees of skill, only when questions triggered this response. Without the teacher or a test, critical reading did not appear to function.

Conclusion

Critical reading involves critical thinking and can be taught at increasingly complex levels throughout the school years. Critical reading is believed to be basic to appreciation of literature, to arriving at sound conclusions about personal and social problems, to scientific investigation and ultimately to education in the broadest sense.

Much more research is needed to isolate and understand fully the processes involved. However, experimentation by able teachers need not wait for all of the insights. Teachers who read critically can help their students do so. Schools that aim to develop critical readers can make their goals explicit and expedite the means for accomplishing them.

Finally, reading tests should incorporate critical reading as one aspect of total reading achievement.

Without conviction and effort, our schools can continue to produce gullible readers. To develop critical readers for our next adult generation is the greatest challenge now faced by every teacher.

References

AUSTIN, MARY C., MORRISON, C., KENNEY, H. J., MORRISON, M. B., GUTMAN, A. R. and NYSTROM, J. W. (1961) *The Torch Lighters: Tomorrow's Teachers of Reading* Cambridge, Mass: Harvard University Press.

CROSSEN, HELEN JAMESON (1946) 'Effect of attitudes of the reader upon critical reading ability', unpublished Ph.D. dissertation, Department of Education, University of Chicago, 95.

DE BOER, JOHN (1946) 'Teaching critical reading', *Elementary English Review*, 23, 251, 252.

DALE, EDGAR (1941) *How to Read a Newspaper* Chicago: Scott, Foresman, 103–13.

GAINSBURG, JOSEPH (1961) 'Critical reading is creative reading and needs creative teaching', *Reading Teacher*, 15, 185–92.

GANS, ROMA (1940) *A Study of Critical Reading Comprehension in the Intermediate Grades*, Teachers' College, Columbia University Contributions to Education, no. 811, New York: Bureau of Publications, Teachers' College, Columbia University.

GRAY, WILLIAM S. (1960) 'The major aspects of reading', *Sequential Development of Reading Abilities*, Supplementary Educational Monographs, no. 90, Chicago: University of Chicago Press, 8–24.

INSTITUTE OF PROPAGANDA ANALYSIS (1937) 'How to detect propaganda', *Propaganda Analysis I*, Publication of the Institute of Propaganda Analysis, 1–4.

LETTON, MILDRED C. (1958) 'Individual differences in interpreting responses in reading poetry at the ninth-grade level', unpublished Ph.D. dissertation, Department of Education, University of Chicago.

LYMAN, R. L. (1924) *The Mind at Work* Chicago: Scott, Foresman, 14.

MCCAUL, ROBERT L. (1944) 'The effect of attitudes upon reading interpretation', *Journal of Educational Research*, 37, 456.

MCCULLOUGH, CONSTANCE M. (1957) 'Responses of elementary school children to common types of comprehension questions', *Journal of Educational Research*, 51, 65–70.

MCKILLOP, ANNE SELLEY (1952) *The Relationship between the Reader's Attitude and Certain Types of Reading Response* New York: Bureau of Publications, Columbia University Teachers' College.

NORDELLI, ROBERT R. (1957) 'Some aspects of creative reading', *Journal of Educational Research*, 50, 495–508.

ROGERS, BERNICE (1960) 'Directed and undirected critical reading responses of high school students', unpublished Ph.D. dissertation, Department of Education, University of Chicago, 209.

RUSSELL, DAVID H. (1956) *Children's Thinking* Boston: Ginn, 292.

SMITH, HELEN K. (1960) 'Sequence in comprehension', *Sequential Development of Reading Abilities*, Supplementary Educational Monographs, no. 90, Chicago: University of Chicago Press, 51–6.

SMITH, MADORA E. (1932) 'The preschool child's use of criticism', *Child Development*, 3, 137–41.

2:14   Speed reading: benefits and dangers

Nila Banton Smith

How the concept of rapid reading originated

Interest in reading rate had its inception in studies of eye-movements which began in the late 1800s. The theory that a reader perceives words letter by letter had been an accepted fact throughout the centuries. The whole methodology of reading was based for many years on the assumption that a person looks at each separate letter as he reads. Hence children were always taught their A B C's as a first step in learning to read.

In 1879 a Frenchman by the name of Javal (1879) became interested in investigating eye movements. He thought that ascertaining exactly how the eye behaves when a person is reading would afford some insight into the mental activities that go on as reading takes place.

First he tried observing the eyes of people who were reading by just looking at them with his own naked eyes. But the eyes of the readers moved so fleetingly that Javal couldn't tell what took place. He then tried placing a mirror in front of the reader, watching the reader's eyes in the mirror. But this didn't work either. Finally Javal concluded that the movements of the eyes could not be detected accurately by another pair of naked eyes.

He continued to work on the problem for some time. His thought was that it might be possible to rig up some sort of contrivance which could be used in obtaining objective evidence in regard to movements of the eyes. He consulted his friends, asking them to help him invent some way of checking the eye movements of a person reading. 'Nonsense,' they said. 'Why bother about something that everybody already knows? The eyes have to look at each letter in every word as they move across a line of print. Otherwise, how could the reader tell one word from another?'

Javal, however, doubted that a person recognized printed sentences letter

BANTON SMITH, NILA (1966) 'Speed reading: benefits and dangers', in Downing, J. (ed.) *The First International Reading Symposium, Oxford 1964* London: Cassell, 211–34.

by letter, so he persisted in trying to figure out some method by which he could detect and record the movement of the eyes under reading conditions. At last he hit upon it—a stick and a drumhead!

In developing his experimental equipment, Javal first fashioned a cup of plaster of Paris which was to fit over the eyeball of the person reading. He made an aperture in the middle of the cup through which the page could be seen. While the plaster of Paris was still damp and pliable, Javal inserted one end of a long, slender stick into the outer side of the cup. When the cup dried, of course, the stick was securely rooted in the plaster of Paris. Next, Javal smoked a drumhead as people sometimes prepare a piece of glass for use in looking at an eclipse of the sun. The smoke left a heavy black coating on the drumhead.

When this equipment was ready, Javal asked a man to sit close to the drumhead and read. The plaster of Paris cup was placed over one eye of the subject, and as he read the stick traced a design in the smoke coating on the drumhead. What did this design reveal? That the eyes did not look at one letter at a time or even at one word at a time. Rather, they proceeded in a series of pauses and jerks, stopping only three or four times in covering an entire line. Thus it was that a startling discovery about reading was made, one that is the very foundation of modern speed reading—namely, that the good reader quickly moves his eyes along over the lines of print, grasping whole meaningful units at each glance, rather than stopping to scrutinize each letter or even each word.

A few years later Ahrens (1891) improved upon the plaster of Paris cup in that he used an ivory cup to which he attached a bristle. The bristle recorded the eye-movements on a smoked drumhead.

Other investigators, stimulated by the experiments of Javal and Ahrens, began to make studies of their own using different kinds of equipment. Finally a huge camera was devised which would actually take photographs of eye movements. This camera was designed by a professor who devoted a year's time to its perfection, and it cost $6,000.

When using this camera, a bead of mercury was placed on the eyelid of the reader. If the reader has ever dropped a thermometer and broken its glass he has seen that little beads of mercury, almost as light as air and as round as balls, rolled about here and there in response to the slightest movement. Because of these properties, mercury was a highly satisfactory medium for this experimental work with eye movements. Furthermore, rays of light were reflected from these bright mercury beads. These rays were photographed as they were reflected on the lines of print while the reader was in the act of reading.

Once this thoroughly scientific procedure for detecting and recording eye movements had been developed, hundreds of studies were made with all kinds of readers at various age levels. Voluminous evidence piled up, showing beyond the shadow of a doubt that there were decided differences between the way poor readers read and the way excellent readers pursue the printed page. These studies revealed that the poor reader perceives just one word or perhaps a part of a word at a time, while the excellent reader takes in an entire group of words at a glance. Obviously, the person who takes in an entire group of words at a glance can read more rapidly than one whose eyes fixate on one word at a time or perhaps on parts of words. This concept was the beginning of a new methodology in rapid reading.

Techniques in teaching rapid reading

Breaking accustomed tempo

The first thing to do is to break the tempo in which you usually read.

An amusing story is told about Puccini, the great Italian composer. One day he dashed out of his flat in Milan, fifteen minutes late for an appointment. As he rushed up the street he encountered an organ-grinder who was drowsily turning the crank of his organ under the spell of the warm Italian sunshine. The disturbing thing to Puccini was that the aria which the grinder was so indolently reproducing was one from his own *Madame Butterfly*. Puccini, deeply irritated by the agonizingly slow movement of his masterpiece, cried out impatiently, 'Heavens, man, faster, faster!' without slackening his pace. As he ran, however, he momentarily attempted to set a tempo by waving his right hand rapidly back and forth in true maestro fashion. The next week Puccini again met this same organ-grinder. This time he was grinding out *Madame Butterfly* in the rapid, sprightly tempo which Puccini's hand had indicated. Even more surprising, however, was the sign suspended from the grinder's neck: 'Pupil of Puccini'.

For you who would speed your reading, this story holds more than passing amusement at the organ-grinder's capitalizing on his brief contact with the great master. Maybe you, too, have fallen into the habit of 'grinding out the tune' in slow tempo when you read. Perhaps you need to be startled out of your lethargy by having someone shout at you, 'Heavens, man, faster, faster!'

Rapid reading is achieved by moving the eyes more rapidly across the page and by taking in more words at each glance. So first of all, set your mind to take in long, meaningful units, with fleeting eye-pauses that gather in everything within the range of vision. Don't point, don't say the words with your lips, and don't move your head. Free your mind from all bodily accompaniments. Let it race ahead unimpeded.

If you are going to practise by yourself, choose the right physical setting for this practice. Don't start your improvement program in the midst of a busy office where phones are ringing, employees are asking questions, and people are coming and going. And don't start it in the living room at home where television is shouting out attention-arresting phrases and the children are playing 'cops and robbers'. You probably can withstand such distractions when you become a highly proficient reader. But to start with, go into a room by yourself—and close the door! Shut out the distractions.

Once you are in a room free from distractions, look for a chair which isn't too comfortable. Your period of reading practice is no time to loll on a chaise longue or to recline on soft pillows in a bed. You have a job to do. You are about to sharpen one of your most important tools. With the importance of your new job in mind, find a straight-backed chair. Seat yourself so that you know you have a spine, square your shoulders, and go to work.

At the beginning easy material should be used. Practice with difficult material will come later on. Easy material will serve best while you are breaking the old tempo and establishing new habits. Consequently, choose something light—so easy that you'll dare to 'let go' and sweep your eyes across the lines with a speed you've never tried before. As you are about to begin the selection, set your own purpose for reading it. A strong purpose helps pull your eyes rapidly along over the lines, and it gives you something to tie to in gathering meanings as you go along.

So when you are ready to read, make up your mind just why you want to read that particular section. Just to follow the plot of the narrative? To get some ideas that might be useful to you? To find out what happened in a current event? Whatever the reason, phrase it concisely and keep it uppermost in your mind throughout the reading of the selection. Your purpose is the pilot light which guides you over the sea of print with a well-filled dragnet of ideas at the end of the journey. It is a magnet which attracts useful information to satisfy your study, business or pleasure needs.

Above all, force your speed! Consciously push your eyes across the line as fast as you can make them go and still know what you are reading about. Across, back, across, back, across, back, in rapid, rhythmic sweeps! Make those eyes leap over each line. They are your servants. You can control them. Don't let them loaf along in the old lazy way.

After each timed trial-run you must check your speed and comprehension. If you are working under an instructor, you will be timed by the instructor and your comprehension will be checked with the use of previously prepared questions which are printed or which he will ask you orally on the content read. If you are working alone, you will need to time yourself, and perhaps check your own comprehension. Checks of speed and content must always follow one another after timed reading practice.

I would suggest practice periods of three minutes each to start with. If you are working alone have someone else watch the time for you, or if that isn't convenient, set an alarm clock for three minutes and stop when it rings.

Speed is ascertained by counting the number of words read during a given time and dividing this number by the number of minutes or number of minutes plus seconds consumed in the reading.

For checking purposes it isn't necessary to count each word on the page individually. An estimate of the number of words on one page of the total number of pages covered may serve as an estimate for all pages in the same selection. In making such an estimate, the number of words in six or seven lines are counted. As a result three or four of the lines may turn out to have the same number of words—let us say thirteen. If this doesn't happen, then words may be counted in several lines and the average found by dividing the total number of words by the number of lines in which words are counted.

Once the average number of words in a line has been ascertained, then you can quickly count the average number of lines covered during a practice period and multiply by the average number of words per line, as:

$$75 \times 13 = 975 \quad \text{total number of words}$$

This number divided by the number of minutes used in the practice yields the number of words per minute read, commonly designated as W.P.M. As an example, if three minutes were used for the practice period, the computation would be:

$$975 \div 3 = 325 \text{ W.P.M.}$$

When practising by yourself, ask someone to question you on what you read after each timed practice to see if you grasped the content. If no one is available to question you, then try to 'tell yourself' what you read. Then check with the content, itself, to find out how accurate you were.

Go on repeating the same procedure over and over again until you finish an article or a chapter. Keep a record of the number of words you read each time and some indication of how well you got the thought. Make comparisons. Strive continuously to beat your own last record.

After you have had some experience in doing what I have suggested up to this point, then begin your speeded reading practice in earnest. This practice should be of two types: 1) general informal practice throughout the day; and 2) specific practice within stated periods of time.

Your general informal practice will consist of forcing yourself to read faster everything that you have to read all day long. Try the same techniques that you used in reading the articles during your practice on *everything* you read. Regardless of whether you are reading chapters in textbooks, memos or ads that are piled up on your desk, news items, or magazine articles, push your eyes along as fast as you can make them go, and speed up your mental process of absorbing meanings rapidly.

You have to work at this business of increasing speed. Nothing short of continuous and abundant practice will develop the new rapid reading habits which you wish to acquire. So jolt yourself out of the old complacency and force yourself to read faster every time you have or can make an opportunity to read. Take in the whole meaningful groups of words at each fleeting glance.

You won't be able to read technical material so rapidly as non-technical material, so while you are breaking old habits and establishing new ones try to devote the bulk of your reading practice to subjects of general interest and material which is easy. Don't shy away from any technical reading that you have to do, however. If this is a 'must' in your daily program, apply the same speed-reading techniques to this that you do to reading easy material. Try to read even technical material at a higher tempo.

At this point, however, let me warn you about a current misconception which many people have in regard to rate of reading. This misconception is that an individual should have *one* fixed rate of reading. When adults come to a reading center they almost invariably ask: 'How many words per minute should I read?' or 'How many words per minute will I be able to read when I finish this course?' or 'I hear that people can learn to read 1,000 words per minute.' All such statements are indicative of a much too prevalent fallacy—the assumption that an individual has just one reading rate that he uses in all situations. As a matter of fact, the expert reader uses many different rates as they accommodate his reading of different kinds of content for different purposes. All of a person's rates can be improved, but improvement in speed alone should not be the goal; flexibility in adjusting speed to different situations is the achievement toward which learner and teacher alike should direct their efforts.

Learning to preview

After the old tempo is somewhat broken, then several new techniques may be introduced and given practice one by one. Among these techniques preview is perhaps the easiest to acquire and at the same time it is very useful.

I might explain this procedure by comparing it to 'window-shopping'. Before you buy a car you shop. You look over the various makes and 'size up' their appearances, special features, colors, promise of performance, price, etc. If you are going to buy a coat you look at the color, the material, the style, the price and consider the purpose for which you wish the coat to serve you. Similarly, you should shop before you select something to read; that is, take a preview. A book, chapter, or article has certain prominent characteristics, just as a car or a suit has outstanding features. If you briefly study these characteristics before you read, your survey may be as valuable to you as your general 'sizing up' of a car or coat before you buy it.

In some cases the preview will provide you with all the information you desire, and you won't find it necessary to read the selection at all. In other cases the preview will 'whet your appetite', increase your interest, and strengthen your motive for reading. In these latter cases, when you actually do begin to read you will find that your prereading insight has paved the way for speedier and more comprehensive coverage of the printed page. Preview is particularly valuable to a student in sizing up a chapter before he studies it or in reviewing a chapter before an examination.

The first step in making a preview is to study the title. The title holds a world of information, for it gives you a quick cue as to what the topic of discussion is. It may be a deciding factor in determining whether or not you want to read the selection. If you decide that you do want to read it, then you have advance information and can read in terms of the promise that the title holds out to you.

Next, glance through the material to see if subheadings are used. If so, a quick survey of them will be valuable to you. You should consider each one for the information it gives or implies. These subheadings reveal to you the trend of discourse in the article as a whole. There will be occasions in which a preview of these subtitles will tell you all you want to know. At other times they will serve as interest-leads to reading the difficult sections and as door-openers to better understanding of the text.

If any visual aids are furnished, study them for their significance. Look at illustrations carefully. They will aid your comprehension by giving you a vivid mental picture of the people, things, and locale dealt with. If maps are provided, study them. Your reading will be more meaningful if you have precise geographical locations in mind. If graphs and charts are provided, study these before you read the article. They will give you a quick grasp of relationships and proportions among data discussed in the text.

Practise previewing whatever you read. Concisely these are characteristics which you will need to observe in making your initial surveys: title, sub-headings, visual materials.

Noting direction-words

Ordinarily when you are driving in unfamiliar territory, you keep yourself on the alert for road signs. You have a definite destination, and you are acutely aware of the fact that the quickest and surest way to reach this destination is to heed the signs which tell you when to turn left, when to turn right, and when to go straight ahead. If you become preoccupied with other thoughts and fail to note the signposts as you roll complacently along, you will later on find that you are on the wrong road. Then time and gasoline and driving energy are all wasted as you retrace the route to the very important sign which you should have observed in the first place.

Printways are similar to trailways in that they, too, are posted with signs which aid the reader in finding his way quickly and surely to his reading destination. If the reader ignores these signs, he, like the motorist, is apt to find it necessary to retrace his steps.

The signposts in reading warn you when to go straight ahead, and when to make a sharp turn. If you pay attention to these signposts, you can read much more intelligently and much more rapidly. They warn you what to expect, and thus you are prepared to anticipate the meaning and to adjust quickly to change in the printed stream of thought.

What are these signposts? Usually they are words; occasionally they are phrases. There are two distinct groups.

One group of direction words tells you to go ahead with speed. These words assure you that there will be no turns, or bends, or obstacles in your printed pathway. They indicate that there will be more and more ideas added which carry forward the same course of thought.

Some of the most commonly used sign words in this group are *and, more, moreover, more than that, furthermore, also, likewise.*

And is the most common of all the go-ahead words. It connects ideas of equal importance, or ideas which occur in a certain order. Notice how *and* signals you to go ahead in the sentence below—to read more and more equivalent ideas.

Mr. Jennings was angry and guilty and apologetic and harassed all at the same time.

The three *ands* in this sentence tell you to race right along, that you will find more and similar ideas about Mr Jennings.

More, moreover, more than that, furthermore, indicate that there is something to be added on the same subject and that the thought will be carried forward in the same direction.

Also literally signifies 'all in the same manner'.

As an example, look at the paragraph below:

> They reported the usual number of hunting accidents this year. They also reported that mistaking men for game came third in all causes of wounds. More than that, they painted a picture of the type of man who usually commits this most inexcusable of hunting accidents. Furthermore, they stated flatly that this type of person ought to stay out of the woods and view television for his recreational diversion.

The go-ahead words *also, more than that, furthermore* carry the same thought forward; they tell you to hasten right along. There will be more of the same thing.

The other group of words are in opposition to the go-ahead words. They turn the thought sharply in a different direction.

The most common of these adversative words is *but*. Literature is filled with laments of writers concerning the effect of this word *but*. As an example, here is a quotation from Samuel Daniel, the English poet:

> Oh, now comes that bitter word—*but*, which makes all nothing that was said before, that smooths and wounds, that strikes and dashes more than flat denial, or a plain disgrace.

If all readers would heed every warning which this little word *but* signals to them, they would read with much greater ease and more decisive understanding.

Read the quotation below. Keep yourself alert for the word *but*. Note how this one word is the harbinger of a complete change in thought.

> Life is like a beautiful and winding lane, on either side bright flowers, beautiful butterflies, and tempting fruits, which we scarcely pause to admire or taste, so eager are we to hasten to an opening which we imagine will be more beautiful still. But by degrees, as we advance, the trees grow bleak, the flowers and butterflies fail, the fruits disappear, and we find we have arrived —to reach a desert waste. [G. A. Sala].

There are other words and phrases which also negate preceding statements with equal effectiveness. Some of these words are *yet, nevertheless, otherwise, although, despite, in spite of, not, on the contrary, however, notwithstanding, rather* and sometimes *still*. When used to divert the current of thought, these words usually occur either at the beginning of a new sentence or in the middle of a two-clause sentence.

When you come upon such words, prepare yourself for an abrupt change. These deflectors tell you to stop going ahead and to change your course to the opposite direction, since the author is about to usher in an idea adverse to those that you have been reading. Don't go jogging along past these signposts on a straight-ahead road. When a signpost says 'Sharp Turn', adjust to the change of course which the author is about to take. Travel with the author, and you'll reach your destination more quickly and more accurately.

Finding the main idea in paragraphs

One of the most useful techniques in rapid reading is that of being able quickly to spot the main idea in a paragraph.

Every selection is made up of paragraphs. Each paragraph is a unit of thought. Quickly grasping the essence of each of these thought units enables you to cover reading materials rapidly and, at the same time, to get the most important ideas which the author is expressing. In a paragraph there is one point of fundamental importance, and the details revolve around this hub idea, expanding upon it.

When you toss a pebble into a pool of water, you immediately perceive a circular ripple at the spot where the pebble came into contact with the water. Then other concentric circles appear, one after the other until there is an entire set of circular ripples. So it is with a paragraph. Figuratively speaking, the author tosses one main idea into a paragraph which sets all the other ideas in motion. It is your job to learn how to find this pivotal idea, swiftly and surely.

In much of the reading that you do you won't care to take time to consider all of the details. You will be satisfied if you can speedily glean the main ideas in the selection. Expertness in 'spotting' the basic thought in each paragraph is the skill that you need to cultivate.

On the other hand, some selections will be of such significance to you that you will want to read and consider the minor ideas carefully. Then you will find that locating the main idea in each paragraph is of major importance because the central thought provides you with a core around which you can organize the details. Whether you are doing cursory reading for the purpose of gathering the larger ideas, or whether you are doing detailed reading for exact information, you will find it to your advantage to acquire the technique of reading paragraphs. In order to do this you must develop a systematic approach to paragraph reading rather than just following along one sentence after the other without effort or thought in regard to paragraph organization.

The position of the key sentence in a paragraph varies. Often the germ idea appears in the first sentence. If so, this is a convenience to the reader because he doesn't have to search through the entire paragraph for the central thought. At other times, the important idea occurs in the middle, at the end, or somewhere else in the paragraph.

In the paragraph above, the most important thought appears in the first sentence. As an example of a different location note the key sentence in the paragraph below:

> 'How can I learn to read better?' There is no quick trick that will enable you to improve your reading ability any more than there is a quick trick that will make you an expert in playing golf. Just reading *about* how to read better won't result in marked improvement, either. The one way to reading improvement is continuous practice with the use of materials designed to develop your specific reading abilities.

In this paragraph the most important thought is given in the last sentence. Because of the variance in the location of the key sentence within a paragraph, position is not a reliable guide in finding the main idea. You must learn to locate the one basic thought wherever it occurs in the paragraph.

The first thing to do is to develop a new concept of paragraph reading— the concept of looking upon each paragraph as a unit. As you encounter a new paragraph, view it as if it were all the reading material you had before you at the moment. Decide what is the *one* important idea this paragraph has to impart.

It takes practice to identify main ideas at a glance while reading, particularly when they do not occur in the first sentence, but this skill is extremely helpful in reading more rapidly and in increasing comprehension.

Skimming

The swallow skims swiftly through the air, catching and devouring insects while simultaneously flapping his wings to propel his body. He even drinks as he skims along over brooks, ponds, and rivers, gathering drops of water in his beak with no cessation in flight. This versatile creature doesn't pause or labor over any one insect or any one pool.

The swallow's mode of skimming for food and water may be likened to the method used by skilled readers who skim over the pages of print, gathering what they want as they 'fly' along. With instruction and practice a reader can become extremely adept in 'catching' what he desires from reading while 'on the wing'. This is the type of reading in which some people cover 3,000 or 4,000 words per minute and are able to repeat the gist of what they have read. They don't really read all of these words. It would be a physical impossibility for the eye to see that many words per minute. These people simply skim and pick up important snatches of content as they do so.

While skimming is the most useful of the reading skills, it is also the most complex. Skimming is a hierarchy built upon and utilizing all other reading skills which I have discussed so far. In skimming you need to force your speed, to accelerate your reading tempo far beyond that used in your fastest reading of even easy material. In skimming you really 'fly' over the pages, but you should learn effective procedures for getting what you want while 'flying', or the flight will be wasted effort.

Recognizing the signposts, finding main ideas and previewing are all techniques which you call into action as you skim for different purposes. Once you have mastered these techniques you can integrate them into your new stepped-up super-speed skimming.

In undertaking to acquire the super-speed of skimming the development of an entirely new attitude is a prime requisite. This new attitude is a combination of resigned willingness to pass hastily over a page without reading all that it has to say and of release from a feeling of guilt because you haven't done thorough reading. For many people, considerable effort and will-power is necessary to 'break loose' and cover quantities of material without reading every word.

There is much reading that must be done meticulously, of course, but most people could skim through, without loss, a great deal of the material they now read carefully. To do this, one must cut all moorings with past reading habits and recklessly take a chance at merely catching snatches of printed symbols here and there. It is necessary to cultivate an attitude of abandon while engaging in the high-powered skill of skimming.

In so far as new techniques are concerned, the first is that of skimming for main ideas *only*. Ignore all content in a selection except the main idea in each paragraph. Do this with no feeling of restraint. Be satisfied to find the main ideas only and rush on.

Another new technique is that of making use of *key words* only. Certain words are important in conveying the general meaning of a selection, and others aren't. Developing skill to read only the key words and omitting all words of lesser importance greatly facilitates skimming. You don't have to stop and tip your hat to the articles *a, an, the*; pronouns such as *you, they, who*; prepositions such as *of, in, at*, etc. Ignore these and pick up only key words—nouns, verbs, sometimes adjectives and adverbs.

And you should use a new pattern of eye movements—the pattern in which you sweep your eyes from the top to the bottom of pages. Let us say you have already developed excellent speed in reading horizontally from left to right. The next step is to develop skill in making fleeting eye sweeps vertically. The old habit of reading from left to right has been ingrained in your nervous system since childhood, and it may be difficult to develop vertical eye movements to a point at which they are as facile and fleeting as your horizontal eye movements.

Normally, our eyes move from left to right across the page, and for this reason all of us are accustomed to using our *lateral* field of vision. We fixate at a point on a line and read all the other words we can see at the left and right of this fixation, then move on to another fixation and repeat the perception process. But it happens that we also possess a vertical field of vision which usually lies dormant in so far as reading is concerned. It is possible to cultivate this to take words above and below the point of fixation, as well as at the left and right of it. Undoubtedly the phenomenal skimmers who claim they can grasp 3,000 or 4,000 words per minute make use of their vertical field of vision.

In summary we may say then that the formerly-learned skills to be integrated into the new procedures are forcing your speed, heeding signposts and finding main ideas. The new attitude and skills which you are to develop are 1) cultivating a willingness to skip large portions of content, 2) making use of key words, 3) developing facility in using a vertical pattern of eye movements, and 4) developing ability to use your vertical field of vision.

I have now discussed the procedures of forcing speed, previewing, heeding direction words, finding main ideas and skimming. These are among the most important techniques in developing speed reading. Just lecturing on these procedures won't do the job. If you wish to improve your own speed, or if you are trying to improve the speed of a student or a class of students, you must realize that practice is necessary. It takes a great deal of practice to become a good piano player, or to become excellent in playing golf. So does it take practice to become a high-speed reader. Most persons make greater gains when under the guidance of an instructor who holds them to rigorous practice and continuously urges them on to higher achievement.

Research on speed reading

The use of instruments

Instruments have been and still are rather generally used in giving speed reading courses in the United States. These instruments are of three types: tachistoscopes, pacers and films.

The tachistoscope is used in flashing series of figures or phrases on a screen or blackboard. The sets of figures or phrases are printed on cards which are inserted in the tachistoscope. The set of cards for figures contains series of numbers of increasing lengths, likewise the set of phrase cards contains phrases of increasing length. The instrument is electrically controlled and can be so adjusted as to flash numbers or phrases in rapid succession and for decreasing lengths of time.

Probably the most widely known of the speed-reading instruments is one which belongs to the family of pacers, accelerators, rate controllers, and 'trainers'. These instruments all operate on the same principle. A platform is provided on which an open book or article can be placed. A metal lever, wire, or beam of light is then moved electrically over the page at any rate desired. As the lever moves along it covers up the lines of print one by one, and the reader has to hurry along in reading each successive line before the lever catches up with him and covers up the line.

One of the latest of these gadgets comes equipped with its own material consisting of eight rolls of programmed lessons. It works automatically without electricity. You pre-set it at your own reading speed and the instrument automatically speeds up the movement of the roll it contains at intervals and you have to read faster to keep up with the rate in which the material on the roll is passing through the instrument. The width of the material on the roll also gradually increases.

Another popular speed device consists of films which are shown with the use of a 16-millimeter moving-picture projector. The films consist of several complete selections. Each selection is flashed on the screen a section at a time. While all the words on the screen are visible, successive phrases stand out more prominently as they are flashed from left to right across the lines until the section is completed. The rate of flashing these phrases can be controlled and varied from slow to high speeds.

The use of instruments is controversial. Many studies have been made of their effectiveness. Traxler and Jungleblut (1960) summarized research in regard to the use of instruments to improve reading and studies in which instruments were not used. They concluded, and I quote their words, 'As was true of a good deal of earlier research, these studies do not indicate that any greater improvement in either speed or comprehension can be obtained through the use of mechanical devices than can be secured with more informal procedures.'

Other facts about rate of reading

Aside from instruments, many, many studies have been conducted to find out other facts about rate of reading. Let us now examine some of these important facts revealed by investigation.

1   Research has shown that speed can be increased with training. Speed evidently is a skill that responds readily to instruction and practice. Reports of practically all studies in which systematic training was given to increase speed resulted in rate increase.

2   Now, how about the assumption that the fast reader reads with the best comprehension? Many of the earlier investigators of reading rate arrived at this conclusion without qualification. Later studies imposed some restrictions on this generalization. Stroud (1942) for example, reviewed the literature on speed and comprehension and concluded that 'published coefficients between speed and comprehension were spuriously high'.

Carlson (1949) concluded that 'At the upper levels of intelligence the rapid readers were more proficient, but at the middle and lower levels of intelligence the slower readers tended to be the better readers.'

Flanagan (1939) had twelfth-grade students read at three different rates —slow, medium and rapid. He concluded that high school students can read with a fair degree of speed without significant loss in comprehension, but when the reading becomes very rapid, comprehension is sacrificed. He also concluded that difficulty of material made a difference.

3   Others have found that many factors affect rate in reading. Intelligence, purpose and relative difficulty of material, all have their effects on rate of reading.

Roesch (1953), as a result of working with college students, found that 'interest in a task, effort and the will to learn' were vital factors in increasing speed.

Reed and Pepper (1941) concluded as a result of their study that 'perhaps most variables governing speed of reading . . . can be accounted for by such factors as rate of concept formation, organizational ability, and general word knowledge'.

In a study involving high school students Bell (1942) found that intelligence, amount of reading and rate of reading are positively related to comprehension. Langsam (1941), in a study with college freshmen, found the following factors to be important in good reading, including rate: a verbal factor 'characterized primarily by its reference to ideas and meaning of words'; 'a perceptual factor which is a function that appears to be a facility in perceiving details'; a word factor which 'seems to have as its principal characteristic a fluency in dealing with words'; 'a factor tentatively identified as seeing relationships . . . possibly involving logical organization and selection of pertinent ideas'.

So it would seem in the light of these studies, that the matter of developing rate is not so simple as we had at first considered it to be. This is a skill which is complicated by many factors.

So much for studies conducted with adults. Not many studies have been conducted with elementary pupils. A few such studies have been made, however, and I will tell you about these.

One of our major concerns at this level has to do with the stage in the elementary school-child's life at which it is advisable to begin systematic training in speed. We need more research in answer to this question. A few very significant studies, however, have been made.

Gray, as early as 1925, reported as a result of research done up to that time that the rate of silent reading increases rapidly throughout the first four or five grades after which gains in rate begin to taper off. This would indicate that rate grows along with other aspects of the reading process while children are mastering the mechanics of reading.

A significant study was conducted by Bridges (1941) with comparable groups of pupils in fourth, fifth and sixth grades. She concluded that '. . . over-emphasis upon speed tended to inhibit growth in reading at this level. With the better readers at about sixth-grade level this did not seem to hold true'.

Baranysi (1941) conducted an elaborate study with 238 pupils. As one of her results she stated that 'the development of the mechanical factors reaches a plateau somewhere between the ages of ten to fourteen'.

A later study which offers clues in regard to levels of maturity was conducted by Ballantine (1957). This investigator checked the eye-movements of children in Grades II, IV, VI, VIII, X and XII. One of the important facts revealed by his study was that growth was much more pronounced beyond the fourth grade than had been reported in earlier findings.

These studies would indicate that up through the fourth grade pupils are still perfecting their control over the mechanics of reading. It appears that it is not until they have reached the fifth or sixth grade and have gained sufficient control over the mechanics that they are freed to make good gains in speed. These, then, are the elementary grades in which it would appear to be appropriate to give systematic training in rapid reading, and then only to the good readers.

These conclusions, of course, have only to do with the matter of giving formal, timed-speed practice. There are many things that can and should be done in the elementary grades with all children designed to lay the foundation for rapid reading.

What can teachers in the elementary grades do to contribute to rate?

Primary grades

In the first three grades rate normally grows along with the other skills. I like to think of reading as consisting of four major growth areas: 1) word identification, 2) getting meanings from reading, 3) study skills, and 4) rate. Whatever the teacher does to improve the first three of these fundamental growth-areas will contribute also to the fourth or rate.

There are many things, however, which the primary teacher can do in developing rate more directly.

1 For one thing, she can give special attention to phrasing.

a In all blackboard and chart work divide runover sentences between phrases, as:
       The big black dog came running
       down the road.

b In all blackboard or chart work assist pupils to read in phrase units by sweeping a pointer or your hand under each complete phrase as it is read, rather than by pointing to each word separately.

c When the children themselves are using a pointer, remind them to 'keep the pointer sliding', thereby preventing the habit of pointing to and seeing just one word at a time.

d Ask children to read as they 'talk' when reading orally, rather than reading one word at a time.

e Read orally in phrases to the pupils occasionally as an example of how they should read.

2 Another thing that a primary teacher can do is to break up habits of bodily movement: lip-reading, finger-pointing, head-movements. The mind can leap ahead much faster than the body can make physical movements. If these movements are permitted to persist, they are bound to impede speed.

3 Encouragement of wide reading of easy material is a must in rate development during the early grades. Studies have shown that much reading of easy, interesting material contributes substantially to the increase of rate in the early grades.

Middle grades

In the middle grades, that is, the fourth, fifth and sixth grades, the teacher may do such things as these:

1 Continue to encourage copious reading of interesting material.

2 Develop in children an awareness of their personal rates by giving an informal rate and comprehension test with the use of regular classroom material. In preparing for this test the teacher should make up ten comprehension questions on the amount of material which she thinks the average child can cover in three minutes (with more pages available to the rapid readers). At a given signal the children start reading and read silently for three minutes. At the end of the three minutes, a signal is given to stop. Each pupil counts the number of words he has read, and then writes the answers to the comprehension questions. The teacher collects the papers and writes on the blackboard both the number of words covered and the comprehension score of each pupil, but without the pupil's name. Each pupil, knowing what his own scores are, may compare his scores with the others without the others knowing what his scores are. If an informal test of this type is given two or three times a year in each of the middle grades, children will become conscious of their respective rates, and perhaps the slower ones will begin to try of their own accord to hasten their speed along.

3 A third thing that the middle-grade teacher can do is to develop the concept of reading in thought units. This may be done by telling the pupils about the early discoveries concerning eye-movements in reading, as discussed earlier in this talk, and lead them to reason why a person could read more rapidly if he took in meaningful groups of words rather than reading one word at a time. The teacher may write a few paragraphs on the black-

board and let the pupils tell where to divide the lines into groups of words each group of which they think a person might read at a glance. (The divisions may be marked with short vertical lines between the word groups.) Later pupils may mark readable word groups in selections which have been reproduced by stencils or otherwise. All such work should be accompanied, of course, with encouragement to pupils to pick up sizeable word groups at each glance as they read.

4 Finally, for those pupils who have a good mastery of the mechanics of reading, timed practice may be given two or three times a week according to the procedure that I described for the informal test, using regular classroom material in their books, or prepared material if desired.

References

AHRENS, A. (1891) *Untersuchungen über die Bewegung der Augen beim Schreiben* Rostac.

BALLANTINE, FRANCIS A. (1957) 'Age changes in measure of eye-movements in silent reading', *Studies in the Psychology of Reading*, University of Michigan Monographs in Education, no. 4, Ann Arbor, Michigan: University of Michigan Press, 65–111.

BARANYSI, ERZSEBET I. (1941) 'Relation of comprehension to technique in reading', *Journal of Genetic Psychology*, 59, 3–26.

BELL, HARRY (1942) 'Comprehension in silent reading', *British Journal of Educational Psychology*, 12, 47–55.

BRIDGES, LUCILE HUDSON (1941) 'Speed versus comprehension in elementary reading', *Journal of Educational Psychology*, 32, 314–20.

CARLSON, THORSTEN R. (1949) 'The relationship between speed and accuracy of comprehension', *Journal of Educational Research*, 42, 500–12.

FLANAGAN, JOHN C. (1939) 'A study of the effect on comprehension of varying speeds of reading', *Research on the Foundations of American Education*, Official Report of the American Educational Research Association, 43–50.

GRAY, WILLIAM SCOTT (1925) *Summary of Investigations Relative to Reading*, Supplemental Educational Monographs, no. 28, Chicago: University of Chicago Press.

JAVAL, EMILE (1879) 'Essai sur la physiologie de la lecture', *Annales d'oculistique*, 82, (Nov.–Dec. 1879), 242–53.

LANGSAM, ROSALINE STREEP (1941) 'A factorial analysis of reading ability', *Journal of Experimental Education*, 10, 57–63.

REED, JAMES C. and PEPPER, ROGER S. (1941) 'The inter-relationship of vocabulary, comprehension, and rate among disabled readers', *Journal of Experimental Education*, 10, 57–63 [sic].

ROESCH, RAYMOND A. (1953) 'Teaching desirable study habits through experimentation', *Catholic Education Review*, 51, 153–62.
STROUD, J. B. (1942) 'A critical note on reading', *Psychological Bulletin*, 39, 173–8.
TRAXLER, ARTHUR E. and JUNGLEBLUT, ANN (1960) *Research in Reading During Another Four Years* New York: Educational Records Bureau.

2:15 Rhetoric and reading comprehension or reading skills in search of a content

Jane H. Catterson

One of the tasks of what Robinson (1969) has called the 'inventive methodologist' is the creation of new teaching models. Such models may be drawn from the original research of the methodologist concerned, or they may be formed by drawing together, from various sources, ideas and principles that seem to provide guidelines for new ways of thinking about teaching. The teaching model discussed in the following paper is based, not on the original research of the writer, but on a drawing together of ideas from such psychologists as Bruner, Ausubel and Robinson, such linguists as Pike, and such inventive methodologists as Herber. The resulting amalgam, it is hoped, will provide a frame of reference for some of the skill-building practice being given in the name of teaching reading, and which, it seems, is seldom translated into 'real' situations because teachers do not understand well enough the context within which they are teaching.

Value of organizing principles in learning

Both Ausubel and Bruner have made important statements about the significant effect on learning of the teacher's conveying to the pupils a sense of the structure of any discipline being studied. In this context, Ausubel (1963) suggests that verbal learning has been unnecessarily maligned and that it need not be so meaningless as some critics would suggest. He makes a number of suggestions, however, about the conditions needed to make verbal learning meaningful and states:

> One important variable affecting the incorporability of new meaningful material is the *availability in cognitive organization of relevant subsuming concepts at an appropriate level of inclusiveness* to provide optimal anchorage.

CATTERSON, JANE H. (1971) 'Rhetoric and reading comprehension or reading skills in search of a content', *McGill Journal of Education*, 6, *ii*, 125–32.

He suggests further that relevant subsuming concepts should be introduced into learning at the beginning of a learning sequence so that these concepts, acting as 'advance organizers', may provide the 'anchorage' needed.

In another context, commenting on the search for 'big ideas' in the development of physics curricula, Ausubel pursues the principle of subsuming ideas:

> The power of the big ideas is in their wide applicability and in the unity they bring to an understanding of what may appear superficially to be unrelated phenomena.

Although Bruner and Ausubel do not agree in all aspects of their thinking about the psychology of cognition, some of Bruner's statements about curricula are remarkably like Ausubel's. Commenting on the problem of constructing curricula, Bruner (1960) maintains:

> The teaching and learning of structure, rather than simply the mastery of facts and techniques, is at the center of the classic problem of transfer.

Applying new organizing principles in new curricula

Statements like those quoted above are widely accepted and are the basis for many developments in 'new' curricula—new science, new math, new social studies. In each of these school subjects, it is considered, there is knowledge to be acquired, knowledge that has structure; and that structure gives the subject its shape. With that basic principle in mind, teachers of physics think that they have failed if they teach their pupils 'bits' of physics knowledge without conveying to them an insight into the structure of the discipline itself. The essence of the revolution in mathematics or science is not, then, that the content of each subject has changed so much but that *approaches* to the content have changed. The thrust has been in the direction of clarifying the subject by putting its content into new frames of reference.

Existing organizing principles in the teaching of reading

Probably the tables of contents of texts on reading are the best source of information about how the reading methodologist presently organizes his subject. Most texts, after saying something about the importance of reading in the world today, make a fairly lengthy statement about 1) readiness (which almost invariably seems to mean readiness for beginning reading and assumes that the child is six years old), and then go on to discuss 2) word skills in the primary grades, 3) comprehension skills in the primary grades, 4) word skills in the intermediate grades, and 5) comprehension skills in the intermediate grades. Of late years, as a recognition of the fact that reading in the subject texts has been neglected, a chapter or two is likely to be included on 'Reading in the Content Areas'.

The impression given by the study of such tables of contents is that reading is a process one can talk about *in general*, without being specific *about what is to be read*. It is assumed, apparently, that reading is simply a process of adapting basic skills already learned to different kinds of material. No wonder teachers in grades four and up wonder why children who have been *A* students in the primary grades cannot read their science or social studies texts. These teachers think that if they use the basal reader[1] regularly they are teaching 'reading'. They leave it to the children to transfer skills to the content areas.

But basal readers are almost entirely made up of narrative materials and, when the child learns to read the narrative pattern and think about it in certain ways, he is not learning to read other patterns which demand quite different ways of thinking. He really must be taught to read *the most common patterns of writing* and develop ways of thinking about them that are appropriate.

The fact is that the skilled reader has as 'advance organizers' his previous experience with patterns of written English. His thought processes are structured, even before he begins to read, by his expectations about the way the pattern will operate to convey ideas. He does not need to read with prior knowledge of the subject matter (although this is, of course, an advantage if he has some), so long as he has prior experience with similar patterns of writing. His advance organizers provide the 'anchorage' Ausubel mentions. The trouble is that good readers have a talent for seeing structure in writing and have taught themselves to use it. Without specific help, some people never learn it.

Proposal for a new organizing principle in reading teaching

The revolution in organizing subjects for teaching is long overdue in reading. 'New' reading should be based on an approach to teaching that uses the common structures of written English as its frame of reference.

1 *Editorial footnote*: Basal readers, basic readers and basals are terms used interchangeably in the United States to identify published reading schemes.

Linguists have moved from word structures to sentence structures. Their move beyond the sentence seems to have moved very little further than the paragraph, it is true, but some of Pike's work (1964), and that of other tagmemicists, seem to bridge the gap between the paragraph and the forms of such whole 'language units' as essays, poems, stories. Obviously the linguists are getting to where the students of literary form have been for some time and reading, linguistics, and literature are finally beginning to coalesce! If it is fair to expand the term 'rhetoric' to include the notions of unity and order within a form, then we can say that the 'new' reading should centre on rhetoric as its organizing principle.

Having studied the teaching of reading with such frames of reference, a teacher would have a precise idea about which reading skills and sub-skills would be needed within each writing pattern and would not give children practice in sub-skills that were not appropriate to the pattern being studied. Teachers could be much more efficient in their questioning if they understood the kind of thinking each pattern of rhetoric demanded.

Interviews with teachers of 'new' reading: building a mind set

Teacher one

Q. What kind of reading are you teaching today?

A. Well, this is a grade two class, so we work mainly in narrative materials.

Q. Do you think that narrative is the most appropriate material to use with beginning readers?

A. That's hard to say. We make the assumption that children want to learn stories when they come to school. Perhaps they are more ready for this form than any other. On the other hand, some children may find it hard to follow a time sequence and remember it. I suppose a different writing pattern might be easier for them.

Q. Why do you mention time sequence in relation to narrative?

A. Oh, mainly because one has to teach reading in relation to the basic organizing principles in the material to be read. The basic skill in comprehending stories is following the plot and using that as the thread around which the concepts about character, setting, and theme are wound.

Q. What materials do you use for teaching narrative reading?

A. I use basal readers for groups and narrative trade books for individual instruction. I try to show them that the same kinds of questions are appropriate in each type of book, so that they are constantly building what I call 'the mind set for reading narrative'.

Q. Are they developing that mind set, do you think?

A. Yes, I think so. Yesterday I gave them a whole story to read by themselves. It was at their independent reading level and I asked them to read and pretend I had asked them some questions beforehand. When they had finished, I asked them what kinds of questions I would ask. They predicted very well the plot, character, setting, theme questions, just from their experience with stories.

Teacher two

Q. What kind of reading are you teaching today?

A. This is a grade four class, so I've been introducing them to the idea of information reading.

Q. How is that different from narrative reading?

A. Well, since information materials are organized in topical outline patterns (that is, a main idea—details pattern) reading in sequence from beginning to end is not appropriate. Robinson (1951) has pointed out that this kind of pattern is much more efficiently read in what he calls the SQR pattern. This involves a *survey* technique, in which one reads title, introduction, summary, headings throughout before attempting to read details at all. This preliminary survey gives one a frame of reference around which to structure one's thinking.

Q. I thought I heard a teacher say last week that she was using the SQR as a pattern for story reading.

A. Yes, unfortunately, that is an example of some teachers' habit of seizing something good in one context and applying it in another where it is not appropriate.

Q. Do I understand, then, that the SQR method of reading is appropriate only for materials organized in a *logical* pattern?

A. Yes.

Q. Does it apply in science books?

A. It did apply in the 'old' science texts, a type still being used a good deal in elementary schools. But it doesn't apply in senior high school in any of the 'new' sciences. Actually, one of the major problems in new biology, chemistry and physics is that the scientist-writers have developed what is essentially a new text-writing pattern. The reader has to be aware that the writer is presenting a 'proposition-proof' kind of thinking and that he must grasp each stage of that proof as he reads.

Q. But can't a reader expect to skip a step or two, just as a reader might skip a detail or two in information reading?

A. No. In information reading, the main ideas are most important and a few details left out are not critical. In new science, every step is important in the development of the single big idea being presented.

Q. How well is this kind of reading being taught? Is it important to students learning the new sciences?

A. From what teachers say, it is absolutely crucial to the subjects, and it may be one of the most important reasons for the admitted difficulty in teaching them. We might note that many lists of reading skills in science are now at least partly out of date. They are built on an analysis of old science texts.

Q. We started talking about your information reading, actually, and I wanted to ask a question about teaching such reading. But perhaps the same question applies in each subject area. Are there materials easily available for practising the reading skills of each subject area?

A. There are some workbooks that give practice in getting main ideas of paragraphs, reading experiments, map reading, and so on, but unfortunately they treat these skills in isolation from the total context of the reading material of which they are a part. The teacher has always to be putting these exercises back into the total frame of reference within a 'real' text.

Q. You don't think, then, that reading skills can be taught unless the teacher understands their application well enough to work into the text regularly?

A. Definitely not.

Q. What do you think about the materials that use a great many pictures and only a little print these days?

A. They seem like a way to get more directly at concepts. The trouble is, they may be difficult reading because a little print with many pictures may mean a good deal of 'gear shifting' mentally and then you have another process to be learned!

Perhaps these two interviews have made the point. The teachers involved have a very clear grasp of the importance to reading of the rhetoric of the material to be read. They know that one cannot talk about the skills of literal comprehension or the skills of critical reading without saying what is to be read.

Explicitness in teaching

As will be evident in the reference to the SQR method above, some books on study reading do suggest that children should be taught to read information in specific patterns. But very little has been done to explore each pattern or writing specifically or to make the concept an important organizing principle in teaching reading. Herber (1970), who has probably been the most innovative of the writers on the subject of reading in the content areas, seems to feel that teachers should not start with statements about structure, or attempt to make explicit the importance of rhetoric in reading. He thinks that teachers should know a good deal about rhetoric, but should convey it to their pupils through carefully structured reading activities called 'reasoning guides'. These reasoning guides, Herber suggests, should be designed to expose the structure of the material without making any statements about it. He insists that a grasp of structure must be gained inductively or not at all.

This attitude seems unnecessarily rigid. In another context, he has found value in advance organizers and others of Ausubel's ideas and so might be persuaded that this statement has merit:

. . . in meaningful learning situations, it is advisable to introduce suitable organizers whose relevance is made explicit rather than to rely on the spontaneous availability of subsumers (Ausubel, 1963).

Even Bruner, who is sometimes thought to be completely committed to the idea of discovery learning, has this to say in a comment on math teaching:

It has also been pointed out by the Illinois group that the method of discovery would be too time-consuming for presenting all of what a student must cover in mathematics (Bruner, 1960).

However the approach is to be made, tangentially or directly, a study of rhetoric would seem to be an important avenue to reading comprehension. The idea is submitted as a new model for teaching reading, for teaching teachers of reading, and for research.

References

AUSUBEL, DAVID P. (1963) *The Psychology of Meaningful Verbal Learning* New York: Grune and Stratton, 28, 78, 84, 85.
BRUNER, JEROME S. (1960) *The Process of Education* New York: Vintage Books, 12, 21.

HERBER, HAROLD L. (1970) *Teaching Reading in Content Areas* Englewood Cliffs, N.J.: Prentice-Hall, chapter 7, p. 131.

PIKE, KENNETH S. (1964) 'Beyond the sentence' in *The Study of Units Beyond the Sentence* Champaign, Illinois: National Council of the Teachers of English, 14.

ROBINSON, FLOYD G. (1969) 'The contribution of educational psychology to teacher training' in David P. Ausubel (ed.) *Readings in School Learning* New York: Holt, Rinehart & Winston.

ROBINSON, FRANCIS P. (1951) *Effective Reading* New York: Harper & Sons.

2:16   What is involved in word perception

William S. Gray

Because their perception of words is usually automatic, few adults have occasion to think of the ways in which they identify words while reading. However, let us take time to consider what enables a mature reader to respond to most printed words accurately and quickly and what additional means he may use to identify an unfamiliar word when he meets one. Once we have determined what the aids to word perception are, we will consider how children learn to use them.

How printed words are identified

Instantaneous perception

In efficient, rapid word perception the reader relies almost wholly on context clues and word-form clues. Awareness of sentence context (and often of general context) and a glance at the general configuration of a word enable the reader to respond instantly with the meaning the author had in mind when he wrote the word. This type of word perception occurs in most of the reading done by experienced, mature readers. For example, you had no difficulty perceiving the words in this and the preceding paragraph. You did not stop to study the form of separate words. Nor did you analyze words by consciously noting root words, prefixes, and suffixes or by 'sounding them out', syllable by syllable. It is highly unlikely that you consulted a dictionary for the pronunciation or the meaning of any word. Why not? Every word was familiar—you have used each one yourself and have seen it in print thousands of times; you know its

GRAY, WILLIAM S. (1960) 'What is involved in word perception', *On Their Own in Reading* (2nd ed.) Glenview, Illinois: Scott, Foresman, 14–31.

meaning (or meanings). Therefore you were free to comprehend the ideas conveyed by the words, react to these ideas, and add them to what you already know about the subject, providing of course you consider them worth while.

Delayed word perception

Suppose, however, you encounter this sentence: 'The annulet on his coat of arms proclaimed him a fifth son'. Unless the word *annulet* is in your vocabulary, it probably stops you, at least momentarily. From sentence context you infer that an annulet is some kind of symbol; in short, you use context clues to get a general meaning for the word. Because a glance at the word does not reveal a word that you know, you may try word analysis. But study of the word form reveals no familiar ending, prefix, suffix, or root (structural analysis); so you divide the word into syllables and determine vowel sound and accent (phonetic analysis). When you arrive at a pronunciation, you wonder about it, since you cannot remember ever seeing or hearing this word. If you are in a hurry, you may be satisfied with your tentative pronunciation and with a general meaning ('some kind of symbol'). Nevertheless your perception of the word *annulet* is uncertain and incomplete. To find out exactly what it means and to check its pronunciation, you will have to consult the dictionary.

If context furnishes no clue to the general or specific meaning of an unfamiliar word, the dictionary is a reader's only recourse. The word *assagai* in the sentence 'Kent showed us the assagai he had brought from Africa' serves as a good example. If you have never seen or heard the word, no amount of guessing or word analysis is likely to reveal its meaning or pronunciation.

Four major aids to word perception

Four major aids to word perception have been mentioned: 1) memory of word form, 2) context clues, 3) word analysis (structural and phonetic), 4) the dictionary. The first two, as already noted, function automatically in most of the reading we do to ensure instantaneous word perception. When fluent word perception is stopped by an unfamiliar word, however, we may consciously use one or more of the four aids.

So far we have been concerned with the way these methods of word perception function in adult reading. Now let us turn our attention to the way children first learn to recognize printed words and to the ways these four methods of perceiving words help young readers grow in ability to remember known words and to identify the new ones.

Promoting growth in word perception

Relationship between a child's oral vocabulary and reading

Although all printed words are strangers to him, a child who is ready to read has learned to respond to and to use hundreds of spoken words. No two children, however, have the same oral vocabulary or the same background of experiences. That is why a teacher of reading devotes a great deal of effort (especially in the primary grades) to helping children enlarge and enrich their oral vocabularies. She knows that if a child, from the very beginning, is to regard reading as something more than merely pronouncing words, he must know the meanings of the printed words that he is asked to read and be able to use them in his own speech. Otherwise, he will have to try to associate an unknown pronunciation and meaning with an unfamilar printed form. We do not expect an adult to make this three-way association of unknowns without the aid of a dictionary. Therefore until a child can use a dictionary, we should not expect him to read words whose spoken forms he has never heard or used. Even though he may 'sound them out' correctly, he is merely exercising his eyes and vocal cords; he is not reading.

How a child first learns to identify printed words

The first printed words a child learns to recognize are usually presented to him as wholes in context. Words that children learn in this way are called sight words. To make sure that every child will associate both sound and a specific meaning with a sight word the first time he sees it, the teacher initiates an oral discussion in which the word is used informally with the same meaning it has in the story that pupils are about to read. During the discussion, as she uses the word in a sentence, the teacher shows its printed form (usually on a word card at early levels). For example, if the new words were *Sandy* and *jump*, she might say, 'One day Jim wanted his dog Sandy to learn a new trick; so he held a piece of meat over Sandy's head and said, "Jump, Sandy, jump".' While saying these words, the teacher would present their printed forms and then ask children to read them with her. Thus direct associations of sound, meaning, and word form are established when pupils see a printed word for the first time.

Importance of an ever-increasing sight vocabulary

For at least two reasons much of a child's early success in reading depends on his mastery of an initial stock of sight words: ability to identify these sight words enables him to read his pre-primers and primer fluently; he will also use his ever-growing stock of sight words as a basis for understanding the relation between letters and sounds (phonetic analysis) and the function of root words, inflectional endings, prefixes, and suffixes (structural analysis). These understandings will enable him to attach sound and meaning to many unfamiliar printed words while reading. At Primer or Book One level when the child has a sight vocabulary of one hundred to one hundred fifty words, he begins to attack new words on his own through the use of word analysis. Even so, throughout the primary grades and until a child can use a dictionary, the teacher should continue to present as sight words those new words that the young reader could not be expected to attack independently because 1) he has not yet developed the prerequisite skills of phonetic and structural analysis or 2) the new words do not lend themselves to word analysis (*aisle, whose, cough*, for example). The teacher will also continue to present as a sight word any word whose pronunciation and meaning are likely to be unfamiliar.

Vocabulary control as an aid to instantaneous word perception

One of the ways that a basic reading program ensures mastery of a stock of sight words (and later of new words that children figure out independently or look up in a dictionary) is by a planned, sequential pattern of introducing and maintaining vocabulary. For example, in one primer that is widely used there is never more than one new word on a page and never more than five new words in a story. Once a word has been introduced, it is repeated at least nine times at spaced intervals in the book, the first five uses being close together as an aid to mastery. Furthermore, words are not dropped but are repeated and maintained in succeeding books in the series of basic readers. This kind of control over the introduction and repetition of printed words, especially in the primary grades, makes it possible for children to bring to the level of instantaneous perception a large number of highly useful words.

In addition to vocabulary control, an effective basic reading program provides specific techniques for helping children remember sight words. It also assumes responsibility for teaching pupils to figure out or analyze new words independently and to use the dictionary. In short, one of the major goals of reading instruction is to help children develop competence in perceiving printed words easily and efficiently. This can best be accomplished by developing the ability to remember word forms and to use context clues, word analysis, and the dictionary.

Memory of word form

When a printed word is completely familiar, we respond to it automatically and are scarcely aware of the details of its form. This kind of response is based on memory of word forms, one of the major word-perception abilities used in rapid, fluent reading. In most instances, memory of word forms is based on 1) the habit of scrutinizing new or relatively unfamiliar word forms, 2) the ability to call up a mental picture or image of a word form, 3) the association of meaning with printed words.

Scrutiny of word form

Before a child can remember a printed word and associate it correctly with its meaning (or meanings), he must look carefully at its details, noting how it differs in form from other printed words that he knows.

Even before a child begins to read, he prepares for scrutinizing printed words by looking carefully at pictured objects on many pages in books especially made to provide readiness for reading. He is led to note and discuss first gross and later minute differences in form, size, position, etc. In so doing, he acquires and refines a vocabulary for thinking about form and arrangement that he will soon apply to printed words. For example, children might be asked to look carefully at a row of pictured chairs that differ only in the way they are facing. As youngsters note and discuss which chair backs are *to the left* and *to the right*, they use the kind of scrutiny and vocabulary they will later use to notice and think about the difference between such letters as *b* and *d* and consequently between such words as *big* and *dig*, *bark* and *dark*.

When a child first begins to read, his attention is called to the spaces between words. He learns to look at a word from left to right: he not only makes gross discriminations between words on the basis of their general configuration but also notes the distinctive characteristics of words. Is the word long or short? Does it have letters that are tall or that extend below the line? The length of the word *grandfather*, the two *e*'s in *feet*, or the first and last letters in *happy* may be the visual characteristics that beginning readers use to identify these words.

As a child begins to encounter words that are very similar in appearance, he learns to compare their details and to note minute differences that distinguish one word from another. Words like *eat* and *cat*, *bean* and *bear*, *but* and *tub*, *then* and *than*, *from* and *form* may be easily confused by a child who is not looking closely or noting the serial order of letters. Because independent word analysis is based on close scrutiny of the arrangement of letters in a word, it is important that pupils form the habit early of comparing the details of printed words and of noting minute differences in form. Obviously, sensitivity to word meaning and sentence context must go hand in hand with such visual discriminations.

As a child matures in reading ability, he uses scrutiny of form to note relationships between such words as *courteous* and *discourteous*, even though the longer word may contain a prefix or suffix with which he is not yet familiar. Words like *different* and *difference*, *establish* and *establishment*, *friend*, *unfriendly*, and *friendship*, he decides, are related not only in form but in meaning.

Imagery of word form

The ability to call up a clear visual image (a mental picture) of a known word is closely related to the habit of scrutinizing word forms to remember details. The child who has carefully observed the details of a known word can usually develop the ability to call up a mental image of that word and to compare its form with that of a word that is before him in print.

In the early stages of reading when a child sees the word *looking* and thinks of *look* with *ing* added or sees *pick* and thinks, 'That word looks like *stick* except at the beginning', a part of a word calls to his mind a known visual form. Then, too, young readers often use the initial consonant as a clue to the whole word. The initial consonant *r*, for example, combined with meaning clues from a picture may be all that a child needs to recognize the word *red* in the context 'a big red car'.

Children learn early to rely on consonant letters as quick clues to recognizing words, since consonants form the distinguishing framework of most words. The ease with which one can image total words from consonant letters alone or from other kinds of partial word forms is illustrated by the following:

Sh_   p_t   tw_   n_ck_ls   _n   h_r   b_nk

She is saving money for a birthday present

As a child progresses, he becomes adept at using imagery of known word forms to help him identify new words. He may recognize the new word *bump* because, as he scrutinizes it, he compares it with his mental image of the known word *jump*. Later, derived forms like *unconcern, adaptation, brilliancy* arouse in his mind images of their roots *concern, adapt, brilliant*. If he misreads a word (*contact* for *contract,* for example), ability to compare his mental image of the word *contact* with his scrutiny of the printed word *contract*, coupled with meaning clues, helps him correct his error.

The ability to image word forms enables a child to think of words that illustrate a particular language understanding or principle. For example, experience with many two-syllable words like *otter, fellow, rudder,* and *channel* helps children generalize that two like consonant letters following the first vowel letter in a word are a visual clue to a short vowel sound in an accented first syllable. Once pupils have made this generalization, ability to image known word forms should help them think of other two-syllable words that illustrate this visual clue to accent and vowel sound.

Association of meaning with word form

If every time a child sees or hears a word in different contexts he associates meaning with it, he automatically strengthens his memory of that word. He might, for example, see the word *line* many times before encountering a sentence like 'The driver grabbed the lines and shouted to the horses', which requires the reader to associate the meaning 'reins' with the word *lines*. Only as a child has many opportunities to encounter familiar words used with new meanings and to meet totally new words will he increase his speaking and reading vocabularies.

Before children begin to read, a teacher helps them strengthen and increase their associations of meaning with spoken words. For example, with the stimulus of pictured situations and their teacher's skillful questions, pupils reinforce understanding of such necessary but abstract words as *good, kind, funny,* and *selfish.*

In the initial stages of learning to read, a child is required to associate only known meanings with printed words; for in his beginning books he meets only printed forms that stand for words he has heard and spoken for a long time. Most of these words have fairly concrete meanings and denote action (*come, run*) and position (*here, there, in*) or name things and people (*car, Mother*).

· Before long, however, a youngster begins to encounter words that are not in his speaking vocabulary. Such words, of course, should be used in oral discussion before pupils are asked to identify them in print. A third-grader, for example, may find authors using the word *scurry* instead of *run, alarm* instead of *frighten*. As he adds such words to his reading vocabulary, he often adds them to his speaking vocabulary. At the same time he is learning new meanings for familiar words. A city child may know the meaning of 'fair play' and 'fair weather' but may need an explanation of *fair* in the phrase 'the county fair'.

Throughout the middle grades, children's associations of meaning with words not only increase rapidly but are sharpened and refined. As sensitivity to shades of meaning develops, boys and girls begin to notice how an author uses particular words to evoke vivid imagery or emotional response. Each of the words *peer, stare, gaze,* and *peek,* for example, denotes a different way of looking at someone or something. *Notorious* and *famous* both mean 'well-known', but the first suggests unfavorable or undesirable qualities that the other does not.

At middle- and upper-grade levels, through discussion of real and fictional situations, pupils become sensitive to the meaning of abstract terms like *responsibility, loyalty, ingenuity,* and *brotherhood*. Many children become curious about words, mull them over, and make deliberate efforts to add them to their speech.

Context clues

The reader who seeks and uses context clues is demanding meaning from the printed page. The use of context clues is based on two understandings of language: 1) a word may have more than one meaning (and pronunciation); 2) meaning (and sometimes pronunciation) must be determined in the light of context. Only through the use of context clues can a reader associate appropriate meaning with visual form like *bank,* as the phrases 'money in the bank', 'on the bank of the stream', 'bank the fire', and 'the third bank of seats' prove. Similarly, meaning and pronunciation of words like *tear*, *wind*, *wound*, and *bow* depend on the context in which they are used—'a tear in the eye', 'a tear in a coat', 'to tear down a building'.

Through the use of pictures at the pre-reading level, children are trained to expect meaning from books. The guidance suggested for many pages in reading-readiness books promotes the kind of thinking that children must engage in if they are to use context clues while reading. One procedure frequently employed is to ask pupils what they think will happen next in a story.

At early reading levels meaning clues furnished by pictures and sentence context are especially valuable to a child as aids to the identification of printed words. A picture of three horses on a page may help the young reader identify the words *three horses* in a story. Should he misread the word *cat* by calling it *eat* in the sentence 'Tom fed the cat', awareness of context helps him correct his error. As soon as a child learns to associate sounds with some of the letters, he uses context clues to check phonetic analysis. The only way, for example, that he can be sure which sound the letters *oo* stand for in the new word *foot* or *boot* is to ask himself, 'Does this sound like a word I know, and does it make sense in the sentence?' Very early, then, children learn to combine scrutiny of form and phonetic clues with context clues and to use the latter as the final check on their identification of new words.

By about third grade most children use the context of both sentence and paragraph to figure out meanings that they have not previously associated with a printed word. They also use context clues to check variant meanings of prefixes and suffixes. When a child first learns the prefix *un-*, for example, he may assume that it always means 'not'. However, meaning clues tell him that in the context 'The boy untied his shoes' the derived form *untied* does not mean 'did not tie' but rather denotes an action opposite to that expressed in the root word *tie*. As his vocabulary grows, a child is increasingly able to use context clues to discriminate between variant meanings and uses of word forms like *pound* and *light* and between forms like *close* and *lead* whose meanings and pronunciations can be determined only in light of context ('close a door', 'close to the door'; 'heavy as lead', 'lead a band').

In the middle and upper grades (indeed, throughout life) a reader continues to use context clues (pictorial and verbal) to check word analysis, to discriminate between similar words forms, and to derive new meanings independently. He uses context clues to determine the accent as well as the meaning of many words—*per'mit, per mit'*; *ob'ject, ob ject'*; *con'duct, con duct'*, etc. When a pupil begins to use a dictionary, he learns that he must use context clues to choose the appropriate definition of a word.

Experience soon teaches the alert reader that an unfamiliar word may be defined or explained in subsequent context. He discovers, too, that the general context or subject matter of a selection is a clue to the meaning of many words. For example, the word *pitcher, batter, plate*, or *rhubarb* would mean one thing in an article about baseball and something quite different in a cookbook.

Context clues are perhaps the most important single aid to word perception. Regardless of whether a child identifies a printed word quickly or stops to figure it out, he must be sure that it makes sense in the sentence. The youngster who is satisfied to read 'Tim went into the horse' for 'Tim went into the house' is obviously not using context clues. However, we should not forget that scrutiny of form must accompany the use of meaning clues. Careful scrutiny of the details of form helps children remember words; and, like the use of context clues, it is fundamental to word analysis.

Word analysis

Word analysis involves analyzing an unfamiliar printed word for clues to its sound and meaning. Frequently instantaneous word perception is blocked by a word that a child cannot readily identify from a glance at its configuration and by the use of context clues. When this happens, he should have at his command systematic methods of attacking the unfamilar word. If the word is in his speech, the child's ability to apply what he has learned about word analysis will often enable him to identify what at first glance appeared to be a totally strange word form.

Word analysis is of two kinds—structural and phonetic. The two are interrelated and are used in combination to attack a new word. A young reader, seeing a word like *leaf* or *buzz* for the first time, uses structural analysis when he decides that the word has no inflectional ending, prefix, or suffix. He is then ready to use phonetic analysis to arrive at its pronunciation.

Frequently, of course, the new words that children encounter are inflected or derived forms. Suppose, for example, a second-grader encounters in context the new word *neatly* ('new' in the sense that he has never before seen it in print). If he has had systematic training in word analysis, he has learned to scrutinize the total word form for familiar meaning units—a root word, an inflectional ending, a suffix (structural analysis). His scrutiny of the word *neatly* reveals the familiar suffix *-ly*. The child then mentally 'takes off' the suffix and searches for clues to the sound of the root word (phonetic analysis). He has learned that when two vowel letters occur together in a word, the first often stands for a long vowel sound and the second is silent. Applying this principle, he comes up with the correct pronunciation of the root *neat* to which he now reattaches the suffix *-ly*. Once he has identified the word *neatly*, he recognizes that it is one he has heard and used many times. The stumbling block in the sentence has been removed; he is free to go on interpreting the printed page. To sum up, the child has successfully used structural and phonetic analysis to identify a word on his own while reading.

Structural analysis

As has been noted, structural analysis is the means by which a child identifies meaningful parts of words—roots, inflectional endings, prefixes, and suffixes. Ability to use structural analysis is based on two fundamental understandings of language. One of these is that a root word retains one of its basic meanings in inflected and derived forms and in compounds. For example, one meaning of the root word *play* is present in its inflected forms *plays* and *playing*; in its derived forms *replay* and *player*; in the compounds *plaything* and *playmate*. The other understanding fundamental to structural analysis is that prefixes, suffixes, and inflectional endings are meaningful parts of words. For example, in the derived form *unable* the prefix *un-* means 'not'; in the derived form *unwrap* it means 'the opposite of'. The suffix *-er* often means 'a person or thing that ————', as in the derived forms *singer* and *freezer*. The endings *-s* and *es* may mean 'more than one', as in the inflected forms *boys* and *bushes*.

The first structural elements, other than root words, that most children learn to recognize in print are such simple endings as *-s*, *ed*, *-ing* added to known roots. . . .

Phonetic analysis

Children use phonetic analysis to associate sounds with the letters in printed words and hence to derive the pronunciation of words. Although English spelling is often inconsistent, there are clues to pronunciation in the spelling of the majority of words—certain types of letter patterns that occur repeatedly. These clues should be presented gradually and systematically as soon as children know a fair number of printed words that illustrate how the clues to sound function.

Ability to use phonetic analysis is based on two fundamental understandings of the relationship between spoken and written language—understandings that children acquire over a period of years as their reading vocabularies increase. One is that consonants, vowels, and accent are basic elements of sound (phonemes) which, when blended in innumerable ways, make words that express meaning. Notice, for example, how changing one consonant or vowel sound or shifting the accent alters meaning in these pairs of words: *run, sun; hat, hut; ob'ject, ob ject'*. The word understanding basic to phonetic analysis is that in printed words there are certain visual clues that aid in determining consonant sounds, vowel sounds, syllabic divisions, and accent. For example:

When final *e* follows the letter *c* or *g*, *c* usually stands for the *s* sound and *g* for the *j* sound, as in the words *dance* and *huge*.

A single vowel letter in the middle of a one-syllable word or accented syllable usually stands for a short vowel sound, as in *had* and *lad'der*.

Two like consonant letters in the middle of a two-syllable word are a clue to an accented first syllable and to a short vowel sound in that syllable, as in *hap'pen, bliz'zard*, and *ten'nis*.

An easy way for children to start using phonetic analysis is to substitute one initial consonant for another in attacking a one-syllable word. A child who has learned to associate sound with most of the consonant letters can identify in context the printed word *hall*, for example, if he knows the word *ball*. . . .

The dictionary

There are many unfamiliar words that children encounter in their reading—especially from middle-grade levels on—to which the application of structural and phonetic analysis will be of little or no help. Word analysis breaks down when an unfamiliar printed word is not in a child's vocabulary. If he has never heard or used the word, he will have to ask someone how it is pronounced and what it means or consult a dictionary. Then, too, some words do not lend themselves to word analysis. If, for example, you had never seen in print the words *sough, hough, sou, chamois*, and *patois*, would you be able to identify them through word analysis?

The dictionary may be used in two ways as an aid in identifying unknown words encountered in reading. It may serve as a check on the meaning and pronunciation of a word that the reader has tentatively arrived at through the use of context clues and word analysis. Or it may be the only efficient method of determining the meaning and pronunciation of an unfamiliar word.

The dictionary, then, is an indispensable aid to word perception as soon as children begin to encounter numbers of words whose pronunciations, meanings, and printed forms are unfamiliar. We must remember, however, that a dictionary is likely to be a mysterious and formidable volume unless children are taught how to use it. Even though the dictionary is not usually introduced until fourth grade, the understandings pupils in the primary grades acquire about the variant meanings of words, the use of context clues, and the use of structural and phonetic analysis prepare them for learning how to use the dictionary. . . .

The importance of word analysis

Thus far we have discussed what is involved in reading and have noted that word perception (attaching sound and meaning to printed words) is a very important component of the reading process. We have also discussed the four major aids to word perception—memory of word form, context clues, word analysis, and the dictionary. . . .

When we remember that the average child in first grade uses hundreds, even thousands, of words in his speech, we realize what an impossible task it would be to expect him to learn the printed form of each one of these words as a separate item. It is not only impossible but unnecessary, since our written language operates on an alphabetic principle. That is, twenty-six letters in various combinations and patterns stand for the sounds in spoken words. If children are to read independently, they must become familiar with the clues to sounds (consonant sounds, vowel sounds, and accent) that occur in the spelling of words. Unless youngsters learn how to analyze words—to see how letters are used to represent sounds, to recognize root words, endings, prefixes, and suffixes as meaningful parts of words—they will be reduced to guessing when they encounter unfamiliar printed words.

Word analysis is not the 'be-all and end-all' of word perception, but it is an important means to that end. To deprive a child of the skills and understandings that enable him to figure out new words on his own while reading is to retard him in reading. A good reading program not only helps children acquire these skills and understandings but also provides youngsters with many opportunities to apply them. For example, there are books in which all the new words can be attacked independently by children who have acquired the skills of structural and phonetic analysis that have been presented by a given level. Such books give young readers a chance to clinch their newly acquired skills while reading interesting stories and provide the teacher with a realistic way of measuring progress.

The ultimate goals in word perception are 1) to bring to the level of instantaneous perception a maximum number of highly useful words that are common to different types of materials that a child wants and needs to read and 2) to develop understandings, skills, and abilities that enable him to attack unfamiliar words independently and thus be on his own in reading.

2:17 Vocabulary growth through the use of context in elementary grades

Paul C. Burns

According to Harris (1962), 'If the total vocabulary of representative children grows 15,000 words or more during the first six grades . . . this means an average of at least 2,500 words a year, 66 words a week, or 13 words a day—excluding vacations, weekends, and holidays.' This statement suggests that although the vocabulary of basal readers [1] may be controlled, the total reading done by children involves a great number of words. The important fact is that if teachers had to teach all the words that children learn, the time required would be exorbitant.

Children who read widely can learn a great many words through use of context. Wide reading provides the opportunity for context, or all of the elements which give support to meaning, to illuminate word meaning when it is essential to the flow of thought. Through wide reading, the reader can begin to recognize the subtleties and varied meanings of words. This idea has its basis in semantics: 'We learn the meanings of practically all our words not from dictionaries, not from definitions, but from hearing these noises as they accompany actual situations in life and learning to associate certain noises with certain situations' (Hayakawa, 1949).

Types and uses of contextual aids

Artley (1962) suggests four types of contextual aids: pictorial context, verbal context, experiential context, and organizational or structural context.

Logical reasoning and research evidence support the validity of pictures as a way of supporting word meaning. Some recent writers obviously ques-

1 *Editorial footnote*: Basal readers, basic readers and basals are terms used interchangeably in the United States to identify published reading schemes.

BURNS, PAUL C. (1967) 'Vocabulary growth through the use of context in elementary grades', in Figurel, J. Allen (ed.) *Forging Ahead in Reading* Newark, Delaware: International Reading Association, 79–85.

tion this premise in favor of children's reading materials which omit pictures presumably to focus attention strictly upon 'decoding symbols'. It is a well established fact that many primary school pupils lack ability to use pictures in constructing the meaning of strange words (Beck, 1940; Miller, 1938a, 1938b). In its broader sense, pictorial context includes maps, charts, graphs, and statistical tables; and inadequate 'reading' and interpreting of these may be hindered by the omission of or de-emphasis of foundational 'picture reading' experience. 'Visual context' examples are emphasized in such programs as Gibson-Richards' *First Steps in Reading English* (1957).

Of verbal context, a distinction may be made between the two types of acts in which context can be used to figure out the meaning of a word: first, using context in figuring out the meaning of a word is (The lecturer leaned upon the ———[podium, lectern, etc.] as he spoke.); and second, in using context in unlocking a word which is strange only in print (Jim opened his ———[book, magazine, etc.] and began to read.). In the first case, context is used as an explainer of a meaning unfamiliar to the reader or as a determiner of which of several familiar meanings is needed for a given word; in the second situation, the reader uses context as a clue which along with his use of sounds represented by letters stimulates the reader to call to mind simultaneously the familiar spoken form and the familiar meaning of a given word (McKee, 1948).

By experience cues, Artley refers to the idea that the reader may rely on his past concrete experience, perhaps to a crow's harsh voice, to help clarify the meaning of the last word in the sentence 'The crow cawed *raucously*'. Organizational or structural context refers to such clues in the presentation of the material as sectional or marginal headings, paragraphing, typographical aids, and those aids that are in the familiar patterns of language as appositive, nonrestrictive, or interpolated phrases or clauses and other language expressions.

A little explored type of context may be referred to as 'spoken context', a foundational experience particularly needed at the beginning instructional levels but appropriate at all grade levels. Examples of use of this orally presented type of context (Bill can play ———[ball, tag, etc.] with me.) can be found in McKee and Harrison's *Preparing Your Child For Reading* (1960).

Another context type may be labeled as 'set context'; that is, the particular circumstances under which the reader does the reading. This type of context provides much of the content of the study of semantics which deals with physical and psychological contexts as well as verbal context.

From consideration of such types of context, it can be reasoned that the uses of context include 1) perceiving new words on the basis of reasoning and logical inference; 2) checking meanings derived through other word analysis skills; 3) checking on word perception, particularly in case of homographs (*tear, hail, lead,* etc.) where one must choose the pronunciation and meaning which makes sense in the sentence; and 4) trying to find a clue to the meaning of a word which leads to sensible use of the dictionary. It would seem that these uses of context are legitimate ones to promote in the elementary school if reading is considered a reasoning act, if multiple tools of vocabulary development are desirable, if the vagaries of our language are to be understood, and if one's reading should make sense.

The importance and need for developing the use of context

Reading authorities have emphasized for many years the importance of developing effective use of context. For example, McKee (1966) writes '... use of context is the chief means for increasing vocabulary through reading. . . .' McCrimmon (1957) states, '... in practice we learn the meanings of words by their context. . . . This is exactly how the writers of dictionaries got their definitions'. Spache (1964) points out: 'Eventually contextual analysis becomes one of the most frequently used methods of derivation of word meanings, as phonics and structural analysis decrease in use.' Leary (1951) advocates, 'Train a child to anticipate probable meaning, to infer an unknown word from its total context, to skip a word and read on to derive its probable meaning, to check the context clue with the form of the word, to search the context for a description or explanation that will identify the word, and he will have acquired the most important single aid to word recognition. For regardless of what word he perceives, if it doesn't make sense in its setting, his perception has been in error.' Fay (1956) and Gates (1947) have made similar statements supporting the use of context. In speaking of the poor reader, Harris (1961) cautions, '... there may be a temptation to assume that pupils who need training in word recognition should be discouraged from attempting to utilize the context at all. Nothing is farther from the truth. . . . All good readers make use of context clues, so there is no reason to discourage poor readers from doing the same. . . .'

Other advantages that accrue to the reader who learns to use context wisely include 1) understanding that a word has no permanent meaning which reflects a *living language*; 2) making use of available material instead of having to go to another source, such as the dictionary; and 3) improving learning to read while reading to learn and thereby facilitating integration of skill learning with content learning.

Classroom experience and research investigations suggest that lack of skill in using context is quite prevalent among elementary school pupils. In an early study, Gray and Holmes (1938) found that when a context clue was available (in this case, an appositional statement), it was not necessarily used to infer a correct meaning. Bradbury (1943) found that in attempting to read his textbooks, the average child in the fourth grade can use the context successfully to construct the meaning of a strange word in about one out of three opportunities. According to Spache and Berg (1955) the average high school graduate uses the context to derive meanings in only about 50 to 60 per cent of the words that are unknown to him. Gibbons (1940) found about the same results for the average college freshman. Several studies give us reason to believe that more guidance in the use of contextual analysis provides for growth in this technique. Porter (1960) found that primary children can learn to use contextual analysis of simple types quite effectively. When words were completely omitted from the context, these pupils correctly deduced the exact word omitted 23 per cent of the time. They were able to deduce probable meanings of the omitted words 83 per cent of the time. In other words they were successful in contextual analysis for meanings in eight out of ten attempts. Harrison (1960) also found that context can illuminate word meaning if the necessary guidance is provided for children. Hafner (1965) concluded that short-term instruction in the use of context aids seemed to hold promise of improving pupil reading comprehension.

Analysis of nature of text material

What are the kinds of situations, oral and verbal, that need to be presented and practised if contextual analysis is to become an important tool and means of vocabulary growth? Types of context clues have been analyzed by Artley, McCullough, and Deighton on the basis of their use in books.

Artly (1943, 1962) has proposed seven types of contextual aids to word meanings from an earlier listing: 1) typographical aids, as parentheses or footnotes; 2) grammatical aids, as appositive phrases or clauses; 3) substitute words, as synonyms or antonyms; 4) word elements, as roots, prefixes, and suffixes; 5) figures of speech; 6) pictures, diagrams, and charts; and 7) inference, as in 'Due to the mountain ranges and the cold climate, the amount of *arable* land is limited.' McCullough (1956, 1958) has categorized types of contextual clues as experience clues, comparison or contrast words or phrases, synonyms, summary clues, reflection of mood of a situation, definition, and familiar expression as 'He kept his *cool.*' Deighton (1959) analyzing the types of context clues found in textbooks on an eighth grade to adult reading level, stated context illuminated word meaning through definition; example, modification, restatement, and inference.

It can be noted that there are similarities and overlappings among these listings. Depending upon one's definition of *context*, some clues may appear more appropriate than others. Other similar classifications of the instructional specifics in this area of context clues are suggested by McKee (1948) and Betts (1957). Which listing or which particular clues are most usable for the elementary school teacher has not been determined. It would seem that inference as a context clue is one of the least used but more promising and that study of word elements (roots, prefixes, and suffixes) has not produced good results. It would be helpful to teachers if they knew the context types which appear most commonly in pupil materials and what degree of difficulty each type of contextual clue presents for the pupil. One study (Wilson, 1947), for example, suggests that the most difficult context situation for sixth-grade children involves use of contrast, such as, 'Is John *clumsy* or is he *agile?*' The connecting word 'or' deserves careful treatment as it can join words of similar meaning or words of different meanings as 'I had never seen him so *depressed* or *melancholy.*' and 'Is Jim *talkative* or *taciturn?*' There is no clue for the reader to use in determining which of the two possible functions *or* is performing. Another problem that has received little study is how to help the young child conceive of an unknown word as referring to a circumscribed meaning rather than to regard the word as carrying with it the whole of a major part of the context in which it appears (Werner and Kaplan, 1950).

Ways of developing effective use of context

It appears to me that there are some basic ideas to be considered in developing the skillful use of context. These would include:

1   Continue to emphasize reading for meaning. While in the strict sense it may be true that context doesn't give meaning to a word any more than the dictionary does, it is safer to suggest that 'symbols signify something' rather than 'symbols signify nothing'.

2 Provide large quantities of readable material appropriate to interests in 'reading class' and in teaching the content subjects (Gray, 1960). The pupil simply *cannot* use context every fourth or fifth word. Content books frequently present such a high vocabulary load that they seriously hinder the use of context clues by the reader.

3 Outline a carefully designed delineation of the set of aids as a context syllabus in the reading area; pre-test to find strengths or weaknesses of the pupils; and then afford practice with the needed abilities through the reading textbooks, workbooks, and other supplementary materials as needed.

4 Provide greater emphasis to context clues development with oral and listening situations, prior to and along with application of verbal reading materials. Further exploration is needed into the area of 'spoken context', for the pupil who cannot use the clues of context in listening will likely have little if any more control of them in the reading act. On the contrary, it has been suggested (Sister Mariam, 1958) that better training in 'spoken-listening context' can be used to improve the pupil's ability to understand adequately what he attempts to read.

5 Teach the child to go beyond the single word in search for the meaning by context. One study (Weaver, 1963) suggests that the words that follow a strange word are more likely to aid in contextual analysis than those that precede it. This study confirms the desirability of teaching pupils to read the entire sentence (or rest of paragraph) before attempting to derive the meaning of an unknown word. The practice of immediately stating, 'Look it up in the dictionary' is a poor one. It would be better to say, 'Try to find a clue to the meaning of the word through the context.' The pupils need to know that the context needed for constructing the meaning of a given strange word may appear before, after, or both before and after the strange word (Godfrey, 1941). It should be recognized that there is some evidence that the influence of context upon word meanings seems to decrease rapidly with the distance of the context, and context more than about five words distant has relatively little effect upon clarifying an unknown word.

6 Provide time for discussion of how meaning can be derived through context. Discuss with pupils what is meant by using context to figure out the meaning of a word, what the helpful parts of the context may be, and where they appear. Also pupils need to recognize the situation where no clue is provided, as in 'Bill was *reluctant* to do it.'

7 Capitalize upon context in all types of content reading situations. Teach pupils the common ways textbooks make new meanings easy to acquire.

Study the content books used to see how the new terms are made under-standable, and let the pupils in on this study.

8 Delay discussion of the meaning of a strange word in the reading material of content subjects if the context is provided by familiar words for building that meaning. Pupils must have an opportunity for applica-tion for taught skills in the normal reading situation. Occasionally the teacher might select a half dozen difficult words from future reading assignments and ask pupils to write their definitions. After the reading, pupils may correct or revise their earlier definitions. This is a particularly applicable assignment at the intermediate school level.

9 Develop a general appreciation for words and language structure. Through experience and instruction the pupil needs to appreciate denota-tions and connotations of specific words and multiple meanings for the same word. He needs to be guided to anticipate the fact that pronunciation and meaning of homographs, such as, *bow, refuse,* and *wind* cannot be verified until seen in 'use situations'. He needs to recognize that homonyms may be spelled alike (cold *hail* or *hail* a cab) or may be spelled differently (*stake, steak*). He certainly should expect irregularities in the alphabetic representations of English sounds (*head, break, early,* etc.). Further, the pupil needs to sense the importance of the order of words to the structure of language and/or meaning, by the position or function of a word in a sentence, and to this extent, its meaning is suggested (McCullough, 1958). 'The igg ogged the ugg' type of presentation may help pupils recognize the 'nounness' or 'verbness' of the words. This feeling helps the pupil sense that nouns and verbs are most essential for meaning. The structure of the phrase, sentence, or paragraph often serves as a clue to the meaning of what is written. Rhetorical terms of coherence are also guids to reading comprehension of a paragraph, pure conjunctions and certain adverbs being very common links (Shaw, 1958). The fact that many of the contextual clues to word meaning have their origin in such concepts provides a strong argument for the development of general knowledge of language structure, and suggests again the interrelationships of the language arts (Zames, 1965).

Cautions in the use of context clues

It is not possible to develop effective use of context clues in situations where the child is bogged down with the mechanics of reading. Wide independent reading—where little difficulty with word recognition or meaning is pre-sented—gives the pupil an opportunity to use contextual aids. But *oppor-*

tunity alone is not enough. As in other skills of reading, children in the intermediate grades vary greatly in their ability to identify words and to derive meaning from context as reaffirmed by studies from Boston University (Burgand, 1950; Butler, 1943; Elivian, 1958; McAuliffe, 1950; White, 1950). Children with poor reading ability usually cannot identify words they do not know. Unless children are taught to notice unfamiliar words and to be alert to the connection between the context and the unknown word it bears upon, they are unlikely to develop large vocabularies from extensive reading.

It must be clear that the child will not always gain the correct meaning of a word from the context. Context always determines the meaning of a word but doesn't always reveal that meaning. Context generally reveals only one of the meanings of an unfamiliar word. It is worth saying to children over and over again that no word has one fixed or unalterable meaning, that no one context revelation will suffice for all the later uses of the word which may be met. Also, context seldom clarifies the whole of any single word meaning. Context will often provide a synonym, but synonyms are never exact equivalents.

Finally, vocabulary growth through context revelation is a gradual one. It is a matter of finding one clue here and another there, of fitting them together, and of making tentative judgments and revising them as later experience requires. It is building meaning into a word over a period of years through the combined experiences of the writer and the reader.

References

ARTLEY, A. STERL (1943) 'Teaching Word Meaning Through Context', *Elementary English Review,* 10.

ARTLEY, A. STERL (1962) 'Developing the Use of Context' in *Developing Vocabulary and Word-Attack Skills, A Report of the Eighteenth Annual Conference and Course on Reading* Pittsburgh: University of Pittsburgh.

BECK, G. (1940) 'The Ability of First Grade Pupils to Use Pictures in Constructing the Meanings of Strange Words', master's thesis, State College of Education, Greely, Colorado.

BETTS, EMMETT A. (1957) *Foundations of Reading Instruction* New York: American Book Co.

BRADBURY, HELEN (1943) 'The Ability of Fourth Grade Pupils to Construct the Meaning of a Strange Word from Context', master's thesis, State College of Education, Greeley, Colorado.

BURGAND, JOAN F. (1950) 'An Investigation of Abilities of Fifth and Sixth Graders to Derive Meaning from Context in Silent Reading', master's thesis, Boston University, Massachusetts.

BUTLER, HULDAH A. (1943) 'Finding Word Meanings from Context in Grades Five and Six', master's thesis, Boston University, Massachusetts.

DEIGHTON, LEE C. (1959) *Vocabulary Development in the Classroom* New York: Teachers' College, Columbia University.

ELIVIAN, JEANETTE (1958) 'Word Perception and Word Meaning in Silent Reading in the Intermediate Grades', master's thesis, Boston University, Massachusetts.

FAY, LEO (1956) *Reading in the High School* Washington: Department of Classroom Teachers, AERA.

GATES, ARTHUR I. (1947) *The Improvement of Reading* New York: Macmillan.

GIBBONS, HELEN (1940) 'The Ability of College Freshmen to Use Context to Construct the Meaning of Unknown Words', doctor's field study, no. 2, State College of Education, Greeley, Colorado.

GIBSON, C. M. and RICHARDS, I. A. (1957) *First Steps in Reading English* New York: Pocket Books.

GODFREY, GRACE (1941) 'A Study of Context as a Means of Explaining the Meanings of Strange Words in Certain Children's Books', master's thesis, State College of Education, Greeley, Colorado.

GRAY, WILLIAM S. (1960) *On Their Own in Reading* Chicago: Scott, Foresman.

GRAY, WILLIAM S. and HOLMES, ELEANOR (1938) *The Development of Meaning Vocabularies in Reading* Chicago: University of Chicago Press.

HAFNER, LAWRENCE E. (1965) 'A One-Month Experiment in Teaching Context Aids in the Fifth Grade', *Journal of Educational Research*, 63, 472–4.

HARRIS, ALBERT J. (1961) *How to Increase Reading Ability* New York: Longmans, Green and Co.

HARRIS, ALBERT J. (1962) *Effective Teaching of Reading* New York: David McKay.

HARRISON, JANICE MANTLE (1960) 'Acquiring Word Meaning Through Context Clues', master's thesis, Ohio State University, Columbus, Ohio.

HAYAKAWA, S. I. (1949) *Language in Thought and Action* New York: Harcourt, Brace and Co.

LEARY, BERNICE (1951) 'Developing Word Perception Skills in Middle and Upper Grades', *Current Problems in Reading Instruction* Pittsburgh: University of Pittsburgh Press.

MCAULIFFE, MARY E. (1950) 'Getting Meaning from Context in Grade Four', master's thesis, Boston University, Massachusetts.

MCCRIMMON, JAMES M. (1957) *Writing with Purpose: A First Course in Composition* Boston: Houghton-Mifflin.

MCCULLOUGH, CONSTANCE M. (1956) 'Recognition of Context Clues in Reading', *Elementary English Review*, **22**, 1–5.

MCCULLOUGH, CONSTANCE M. (1958) 'Context Clues in Reading', *The Reading Teacher*, **11**, 225–9.

MCKEE, PAUL (1948) *The Teaching of Reading* Boston: Houghton Mifflin.

MCKEE, PAUL (1966) *Reading: A Program of Instruction for the Elementary School* Boston: Houghton Mifflin.

MCKEE, PAUL and HARRISON, LUCILLE (1960) *Program in Skills Basic to Beginning Reading* Boston: Houghton Mifflin.

MILLER, W. (1938a) 'Reading With and Without Pictures in the Primary Grades', doctor's field study, no. 2, State College of Education, Greeley, Colorado.

MILLER, W. (1938b) 'What One Hundred Third Grade Children Saw in Six Pictures', doctor's field study, no. 2, State College of Education, Greeley, Colorado.

PORTER, DOUGLAS (1960) 'The Instrumental Values of Sound Cues in Reading', paper read at the AERA Convention, Atlantic City, 17 February.

SHAW, PHILLIP (1958) 'Rhetorical Guides to Reading Comprehension', *The Reading Teacher*, **11**, 239–43.

SISTER MARIAM, O.P. (1958) 'Context Clues in Primary Reading', *The Reading Teacher*, **11**, 230–34.

SMITH, HENRY P. and DECHANT, EMERALD V. (1961) *Psychology in Teaching of Reading* Englewood Cliffs, N.J.: Prentice Hall.

SPACHE, GEORGE D. (1964) *Reading in the Elementary School* Boston: Allyn and Bacon.

SPACHE, GEORGE D. and BERG, PAUL C. (1955) *The Art of Efficient Reading* New York: Macmillan.

WEAVER, WENDELL (1963) 'The Predictability of Word Meaning', *New Developments in Programs, Training Aids and Procedures* National Reading Conference Proceedings, **12**, 152–7.

WERNER, HEINZ and KAPLAN, EDITH (1950) 'Development of Word Meaning Through Verbal Context: An Experiental Study', *Journey of Psychology*, **29**, 251–7.

WHITE, LORETTA M. (1950) 'The Ability of Fifth Grade Pupils to Get Word Meaning from Context', master's thesis, Boston University, Massachusetts.

WILSON, FRANK E. (1947) 'The Ability of Sixth Grade Children to Acquire the Meaning of a Strange Word from Context', master's thesis, State College of Education, Greeley, Colorado.

ZAMES, WILBUR S. (1965) 'A Study of the Process By Which Readers Determine Word Meaning Through the Use of Context', unpublished doctoral dissertation, University of Missouri, Columbia, Missouri.

Part 3 What is diagnostic teaching of reading?

Introduction to Part Three:
What is diagnostic teaching of reading?

In the past, diagnosis has largely been associated with clinicians, backward readers, and the use of specialized testing instruments to study causes of reading failure. Today, expanded knowledge of the reading process and concern for the continued improvement of reading competence at each level of development has led to the recognition that systematic instruction *based on continuous assessment* is essential for the attainment of higher standards of reading for all pupils. Thus, the new term 'diagnostic teaching of reading' suggests that diagnosis is an intrinsic part of the teaching process. It is not an end in itself; it is a means to more effective teaching and more efficient learning. Diagnostic teaching should be used for reading development in the middle years of schooling and later, just as much as in the beginning years, for it is no longer a question of 'Learning to read in the primary grades and reading to learn thereafter'. The teacher need no longer wait for a specialist to give him diagnostic information, which he himself can obtain in the classroom through observation and teaching.

According to Early (3:1), diagnostic teaching begins with the teacher's careful analysis of classroom reading material to identify the types of reading skills required to understand it. Diagnostic teaching is skilful observation and analysis of how children should and actually do approach various types of printed media, and how they respond to questions phrased in different ways for different purposes.

> As the teacher collects information about the student, he interprets, synthesizes, and uses it to help him improve his reading. Recognizing the individual's present powers, he tries to adjust the curriculum and his teaching procedures to the child's competencies, needs and interests at the moment. (Strang, 3:2, p. 311.)

On the basis of pupil observation and analysis of reading tasks, teachers formulate relevant instructional questions and comments to guide and develop pupils' reading and understanding of the content of the material.

Their responses to his questions provide the teacher with an immediate feedback on which his continued instruction is based.

The role of the teacher in diagnostic teaching of reading is further expanded by Strang (3:2) who outlines the various kinds of understanding which teachers may gain through diagnostic teaching in informal classroom situations. 'Without these kinds of understandings, the teacher may either neglect practice and instruction on skills badly needed or give unnecessary instruction' (p. 321). To help the extension of teachers' observations beyond the mechanical level of 'seeing' to the level of penetrating analysis, Strang (3:3) presents and discusses various charts to guide observations that can be made during pupils' oral reading, silent reading and group discussion.

Questions play a central role in a diagnostic teaching. '. . . the asking of questions is "one of the basic ways by which the teacher stimulates student thinking and learning" ' (Gall, 3:4, p. 344). Needless to say, effective questioning should reflect the purposes and skills needed to develop competence in reading. The types of questioning strategies teachers use indicate their own understanding of the reading process, and influence the quality of reading guidance they provide pupils. Since little is available on the use of questions to teach reading, we have drawn on research dealing with questions in relationship to general teaching practices, and readers will have to apply the general principles to their own teaching of reading. Gall's (3:4) comprehensive review of research on the use of questions in teaching during the past fifty years provides the necessary background to appreciate the importance of questions in diagnostic teaching. Up until now, questions in class have emphasized facts; what is important now is the development of pupils' critical reading skills.

Recent studies on the nature of classroom interaction have provided teachers with an opportunity to analyse and improve their questioning strategies and thus the quality of their teaching. Blackie's report (3:5) of her own experience in this type of study indicates the kinds of significant insights that teachers may gain from analysing transcriptions of tape-recorded classroom discussion.

We end our discussion of the function and use of questions in diagnostic teaching of reading, with Buton's (3:6) practical suggestions for improved questioning procedures which should be a helpful guide to teachers wishing to increase their teaching competence.

Although there have been a number of studies of classroom interaction, all of which point to the importance of the teacher's questions, few training programmes have been designed to develop effective questioning techniques in the classroom. If, as Early (3:1) states, diagnostic teaching begins with the teacher's careful analysis of printed material which pupils are required to read in the classroom, it may well be that guidance in this type of reading analysis should be the first step towards improved questioning practices. Increasing teachers' knowledge and awareness of their own reading approach and skills could have a significant impact on the kinds of questions and interaction stimulated in the classroom.

3:1   Diagnostic teaching in upper elementary grades

Margaret J. Early

How will teaching reading in the upper elementary grades be affected by the overwhelming attention currently being paid to beginning reading instruction? How will it be affected by changes in curriculum and organization such as the middle school, non-graded programs and varying degrees of departmentalization?

There is the possibility that upper elementary teachers will once again listen to the siren song of 'learning to read in primary grades and reading to learn thereafter'. The grain of truth in this cliché seems to be supported by claims of newer basal programs[1] and linguistic-phonics approaches that all the word-analysis skills, from letter-sound relationships through use of the dictionary, can be learned by the end of third grade. Suppose that excellent teaching in the primary grades did indeed insure mastery of this stepped-up program, so that by fourth grade most children could decode any printed word and use context and other comprehension skills to discover meanings. Would teachers in grade four and beyond then be justified in adopting 'reading to learn' as their watchword? No, not if that slogan is interpreted as assigning students to read without teaching them how. But if 'reading to learn' is interpreted as teaching youngsters *how* to learn through reading, there is reason to believe that reading programs in upper elementary grades may be greatly strengthened. Real improvements in materials and methods of teaching beginning reading have appeared in this decade. Teachers in grades four to six now have the

1   *Editorial footnote*: Basal readers, basic readers and basals are terms used interchangeably in the United States to identify published reading schemes.

EARLY, MARGARET J. (1967) 'Diagnostic teaching in upper elementary grades', in Figurel, J. Allen (ed.) *Vistas in Reading* Newark, Delaware: International Reading Association, 245–8.

chance to build stronger programs on the improved foundations of primary reading instruction if they refuse to believe that a good start means that 'reading to learn' just happens.

Upper elementary teachers who have learned to analyze the reading process and to observe its development in individual children are prepared to teach reading-to-learn skills or to re-teach learning-to-read skills. They know that some children who have 'been through' a reader have not necessarily mastered skills of beginning reading. On the other hand, they know that some children at the beginning of fourth grade have not only mastered beginning skills but are able to apply these skills in increasingly complex materials. Diagnostic teaching is as vital a service to advanced students as it is to the retarded.

A second influence on teaching reading in upper elementary grades—the burgeoning curriculum and new organizational patterns—may be positive or negative. Teachers' skills in diagnosis can determine which. Surely the reading program stands to suffer from increasing specialization in the upper elementary grades if the experience of the junior high school is duplicated. Here we have seen departmentalization make every teacher a subject specialist (in intent, if not in fact) and none a teacher of reading. We have tried to patch up the situation by creating 'extra' reading classes that isolate skills instruction from the learning of subject matter, or we have tried without notable success to train subject specialists in methods of teaching reading.

The way to avoid similar problems in the elementary school is to keep the self-contained classroom, bringing subject-matter specialists to the children instead of dispersing them on a fixed schedule to teachers who lose track of individuals when they have pupil loads of one hundred or more. In a design that allows for specialization without departmentalizing, language learning (including reading) is central to the whole curriculum and the core of the classroom teacher's education. The help he needs in teaching math and science, social studies, art, and music comes into the classroom in the person of the teacher-consultant who adds depth, richness, and accuracy to the curriculum. But the children continue to be observed and guided by the one who knows most about their learning processes. I am suggesting that reading specialists in the intermediate grades should be the classroom teachers. The subject specialists should be the 'floaters', working with teachers and pupils but without permanent relationships with or responsibilities for grading any groups.

What turns a classroom teacher into a reading specialist? More than anything else, it is the ability to diagnose and to develop strengths and correct weaknesses. Any teacher can distinguish good readers from poor and fair-to-middlin' ones. During the first week of school, without consulting the cumulative folders or the standardized reading-test scores, Miss Jones can tell which of her students can read the fourth grade texts with ease and which cannot. But so could any layman. What makes Miss Jones a professional is her skill in analyzing *why* pupils can read some books fluently and with understanding and others haltingly and without comprehension. We mean 'why' in the sense of what specific reading skills are present or lacking. The deeper 'why' of causation is one that Miss Jones should also explore, with help from the school psychologist, physician, the child's family, and others; but when she finds pupils who are severely and inexplicably retarded, she will have to refer them for clinical diagnosis and treatment.

Determining the readability level at which a child can learn through reading is a necessary first step. It is accomplished through the informal inventory based on graded selections from basal readers, which serve also as a limited vehicle for analyzing the reading performance. This crude instrument allows a sensitive teacher to guess at how a child normally attacks silent reading by sampling how he reads at sight and by comparing comprehension after silent and oral reading. Analysis of oral-reading errors can reveal specific weaknesses in word attack—errors on medial sounds are most common among poor readers in intermediate grades and in use of context. But the significance of specific errors varies widely. A meaningful substitution is a far different order of error from a mispronunciation or wild guess. Refusal to try a word indicates the most serious weakness. Similarly, comprehension errors vary in significance. Accurate comprehension after silent reading alters our evaluation of the oral-reading performance.

So, merely quantifying errors on an informal inventory is no more revealing than on a standardized-test score. Each error must be weighed sensitively if appraisal is to be accurate. Even so, an informal inventory, like any other test, only starts a series of hypotheses. Diagnostic teaching is the process of continuously checking hunches.

The classroom teacher uses the informal inventory only on those pupils he suspects of reading below grade level. He identifies these through testing oral reading in small groups and notes on index cards the nature of each child's performance. Children who read a sample passage from a grade-level reader with at least 70 per cent comprehension and few gross oral-reading errors may be grouped for instruction at this level. Excellent readers form another group, perhaps to be instructed from a higher-level basal. After individually testing the poorest readers, the teacher knows the level where developmental-reading instruction can safely begin for them, and he knows the types of weaknesses that require supplemental skills instruction. Moreover, through individual and group testing of this kind he acquires a first rough estimate of the independent-reading levels of average and poor readers.

Since the basal program is but one phase of teaching reading, diagnosis extends to the subject texts and to analysis of study skills. (Children reading on primary levels are excused from this phase of the diagnosis. They are not yet ready to learn very much through reading; their study of math, science, social studies, and literature must be largely accomplished through listening and oral participation, with tape recordings and visuals supplementing class discussions.) We cannot assume that children capable of reading grade-level basal readers will learn through reading subject texts at corresponding levels.

Diagnosis should begin with the teacher's careful analysis of these textbooks, which will reveal the need for types of reading not ordinarily encountered in basal readers, workbooks, or skills exercises. For example, successful reading of science texts requires initial understanding of the organizational pattern of the whole book and of individual chapters, the ability to integrate the reading of experiments (following directions, using diagrams and pictures) with the basic text, skill in noting details, ability to construct concepts and to hypothesize, ability to evaluate and revise generalizations, and habits of flexible reading. Skill in identifying major and minor ideas, which is developed on well-structured expository prose in reading workbooks, must often be abandoned or greatly modified for reading science, math, and even social studies books, which employ single-sentence paragraphs, omnibus paragraphs containing more than one main idea, and transitional paragraphs that express no main idea. Outlining based on following the author's organization does not work in many textbooks which instead require the student to reorganize the author's ideas into a logical, easily retained structure.

Analysis of subject texts will convince the teacher that the spectrum of reading skills to be developed in upper elementary grades extends far beyond the basal. Thoroughly acquainted with the styles of textbook writing and publishing, the teacher will observe carefully how students respond to problems such as those noted above, will estimate how much assistance they need, and will decide when and how to offer it.

The diagnosis which precedes teaching will have to be limited. One clue to the readability of a specific text may be obtained by duplicating a passage omitting every fifth or seventh word. Children who can restore about 70 per cent of the deleted words (or their equivalents) can probably learn from this text.

Teaching the overall structure of the whole book should be a first step, followed by frequent checks of ability to use the table of contents, index, glossary, and special features. Diagnosis continues as the teacher evaluates children's readiness for each assignment in a subject textbook, observes their attack, and listens to their discussions of what they have read.

Since there will be differences in the abilities of a group of children for whom a single textbook is a reasonably good choice, differentiated study guides will provide more direction for some, less for others. A study guide for one group may re-word complex passages or supply help with concept formation or call attention to context clues. For another group using the same text, the study guide may call for more subtle inferences or may challenge pupils to question facts and generalizations.

In the upper elementary grades, children of comparable abilities in word skills and basic comprehension develop divergent rates of reading. Diagnostic teaching uncovers such differences and makes provisions for them.

Diagnosis of reading and study skills means probing children's responses to reading and their uses of ideas obtained from reading. Comparisons must be made between the ability to recognize ideas on objective-type tests and to reproduce them in free responses and the ability to interpret and extend ideas. Since facility in expression is critical in measuring comprehension, written and oral responses should be compared.

Yet diagnostic teaching is not simply a matter of varied testing procedures. It is more a matter of observing how children respond to various approaches, how they answer questions phrased in different ways, and how they react to different degrees of teacher direction. Diagnostic teaching means observing how a child attacks an assignment in a textbook, how he uses references, how he chooses books, how he behaves while reading, and what his attitudes are.

The object is to find out what lies behind a test score and how a pupil learns best in order to facilitate learning to read and to make learning through reading not merely possible but desirable in his eyes.

3:2   The role of the teacher in diagnosis

Ruth Strang

Introduction

In the discussion of reading problems, we often hear the words *identification, appraisal, diagnosis,* and *evaluation.*

Identification determines a student's reading status. It is a first step toward grouping pupils either within a class or in separate sections. Without identification of some kind, individualization of instruction is impossible. Many schools have not gone far beyond the process of identification.

An *appraisal* of a student's reading ability gives a more complete positive picture of his reading status and development. It emphasizes his potential in relation to his performance; it helps him to set attainable goals.

Diagnosis puts more emphasis on defining the nature of the individual's reading difficulties and the conditions causing them. Diagnosis is also concerned, however, with positive factors on which one may build. Even a tentative diagnosis gives the teacher a sense of direction and confidence in working with the individual. Without diagnosis, the teacher may miss important areas, may over-emphasize others.

Evaluation stresses the desirability and worth of the reading instruction. It not only ascertains the progress that has been made toward specified objectives but also asks questions such as: 'Are the changes that are being effected worthwhile?' 'What values have they to the students and to society?' Evaluation looks beneath certain obvious or superficial results of reading instruction. For example, suppose a student brings his reading rate up to 400 words per minute. Looking at the student's improvement in rate, the teacher who evaluates this change may ask: 'What purpose did the increase in speed of reading serve?' 'At what cost has speed been gained?' 'What has happened to the reader's habit of reflective thinking?' 'How

STRANG, RUTH (1969) 'The role of the teacher in diagnosis', *Diagnostic Teaching of Reading* (2nd ed.) New York: McGraw-Hill, *v–vi*, 31–43, 44–6.

much strain or tension was involved?' 'How much does such rapid reading contribute to his personal development?'

Appraisal, diagnosis, and evaluation have much in common. All involve 1) getting facts about the individual and his reading, 2) synthesizing and interpreting these facts, 3) arriving at hypotheses that are modified as new information is obtained, and 4) using the understanding gained to help students improve their reading.

Diagnosis is never an end in itself; it is only a means to more efficient learning. Gaining an understanding of the student's reading proficiency and difficulties takes time, but it also saves time. It saves time by enabling the teacher to focus his attention on the specific help the student needs, thus avoiding trial and error and unnecessary instruction and practice.

In this book diagnosis is viewed as an intrinsic part of teaching. Most of the information a teacher gains about a student's reading is not recorded; it is used immediately in helping the student to improve. The more familiar a teacher is with factors that may influence a student's reading development, the more alert he will be to note their presence as he works with individuals and with groups.

Another important emphasis is on student's self-appraisal. Diagnostic information is for the student as well as for the teacher or reading specialist. Increasing proficiency in self-appraisal is a major goal throughout school years.

Any teacher can gain an understanding of his students that will help him to reinforce their desirable attitudes and competencies and to develop those which they lack. He need not wait for a specialist to give him diagnostic information; it is available to him in his daily work. According to Lytton (1967) an adequate basis for preventive and for remedial teaching is provided by a continuous analysis of students' classroom behavior. He found that teachers trained to detect individual differences have been as accurate in selecting retarded readers for remedial education as were group tests yielding IQs and AQs (accomplishment quotients). Haring and Ridgway (1967) likewise concluded that a battery of diagnostic tests does not predict as effectively as does trained teacher observation of the individual child.

Such teachers diagnose as they teach. They note individual pupils' reading performance. In their daily contact with children they also gain an understanding of *how* the individual acquires certain reading skills and *why* he makes certain errors. In diagnostic teaching, reading difficulties are recognized, understood, and, as far as possible, remedied. This should be an intrinsic part of the teaching process.

To obtain diagnostic information the teacher observes, listens, gives informal tests, and uses available standardized test results. He may make a case study of a particularly baffling problem.

It is only through working with an individual child who has a reading problem that a teacher truly learns *how* to teach reading. Every teacher of reading should have such an experience, for it is through teaching individual children to read that teachers gain insight into the intricacies of reading instruction. Such work makes any teacher a better teacher of reading (Cutts, 1964, p. 97).

As the teacher collects information about the student, he interprets, synthesizes, and uses it to help him improve his reading. Recognizing the individual's present powers, he tries to adjust the curriculum and his teaching procedures to the child's competencies, needs, and interests at the moment.

Instruction is guided by the student's own evolving curriculum and by the teacher's knowledge of a psychological sequence of reading skills. (For a comprehensive chart of sequential development of reading abilities see Strang, McCullough, and Traxler, 1967, pp. 131–144.) As the teacher continues to appraise the student's progress and to work with him on his reading improvement, he obtains additional information that suggests to both student and teacher further methods and materials to be employed. Thus diagnosis and teaching are fused into a single process.

The teacher also works indirectly through the environment, which he often can manipulate so that the student will be successful. With the younger children, he will work with parents in creating a more favorable home environment.

Understanding gained incidentally

Much understanding is gained incidentally. For example, when the principal assured Pat and another first grader that he had not accused them of walking on the grass, Pat said to her boy friend, 'Percy, we are exonerated'. In response to the teacher's question, 'What is the opposite of *tame*?' another first-grade child said, 'Ferocious'. Both children gave indications of an unusual speaking vocabulary for their age. General diagnostic signs of reading difficulty that teachers observe are:

A dislike of school and especially of reading.

R.C. – 17

Frequent absence for no good reason and other evasive methods of avoiding failure.

Apparent effort, but lack of learning.

Frequent wrong answers, showing lack of comprehension of the selection read.

Immature sentence structure and inaccuracy of descriptions.

Signs of fatigue, in one case the result of a 4 a.m. newspaper round.

A casual remark such as, 'Now I'll find out who in the class likes me'. This may indicate the child's concern about his social relations.

A child may also reveal his personal feelings and interests in the accounts of his own experience or in his stories and poems.

Understanding gained during a reading lesson

The teaching of any story or article offers opportunities for an informal kind of diagnosis. The following description of a reading lesson shows ways in which the teacher can learn about the student's vocabulary knowledge, his reading habits, his comprehension of the selection, his specific difficulties, and the background of experience that he brings to his reading.

Obtaining understanding

In orienting students to a selection, the teacher encourages them to talk about experiences they have had which are relevant to the story. He notes background knowledge that they bring to the interpretation of the selection. The extent and quality of their speaking vocabulary, sentence structure, and speech habits also become evident. This preliminary discussion may indicate the need to enrich the students' previous experience with pictures, explanations, or descriptions of the author and the setting. Before reading the selection, the teacher may help students set up a target or purpose for reading and discuss the unfamiliar words and concepts that they will encounter.

While the students are reading silently, the teacher will note that some seem to be reading rapidly with interest and attention. Others read slowly and show signs of difficulty—inattention, frowning, lip movements. A few ask questions that indicate the particular difficulties they are having. The poor readers usually are easily distracted. Their resistance to distraction is an index of their reading proficiency and their interest in the book.

The group discussion that follows the silent reading will give additional information: How well have individual students accomplished their purposes for reading the selection? Were they able to comprehend the selection accurately and easily? Did they comprehend what the author said? Did any of them make creative comments and applications? Did they profit by the instruction given? How did they answer the question, 'How might you apply this story to your own lives or to the world today?' Class discussions also give clues as to students' ability to learn from listening. In some discussions they spontaneously give information about family reading habits, their favorite TV programs, and other home conditions.

To obtain more specific information about their vocabulary and word recognition and comprehension skills, the teacher may ask individual students, while the others are still reading, to read a paragraph aloud, to state its main thought, to give the meanings of certain words in context, and to point out relationships or sequences.

If the teacher allows ample time for reading the selection, some students will finish before the time is up. How do they spend their free time? What initiative and self-direction do they show in finding something worthwhile to do? Some may begin reading another book; others may draw an illustration or write a poem or story suggested by the selection.

Using understanding

The teacher may use information of this kind immediately or later in planning individual and group instruction. He will vary individual assignments as to length and difficulty. To help each student progress at the rate and on the level appropriate for him, the teacher may use multi-level material such as The Science Research Associates Reading Laboratories (Science Research Associates, Chicago). To students who have similar difficulties he will give instruction and practice in small groups. To meet the needs of all students, he will draw on his reservoir of instructional procedures, materials, and ideas for creative activities. For the able learners he will provide some challenging books in different fields, plays for dramatized reading, and opportunities to prepare and present special reports and programs.

For poor readers the teacher will supply study guides, books, and other reading materials that are on their level. They need much easy supplementary reading to give practice in basic sight vocabulary and in the use of word recognition skills in context. Interesting books also serve as an incentive to acquire the reading skills that they need. To obtain additional practice, they may play vocabulary and word recognition games such as those published by the Garrard Press, Champaign, Illinois. Poor readers especially enjoy participating in choral reading and taking minor parts in the dramatized reading of plays. In interest groups, they can contribute to the study of special topics or problems by reading and reporting on a simple book, even a picture book. Motivated by a need to find out, a retarded reader sometimes makes sense out of material that the teacher thinks is too difficult for him. He uses clues the teacher may not recognize and puzzles out meanings in ways known only to himself.

The most seriously retarded readers cannot comprehend the texts provided for their grade. For these students the teacher may present orally the science and social studies content that is too difficult for them to read. He may make his presentation more vivid by the use of audio-visual aids. The students then dictate the main points, which the teacher will write on the board and type for them to read. In the stories they write or dictate, they often disclose their personal feelings and interests as well as vocabulary, sentence structure, and sense of sequence. If special reading classes are available, the teacher will refer these students for special instruction.

Diagnostic teaching becomes a process of continuous adjustment to individual pupils. The teacher accepts a bright student's comment, but gives special recognition to another student who needs encouragement. He may offer help to a student who is on the verge of frustration, but leave another who needs to develop independence to arrive at the solution himself. By adjusting the difficulty of his questions to the ability of his students, he challenges the gifted and helps the slow, shy individual to gain self-confidence. He helps the student to view mistakes as an opportunity to identify his errors and learn how to correct them.

Understanding individual differences

In any class, many kinds of reading behavior may be noted:

1   Charles, age nine, tries to escape any type of reading. When he is called upon to read, he excuses himself by saying that he has not studied the lesson. During silent reading periods he stares at the page, but makes no effort to read. He likes to go to the library just to look at the pictures in books. The teacher reinforces his reading interest of the moment, which may eventually lead to other interests. By adjusting the length and difficulty of the reading selection to Charles's present ability, the teacher avoids confronting him with a task too difficult and complicated for him even to

attempt. A certain degree of difficulty and novelty attracts attention; too great a degree of either causes anxiety or frustration or withdrawal.

2 Sue, age twelve, does not like to read aloud for fear of making a mistake. While reading, she frequently clears her throat. Words of encouragement work like magic. With students like Sue who show extreme lack of confidence in their reading ability, the teacher avoids making value judgments. Instead, he might ask, 'How did you get the main thought this time?' or 'How might you use a better method next time?'

3 Karen, age twelve, signs up for all school activities and then backs out or forgets. She displays much assurance and is inclined to brag often. In her reading she guesses wildly. Before Karen starts to read, the teacher may suggest several things to look for. When she makes a generalization, the teacher may ask her to state the ideas that support it. As the child learns to read more thoughtfully and deliberately, she will become less impulsive.

4 Mike, age eleven, will not read of his own accord unless the assignment is very simple. If the work is a little difficult and he does not get help immediately, he slams his book down with, 'Oh, I can't do that.' In silent reading he mutters continually. He is a discipline problem and often in trouble for bullying the smaller children. But he likes to help the teacher, and if he is kept busy enough, he does not get into trouble.

5 Randy, age nine, is apathetic toward reading. He does not even wish to have stories read to him. When the other children read, Randy looks off into space. His attitude toward reading is changing now that the teacher is reading with him alone.

6 Fred, age seven, is always squirming in his seat, playing with his ears, and daydreaming. He talks in such a soft voice that he can hardly be heard. When reading, he gives up at the slightest error. Fred was retained in first grade, and this seems to bother him very much.

7 Cathy, age seven, is inclined to daydream during reading periods, but makes an effort when called upon. She often substitutes a story of her own, which may or may not have anything to do with what the group is reading. She is so successful in other things that she is not concerned about her failure in reading.

Having noted conditions that seem to be interfering with students' progress in reading, the teacher may say or do something to reinforce their strengths and overcome their weaknesses. He would reward Sue's successful attempts, insist on Karen's substituting systematic word attack for guessing, and give Mike much easy reading material before gradually increasing its difficulty.

Building readiness for reading

Early identification of children with learning disabilities and the correction of remediable deficits will make the teaching of reading much easier for first-grade teachers. At home, at nursery school, at kindergarten and beginning first grade, parents and teachers can provide games that will develop eye-hand coordination, facility in the use of language, visual and auditory perception, discrimination, and memory. Practised in a natural setting, these skills become immediately functional (Haring and Ridgway, 1967; Early, 1962). Reading aloud to children acquaints them with the sound of language and introduces them to the delight that books may give. Providing them with varied experiences and talking with them build their speaking vocabulary of meaningful words. In a reading environment, they acquire a love of books and an eagerness to learn to read. If these experiences have been lacking during preschool years, they may be supplied to some extent in the kindergarten or at the beginning of the first grade.

The first-grade teacher may diagnose the child's readiness to learn to read informally and by the use of a readiness test such as the Metropolitan Readiness Tests, 1965 revision (Harcourt, Brace & World, Inc.), and the Lee-Clark Reading Readiness Test, 1962 revision (California Test Bureau). Dykstra (1966) concluded that thirty minutes of testing in addition to the teacher's day-to-day observation would give an adequate diagnosis of readiness. The diagnosis of readiness at any age level makes possible a good match between the child's development and the reading task. A good match, in turn, results in intrinsic satisfaction in the experience.

Teachers may fail, too

Often diagnostic information is acquired too late. It was only after several weeks that a classroom teacher realized fifteen-year-old Dan needed special help. In his silent reading assignments and on tests he was always the last to finish. As the weeks passed, his scholastic standing decreased and his misbehavior increased. One day when the teacher, after an enthusiastic introduction of 'The Great Stone Face', asked the class to read it silently, she saw that Dan was the only student not reading. His head was on the desk. The teacher quietly moved to his desk and touched him on the shoulder. 'Dan, won't you try? It's a wonderful story.'

'Are you kidding?' he replied, almost in tears. 'Do you know how long it would take me to read one page? I wouldn't finish it before the others had read all twenty pages.'

It was not until then that the teacher checked the school records. Although average in intelligence, his grades in the academic subjects were low, and his reading score still lower. The teacher had not realized that the boy's apparent indifference, restlessness, attention-seeking behavior, lethargy, withdrawal, slow performance, and disheveled appearance all signaled for help. He did get help, but much too late.

Understanding gained in special reading classes

A period with a special reading class in a junior high school further illustrates how the teacher may gather information about individual students while teaching. According to group reading tests, the boys in this class were three or more years below their seventh-grade placement. Each boy was given a copy of the third-grade *Reader's Digest Skill Builder* to read. When they had finished the story, the teacher discussed it with them.

One boy, whom we shall call Bert, apparently had comprehended very little of it. Although he spoke glibly, he had little to communicate. When later asked individually to read a few paragraphs aloud, he stopped at every word of more than three letters. When asked if he did much reading, he merely shrugged his shoulders. When sports were mentioned, he showed a little more interest. When asked if he liked animals, he became excited and took from his pocket two photographs of bears taken by his brother who had a job feeding animals at the zoo. Although Bert was enthusiastic about animals, he showed no interest in reading books or articles about them.

Near the end of the period Bert asked if they could do the *Reader's Digest* exercises next week. He told the others that he had got 100 per cent on the SRA Reading Laboratory's Power Builder Test. Actually, the teacher discovered, he had left the spaces blank and filled in the correct answers by consulting the scoring key; then he had proudly claimed to have scored 100 per cent.

He was very slow in all his reading and was extremely restless. He distracted others by his wisecracks and useless questions.

It became obvious in this single period that Bert could not comprehend second-grade material, that he needed to build up his basic sight vocabulary and acquire effective word recognition skills. He revealed his need to succeed in the group by making wild guesses and by copying the answers so that he could boast about getting 100 per cent. His tension showed in restlessness and nail biting.

Using the understanding gained from this preliminary appraisal, the teacher planned to help Bert build a basic sight vocabulary and acquire word recognition skills so that he could achieve some real success. He could get this practice through drill on sound-letter associations, through reading easy material, and through a variety of games and activities that would also help to relieve his physical tension. The teacher planned to interest him in keeping a record of the words he learned so that he could see his progress. As he acquired sufficient reading ability, she would provide animal stories he might enjoy if he could read them without frustration. Since recognition in the group was so important to him, the teacher planned to teach him the skills needed to participate successfully in some group activity such as reading a few lines in a play. If Bert did not respond to this instruction in reading skills in which he was deficient, the reading teacher would move to a deeper level of diagnosis.

Understanding gained through individualizing instruction

In one fifth-grade class the last twenty minutes of each reading period was used for free reading. Pupils kept a record of their reading by writing on a card a few sentences telling what the story was about. Since this requires the ability to summarize, which is a difficult skill to master, the teacher demonstrated and went through the process with them several times.

She noticed one boy frowning over his card when he had just finished a simple story. He hesitated for quite a while as though he did not know what to write; then he started copying parts of the first page word for word. The teacher sat down with him and asked him to tell her what happened in the story. She led him along with such questions as 'What happened first? Then? What happened at the end?' She also asked other questions to test his comprehension of details. His general comprehension was good. It became clear to him that the story had four main parts or happenings. The teacher asked him to think of one sentence that would tell what happened in each part. Once he sensed the structure of the story, he was able to write several sentences telling what happened. All he needed was instruction and practice in telling a story in sequence.

While members of the class are independently reading suitable interesting books of their own choice, the teacher has time for individual conferences. In these conferences she may ask the student to read a paragraph or two aloud. She first notes and approves something the student does well or better than he did before. Then she may analyze a task which the student needs to improve and go through the process with him. With another student, the teacher may spend his ten-minute conference in finding out how well he has comprehended the selection and in helping him to discover ways of improving his comprehension. With a student who can read but does not, the teacher may spend the time introducing this reluctant reader to a book that he may be persuaded to read outside of class.

Sometimes the teacher may give a larger amount of time to an individual student whose lack of improvement is baffling. Group methods have not reached him. For example, Alice, an apathetic, slow-learning girl, seemed to have only one interest—her dog Blackie who had died. She still felt very sad about it. 'Blackie was my best friend', she said. As she told about Blackie, the teacher wrote the story, typed it, and gave it to her to read. Alice found little difficulty in reading her own language patterns and words whose meaning she already knew. This experience encouraged her to make a book about the care of dogs. She visited a friendly veterinarian who gave her some first-hand information as well as a pamphlet on selecting, feeding, and caring for dogs. As Alice read this pamphlet aloud the teacher observed:

Which words Alice knew at sight.

How she attacked the pronunciation of unfamiliar words.

Whether she understood the meaning of certain words and phrases: 'Substantiating your claims' she explained as 'showing the reasons for your claims'; 'grooming the dog', as 'making the dog look nice'.

How quickly she learned and how permanently she remembered the meaning of the new words she was being taught.

Whether she could get the main thought of paragraphs.

What her attitude was toward reading.

How spontaneously she was able to express her feelings.

In the individualized reading periods the teacher may also uncover sudden changes in a child's performance that call for further study. A third grader, Patty, previously at the top of her class, seemed overnight to go rapidly downhill. She appeared to pay attention in class, but her expression and her responses gave the impression that her thoughts were elsewhere. The teacher observed her behavior and work habits to see if there might be something in the school situation that was disturbing her. There were no signs of visual, auditory, or nutritional problems. The teacher did not think the child's difficulty stemmed from her home, which was one of the best. However, from a home visit the teacher learned that Patty's mother was going to have another child and that Patty was afraid something might happen to her mother. After the baby arrived and the mother returned home well and happy, Patty's work again reached its former superior quality.

An individualized reading program gives teachers more time to synthesize information from a number of sources. For example, it became apparent to a first-grade teacher that Jack was not reading up to his capacity. He tested in the average range on the Lorge-Thorndike Intelligence Test and above average on the Metropolitan Reading Readiness Test. He could recognize all the Dolch Basic Sight Vocabulary and always received 100 per cent on his phonics worksheets. When the vowel sounds were introduced, Jack was delighted to find that he could read and spell new words by inserting the short vowel sound, for example, *h-t, hat; c-n, can*. But he could not read from the first-grade book.

After eliminating possible visual and emotional causes of his difficulty and closely observing his oral reading, the teacher came to the tentative conclusion that Jack could not transfer the phonics skills he had learned in isolation to the reading of the printed page. On the basis of this hypothesis the teacher, with the cooperation of the boy's parents, presented all new words to him in context. In reading each story he systematically used his word attack skills to pronounce the unfamiliar words. The teacher helped him only with the words he could not figure out for himself. His progress was amazing.

Diagnosis and instruction in reading on the first day of school

One teacher described her method of gaining an understanding of a middle-class fifth-grade group on the first day of the school year. Beforehand she gets information about each child that is available on his cumulative record: his achievement as measured by tests and school marks, and any outstanding physical, emotional, social, or learning problems that might need her special attention.

On the first day she asks pairs of children to interview each other and then introduce their partner to the class. Thus she learns their interests, linguistic abilities, speech difficulties, and poise. To assist her in remembering names and faces she asks each child to fill out a card with his name, address, family composition, main interests and hobbies, favorite TV programs, the books he has read during the past year, and his educational plans. The pupils usually enjoy writing the answers to the question, 'If you had three wishes, what would they be?' These cards form a convenient basic information file for each class.

In their first reading lesson the teacher selects a story from one of their fifth-grade books. They read it silently. She asks questions to check their understanding of the story. She also notes how well they express their ideas: Can the rest of the class understand what they are saying? Are the ideas well organized? Which students are eager to answer? Which seem too shy to speak up? Which seem to be paying no attention at all?

By reading a short story or article aloud to the class, the teacher tests their listening comprehension and ability to discuss the selection.

From these informal diagnostic methods the teacher gains initial understanding of individuals who need special attention because of reading deficiencies or because the average work of the grade may not be stimulating to them.

Values of teacher diagnosis

Without these kinds of understanding, the teacher may either neglect practice and instruction on skills badly needed or give unnecessary instruction. He may also unwittingly reinforce an undesirable response as, for example, when he accepts and apparently approves word calling, i.e., without comprehension, or when he tells the student the meaning of a word he could have solved himself if he had used his newly acquired word recognition skills. There is a nice balance between the extremes of 'accentuating the positive' and insisting upon 'errorless learning'.

The information obtained in appraising the progress of individual students can also be used in evaluating the reading program as a whole. Is it balanced? Does it use the best features of various methods and materials as they are appropriate, e.g., drills from a phonic system if they are needed by some children and wide, challenging reading for the able learners? Are combined instruction and appraisal an essential part of the program?

Concluding statement

There is a reciprocal relationship between diagnosis and teaching. The teacher analyzes each behavioral objective into steps, beginning with the student's concrete experience and leading into the more complex and abstract process of reading.

As he teaches, he notes which children progress easily and which encounter difficulty at certain stages. He may ask successful students to describe their methods of learning so that others may apply them; e.g., how did they manage to pronounce a word? how did they come to know its meaning? how did they get the author's thought so clearly?

For those who have special difficulty the teacher provides special instruction individually or in small groups. While the class as a whole is working independently, the teacher holds conferences with individuals in the most private part of the room to obtain more specific diagnostic information and to help them with their immediate reading problem.

The teacher has in mind characteristics and conditions that influence individual students' reading achievement: mental alertness; learning capacity; listening comprehension; visual and auditory acuity and discrimination; previously acquired reading abilities; needs, interests, and attitudes toward themselves and toward reading. He is aware of conditions and attitudes in the home and community that affect the child's interest and effort.

Too many teachers think that they must depend upon test results. It is better to select a few reliable instruments that the teacher can interpret and apply them to administer many tests whose results are poorly interpreted and used unwisely. Many teachers underestimate the diagnostic possibilities of their day-by-day contacts with students. Many do not realize that they themselves are the most important influence on students' reading achievement.

Fortunately, the teacher does not bear the entire burden of helping a student improve his reading. Administrators, counselors, librarians, and other staff members all make some contribution to the diagnosis and remediation of reading difficulties and to the appraisal of students' progress in reading (Early, 1962, pp. 1–6). The teacher is the most important member of a team that is concerned with making better readers and better persons.

References

BOND, GUY L. (1966) *The Coordinated Phases of the Reading Study,* progress report presented at the Annual Conference of the International Reading Association, Dallas, Tex., May.

BURNETT, RICHARD W. (1963) 'The Diagnostic Proficiency of Teachers of Reading', *The Reading Teacher,* 16, 229–34.

CAPOBIANCO, R. F. (1964) 'Diagnostic Methods Used with Learning Disability Cases', *Exceptional Children*, 31, 187–93.

CUTTS, WARREN G. (1964) *Modern Reading Instruction* Washington, D.C.: Center for Applied Research in Education, Inc.

DYKSTRA, ROBERT 'Auditory Discrimination Abilities and Beginning Reading Achievement', *Reading Research Quarterly*, 1, 5–34.

EARLY, MARGARET J. (1962) *Providing Leadership for Secondary Reading Programs* Albany, N.Y.: Council for Administrative Leadership.

HARING, N. G. and RIDGWAY, R. W. (1967) 'Early Identification of Children with Learning Disabilities', *Exceptional Children*, 33, 387–95.

LYTTON, H. (1967) 'Follow-up of an Experiment in Selection for Remedial Education', *British Journal of Educational Psychology*, 37, 1–9.

STRANG, RUTH, MCCULLOUGH, CONSTANCE M. and TRAXLER, ARTHUR E. (1967) *The Improvement of Reading* (4th ed.) New York: McGraw-Hill.

3:3   Observation in the classroom

Ruth Strang

An elementary school teacher who stays with his class four hours a day for over 150 days has a total of about six hundred hours of possible time for observation. If he has fifty pupils in his class (which, heaven forbid!), theoretically he would have twelve hours to devote to each pupil. Of course he must spend some of his time in giving instruction to the class as a whole. But even then he may be noticing how the class and certain individuals in it are responding to the instruction. A teacher readily identifies a student who has reading difficulties: he often looks away from his book; he tries to avoid reading; he gets better marks in subjects that do not require reading. Sometimes he comprehends what he hears better than what he reads. As the teacher observes more closely, he discovers specific difficulties in visual and auditory acuity, perception, discrimination, and memory; in vocabulary, word recognition, comprehension, and logical thinking. From further observation in the classroom and from interviews, he may infer that certain emotional difficulties are interfering with the student's achievement in reading. It seems possible that most teachers can develop greater skill in understanding their pupils through observation, specific and objective.

Observation is a basic technique (Cronbach, 1960; Strang, 1953; Thorndike and Hagen, 1961; Withall, 1960). It is employed every day by every teacher. It does not require extra time or materials. Day by day the teacher observes pupils in his classes as they engage in learning all the language arts.

Teachers and clinicians should have 1) a background knowledge of behavior and of conditions frequently associated with reading achievement,

STRANG, RUTH (1969) 'Observation in the classroom', *Diagnostic Teaching of Reading* (2nd edn.) New York: McGraw-Hill.

2) techniques of accurate, insightful observation, and 3) ability to under-stand the behavior they have observed. The traditional diagnostic approaches have focused too exclusively on pathological conditions and on what an individual *cannot do* rather than on what he actually *does* under certain conditions. Teachers' observations usually have the same tendency.

With training in methods of observation, teachers learn to observe behavior involved in classroom learning tasks. From an experiment in training teachers in forty-eight kindergarten classes, Haring and Ridgway (1967) concluded 1) that the teacher plays a key role in the early identifica-tion of children with learning disabilities and 2) that even a battery of tests does not predict as effectively as does teacher observation of the individual child. Trained teachers who observe and respond appropriately to pupils' reading strengths and difficulties bridge the gap between diagnosis, classroom teaching, and remedial work.

Most of the teacher's observations are never recorded; they are used immediately or at the first opportunity to help the student. For example, a child hesitates over the initial sound of an unfamiliar word. The teacher says, 'What other words do you know that begin with the same letters?' Thus the child identifies the initial sound of the word. This clue may enable him to pronounce the word. As a check on the correctness of his pronunciation, the teacher asks, 'Does the word you pronounced make sense in the sentence?'

Limitations of observation

Although individual teachers' appraisals of a child's reading development are often remarkably accurate, not all teachers have the training, intuition, or experience that would enable them to make a reliable evaluation (De Hirsch *et al.* 1966). And while observation is excellent for gaining understanding of the way a student reads, it does not directly tell us why he reads this way. From our observation we can only make inferences about the causes of the student's reading failures or successes. To guide the student in improving his reading, we need inferences or hypotheses based on a number of observations plus all the other relevant information that is available.

As safeguards against misinterpreting recorded observations, four prin-ciples should be kept in mind:

1 Since the student is always changing and growing, an observation that was made last year may not describe his present reading performance.

2 A teacher can observe only a small part of a student's total behavior. On the basis of such limited information the teacher can make only tentative generalizations about the student's reading.

3 Observations made by a teacher may tell more about the teacher than about the student. What the teacher sees may be influenced by his beliefs and biases, by his interest in the children observed, and by a subtle expectancy of a child's success or failure. His first impression of the student, his philosophy of education, and many other factors may color what he sees. What he looks for may be only what is already in his mind. It is therefore very important that the teacher understand the reading process and common causes of reading difficulty, and that he be receptive to what the child is trying to communicate through his behavior.

4 Ideally, observations should be interpreted in conjunction with interview, test, and other data. However, observations often are the only data that are available at the moment, and sometimes action should not be deferred.

Opportunities for observation

The classroom is a normal situation in which conditions are significant for the child. The teacher's opportunity to make many observations over a long period of time enables him to recognize typical behavior and temporary deviations from that behavior. In his role as teacher, his observations are unobtrusive; they do not alter the behavior observed. The teacher's observation and appraisal are a regular part of classroom procedure.

Any test administered individually, whether an oral reading test, an informal reading inventory, or a standardized individual intelligence or achievement test, offers excellent opportunities to see how an individual's mind works. One child will impulsively guess at the meaning and pronunciation of a word; another will use a trial-and-error approach instead of reasoning. One child may refuse to give any answer unless he is sure he is right, while another will glibly give answers to questions about which he has no knowledge. The individual's responses may also indicate disturbed thinking and disclose attitudes and values (Cronbach, 1960).

Detailed analysis of classroom situations

Teachers are daily confronted with many common classroom situations in which they may gain much understanding of their students' reading (Wright, 1969). A detailed analysis of these situations serves as a guide to observation; it alerts the teacher to significant reactions which he might not otherwise notice. We may either start with the situation and describe the kind of understanding we can obtain from it, or start with the kind of understanding we need and indicate the situations in which such understanding can be obtained.

The analyses on the following pages show kinds of information that may be significant for students' progress in reading. This information often raises the question 'Why?' which can be answered only by further observation and conversation with the student. Such understanding may be obtained in different classroom situations. To save space we have run the items on the same line; however, it would be easier for the teacher to select the items he wants to observe and record each one on a separate line, e.g.:

LANGUAGE ABILITIES

Vocabulary	*Sentence structure*	*Speech*
Meager ____	Incomplete sentences ____	Distinct ____
Rich ____	Simple sentences ____	Inaudible ____
Accurate ____	Complex sentences ____	Monotonous ____
Incorrect ____		Expressive ____
		Defects ____

Oral report periods

In kindergarten and the lower grades and in oral English periods in the upper grades, students are offered many opportunities to relate their experiences. As the teacher listens, he learns about their vocabulary and language patterns, their interests and personality traits. Glimpses of home conditions also are frequently revealed.

In making and giving oral reports individually or in a small group, the students may show their interest in certain topics; their acquaintance with sources of information; and their ability to evaluate and compare sources, extract relevant information from them, organize it, and report it effectively. Observation of the audience gives indication of the speaker's effectiveness and of the audience's ability to listen and evaluate tactfully the reports given.

Specific observations:

Vocabulary: meager _____, rich _____, accurate _____, incorrect _____, words mispronounced _____

Sentence structure: incomplete sentences _____, simple sentences _____, complex sentences _____, says little _____, is very voluble _____

Imagination: creative____, bizarre ____

Organization: events recounted in proper sequence _____, well organized _____, disjointed _____, repetitive _____

Sense of humor: enjoys humor _____, makes others laugh _____

Intelligence: is alert mentally _____, sees relations _____, solves problems _____, learns slowly _____

Interest: wholehearted _____, indifferent _____, apathetic _____

Personality: self-confident _____, shy _____, socially poised _____, embarrassed _____, tense _____, hostile _____

Family relations and background: affectionate home relations _____, unhappy home _____

Relations with parents: constructive _____, detrimental _____

Relations with siblings: congenial _____, rivalrous _____

Peer reactions: interested _____, friendly _____, sympathetic _____, uninterested _____, critical _____

Appearance: happy _____, sad _____; well dressed and well groomed _____, poorly dressed _____, inappropriately dressed _____, disheveled _____

Listening to the teacher read a story

Note degree of interest evoked: keenly interested _____, eager to talk about it _____, indifferent _____, bored _____

Comprehension: accurate _____, detailed _____, inadequate _____

Students reading aloud

This situation gives the teacher opportunity to observe each student's word recognition skills, pronunciation, phrasing, and expression. One can quickly detect word callers by asking several searching questions on the selections they have read. The student may also reveal his attitude toward reading and toward himself as a reader. It will be evident whether he approaches reading with enjoyment, indifference, dislike, anxiety, resistance, or hostility.

Dramatized reading of a story or play shows still more clearly the student's ability to read aloud with expression, to bring out appropriate feeling and meaning, to interpret clues of character, and to evoke the interest of the audience.

Types of observations:

Familiarity with phonics: _____
Method of word attack: sounds out words _____, uses syllabication _____, tries to analyze structure _____, uses context clues _____
   Word recognition problems: skips words _____, reverses letters, words, phrases _____, substitutes words _____, guesses wildly _____
   Rate of reading: appropriate to material _____, too slow _____, too rapid _____

Substitutions yield valuable clues. If the student substitutes a word that makes sense in the sentence, we may infer that he is reading for meaning. If, however, the word he substitutes makes no sense, we may infer that he is merely pronouncing words with little concern for the meaning of what he reads. The teacher should also note what kinds of words cause the student difficulty. Are they short common words such as those in the Dolch basic vocabulary, or longer words; words within his experience or words foreign to him? It is also important to observe how he goes about getting the meaning of unfamiliar words.

Phrasing: reads word by word _____, reads in phrases or other thought units _____, loses place easily _____, reads clearly and with expression _____
   Closure: cannot blend sounds _____, has difficulty in supplying missing letters, words, sentences_____
   Sequence: difficulty in retelling story in sequence _____, following series of directions _____, remembering order of letters _____, of words _____
   Comprehension: recognizes basic vocabulary at sight _____, gives good answers to questions _____, gives irrelevant answers _____, sees relationships and sequences of ideas _____, can recount or discuss what he has read _____, shows originality in interpretation _____, relates reading to experience _____
   Attitudes: volunteers to read orally _____, reads only when called upon _____, appears to enjoy reading orally in audience situations _____, reads aloud to others in free time _____, makes excuses to avoid reading aloud _____
   Reaction of classmates to student's oral reading: are eager to have him read _____, show interest _____, attention wanders _____, are restless _____, are disinterested _____, rudely interrupt _____

Silent reading in library, free-reading, and study periods

The student's choice of books in a free-reading or library period may show his reading interests and level. His behavior during the period indicates his silent reading habits and power of concentration. In addition to the specific observation, teacher or student may make an attention-distraction chart. Such a chart may make the students more aware of the time they are wasting. Of course, it would be necessary for the students to have a chance to discuss what goes into their attention-distraction charts. Were they just idly daydreaming, or were they staring into space while pondering thoughts evoked by their reading? If they were distracted, what caused it? Was the book too hard? Were they thinking about tonight's party?

Types of observations:

Approach to books: does not enjoy books or pictures _____; leafs through many books _____, chooses quickly _____; looks first at chapter titles and/or table of contents _____, pictures _____, printed pages _____; tends to choose small books _____, large books _____, one kind of book _____, a particular author or series _____; is rather uniform in choices _____, chooses a variety of books _____; chooses books at his own age level of interest _____, below _____, above _____; takes books home often _____, seldom _____, never _____; reads them through _____; can discuss what he has read _____; returns books on time _____, undamaged _____; asks for books he does not find on shelves _____; is unable to find any book of interest to him _____

Uses library just to look at magazines _____; reads little of newspapers except the sports page and 'funnies' _____; always carries a big stack of books home _____; asks for permission to take a new book home over the weekend _____

Can locate sources of information _____, uses index _____, table of contents _____, finds suitable material _____, makes useful notes on relevant material _____

When a new book is distributed, receives it enthusiastically _____, groans and shows other signs of rejection _____, turns pages aimlessly _____, systematically examines book _____, asks questions about book _____

Voluntary reading: does no voluntary reading _____, reads more than required _____, includes a variety of material _____, makes clear, original, thoughtful comments on reading _____, shows depth of appreciation beyond his grade level _____

Visual habits and posture: frowns _____, blinks often _____, squints _____, rubs or wipes eyes _____; holds book at average distance _____, too close _____, too far _____; has good general posture _____, complains of headache _____

Uses reference tools such as glossary and dictionary: freely _____, seldom _____, never _____, effectively _____, as an excuse for leaving seat (as evidenced by attitude, approach, results) _____; independently _____, with assistance _____

Reads by himself _____, talks to others _____; if the latter, in cooperative study _____, as a disturbance _____

Amount of work completed; about same as classmates _____, noticeably more _____, noticeably less _____; if assignment is completed early goes on to more of the same _____, stops and is idle _____, does something else _____, related (such as drawing pictures to illustrate the story) _____, unrelated _____; disturbs others _____

Asks for teacher's help _____

Group instruction and discussion

The teacher will observe that some students 'catch on' quickly while others need to have an explanation repeated several times. The student who learns quickly should not have to mark time while the slow learners gain sufficient comprehension to go on. Sometimes, in a question or comment, a quiet student will reveal undetected ability. In response to a picture or incomplete story, a student may show exceptional originality.

Interaction in the group also may be observed. A great deal of learning takes place as a result of group interaction. Students may stimulate and encourage one another to read better; they may share their most effective reading methods, recommend stories they have liked, and otherwise facilitate each other's learning. On the other hand, interaction in some groups may be detrimental to growth in reading. Many retarded readers have told of being embarrassed when classmates shouted out the words they did not know, laughed at their mistakes, or made fun of the easy books they were reading. The bright child who enjoys reading may suffer in equal measure from an anti-intellectual spirit.

In informal discussions, students may show what they are learning through television, radio, and part-time work and indicate its relevance to what is going on in school. The teacher who is receptive will be able to enter at least a small part of his students' world and see where reading fits into it.

Types of observations:

Attitudes: eager to participate _____, interested _____, indifferent _____, withdrawn _____

Work habits: works well alone, _____, with others _____

Thought habits: follows sequence of story or discussion _____, organizes thought well _____, recognizes cause and effect relations _____, summarizes well _____, does not understand questions or directions or the significance of what is said _____, is confused in his thinking _____

Learning capacity: quick to catch on _____, needs to have directions or questions repeated _____, asks searching questions _____, relates ideas _____

Oral expression: expresses thought clearly in well-constructed sentences _____, uses words accurately _____, has good enunciation _____, uses a wide range of oral vocabulary _____, is halting _____, is incoherent _____

Discussion techniques: contributes relevant facts _____, analyzes the situation _____, shows breadth of information _____, listens to others and builds on what they have said _____, does not participate _____, makes irrelevant comments _____

Creativity: is inventive _____, shows imagination _____, is intellectually curious _____, shows maturity of interests _____, shows little or no originality _____

Personal involvement: tense _____, noncommittal _____, nervous and ill at ease _____, self-conscious _____; enjoys discussion _____, listens well but contributes little _____, applies vicarious experience to himself _____, displays wholehearted participation _____

Quality of comprehension: accurate _____, well-organized _____, factual ——————, inaccurate _____, incoherent _____, creative _____

Whole observer _____, part observer _____

Other activities during the day

Types of specific observations:

Positive attitudes: toward school _____, toward reading _____, toward self _____, toward parents _____

Negative attitudes: toward school _____, toward reading _____, toward self _____, toward parents _____

Difficulty in physical activities: in sports and games _____, in coordination

Favorite school subjects: _____

Subjects disliked: _____

Best friends: younger _____, older _____, brighter _____, duller

_____

Significant events in the student's past: _____

Some teachers may think this detailed analysis of observation in class-room situations is bewilderingly complex. Others may think it is 'much ado about nothing'. Obviously, a teacher cannot observe all the items about every student. But if he is familiar with the kinds of understanding of students' reading that a teacher may gain during the school day, he becomes more alert to significant responses that individual students may make.

Observation during play periods

Observation of children on the playground may yield helpful information about psychomotor abilities related to the reading achievement especially of younger children. It is easy to spot the children who are lacking in motor and eye-hand coordination and those who exhibit 'directional con-fusion' (inability to discriminate right from left parts of the body). Less important is observation of lateral preferences, which are no longer con-sidered of much significance in reading disability. The incidence of incon-sistency in hand and eye preferences changes with age—around 42 per cent for six-year-olds and only 18 per cent for seven-year-olds.

On the playground a child's interest in sports, the quality of his participation, leadership, and initiative, the tendency to get into trouble, and the rejection or acceptance by classmates may all be indirectly related to his reading achievement.

Tape recordings of spontaneous conversations of children in groups yields valuable information on proficiency in vocabulary, sentence struc-ture, and logical thinking. Most useful is an observation and analysis of the setting in which children experience success or failure in various reading tasks.

Observation over a period of time

Joe, a third-grade boy, comes from a non-English-speaking home. He is just beginning to read with difficulty at a primer level. His speaking vocabulary is meager; his enunciation, poor; his sentences, incomplete and poorly organized. When he reads orally, he stumbles over basic sight words in the Dolch vocabulary. He lacks word attack skills. His substitution of wild guesses for the words he does not know suggests that he is not reading for meaning. In relating a story, he relies heavily on the pictures.

During a free-choice reading or library period, Joe resists teacher guidance in selecting appropriate books. He chooses books that are too difficult for him and merely goes through the motions of reading them. Whenever possible, he avoids reading and prefers to draw pictures during reading time.

Listening in a group situation is one of Joe's main problems. He is restless and seems preoccupied, listens only part of the time, and is easily distracted. His work habits are poor, and he often disturbs others.

Both the teacher's observation and the results of psychological tests indicate more technical potential than he is demonstrating. He can see relationships and answer inference questions. If he is given individual attention, his comprehension is much better.

His background of experience is quite different from school experiences, and there are emotional problems in the home. His failure in reading, together with home problems, has made him tense and anxious and lacking in self-confidence. The amazing thing is that although he has had so little success in his past reading experiences, he seems willing and determined to overcome his deficiencies.

Since he responds so well to individual attention, even a few minutes of the teacher's exclusive attention would be helpful. In these brief individual conferences, the teacher could stress his good qualities and evidences of progress, and give him specific instruction in pronouncing English words that cause special difficulty. In class the teacher could use choral reading and dialogues to give him fluency in speaking a selection before he attempts to read it. Encouraging verbal interaction with English-speaking children on the playground and in class would increase his facility in speaking English.

Observation of children with severe reading disability

The teacher's classroom observation is important in the initial screening of problems referred to as 'developmental lag', 'minimal brain damage', or 'sensorimotor immaturity'. The following clues may alert the teacher to possible neurological deficits:

Extreme difficulty in learning to read and spell

Awkwardness in finger and hand movements, difficulty in coloring between lines, inability to copy a simple geometric form

Difficulty in balancing, in riding a two-wheeler or a skateboard, in skipping or hopping

Reversing letters or numerals: reading *was* for *saw*, *12* for *21*

Hyperactivity, short attention span

Apparent anxiety and insecurity about school

Many kinds of behavior measured by standardized tests can be observed by the classroom teacher if he knows what to look for. For example, the teacher can observe day-to-day kinds of responses measured by the Illinois Test of Psycholinguistic Abilities. Among those most closely related to reading development are understanding the significance of what he hears, reproducing and identifying what he has been shown and relating it to his past experience; seeing similarities, completing missing parts of a sentence or figure, retelling a story in sequence, and duplicating and remembering a sequence of numbers or forms presented to him orally and visually. Having recognized a difficulty or deficit, the teacher can give the child practice in that kind of ability.

If such difficulties are observed in preschool, kindergarten, and early in first grade, they might be corrected by games and other activities that children enjoy: skipping to music, jumping rope, playing hop scotch, finding missing elements in pictures, playing 'Simon Says', etc. Practice in auditory discrimination and memory is given by tapping two rhythms and asking the child to tell whether they were the same or different, asking him to repeat interesting sentences, letting him watch a simple experiment and tell what happened. First-grade children who have not developed tactual, motor, visual, and auditory discrimination and integration need special practice. For them activities such as have just been suggested are not just play; they are essential to success in learning to read.

Observation of interaction between student and teacher

Since the influence of teacher behavior on children's spontaneous, co-operative, and self-initiated behavior and on their learning and achievement has been demonstrated by a number of research studies (see Anderson, 1939, 1954; Withall, 1960; Flanders and Havumaki, 1960; Moustakas *et al*, 1956), we should observe not only the individual student or teacher, but also the interaction between them. In this way teachers can gain an understanding of the effect of their behavior and methods on students' attitudes and efforts. They can see the results of their words and action. By observing interaction among students, the teacher can gain insight into the influence of peer relations and values.

Observation varies in breadth and depth. Separate observations of behavior and errors become more meaningful when grouped into patterns. For example, omission of one or more words may be related to inability to comprehend and that, in turn, to inability to recall the author's ideas. Repetition of words or parts of words becomes more meaningful when it is seen as a way of stalling for time while trying to pronounce a different word or to relate an idea to the first part of the sentence. The observed behavior is not so important as the motivation and sequences that lead up to it. It is possible to observe clues to the individual's cognitive style in reading. In other words, what is his thinking process in various types of reading—why and how does he arrive at certain responses? Such understanding can be obtained only by a person who is able to think and feel with another individual and to sense why he is acting as he does at a given moment.

Examples of observation during an individualized reading period

Sixth-grade boys were reading books of their own choice during an individualized reading period. Bruce, a large boy who was repeating the grade, laughed out loud as he was reading *Rufus M.* by Eleanor Estes. Most of the other students paid no attention to him; a few of his immediate classmates looked up, some annoyed, some amused. Occasionally he smiled to himself. It was almost four minutes before he turned the page. His lips were moving as if he were pronouncing each word to himself. In the second period he was still struggling through his book; he had completed two-thirds of it, still reading in the same slow way.

This observation raises questions about the meaning of Bruce's behavior: did he really appreciate the humor of the book, or was his loud laughter an attention-getting device? Do his classmates tolerate, ignore, or reject him? What are the causes of his slow reading—lack of a basic sight vocabulary? Inability to apply the word recognition skills he has been taught? Poor reasoning ability? Failure to use his knowledge of sentence structure to get meaning? Overemphasis on phonics that has led to persistence of the habit of sounding out every word? Further observation and conversation with Bruce are necessary to answer these questions.

Mack, the slowest student in the group, sat with the open book he had chosen, *Kidnapped*, looking into space. He did not get beyond page 9. He had previously read and enjoyed a simplified version of *Treasure*

Island and wanted to read another book by the same author. But this time he had got hold of the original edition and could not understand it. Once in a while he roused himself and tried hard to read it, but made little progress. He seemed glad when the period ended. Next time he chose an easy, new, illustrated book and enjoyed looking at the pictures. This observation made the teacher realize the importance of helping Mack choose a book that he could read independently without frustration. A too difficult book might destroy his recently acquired interest in reading and his effort to improve.

John had selected *Robinson Crusoe*. He squinted and grimaced as he read. He told the teacher he had a headache. He said he often got a headache when he read in school. Although he said he had been to an eye doctor who told his mother there was nothing wrong with his eyes, in view of these signs of visual discomfort the teacher decided to ask the school nurse to make a follow-up of his eye examination. The teacher also recognized that John's inability to read the books that his friends were reading might account for symptoms he had observed.

These examples illustrate a few kinds of understanding that a teacher may gain from observation. They also show the limitations of observation alone; one needs additional information to interpret most observations.

Recording of teacher observations

Although most teachers' observations are not recorded, some systematic recording of the most significant student behavior is useful to the teacher, the student, the parent, and the student's next teacher.

The recording may take either of two forms: 1) dated observations of individual students or anecdotal records that are recorded and then may be collected in each child's cumulative record folder and summarized periodically or 2) a checklist. The checklist may be used for a single pupil or as a record for the entire class. A checklist may contain some blank spaces for recording additional observations or explaining items checked.

A checklist record form

A checklist type of guide to observation in the classroom may be judged by these criteria:

1 It is organized around classroom situations with which the teacher is confronted.

2   Its items refer to specific behavior that can be observed rather than to generalizations or inferences about behavior.

3   It provides space to add further observations, impressions, and insights.

4   It is selective; i.e., it does not contain so many items that it becomes unwieldy.

The following directions for using this form of record are suggested:

1   The teacher will have one of these checklist forms for each student. He will include the most significant kinds of observation that may be made in different classroom situations.

2   In each of the situations described, the teacher will record his observations of each student's performance. For example, it is Mary Jones's turn to tell about her weekend. The teacher takes Mary's checklist from the pile, listens and observes as Mary gives her report. He makes these comments on it: 'Mary spoke very clearly and distinctly. I liked the way she told about each event in her weekend in just the order in which it happened—what happened first, next, and last. You were all interested in her story, weren't you? There was one new word she used that we can all learn to pronounce correctly. . . .' As the teacher summarizes the good points and the criticisms, he makes a tally on Mary's record as follows:

Speech	*Language patterns*	*Reaction of peers*
1____Distinct, clear	1____Good organization	1____Interested

In the blank space provided, the teacher may write the word that Mary mispronounced and his impression of progress she has made.

By putting the first tally to the extreme left and the tallies for each subsequent observation a little further to the right, the teacher can get some indication of the student's progress.

In each period the teacher will not attempt to record his observations of all the students. Instead he will focus his attention on a few students and record his observations on their records. Thus, in time the teacher may systematically accumulate observations of behavior significant for reading improvement. In some instances it may be easier for the teacher to jot down his observations on a scratch pad and tally them later on the checklist.

If, as suggested, the teacher calls attention.to or asks the students to point out the individual's strengths, he will reinforce the good reading habits of the other students. If he gives instruction in an error noted, as when the teacher taught the pronunciation of a new word, the entire class profits by the analysis of one student's performance.

In addition to this immediate use, the checklist serves as a periodic appraisal of a student's progress. The teacher may go over the record with the student, who thus becomes more aware of his reading goals, the progress he is making toward them, and the practice he needs to correct certain faults or deficiencies. Such a record, passed on to the next teacher, supplies a wealth of initial understanding of the students in the new class.

Various checklists have been developed. A one-page form that is remarkably concise and at the same time cumulative and comprehensive in its coverage of significant diagnostic information was developed by Newman and is published by Science Research Associates. It includes 1) a scale of recreational reading fluency from readiness to high sixth grade, 2) a rating scale of interest in pleasure reading, 3) three estimates of voluntary reading, 4) titles of favorite books, and 5) results of academic aptitude and achievement tests.

A much more detailed checklist based on an analysis of reading skills, beginning with the readiness level and continuing with one page for each grade through sixth, is published privately by Barbe, 3124 Harriet Road, Silver Lake, Cuyahoga Falls, Ohio. Each grade level includes details on vocabulary, word analysis, comprehension, and oral reading.

As a guide to high school students' own analysis of their reading development, Ellen Thomas, Reading Consultant of the University of Chicago Practice School, has prepared a unique series of sheets that invite students to explore their educational and vocational plans as these may affect their reading performance, their purpose in coming to a reading class, their present reading interests. This first page is followed by a checklist of skills that they want to improve. Having thus set their goals, tentatively, they may obtain more information from standardized and informal tests. On the basis of their test results they list the reading areas and skills which they would like to improve. The students also estimate the amount of time they can devote to practice outside of class and other values they would like to gain from the class. This analysis is made in the form of a letter to the instructor. The students are then provided with a form having three columns: 1) skills to be improved, 2) practices to do, and 3) record of results. In the column 'Practices to Do' the teacher suggests practice material and effective ways of using it. These forms, which may be adapted to the elementary school, encourage students' initiative in planning and carrying out their own reading programs.

To aid in the diagnosis of emotionally disturbed children, Llorens *et al.* (1964) made a comprehensive list of primary, cognitive, perceptual, and motor correlates of behavior. They also included and evaluated tests used to measure these functions and suggested training procedures.

A global approach

What might be called a 'global approach' is another possible way of recording observations, plus interpretation, plus recommendations. It describes the most significant aspects rather than checking separate items.

This method is most effective when used by an experienced person, one who has gone through the process of specific analysis many times and is thoroughly familiar with the detailed guide to observation. He should also be skillful in seeing relationships and drawing inferences from the observed behavior. Such a person can sense the central factor and the related factors that are affecting the students' responses.

For example, the teacher might write about Mary Brown's oral report: 'Mary speaks clearly and distinctly. This ability and her sense of sequence in reporting her stories help her to hold the attention of the class. She likes to use new words but does not always pronounce them correctly. We shall encourage her to listen carefully to new words and to be precise in her pronunciation of them.'

Interpretation of observations

The most difficult part of the technique of observation is interpreting what one sees. For example, it is easy to observe that a poor reader wants to read aloud at every opportunity and attempts to answer questions that are too difficult for him, but what is the motive underlying this observed behavior? Is it family pressure to be an outstanding student? Desire for attention? An inaccurate self-appraisal? Or is there some other explanation?

Manifestations of inattention may indicate language difficulty, visual or auditory defects, resistance to authority, inner conflicts, lack of immediate as well as long-term goals, or failure to recognize one's need for the knowledge and skills that are being taught—to mention only some of the many possible interpretations.

Ideally, interpretation should be attempted only after a number of observations have been made, and then it should be supplemented by interviews and other sources of information. Actually, however, an experienced teacher, against the background of his accumulated impressions, often may use a single observation as the basis for giving immediate help to a student.

Concluding statement

There is no substitute for skill in observation. The understanding of students' reading development and difficulties that can be obtained by this technique is pertinent, specific, and often immediately applicable to the instruction being given.

However, the prerequisites for and the limitations of observation should be recognized. First, descriptions of typical behavior can be obtained only by a sufficient number of pertinent, systematic observations. Several observations may indicate merely a temporary deviation from the individual's usual behavior. Second, knowing that the teacher is observing may alter the behavior observed. This is all to the good if observation is a regular part of the school day and motivates the student to do his best. Third, occasionally each student may be placed in essentially the same situation, e.g. oral reading of a given paragraph, which permits comparison with other students doing the same reading task. Observation of the student under natural classroom conditions that are significant to him often elicits diagnostic information most important for practical purposes.

Other sources of information are needed to interpret the facts and to answer questions raised by observation of the students' behavior. What appears to be the same behavior may have different meanings to different students.

Although the teacher uses most of his daily observations immediately in instruction, or merely adds them to his general impression of his students, there are some items significant enough for him to record. The checklist form of record serves both as a guide to classroom observation and as a summary of information he has gained from day to day. The global or descriptive account is the more dynamic form of cumulative record; it is more effective after the teacher has become familiar with the kinds of details that may be most significant. Then he may prefer to write a brief description of the highlights of his observation and interpretation. Both types of records are of value only insofar as they are used in helping students to improve their reading. Neither should become a burden to the teacher or usurp time he might be spending in giving instruction that the student needs immediately. As the student grows older he should increasingly participate in the appraisal of his reading. Tape recordings, sound motion pictures, and video tapes make possible the most precise basis for appraisal of samples of teacher and student behavior and interaction.

There is some research evidence (Haring and Ridgway, 1967) that day-by-day observation by trained teachers who respond appropriately to the information gained may be as effective and more practical than elaborate test batteries. If generally applied, observation so used would diminish the distinction between classroom teaching and remedial teaching. Observation would then become a method of diagnosing the efficacy of teaching methods as well as the abilities, attitudes, and interests of the students.

References

ANDERSON, HAROLD H. (1939) 'The Measurement of Domination and Socially Integrative Behavior in Teachers' Contacts with Children', *Child Development*, 10, 73–89.

ANDERSON, HAROLD H. (1954) 'A Study of Certain Criteria of Teaching Effectiveness', *Journal of Experimental Education*, 23, 41–71.

CRONBACH, LEE (1960) *Essentials of Psychological Testing* (3rd ed.) New York: Harper & Row.

DE HIRSCH, KATRINA, JANSKY, JEANETTE J. and LANGFORD, W. S. (1966) *Predicting Reading Failure* New York: Harper & Row.

DRISCOLL, GERTRUDE P. (1956) *How to Study the Behavior of Children* New York: Teachers' College Press, Columbia University.

DURKIN, DOLORES (1962) *Phonics and the Teaching of Reading* New York: Teachers' College Press, Columbia University.

FLANDERS, NED A. and HAVAMARKI, SULO (1960) 'The Effect of Teacher-Pupil Contacts Involving Praise on Sociometric Choices of Students', *Journal of Educational Psychology*, 51, 65–8.

HARING, N. G. and RIDGWAY, R. W. (1967) 'Early Identification of Children with Learning Disabilities', *Exceptional Children*, 33, 387–95.

LLORENS, LELA A. *et al* (1964) 'Cognitive-Perceptual-Motor Functions', *American Journal of Occupational Therapy*, 18, 202–208.

LYTTON, H. (1967) 'Follow-up of an Experiment in Selection for Remedial Education', *British Journal of Educational Psychology*, 37, 1–9.

MOUSTAKAS, CLARK E. *et al* (1956) 'An Objective Method for the Measurement and Analysis of Child-Adult Interaction', *Child Development*, 27, 109–134.

STRANG, RUTH (1953) *The Role of the Teacher in Personnel Work* (4th ed.) New York: Teachers' College Press, Columbia University, ch. 8.

THORNDIKE, ROBERT and HAGEN, ELIZABETH (1961) *Measurement and Evaluation in Psychology and Education* (2nd ed.) New York: John Wiley & Sons, 399–421.

WITHALL, JOHN (1960) 'Research Tools: Observing and Recording Behavior', *Review of Educational Research*, 30, 496–512.

WRIGHT, E. and MURIEL M. (1959) 'Development of an Instrument for Studying Verbal Behaviors in a Secondary School Mathematics Classroom', *Journal of Experimental Education*, 28, 103–21.

3:4 The use of questions in teaching

Meredith D. Gall[1]

It is a truism for educators that questions play an important role in teaching. Aschner (1961), for example, called the teacher 'a professional question maker' and claimed that the asking of questions is 'one of the basic ways by which the teacher stimulates student thinking and learning'. Also, asking questions is one of the ten major dimensions for studying teachers' behavior in the widely used System for Interaction Analysis (Flanders, 1970).

Certainly teachers ask many questions during an average school day. A half-century ago, Stevens (1912) estimated that four-fifths of school time was occupied with question-and-answer recitations. Stevens found that a sample of high-school teachers asked a mean number of 395 questions per day. High frequencies of question use by teachers were also found in recent investigations: ten primary-grade teachers asked an average of 348 questions each during a school day (Floyd, 1960); twelve elementary-school teachers asked an average of 180 questions each in a science lesson (Moyer, 1965); and fourteen fifth-grade teachers asked an average of sixty-four questions each in a thirty-minute social studies lesson (Schreiber, 1967). Furthermore, students are exposed to many questions in their textbooks and on examinations.

Granting the importance of questions in teaching, researchers still do not know much about them. What educational objectives can questions help students to achieve? What are the criteria of an effective question and how can effective questions be identified? How can teachers' question-framing skills be improved? Until researchers find answers to questions such as these, hopes for a viable behavioral technology of teaching will remain unrealized. The purpose of this paper is to define the present state

1   The author wishes to thank Dr Walter R. Borg for his helpful suggestions and criticism during the writing of this paper.

GALL, MEREDITH D. (1970) 'The use of questions in teaching', *Review of Education Research*, 40, v, 707–20.

of research knowledge in this area and to suggest some contributions which can be made by researchers who are interested in improving the quality of classroom teaching. Although textbook and examination questions undoubtedly make a contribution to the learning process, I will limit my review for the most part to studies of spoken questions which occur during regular classroom teaching, particularly classroom discussions.

The classification of questions by type

Many researchers have attempted to describe the types of question asked by teachers. To quantify their descriptions, some have found it helpful to develop sets of categories into which teachers' questions can be classified. At least eleven classification systems have been proposed in recent years (Adams, 1964; Aschner, 1961; Bloom, 1956; Carner, 1963; Clements, 1964; Gallagher, 1965; Guszak, 1967; Moyer, 1965; Pate and Bremer, 1967; Sanders, 1966; Schreiber, 1967).

Several systems, such as Bloom's, Gallagher's, and Carner's, consist of a limited number of general categories which can be used to classify questions irrespective of context. This feature enables the researcher to investigate issues such as the different types of question emphasized in various school curricula (Pfeiffer and Davis, 1965) or in traditional or new curricula (Sloan and Pate, 1966). However, these systems are of limited utility if the researcher is interested in more detailed descriptions of questions asked in a specific context.

For detailed descriptions a classification system developed for a specific curriculum is preferable. One such system (Clements, 1964) was designed to classify the questions asked by art teachers as they talked with students about their artwork. For example, the 'suggestion-order' category includes questions such as: 'Why don't you make the hands larger?'; 'Why not put some red over here?'; 'Why don't you use freer lines?' This type of question, which occurs frequently in art classes, is not adequately described by any of the categories in the more generalized systems.

Guszak's Reading-Comprehension Question-Response Inventory is a specific classification system designed for the analysis of questions that teachers ask elementary school reading groups. The specificity of the categories is typified by the 'recognition question' category, which includes questions requiring students to locate information from the reading context (e.g., 'Find what Little Red Ridinghood says to the wolf.') In Schreiber's system for classifying social science questions, there are also a number of fairly curriculum-specific categories, such as Use of Globes (e.g.,

'Will you find Greenland on the globe?') and Stating of Moral Judgments (e.g., 'Do you think it is right to have censorship of the news?').

Most of the question-classification systems are composed almost entirely of categories based on the type of cognitive process required to answer the question. For example, in Bloom's *Taxonomy*, the question, 'What is your opinion of our present stance on the Vietnam War?' is classified an Evaluation question because it requires evaluative thinking, whereas 'What assumptions does the author make in criticizing New Deal politics?' is classified an Analysis question because it required that students engage in analytic thinking. The categories of representative question-classification systems are shown in Table 1. I have organized the categories to show similarities between the systems. It appears that Bloom's *Taxonomy* best represents the commonalities that exist among the systems.

A weakness of the cognitive-process approach to question classification is that these processes are inferential constructs. Therefore, they cannot be observed directly. Bloom (1956) acknowledged this difficulty in his statement that it is not always possible to know whether a student answered a particular question by using a high-level cognitive process, such as analysis or synthesis, or by using the relatively low-level process of knowledge recall. The question, 'What are some similarities between the Greek and American forms of democracy?' probably stimulates critical thinking in some students. However, this question may only elicit rote recall if students answer by recalling similarities they have read in a textbook.

To deal with this problem, the researcher can control the lesson material on which the teacher bases his questions. For example, he might have a sample of teachers give the same reading assignment to their students. Preferably the assignment would be on a subject new to the students. The teachers would then ask discussion questions on this assignment and the questions could be classified as recall or higher-cognitive depending on whether the answer was given directly in the assignment. Furthermore, if the researcher is studying differences between teachers in question-asking skill or is studying improvement in this skill as a result of a training program, the use of a constant lesson topic makes it possible to attribute variance in question-asking to the teachers rather than to differences in the lessons. With two exceptions (Gall, Dunning, Galassi and Banks, 1970; Hunkins, 1966, 1967), the studies reviewed here did not make use of this important control technique.

It seems evident that existing taxonomies classify questions which cover only a few important educational objectives. These are the types of questions which teachers ask to test students' recall of information and to

TABLE I. *Representative Question-Classification Systems*

| | CLASSIFICATION | | | | |
AUTHOR	*Recall*	*Analytic thinking*	*Creative thinking*	*Evaluative thinking*	*Other*
Adams (1964)	Memory	Ratiocinative (logical reasoning)	—	Evaluative	Associative, clarifying, neutral
Aschner (1961)	Remembering	Reasoning	Creative thinking	Evaluating	—
Bloom (1956)[a]	Knowledge	Analysis	Synthesis	Evaluation	Comprehension, application
Carner (1963)	Concrete	Abstract	Creative	—	—
Clements (1964)	Past experience, process recall	—	Planning	Product judgment	Present experience, rule, opening, identification, suggestion, order, acceptance
Guszak (1967)	Recognition, recall	Explanation	Conjecture	Evaluation	Translation
Pate & Bremer (1967)	Simple recall of one item, recall-choice of multiple items	Principle involved, concept analysis	Divergence	—	Determination of skills abilities (demonstrate), skills demonstration (verbal), example-singular, examples-multiple
Schreiber (1967)	Recall of facts, arranging facts in sequential order	Making comparisons, identifying supporting facts, drawing conclusions	Speculating on outcomes	Identifying main part and important parts, stating moral judgment, stating judgment based on personal experience, evaluating quality of source material, evaluating adequacy of data	Describing situations defining and clarifying information, using globes, using maps, uncovering information and raising questions for study

a In the complete system, each category is divided into sub-categories.

develop their critical thinking processes. Yet there are several other worth-while question types which are treated scantily, if at all, in existing tax-onomies: *a*) questions which cue students to improve on an initially weak response to a question ('Can you tell me a little more?'; 'What do you mean by that?'); *b*) questions which create a discussion atmosphere 'Billy, do you agree with Sue's position?'); *c*) questions which stimulate students' sense of curiosity and inquiry ('What would you like to know about this manuscript?'; 'How would you propose to find an answer to this question?'); and *d*) questions which guide students' learning of a problem-solving, behavioral or affective skill ('What do you think we do next to solve this problem?'; 'Mark, what is your response to these drawings?').

Another limitation of existing classification systems is that they were designed primarily to investigate the types of question which teachers actually use in the classroom, not the types of question which teachers should use. Researchers have shown relatively little interest in identifying effective types of questions. There have been only a scattering of opinion articles, and these have emphasized the formal characteristics of a 'good' question, e.g., clarity of phrasing, rather than the educational purposes which good questions serve.

Much of what has been learned about the merits and pitfalls of descriptive systems should provide guidance for identifying effective question types. For example, it would seem preferable to identify questions which are effective for a specific curriculum and classroom setting rather than to search for general question types. Research might be done to identify effective question types in mathematics tutoring, introducing concepts in the science curriculum, discussing controversial issues, role playing in social studies, etc., These specific question types, as compared to the categories of a general classification system such as Bloom's *Taxonomy*, would have two advantages: they would provide a more precise and possibly clearer description of what constitutes effective questioning in a particular teaching situation; and they would be more useful than general question types in training teachers to improve their classroom instruction.

Prior to defining effective types of question, the researcher needs to identify valued educational objectives in a specific setting. Once objectives are identified, the task of constructing questions which enable the student to reach each objective can be started. It would help in this task if groups of expert teachers and curriculum developers composed questions for each objective and then selected the most effective questions. In this type of research, effective question types would be defined in terms of whether or not they enabled the student to achieve desired educational objectives.

Another task for the researcher is to consider whether there are effective question sequences. Should teachers start a discussion by asking recall questions to test students' knowledge of facts and then ask higher-cognitive questions that require manipulation of these facts? This was the approach taken by Taba (1964, 1966), who attempted to identify questioning strategies that stimulate students to reflect on curriculum materials on an increasingly abstract level. In Shaver's model of Socratic teaching (1964), another type of question sequence was proposed: the teacher asks the student for a statement of his position on an issue, then asks appropriate follow-up questions to probe the student's stated position.

Further research on teachers' 'follow-up' questions is needed. Consider a typical situation which occurs in classroom discussions. The teacher asks a question such as, 'What do you think can be done to solve the problem of air pollution?'; this would be classified as a higher-cognitive question in most question-classification systems. A student answers, 'Make sure all cars and trucks have smog control devices.' Did the student really have to think to answer this question? He may have considered the problem in depth and decided that smog control is the best solution. However, it is more likely that the student is repeating a solution he has heard or read about. To really test the student's ability to think about the problem and to stimulate the development of his thinking processes, the teacher should probably ask follow-up questions such as, 'How would that solve the problem?'; 'Isn't that being done already?'; 'Is that a better solution than converting to electric or steam-powered cars?' We know very little about teachers' use of such questions in discussions. In fact, most question-classification systems do not take them into account since the systems are not concerned with question sequence. However, I suggest the hypothesis that follow-up questioning of the student's initial response has substantial impact on student learning in classroom teaching situations.

Studies of teachers' questioning practices

Educators generally agree that teachers should emphasize the development of students' skill in critical thinking rather than in learning and re-calling facts (Aschner, 1961; Carner, 1963; Hunkins, 1966). Yet research spanning more than a half-century indicates that teachers' questions have emphasized facts.

Probably the first serious study of this issue was done by Stevens (1912). She found that, for a sample of high-school classes varying in grade level and subject area, two-thirds of the teachers' questions required direct recall of textbook information. Two decades later, Haynes (1935) found that 77 per cent of teachers' questions in sixth-grade history classes called for factual answers; only 17 per cent were judged to require students to think. In Corey's study (1940), three judges classified all questions asked by teachers in a one-week period in a laboratory high school. The judges classified 71 per cent of the questions as factual and 29 per cent as those which required a thoughtful answer.

Studies conducted in the last several years indicated that teachers' questioning practices are essentially unchanged. Floyd (1960) classified the questions of a sample of 40 'best' teachers in elementary classrooms. Specific facts were called for in 42 per cent of the questions. I summed Floyd's percentages of questions in categories which appear to have required thoughtful responses from students; these accounted for about 20 per cent of the questions asked. In two other studies conducted at the elementary-school level (Guszak, 1967; Schreiber, 1967), similar percentages of fact and thought questions were asked. At the high-school level, Gallagher (1965) and Davis and Tinsley (1967) classified the questions asked by teachers of gifted students and by student teachers. More than half of the questions asked by both groups were judged to test students' recall of facts.

The findings in studies on teachers' questioning practices are fairly consistent (though in some instances there are methodological flaws such as failure to report inter-rater reliability in classification of questions and lack of clarity in the definition of question categories). It is reasonable to conclude that in a half-century there has been no essential change in the types of question which teachers emphasize in the classroom. About 60 per cent of teachers' questions require students to recall facts; about 20 per cent require students to think; and the remaining 20 per cent are procedural.

Why has the primary objective of American education, as revealed by an analysis of teachers' questions, been the learning and recall of facts? One explanation is that although higher-cognitive objectives are valued in American education, teachers need to ask many fact questions to bring out the data which students require to answer thought questions. Even though this explanation has merit, it can be argued that instruction in facts is best accomplished by techniques (such as programmed instruction) that do not require teacher intervention. The teacher's time is better spent in developing students' thinking and communication skills during discussions after the students have demonstrated an acceptable level of knowledge on a written test.

Another explanation of the research findings is that although educators have for a long time advocated the pursuit of objectives such as critical thinking and problem solving, only recently were these objectives incorporated systematically into new curricula. The relationship between curriculum change and teachers' questioning practices is illustrated in a recent study comparing teachers in the School Mathematics Study Group (SMSG) with teachers in a traditional mathematics program (Sloan and Pate, 1966). The researchers hypothesized that the two groups would differ in their patterns of questioning since the SMSG program emphasizes the objectives of inquiry and discovery. They found that, compared to the traditional math teachers, the 'new math' teachers asked significantly fewer recall questions and significantly more comprehension and analysis questions.

Sloan and Pate's study suggested the interesting hypothesis that teachers' use of fact and higher-cognitive questions is dependent on the type of curriculum materials available to them. This hypothesis could be easily tested by asking teachers to lead discussions based on different lesson topics assigned to students: for example, a poem, a traditional textbook chapter, a newspaper editorial, a film. On the basis of my own preliminary research findings, I hypothesize that teachers ask more higher-cognitive questions about primary sources, e.g., poems and newspaper editorials, than about secondary sources (most school textbooks).

Still another reason why teachers have emphasized fact questions over a half-century, as indicated in research findings, is the lack of effective teacher training programs. In their study of questions in mathematics teaching, Sloan and Pate (1966, p. 166) observed:

> Although the School Mathematics Study Group teachers' use of questions evidenced their awareness of the processes of inquiry and discovery, these processes had not been fully implemented, as shown by the fact that these teachers used so few synthesis and opinion questions that the pupils were denied the opportunity to develop inferences from available evidence.

Therefore, Sloan and Pate advocated training teachers in effective questioning practices so the objectives of the 'new math' can be realized. The issue of teacher training in questioning skills is discussed later in this paper.

Effect of teachers' questions on student behavior

Teachers' questions are of little value unless they have an impact on student behavior. Yet very few researchers have explored the relationship between teachers' questions and student outcomes.

The most important work in this area to date is the research by Hunkins (1967, 1968). The purpose of his research was to determine whether the variable of question type bears any relationship to student achievement. Two experimental groups of sixth-grade students worked daily for a month on sets of questions which were keyed to a social studies text. In one group the questions stressed knowledge; in the other analysis and evaluation questions were stressed. Question types were defined in terms of Bloom's *Taxonomy*. Hunkins found that the analysis-evaluation group earned a significantly higher score on a specially constructed post-training test than did students who answered questions that stressed knowledge. The performance of the two groups was also compared on the six parts of the test which corresponded to the six main types of question in Bloom's *Taxonomy*: the analysis-evaluation group of students did not differ from the comparison group in achievement on subtests containing knowledge, comprehension, analysis, and synthesis questions; they scored significantly higher on the subtests containing application and evaluation questions.

Before the implications of these findings are considered, some possible limitations of Hunkins' research design should be noted. First, whereas the daily sets of questions required students to write out their answers, the students responded to multiple choice questions on the post-training test. Therefore, one may question whether the achievement test provided an adequate comparison of the effectiveness of the two experimental conditions. Second, it seems a distortion of Bloom's Taxonomy to put the question types into a multiple-choice format since some types, such as evaluation questions, do not really have a 'correct' answer. In other words, practice in answering certain types of questions may affect the quality of students' responses rather than their correctness. Third, students monitored their own responses using answer sheets provided with the daily sets of questions. Teacher monitoring of at least some of the students' responses might have enhanced the differences found between the experimental conditions.

In view of these methodological limitations, the Hunkins' findings should be viewed as only suggestive. It seems to be a reasonable hypothesis for further investigation, however, that if a group of students is exposed to certain types of question and if their responses are monitored to improve their quality (rather than correctness), then they will be able to answer similar types of question better than a group of students who have not had this exposure.

In testing this hypothesis, the researcher is confronted with the problem of defining qualitative differences in student responses. This is one of the important unsolved problems in the study of teachers' questioning practices. Although much is known about higher-cognitive questions and their classification, little is known about what constitutes good answers to these questions. It seems reasonable to state, though, that responses to fact questions can be evaluated by the simple criterion of correctness, but responses to higher-cognitive questions require several criteria to measure their quality. On the basis of exploratory work on the problem I suggest these criteria as possibilities: a) complexity of the response; b) use of data to justify or defend the response; c) plausibility of the response; d) originality of the response; e) clarity of the phrasing; and f) the extent to which the response is directed at the question actually asked. It would seem reasonable to expect at least a moderate correlation between length of the response and its quality, particularly as judged by criteria a) and b). Dealing with a related problem, Corey and Fahey (1940) obtained a correlation of +.50 between judges' ratings of the 'mental complexity' of student questions and number of words in the question.

Students' questions

Some educators contend that our attention should be focused on questions asked by students rather than on teachers' questions (Carner, 1963; Wellington and Wellington, 1962). Certainly, it seems a worthwhile educational objective to increase the frequency and quality of students' questions in the context of classroom interaction. However, research findings consistently show that students have only a very limited opportunity to raise questions.

Houston (1938) observed eleven junior-high-school classes and found that an average of less than one question per class period was student-initiated. Corey (1940) recorded all talk in six junior-high and high-school classrooms for a period of one week. The ratio of student questions to total questions varied considerably between classes: in two English classes, students accounted for 1 per cent of the questions asked; seventh-grade and ninth-grade science students asked 17 per cent and 11 per cent of the questions respectively. At the primary-grade level, Floyd (1960) found that student questions were 3.75 per cent, 5.14 per cent, and 3.64 per cent of the total number of questions asked during a taped class session for samples of first-, second-, and third-grade classrooms respectively. A low incidence of student questions was also reported for high-school English classes (Johns, 1968) and for social studies classes at the elementary-school (Dodl, 1966) and senior-high-school levels (Bellack, Kliebard, Hyman and Smith, Jr., 1966).

In investigating student questions in the classroom, researchers need to undertake several important tasks. First, although it would be of interest to investigate the types of question students ask (Gatto, 1928), the more important task is to identify the types of question which students should be encouraged to ask. For example, when introducing a new topic for study, teachers should probably ask students what they want to know about it. Finley (1921) found that elementary-school students had an average of about five questions each to ask when presented with an unfamiliar animal in class. Another classroom situation in which student questions should probably be elicited occurs when a teacher has explained a new subject. Students should be queried about possible lack of understanding. In fact, one might offer the hypothesis that students encouraged to ask questions in this type of situation will learn more than a group of students deprived of this opportunity.

Another key area for educational innovation is the training of students in question-asking skills. For example, what types of question should students ask themselves when they read a poem, a social studies textbook, or a science lesson? It seems that the shaping of student questioning skills has been a neglected feature of classroom learning. There has been increasing attention given to this problem since inquiry and discovery methods of teaching became prominent, but as Cronbach (1966) and others pointed out, research and training in these methods remain limited by the failure adequately to operationalize the concept. Perhaps the approach of focusing on specific questioning skills in various classroom situations, as I did above, would provide the clarity needed to operationalize the inquiry method.

Programs to change teachers' questioning behavior

I have shown that the importance of questioning skills in teaching has been recognized by educators for more than a half-century. Yet relatively few programs have been implemented for the specific purpose of improving teachers' questioning practices. This does not mean that the need for such programs has been ignored. More than thirty years ago, Houston (1938) developed an in-service education program for the purpose of changing teachers' questioning practices. Among the techniques Houston used to effect behavioral change were group conferences, stenographic reports of each teacher's lessons, self-analysis, and supervisory evaluation. Examination of quantitative data yielded by pre- and post-training evaluations of eleven teachers indicated that most of the teachers were able to effect substantial changes in specific aspects of their questioning behavior. As a group the teachers increased the percentage of questions relevant to the purpose of the lesson from 41.6 per cent to 67.6 per cent, the percentage of student participation from 40.4 per cent to 56.1 per cent, and the percentage of questions requiring students to manipulate facts from 10 per cent to 18 per cent. There was also a reduction in a number of bothersome teaching habits such as repetition of one's questions (from 4.8 occurrences to none), repetition of students' answers (from 5.5 to .6 occurrences), answering of one's own questions (from 3.5 to .3 occurrences), and interruption of student responses (from 10.3 to 1.5 occurrences).

Recently a program was developed at the Far West Laboratory for Educational Research and Development (Borg, Kelley, Langer and Gall, 1970) to help teachers achieve similar changes in their questioning behavior. Called a minicourse, it is a self-contained, in-service training package requiring about fifteen hours to complete. The minicourse relies on techniques such as modeling, self-feedback, and microteaching (Allen and Ryan, 1969) to effect behavioral change. In a field test with 48 elementary-school teachers, the minicourse produced many highly significant changes in teachers' questioning behavior, as determined by comparisons of pre- and post-course videotapes of twenty-minute classroom discussions: increase in frequency of redirection questions (questions designed to have a number of students respond to one student's original question) from 26.7 to 40.9; increase in percentage of thought questions from 37.3 per cent to 52.0 per cent; and increase in frequency of probing questions (questions which require students to improve or elaborate on their original response) from 8.3 to 13.9. As in Houston's program (1938), there was also a reduction in frequency of poor questioning habits: repetition of one's questions (from 13.7 to 4.7 occurrences); repetition of students' answers (from 30.7 to 4.4 occurrences); and answering of one's own questions (from 4.6 to .7 occurrences). The Far West Laboratory now supports the development of about twenty additional minicourses to deal with other types of classroom teaching such as tutoring, role-playing, lecturing, and the inquiry method. Many of these courses include training in questioning skills that are appropriate to the particular teaching-learning context.

Other programs for improving teachers' questioning practices have been developed, though these have generally had more limited objectives than the programs of Houston (1938) and Borg (1970). Shaver and Oliver (1964) trained teachers in the use of questioning methods appropriate to discussion of controversial issues in the social studies. Suchman (1958) identified inquiry skills for science classes; training teachers in their use resulted in a significant increase in the number of questions asked by students. In social studies, Taba (1966) and her co-workers (1964) developed a system of teacher training centered around questioning strategies. These questioning strategies were viewed as techniques which teachers could use to develop their students' abilities in forming concepts, explaining cause-and-effect relationships, and exploring implications.

Discussion

This survey of research on questions over a fifty-year period reveals that the main trend has been the development of techniques to describe questions used by teachers in classroom practice. There is now considerable data regarding the incidence of teachers' questions and the relative frequencies with which various types of questions are asked. I expect that researchers will now turn their attention more toward the improvement of teachers' questioning practices.

Efforts to improve existing practices will probably move in several directions. First, whereas in the past researchers have developed taxonomies to describe questions which teachers ask, they need now to develop taxonomies based on types of question which teachers *should* ask. This means that increasing attention must be paid to the definition of desirable educational objectives and to the identification of questions and question sequences which will enable students to achieve these objectives. It was pointed out above that there are certain advantages to developing systems of question types which are curriculum- and situation-specific. The chief advantage is that teacher training in questioning methods is likely to be facilitated if specific rather than general types of questions are learned.

It is important that teachers' questions should not be viewed as an end in themselves. They are a means to an end—producing desired changes in student behavior. Therefore, researchers should give high priority to the tasks of identifying what these desired changes are and of determining whether new questioning strategies have the impact on student behavior which is claimed for them. Hunkins' investigation (1967, 1968), discussed above, may serve as the prototype for future research in this area. In line with the concern with student behavior, researchers should develop more programs directed at the shaping of student skills in questioning.

I would like to stress again the need for effective teacher training programs to implement desired questioning strategies in the classrooms. Sloan and Pate (1966), for example, called for strong in-service training programs in the questioning skills necessary for teaching the 'new mathematics' (SMSG) curriculum. If these programs are to succeed, they need to incorporate two important features. First, teacher training should involve not only study of questioning strategies, but also guided practice in their use. As the findings of Borg and his colleagues (1970) seem to indicate, microteaching is an effective technique for providing this practice. Second, teachers cannot be expected to learn the inquiry method or any new pedagogy if it is presented to them in vague, general, undefined terms; they can be expected to learn new methods if the methods are presented, at least in part, as sets of specific types of questions asked in specific classroom situations.

In the last analysis, the value of focusing on teachers' questions is that they are the basic unit underlying most methods of classroom teaching. If this is true, then their continued study deserves the strong support of researchers.

References

ADAMS, T. H. (1964) *The development of a method for analysis of questions asked by teachers in classroom discussion* (Doctoral dissertation Rutgers University) Ann Arbor, Mich.: University Microfilms, no. 64–2809.

ALLEN, D. and RYAN, K. (1969) *Microteaching* Reading, Mass.: Addison-Wesley.

ASCHNER, M. J. (1961) 'Asking questions to trigger thinking', *NEA Journal*, 50, 44–6.

BELLACK, A. A., KLIEBARD, H. M., HYMAN, R. T. and SMITH, F. L. Jr. (1966) *The language of the classroom* New York: Teachers' College Press, Columbia University.

BLOOM, B. S. (ed.) (1956) *Taxonomy of Educational Objectives: Handbook 1: Cognitive Domain* New York: David McKay.

BORG, W. R., KELLEY, M. L., LANGER, P. and GALL, M. (1970) *The Minicourse: A Microteaching Approach to Teacher Education* Beverly Hills, Calif.: Macmillan Educational Services.

CARNER, R. L. (1970) 'Levels of questioning', *Education*, 83, 546–50.

CLEMENTS, R. D. (1964) 'Art student-teacher questioning', *Studies in Art Education*, 6, 14–19.

COREY, S. M. (1940) 'The teachers out-talk the pupils', *The School Review*, 48, 745–52.

COREY, S. M. and FAHEY, G. L. (1940) 'Inferring type of pupil mental activity from classroom questions asked', *Journal of Educational Psychology*, 31, 94–102.

CRONBACH, L. J. (1966) 'The logic of experiments on discovery', in Shulman, L. S. and Keislar, E. R. (eds), *Learning by discovery: A critical appraisal* Chicago: Rand McNally.

DAVIS, O. L. and TINSLEY, D. C. (1967) 'Cognitive objectives revealed by classroom questions asked by social studies student teachers', *Peabody Journal of Education,* 45, 21–6.

DODL, N. R. (1966) *Pupil questioning behavior in the context of classroom interaction* (Doctoral dissertation, Stanford University) Ann Arbor, Mich.: University Microfilms, no. 66–2512.

FINLEY, C. (1921) 'Some studies of children's interests in science materials', *School Science and Mathematics,* 21, 1–24.

FLANDERS, N. A. (1970) *Analyzing teaching behavior* Reading, Mass.: Addison-Wesley.

FLOYD, W. D. (1960) *An analysis of the oral questioning activity in selected Colorado primary classrooms* (Doctoral dissertation, Colorado State College) Ann Arbor, Mich.: University Microfilms, no. 60–6253.

GALL, M. D., DUNNING, B., GALASSI, J. and BANKS, H. (1970) 'The relative effectiveness of perceptual versus symbolic modeling in a teacher training program on higher-cognitive questioning', unpublished manuscript, Far West Laboratory for Educational Research and Development, Berkeley, California.

GALLAGHER, J. J. (1965) 'Expressive thought by gifted children in the classroom', *Elementary English,* 42, 559–68.

GATTO, F. N. (1928) 'Pupils' questions: Their nature and their relationship to the study process', unpublished doctoral dissertation, University of Pittsburgh.

GUSAK, F. J. (1967) 'Teacher questioning and reading', *The Reading Teacher,* 21, 227–34.

HAYNES, H. C. (1935) 'The relation of teacher intelligence, teacher experience, and type of school to types of questions', unpublished doctoral dissertation, George Peabody College for Teachers.

HOUSTON, V. M. (1938) 'Improving the quality of classroom questions and questioning', *Educational Administration and Supervision,* 24, 17–28.

HUNKINS, F. P. (1966) 'Using questions to foster pupils' thinking', *Education,* 87, 83–7.

HUNKINS, F. P. (1967) 'The influence of analysis and evaluation questions on achievement in sixth grade social studies', paper presented at the annual meeting of the American Educational Research Association, New York.

HUNKINS, F. P. (1968) 'The effects of analysis and evaluation questions on various levels of achievement', paper presented at the annual meeting of the American Educational Research Association, Chicago.

JOHNS, J. P. (1968) 'The relationship between teacher behaviors and the incidence of thought-provoking questions by students in secondary schools', *Journal of Educational Research,* 62, 117–22.

MOYER, J. R. (1966) *An exploratory study of questioning in the instructional processes in selected elementary schools* (Doctoral dissertation, Columbia University) Ann Arbor, Mich.: University Microfilms, no. 66-2661.

PATE, R. T. and BREMER, N. H. (1967) 'Guiding learning through skilful questioning', *Elementary School Journal*, 67, 417-22.

PFEIFFER, L. and DAVIS, O. L. (1965) 'Teacher-made examinations: What kind of thinking do they demand?', *NASSP Bulletin*, 49, 1-10.

SANDERS, N. M. (1966) *Classroom questions: What kinds?* New York: Harper & Row.

SCHREIBER, J. E. (1967) *Teachers' question-asking techniques in social studies* (Doctoral dissertation, University of Iowa) Ann Arbor, Mich.: University Microfilms, no. 67-9099.

SHAVER, J. P. (1964) 'Ability of teachers to conform to two styles of teaching', *Journal of Experimental Education*, 32, 259-67.

SHAVER, J. P. and OLIVER, D. W. (1964) 'Teaching students to analyze public controversy: A curriculum project report', *Social Education*, 28, 191-4.

SLOAN, F. A. and PATE, R. T. (1966) 'Teacher-pupil interaction in two approaches to mathematics', *Elementary School Journal*, 67, 161-7.

STEVENS, R. (1912) 'The question as a measure of efficiency in instruction: A critical study of classroom practice', *Teachers College Contributions to Education*, no. 48.

SUCHMAN, J. R. (1958) *The elementary school training program in scientific inquiry* United States Office of Education Cooperative Research Project no. 216, Urbana: University of Illinois.

TABA, H. (1966) *Teaching strategies and cognitive function in elementary school children* United States Office of Education Cooperative Research Project no. 2404, San Francisco: San Francisco State College.

TABA, H., LEVINE, S. and ELZEY, F. F. (1964) *Thinking in elementary school children* United States Office of Education Cooperative Research Project no. 1574, San Francisco: San Francisco State College.

WELLINGTON, J. and WELLINGTON, B. (1962) 'What is a question', *The Clearing House*, 36, 471-2.

3:5   Asking questions

Penny Blackie

When *Language, the Learner and the School* (Barnes *et al.*), came out in 1968, I had been teaching for two years and it threw me completely. Page after page I saw, with guilty recognition, how it all applied to me. It was little comfort to know that it also applied to most other teachers I knew. For weeks I was unusually self-conscious in the classroom—everything I said seemed to ring louder in my ears and I started leaving a tape-recorder running to see how much I did actually talk. The tapes bore out my fears —I like the sound of my voice too much.

Being aware of the problem didn't help . . . enough. I became increasingly interested in the now-often quoted paradox about asking questions. When we, as adults, want to know something, we ask someone who might know the answer. In schools, when we, as adults and teachers, often (though not always) know more than our pupils, it is we who ask the questions. The answers we already know, or, even if the question is genuinely open-ended, there is a range of possible answers in our minds. There is much evidence, in *How Children Fail* (Holt, 1964) especially, to show that teachers somehow indicate to their pupils which is the right or most acceptable answer, by leaning towards it, by an inclination of the head or a particular tone of voice. In my case, this is a hypocritical acceptance of a given answer, followed shortly by a hopeful 'Anything else?' I find myself saying this time and time again. So, in fact, what we are asking children to do is to play a game called Read My Mind.

Teaching in a secondary school has made me notice that whereas the eleven- and twelve-year-olds are often prepared to ask questions, the natural curiosity and exuberance of most children dies away in the next year or two. One can only speculate about the causes for this, but at quite an

BLACKIE, PENNY (1971) 'Asking questions', *English in Education*, 5, iii, 77–96.

early age small children find their parents fobbing off their questions because they cannot cope with the interminable 'Why?' It is likely that in their first years of schooling this crushing of questions becomes more widespread until, in the setting of the more rigidly structured secondary school, teachers find the questions irritating: they are asked just as the bell goes, or there isn't time anyway—we have to get through the syllabus. Another factor that might affect this directly is the greater willingness of younger children to put themselves at risk. The adolescent will go to enormous lengths to avoid any kind of threat, whether it be making a fool of himself, or risking direct scorn and wrath or polite dismissal from his teacher. Richard M. Jones (1968) says:

> Teachers know that the proofs of well-composed and well-conducted lessons are more often found in the questions raised than in the answers given. Moreover, one has only to spend some time as a professional outsider in an elementary school to know that children will share their answers with almost anyone who asks the right questions; but they will only share their questions with their own teachers—and then only if they love them. After all, there is little risk in giving an answer, it is either right or wrong and that is usually the end of it. But to share a question is often to invite inspection of one's tenderer parts. Like other loving acts this is not something we do with strangers.

It was with great interest and something like relief that I decided to follow up a suggestion for a possible group study in Bulletin 7 of the 'Children as Readers' project (N.A.T.E. 1971):

> One of the more disappointing aspects of the traditional classroom is the relatively small number of questions asked by the pupils themselves; and these probably become even fewer as children move into adolescence. This has two implications for any study of children's questions: it raises the problem of what determines the rate of question-asking; and it makes it impossible to collect children's questions just by recording ordinary lessons. Thus it becomes necessary to design situations that positively encourage children to ask questions—both because the habit of questioning is educationally valuable to children, and for research purposes.
>
> What is required is a collection not just of children's questions, but of questions gathered in a prearranged sequence of teaching.

The 'Children as Readers' Panel, with the approval of Dr W. P. Robinson (Director of the Schools Council Project on 'Children's Questions'), then suggested a procedure for following up this idea. I have used this procedure (slightly adapted for convenience) with a first-year class, two third-year classes, a fifth form and more frequently with the Sixth Form 'A' level group. In describing some of the work I should like to stress that any conclusions or hypotheses are very tentative as I have only worked on this for one term and have several tapes which I have not yet examined very closely.

After some preliminary work I thought that the procedure for 'Training Pupils to ask Questions about Poems' was particularly suitable for the Sixth Form. I teach in a girls' comprehensive school in a rural area, and although we have a group of twenty-three in the Lower Sixth taking 'A' level English, few of them will go on to university and only one or two to read English. Many of the students might be included in what is loosely termed the 'New' Sixth Form, in that it is not important for their future careers that they pass 'A' level but they either want to, or are required to, follow an 'A' level course. For this reason we try to make our 'A' level course as flexible as possible—set books are chosen to fit into themes and we have lectures, play-readings, poetry readings, seminars, smallish tutorial groups twice a week and a good deal of individual work based on worksheets[1]. The tutorial groups range from six to nine students. We have been studying the theme of 'War' with the Henry IV plays, Graves, *A Farewell to Arms* and war poets including, recently, Wilfred Owen. Because of the departure of a member of the English department, I found myself with three Lower Sixth tutorial groups all studying Owen. Much as I like his poetry, I was somewhat daunted by the prospect of six sessions a week, two with each group. Therefore, to experiment with the

---

1 Since worksheets are another way of asking questions, it might be worth saying a word about those we use. The idea of the worksheets for our Sixth Form course is that they should provide an occasion for writing—it is always stressed that although there are certain minimum requirements, the students are free to use or reject the worksheets as they wish. As long as they do write, they are invited to formulate their own questions or write about any aspect of the text or theme that interests them. However, few of them take this opportunity, so we try to provide a variety and range of questions. For example in a worksheet on *The Rainbow* by D. H. Lawrence, the students are required to prepare notes for discussion on a few questions such as:

Examine the three major symbols of the novel. Make notes on their significance and effects:
the arch (pp. 65, 202)
the rainbow (pp. 97, 202, 496)
the cathedral (pp. 200+, 456)
(page references are always a guide).

Also, along with a fairly wide choice of other questions there are traditional 'A' level-type essay questions, and also questions like:

Lawrence is very concerned with the place of woman, both in her relationships with men and in society as a whole. Examine this concern. You might like to compare the position he takes with Women's Lib., but find out about Women's Lib. first (there are newspaper articles available if you ask for them, or read *The Female Eunuch* by Germaine Greer). (Pp. 9, 11, 19, 334, 343, 353, 406).

'Children as Readers' suggestion of asking questions about poems seemed a good way of tackling the problem.

This account will deal with three or four lessons (of thirty-five minutes each) with two of the groups. Group 1 contains six students, grouped according to their subject choices, containing only one student likely to go to university. Four students in the group have very little chance of passing 'A' level. Group 1 started by splitting into two groups of three, with copies of two poems by Owen: 'Shadwell Stair' (an early poem) and 'The Promisers' (written shortly before Owen's death).[2] They were asked to look at and talk about the poems, either or both, and set out to formulate questions about them. The stipulation was made that the questions should be a) questions to which they did not already know the answers, and b) questions to which they would *like* to know the answers. They took one lesson to formulate their questions, to be followed by a discussion by both sub-groups of all the questions.

Group 1 Questions

Sub-group A:

1 Where/what is Shadwell Stair? Is it a real place or is it somewhere imaginary?
2 What is the point of 'Shadwell Stair'? He is trying to say something, but what?

Sub-group B:

3 Where or what is Shadwell Stair?
4 Is it a ghost or memory or what?
5 What does 'and after me a strange tide turns' mean?

(At all stages I shared with the students the approach to this work as an experiment, and at appropriate moments we had very full 'post mortem' discussions [to which I shall refer later], quite separate from the work itself, about what was happening to them and how and what they were learning.)

The next lesson the questions were put on the blackboard and the two groups discussed them all while I acted as an impartial Chairman. My explicit aim and intention was to act as Chairman, not as a teacher and not to intervene unless it was absolutely necessary. As will be seen to some extent from the transcripts, I find this extremely difficult to do. The transcript of Group 1 that follows is made from detailed notes as the

2 For the text of 'Shadwell Stair' see Appendix, p. 377.

students were not happy about recording it. (I did not think to identify speakers at that time.)

Group 1—the whole lesson (from notes)[3]

Teacher: Which questions are most important?
Student: 1 and 5.
No response
Teacher: Well, if it's real ... ?
Student: Hotel stairs.
Student: It might be coming up from an embankment.
General agreement
Silence
Teacher: What time of day is it?
Student: Evening.
Long silence
Teacher: What sort of mood is he in?
Student: Reflective.
Student: Pensive.
Pause
Teacher: Why does he go out?
Student: To think about something.
Pause
(This part of the transcript took ten minutes and was very slow)

a Teacher: (with some frustration) I refuse to barrage *you* with questions. Start talking through your questions.
Student: Why does he go out every night?
Student: Possibly he's a tramp.
Student: In the third stanza it says 'always'—gives the idea that he *lives* there—and 'I walk' as if it *always* happens.
Student: Is he waiting for something or somebody?
Student: What does he do during the day?
Student: Perhaps he's escaping from some world ... wants to be alone.
Pause
Teacher: What about the last two lines? What are the 'crowing syrens'?

bi Student: Work syrens?
Student: Bombing syrens?
Rest: No.
Student: When the rest of life wakes up he disappears 'like a ghost'. Perhaps he can't stand the daily life.
Student: If it's a person why does he call himself a ghost?
Student: He might be comparing ...
Student: If it's a ghost, it can be a shadow ...
Student: Do you think he's mad?

3   The letters *a* to *j* will be referred to later in detailed comment.

bii Student: We still don't know what he's doing?
 c Student: Someone suggested he was waiting.
   Student: Why the last line?
   Student: Perhaps inspiration only comes at night?
   Student: What is 'the other ghost'?
 di Student: That part of his life is finished.
   Student: Can't be.
dii Student: Perhaps the part of life he doesn't want to know about is during the day?
   Student: Is he asleep all day?
   Student: There must be two ghosts.
   Student: Which is the other ghost?
   Student: Look at the notes, it says 'For "crowing syrens" in the last line but one, "morning hooters" is written in another version'.
   Student: Night has put a stop to people working on ships. Everything is still except for him waiting.
 e (After this, four out of five students thought Shadwell Stair was a real place. All thought they hadn't got anywhere—yet the first four questions had been answered after a fashion.)
   Teacher: Let's sum up: Where is it? [Bank of Thames].
                What is it? [Steps leading up from embankment].
                A real place? [Yes].
   Student: Couldn't it be imaginary?
   Pause
   Teacher: Therefore we have answered 1 and 5. Have we answered 2?
   Students: No.
   Teacher: Have we answered 6?
   Students: Yes—he is not a ghost or a memory.
   (One student disagrees.)
   Student: He is a troubled man out walking.
   Teacher: Let's look at question 2.
   Student: In the morning he has to live like others, at night he is someone else.
   Long silence
 f Teacher: Why is it more difficult to answer question 2? What is it about the question.
   Student: In question 1 there is more to go on.
   Student: Greater possibilities.
   Student: This drift . . . becomes a thought in his mind . . . other things are definite . . . We won't know how his mind works . . . we can think but we can't know.
   Student: Yeah . . . we can't generalise.

g {
Teacher:	Can we imagine it? Can we each interpret it our own way?
Silence	
Teacher:	What will affect the way we interpret it?
Student:	The mood you're in.
Student:	Whether you've done it yourself.

h Student: Yeah ... your past experience.

The next week we talked about 'The Promisers'. In fact I am only going to deal with 'Shadwell Stair' in detail, but include this linking piece:

j Sue:	If he's dead, at night, the ghost comes back when it's dark and then it links up with 'Shadwell Stair'.
Jeni:	Yes it does, he's waiting for something.
Faith	The man in 'Shadwell Stair' is always out at night.
Liz:	He's been expecting him all day.

BELL (for end of lesson)

Teacher:	What about the other questions? (on 'The Promisers') Are they important?
Jeni:	No, not really.
Teacher:	Why not?
Jeni:	We seem to have got at the poem more.
Teacher:	Which parts?
Jeni:	The bits that were puzzling us.

Group 1 find it difficult to talk. After the first stultifying ten minutes up to (*a*), it became much easier, because I abdicated my role of impartial Chairman and took over the habitual role of the teacher, i.e. choosing or directing questions to act as starting points. More of this later. Looking at contrasting questions helped (I certainly wouldn't have thought to ask whether 'Shadwell Stair' was an imaginary place) and we would not have had *this* discussion without that question. The choice of the question raises important points because it appears that the teacher does not always choose the question the students would most like to know or talk about.

In our post-mortem discussion, the group said that if I had gone on asking the questions they would have been silent (as indeed they were at the beginning) or would have given monosyllabic answers, often using the opt-out 'I don't know'. As they became more relaxed as a group, the answers became fuller, although it was noticeable how short the answers still were. It would have taken us longer perhaps to get round to the purposeful and insightful observations, but I am sure that this is because a measure of exploratory talk had already taken place and had an important function for the students' learning. Sue had been away for the formulation of the questions, and came into the session feeling it was all rather strange. She thought she wouldn't 'catch on, but it was better than I expected—I didn't feel I'd missed anything'.

I haven't space to discuss the talk about 'The Promisers' in detail, but this was even more useful and relaxed. I should like now to take up some specific points marked *a* to *j* on the transcript.

a This sort of statement might normally be expected to have the opposite effect on a group than that of making them talk more freely. The only reason why I think it did not have this dampening effect is that in four previous tutorials I had opted out of the discussion completely because of their reluctance to talk to each other. Each student had chosen a poem and led discussion on it, and therefore this statement was what they had come to expect of me at this time.

bi to *bii* At first sight this appears to be a series of unconnected thoughts with no-one listening to anyone else or taking up points that are made. There is certainly none of the sort of organized sequence that a teacher might have encouraged when taking an active role. However, this may be a very necessary kind of 'talking around' the question, exploring through talk.

c This is the first indication that any student has actually taken any notice of what has already been said, but even this is not pursued.

di and *dii* Both of these are the sort of statement that are just bordering on the verge of an insight into the poem. A teacher who did not have my aims in this situation would probably have followed up both these points, making more of them. In this kind of talk, how can we ensure that important observations are not left floating? Does it matter if they are? Perhaps George Kelly helps here:

> The confirmation of our local predictions, equivocal as that may be, is about the most we can expect. No, there is one thing more, vastly important —our ability, while alive, to pose further questions by our invested behaviour, and thus to enter the stream of nature's fluid enterprise as an entity in our own right (Maher, 1969, p. 39).

e The tentative nature of the talk and the lack of a very clear directive had led the students to think that they had achieved nothing, whereas in fact they had had some purposeful discussion and had certainly answered some of their questions. Once they became used to this sort of working, it might be reasonable to think that they might explore certain points more deeply because they thought they were getting somewhere and achieving something positive.

f Question 2 is a much larger question than the others, and this has affected the group's ability to handle it profitably. They should, with practice, be able to work towards tackling questions like it more successfully.

g Teachers often use this method of asking questions—re-phrasing the question when there is no immediate response. Students don't appear to do it in their own questioning—what effect does it have?

h Here the student is coming to terms with an important way of approaching literature. She is making explicit the realisation that one's own experience affects one's interpretation of literature and from that follows the corollary that one's experience of literature in some way changes, as Kelly puts it, 'one's perception of himself and his world' (Maher, 1969, p. 39). This seems to be continued from what they were saying earlier, and not to be entirely due to the teacher's question.

i This lesson a week later shows the link the group made after their discussion on the questions about 'The Promisers'. Here, two important things seem to be happening—the first part of their talk is more confident and assertive once they have understood what this method of working is all about (they decide the priorities); and they are also making the point that they are tackling the bits that puzzle *them*, not the parts that the teacher would necessarily have emphasised or thought they ought to know.

Group 2 consists of nine students, who although they are also grouped according to their other subjects at 'A' level, contain most of the really able students. At least four will probably go on to university, three to colleges of education and only one is likely to have any real difficulty passing 'A' level English. I had taught this tutorial group all through the year (and several of them for four years previously) and knew them very well. They had had no difficulty up till now in talking freely and openly.

Group 2 started asking questions about three other poems by Owen—'The Show', 'Mental Cases' and 'Spring Offensive'. The questions, I was interested to see, were very different from those of Group 1 on 'Shadwell Stair' and 'The Promisers'. I did not know why. Was it because the poems were intrinsically of a different nature? Were three poems too many? Was it because these students were more able? (Although they had the option to talk about one or two poems, all three sub-groups talked about all three poems.) The first full group discussion on 'The Show' was a disaster—we all ended up knowing far less about the poem than we had to start with, and we were all thoroughly confused. When we discussed why this was in a post-mortem, we started to analyse the questions.

We developed the categories of a) imagery; b) semantics; c) whole poem —background. Out of eighteen questions, ten were category a), five were category b) and three were category c). At the time I did not comment on this, but we all decided that to pursue these poems would do more harm than good. Therefore it was in this rather dispirited and muddled frame of mind that Group 2 came on to 'Shadwell Stair' and 'The Promisers'. Instead of having three groups of three as we had had before, this time we had one group of three and one of six. The larger group recorded their discussion, and the full group discussion of 'Shadwell Stair' was also recorded.

Group 2 Questions

Sub-group A (three students):
1 Who is the ghost?
2 Where is Shadwell Stair? In London, but what is it?
3 What do the last two lines mean?

Sub-group B (six students):
4 What was his job?
5 What does 'after me a strange tide turns' mean?
6 What does the last line mean?

(The similarity in the questions between sub-group and sub-group and, in fact, between group and group does not need labouring—but would I, preparing that poem to teach, have asked those questions?)

Here follow certain extracts from the transcript of the full group discussion on 'Shadwell Stair', which I feel have interesting points to offer.

Group 2—extract A of lesson transcript

Talking about Question 1:
Teacher: (summing up) So, it's this person anyway who looks like a ghost because he's seen from a distance, but who is he do you think?
Sue: A watchman.
Teacher: A watchman?
Several: Mmm.
Long pause
Teacher: A night watchman? What an interesting idea. What do you think of that? I never thought of that. . . . Go on.
Susan: We talked about it last week . . . being a watchman.

Teacher: What, among yourselves? Yes, of course, Vicki wasn't here and
I wasn't here. You talked about it yourselves. Margaret wasn't
here either.
Pause—followed by discussion about absence
Teacher: So you decided he was a watchman did you?
Susan: We talked a lot about it and thought he probably could be . . .
Marion: Because he goes *through* the slaughter-house and not round it
and he'd . . .
Teacher: Oh, yes . . .
Marion: He's just in one part all the time.
Yvonne: Stays in one place . . . 'where I watch *always*'.
Teacher: Yes . . . 'where I watch always'.

I am particularly interested in this piece of talk for two reasons. First, at
the time, I felt very excited about this idea (the night watchman) and the
detail with which its exponents tried to convince us. I no longer felt
myself to be in the role of the Chairman, nor did I feel remotely like a
teacher, but was with them as a member of the group. (The intrusiveness
comes out as excitement on the *tape* although I realise that it is not so
evident from the words of the transcript.) Although we were discussing a
minor point in the poem (and it was quite probably an incorrect assumption to make about the 'ghost'), the teacher here was clearly a learner in
every sense as much as any other member of the group. If the teacher can
be seen to be learning with the group this must have important effects on
the atmosphere and relationships within the group. By extending the
discussion on Question 1 in this way, we partly answered Question 4.

Secondly, the extract makes me feel simultaneously ashamed and interested. When I played the tape of the group formulating their own
questions, I found that I had not remembered participating in that discussion right at the end when I returned to take away the tape recorder.
In fact, the tape shows that we talked, then, about the watchman and
that I had tentatively suggested framing a question on that idea as the
group was puzzled about it. Yet a week later, when the question arose,
I felt I was genuinely learning something and had no recollection of the
previous conversation. Nor, from their tone, had the group remembered
that I had been there. This has implications for learning—possibly self-
evident ones. The mood and attitude of the learner directly affects how
much he retains. On the first occasion, I had felt like an intruder in their
group discussion and was loath to be drawn in: I therefore somehow shut
out the part I had played in their formulation of that question. What implications does this have for how children learn—or don't learn?

Group 2—extract B

Teacher: What do the last two lines mean? Are you happy about them?

Vicki: Well, I can get the bit when he's the night watchman and he's tired when morning comes and his work ends and he goes home to sleep and the ordinary people come out to do their ordinary work . . . you know, in the day time . . . normal, more or less . . . and he has to go back to sleep; that's the wrong way round isn't it, for human beings who should sleep at night . . . but I can't, I still can't see the ghost—'another ghost' fits in . . .

(never resolved)

* * * * * *

(In answer to the question 'Who is the ghost?')

Yvonne: Well, I looked at it like this, like down there at night and anybody watching from a fence, that sort of thing, would only see sort of shadows, a dark thing moving and wouldn't be able to identify it really, so he's just got a ghost-like appearance.

These pieces are by far the longest speeches that were made in a tape that lasts twenty-five minutes. It is worth noting that both of them are the sort of exploratory talk that tries to build up a context in which the poem might fit. The West Suffolk 'Children as Readers' group has been studying transcripts of tapes of children talking about poems when the teacher is not present. In two tapes of eleven-year-olds, the children use this technique of building up a context much more often and it does help them to see how the poem might work. Why, with seventeen-year-olds, is there so little of it?

Group 2—extract C

Teacher: (as Chairman) Right, then, what does 'after me a strange tide turns' mean?

Yvonne: Could it mean when a ship goes past and sends a sort of tidal wave type thing as he turns away to go back home?

Teacher: In what sense 'turns' and 'tide'? You mean literally?

Yvonne: It's the only thing I could see clearly.

Carmel: I don't think the tide's turning literally . . . on the whole it's a 'strange tide' . . . in his mind.

Long pause

Teacher: Well . . . yes . . . well, let's carry on with that idea.

Long pause

This extract raises a point we have discussed earlier. Carmel is making a significant and insightful observation which is not taken up by any of the others. After her interjection, made very quietly and hesitantly, there is a long and unresponsive pause. The teacher, unable to resist the potential of a comment like this, tries to get the group to consider it still further; but within the brief of acting as an impartial chairman, insistence on it cannot be justified. Therefore, the insight is not pursued and all discussion of this point collapses. How can this be overcome? (Should it be?)

Group 2—extract D

Teacher: Do you feel happy with the poem now looking at it like that?
All: Yes.
Vicki: What do you think 'dolorously' means though?
Teacher: Anybody? Dolorously?
Susan: Grief.
Teacher: Something to do with grief, sadness, very depressed, yes. Well, I think this is very interesting you know, because we've spent now three, some people have spent four sessions on these two poems and certainly with *this* poem ['Shadwell Stair'—we hadn't yet discussed 'The Promisers'] I think we wouldn't have got anywhere near where we've got if we hadn't been working in this method? What do you think?
Jane: Mm.
Pause
Teacher: Because, let's face it, you thought of things which I didn't think of, and if you, if I had been asking the questions I would have been asking questions of things that *I* was thinking about whereas you were asking questions that *you* were thinking about . . . right?
Yvonne: Yes.
Teacher: It never occurred to me perhaps to say 'What is his job?' whereas you formulated that question because you had talked about what his job was which confirms me in my belief that half of the time, probably all of the time, I am asking the wrong questions.
Long pause
Teacher: What do you think?
Reflective pause
Teacher: What do you feel about this asking questions? Do you feel sceptical about it or do you think you've learnt something? Do you think it's a useful thing to do?
Several: Yes.
          Mmm/Yeah.

Teacher: Is it?

Susan: I was a bit muddled at first but we've got the result now. I thought, you know . . . the first couple of times we were thinking differently . . .

BELL

Teacher: Yes, I'm very interested in this you see because as a group you have not liked doing this at all, or up till now perhaps; I don't know if you even like doing it now but at least you feel a sense of achievement . . . or do you?

Several: Mmm.

Teacher: Does everybody?

Several: Yes . . . I do . . . Mm.

Teacher: But I sense that you didn't until now. And I certainly didn't with you till now. Right? With the other groups, particularly one group I'm thinking about, they felt it was important right from the start, very exciting . . . and they felt it was a new way of looking at things and felt very satisfied the very first time they did it. Now I wonder if we can account for at all why you took such a long time.

Pause

I really don't know the answer. I'm just wondering about this . . .

Yvonne: I don't think we've . . . *I've* never disliked doing it.

Teacher: You didn't dislike doing it?

Yvonne: No.

Teacher: (to the rest) Did you?

Sandra: I didn't mind.

Teacher: You felt indifferent?

Several: Yes.

Teacher: All of you?

Marion: We had to start off without any questions whereas usually we start off with something to work on.

Teacher: What, from me?

Marion: Yes.

Teacher: Did you find starting off, then, very difficult?

All: Yes.

Carmel: We've got to think what to look at first.

Teacher: Yes. Well, in that case, do you think you've progressed because the questions you've asked in the first lot of poems ('Mental Cases', 'The Show' and 'Spring Offensive') were in fact very particular questions? They were all sort of imagery or semantic questions. And remember that we talked about this on Monday [3rd session] that it wasn't until you started finding questions on *these* poems [nearly all category (c) questions] that you started looking at the key parts of the poem . . .

Student: Mmm.

Teacher: And it's on your own (I mean I hope I didn't point this out to you, I spotted it at the beginning and was a bit worried about your kind of questions . . . which is in fact why I got you to categorise them but I don't think that at the time I drew any conclusions from it, did I?)

Student: No.

Teacher: Until after you'd done those questions. Now somehow on your own you got these questions which were what was needed to break it open, which I think is very interesting.

I am not at all happy about the intrusive role played by the teacher here. In explanation I must point out that this whole conversation took place in three minutes at the end of the last lesson before school examinations, and in the knowledge that there would be no opportunity to come back to it for three weeks. This is not offered as an excuse because I feel very conscious of its limitations—for example, many of the affirmative mutters could simply be the sort of agreement one finds in polite society. The reason for bringing the extract in at all at this stage is to point out how seriously I took the factor of awareness in what was happening. I wanted the students to be critical and analyse what was happening to them in this situation. It also reveals a misunderstanding on my part—in the earlier work when we had achieved little, I had been disappointed and thought the group shared this feeling. They obviously didn't, at least not to the same extent. Possibly this more positive viewing of events by the students happens more than we think it does. Sometimes teachers are disappointed in lessons that students may have found more rewarding.

However, the key point is made by Marion when she says, 'We had to start off without any questions', and by Carmel when she says, 'We've got to think what to look at first'. This has been exactly the situation found to exist in the transcripts of the tapes of younger children studied by the West Suffolk 'Children as Readers' group. There, we found that there is either a panic response, where the only way out is to examine bits of the poem in isolation (as Group 2 did in their earlier work on 'The Show') or a more ordered response where the group talks through the problem slowly and carefully, not feeling threatened if they cannot reach immediate conclusions. In 'Shadwell Stair' and 'The Promisers', the questions were much more 'background' questions than 'meaning' questions in the sense of merely pertaining to imagery or semantics.

General observations

Group 1, ostensibly the weaker group which had always had difficulty in talking easily, coped much better at first with this work. Why? Does the size of the group affect this? Or their relationship with the teacher? (I had worked with Group 2 for a year, and Group 1 for six weeks.)

All the tapes show horrifyingly and abundantly clearly that I tend to pause for far too short a time between question and answer, or statement and follow-up. The pressure for someone to say something (*anything?*) leads to embarrassed and uncomfortable silence which might account for the rather slow and dead response in the first part of Group 1's discussion. Worse still, this anxiety to have someone talking cuts down the opportunity for exploratory thought and talk. This is shown to be crucial in the tapes made of the groups discussing alone, where points are often discussed slowly and thoughtfully with many long, relaxed pauses. This carries implications for all forms of teaching and Douglas Barnes in his latest work is further emphasising this need for exploratory talk (N.A.T.E., 1971)—it is depressing to find that one makes too few allowances for it, even when trying consciously to opt out of the role of teacher.

Many times in the tapes of full group discussion I find that I repeat the students' contributions. Why is this? Is it necessary for reinforcement or consolidation or reassurance (mine or theirs), or is it for the benefit of the tape recorder? A more serious possibility – does this repetition destroy the students' own language, especially if the teacher paraphrases their contributions?

Is there any pattern in the initiation of responses after a pause? If the pause is uncomfortable *and* too short, it is usually the teacher who interrupts it. If a student assumes this role, does it happen in the same way as when a teacher interrupts? If the pause is not threatening, what is the nature of the initiation of the next point? I know little about this.

There are places where the teacher could (and normally would?) help by providing information, but this does not occur here because of the impartiality of the teacher's role. For example, a copy of the *A to Z* (which most of our students, living in Suffolk, don't know) would have told them where Shadwell Stair was. By not having recourse to an authority, in the shape of person or book, they worked it out for themselves and I feel sure that this was of greater educational value in the end. However, it is important that this authority (where it exists) is eventually recognised and that we don't rely only on guess-work. I did, in fact, show both groups where Shadwell Stair was on the map after they had reached their conclusions. Points which did not come out in full group discussion sometimes do in the smaller sub-groups; e.g. in one full discussion the assumption was made that 'Shadwell Stair' must be a war poem since Owen wrote war poetry, and the fact that 'Shadwell Stair' is an early poem was not raised. However, in one of the Group 1 sub-groups, this very point was discussed fully by some of the students with references to technique to back up their conclusions. The teacher might have pointed out this fact in a traditional lesson—here again the students work it out for themselves, a fact which was not immediately apparent until the tape of their own discussion was played. All these processes take a great deal of time. In a normal study of Owen, a poem like 'Shadwell Stair' might be lucky if it were discussed for one thirty-five minute session. *In fact, this work in both groups took four times as long as this.*

Asking questions of themselves and each other seems to ensure that the questions discussed are those the students really want to know about, rather than those the teacher might think they want/ought to know about, although usually one could expect certain questions to straddle both choices. This is not merely a question of relationship with the teacher – in many cases the students did not themselves know what questions they would like to ask until they had discussed the poems at some length.

Certain levels of enquiry do not seem to be satisfactorily achieved with this method. Insights are not thoroughly pursued, and sometimes seemingly trivial data overshadow the key points. However, I feel reluctant to do more than state this as a problem at this stage. The work the Leeds 'Children as Readers' group has done points to the possibility that this 'sorting-out' process may be a necessary stage for students working on their own. Furthermore, more practice in this kind of independent work might well lead to a deepening response to the real insights that occur.

I throw out questions and problems deliberately, and do not attempt to attach weight to the few conclusions I draw. Carried out as a serious research project, the whole problem of children asking questions will be sure to raise important implications for teaching. I do not pretend to do that here, but simply raise a few points which I found to be interesting in a very limited study.

Appendix

SHADWELL STAIR

I am the ghost of Shadwell Stair.
  Along the wharves by the water-house.
  And through the dripping slaughter-house,
I am the shadow that walks there.

Yet I have flesh both firm and cool,
  And eyes tumultuous as the gems
  Of moons and lamps in the lapping Thames
When dusk sails wavering down the pool.

Shuddering the purple street-arc burns
  Where I watch always; from the banks
  Dolorously the shipping clanks
And after me a strange tide turns.

I walk till the stars of London wane
  And dawn creeps up the Shadwell Stair.
  But when the crowing syrens blare
I with another ghost am lain.

WILFRED OWEN

From *The Collected Poems of Wilfred Owen*. Reprinted by permission of
Chatto and Windus Ltd.

References

BARNES, D., BRITTON, J. and ROSEN, H., and the L.A.T.E. (1968 rev. edn, 1971)
    Language, the Learner and the School Harmondsworth: Penguin Educa-
    tion.
HOLT, JOHN (1964) *How Children Fail* New York: Pitman.
JONES, RICHARD N. (1969) *Fantasy and Feeling in Education* London: Uni-
    versity of London Press.
MAHER, BRENDAN (1969) *Clinical Psychology: the Selected Papers of George
    Kelly* New York: John Wiley.
N.A.T.E./Schools Council Project (1971) 'Children as Readers', Bulletin 7.
N.A.T.E. (April 1971) from a talk to the Projects Commission Annual Con-
    ference on 'Language across the Curriculum'.

3:6 Improvement in the use of questions

William H. Burton

The results of early investigations of the teacher's use of questions somewhat shocked educational leaders. Teachers were found asking regularly 150 questions per class hour. In a class of twenty-two pupils, one was questioned twice in two weeks, whereas a classmate was called on eleven times in the same period. In a small class of thirteen, one pupil was questioned four times, whereas another was called upon eighteen times. These facts should not have shocked those who discovered them. They evidently do not shock thousands of so-called practical teachers, since the practices described are in common use. And why not? As long as the aim of education is believed to be the mastery of content, the memorization of masses of unrelated, fragmentary facts, a barrage of minute fact questions is a natural and legitimate procedure. As long as the school is not concerned with causes of failure, nor with adaptation to individual differences, accidental and uneven distribution of questions will be found.

In a recent investigation (soon to be published) 2600 tape recordings were made of class sessions in over forty rooms. In one room only, were students asked thought questions! Students were clearly trying to formulate their own conclusions and reactions, to figure out answers, to use various sources, to critically evaluate. In the other thirty-nine rooms, impossible though it seems, the questions were all similar to: 'What did the book say about this?' 'What can you remember about this?' Other types of questions, or pupil response, did not appear. The criticism is again, not altogether of the teachers, but of the institutions which trained them.

When the aim of education is conceived not as memorization of fact but as the development of complex controls of conduct—understandings, attitudes, appreciations, skills, and special abilities—a wholly different technique of questioning becomes imperative. A questioning technique

BURTON, WILLIAM H. (1962) 'Improvement in the use of questions', *The Guidance of Learning Activities* Appleton-Century-Crofts, 436–47.

suitable to the older method of learning cannot develop pupil judgment, independence in study, suspension of judgment, or abilities to analyze and discriminate.

Sound conception of aim: good general education necessary for improvements of questioning

Butler calls attention sharply to the error of earlier writers on questioning. They endeavoured to improve questioning by improving the wording, the form, the mechanics—that is, the technique. The *chief* weakness lies, however, not in the technique but in the teacher's conception of the purpose or aim. If his aim is pupil mastery of facts, then his rapid-fire questioning technique cannot be condemned. It is well fitted to his aim. To improve questioning, the teacher's knowledge of aims must be improved. A *secondary*, allied weakness is lack of knowledge of the mental processes of learning. A *third* important weakness is often found in the teacher's own lack of general education and intellectual interest. Teachers cannot ask questions which lead the child to develop values or appreciations if they have never achieved values or appreciations of their own. Individuals who have not read critically and endeavored to interpret a number of conflicting statements cannot ask interpretive questions. The writer recently observed a high school teacher stumble through an atrociously incompetent lesson in modern literature. Later in conversation the teacher quite casually said that she had not had time for several years to read any of the books 'on the list'. No wonder her questions designed to guide pupils in evaluation, in discrimination, and toward appreciations were peculiar!

Butler's (1939) blunt indictment is worth repeating:

> When we say that a teacher's questions are poor, we actually mean that her knowledge and thinking are poor. Why not be honest and call a spade a spade? We endeavor to do everything by techniques; on the contrary the source responsible for the weakness should be strengthened and invigorated. . . .
>
> It is essential that beginning teachers and experienced teachers realize the importance of developing their own minds before their teaching can be improved. The person who has ideas, thoughts, different viewpoints, notions of genuine values, and real purposes and aims in mind will ask questions in keeping with profitable achievement without seeking a mechanical clue in the

specific words or forms in framing questions. The purpose of the question, rather than its form or wording, is the all-important factor. A thought question is a thought question regardless of the vocabulary used. Purposes pull in words needed to give the purpose proper expression (pp. 195, 197).

This is excellent. Nevertheless, considerable assistance can be given to teachers about wording and form after purposes have been clarified. To this we will turn later.

Good native ability to think and teaching experience are necessary for improvement of questioning

As was said of the socialized techniques in the section on the recitation, no one can tell another how to concoct good questions. Advice almost reduces itself to the equivalent of telling students and teachers to lift themselves by their boot straps! Expert or even passable questioning and the ability to lead discussion by means of questions is greatly affected by native ability and by experience. The actual development of the art of questioning is one of the most difficult and, oddly enough, one of the most neglected problems in teaching. It remains a constant problem for many good teachers. Good questioning requires the ability, native or acquired, to think quickly and easily while facing a class, to shift and change as thought progresses, and to phrase questions in clear and unambiguous terms.

The teacher must also be able to sense quickly the causes of misinterpretation of his questions. For every curious answer, 'schoolboy howler', or simple misinterpretation, there is good reason in the mind of the pupil. The ability to direct thought by questioning is one of the most valid proofs of teaching skill known. Through it all, the teacher has to move with the thought of the group, guiding but not dominating.

These requirements puncture in some measure the pleasant fiction that the slow but efficient thinker can, in the end, do anything that the quick person can. A slow thinker, no matter how efficient and conscientious, will always have difficulty with a class of normal pupils. The quiet, retiring, scholarly young person who often goes in for teaching so often turns out to be a misfit because he lacks these very requirements.

Planning is clearly demanded. Few persons are gifted enough to be able without some previous preparation to follow the thought of a group, to shift and turn quickly enough, to guide the lesson coherently without domineering. A preview which is not the formulation of a rigid sequence will be helpful. In fact, the writer, after some years of minimizing lesson planning, has returned to it in flexible form. Practice teachers for several years now have been unanimous in declaring that being forced to write out some questions in advance with probable answers, and to plan continuity thus, was one of the most helpful devices given them. One brilliant student who was about to fail in his practice teaching rejected this suggestion for some time. He was not required to accept it. Finally, in desperation he tried it. Within ten days he, his supervising teacher, and several members of his high school class were astonished at the change.

Learning to concoct good questions is not, however, quite so difficult as lifting oneself by the boot straps. Native knack and experience are vital, but one can profit from advice and training. Plato, probably reflecting his training under the great questioner, Socrates, wrote in *The Republic*, 'Then you will enact that they [the rulers] shall have such an education as will enable them to attain the greatest skill in asking and answering questions.'

The purposes to be served by questions

The aims and purposes to be served by questioning are obviously fundamental. The number would be large if all subpurposes were included. The most important are:

1   *To stimulate reflective thought*
This is, of course, a blanket term. The various elements include analysis, comparison, definition, judgment, and interpretation.

2   *To develop understanding*
Questions may direct attention to important elements basic to the understanding. The pupil's own experience can be searched, analyzed, and organized through questioning.

3   *To bring about the emergence of new concepts*
This may call for comparisons with simple known facts, for pointing out of analogies.

4   *To apply information*
Good problem questions and certain 'exercises' in texts and syllabi illustrate this. Many exercises are unfortunately composed of memory questions or call for the following of recipes.

5   *To develop appreciations and attitudes*
Analytic questioning, so widely used for this purpose, is definitely detrimental. The teacher should provide opportunities for appreciation to emerge.

6   *To develop the power and habit of evaluation*

7   *To change beliefs or attitudes*
This is a delicate matter. Beliefs acquired in emotional settings cannot be changed ordinarily by fact or logic. Hence the questions which encroach upon an emotionally held belief must be indirect and free from emotional content. In fact, education should first attempt to train persons in knowledge of mental and emotional processes before attempting to change beliefs.

8   *To focus attention on cause-and-effect relationship*
This aim, of course, overlaps with two or three others. Socratic, conversational questioning of the 'if this, then that' type is valuable.

9   *To determine the informational background, interests, and maturity of individuals or class groups*
General techniques for pretesting listed in the chapter on the assignment supply guidance here. Here, if anywhere, direct fact questions might play a legitimate part along with other forms.

10   *To create interest, arouse purpose, develop mind-set*

11   *To test directly for designated achievements*

Illustration of contrasting purposes revealed by questions

The story of the boy whose composition about the Washington monument was rejected illustrates the different purposes which a question may serve. The teacher aimed the question at a series of facts. The boy assumed that the question was aimed at understandings and attitudes, and answered accordingly.[1]

Butler (1939) gives a simple and explicit illustration. Two sets of questions

---

1   *Editorial footnote* : See chapter 5 of Burton, W. H., *The Guidance of Learning Activities*, Appleton-Century-Crofts, for this story.

about Lincoln's Gettysburg Address are contrasted to show how aims vary and how the variation determines the quality of the questions.

In one classroom:

1   Where did he give it?
2   When did he give it?
3   What was the occasion?
4   How many years are there in a score?
5   How many years are there in four score and seven?
6   Who is ready to recite the Address?

In another classroom:

1   What was the basic principle upon which Lincoln developed the Address? Did Lincoln think of the principle first or did others before Lincoln believe in it?
2   Did you notice any time sequence?
3   What message did Lincoln leave for his fellow-citizens?
4   What feelings would you have had if you were at the dedication and heard Lincoln?
5   Suppose you had never heard Lincoln, do you think you could tell something about his character from just reading the Address? (p. 198)

The second set is by no means perfect, but the difference between the two sets is too striking to need extended comment. The difference is not in the words, both vocabularies being simple; it is in the purposes served.

The following interpretive questions listed by a practice teacher are in pleasing contrast to the typical 'who, what, when, how many, and what happened next' questions.

Questions to be used as a basis for discussion of Carl Sandberg's 'Abraham Lincoln'

1   Through Chapter 18, page 41
a   Why was Nancy Hanks called a pioneer sacrifice? What are the implications?
b   Do you agree with Dennis Hanks' statement, 'Exceptin' for an interest in politics and religion, they lived just like Injuns'? Why?
c   Why does Sandburg keep repeating 'the wilderness is careless'?

d Where and how would you say that Lincoln got his real education?

e Is the style of writing suitable to the subject?

2   Through Chapter 29, page 82

a In the various jobs that Lincoln had, what could he have learned which would later help him?

b Jefferson said, 'Sometimes it is said that man cannot be trusted with the government of himself. Can he then be trusted with the government of others?' Apply this to Lincoln. Apply it to Andrew Jackson.

c Does Sandburg give the historical background of these times? Give instances.

d How did Lincoln's idea of God affect his actions?

e What did Lincoln's first election speech show of his character?

f Find instances of symbolism in these chapters.

g Could you tell from reading this book that Sandburg is a poet? How?

h What is the relation of this book to the school of interpretive biography?

Knowledge of purposes is then the first step in preparing good questions. Attempting to aim the wording directly at the purpose to be served will help to prevent pointless questioning.

General principles basic to good questioning

With the place or purpose clear as one important guidepost and before turning to the details of wording and form, we may set up a list of general principles.[2]

1 *The general sequence of questions should be organized around a thread or core*

This refers to the general continuity of the lesson and not to the minutiae which are arranged as the lesson progresses. The evils of rambling discussion have already been mentioned in the section on recitation. Maintaining reasonable continuity is extremely difficult for beginning teachers. Practice teachers who are unable to make progress in developing this ability should doubtless be discouraged from continuing in the profession. The development of the particular objectives of the unit or lesson series—understanding, appreciation, or attitude—furnishes the thread.

2 The writer's original list was improved by some items and wordings adapted from other authors. Grateful acknowledgment is made to Bossing, Frederick, Ragsdale and Salisbury, and particularly to Butler.

2   *Answers, to be acceptable, should be reasonably full, rounded replies*
Short, choppy questions invite short, choppy answers. Probably as an
outcome of the rapid-fire fact question, there has grown up in schools of
the United States a thoroughly reprehensible practice, namely, the acceptance from pupils of fragmentary one-point answers. Our typical procedure
is to secure one point from the first pupil, a second point from another,
and so on until several pupils have contributed enough fragments to complete a reputable answer. This is true from elementary school through
college. Genuine effort is necessary to break it up, and so far little progress
has been made. The modern school, because of the different setting of
questions and discussion, cares for the matter properly for the most part.
     The writer had a most revealing experience while teaching in the
University of Puerto Rico. After the usual preliminary days of explanation,
defining of problems by the students, planning methods of procedure,
and so on, the day came when the first set of the study questions was to be
analyzed in class. The first student called upon glanced at some notes,
laid them down, and proceeded to speak without interruption for nine
minutes! There was nothing much to be said further and everyone knew
it. Thinking he had by accident called upon a local honor student, the
writer studied his class to find a student who seemed to be average or
poorer. He fell into the ancient error of assuming that the beautiful are
dumb and assigned the next question accordingly. The young lady looked
at her notes, rose, and spoke for six minutes! Again there were no cor-
rections or additions warranted. It should not be assumed that this formal
procedure was used exclusively. Many of the questions called not for
summaries but for comparison of views, whereupon the discussion was fast
and furious—so fast, in fact, that the Spanish-speaking students asked
permission to carry on in Spanish because thinking in English slowed
them down! The argument was then summarized in English for the
instructor, who guided the continuing analysis. The point to be emphasized was that these Puerto Rican students had been thoroughly trained
to answer in adequate, coherent summaries. In this one respect at least,
these students are superior to ours.

3   *Accept any answer or part thereof which can be used*
If reasonably full responses to questions are not, for any reason, obtainable, it is well to encourage pupils by attempting to use, with proper
comment, any contribution. This begets more and better volunteering.
Even an answer which is not too close to the point should not be just
ignored. A comment or question may aid the pupil in seeing how he

missed the objective. Rarely should a teacher flatly reject an answer, possibly never reject without explanation. 'That's part of it, let's see if you (or anyone else) can elaborate it.' 'That's on the point, but it's a minor point which supports another major idea—what might the latter be?' 'Hold that a moment; we will use it later.' A teacher who says that an answer is 'dead wrong' or otherwise ridicules an honest effort is preventing the very thing he is there to encourage—learning activity.

4   *The questions should be within the pupil's experience and knowledge*
It is difficult for students fresh from high-grade liberal arts colleges to realize that what is everyday knowledge to them is utterly and completely unknown to high school pupils. The differences in experience and knowledge between high school pupils of the same age but of different socio-economic backgrounds are enormous. Differences in maturity and special interests also affect this matter vitally. Some specific suggestions for the improvement of questioning will be made in later pages when discussing the vocabulary of questioning. For the moment, the general principle is important.

The writer observed a high school teacher present to a class an exhibit of extensive statistical material. He repeated several times that *'no one except a trained expert* in statistics could understand these statistics and their implications'. Without pausing for breath, he then assigned the tables to the class for overnight study, full explanation to be brought to class next morning! No one else saw the joke, least of all the teacher. The class naturally did not see the joke—such things are no joke to them!

5   *Allow time to think of an answer and to put it into words*
It is difficult for an eager, quick-thinking teacher to remain silent while a slow-thinking, or even a quick, pupil figures out an answer. The pressure on the teacher is increased because the answer is already in his mind, full-formed and 'perfect'. It is in the forefront of his consciousness, and he completely forgets that a pupil may have to recall data, try to relate them to the question, think of words or perhaps illustrations. The teacher must simply school himself to stand quietly while thinking takes place.

To insist on quick answers gives excellent training in superficial, inaccurate thinking. It encourages the practice, too common in adult life, of stating ignorant and half-formed opinions as if they were important contributions to conversation.

Time should not be wasted, however, attempting to extract from a pupil an answer which he does not know, but which the rest of the class does. Many teachers think it an index of pedagogical expertness to pursue a child with a volley of questions in an effort to secure a desired response. They say, 'It makes him think; he must get it himself.' Anyone who has seen a blushing, stammering child subjected to this knows that the opposite is true. The procedure clearly embarrasses and muddles the poor child so that he cannot think. If the rest of the class knows, and the question is simple, another child should supply the information immediately and let the thinking move forward. When the learning situation is complex and most of the class needs guidance in analysis, then a series of questions slowly and sympathetically given, with class participation, is valuable.

6 *The teacher's attitude during questioning should be natural, friendly, and conversational*

This is merely in keeping with the practice of both old and new schools which are trying to apply modern psychology. Its effect on pupil attitudes and upon learning has been discussed earlier in several places.

7 *Pupils should be encouraged to ask questions*

Good teachers encourage and welcome questions from the class. To secure interested, competent response is an index of high teaching skill. The best type of pupil participation is being secured. Careful distinction should be made, of course, between the interested, alert pupil who asks intelligent, legitimate questions, and the bluffer who wastes time with many foolish and irrelevant ones. Good teachers attempt to use any part of a question which will contribute to class thought. Even a pointless question should not be summarily dismissed if further conversation may bring the pupil to see wherein his question is useless. Recurring pointless questions from the same pupil call for individual assistance outside class time.

Unfortunately, some teachers dislike pupils who ask questions. They strive to discourage such activity. Teachers who consistently discourage the alert questioning child are either very lazy or completely misunderstand their functions as teachers. Teachers who will not or cannot encourage, guide, and enter into the learning processes of the pupils should be removed, if possible.

8 *Develop an attitude of pupil responsibility for answering questions from the class as well as those from the teacher*

Again this is but good modern psychology. Children are not to look to the teacher as final and unanswerable arbiter. They are to take responsibility, come to conclusions, and support them.

9 *Do not hesitate to say, 'I do not know' to a pupil's question*

Many traditional teachers were as bad bluffers as some of their pupils! No one is supposed to know everything. Learning is continuous for all of us. Teachers who feel they 'lose face' by not answering lose much more, if they only knew, when they pretend to answer everything. Questions for which the teacher does not have an immediate answer can be made the subject of discussion, of minor assignments to individuals or to small committees. Sometimes, the teacher alone will be able to get the answer, and he should volunteer to bring it in when available.

The wording and form of questions

With purpose-to-be-served and other major principles understood, we may turn to some of the minutiae. The following suggestions will aid in the actual construction of questions.

1 *The objective of the question should be clear and definite*

If the objective is not clear, there is no fair criterion for judging the answer. The chief errors here are the 'discuss', 'what about', 'tell about', 'what can you say' questions. These are vague and general and unfair to the student. They indicate lazy, inexact thinking or no preparation on the part of the teacher.

a Avoid 'discuss' questions. This type abounds in high school and college: 'Discuss the reign of Nero', 'Discuss the results of the Westward Movement', 'Discuss the Missouri Compromise', 'Disuss the novel as a literary form'. The following are culled from recent examinations. 'Discuss a speech on ceremony', 'Discuss eavesdropping as a device in *Much Ado About Nothing* and in *Twelfth Night*', 'Discuss the arithmetic mean, the probable error, and the mean error', 'Discuss the thermodynamic principles involved in the determination of the Heat of Combustion of a substance with the Bomb Calorimeter', 'Discuss the Federal Reserve Act', and 'Discuss:

> Let music sound while he doth make his choice;
> Then if he lose, he makes a swan-like end,
> Fading in music.'

These questions are absurd. They indicate no beginning, no end, and no organization for the answer. Some could be 'discussed' for six months. Some have been 'discussed' for years. There is no guidance or stimulation of any sort. Such questions are responsible for much harsh unfairness in marking pupils.

For instance a pupil might answer the question 'Discuss Roosevelt's silver policy' with one sentence: 'The policy was one of expediency, unjustified, and detrimental to our economy.' He has fulfilled the conditions of the question. 'But,' says the instructor, 'I meant that he was to outline the circumstances leading to the emergence of the policy, the events following its announcement, results to date, and the probable future developments. I wanted a detailed, organized discussion.' The pupil cannot be a mind reader. The question neither demands nor implies anything of the type of answer concealed in the instructor's mind. It suggests no such beginning, sequence, or terminus. The pupil cannot with any honesty be held for such an answer. As the question stands any 'discussion' is satisfactory: lengthy, brief, organized, or unorganized. An ancient schoolroom joke illustrates the point. A student was confronted with the question, 'Discuss the reign of Caligula', and realized he knew nothing whatever about this reign. Purely as a shot in the dark, or perhaps as a satire on his own state of mind he wrote, 'The less said about the reign of Caligula the better.' This is said to have been accepted.

High school teachers and college professors addicted to use of 'discuss' questions follow the argument further. They claim that such questions teach pupils to organize. Not at all; they may equally teach them to make rambling incoherent presentations. If the instructor refuses to accept a poor organization, he is marking by a criterion not implied in the question and not within the knowledge of the pupil. As indicated above, the crux lies just here. Most instructors do have in mind a type of organization and treatment they wish reproduced when they ask 'discuss' questions, but the type accepted varies from instructor to instructor. Students can be taught to organize by far better devices than vague, indefinite questions. In fact, there is much material available in the literature on study skills showing how to do this. Further, pupils should have been taught to organize long before test or summary questions appear.

Again, the instructor may desire a critical comparison. He may reject not only a rambling discussion but the expository organization acceptable to another professor. Again the pupil cannot be clairvoyant. If the instructor means by 'discuss' a critical comparison thrown into certain form, he should ask for it.

The question stated above may be thrown into better form, 'Present in organized form, the origin, development, present status, and probable future of Roosevelt's silver policy.' This by no means 'gives the answer away' but it implies a definite type of answer which can be marked under a criterion clear to any honest pupil. One teacher, defending the 'discuss' question as a stimulus to thinking, criticized the form of the 'Roosevelt silver policy' question just given by saying that all it did was call for repetition of assigned text. Certainly it does! That is exactly what the majority of secondary and college teachers want, especially when they ask 'discuss' questions. Training pupils to think demands not only a change in the form of question but in the teaching. Several sources may be assigned, controversial data should be introduced, reference to related material included. The question to stimulate thinking will not be the sloppy 'discuss' question, but perhaps, 'Present in organized form the origin, development, present status and probable future of Roosevelt's silver policy as you derive it from the readings and class discussion. Indicate clearly why you accept certain data and views, rejecting others. Support your summary with argument at all points.'

Some teachers instruct and drill their pupils in the desired type of answer to 'discuss' questions. Under specific, limited conditions of this sort the question is fair, but this procedure seems a long way around a simple point. Ordinarily, this type of question is a shot in the dark, a 'sloppy' device, a lazy teacher's refuge.

Stimulated evidently by the sharp criticisms made of such questions by psychologists, there have recently appeared some paragraphs in defense of 'discuss' questions. Most of them are more indicative of hurt surprise that a time-honored technique should be assailed than they are of any critical analysis of the issue. Are not 'discuss' questions used by the best professors, and in respectable schools, forsooth! Some of the comments are quite transparent defense mechanisms. Nothing has yet appeared which invalidates the criticisms.

b Avoid 'what about', 'what can you say about', 'talk about', questions. These are but variations of the 'discuss' procedure. The same analysis applies. Such questions have no clear objective; they give the pupil no guidance whatever; the answers cannot be marked with fairness. They indicate complete failure on the part of the teacher to give attention to analysis of his objectives and to the wording of his questions.

c Avoid leading questions. The opposite of the discuss question is the question which gives too much guidance, the type condemned in courtrooms as 'leading' questions. This error is so obvious and simple that it should not need mention. Teachers everywhere, however, use such questions. 'Pericles was banished from Athens, was he not?' 'Lincoln was right in freeing the slaves, was he not?' Pupils are constantly crowded into a desired answer by questions which contain within them such phrases as 'don't you think so?' 'it is true, isn't it?' 'you would have to agree, wouldn't you?' Leading questions result sometimes from poor ability to think and to phrase questions but sometimes from the teacher's insistence that a predetermined answer be forced upon the class. In the social studies, such questions are very serious blunders.

d   Avoid catch questions. Most of us have been caught by such questions as the following:

> An athlete is to run around a square field. It takes him 40 seconds to run the first side which is 140 yards. It takes him 50 seconds to run the second side. How long is the second side?

> A train leaves Chicago for New York traveling 50 miles an hour. At the same time a train leaves New York for Chicago going 65 miles an hour. Which will be the farthest from New York when they meet?

Following normal and sensible mathematical attitudes and precedents, many pupils will try to work such problems. The catch is then explained.

Intrigued by the trick, one tends to say, 'Such problems make one think.' The direct opposite is true. Such questions confuse thinking by making one 'think' in ways which are not valuable in real problems. The uncritical teacher confuses 'hunting for the catch' with true 'analysis of a problem'. Real thinking has to do with ferreting out true and logical connections, not with discovering odd and bizarre tricks which rarely appear in real problems. The mental attitude engendered by catch questions is inimical to analytic thinking. Looking for the catch prevents one's seeing the logical connections. These questions are good parlor entertainment and are prominent in many intellectually perverted radio programs.

2   *The question should be directed at attainable objectives*

Certain questions, although clearly stated, are confusing because they call for more or less final answers when such answers are either not available, or can only be guessed at by the pupils. They are directed at the causes or solutions of certain historical events—wars, revolutions, economic upheavals, political movements—or call for moral judgments to be passed upon such events. If the teacher accepts superficial answers, his pupils are receiving training in poor thinking. They all too often feel a smug and ignorant satisfaction when their simple answers are accepted for complex problems. The real answers to some of these problems have puzzled the best thinkers we have. Such questions are clearly permissible when it is understood that the objective is to stimulate discussion, the search for and organization of data, and the suspension of judgment. Wide difference of opinion regarding final answers should be permitted and encouraged.

3   *The wording of the question should be precise and direct*

a   *Avoid digressions and involved statements.* If questions are to direct thought they must be to the point, avoiding long involved phrases, or supposedly facetious or even explanatory digressions. Many teachers believe they are engendering good feeling in the class when they interlard the question with humorous commentary. A college professor was heard to ask, 'A group of bright young men such as we have here must in their previous variegated academic careers have met the Law of Parsimony—sometimes called Occam's razor—and why do you suppose it was called Occam's razor—and have some dim realization of its application to thinking and so we will have Mr Blank apply it to the several explanations which seem derivable from the pedagogical experiment upon the efficacy of several ways of increasing the vocabulary.'

b   *Avoid ambiguity.* The difficulties inherent in using language carefully have been discussed earlier. The young teacher and the hurried older teacher often use words which may be interpreted quite honestly by pupils in several different ways. A teacher, developing concepts of latitude and longitude by means of street directions in a small town, asked an inattentive boy how he would get from the depot to the hotel and received the reply, 'I'd walk.' The teacher, desiring the reply, 'One block south and four blocks west', became very angry, failing to realize that the boy's interpretation of his question was honest. With more mature bright students, words must be chosen with real care.

c   *Avoid asking the question two or more ways in one statement.* Teachers often fall into this error in a sincere effort to aid the pupil. 'What is a ballad, or can you define this type of poetry?' It is better to ask it one way and give time for recall or volunteer answers before changing the wording. It is good practice to rephrase a question in different words, since different wordings strike responses in different minds; an interval, however, should elapse.

d   *Avoid calling for more than one unified reaction at a time.* This is sometimes called a 'double' question. 'Why is alcohol not a food and why is it bad for us?' 'Did the belligerent submarine have a right to enter our neutral port to exchange goods, and what should we have done about it?'

A more complicated form of the double question is one that states alternatives. 'Is there great rainfall or not in Western Oregon?' 'Was Pizarro a Spaniard or a Portuguese?' Questions may legitimately present alternatives when controversial issues are involved and when the question is designed to initiate a continuing comparison and evaluation of data.

4   *The vocabulary should be within the comprehension of the pupil*
The case is cited of a junior-high school history text which included on one page in the first chapter such words as *embryonic, vicissitudes*, and *economic stability*. The writer observed a teacher who asked a junior-high school class, 'Did not the group of signers to the Declaration of Independence constitute a *felicitous galaxy* of statesmen?' Still another asked a pupil to '*embroider* on the theme'. 'Did the conference *culminate* in *unification*?' 'What is the *thesis* of the book you are reading?' Such words as *mercenary, romanticist, mores*, have little meaning for young pupils. Many children are even confused by being asked to 'Tell the *influence* of' or '*Compare* the industries of' since the words *influence* and *compare* have not ordinarily been used that way by them. One class failed to answer a question which included the word *semester* because they had never heard the word before, *term* being the usage in their school.

The question may be asked whether extension of vocabulary is not one aim of teaching. Assuredly. In all educational procedure, questioning included, the pupil's vocabulary—as well as many other achievements—is to be improved. This is done in questioning as in reading, through contextual clues and through direct study. New words which can be properly interpreted by ordinary pupils may be used freely. The criticism refers to words which have not, and cannot have, meaning for the pupil.

Mechanical features of questioning

Before we list the mechanical features of questioning, note that we are referring to the improved recitation period and not to the completely modern working period of a unit. Frederick, Ragsdale, and Salisbury (1938) poke considerable fun at certain of the advices commonly given about the actual mechanics of presenting and distributing questions. Their criticisms are quite correct if we abandon the typical formal recitation. But since the recitation will be common practice for some time to come, attention is still necessary to the improvement of a practice which is not itself basically sound.

1   *Present question to class before calling upon someone to answer*
This tends to secure attention from all, and all at least start thinking about an answer.

2 *Distribute questions*

Teachers tend naturally to favor those pupils who volunteer, who contribute, and who themselves ask questions. Some device to insure distribution of opportunity to participate is necessary. Alphabetic or other fixed orders for calling upon pupils should be avoided. These are too useless even for the traditional recitation. Glancing over the roll just previous to class and noting those who have not contributed recently will help. Writing those names on a card is even better. Shuffling class cards is another recommended device.

Suggestions 1 and 2 are those chiefly ridiculed by Frederick, Ragsdale, and Salisbury as being wholly out of line with reputable learning situations and as provocative of undesirable attitudes. This is correct unless, as stated, we are already operating under a system which makes forced attention necessary.

3 *Do not repeat questions*

Questions should not be repeated habitually, because this makes for lack of attention. Care should be taken not to offend or embarrass the conscientious pupil who occasionally asks for repetition of a question which he does not understand. In the case of consistently inattentive pupils a sharp refusal to repeat is legitimate—if such an attitude is ever legitimate.

This suggestion, also, is one which would be ridiculous under modern teaching conditions.

4 *Do not repeat answers*

This is a seriously bad habit, one easily acquired and most difficult to overcome. It arises from the teacher's natural desire to emphasize, to interpret, and to extend thinking. Teachers should be rigidly on guard against this, as it encourages fragmentary, incomplete, and poorly worded answers from pupils.

5 *With certain exceptions, secure answers in complete sentence from*

Complete answers in good English are ordinarily desirable. This is particularly true during important class discussions. Otherwise, bad habits in expression arise and misunderstandings occur. Answering in complete and coherent form should be a matter of course. In some kinds of discussion, as in real life, this type of answer would slow thinking, if not actually confuse it. Contrary to the opinions of some teachers, it is quite all right to ask 'yes or no' questions. Criticism should be directed at the teacher's failure to follow up with other questions aimed to secure reasons and argument.

Adapt to individual differences

Adaptation of all procedures to individual differences has been stressed throughout this volume as a prime characteristic of modern teaching. This is particularly true of questioning. Teachers should make earnest, reasonable effort to take into consideration pupils' abilities, special interests, personal characteristics, and so forth, in distributing questions.

The distribution of difficult thought questions has caused some debate among teachers. Some hold that these should be given to the weaker pupils in order to spur them to effort and to give them practice in analyzing difficult problems. Success is said to bring satisfaction and confidence. Others maintain that the poor pupil is not able to solve difficult problems, and that instead of getting practice in thinking, he is more likely to become confused and embarrassed. Instead of confidence, he suffers the opposite and avoids participation. A waste of class time also results. It seems better to distribute difficult problems to brighter children. Their analysis is of value to slower pupils, who can often understand their fellows better than they can the teacher. Weaker pupils would then be given easier questions which they can solve with some degree of facility. Properly adjusted to levels of ability, such questions will probably afford all the opportunity for thinking these pupils can use. The flashy, superficial pupil may be given difficult questions and held firmly to results in order that he may appreciate and experience the value of good work.

Common weaknesses in pupil answers

Observation and teacher reports indicate certain typical weaknesses in answering which can be remedied.

1 Pupils begin to answer before thinking out the complete implication of the question.
   A fragmentary answer results.
   Minor points may be magnified and major points neglected.
2 Pupils seem to expect continued stimulation from the teacher.
   Fragmentary, choppy, one-point answers are given.
3 Pupils believe that they have answered a question if they give any one or two of several points which could be given.
   Inadequate, unorganized answers are given.

4   Pupils take no responsibility for organization, sequence, and coherence. *Rambling, discursive answers result.*
Relative values are neglected.
5   Pupils seem to be seeking to discover what the teacher wants, rather than to evolve answers based on the data and implications.
Answers are dictated by suggestibility rather than by analysis and thought.

These points overlap but are listed separately for emphasis. It is clear that the teacher's mode of questioning and the type of answer accepted will contribute to the development of good or poor habits of answering. An analysis of pupil answers and habits of answering supplies guidance toward the improvement of questioning.

Discussion questions

1   For each of the faults listed above show briefly how the teacher may unwittingly contribute to their development; how he may help eliminate them.
2   Give examples, if you can recall them from your own school experience (or watch for them now in observing), of particularly skillful guidance of class discussion by questions either prepared in advance or developed in terms of class-hour demands. (Several reports may be made on this to illustrate different points.)
3   Do the same thing for cases of particularly poor practice. Could you suggest improvements?
4   How will you probably learn to construct good questions?
5   In general, how would you handle a bright pupil who rarely studies carefully and who is a good bluffer?
6   List a number of suggestions for stimulating pupils to ask questions.

Exercises and reports

1   Secure a lesson plan, or lesson report, or unit plan or log, containing a fairly detailed account of the question-and-answer procedure in the class period. Accounts of traditional daily lesson plans are to be found in practically every text on general method or principles of teaching. Both traditional and modern plans appear in the periodical literature and in

books on unit teaching. Instructors should have built up a large personal collection of plans and unit outlines.

Read the general questioning sequence carefully and analyze critically in the light of the principles and suggestions summarized in this chapter. Prepare an organized, detailed critique.

2 Select a typical segment of material used as the basis of a traditional recitation. Organize a general sequence of major questions based upon it but designed to get as good learning as is possible under formal conditions.

3 Do the same thing for the approach or initiation of a typical experience unit.

References

FREDERICK, ROBERT W., RAGSDALE, C. E. and SALISBURY, RACHEL (1938) *Directed Learning* New York: Appleton-Century-Crofts, 170–1.

BUTLER, FRANK A. (1939) *The Improvement of Teaching in Secondary Schools* Chicago: University of Chicago Press, 195, 197, 198.

Part 4   How is reading assessed?

Introduction to Part Four:
How is reading assessed?

Both printed media and the reader need to be properly evaluated if the reading curriculum is to provide a suitable range of reading experiences appropriate to individual needs and levels of reading competence for all pupils.

In an overview of the concept and content of readability measures designed to assess the level of difficulty of printed material, Gilliland (4:1) brings to our attention the kinds of practices and problems involved in attempts to secure a precise measurement of both conceptual and textual aspects of printed material. To overcome some of these difficulties, researchers have recently emphasized the use of the cloze procedure, which is described and demonstrated by Moyle (4:2). The emergence of yet another new technique and theoretical frame of reference emphasizes the use of recent linguistic knowledge of children's oral structural patterns as a basis for assessing readability. Reid's (4:3) linguistic analysis of four reading schemes concludes with valuable practical suggestions for the production of reading materials and methods which match more closely children's oral linguistic resources.

Assessment of pupil reading performance has also shifted in emphasis and approaches within recent years. In their concern for reading progress as well as achievement, educationists are advocating the increased use of informal procedures of appraisal by the classroom teacher. Using these informal inventories, teachers are guided in more systematic observation of pupils' reading competencies in natural classroom situations. In this way, teachers are more likely to provide immediate relevant instruction based on first-hand evidence rather than on the delayed and limited information provided by the statistical results of standardized reading tests.

In the area of reading readiness, Downing and Thackray (4:4) present a thoughtful explanation of the development of and need for their own proposed Reading Readiness Inventory, which can serve as a useful starting point for determining pupils' introduction to beginning reading. Their inventory suggests that readiness is not a magic moment of mere biological maturation, but a result of trained experience which both teachers and parents can influence.

Like readiness, attitudes toward reading also affect pupils' development in reading. Pumphrey and Dixon's (4:5) analysis of three attitude scales provide useful suggestions of ways teachers may informally study and influence pupils' attitudes toward reading, which many consider have been neglected in our preoccupation about reading attainment. What have we achieved if we develop capable readers who do not like, want, or choose to read?

Negative attitudes toward reading are more likely to develop if pupils' reading needs and abilities are not matched with appropriate kinds and levels of reading material. Informal reading inventories help teachers to determine more precisely the kinds of reading guidance needed in the classroom and the types and levels of reading materials suitable for their pupils' levels of attainment.

Inventories of this kind consist of a graded series of paragraphs as determined by readability formulae. As the pupil reads these paragraphs orally and responds to questions, teachers can observe and record information about the individual's approach to reading, his methods of word analysis, and the quality of his comprehension levels and skills. From an analysis of this data, the teacher can ascertain: 1) the level of the pupil's reading competence; 2) his specific strengths and weaknesses in word analysis and comprehension skills; 3) the readability level of the material which reflects his independent, instructional, frustrational, and capacity levels of reading performance (Johnson and Kress, 4:6). Through this approach pupils also can become more aware of the reading methods they use.

Although teachers are recommended to prepare their own inventories, several examples are provided by Strang (4:7) to introduce teachers to the format and use of these instruments which combine the diagnostic values of observation of both oral and silent reading with teaching. Suggestions for the formulation of questions designed to reveal various kinds of comprehension skills are provided by Valmont (4:8) as a helpful aid for the teacher who wishes to construct or review an inventory of her own. Constructing and using informal reading inventories contributes to the development of diagnostic teaching of reading.

If an adequate and balanced reading programme is to permeate the curriculum, then all aspects of pupils' reading competence should be evaluated by teachers, administrators, and pupils themselves. Comprehensive guidelines and practical procedures to implement such a view are provided by Strang (4:9), who considers evaluation as essential to learning. 'It is an incentive to students, an intrinsic part of teaching, and an aid to the administrator and the specialist in improving the [reading] program' (p. 508).

Classroom performance is significantly influenced by the social climate, conditions, and experiences through which learning takes place. For this reason, increasing recognition and respect is being given to the role and responsibility of the teacher. According to Harris (4:11), '. . . differences among teachers are far more important than differences among methods and materials in influencing the reading achievement of children' (p. 541).

What are the characteristics of effective teachers of reading? What are the characteristics of professional training programmes which develop effective teachers of reading? What can we do to help teachers become more effective teachers of reading?

Appraising the reading programme as a whole, Rauch (4:10) considers that 'The purpose of evaluation is to take a comprehensive, unbiased and cooperative look at the reading program and to decide what modifications or changes, if any, should be made to improve the program' (p. 524).

4:1   The assessment of readability—an overview

Jack Gilliland

Introduction

All teachers are concerned, in different ways, with the problem of matching a variety of printed materials to a variety of children with specific reading abilities. Usually, an attempt is made to minimize the difficulties which a given child will encounter so that the reading undertaken will be efficient, profitable and enjoyable. The problem is that the reading materials are extremely varied as are the characteristics of the children for whom the material is to be chosen.

Amongst the various kinds of reading materials, conventional reading schemes present the least problem. In most cases teachers' manuals, giving details of vocabulary control, levels of difficulty and graded alternative readers, provide evidence upon which the suitability of the scheme for given children may be judged. However, either by choice or by direction, children will be looking at a range of reading materials for pleasure, for projects and assignments, about which little evidence is available upon which to pass judgment. Publicity material may be available but all too often this is inadequate. Matching a book to a child can hardly be reliable when based upon such comments as 'suitable for eight years and above' or 'for boys and girls aged six to sixteen years'. One's personal reading offers some basis for subjective judgment, but the unreliability of subjective judgments in many spheres has been well established, and no less so in the selection of reading materials. Chall (1958) has shown that while experienced teachers were able to rank reading material in an order which

GILLILAND, JACK (1970) 'The assessment of readability—an overview', in Merritt, J. (ed.) *Reading and the Curriculum* London: Ward Lock Educational, 144–58.

corresponded closely to objective measures of difficulty, these rankings were inaccurate and inadequate when matched with children. Researchers into readability are attempting, however imperfectly, to produce objective and reliable means by which the levels of difficulty in texts can be measured, and matched to levels of reading ability in children.

Definitions of readability

Readability has been variously defined but two typical definitions, given below, indicate the essential attributes which are included in the concept of readability:

> 1 In the broadest sense, readability is the sum total (including interactions) of all those elements within a given piece of printed material that affects the success which a group of readers have with it. The success is the extent to which they understand it, read it at optimum speed, and find it interesting (Dale and Chall, 1948).
>
> 2 The quality of a written or printed communication that makes it easy for a given class of persons to understand its meaning or that induces them to continue reading (English and English, 1958).

Although ease of reading and speed of reading have been incorporated into the Dale-Chall and other definitions, the most frequent and most heavily emphasized elements have been comprehensibility and interest. McLaughlin (1968) extends the English and English phrase 'that induces them to continue reading' and makes 'compellingness' an essential part of his definition. He argues that compellingness is a necessary component in any measure of readability, and his suggestion for the use of readability tables, incorporating this factor, rather than the use of formulae will be discussed later.

Following these definitions, the many variables which contribute towards the comprehension and interest of a passage may be conveniently grouped under four main headings:

1 factors in the reader, e.g. age, sex, motivation, state of knowledge
2 factors in the print, e.g. type size, leading, format
3 factors in the content, e.g. fact, fiction, topic
4 factors in the language, e.g. vocabulary, grammar, style.

This picture is complicated by the fact that these do not merely make an independent contribution but interact with each other to influence readability. For example, the format and style of a scientific paper may be affected by the subject matter and details given, and a reader's state of knowledge may affect his response to vocabulary factors.

Methods of assessing readability

Attempts to evaluate the factors affecting readability, singly or in combination, have involved comparing an assessment with a criterion measure. The three measures most commonly adopted in the past have been:

1 visibility of print, as measured by visual acuity tests and number of fixations
2 ease of reading, as reflected in speed of reading and
3 ease of understanding, as measured by tests of comprehension.

Each of these criterion measures incorporates only one of the alternatives involved in the definitions of readability described earlier, and clearly different assessments of readability may not be comparable if they have been matched against different criteria, since the criteria themselves are not equivalent. Reading speed, for example, cannot be equated with reading comprehension. Visibility of the print, on the other hand, measures an important but subsidiary element which is common to both. Even within one kind of measure, there are many practical problems.

For example consider the difficulties involved in producing satisfactory measures of comprehension. The question and answer technique, although frequently used, is of little use to readability research since it is impossible to establish whether difficulties in understanding are due to difficulties in understanding the passage or the questions. Answering difficult questions about an easy passage cannot be compared with asking easy questions about a difficult passage.

Again, the conditions of testing may be critical. If the text is removed, memory factors and reliance upon cues in the questions will influence the result, and this cannot be regarded as a comparable exercise to matching cues in the questions with cues in the context when the passage is retained.

The utility of 'objective' measures such as multiple choice test items is also limited. Here responses of items may be influenced by the range and type of alternatives given, as well as by guessing.

An interesting and potentially very useful variation of the sentence completion principle has been developed by Taylor (1953) and labelled the 'cloze procedure'. Bormuth (1966) argues that it has fewer limitations than other methods and its potential as an improved measure of comprehension is now being examined by several researchers. Although in readability studies it is being used mainly as a criterion measure against which other measures are compared, it will be argued later that it could be used as a readability measure itself.

In general it may be said that the concept of readability and the problems involved within it are now fairly clearly established. Recent research is less concerned with redefining the concept than with increasing the accuracy of measurement by the refinement of existing procedures or by the introduction of new bases for measurement. Many different procedures are available and like the criterion measures reflect the various components in the definitions. Attention is now directed to an evaluation of some of these methods used in the assessment of interest, language and legibility.

The assessment of interest

Attempts to define and quantify the degree to which a given text is compelling to a given reader are not numerous, perhaps because the problem is more daunting than that of dealing with textual factors or legibility. Yet, as has been seen, interest or 'compellingness' is an essential factor in the concept of readability and, as mentioned earlier, McLaughlin has argued that any measure of readability should use as a basis those materials which children have chosen to read.

One basis for the selection of types of reading material has been the frequency with which books in libraries have been used. Lists have been prepared upon this basis but few attempts seem to have been made to follow up the use of selections made or to relate the selections to other measures of readability. Although of only general application, surveys of this kind into children's interests have provided crude guides as to the likely use of books. Analysis of subject matter and themes, reported by Chall (1958) led to some easily anticipated generalizations in that interests were largely individual and showed large differences in the groups studied. Some trends in choices were related to maturity and sex.

1 Children between six and eight years were found to be interested in stories of animals, children, familiar experiences, nature, fairies and lively stories containing elements of surprise and humour.

2 Between eight and twelve years, boys showed preference for adventure, mystery, sport and realistic animal stories, while girls preferred stories of

home and school life. Action and humour were the factors found to exert the greatest common influence.

3   Over twelve years boys and girls showed preferences for adventure and humour while girls also showed an increased interest in love stories.

In addition to the low predictive value of such generalizations concerning American children, cultural differences in the amount and types of reading interest reduce considerably the use to which these conclusions might be put in this country.

McLaughlin's idea of collecting lists of books actually read and enjoyed by children of different ages, rather than searching for areas of interest, may be more relevant to the precise assessment of readability. Also Abernathy *et al* (1967) report an investigation into the reading habits of Belfast school children. If extended, this type of survey could provide a series of reading materials to be used as a basis for a measure of readability reflecting interest, particularly in the choice of fiction.

Chall (1958) reports findings of a series of studies which investigated the relative importance of content, style, format and organization. Leary and Strong in separate studies reported by Chall both found content and style to be stronger influences than format and organization and she also reports a study by Engelman in which conversational style was preferred to narrative expository style. As far as is known, only two studies appear to have quantified this type of factor and applied them in the assessment of readability.

Flesch (1948), using the frequency of personal pronouns and the number of personal sentences in the sample, devised a 'human interest' formula, which was claimed to be measuring the level of abstraction. This, with his reading ease formula, was very widely used but has since been superceded by more recent formulae.

In a study reported by Klare (1963), Morriss and Halverson used a method of analyzing 'content' words in context, thus attempting to measure the relationship between 'ideas' and reading difficulty. This technique, so different from others of the time, has been found cumbersome to apply and has been criticized for its lack of validity and applicability, though Klare reports a study which examined this system and found a significant correlation between the word classifications and the McCall-Crabbs Standard Test Lessons in Reading. The significance of this study lies in the attempt to produce an assessment of readability which reflected the effect of word meaning and context.

Interest and ideas reflect the meaning or significance which the words have for individuals. Many psychologists have examined the learning of verbal material and the meaning which individuals attach to words. In particular, Osgood *et al* (1957) devised a measure of meaning, the 'semantic differential'. While this tool does not yet seem to have been used in the assessment of readability, the principles involved seem applicable and its use has been advocated.

Although there is an absence of detailed and systematic research, two general factors related to interest and readability have been examined and are relevant to this section of the overview. The effect of motivation upon reading speed and comprehension has been reported by Klare. Examining the truism that motivation is necessary to achievement in the context of reading, he suggests that a specific kind of motivation, a 'set to learn', has a noticeable effect upon readability scores. He found that while the presence of a strong set to learn had little or no effect upon the number of words read per second or the words read per fixation, this strong set to learn produced significantly higher scores in a recall comprehension test.

The second general factor considered relevant is the 'principle of least effort' expounded by Zipf (1949). This 'principle' involves the notion that a human being will minimize the amount of work necessary to reach a certain goal. Preferences for reading material have been shown to be governed by the simplicity of the text, and the fact that the reader usually reads more of simpler texts than he does of harder. This does not mean to say that the reader will never tackle something difficult, it means that he will only do so when motivation is high. What the reader *chooses* to read will therefore be generally below the level which he *could* read.

It may be concluded that measures of readability based upon free choice and reading for pleasure will involve a reading level determined by the principle of least effort and which may be noticeably below the potential reading level of an individual when motivated. The assessor of readability has the problem of deciding which of these two general factors he bases his work upon, since texts read on the basis of choice and those read under a a strong 'set to learn' will produce different patterns of results when assessed for readability.

The difficulties posed by these points may be reduced by the consideration of two possible approaches to measurement. Firstly, following McLaughlin's argument in favour of readability tables. Such a table would be constructed from the selection of books which children at different ages had actually read and enjoyed, and would indicate the proportion of a particular group of readers who find a specific kind of material compelling. Secondly, the extended use of 'cloze' passages to include children's ranking as well as reading performance might permit the incorporation of interest factors without involving cumbersome analyses of texts.

The measurement of language

No other basic factors involved in the assessment of readability have pro-duced so many variables used in measurement as language. Since the characteristics of paragraphs, sentences and words are numerous and easily quantifiable, it is perhaps inevitable that the study of language should provide so many measures. More than 150 different linguistic variables have been examined and found to be related to reading diffi-culty. Happily, most of these factors vary together because of underlying relationships between them, and so only main groupings will be referred to. Variables have been sought which relate to reading difficulty at passage, sentence and word levels. The largest groupings involve sentence and word factors.

An interesting attempt to classify paragraphs in a way which reflects their structure has been made by Bissex (see Strang and Bracken, 1957). Developing the idea from his teaching, he has produced a system of visualizing paragraphs and grouping them under main and subheadings. Three theoretical forms of a paragraph (inductive, deductive and balanced) are proposed and broken down into subtypes. Bissex points out that variations in the structure of paragraphs, though great, are not infinite, and that examining the structure of a piece of writing can assist in the comprehension of it. Plotting the ranges and frequencies of occurrences of these types of paragraph, if they are found to be linked to understanding, might well be of use in the assessment of the readability of a text. This approach is particularly valuable, in view of its potential as a means of quantifying organization of the paragraph and thought structures involved in a text, an aspect of readability which seems to have received scant attention. Hopefully, it might even lead to the adoption of a more systematic approach to paragraph structure!

Measures of readability incorporating sentence and word factors have conventionally been expressed as a formula which has been used to produce a reading grade (since all the published work of note with one exception has been related to the American situation). The application of the formula usually involves the teacher in the selection of a sample of the text, count-ing some characteristic of sentences and words (for examples see below), and then a calculation which produces the level of difficulty in the form of a reading grade. The constructors of measures have frequently had to resolve the problem of choosing between a formula which was easy to calculate but low in reliability and validity or a complicated formula which is unwieldy and difficult to apply but reliable and valid.

Two typical and frequently used formulae are given below. The frequent use of both word and sentence variables in the formula is reflected in each example.

1 *Dale and Chall readability formula (1948)*

$$X_{c50} = 0.1579X_1 + 0.496X_2 + 3.6365$$

where X_{c50} is the reading grade score of a pupil who could answer one half of the series of test questions correctly.

X_1 is the Dale score (the relative number of words outside the Dale list of 3,000 words)

X_2 is the average sentence length

3.6365 is a constant

2 *Farr-Jenkins-Paterson*

New reading ease index $= 1.599$ nosw $- 1.015$ sl $- 31.517$

nosw $=$ number of one syllable words per 100 words

sl $=$ average sentence length in words

31.517 $=$ constant

Most formulae incorporating a sentence factor have used the length of the sentence as a measure of its readability. Research has repeatedly shown that there is a sentence factor affecting readability. Since it is easy to accept that the longer a sentence becomes the more difficult it is to read and understand, sentence length has continued to be used, particularly as it is a variable which is easily measured. It is arguable, however, whether this measure can be regarded as adequate in the light of more recent linguistic analyses.

In an article concerning the structure of language, Yngve (1960) quotes two sentences which are of use in this context:

1 If what going to a clearly not very adequately staffed school really means is little appreciated, we should be very concerned (21 words).

2 We should be very concerned if there is little appreciation of what it really means to go to a school that clearly isn't very adequately staffed (26 words).

Using sentence length as a measure, one might be led to expect that sentence 1 would be easier to read and understand than sentence 2! These, and many other examples, indicate clearly that difficulty at the sentence level may have more to do with grammatical complexity than with simple sentence length, and that an assessment of readability should reflect the complexity variable as well as length. The former measure may reflect the linguistic capability of the reader while the latter measure reflects memory span.

In the paper referred to above, Yngve has proposed a model for language structure based upon certain assumptions concerning the production of sentences. A counting system is applied to the syntactic structure and relationships in a sentence. This quantification of sentence complexity enables one to use it in the assessment of readability.

Bormuth stated, as a result of his research, that 'word depth' as defined by Yngve seemed a useful readability measure which correlated highly with difficulty of comprehension. 'Word depth analysis' is difficult to grasp and apply and so for practical reasons may find less favour than traditional and other more modern techniques.

McLaughlin cites another recent form of linguistic analysis which he considers suitable for readability measures. He uses Harris's string analysis to produce a measure of 'separation'. He devised an experiment using original passages and rewritten passages with varying degrees of 'separation'. Using the cloze procedure as a measure, he found significant differences in comprehension related to the degree of separation and not simply to sentence length. He goes further and offers a theory to explain the psychological difficulty involved in separation, in a way which takes account of linguistic and memorizing phenomena which affect reading performance. While extremely valuable at an explanatory level and in research contexts, in terms of practicability both word depth and analysis and string analysis require simplification. Using different approaches, they appear to be reflecting the same aspect of reading difficulty, namely sentence complexity.

Bormuth also highlighted the possibility that the examination of independent clause frequency may give higher predictions of readability than other sentence measures used in his study. He reported that six of the eight highest predictors of difficulty involved independent clauses, and that the most successful traditional sentence measure (syllables per sentence) was ninth. The ease of counting and sorting independent clauses may make it preferable to word depth analysis for many readability assessments. A further conclusion from Bormuth's results was that though sentence length and complexity are correlated, they each have an independent correlation with difficulty.

Memory span and its effect upon the recall of sentences has been examined. Memory span for sentences has been found to be related to the degree of approximation to English. Approximations to English have been described and evaluated by Miller (1951) and also by Carroll (1964). Essentially, higher approximations to English enable a reader to use his previous learning and increase the predictabality of words and phrases. The more he can predict, the fewer words the reader has to read carefully in order to proceed. In this way, a proportion of words in the text become redundant. The response to contextual clues in this way may have more to do with the reader's linguistic competence than with the 'meaning' of the passage. It is nevertheless a significant variable in the assessment of readability.

Redundancy has received little attention to date. Klare argued that while redundancy is closely related to readability, its inclusion as a factor would rob readability formulae of their usefulness, since redundancy can only be estimated through a try-out of written material on subjects. Bormuth, on the other hand, suggests that if some of his correlations are to be believed, then redundancy variables (letters not words) may be among the best used in his study. Results from the use of the cloze procedure, which permits redundancy to have an effect upon scores, also suggests that readability measures may reflect a reader's response to this linguistic factor without affecting the measure of comprehension.

The importance of the continued attention to measures of sentence difficulty is supported by such reports as that of Strickland (1962), which indicates relationships existing between the language of children's textbooks, the spoken language of children and reading attainment.

Word factors used in the measurement of readability have usually been based upon word frequencies, word length or grammatical classifications. Word frequency indices most commonly used have involved reference to the word lists compiled by Thorndike and Dale. It is considered that the more infrequent words there are in a passage, the more difficult comprehension will be.

However, it is unlikely that a general frequency count such as Thorndike's will reflect the word frequencies peculiar to an individual. The use of such a count will more often than not lead to an underestimation of frequencies, and thus level of comprehension, of specific individuals. Additionally, the frequency of a word is not the same as its familiarity to a given individual. Frequency and familiarity do not share a one-to-one relationship and therefore readability formulae using the former will be sampling imperfectly the familiarity of the words used. A more accurate prediction of readability would involve familiarity as a measure.

Finally, the use of word frequency has been justified in measures of readability using ease of reading as a criterion, since this factor has been found to be related to speed of word recognition. These results reflect the influence of word and letter redundancy which has already been discussed. Readability of texts has been found to be influenced by the length of the words used. This measure of difficulty has usually involved counting the frequency of polysyllabic words or the calculation of an average word length expressed in syllables or words. Such measures have the advantage of being easy to work out and seem to retain acceptable levels of reliability and validity. In the past, as isolated measures, they have not been found very useful, though recently McLaughlin (1969) has proposed a formula using a polysyllabic count as the sole variable.

Assessments of word length and word frequency would appear to be different reflections of two characteristics of language. Firstly, much of the grammatical glue which holds sentences of English together is composed of short words of Anglo-Saxon derivation referred to as 'function' words. These 'function' words occur very very frequently. By contrast, 'content' words tend to be derived from the Romance languages in which words are very frequently polysyllabic and so tend to be long. Secondly, words are affected by a 'law of abbreviation', described by Zipf (1935). This law refers to the tendency for words to be abbreviated with frequent usage, e.g. 'tele' for 'television' and 'bus' for 'omnibus'. Measures of word length and word frequency therefore reflect a common element in language—either abbreviation through usage or origin and grammatical function.

Few assessments of readability have yet incorporated a measure based on grammatical class. Bormuth did include a number of such variables in his research. Among other things he compares the frequency of occurrence of certain classes of word and parts of speech ratios with previous word measures. His correlations, if reliable, showed that this type of predictor may be worthy of further investigation. He predicts that major advances in the assessment of readability will stem from the further study of the new linguistic variables referred to here and more fully in his article.

The measurement of legibility

An overview of readability must necessarily include a reference to studies of legibility and situational conditions which affect visibility. However, although some definitions of readability include ease of reading as a factor, and although there is much useful research available, legibility will not be dealt with to the same extent as other factors referred to. Firstly, the experiments and evaluations are thoroughly reported by Tinker (1963, 1965 and 1966). Secondly, control of many variables is outside the direct sphere of influence of teachers. Thirdly, recent developments do not have the same application to readability measures as others mentioned in this paper. Fourthly, the technical nature of the forms of measurement of such perceptual processes as visual acuity and saccadic movements involved in legibility cannot be readily utilized by a teacher. This section will therefore be confined to a description of the main conclusions considered relevant to an overview of readability measures.

Studies of legibility have involved the investigation of the following major factors:

1 the visibility and legibility of letters, digits and other symbols
2 the influence of type faces
3 the size of type, line width and leading
4 the influence of colour of print and background
5 the influence of printing surfaces
6 the influence of illumination and other situational conditions.

The findings of Vernon (1929) and Shaw (1969) support Tinker's conclusion that such factors as simplicity of outline, serifs, and the way they are used affect the readability of the text. It has long been recognized that the upper coastline of print is more informative than the lower, and more recently Kolers (1969) has shown that a fluent reader finds the right hand side of letters more informative than the left. Also the presence of single distinguishing features—areas of white space enclosed in outlines and heaviness of stroke—will be critical in children's reading, particularly under non-optimal reading conditions and also where little contextual meaning is being extracted.

There are literally dozens of studies investigating the other factors referred to above. Singly, each of these factors has been found to affect readability but interaction effects have also been found which further affect reading ease. Findings from researches have led Tinker to establish 'safety zones'. These are limits within which variables may be altered without significantly affecting the legibility of type. Tinker particularly stresses the effect of introducing non-optimal features into a reading situation. He states that a combination of non-optimal factors produces a severe disorganization of the oculomotor system which does not seem to occur when an optimal set up is used.

Spencer (1968) has vividly illustrated the effect of angles of vision, curvature of the page and vibration upon visibility. Glazing of paper and directional lighting have also been shown to seriously reduce the efficiency of capable readers. In these respects knowledge of legibility studies can have a direct effect upon the work of a reading teacher.

Second thoughts on measures of readability

After a period of stagnation the renewal of interest in readability would seem to be accounted for by the increased interest in psycholinguistics and by the improvement of measures of comprehension.

Studies of psycholinguistics and the development of theories to account for levels and processes involved in language behaviour have provided new tools with which to describe and quantify characteristics of different readers and texts. Bormuth's thorough examination of the correlations between comprehension difficulty of texts and new and traditional linguistic measures indicates that several new factors might be utilized to provide new improved formulae and refine existing ones.

Of the new measures of reading comprehension, Taylor's cloze procedure, referred to earlier, has proved most interesting to researchers in readability. This procedure involves the preparation of a sample of text by removing every 'nth' word (usually the fifth) and replacing it with a blank of standard size throughout the passage. The subject then has to attempt to replace the deleted words. The subject's score reflects the extent to which he has used the exact words of the author and thus is a measure of the subject's ability to estimate the author's intentions as well as to respond to purely linguistic factors. The methods of testing and scoring, together with the use of the actual readers for whom readability is being measured, make this procedure the measure which, to date, most adequately reflects the elements and interaction defined by Dale and Chall. It has in addition several practical advantages such as ease of preparation and simplicity in scoring which are likely to make it of interest to teachers.

Conclusion

In a society becoming increasingly aware of the necessity for efficient and pleasurable communication through print, the control of difficulty of comprehension is critical, particularly in educational situations.

The concept of readability is now clearly defined. In view of its relevance to the problem of selecting reading materials, it should be an essential part of the body of knowledge of anyone concerned with reading. Teachers and children could profit from the use of readability measures. This argument has been accepted in the USA but regrettably it has been given much less consideration in this country.

The traditional approach to readability assessment has been through the production of formulae. Alternatives such as the cloze procedure and the construction of readability tables have been suggested which may provide the accuracy and ease of application required by teachers which readability formulae do not yet have.

In addition to removing the need for a reliance upon traditional testing procedures, recent methods of linguistic analysis have produced a number of variables and measures likely to improve the assessment of readability. The explanations of the generation of language offered may also be utilized in the prediction of reading difficulty.

References

ABERNETHY, D., FERGUSON, S., MCKAY, Y. and THOMPSON, D. F. (1967) 'Children's in-school reading in Belfast—A suggestive survey', *Reading*, 1, iii.

BORMUTH, J. R. (1966) 'Readability: A new approach', *Reading Research Quarterly*, 1, 79–132.

CARROLL, J. B. (1964) *Language and Thought* Englewood Cliffs, N. J.: Prentice-Hall.

CHALL, J. S. (1958) *Readability: An appraisal of research and application,* Bureau of Educational Research Monographs no. 34, Ohio State University.

DALE, E. and CHALL, J. S. (1948) 'A formula for predicting readability', *Educational Research Bulletin*, 27, 11–20.

ENGLISH, H. B. and ENGLISH, A. C. (1958) *A Comprehensive Dictionary of Psychological and Psychoanalytical Terms* London: Longman.

FARR, J. N., JENKINS, J. J. and PATERSON, D. G. (1951) 'Simplification of Flesch Reading Ease Formula', *Journal of Applied Psychology*, 35, 333–7.

FLESCH, R. (1948) 'A new readability yardstick', *Journal of Applied Psychology*, 32, 221–33.

KLARE, G. R. (1963) *The Measurement of Readability* Iowa State University Press.

KOLERS, P. A. (1969) 'Clues to a letter's recognition: Implications for the design of characters', *Journal of Typographical Research*, 3, 145–67.

MCLAUGHLIN, G. N. (1968) 'Proposals for British Readability Measures', in Brown, A. L. and Downing, J. (eds) *Third International Reading Symposium* London: Cassell.

MCLAUGHLIN, G. N. (1968) 'SMOG grading—A new readability formula', *Journal of Reading*, **12**, 639–46.

MILLER, G. A. (1951) *Language and Communication* New York: McGraw-Hill.

OSGOOD, C. E., SUCI, G. J. and TANNENBAUM, P. H. (1957) *The Measurement of Meaning* Urbana: University of Illinois Press.

SHAW, A. (1969) *Print for partial sight—a research report* London: Library Association.

SPENCER, H. (1968) *The Visible Word: Problems of Legibility* London: Lund-Humphries.

STRANG, R. and BRACKEN, D. K. (1957) *Making better readers* Boston: D. C. Heath and Co.

STRICKLAND, R. G. (1962) 'The language of elementary school children: Its relationship to the language of reading textbooks and the quality of reading of selected children', *Bulletin of the School of Education* Indiana University, **38**, *iv*.

TAYLOR, W. L. (1953) 'Cloze procedure: A new tool for measuring readability', *Journalism Quarterly*, **30**, 415–33.

TINKER, M. A. (1963) *Legibility of Print* Iowa State University Press.

TINKER, M. A. (1965) *Bases for Effective Reading* University of Minnesota Press.

TINKER, M. A. (1966) 'Experimental studies in the legibility of print: An annotated bibliography', *Reading Research Quarterly*, **1**, *iv*, 67–118.

VERNON, M. D. (1929) *Studies in the Psychology of Reading: A—The Errors made in Reading* London: HMSO, 5–26.

YNGVE, V. H. (1960) 'A model and hypothesis for language structure', *Proceedings of the American Philosophical Society*, **104**, *v*, 444–66.

ZIPF, G. K. (1935) *The Psycho-Biology of Language* Boston: Houghton-Mifflin.

ZIPF, G. K. (1949) *Human Behaviour and the Principle of Least Effort* Cambridge, Massachusetts: Addison-Wesley.

4:2   Readability—the use of cloze procedure

Donald Moyle

Cloze procedure, as a new approach to the assessment of readability, was first used by Taylor (1953). It is an empirical measure which uses the performance of children upon the text being measured to obtain the readability level. Though it would seem obvious that an examination of the performance of children on the actual text has more face validity than the use of formulae, it has as yet been employed infrequently. In the USA, where both reading materials and subject texts are often assessed for readability before publication, formulae are normally employed no doubt due to the greater expense and trouble which would be occasioned if an empirical measure were used. In Britain there has to date been little interest in measures of readability other than the grading of books by committees of experienced teachers using subjective judgments, e.g. Pascoe (1962) and Lawson (1967). Cloze procedure has to date been employed only experimentally and even here usually at high levels of reading attainment.

Cloze procedure: what is it?

Gestalt psychologists applied the term 'closure' to the tendency to complete a pattern which has a part missing. Thus we tend to see a circle even when a small gap is left in the drawing. The fluent reader will often substitute a word of similar spelling and meaning to the one in the text or read correctly a word from which a letter has been omitted. A current advertising stunt to promote pre-packed bacon is based upon this principle. Spelling errors are to be located, one being the omission of

MOYLE, DONALD (1970) 'Readability—The use of cloze procedure', in Merritt, J. (ed.) *Reading and the Curriculum* London: Ward Lock Educational, 159–68.

the 'h' from the word 'when'. Though this appears in large print in a four word sentence a group of intelligent adults took on average three and a half minutes to locate the error.

Cloze procedure, applied to reading, requires the subject to fill in a gap, usually a whole word, which has been left in the text. In order to do this the subject must complete the language pattern of the writer by filling the gap, e.g. by supplying 'ran' in 'The dog — after my cat'. In order to complete such blanks in an extract from a book, the child must be able to react according to a number of criteria:

1   select a word according to grammatical rules
2   select a word with the correct meaning
3   choose a word which fits in best with the language patterns and vocabulary employed by the author.

For example, in the sentence given above the word omitted could equally well have been 'runs'. However if the sentence had been preceded by 'Yesterday my cat scratched a dog' the word 'runs' would no longer be acceptable for the omission must be a verb in the past tense. The synonym 'chased' could possibly be employed but is perhaps less likely to occur than 'ran' in the given text.

Cloze procedure involves accuracy, in that the child cannot hope to fill in the blanks if he cannot recognize the majority of words given. It also involves fluency and a knowledge of grammatical structure. Further, it necessitates understanding the text and therefore comprehension. As such it would seem to measure total readability much more nearly than any of the formulae or other measures so far developed.

Cloze procedure: how does it work?

There are a number of alternative approaches to the application of cloze techniques. It is usual to sample the text by taking a short passage from the early pages, another midway through the book and a third from near the end. This gives some idea of the internal consistency of the book with regard to reading level. Sampling of course has the danger that the extracts used may not be fully representative of the level of the book as a whole. It is necessary therefore to examine the complete text subjectively to assess whether the extracts used are representative.

Passages can be presented either with deletions, i.e. the use of the original text with chosen words obliterated, or with omissions, i.e. with the passage retyped, each word omitted being represented by a blank of equal size. Both methods have their advantages and disadvantages. In the former the presence of illustrations and the clue given to the size of the word omitted may influence results. In the latter the use of a different type face may alter the difficulty of the task, especially among very young children.

Omissions or deletions from the text can be selected on a structural or lexical basis. Rankin (1959) found structural deletions correlated at a significantly higher level with vocabulary and reading comprehension scores than did lexical deletions.

In structural deletion a certain percentage of words are removed from the text no matter what words these prove to be. In lexical deletion certain parts of speech are omitted, e.g. nouns or verbs.

Structural deletions can be determined by a table of random numbers or the omission of say every tenth word. Taylor (1953) found that though both methods achieved a similar grading of the passages he employed, the deletion of every fifth word gave the best discrimination between passages. It must be added, however, that Taylor was working with adult subjects and it may be that there will be differences from one age to another in the deletion rate which gives the best discrimination. Indeed Smith and Dechant (1961) suggest that among young children a passage cannot be understood if more than one word in ten cannot be read. If this is so then to omit more words than one in ten would prevent the child using his ability to understand the text in order to fill in the blanks.

The two passages below have been treated in an identical manner, every tenth word being deleted. Actual deletions are shown in italics. Quite by chance the parts of speech selected are heavily different and it could be that the difficulty of the passages presented as cloze tests could be significantly affected by the nature of the words selected. The two passages are graded by their respective authors as having a reading level of nine years. No information is available on how this grading was achieved.

Passage 1 From *The Village That Was Drowned* by P. Flowerdew (Oliver and Boyd, 1965)

'You haven't seen Foxy. Isn't he a pretty little *thing*?'
Carol gave the animal scarcely a glance. She was *bursting* with news of her own.
'Have you heard?' she *asked*.
'Heard what?'
She paused to give full effect to *her* coming announcement.
'This village,' she said in a dramatic *voice*, 'this village is going to be drowned.

All the *houses* will be covered by water. The church will be *covered*. The school will be covered. The whole valley will *become* one great lake.'
'What do you mean?'
'What are *you* talking about?'
'It's true. People in the town of *Westhill* haven't enough water, so it's going to be stored here for them.'

Passage 2   From SRA International Reading Laboratory IIA

About forty men live on this island, each man *an* expert in one of the many jobs there are *to* do.
'Any luck yet?' Bill asks, as he and *his* team get ready to take over from another drilling *team*.
'No,' one man tells him, shaking his head. 'And *you* won't find gas on your shift. Rock's hard now *and* there's still half a mile to go.'
The experts *had* said that there might be gas at this point, *but* it would be two miles under the sea. Bill *and* his team take over.
To reach the place under *the* sea-bed where the gas is trapped, great drills are used.

Cloze procedure: possible uses

1 The method would seem to commend itself to authors and publishers as a realistic means of assessing the reading level of books of all types prior to publication.
2 The teacher could employ the technique for grading the books within his/her own classroom.
3 Teachers might well find that a brief cloze test taken from the text of a given book and administered to the child before he reads the book itself would prevent a child experiencing failure through reading a book that is too difficult for him.
4 Cloze supplies a quick and easy way of checking important aspects of comprehension.
5 A battery of standardized cloze tests could simplify attainment testing in reading.

Preliminary report on a pilot study using cloze procedure in assessing the readability of a reading scheme

The purpose of this pilot study was simply to obtain evidence on the possibility of using cloze procedure in the grading of books for children in the early stages of reading. The Griffin and Dragon Books written by

S. K. McCullagh and published by E. J. Arnold were selected. These books were chosen as they have proved popular with children and are well graded. The only criticisms heard have been that the Griffins are heavily weighted towards the interests of boys and that the scheme is rather steeply graded at certain points.

Estimates of the difficulty of the books by teachers' committees have varied somewhat. For example, *Griffin Book 1* has been given reading levels varying from five to more than six years.

The Griffin Books present a single story in twelve parts which tell the adventures of three pirates. The Dragon Books were added as supplementary readers at a later date. Again there are twelve books but each presents a complete story. Here the characters are more numerous and the content would seem equally attractive to girls and boys.

Two passages of 100 words were selected from each of the twenty-four books, one beginning with the first complete sentence on the second page of the text and the other ending at the last complete sentence on the next to last page of the text. Structural deletion was employed and every tenth word was covered with masking tape. Children read the passages orally from the actual text and the actual responses were recorded though in fact only the author's original words were counted as correct responses for the purposes of the analysis which follows. All the children were given a practice passage before they used the Griffins and Dragons and all read the page before the one containing the cloze test. The books were presented in the order suggested by the publishers and therefore practice in using the cloze technique may have reduced the discrimination of the tests between the early and later books.

Children from two schools varying in age from 6.0 years to 9 years 10 months were used as subjects. The schools were chosen to represent a wide range of ability and socio-economic status. Ninety children were tested on the Schonell Graded Word Recognition Test and the Schonell Silent Reading Test R4B. Thirty-eight children were eventually selected for the evaluation of cloze results on the basis that the mean chronological age of each of the four age groups was equal to the mean reading age.

A further eighteen children were matched with the eight-year-old group and these children read the same passages without deletions. Their total reading errors were recorded.

A third measure was obtained by submitting the passages used for the cloze tests to analysis using the Fry (1968) Readability Graph. This computes a reading level from a combination of the number of syllables and the number of sentences per 100 words.

Results

TABLE 1   *Reading age levels of Griffin Books 1 to 6 according to the Fry Readability Graph*

Griffin Book	Reading age
1	6 yrs 11 mths
2	8 yrs 10 mths
3	8 yrs 1 mth
4	9 yrs 8 mths
5	7 yrs 6 mths
6	7 yrs 5 mths

TABLE 2   *Results of cloze tests*

Book		Percentage correct: closures				Total closures (possible 760)	Mean (possible 20)
	Average age	9·6	8·6	7·6	6·6		
	N	5	17	11	5		
Griffin	1	76	74	55	53	503	13·24
	2	72	71	49	35	457	12·03
	3	70	68	39	25	412	10·84
	4	70	67	39	17	403	10·61
	5	64	51	23	9	337	8·86
	6	67	66	31	12	372	9·79
	7	64	54	26	9	313	8·24
	8	54	41	15	5	231	6·08
	9	50	39	14	8	223	5·87
	10	44	35	13	2	193	5·08
	11	39	30	8	0	160	4·21
	12	36	25	6	0	134	3·53
Dragon	A1	79	71	49	62	490	12·89
	A2	81	75	51	52	501	13·18
	A3	73	69	48	35	447	11·76
	B1	72	63	44	29	411	10·82
	B2	70	69	39	21	412	10·84
	B3	65	46	26	13	291	7·66
	C1	68	49	26	11	305	8·03
	C2	60	39	21	6	244	6·42
	C3	61	37	16	4	227	5·97
	D1	50	33	15	2	198	5·21
	D2	44	25	12	0	157	4·13
	D3	39	28	9	0	152	4·00

Until applying this formula to the Griffin Books, I had found it to be reasonably reliable considering its simplicity. The weaknesses of assessing readability by sentence and syllable length are fully shown up here. One of the very strong points of McCullagh's writing is her ability to produce vivid description within the limits of a restricted vocabulary. However, descriptive writing usually employs long sentences and this explains in part the high reading levels given throughout. A second feature of course is the fact that American children start school, and usually therefore reading, later than British children.

The sudden jump of two years from Book 1 to Book 2 is interesting, for the passage selected in Book 2 consisted of the pirate's song. This has rhythmic repetition and children usually read it easily. However, it has very long sentences and the name 'Acrooacre' occurs frequently. Thus the Fry score is raised considerably on both items which it measures. It will be noted that the cloze test did not suffer any distortion because of this passage.

TABLE 3 *Results of estimating difficulty by counting the number of errors made in oral reading of the passages employed in the cloze tests of Griffin Books 1–6*

This table is based on the performance of 18 children—average chronological and reading age 8 years 6 months.

Griffin Book	Average number of errors
1	3·7
2	4·9
3	5·1
4	6·2
5	9·9
6	9·6

The results of the counting of errors method suggested by McLeod (1962) is shown for the first six books of the Griffin series. It will be seen that the grading of the books is identical in order to that given by the cloze procedure results. All three measurements used in fact suggest that Book 5 is more difficult than Book 6. Certainly teachers have often commented that Book 5 causes difficulty for children and it has been suggested that the high literary quality of the language used to describe the storm involves sentence constructions and figures of speech which are rather difficult at this reading level.

TABLE 4   *Griffin and Dragon Books in publisher's suggested order*

Main scheme (*Griffin*)	Supplementary (*Dragon*)
Book 1	
Book 2	
Book 3	
	Book A1
	Book A2
	Book A3
Book 4	
Book 5	
Book 6	
	Book B1
	Book B2
	Book B3
Book 7	
Book 8	
Book 9	
	Book C1
	Book C2
	Book C3
Book 10	
Book 11	
Book 12	
	Book D1
	Book D2
	Book D3

The counting of errors procedure would seem to have two weaknesses as a measure of readability. Firstly, it emphasizes reading accuracy rather more than comprehension, and secondly it demands individual application whereas the cloze procedure test can be given as a group test.

The cloze tests seem to suggest that with the exception of Book 5 the Griffin scheme is extremely well graded.

Contrary to expectations the cloze tests did not show any difference in readability levels between boys and girls. However one cannot rule out the possibility of a cumulative effect where, on reading the whole series, boys may eventually gain from the exercise because they find the subject matter of the books more attractive.

The Griffin Books were written specifically for the retarded reader in the junior school. It seems significant therefore that the only break in the smooth gradient from book to book at all age levels and between the age groups is shown in the difference between children in the 7 years 6 months and 8 years 6 months groups. The big jump in scores on the cloze tests between two age groups is so marked that it could hardly have occurred by chance. It could be that the concepts and language used are more related to those of the older child. If this is so then there is a further argument for not using remedial readers in the infant school, no matter how attractive they may seem to the teacher.

As the Dragon Books are a series of supplementary readers and are individual stories grouped in sets of three, their precise positioning from a readability point of view is perhaps not quite so important within each set of three books.

The cloze tests suggest only minor modifications in the order planned by the publishers. On only one occasion, namely the case of B3 and C1, is there a suggestion that the presentation in groups of three is incorrect.

TABLE 5 *Reordering of the scheme based on results on cloze procedure tests.*

Griffin	Dragon
Book 1	
	Book A2
	Book A1
Book 2	
	Book A3
Book 3	
	Book B2
	Book B1
Book 4	
Book 5	
Book 6	
Book 7	
	Book C1
	Book B3
	Book C2
Book 8	
	Book C3
Book 9	
	Book D1
Book 10	
Book 11	
	Book D2
	Book D3
Book 12	

It should be noted that the reordering based on the results of the cloze tests is not a plan for action by teachers. To suggest for example that Griffin Book 5 should be read before Book 6 would make nonsense of the story content of the readers. Rather, the teacher should ensure that children have adequate help to overcome any difficulty they might experience with Book 5. In the case of the Dragon Books certain reordering in the placement could be made without any real damage to the scheme as a whole. However it must be remembered that the scheme has been constructed around a system of vocabulary control. Thus any change in order suggested by total readability must be weighed against a break in the sequence of vocabulary growth provided by the scheme.

Cloze procedure commends itself as an empirical measure of readability which would provide information complementary to the teacher's own subjective assessments of printed materials. There are however a number of aspects upon which we need further information:

1　What is the appropriate number of deletions for each age group?
2　Will deletion or omission have an effect upon results gained and might this vary as to whether the test is given orally or in group form?
3　What variables affect performance e.g. vocabulary, sentence completion or comprehension attainment, intelligence and socio-economic status?
4　What effect on cloze scores is observed when there are heavy deletions of particular parts of speech?
5　Can a percentage score be suggested which can be equated with an individual's frustration or independent reading level?

Some work on the analysis of cloze procedure as a measure has been undertaken in the USA e.g. the factor analysis studies of Weaver and Kingston (1963) and Bormuth (1969). The writer hopes to report on some of the above questions in the near future as a result of work which is at present in hand.

References

BORMUTH, J. R. (1969) 'Factor validity of cloze tests as measures of reading comprehension', *Reading Research Quarterly*, 4, *iii*, 358–65.
FRY, E. A. (1968) 'A readability formula that saves time', *Journal of Reading*, 11, *vii*, 513–16.
LAWSON, K. S. (ed.) (1968) *Children's Reading* University of Leeds Institute of Education.

MCLEOD, J. (1962) 'The estimation of readability of books of low difficulty', *British Journal of Educational Psychology*, **32**, 112–18.

PASCOE, T. O. (ed.) (1962) *A Second Survey of Books for Backward Readers* London: University of London Press.

RANKIN, E. F. (1959) 'The cloze procedure—its validity and utility', in *Eighth Yearbook of the National Reading Conference*, 131–44.

SMITH, H. P. and DECHANT, E. (1961) *Psychology in teaching reading* Englewood Cliffs, N.J.: Prentice-Hall.

TAYLOR, W. L. (1953) 'Cloze procedure: A new tool for measuring readability', *Journalism Quarterly*, **30**, 415–38.

WEAVER, W. W. and KINGSTON, A. J. (1963) 'A factor analysis of the cloze procedure and other measures of reading and language ability', *Journal of Communication*, **13**, 252–61.

4:3   Sentence structure in reading primers

Jessie F. Reid

Introduction

The notion of deliberate control of the language of reading material for learners is now a commonplace. But it is relatively new, especially in its application to the very earliest stages of reading. The description given by Huey (1908) of the content of Webster's first school reader, published in America in 1783, contains the following statement:

> Besides selections intended directly to instruct the youth in morals and religion, it contained dialogues, narratives, and many selections from American statesmen and patriots of these revolutionary times (p. 249).

Later, discussing other American readers produced as rivals to Webster's, he talks of 'the preference of their makers for the productions of American genius'; and remarks of a very popular one—the English Reader of Lindley Murray—that it showed 'little adaptation to the needs of the young'. He notes that Cobb, who began to publish about 1831, was apparently the first to attempt to 'interest the child by means of stories, information about animals, etc.' (p. 251); and that Keagy, in his Pestalozzian primer of 1826, first tried 'to make use of the child's environment in an educative manner'. None of these books, of course, was intended for a beginner: the first stages of reading were concerned with the alphabet, with syllables, and with words either out of context or illustrated by pictures, in the manner of the *Orbis Pictus*.

The position in Britain seems to have been similar. But in 1857 a reading series called *Reading without Tears* was published. Diack (1965) describes Part One as having the first 117 pages devoted to practice with letters, syllables, short words and sentences, in the familiar manner. The

REID, JESSIE F. (1970) 'Sentence structure in reading primers', *Research in Education*, 3, 23–37.

first 'story', however, is worth noticing, for it began with sentences composed entirely of phonically regular words of not more than three letters. The book was in fact one representative of a new species, and by the time Huey was actually writing (i.e. by 1908) the situation in both Britain and America had greatly changed from what it had been some sixty or seventy years before. Primers were now common—books with the avowed aim not only of providing content suitable for five- or six-year-olds, but of deliberately simplifying in some way the language in which that content was couched.

The bias of a given scheme towards a phonic or a look-say (whole word or sentence) method determined the form of simplification which operated and the kind of reducing process to which language was subjected. In material produced as part of a phonic approach, the essential 'simplicity' was the phonetic structure of the vocabulary—that is, in its spelling patterns. The look-say methods simplified by having a restricted (though not a phonically regular) vocabulary, with many repetitions. They made sparing use of morphological variants, and tried to use words which 'interested' children. In a language-experience approach where textbooks were not used, or used much less, the simplicity was conceived of not so much as imposed from without as emerging naturally in material produced by the children themselves (Huey, 1908, p. 273–4).

By 1908, however, no empirical identification of words in common use by five- or six-year-old speakers of English had been undertaken in any systematic way. The control of the vocabulary of primers was still intuitive, non-quantified, and not susceptible to deliberate manipulation. This in itself might have been thought likely to lead to misjudgements in the choice of language. But a study of Huey's comments on the primers of his day shows that, as he saw it, much more was involved than merely vocabulary. Having remarked on the high standard of the illustrations in these books, he goes on :

> Next to the beauty of the primers, the most striking thing about at least three-fourths of them is the inanity and disjointedness of their reading content, especially in the earlier parts. No trouble has been taken to write what the child would naturally say about the subject in hand, nor indeed, usually, to say *anything* connectedly or continuously, as even an adult would naturally talk about the subject. (p. 279)

Huey is here objecting to the language of primers on syntactic and semantic grounds. He goes on to give numerous examples of the way in which, even when they intended to write naturally, authors of these primers have come, through their very preoccupation with simplicity, to produce stilted, artificial and inane phraseology, and shows very clearly that no notion of 'getting down to the child's level' by means of a formula of easy words in short sentences can take account of the complicated ways in which words, syntax and sense are bound up with one another.

Fourteen years after the publication of Huey's book, interest in children's vocabulary and in 'readability' was aroused by the appearance of Thorndike's *Teacher's Word List* (1922). After an initial concentration on vocabulary, readability studies were extended to the measurement of a great variety of factors, such as sentence length, sentence complexity, number of prepositions, and idea density (see Chall, 1958, for a comprehensive account of this work).

Readability formulae produced by combining these measures in the best weighting (as given by a regression equation) appear to have been used widely in the United States in the grading of existing textbooks and reading schemes, and in the assessment of new manuscripts submitted to publishers. More recently, word counts based on samples of either the oral or written language of children in the early school years have added to the store of precise information about words in common use (S.C.R.E., 1948; Rinsland, 1945; Burroughs, 1957; Edwards and Gibbon, 1965). Lists based on the vocabulary of existing reading primers were compiled by Gates (1935), Dolch (1942) and Fry (1960).

Reading as language learning

The aptness of Huey's strictures is borne out, however, by the fact that all the work on vocabulary and readability undertaken since his time has not removed the grounds of his criticism. Lefevre (1963), discussing the learning of reading as a form of language learning, deplores the 'fractured English and idiotic story line built into the controlled-vocabulary attack on primary reading' (p. 37). 'These materials', he says, 'have become a chronic national pain.' He asserts that one of the chief sources of error has been the concentration by the writers on vocabulary instead of on language structure, and draws attention to a fact that is symptomatic of this error, namely that the important distinction between 'content' words (or 'full' words) and 'structure' words (or 'empty' words) has been ignored by some of those who have drawn up basic word lists for initial reading material.

As examples, he cites the Dolch basic word list (Dolch, 1942) which contains 220 words, of which 107 are structure words, and the Fry list of 300 instant words (Fry, 1960), of which 129 are structure words. Both these writers, he points out, argue that the lists are to be taught as sight words, though Fry notes the difficulty of achieving this with words which are 'largely devoid of subject-matter meanings or object reference' (p. 141). Neither writer, Lefevre says, is regarding reading as a language-related process, but rather as a process of learning isolated words, which are then combined into 'arbitrary segments of print'.

Lefevre goes on to develop the view that since reading is one mode of linguistic behaviour, the learning of it by the child must be based on 'the language patterns he brings to school'. He abstracts, as the significant features of these patterns, four components: intonation and stress, functional word order, structure words, and word-form changes, and his subsequent discussion is based on the utilisation of these features of language in the teaching of reading and writing.

Fries (1962) makes a similar emphasis, though more briefly. Criticising W. S. Gray (1956) for stating that 'The final idea [as given by a sentence] is the result of the fusion of the meanings of the separate words into a coherent whole' (p. 69), he goes on:

> There is a layer of meanings apart from those of the words as separate lexical items. These meanings can be called *grammatical meanings* [his italics] . . . They are definite and sharp, essential features of every utterance . . . Since the connections of these 'meanings' with the patterns of contrastive arrangement and form are arbitrary *they must be definitely learned* [my italics]. (p. 70)

What is being said by both these authors is in some ways very similar to what Huey said fifty-five years before. What is new, however, is the availability of a theoretical frame of reference by means of which features of language may be specified, and an increased recognition of the need to think in terms of learning to *read structures*. The shift of emphasis to structure, and to meaning as conveyed by structure, does not of course dispense with the need to consider vocabulary; but it has immediate implications at the level of word choice. For one thing, it means that the question of the choice of structure words becomes a question not about 'lexical units' but about syntax and 'grammatical meanings'.

Among recent producers of reading schemes in Britain, Schonell (1959) makes explicit reference to features of language other than vocabulary, and it is interesting to look at what he says in the light of the views of

Fries and Lefevre. He describes the material of the *Happy Venture Readers* as embodying '. . . a variety of simple sentence patterns, adroitly repeated and increasing in length' (p. 27). He goes on to mention '. . . simple and complex sentences . . . a variety of opening phrases, . . . new joining words which are employed in the material in accordance with the order in which they emerge in their [i.e. the children's] speech'. In short, he claims to have controlled syntactical complexity on a developmental basis, though he presents no empirical data in support. In an earlier reference to 'linking words' (p. 14) he says these are 'kept to a minimum' and that prepositions, in particular, are 'sparingly introduced'. This way of speaking strongly suggests that in spite of his reference to patterns he, too, fails to sense fully the connection between the choice of structure words and the syntax they help to constitute, and in fact some of the sentences in the *Happy Venture Readers* tend to bear this out. For instance, the first sentence on page 5 of Book 2 runs: ' "Dick, this seat by you is for Jack," said Mother.' The five structure words *this, by, you, is* and *for* are all in the first 200 words of both Dolch's and Fry's lists. But the syntax of the sentence is sufficiently unnatural to suggest that the selection of words was made at a lexical level only.

At another point in the discussion, however, Schonell expresses a view about the function of an early reading book that bears importantly on the question of the selection of patterns:

> It is through early reading experiences that young children develop their first language patterns—appreciation of simple sentences, the form of statement and question, the meaning of an attractive word or a common phrase, a sense of balance, of rhyme and of rhythm—all of these, and other facets of language, are subtly and cumulatively learnt by children through their early reading. For this reason the material of first reading books should be of the highest merit, within the limits of the vocabulary, in style and in pattern of language. (p. 26)

Interpreted literally, the first part of the first sentence is patently not true, if by 'develop' is understood 'come to have in their speech' or 'achieve competence in'. But the remaining items in the list ('the meaning of an attractive word', etc.) suggest that Schonell is referring to the ability to manipulate structures consciously in order not just to convey meaning but to achieve variety and elegance. If this is a correct interpretation, there emerges at once a sharp contrast of emphasis between Schonell and Lefevre with regard to the purpose of a reading primer and therefore its linguistic content. Schonell sees one of the main functions to be the teaching of the elements of literary sensitivity—of a command of stylistic variation. Lefevre sees it as teaching the child to recognise, on the printed page, the 'graphic counterparts of entire spoken utterances' (1963, p. 39).

It is important to note that both these views concern ways in which learning the writing system of a language involves some kind of language learning. But whereas one is concerned mainly with 'merit' and the development of standards, the other is concerned with the ways in which the child comes to understand the actual features of the communication system—those means by which, in Fries' words, it conveys 'grammatical meanings'. The exploration of this aspect of learning about language is still far from complete. Lefevre, for instance, in discussing the learning of patterns of functional word order (chapter 5) does not deal with the question of how children arrive at the notion of 'a word' in the first place. But Reid (1966) and Downing (1969) have shown that the attainment of this concept can be a source of considerable difficulty and confusion. The implications for the teaching of initial literacy of Reid's findings, and of the differences between written and spoken language, have been discussed recently by Mackay and Thomson (1968).

The need for empirical study—Strickland

Before recommendations about taking account of structural patterns in reading can be fully implemented, there must be information about those which children of different ages actually use and about the order in which they appear. On the basis of this information, hypotheses should then be formulated and tested experimentally. Reference has been made earlier to the large amount of work done in the area of readability studies, and to the apparent failure of these to effect improvement in the syntax of early reading material. It seems very likely that the reason for their failure is to be found in the fact that these studies did not fulfil either of the requirements just mentioned. Chall (1958) notes that, up to the time of writing, practically no experimental evidence had been collected about optimum values for the many variables isolated. More recently, Schlesinger (1969) has observed that readability studies have been used to produce '. . . a yardstick by means of which the reading ease of a given text can be conveniently measured', and that the work 'has been lacking in theoretical orientation'. And none of it appears to have been based on observation of the syntax of children's speech.

It is this latter omission that is the starting-point for the study by Strickland (1962), who investigated the relationship between speech structures of children and those in the textbooks by which they were learning to read. In the introduction, discussing previous studies of the difficulty of children's readers, she writes: 'There is no evidence that such studies give attention to structure of sentences or to the familiarity of such structures to the readers for whom the material is written.'

The speech samples used by Strickland were obtained from contrived but informal conversations. They were segmented into 'phonological units', a phonological unit being defined by Strickland as '. . . a unit of speech ending with a distinct falling intonation which signals a terminal point' (p. 16). Strings of twenty-five such units were then submitted to a two-stage analysis. In the first stage, each unit was analysed into its syntactic constituents, following a scheme and a labelling system developed by a panel of linguists. The constituents isolated at this stage were:

1   *The fixed slots.* These correspond roughly to what traditional grammatical terminology calls the subject, the verb, the copula (e.g. 'is'), the indirect object, the direct object, and the complement. In the labelling system, the symbols 1, 2, 2b, 3, 4 and 5 were allotted to these elements, so that the pattern of any sentence—or clause in a sentence—could be indicated. For example, sentences with a transitive verb (e.g. 'I saw a cat') have the form 124; those with an intransitive verb (e.g. 'John ran') have the form 12; those like 'Mary is pretty' have the form 12b5; those with an indirect and a direct object (e.g. 'He gave me a sweet') have the form 1234. The term 'fixed slot' refers to the fairly severe restrictions which obtain concerning the order in which these elements may correctly appear. The transposition of the occupants of slots 1 and 4 in a 124 sentence will in most cases change the meaning: 'John told Mary' becomes 'Mary told John'. And word orders of the form 'John Mary told' or 'Told John Mary' are inadmissible.

'Question words' (e.g. 'where'), labelled W, also come in this category.

2   *Movables.* These are modifiers—adverbial words, phrases and clauses. The term refers to the fact that, in contrast to the fixed slots, they are subject to much less restriction in respect of position. It would, for instance, be quite correct to put the word 'immediately' either at the beginning, or in second position, or at the end of the sentence 'John told Mary'.

3   *Sentence connectors.* These are conjunctions, like 'and', 'but' and 'because'.

The second stage of analysis looked into the types of 'filler' found in the fixed slots and movables. It was concerned, for instance, with the different kinds of noun phrase that were used to form the subject of a sentence, and with the range, in type and complexity, of subordinate clauses.

For first-grade children, stage (1) analysis yielded 658 different patterns, produced from the four basic fixed slot combinations mentioned in (1) above, together with a variety of movables, and the common sentence connectors. Some patterns occurred many times; others were only sparingly used. In a study of language development these rare forms are of great importance, because they testify to what Halliday (1968) calls the range of 'syntactic options' at the subject's disposal. But here it is the most commonly recurring patterns and tendencies that are of chief interest. Strickland's figures showed that:

1 The five most common types of pattern had no movables.
2 Overall, the most common pattern was that employing a transitive verb.
3 Sentences involving the combination of two or more basic patterns were about half as frequent again as those involving one only (see table 13 on p. 29 of her report).

Her comparative analysis of the structures found in early reading material took account only of the overlap between that material and the speech of children at the grade levels corresponding to the books examined. It did not deal either with the frequency of the structures in the books or with structures that occurred in the books but not in the speech sample, and it took account of level (1) analysis only. Within these limits the main findings were:

1 Books for first-grade children differed widely in the patterns they used.
2 Use of movables was scattered, and most were movables of place.
3 Little or no use was made of the combination of two or more basic patterns in one sentence. The word 'and' was used almost exclusively to produce a compound nominal (e.g. 'Tom and Betty') or to co-ordinate verbs (e.g. 'come and see').

Strickland's general comment was that there seemed to be no scheme for the development of command in reading of sentence structure which would parallel the generally accepted scheme for the development of command in vocabulary, and the whole tenor of her argument is that schemes of this kind, based on empirical findings, should be developed and tried out.

Report of analysis of reading primers

The pilot investigation now to be described was undertaken in order to discover what differences, if any, appeared between four basic schemes at present widely used in Britain, and between these schemes and Strickland's speech sample, when the following questions were asked:

1 In what proportions do the basic fixed-slot patterns, compound patterns and movables occur, and how do these proportions compare with one another and with estimates from Strickland's findings?

2 What structures not commonly found, or not found at all, in the speech sample, occur in the early reading books?

Procedure

In order to answer the first of these questions it was necessary to render some of Strickland's findings as percentages; and here difficulty was encountered. In the first place, the various tables containing frequencies of pattern found for Grade I do not correspond exactly, because they are cut off at different points in the frequency distribution. Second, compound structures have been coded by using the symbol 'T' for all but one of the patterns. Estimates have been based on the figures in table 30 (see p. 63 of her report). They are presented and used here as having been judged the best available, but with some reservations.

The books from the four reading schemes were matched by vocabulary load. Although a good match was obtained for the earlier book in each pair, the step to the next in the series (next but one in the *Downing Readers*) involved increases of very varying amounts. The figures, together with the total number of structures found in each pair,[1] are given in

TABLE I

Title	Level	Vocabulary	Structures in sample
Happy Trio	Pre-primer 3	60	55
	Primer 1	115	72
Happy Venture	Book 1	62	61
	Book 2	165	70
Janet and John	Book 1	59	31
	Book 2	183	57
Downing Readers	Book 5	64	28
	Book 7	122	41

1 This figure includes non-sentences and short utterances as well as fixed-slot patterns.

Table 1. The sampling procedure followed Strickland exactly, and the analysis followed the scheme developed for use by Strickland and Loban (1963), except that some additions were made to the coding system in order to make extra distinctions, and to deal with patterns that had not occurred in the speech sample.

Results: basic fixed-slot patterns

The percentage occurrence of each of five 'fixed-slot patterns' in the four samples, together with the estimated percentages from Strickland's speech sample, are given in Table 2. The total number of these patterns is shown in the final column. Structures in question form are not included here, but questions are discussed on pp. 441–2.

It will be seen that pattern 124 is represented much less in all four than in the speech sample. *Happy Trio* and *Happy Venture* make very little use of 12b5 but the *Downing Readers* use it one-fifth of the time. *Happy Venture*, *Janet and John* and the *Downing Readers* use a much larger proportion of 12 than appears in the speech sample, whereas *Happy Trio* does not. But perhaps the most striking pattern is 2c(4) (i.e. the imperative, with or without an object). This is the pattern not only of the true imperative, but also of all the exhortations to 'see' and 'look' which have been such a focus of controversy and ridicule. The four schemes vary enormously in the use they make of it, and it often appears in a peculiar variant, typified by 'see Janet play'. The 24 pattern is rare in Strickland's sample,

TABLE 2   *Proportions of basic patterns in four schemes patterns (%)* *

Scheme	124	12b5	12	2c(4)	123(4)	Total N
Happy Trio	28·2	5·6	22·5	43·7	0	71
Happy Venture	30·8	14·8	46·8	4·9	2·5	81
Janet and John	23·5	10·3	36·7	29·4	0	68
Downing Readers	21·5	19·0	40·5	19·0	0	42
Average % (weighted)	26·7	11·9	36·6	24·0	0·7	262
Strickland's sample	60·6	13·1	23·2	1·3	1·8	1,910

Between schemes:

$x^2 = 36·684$ (on raw frequencies omitting col. 5.)   9. d.f.

$p = <0·001$

**Key to fixed slots*

1 = subject; 2 = verb; 2b = copula or passive; 2c = vb. imperative; 3 = indirect object; 4 = direct object; 5 = complement after 2b.

but O'Donnell *et al.* (1967) note that Hocker (1963) (who called it a 'hortatory' structure) found it ranking fifth in order of frequency in her sample of the speech of first-grade children. There are obvious implications here, as O'Donnell *et al.* remark, for the conditions under which speech samples are obtained.

Compound structures

Table 3 shows, for each of the four schemes, the number of compound sentences in the sample pages. It is immediately clear that all the schemes make only minimal use of the compound sentence form.

TABLE 3   *Number of compound sentences per sample*

	Book 1	*Book 2*	*Total*
Happy Trio	1	2	3
Happy Venture	3	5	8
Janet and John	0	3	3
Downing Readers	3	5	8

Direct speech

The structure by which direct speech is indicated in printed material may take one of four forms. These have been coded in this study as follows:

D21, in which the structure 'said+S' ('S' being the subject, e.g. 'Mother') follows the segment of direct speech. This is one of the standard literary forms, but is not used at all in oral reporting.

D12, in which the structure 'S+said' follows the direct speech. This is also literary, and seldom used in oral reporting.

12D, 123D, in which the structure 'S+said' or 'S+said+to+O' (e.g. 'Mother said to Dick') precedes the direct speech. This may be found in written conversation, but it is much less common than the other forms, whereas it is by far the commonest form in speech.

Table 4 shows the number of each of these four forms occurring in each sample. The percentage which these figures form of the grand total of structures is given in brackets. Once again the samples differ a great deal from one another. Moreover, the two forms that are natural in speech are hardly used at all, except in *Happy Trio*, while D21, the inverted literary form, is by far the most common.

TABLE 4   *Structures signalling direct speech*

Scheme	$D\,12$	$D\,21$	$12\,D$	$123\,D$	Total structures
Happy Trio	0(0)	16(12·6)	9(7·1)	0(0)	127
Happy Venture	0(0)	22(16·8)	5(3·8)	5(3·8)	131
Janet and John	2(2·3)	6(6·9)	1(1·1)	0(0)	88
Downing Readers	2(2·9)	13(18·8)	1(1·4)	0(0)	69
Average %	0·96	13·7	3·9	1·2	

Figures in brackets indicate percentage of total structures

Movables

Table 5 shows *a)* the number of movables in each of the two levels of the four schemes sampled, and *b)* the types represented. Wide divergences are again present, in type used and in numbers, and there are discrepancies with the findings on speech, especially in the early use of M_4 and M_5. Moreover, this analysis takes no account of the range of variation of movables which the schemes may exemplify.

TABLE 5   *Movables*

Scheme	Book	Number of movables	Type*
Happy Trio	1 (p. 3)	7	M_1
	2 (p. 1)	15	M_1, M_3, M_5
Happy Venture	1	19	M_1, M_2, M_4, M_5
	2	27	$M_{,1}$ M_2, M_3, M_4, M_5
Janet and John	1	5	M_1, M_2
	2	13	M_1, M_3, M_5
Downing Readers	1 (5)	11	M_1
	2 (7)	18	M_1, M_2, M_3, M_5

*M_1 = place; M_2 = manner; M_3 = time; M_4 = reason or condition; M_5 = preposition + slot 3, e.g. 'for me'.

Questions

The direct speech in all four samples contained some questions. *Janet and John* had three, *Happy Trio* two, *Happy Venture* nine, and the *Downing Readers* six. Since these showed great diversity of form, they were not analysed in detail. They do of course contain the 'fixed-slot' elements as do declarative sentences, and it is worth noting that out of the total of twenty only eight contained transitive verbs. Question forms are not scored at all in Strickland's speech sample, so no comparison is possible.

Discussion

The four schemes examined have been shown to differ substantially, in a number of ways, from a sample of the speech of American first-grade children. They employ fixed-slot patterns in different proportions; they make hardly any use of compound sentences; they use a great deal of direct speech, signalled in a variety of ways, but mainly by the literary inversion transformation 'said+S'; and they make extensive use of types of movables not common in the speech sample. Within this general divergence from speech they differ greatly from one another, so that a scheme resembling the speech sample in one respect may well diverge markedly from it in another.

Perhaps this analysis may be regarded, then, as going some way towards specifying the features of the 'fractured English', the 'inanity and disjointedness', deplored by Lefevre and Huey. It would of course be naive to try to maintain the view that even early reading books could exactly reproduce the spoken word. As Dakin (1969) put it 'Written language is not just recorded speech', and the problem of producing suitable texts then resolves itself into that of reconciling the requirement that the language should be 'natural' with the exigencies of written language and of the writing system.

On the basis of the findings described above it is possible to make suggestions for experimental work with reading materials in which the discrepancies between the schemes studied and the data on speech would be minimised, while at the same time the essential differences between spoken and written language would be dealt with systematically in some way that made them accessible to the learner.

1 Material should be prepared with much more use of transitive verbs. This, of course, is a statement not just about structures but about content. What is written about determines in part what structures will be obligatory; and it may be the case that five- and six-year-olds talk mostly about 'transitive' situations. Note, however, that English lends itself to a duality of structure in which, by using a few verbs like 'have', 'take', 'make', etc., a transitive form may often be substituted for an intransitive one. We can say either 'He slept' or 'He had a sleep'; either 'I have not eaten' or 'I

have not had any food'. This is, in fact, part of the principle of 'Basic English'. It might be worth studying in detail the frequency of these transitive alternatives in children's speech. They require more words, but they may well be 'easier' than their briefer counterparts.

2   The use of compound sentences should be explored. The necessity for short sentences has been taken as axiomatic for the last hundred years, but the notion that 'short equals simple' must be questioned. Methods of teaching, and of presenting print (such as the use of unjustified setting), which may help to maximise awareness of constituent breaks, should be seriously investigated, and the effect of the various transformations found in compound sentences should be studied.

3   The teaching of important graphic signals, such as inverted commas, should be sharply distinguished from the teaching of literary conventions like the inverted 'said + S'. The use of indirect speech, by far the most common mode of oral reporting, should be tried out. Again, it appears less 'simple' than direct speech, but perhaps by a mistaken criterion.

4   The type, frequency, and position in the sentence of the 'movable' elements, and the types of 'filler' (nominals and verbs) used for the fixed-slot positions, should be the subject of experiment. Schonell's grading principles, discussed earlier, rest to a great extent on these elements, apparently without empirical support. Yet it is surely of great importance that in Strickland's survey those Grade 1 children with fathers in the two lowest occupational categories used hardly any movables at all, and none of types 4 and 5; and that, over all the grades studied, children in the upper quartile of reading age used some types of subordination as many as *forty-two times* more than children in the lower quartile.

5   The difficulty presented by different question forms should be explored. For instance, comparison should be made between forms containing simply inversion (e.g. 'have you . . .'), forms introduced by question words (e.g. 'where'), forms introduced by locutions such as 'is there', and forms containing 'do' (e.g. 'do you like . . .').

In general, experiment should be undertaken in ways that make it possible to give an account of the syntactic content of trial material, and hence to manipulate it in known directions and amounts. The different kinds of teaching about language that any given reading material may do should be distinguished and specified, so that teachers may be clear in their minds about the kinds of understanding they are trying to bring about. The final aim should be to produce materials and methods by means of which children's linguistic resources, in their strengths and their limitations, may be first matched and utilised, and then carefully extended in ways which not only follow the chronology of acquisition but are of maximum usefulness in all aspects of communicative behaviour.

References

BURROUGHS, G. E. R. (1957) *A Study of the Vocabulary of Young Children* Edinburgh: Oliver & Boyd.

CHALL, JEANNE S. (1958) *Readability: an appraisal of research and application* Bureau of Educational Research Monographs, no. 34, Columbus, Ohio: Ohio State University.

DAKIN, J. (1969) 'The teaching of reading', in Fraser, H. and O'Donnell, W. R. (eds), *Applied Linguistics and the Teaching of English* London: Longman.

DIACK, H. (1965) *In Spite of the Alphabet* London: Chatto & Windus.

DOLCH, E. W. (1942) *The Basic Sight Word Test* Champaign, Ill.: The Garrard Press.

DOWNING, J. (1969) *How children think about reading,* Distinguished Leader's Address, Annual Convention of the International Reading Association, Kansas City, May 1969.

EDWARDS, R. and GIBBON, V. (1955) *Words Your Children Use* London: Burke.

FRIES, C. C. (1962) *Linguistics and Reading* New York: Holt, Rinehart & Winston.

FRY, E. (1960) 'Teaching a basic vocabulary', *Elementary English*, April, 41.

GATES, A. I. (1935) *A Reading Vocabulary for the Primary Grades* New York: Columbia University Press.

GRAY, W. S. (1956) *The Teaching of Reading and Writing*, UNESCO Monographs on Fundamental Education, no. 10.

HALLIDAY, M. K. (1968) 'Language and experience', *Educational Review*, 20, ii, 95–106.

HOCKER, MARY ELSA (1963) *Reading materials for children based on their language patterns of syntax, vocabulary and interest*, unpublished Master's thesis, University of Arizona.

HUEY, E. B. (1908) *The Psychology and Pedagogy of Reading* Paperback edition 1968, Cambridge, Mass.: M.I.T.

LEFEVRE, C. (1963) *Linguistics and the Teaching of Reading* New York: McGraw-Hill.

LOBAN, W. D. (1963) *The Language of Elementary School Children* Champaign, Ill.: NCTE research report no. 3.

MACKAY, D. and THOMPSON, B. (1968) *The initial teaching of reading and writing*, Programme in Linguistics and English Teaching, paper no. 3, London: Longman.

O'DONNELL, R. C. *et al* (1967) *Syntax of Kindergarten and Elementary School Children: a transformational analysis* Champaign, Ill.: NCTE research report no. 8.

REID, JESSIE E. (1966) 'Learning to think about reading', *Educational Research*, 9, *i*, 56–62.

RINSLAND, H. D. (1945) *A Basic Vocabulary of Elementary School Children* New York: Macmillan.

SCHLESINGER, I. M. (1969) *Sentence Structure and the Reading Process* The Hague: Mouton.

SCHONELL, F. J. (1959) *Happy Venture Teacher's Manual* Edinburgh: Oliver & Boyd.

SCOTTISH COUNCIL FOR RESEARCH IN EDUCATION (1948) *Studies in Reading*, I, London: University of London Press.

STRICKLAND, RUTH G. (1962) *The language of elementary school children: its relationship to the language of reading textbooks and the quality of selected children* Bloomington, Indiana: Bulletin of the School of Education, Indiana University, 38, *iv*.

THORNDIKE, E. L. (1922) *Teacher's Word Book* New York: Columbia University Press.

Acknowledgements

The author gratefully acknowledges the help given, in the gathering of data for this enquiry, by the headmasters and infant teachers of Drylaw Primary School, Edinburgh, St Ninian's Primary School, Edinburgh, and Campie Primary School, Musselburgh.

4:4   An appraisal of reading readiness

John Downing and D. V. Thackray

The discussion in the preceding chapters of the main factors involved in reading readiness and the ways in which they may be taken into account by teachers and parents indicates the complexity of the concept and the practical difficulty of determining any one point in time at which a child is ready for reading. The magic 'teachable moment' for beginning reading seems impossible to find.

There can be no decisive answer to the question. 'When is a child ready for reading?' because there is no single criterion that applies to all children or to all learning situations. Children grow towards readiness for reading at different rates and vary widely in the various abilities, skills and understanding which make for reading readiness; again, reading methods and materials differ from classroom to classroom affecting the threshold requirements of readiness. A more reasonable question would be 'When is *this* particular child ready for *this* particular reading programme?'

However, when classes are large in number, any help the teacher can be given in her task of appraising reading readiness is valuable; in such appraisal it is necessary to consider the many and varied items which contribute to readiness. The three main methods by which teachers in many American schools gather information concerning readiness are:

The use of a reading readiness test.
The use of an intelligence test.
The directed observation of each pupil's behaviour.

Investigations by Robinson and Hall (1942), Kottmeyer (1947), and Henig (1949), among others, have been made to find out which of the above methods is the most predictive if only one is used, and secondly whether a combination of two or all three of the methods is more valid.

DOWNING, JOHN and THACKRAY, D. V. (1971) 'An appraisal of reading readiness', *Reading Readiness* London: University of London Press, 89–99.

The research findings are not clear cut, but indicate that when methods are combined the correlation figure is altered by a minimal amount. As to which method is the most predictive, the findings of Robinson and Hall, who analysed the data of over twenty investigations, are still valid as shown by the more recent investigations by Spaulding (1956) and by Bremer (1959) in America, and by Thackray (1965) in Britain. Robinson and Hall found that the median correlation between reading success and these three types of predictive measures were: reading readiness tests ·58, intelligence ·51, and teachers' rating scales ·62. It is notable that the teachers' judgments scored highest in this comparison. However, let us examine each type of measure in turn.

1   Reading readiness tests

Since 1930 in America reading readiness tests have become more numerous and are now quite widely used there. These tests are usually group tests consisting of a number of sub-tests of the pencil and paper kind; they are similar to intelligence tests but they differ in that they are directed specifically at skills which the research literature shows are connected with reading. Standish (1959) has analysed eight American reading readiness tests and finds that, of the eight, all use a test of visual discrimination, six use tests of vocabulary, three use motor tests, two use tests of the reproduction of patterns and shapes from memory, and two make use of tests of relationship. Other tests used include: ability to recall a story, ability to remember ideas in sequence, pronunciation, rhyming of words, auditory discrimination, and handedness and eyedness. Examples of some of these devised by Thackray are shown on pp. 91–3 [in *Reading Readiness*].

The most widely used reading readiness tests in America are the *Gates Reading Readiness Tests* (Gates, 1939), the *Harrison–Stroud Reading Readiness Profiles* (Harrison and Stroud, 1956), the *Metropolitan Readiness Tests* (Hildreth and Griffiths, 1948) and the *Monroe Reading Aptitude Test* (Monroe, 1935). In addition to general reading readiness tests there are a number of tests used in America which are connected with a basic reading series; these tests are composed of sub-tests and some items relate to the material to be found in the basic readers.

Gates, Bond and Russell (1939), Betts (1948) and Harrison and Stroud (1956), have emphasised the diagnostic value of reading readiness tests. Betts feels that these tests have been a potent factor in furthering interest in reading readiness problems. He argues that, firstly, they make it possible for the teacher to identify specific strengths and weaknesses in certain areas, such as visual and auditory discrimination, background of information, vocabulary, perception of relationships, and secondly, that the fairly specific nature of the tests makes it possible to suggest relevant procedures for developing reading readiness sub-skills.

Another obvious and practical way of finding out if a child is ready to learn something is to try him out on a sample of the learning task and see if he can do it. We might call this the 'try him and see if he can' method. Durrell (1956) although admitting that reading readiness tests predict readiness fairly well suggests a very simple alternative method; he recommends teaching the child some words and then seeing if he can remember them. He suggests that children should be taught from three to ten words, printed on individual cards which bear no identifying marks that may be associated with individual words; after an hour each child is tested individually to see how many words he can remember. Durrell called this measure the 'learning rate' and feels that a child who can remember the words is ready for reading. It is interesting to note that teachers in Britain generally use a similar measure as a guide, though not in any structured way; they introduce the words of the introductory reader to the children and one criteria of readiness for reading is if they can remember the words.

There are no British reading readiness tests, and according to Morris (1959), who investigated reading in sixty Kent primary schools, although the Kent teachers interviewed had considerable experience in measuring ability and attainment by means of standardised tests, they were unfamiliar with reading readiness tests. However, Thackray's (1965, 1971) investigations have shown that five-year-old children can be tested successfully in small groups, and secondly that visual and auditory discrimination are the most important of the reading readiness skills which he included; this means that simple tests of auditory and visual discrimination given soon after school entry could be a valuable aid to the teacher in determining whether each individual child in her class is ready to read. As reading readiness tests become more diagnostic, they can be used not only to discover how ready each child is for learning to read but what activities are needed to cultivate readiness. When the classes are large it is difficult for a teacher to gain a knowledge of each child's strengths and weaknesses in various directions. The results of administering a simple reading readiness test can give the teacher an immediate impression of each child's abilities and enable her to plan reading readiness activities for children who need them, as well as giving her an indication as to which children are ready to start reading as soon as they enter school.

2 *Intelligence tests*

Since general intelligence is an important factor in readiness for reading, and since many have indicated that a certain minimum mental age is necessary for success in reading, group or individual intelligence tests are often used in American schools for appraising readiness for reading. Schonell (1961) feels that for the appraisal of reading readiness with British children, too, mental age is useful. He recommends as possible individual tests the *Stanford–Binet Intelligence Scale* (Terman and Merrill, 1961) and the *Wechsler Intelligence Scale for Children* (1955), and as a group test the *Moray House Picture Intelligence Test* (Mellone, 1944). These recommendations are not realistic, however, as British teachers are not permitted to use either the *Stanford–Binet* test or the *Wechsler Intelligence Scale for Children*, and the *Moray House Picture Intelligence Test* is too difficult for children below the age of six.

3 *Directed observation of pupils' behaviour*

Teachers' judgements regarding a child's readiness for reading have been shown to be very sound; as already noted, Robinson and Hall (1942) found a higher median correlation between teachers' ratings and reading success than between the latter and either reading readiness tests or intelligence tests.

The reasons for this are likely to be complex. But obviously a teacher who gets to know her pupils personally soon becomes sensitive to each individual's development in a wide range of aspects of growth—a much wider range than is sampled by either reading readiness tests or tests of general intelligence. Furthermore, our review of the research on intellectual factors in readiness brought out an important area of children's development which is hardly touched on directly by these tests. We are referring to children's cognitive development, and in particular their growth of cognitive clarity regarding the functions and processes of reading. Reading readiness tests are generally deficient in this respect, and intelligence tests are not sufficiently specific to bring out this aspect of readiness. New tests should be developed for this purpose.

Meanwhile the teacher's judgement can include such considerations, although, again, the published guides and inventories are also rather vague as regards this important aspect of child development for reading readiness.

Gray (1956) points out that teachers can observe their children's behaviour in the following ways:

1 Observing the characteristics and behaviour of children in their play activities;
2 Studying during class periods their responses in various learning activities;
3 Getting reports from parents and previous teachers, if any, concerning their interests, language ability, and the general status of their mental, physical, social and emotional development.

Most American writers of books on reading instruction and writers of basal reading schemes, have suggested the form a teacher's record sheet for each child might take, and the ways in which notes on all the important abilities and skills involved in reading readiness, could be recorded. Some useful forms have been suggested by Lamoreaux and Lee (1943), Betts (1946), Russell (1949), Gray (1956) and Harris (1961).

Some of these observation lists are very detailed, others more simple. For example Betts' list is very detailed and covers several pages; the list is divided into major divisions as follows:

1 Social adjustment, which includes checks on attitudes, emotional stability, interests and work habits;
2 Mental maturity, which includes checks on general alertness and ability to relate language and experience;
3 Background of experience, which includes checks on literature, information, school experience and home background;
4 Language adjustment, which includes checks on speech, language usage and reading and writing;
5 Physical qualifications, which includes checks on visual sensation and perception, auditory sensation and perception, nutrition, glandular balance, dentition and health habits;
6 Motor development, which includes checks on rhythm, balance and co-ordination.

A list of a simpler nature is that of Harris, which covers the following:

NAME

AGE

Mental Ability
General Mental Maturity (MA)
Brightness (IQ)

Visual Perception
Auditory Perception

Health
Vision
Hearing
General Health
Physical Maturity
Lateral Dominance

Experience
Cultural Level of Home
Richness of Experience

Language
Vocabulary
Use of Language
Clearness of Speech

Social and Emotional
Family Relationships
Emotional Stability
Self-Help
Group Participation

Interest in Books

Overall Rating

Schonell (1961) has produced a check list in the form of a printed card for use in British schools which he calls a *Reading Readiness Chart*. It is divided into eleven sections under headings as follows:

1 Mental level
a Remarks based on class observations
b Supplementary data—IQ, mental age
2 Reading Readiness Abilities
a Remarks based on class observations
b Reading readiness test results (or results from the use of a reading readiness book)
3 Estimate of experiential background
4 Extent and quality of play with other children
5 a Ability to listen to what is read

b   Ability to attend to instructions
6   Extent of vocabulary and talk with others
7   Attitude towards books and printed words
8   Social and emotional attitudes
9   Physical Equipment
a   Vision
b   Hearing
c   Speech (accuracy)
d   Physical state (energy)
10   Recommendations as a result of Sections 1 to 9
11   Further progress

Conspicuous in these three examples is the absence of any mention of children's concepts and reasoning abilities of specific importance in the learning-to-read process.

To the best of the authors' knowledge, Schonell's card is not used very widely in Britain, but most infant teachers do make notes of their day-to-day observations of the children in their classes and these records prove very helpful. A more structured form of observation and recording however could prove a valuable aid in judging readiness, particularly if it took more account of the cognitive factors which have been recognised as more important since the work of Piaget. For British teachers, however, such a list still would have to be short and simple. Bearing in mind the relative importance of the factors involved in reading readiness already discussed it should be concerned primarily with general mental ability, the specific abilities of visual discrimination, auditory discrimination, specific cognitive development as regards concepts and reasoning skills required in learning to read, and the cultural aspects of home background.

Many groups of teachers are at present working together to develop different aspects of the curriculum for all types of school. Reading readiness is a very important area of concern to infant teachers, and study groups of infant teachers should be encouraged to draw up simple reading readiness charts embodying the common experience and knowledge of its members; such charts would be readily accepted and of real value.

To provide a starting-point for teachers who wish to develop their own reading readiness chart we propose tentatively the following inventory of factors to be considered in judging a child's preparedness for the tasks involved in the beginning stage of learning to read.

Reading readiness inventory

CONFIDENTIAL RECORD   NAME   AGE

1 *Physiological Factors*
a Boy or girl?
b Vision
    i Have eyes been tested?
    ii With what result?
    iii What has been prescribed?
    iv Does child show any signs of visual discomfort?
c Hearing
    i Has hearing been tested?
    ii With what result?
    iii What has been prescribed?
    iv Does child show any signs of hearing problems?
d Speech
    i Does the child lisp?
    ii Does the child stutter?
    iii What treatment has been prescribed?

2 *Environment*
a Home experiences
    i Does the child have contact with books at home?
    ii Does someone read to him/her at home?
    iii Do the parents try to help?
    iv *How* do they attempt to do this?
b Cultural affiliation
    i Do the parents speak English at home?
    ii If not, what is their language?
    iii Does the child speak in a dialect, other than standard English?
    iv If so, which?

3 *Emotional, Motivational, Personality Factors*
a Does the child have any *very severe* emotional problem?
b Does he/she have an *exceptional* distaste for books or written language?
c Is the child being treated for a *serious* maladjustment of personality?
d What are his *special interests* which could be tapped to get him motivated to use books?
e Does he recognise that good things can be found in books?
f Does he know the fun that can be got from writing?

4   *Intellectual Factors*

a   General intelligence
- *i*   Mental age (if known)
- *ii*   IQ (if known)
- *iii*   If above not known, how quick is he at learning new things generally?

b   Cognitive development
- *i*   Does he *understand* why we have written language?
- *ii*   Does he *understand* the difference between a written word and a picture?
- *iii*   Does he *know the meaning* of 'word', 'letter', 'number', and other technical terms of written language?
- *iv*   Does he *understand* that spoken language can be divided up into words and sounds?
- *v*   Does he *understand* that words can be built up from sounds?

c   Auditory discrimination
- *i*   Can the child *hear* that two or three words begin with the same initial sound?
- *ii*   Can he hear that two or three words rhyme in their final sound?
- *iii*   Can he hear that two or more words contain the same sound in a middle position?
- *iv*   Can he detect that sounds are different in these three positions, beginning, ending, middle?

d   Visual discrimination
- *i*   Can the child match identical sentences in print?
- *ii*   Can he match printed words?
- *iii*   Can he match printed letters?
- *iv*   Can he find small differences in rather similar words, e.g. *kit*, *kite* or *bog*, *dog*?

e   Language development
- *i*   In his own language or dialect, how fluent is the child?
- *ii*   How extensive is his talk with others who have his same language or dialect?
- *iii*   How extensive is his vocabulary in his own language or dialect?
- *iv*   Fluency in standard English?
- *v*   Vocabulary in standard English?

In effect, the above represents a summary of what we have found in reviewing the factors related to reading readiness. But it presents more the fitting the child for the reading side of the readiness coin. In our final conclusions now we shall emphasise the other aspect—fitting the reading to the child, although, clearly, in using the above readiness inventory, the teacher will not be seeking the impossible 'magic moment' to begin. She will use it more to determine what kind of readiness or reading activities each child needs to make further progress.

Conclusions and summing-up

We have just proposed a new 'Reading Readiness Inventory' which teachers can use to organise their knowledge of each child's development in the learning-to-read process. As we pointed out, this inventory is also a summary of our findings from our review of research on this topic. It lists the factors we have found to be important in fitting the child for reading.

We have also concluded that readiness does not need to wait for mere biological maturation. There are many ways in which teachers and parents can help their children develop the understandings and sub-skills which are the basis of learning to read. Research has found quite clearly that readiness can be trained to a useful extent.

But we need to reiterate some of the warnings derived from our review of the research. In particular, teachers should beware of naïve conclusions drawn from correlational studies. The outstanding example in the literature of reading readiness is the letter-names fallacy. Although a child's knowledge of letter-names is a good guide to his general level of progress towards readiness, teaching children the letter-names has no effect in improving their abilities in learning to read. A more appropriate type of training would be to provide those rich experiences of natural language which are the probable cause of a child being both good at naming letters at the pre-school stage and good at learning to read when he comes to school. Such language experiences must be *natural*, not the artificial questioning procedures recommended by many teachers' manuals for American reading programmes. Language growth depends on experiences which are really relevant to the child—language which is integrated with his own interests and activities in his natural environment.

Teachers and parents also should view commercial claims for readiness materials or readiness tests with a degree of caution. With regard to published tests, none have proved superior to the professional judgement of the teacher. Indeed, teachers' assessments have been found to be slightly better. Readiness programmes which have been published have also been found in research to be no more than *as good as* informal procedures invented by individual teachers for their own classrooms. We must add that formal readiness programmes are equal to teacher-devised informal activities only as regards formal tests of reading readiness. The informal activities may have other valuable effects, besides.

Our final word must be to emphasise the direction in which educational thought seems to be moving as regards the reading readiness concept. In recent years it has been increasingly recognised that the teacher is the one whose readiness needs evaluating, perhaps even more than the child's. A *teacher's* readiness test would check such questions as:

1 How am I fitting my demands in reading to the child's level of readiness?

2 Do the reading books fit the child's experiences of life in his particular environment?

3 Do the books fit his language or dialect?

4 Do the teaching methods fit the child's level of ability?

5 Does the alphabet in which the child's books are printed fit his needs in cognitive development?

Although they have not applied their theories directly to the teaching of reading, two of the world's leading psychologists have given the lead in developing this more dynamic view of readiness for education in general, Vygotsky (1963) in Russia, and Bruner (1960) in America.

Vygotsky's important contribution is his concept of 'the zone of potential development'. He points out that the usual objective tests of general intelligence or some more specific ability only gives us a *static* picture of the child's actual development at one moment in time. This is useful, but it does not tell us the child's potential in making the next step in developing this ability. Two children may both score the same on such a test. Yet, if we give each of them the same amount of help, one might leap ahead while the other remained at the same level. The difference lies in the 'zone of potential development'. Vygotsky proposes that we can measure this by giving the test twice, once without help, and then with a given amount of assistance. Then we can gauge the child's potential for new learning.

This is rather like Durrell's method which we labelled the 'try him and see if he can' approach, and which many practical teachers have used intuitively. The important lesson we as reading teachers learn from this is that readiness is a dynamic condition *depending upon flexible features of the child and flexible features of the teacher and her methods and materials.*

Bruner begins by attacking the conventional view of readiness as some 'magic moment' before which it is useless to even try to teach the child:

> Experience over the past decade points to the fact that our schools may be wasting precious years by postponing the teaching of many subjects on the ground that they are too difficult.

Bruner asserts, then:

> The foundations of any subject may be taught to anybody at any age in some form. . . The basic ideas that lie at the heart of all science and mathematics and the basic themes that give form to life and literature are as simple as they are powerful. To be in command of these basic ideas, to use them effectively, requires a continual deepening of one's understanding of them that comes from learning to use them in progressively more complex forms. It is only when such basic ideas are put in formalised terms as equations or elaborated verbal concepts that they are out of reach of the young child, if he has not first understood them intuitively and had a chance to try them out on his own. The early teaching of science, mathematics, social studies, and literature should be designed to teach these subjects with scrupulous intellectual honesty, but with an emphasis upon the intuitive grasp of ideas, and upon the use of these basic ideas.

We believe that Bruner's words apply with the greatest possible force to the early stages of learning to read. The teacher who keeps in mind this quotation from Bruner will be constantly aware that reading readiness is a state of the teacher as well as of the child. She will take care, not only to fit the child for reading, but also to fit the reading to the child.

References

BETTS, E. A. (1946) *Foundations of Reading Instruction* New York: American Book Co.

BETTS, E. A. (1948) 'Remedial and corrective reading: content area approach', *Education*, 68, 579–96.

BREMER, N. (1959) 'Do readiness tests predict success in reading?', *Elementary School Journal*, 59, 222–4.

BRUNER, J. S. (1960) *The Process of Education* New York: Vintage Books.

DURRELL, D. D. (1956) *Improving Reading Instruction* New York: World Book.

GATES, A. I. (1939) *Gates Reading Readiness Tests* New York: Teachers' College, Columbia University.

GATES, A. I., BOND, G. L. and RUSSELL, D. H. (1939) *Methods of Determining Reading Readiness* New York: Teachers' College, Columbia University.

GRAY, W. S. (1956) *Teaching of Reading and Writing: An International Survey* Paris: UNESCO, and London: Evans Bros.

HARRIS, A. J. (1961) *How to Increase Reading Ability* (4th edition) New York: Longmans, Green.

HARRISON, M. L. and STROUD, J. B. (1956) *Harrison–Stroud Reading Readiness Profiles* New York: Houghton Mifflin.

HENIG, M. S. (1949) 'Predictive value of a reading readiness test and of teachers' forecasts', *Elementary School Journal*, 50, 41–6.

HILDRETH, G. M. and GRIFFITHS, N. L. (1948) *Metropolitan Readiness Tests* Yonkers, N.Y.: World Book.

KOTTMEYER, W. (1947) 'Readiness for Reading', *Elementary English*, 24, 355–60.

LAMOREAUX, L. A. and LEE, D. M. (1943) *Learning to Read Through Experience* New York: Appleton-Century Crofts.

MELLONE, M. A. (1944) *Moray House Picture Intelligence Test* London: University of London Press.

MONROE, M. (1932) *Children Who Cannot Read* Chicago: University of Chicago Press.

MONROE, M. (1935) *Monroe Reading Aptitude Tests* New York: Houghton Mifflin.

MORRIS, J. M. (1959) *Reading in the Primary School* London: Newnes.

ROBINSON, F. P. and HALL, W. E. (1942) 'Concerning reading readiness tests', *Bulletin of the Ohio Conference on Reading*, no 3.

RUSSELL, D. H. (1949) *Children Learn to Read* Boston: Ginn.

SCHONELL, F. J. (1961) *The Psychology and Teaching of Reading* (4th ed.) Edinburgh: Oliver and Boyd.

SPAULDING, G. (1956) 'The relationship between performance of independent school pupils on the Harrison-Stroud reading readiness profiles and reading achievement a year later', *Educational Records Bulletin*, no. 67, 73–6.

STANDISH, E. J. (1959) 'Readiness to read', *Educational Research*, 12, 29–38.

TERMAN, L. M. and MERRILL, M. (1961) *Stanford-Binet Intelligence Scale* London: Harrap.

THACKRAY, D. V. (1965) 'A study of the relationship between some specific evidence of reading readiness and reading progress in the infant school', *British Journal of Educational Psychology*, 35, 252–4.

THACKRAY, D. V. (1971) *Readiness to Read with i.t.a and t.o.* London: Geoffrey Chapman.

VYGOTSKY, L. S. (1963) 'Learning and mental development at school age', in Simon, B. and J. (eds) *Educational Psychology in the U.S.S.R.* London: Routledge and Kegan Paul.

WECHSLER, D. (1955) *Wechsler Intelligence Scale for Children* New York: Psychological Corporation.

4:5 Junior children's attitudes to reading: comments on three measuring instruments

P. D. Pumfrey and Elsie Dixon

Introduction

The majority of junior school teachers are versed in the measurement of attainment in reading using standardised tests. Far fewer are aware of the use of techniques to measure children's attitudes towards reading. This article is concerned with describing three such measures and considering their possible uses in school.

Attitude scales

Attitude is a complex concept. Its measurement in relation to reading presents considerable, but not insurmountable, difficulties. The responses of a child to a situation requiring him to agree or disagree with certain statements are likely to be influenced by a variety of pressures and the reliability of such responses are lower with younger children. The honesty of the child's opinion can be affected by a desire to give responses that will please the questioner, by fear of consequences and by the relationship between the teacher and the child. Despite the inherent difficulties in attitude measurement, there have been several attempts to measure attitude to reading. The following three scales developed in England were designed to measure this aspect of children's behaviour. They are briefly described and appropriate references are given for the benefit of those who wish to know more.

a Dunham reading attitude scale

Dunham wished to obtain evidence concerning the effect of the remedial teaching of reading on the attainment in and the attitude towards reading

PUMFREY, P. D. and DIXON, ELSIE (1970) 'Junior children's attitudes to reading: comments on three measuring instruments', *Reading*, 4, *ii*, 19–26.

of a group of retarded juniors. To do the latter, he had to construct an attitude scale (Dunham, 1959). The method he chose was that described by Thurstone and Chave (1929). In essence, this consists of collecting from a number of judges a wide range of statements describing attitude towards reading ranging from extremely negative to extremely positive. These statements are then individually sorted into eleven categories ranging from the most positive, through neutral, to the most negative, by other judges. Judges are not required to show their own attitudes, only to classify the statements. Each statement is then analysed in terms of the judges' classification. The scale value of each item, ranging from 0 to 11, is determined by the median position assigned by the judges. The variability of the judges in placing the item is also calculated. The more the judges agree, the less ambiguous is the item. The relevance of the items is also assessed. The items that are selected to comprise the scale must be shown to be relatively unambiguous, relevant and evenly distributed over the range of scale values. In taking the scale, the child marks all the statements with which he agrees. His score is the median scale value of the statements he endorses. In Dunham's scale there are twenty statements and the scale values of the items range from 0·4 to 10·4, the higher the score the more favourable the item. The following three items indicate the range of attitude to reading covered by the scale:

item 18 (scale value 0·7) 'John thinks reading is horrible.'
item 9 (scale value 5·0) 'Bill likes reading better than anything else.'
item 19 (scale value 10·4) 'Margaret only likes to read comics.'

The test-retest reliability of the scale was found to be 0·77. Its validity as indicated by agreement with teachers' opinions of children's attitudes to reading was 0·59. Bearing in mind the limitations of the study, these figures are reasonably acceptable.

The principal defects of Dunham's scale are that it is 'visible' (the children know what is being assessed) and that it is rather difficult to use as a scale for both boys and girls. Children sometimes have difficulty in responding to statements referring to a child of another sex.

b Williams reading attitude scale

Williams was interested in examining the often stated belief of teachers that junior children's failure in reading was caused by the children's lack of interest (Williams, 1965). She appreciated the need to present a measure of children's attitude to reading as a game so that aversion and test anxiety would not influence the results. Her scale was also constructed on the Thurstone-Chave model used by Dunham. The scale comprises twenty-five items with a range scale value between 0·5 and 10·5; the lower the score the more favourable the item. The following three items indicate the range of attitude covered by Williams' scale:

item 6 (scale value 0·5) 'Marly likes reading best of all the lessons.'
item 12 (scale value 3·75) 'Peter sometimes goes to the public library.'
item 24 (scale value 10·5) 'Tom thinks reading is horrible.'

Using small groups of various subjects, Williams examined the reliability and validity of the scale and the relationship between attitude to reading and attainment. The results were satisfactory.

Williams was anxious to ensure a favourable response to the orally administered test and she therefore devised the use of coloured counters to indicate children's choices. A red counter placed in a container indicated a 'no' response; a yellow counter indicated a 'yes' response. Thus the use of this scale involves having fifty counters for each child. Its administration involves a considerable amount of preparation if one is dealing with class-size groups.

The main weaknesses of the Williams' scale are its 'visibility', the assumption that children will be able to make appropriate responses to statements relating to a child of another sex and the difficulty of administration to large groups.

c Georgiades reading attitude scale

Georgiades was concerned with a remedial education scheme and wanted an objective means of assessing the children's motivation towards reading. He required an orally administered instrument to be able to measure the slight shifts in attitude that might occur. As he was dealing with children who had experienced failure in reading, Georgiades was anxious to produce a technique requiring minimum verbal ability. A colleague suggested that, when lost for words, children often expressed their likes and dislikes by an expanse of arms. A wide spread usually indicates a favourable response and a small spread a less favourable one. Puppets, John and Judy, with arms pivoted at two points to allow lateral extension were used to demonstrate the technique to children. The extreme positions, that is, hands wide apart for most favoured and very near for least favoured were demonstrated first. Strips of paper were placed between the puppet's hands and then transferred to the blackboard. Subsequently, a seven-point scale was built up on the blackboard related to the puppets' agreement or otherwise with given statements.

The children are then presented with a booklet containing twenty-three pages. They are given a further three practice questions to ensure that they have understood the technique. Then they are required to place a large pencil dot on whichever of the seven columns of increasing size represents what they consider the attitude of the puppet to be towards a given statement. The initial practice question is 'John/Judy always goes to the pictures once a week. How much does he/she like this?' When it has been ascertained that the children understand the response technique, they turn over a page and are on the correct page for the first question on the scale. The following four items give the flavour of the scale:

item B (practice)	'Last week J. had to go to the dentist. How much did he enjoy this?'
item 21	'Once a week J. was asked to read aloud to the class. How glad was he?'
item 7	'How glad was J. when he found he could read?'
item 11	'Sometimes J. was allowed to stay up late and watch television. How much did he enjoy this?'

Although there are twenty-two items on the orally administered test, only seven are related to reading. Thus Georgiades has produced a test that children enjoy, that does not reveal its purpose and is easily administered to children of both sexes. Total administration time is about twenty-five minutes. No index of reliability is given by Georgiades in his 1967 account, but with a sample of forty-nine children he reports a Spearman rank order correlation of 0.361 between reading age and total score on the scale. He also checked that the relevant items of the attitude scale discriminated between good and poor readers. Georgiades notes that the technique appears relevant to the assessment of change in a child's attitude to reading. Although in its early stages, the technique is one that can be readily developed.

Georgiades does not specify the technique used in constructing the scale but indicates that Osgood's Semantic Differential (1953) and the Thurstone-Lickert techniques have influenced the way in which the scale was developed. The child can obtain a score ranging from 7 to 49 points. The former indicates a negative and the latter a positive attitude towards reading. This is Lickert Scale type scoring (Lickert, 1932).

Use of the scales

The three attitude scales described were administered by E. Dixon to 304 second- and third-year pupils of two large mixed primary schools, one streamed and one unstreamed. Measures of intelligence and reading attainment were also obtained. The preliminary findings of the study are reported elsewhere (Dixon, 1969).

The above details have been given so that the basis of experience for the following observations can be appreciated.

Children's opinions of the scales

These comments are subjective but nonetheless likely to be of value. In general the attitude scales were tasks which the children enjoyed and carried out successfully except for six children in the total sample of 304. As there were no right and no wrong answers, failure was not an inherent threat in the situation. The children enjoyed completing the scales and asked for more. As one boy said, 'I've never been asked my *opinion* before.'

The mose popular of the three was the Georgiades scale. The children readily understood the ideas of graded responses and did choose over the seven-point scale. It was not apparent to the children what was being tested in this scale other than their feelings about certain statements covering a variety of activities.

The able children enjoyed the written presentation of the Dunham scale. Its quickness and simplicity appealed to them and they would have preferred to answer on their own. However, although the scale was orally administered there was still some hesitation by the non-readers who were aware that they were dependent upon the teacher. It was clear to most of the children that feelings about reading were being requested. Because the scale's purpose is fairly obvious, some defensive reaction is likely to have taken place particularly amongst the poor readers. The test is probably best suited to good readers who already have positive attitudes towards reading in any case.

Somewhat different in its approach, the Williams scale involves much preparation both of materials and of the children. It is not easy to administer to large groups as each child has fifty differently numbered counters to sort. This sorting process presented considerable difficulties, particularly to the dull children. If, however, the scale is administered to small, highly supervised groups as was originally intended by Williams, these difficulties are likely to be less marked. Because, in this test, children can see which coloured counter is placed in the container, copying of responses between children can occur.

Many boys *hated* being like 'Elizabeth', irrespective of the content of the accompanying statement. Similarly, some girls were averse to identifying with a boy's name. The Williams and Dunham scales were equally weak in this respect. It would seem both feasible and desirable to produce separate forms for boys and girls for each test using suitable names but otherwise keeping the content the same. Georgiades had foreseen the problem and so his test must, according to the instructions, be administered to single sex groups containing not more than twelve children—a tedious and impracticable task for most teachers.

All three scale constructors are convinced of the value of the child relating through the third person. The children did not find this quite so relevant or needful and many queried 'Why do you say "Are you like Tom?"; why don't you say "Tom thinks reading is horrible. Do *you*?"' Possibly children at the second- and third-year junior stage appreciate a measure of direct self-involvement. The instructions to Dunham's scale are the most helpful in this respect.

The above opinions were carefully gathered in the hope that they will prove useful in further work with the scales. The children were generally anxious to convey that their praise far outweighed their criticism of the scales.

The use of attitude to reading scales

Most teachers would expect attitude to reading and reading attainment to be closely related. Indeed, the expected positive relationship does exist. Is it possible that the measurement of both aspects of reading could help a teacher to help a child? Or is the measurement of reading attitude an unnecessarily roundabout and less reliable way of assessing attainment in reading?

From the evidence available, it seems fairly certain that attitude to reading is not identical with attainment in reading. Good readers can have poor attitudes to reading and vice versa. And attitudes may be less easily changed than attainment. Dunham (1959) found that it was possible to improve the reading attainment of severely retarded readers by the remedial teaching of reading for a limited period, but that a significant improvement in their attitude to reading did not occur. Possibly a combined attack on both attitude and attainment would be even more effective than the considerable benefits reported by Ablewhite (1967) in switching emphasis from diagnosis and remedial treatment of slow learning children to their involvement in activities likely to generate a more positive attitude to literacy.

If we, as teachers, are concerned with children's attitudes as well as their attainments, the value of sensitive measures of attitude to reading will be apparent. Most teachers are concerned with *more* than attainment. Many teachers judge their schools' and their own effectiveness more in terms of children's attitudes than of their attainments. This is particularly so with the less able children. It follows that the measurement of attitudes to various subjects will be one way of assessing the effectiveness of our teaching rather more efficiently than by impression. Knowledge of our effectiveness, or otherwise, is the only way of improving the service education offers to children. The use of scales such as those mentioned is likely to be of interest to the class teacher and of value in planning work and assessing progress. Further work will have to be done to develop our measurement instruments in this area. The use of more specialised techniques such as the semantic differential and repertory grid measures may also have something to offer here and it is hoped to discuss these in a possible later article.

References

ABLEWHITE, R. C. (1967) *The Slow Reader* London: Heinemann.

DIXON, E. (1969) *A Comparative Analysis of Three Reading Attitude Scales*, unpublished study.

DUNHAM, J. (1959) *The Effect of Remedial Education on Young Children's Reading Ability and Attitude to Reading*, M.Ed. thesis, Manchester University.

GEORGIADES, N. J. (1967) 'A report of a pilot study on the development of an instrument to investigate the attitude of children to reading', in Downing, J. and Brown, A. L. (eds) *The Second International Reading Symposium* London: Cassell.

LICKERT, R. (1932) 'A technique for the measurement of attitudes', *Arch. Psychol.*, 40.

OSGOOD, C. E. (1953) *Method and Theory in Experimental Psychology* London: Oxford University Press.

THURSTONE, L. L. and CHAVE, E. J. (1929) *The Measurement of Attitudes* Chicago: University of Chicago Press.

WILLIAMS, G. M. (1965) *A Study of Reading Attitude Among Nine Year Old Children*, unpublished dissertation, University of Manchester.

4:6   Why informal reading inventories?

Marjorie Seddon Johnson and Roy A. Kress

'Should I move Jane into the third-level reader?'

'I wonder why Rob is having so much trouble keeping up with his group?'

'Frank's permanent record card says he'd finished the first reader in June, but he can't seem to read the second reader now at all. What should I do with him?'

'I have eleven children who hit between 4.7 and 4.9 in reading comprehension on last year's achievement tests. Do you think they'd make a good reading group?'

Possibly these are not your exact questions, but they do have a familiar ring. Most teachers show a real concern for their pupils' achievement in reading. They also realize that good teaching is dependent upon understanding those to be taught. Planning for reading instruction is, therefore, impossible for them without thorough investigation of each pupil's present level of achievement, his capacity for achievement, and his specific strengths and weaknesses. The classroom teacher must evaluate each of his pupils in all of these areas. He can accomplish this task most efficiently through the use of informal inventories, which are actual structured observations of reading performance. The problems teachers face arise not out of lack of recognition of the need, but out of uncertainty about determining the correct instructional levels.

Various methods are frequently used to attempt to determine the proper level for a child's reading instruction. Prominent among them are standardized tests. For many reasons, such tests prove inadequate for this particular purpose. They are designed for group measurement and give information about the child in terms of group achievement. Standardized

JOHNSON, MARJORIE SEDDON and KRESS, ROY A. (1965) 'Why informal reading inventories?', *Informal Reading Inventories* Newark, Delaware: International Reading Association, 1–14.

tests rate an individual's performance as compared to the performance of others. By contrast, an informal inventory appraises the individual's level of competence on a particular job without reference to what others do. It is designed to determine how well the individual can do the job. Materials of known levels of difficulty are used to find out if he can or cannot read them adequately. Inventories can be administered on an individual or a group basis. For general classroom use, the group inventory is more efficient except for those pupils whose status cannot be appraised adequately without a complete, clinical-type inventory. The evaluation of the reading of children in this latter group may depend on an individual word recognition test and reading inventory.

The purpose of this bulletin is to suggest criteria for evaluating a pupil's achievement levels in reading and methods the classroom teacher may use to find these levels. Techniques applicable to both individuals and groups will be considered.

In both the group and individual inventories, the child reads material at known levels and responds to questions designed to measure his understanding of what he has read. Material at one level only is usually employed for each test when group procedures are used. In administering an individual inventory, the teacher has the pupil read materials at successively higher levels until he reaches the point at which he can no longer function adequately. In both cases, specific abilities can be evaluated at the same time that information is obtained on the appropriate difficulty level of materials for independent reading, for instruction in reading, and for listening activities. Getting all this information through group inventory techniques may require a number of reading sessions at various levels. However, with either procedure the teacher has an opportunity to determine levels and needs in the most logical way—by seeing how the pupil functions in an actual reading situation.

Nature of an informal reading inventory

Basic concepts

The term *informal reading inventory* is one in our language which expresses three fundamental concepts with three words. Consider first the basic noun in the title. This technique of evaluating a child's performance is an inventory in the sense that it is a detailed study of his whole performance in the reading area and those language and thinking functions related to reading. The second major concept is that of reading itself. In the label *informal reading inventory*, the function reading is widely conceived. The interest is not in mere pronunciation of words, but also in the manipulation of ideas which are represented by these words. Finally, the technique is an informal one in that specific methods are not standardized, and no norms have been established for performance to be compared with what other students can do. Instead, evaluations are made in terms of absolute standards. A child's performance is judged against virtual perfection rather than compared with what the majority of children might do if given the same job.

An informal reading inventory, therefore, offers the opportunity to evaluate a child's actual reading performance as he deals with materials varying in difficulty. While an appraisal of these specific reading abilities is being made, opportunities also arise for making informal evaluations of his expressive and receptive abilities in the oral language area, for reading is only one facet of verbal communication. As such, it is inextricably bound in with listening, speaking and writing—the other facets. An effective evaluation of a child's ability to read must take into consideration this interrelatedness of the receptive and expressive functions of total language performance.

Specific purposes

A number of very specific kinds of information can be obtained from careful administration of an informal reading inventory. Accomplishing these purposes is inherent in the administration of the informal reading inventory provided a competent examiner makes the evaluation. Because the usefulness of the inventory depends on accurate observation of the individual's performance in the testing situation, and interpretation based on these observations, only a competent examiner can accomplish the purposes.

Careful administration of an informal reading inventory can determine the level at which the child is ready to function independently, the point at which he can profit from instruction, the level where he reaches complete frustration with the material, and his level of hearing comprehension. Three of these four levels have special significance for the teacher. It is necessary to know the level of material the child can handle adequately when working on his own. Much of the child's school work, and certainly that reading which will make him a mature and avid reader, is done on an independent basis. Unless materials at the proper level are provided, the child can hardly be expected to do an adequate job in independent work and thereby establish for himself high standards of performance. All instructional work must be provided at a level where the child meets sufficient challenge to learn and yet has adequate readiness for learning. This means that he must achieve well enough to be able to absorb the instruction which is being given. However, to give instruction in materials which the child can handle virtually independently would be foolhardy. Finally, for oral activities it is important to know the child's hearing comprehension level. Too often the false assumption is made that if material is read to the child, he will be able to understand it regardless of the level of complexity it represents. For profitable listening activities one must know the hearing comprehension level.

A second purpose to be served by the informal reading inventory is the determination of the child's specific strengths and weaknesses. Only in terms of such analysis of specific skills and the pupil's adequacy of achievement in these skills can a suitable instructional program be planned. Teaching at the right level is not enough. It must be directed toward overcoming any specific weaknesses that exist. It must also be given in areas where the child has adequate readiness for learning.

For instance, a child may be weak in auditory discrimination of long vowel sounds and show no appreciation of vowel digraphs which represent such sounds. Readiness for the second area involves the first. It might well be possible to teach, at this time, to overcome the lack of auditory perception. However, it would be foolish to launch a program of instruction on the vowel digraphs before readiness is established.

A third purpose of the inventory is to help the learner himself become aware of his levels of achievement and his specific strengths and weaknesses. As he works with materials of increasing difficulty, he should be able, with the aid of the teacher, to determine where he functions well and where he needs assistance. In the same fashion, he should develop an awareness of the kinds of thinking and word recognition which he is capable of handling, and those in which he needs to improve. Without adequate learner awareness, instruction becomes exceedingly difficult if not impossible.

A final purpose to be accomplished by an inventory is that of evaluation of progress. Repeated inventories at periodic intervals should make it possible to determine changes in levels and in the handling of individual skills and abilities. In this way a true measure of the child's growth can be obtained.

Criteria for levels

One of the problems in determining independent, instructional, and hearing comprehension levels is the variability which exists in the criteria used for judgment. All too often, the criteria are quite low. Consequently, the level at which a child's performance is judged adequate for independent work often turns out to be one at which he has many problems. Instead of doing a high quality job with the material, he is perhaps operating at something close to the old seventy-percent-passing level. In the same fashion, children are often considered ready for instruction when they have a great many deficiencies in their operating patterns at a particular level. Experience has shown that when there is too much to be accomplished through instruction, the child does not adequately profit from instruction and retain those things which are taught. In order to overcome these weaknesses, high standards must be used for judging the achievement levels. In the following paragraphs, each of the four levels previously noted is discussed in terms of the specific criteria to be applied.

Independent level. This is the level at which a child can function on his own and do a virtually perfect job in handling of the material. His reading should be free from observable symptoms of difficulty such as finger pointing, vocalization, lip movement, and other evidences of general tension in the reading situation. Oral reading should be done in a rhythmical fashion and in a conversational tone. Materials, in order to be considered to be at an independent level, should be read with ninety-nine per cent accuracy in terms of word recognition. This does not mean merely final recognition of the words in the selection. Rather, this means that even in a situation of oral reading at sight, the child should be able to handle the material accurately, making not more than one error of even a minor nature in one hundred running words. In terms of comprehension, the score should be no lower than ninety per cent. Whether the reading has been done silently or orally at sight, the child should be able to respond with the same degree of accuracy to questions testing factual recall, ability to interpret and infer, and should have the comprehension ability required for full understanding of the material. He should be able to respond adequately to humor, for instance, or to follow any sequence of events involved in the material. In addition, the child should be able to make adequate applications of information and ideas to other situations.

INDEPENDENT LEVEL

Criteria * Word recognition: 99% Comprehension: 90%

Related behavioral characteristcs
Rhythmical, expressive oral reading
Accurate observation of punctuation
Acceptable reading posture
Silent reading more rapid than oral
Response to questions in language equivalent to author's
No evidence of:

lip movement	vocalization
finger pointing	sub-vocalization
head movement	anxiety about performance

* Must be met without aid from the examiner.

Attention to the independent level can be a key point in the determination of progress in reading. The child, his teacher, his parents, and the librarian should all be concerned with this level. All are involved in the process of selection of materials for his independent reading. Books bought for his own reading, his personal library, should be ones he can read well. References suggested to him by the librarian, as she helps him get resources for carrying out a project, must be ones he can use successfully. Homework assignments should be ones he can read without assistance. It is through wide reading at the independent level that the child has opportunities to apply the abilities he has acquired, to learn through his own efforts, to increase the rate and flexibility of his reading—in short, to bring his reading ability to the point that it provides him with real satisfaction. Only through his independent reading will an individual become a 'spontaneous reader', one to whom reading is a natural part of living.

Instructional level. This is the level at which the child should be and can profitably be instructed. Here again the child should be free from externally observable symptoms of difficulty. Again, as at the independent level, he should be able to read rhythmically and in a conversational tone. One would expect that certain difficulties might arise in the course of oral reading at sight; however, when the child has a chance to read the material silently, most of these difficulties should be overcome. Consequently, oral rereading should be definitely improved over oral reading at sight. The child, in order to profit from instruction, should encounter no more difficulty than can reasonably be expected to be overcome through good instruction. In terms of specific criteria in word recognition, this means that he should perceive accurately at least ninety-five per cent of the words in the selection. In terms of comprehension, he should attain a seventy-five per cent level of understanding of the material without instructional aid. When these criteria are met, the child in all probability will be able to reach, with teacher help, the same high levels of performance as were indicated as criteria for the independent level. In general, one should strive in instruction to have the child handling the material independently by the time the lesson is completed. If he begins the lesson with less adequacy than ability to get ninety-five per cent word recognition and seventy-five per cent comprehension, there is very little likelihood that he will overcome all of his problems.

Certain other evidences of ability to profit from instruction can be observed at this level. The child should know, for instance, when he is running into difficulty. He should be able to profit from minimal clues offered by the teacher to help him overcome any difficulties he may encounter. He should also know when he needs to ask for direct help because he lacks the skills necessary to solve problems he meets in reading. Here, as at the independent level, the child should be able to set continuing purposes for reading once he has been helped to develop an initial readiness.

INSTRUCTIONAL LEVEL

Criteria * Word recognition: 95% Comprehension: 75%

Related behavioral characteristics

Rhythmical, expressive oral reading
Accurate observation of punctuation
Conversational tone
Acceptable reading posture
Silent reading more rapid than oral
Response to questions in language equivalent to author's
No evidence of:

lip movement	vocalization
finger pointing	sub-vocalization
head movement	anxiety about performance

* Must be met without aid from the examiner.

It is in guided work at the instructional level that the child will have the opportunity to build new reading and thinking abilities. Building on the foundation of his previously acquired skill, he can profit from teaching and thus extend his concepts, his word analysis skills, and his specific comprehension abilities. Extension of these skills through both increased range of abilities and greater depth of applicability is the purpose of instruction. If this is to be accomplished, knowledge of the child's instructional level is essential to the teacher.

FRUSTRATION LEVEL

Criteria   Word recognition: 90% or less   Comprehension: 50% or less

Related behavioral characteristics

May show one or more of the following:
abnormally loud or soft voice
arhythmical or word-by-word oral reading
lack of expression in oral reading
inaccurate observation of punctuation
finger pointing (at margin or every word)
lip movement—head movement—sub-vocalization
frequent requests for examiner help
non-interest in the selection
yawning or obvious fatigue
refusal to continue

Frustration level. The point at which the child becomes completely unable to handle reading materials is of more clinical than classroom importance. For the classroom teacher, however, knowing this level may serve two purposes. Information on the frustration level may give the teacher some guidance about the kinds of material to avoid for this child's work. It may also give him some indication of the rate at which the child might be able to progress when he is taught at his proper instructional level. If a child is ready for instruction at one level and completely frustrated at the next, there is clear-cut evidence that he has many problems to be overcome at the appropriate instructional level. It is not likely that this instruction will progress rapidly because of the complexity of problems. On the other hand, if there is a considerable spread between the instructional and the frustration levels, a better chance for fairly rapid progress exists. There is evidence that a child can continue to use his reading abilities with fair effectiveness when he meets more difficult material than that truly appropriate for instruction. This fact would seem to indicate that the needs to be met at the instructional level and somewhat above are not terribly serious or complex ones. Consequently, he might be expected to solve any problems encountered relatively rapidly with good teaching to help him.

Specific criteria for the frustration level are these: comprehension of fifty per cent or less and word recognition of ninety per cent or less. Failure to meet the other criteria already described for independent or instructional level would also be indicative of frustration.

Hearing comprehension level. This is the highest level at which the child can satisfactorily understand materials when they are read to him. The hearing comprehension level can serve as an index to the child's current capacity for reading achievement. It indicates, in other words, the kinds of materials that he would be able to understand if his reading levels were at this moment brought to a maximum point. Criteria for judgment of adequacy of hearing comprehension are similar to those for the establishment of the instructional level. The child should be able to understand at least seventy-five per cent of the material when it is read to him. A second measure, and a very important one, is the index given by his own speaking vocabulary and language structure. He should, in responding to the material, show an oral language level which is comparable to the language level of the material which has been read to him. The necessity for the examiner to translate questions down in language level or for the child to answer in a lower level of language would indicate that he is not comprehending fully at this point.

All instructional activities involving listening should take into account each child's hearing comprehension level. Whether materials are being read to the class or spoken, there can be no real profit to an individual if they are beyond his hearing comprehension level. He may simply tune out when he finds himself failing to understand. Knowing the appropriate levels of oral language activities can lead, then, to better classroom attention and thus to greater learning.

The hearing comprehension level has one other kind of significance for the teacher. It gives him an indication of the level at which the child *should be reading*. The criteria in terms of comprehension are the same for the instructional reading level and the listening level. One should not feel completely satisfied until the child can do as well with the material when he reads it himself as when it is read to him. Therefore, a goal to aim for is equivalence of the reading instructional and the hearing comprehension levels.

HEARING COMPREHENSION LEVEL

Criteria *   Comprehension : 75%

Response to questions in language equivalent to author's

* Must be met without aid from the examiner.

Materials

The types of materials to be used in an informal reading inventory are dictated by the purposes of the inventory itself. Because the establishment of levels is one of the expected outcomes of the administration, it is obviously necessary that the materials represent a variety of levels. In a clinical instrument, for instance, it is usual to have the difficulty level of the material progress from preprimer level to the highest point that one is likely to need. These materials may represent a variety of subject areas and types of writing. However, if one were interested primarily in the achievement levels of the child in the science area, then materials relevant to this content field should be used for the inventory. Because an evaluation of competency in handling specific skills and abilities is the desired outcome, the materials of the inventory must present the opportunity for evaluating this competence. Obviously, not every ability which is a part of reading comprehension could be tapped in the course of each inventory; however, an adequate sampling should certainly be made.

The length of materials must be controlled sufficiently to allow the inventory to be administered without undue fatigue on the part of the child. In general, selections of increasing length can be handled as the difficulty level of the material increases. As few as thirty words might be used at preprimer level and yet 250 to 300 at ninth-reader level. Specific materials and arrangement of them for the inventory depend, to some degree, on whether the evaluation is to be in an individual or group situation. For an individual inventory, most frequently used on a clinical basis, two selections, preferably connected, should be chosen for each level, from preprimer to the highest level to be tested. One of these is used for oral reading at sight and the other for silent reading. Oral rereading ability is evaluated by having the child reread aloud a portion of the material designed for silent reading. For a group inventory, one level at a time might be handled in a directed reading situation slanted toward evaluation or, at most, possibly two or three levels of material incorporated into one directed reading activity. It is very unlikely that a full range of materials from preprimer level on would be used in one group inventory. Instead, the total inventory process might continue over a number of related sessions. In the group inventory, definite portions of the materials would possibly not be set aside for silent oral reading. When the children are operating in a group situation, there appears to be no justification for asking them to do oral reading at sight. Rather, materials should first be read silently as in any good instructional situation. Portions to be used to evaluate oral rereading should be selected so that the rereading is a natural part of the evolving group activity.

Ideally, the materials chosen for the inventory should parallel as closely as possible those materials which will be used for instruction. However, they should not be materials which the child has actually encountered in his instructional program. The inadequacies of the material which has been used for instruction seem obvious. There would certainly be the real possibility that the child would respond in terms of what had gone on in the classroom rather than in terms of what he was reading at the moment.

4:7   Informal reading inventories (IRI)

Ruth Strang

The individual reading inventory combines the diagnostic values of oral reading and observation. It is administered to individuals while the rest of the class are working independently. As described here, the individual reading inventory is informal and flexible. The teacher may modify it in numerous ways to explore with the student his reading performance and process. The IRI is specifically useful in the appraisal of proficiency in basic vocabulary, word recognition, and comprehension of paragraphs of different levels of difficulty. Every reading teacher should be prepared to use it.

Construction of an IRI

The informal reading inventory consists of a series of graded paragraphs which the student reads aloud; he then answers questions about their content. The paragraphs may be selected from various sources: from a graded basal reading series the student has not read, from *My Weekly Reader* (as are the extracts in the examples on pp. 478–81), or from any other kind of graded reading material. The teacher may also write paragraphs especially for this purpose and check them for reading difficulty.

As in other testing situations involving achievement and capacity, it is desirable to elicit the optimum response from the individual. Since reading requires effort, and since effort can be motivated by interest, the material chosen obviously should be as interesting as possible. Otherwise, lack of achievement is confused with lack of effort. Paragraphs from primary basal readers often are too childish in content for the bright child or the older retarded reader; he may resent being given such 'baby stuff' and may not even try to read it.

STRANG, RUTH (1969) 'Informal reading inventories', *Diagnostic Teaching of Reading* McGraw-Hill, 192–204.

The comprehension questions for an IRI should be of four kinds at least: questions of fact, questions requiring a grasp of the main thought, questions of inferences or conclusion, and questions of word meanings.

The following is an example of an individual reading inventory such as any teacher might make, selecting paragraphs of special interest to his students and asking questions appropriate to their level of understanding.

INFORMAL READING INVENTORY *(Teacher's Record Form)*

Some seeds travel
in the water.
Some seeds travel
in the air.
Some seeds travel
on animals.
Some seeds travel
on people's clothes.
(My Weekly Reader, 39, i, 3.)

First Grade: 'How Seeds Travel'

Questions:

1   What are these sentences about? (2 points)
2   How do some seeds travel? (4 points)
3   Why is it good for seeds to travel? (2 points)
4   What does *travel* mean? (1 point)
5   Give a sentence using the word *travel*. (1 point)

Total no. words: 23	Accuracy:
No. words correct:	90% (21)[1]
No. errors:	95% (22)
Reading time (wpm):	Comprehension score:

Autumn is a busy time
in the north.
Autumn is harvest time.
Potatoes are dug in autumn.
Corn is picked in autumn.
Many crops are being harvested.
(My Weekly Reader, 31, ii, 1.)

Second Grade: 'Autumn's Harvest Time'

Questions:

1   What are these sentences about? (2 points)
2   What kind of a time is autumn in the north? (1 point)

1   The figures in brackets are the number of words correct to make 90 and 95 per cent accuracy.

3 What is dug in autumn? (1 point)
4 What is picked in autumn? (1 point)
5 Why is autumn a busy time? (2 points)
6 What does *harvest* mean? (1 point)
7 Use *harvest* or *harvested* in a sentence. (2 points)

Total no. words: 27   Accuracy:
  No. words correct: 90% (24)
  No. errors: 95% (27)
Reading time (wpm):   Comprehension score:

> The U.S. Army has been buying dogs. The dogs are German shepherds. The Army needs 200 dogs. The dogs will help to guard top-secret Army camps.
>
> The Army tests the dogs before buying them. Army dogs cannot be afraid of noise. They must be smart and able to obey orders.
>
> (*My Weekly Reader*, 31, *iii*, 13.)

Third Grade: 'Dogs Guard Army Camps'

Questions:
1 What are these paragraphs about? (2 points)
2 How many dogs does the Army need? (1 point)
3 What kind of dogs does the Army buy? (1 point)
4 What must the dogs be able to do? (2 points)
5 Why does the Army need dogs? (1 point)
6 What does *guard* mean? Give a sentence using the word *guard*. (1 point)
7 What does *top-secret* mean? (1 point)
8 Use *top-secret* in a sentence. (1 point)

Total no. words: 51   Accuracy:
  No. of words correct: 90% (46)
  No. errors: 95% (48)
Reading time (wpm):   Comprehension score:

> A giant, four-engine airplane swoops low over a burning forest in California. A 'water bomb' drops from the plane. Soon, the roaring blaze is out.
>
> A helicopter flies slowly over a newly cut forest in Minnesota. As the helicopter moves, it leaves behind a trail of small seeds.
>
> (*My Weekly Reader*, 43, *iv*, 1.)

Fourth Grade: 'How Airplanes Help'

Questions:

1   What are these paragraphs about? (2 points)
2   What does the airplane drop on the burning forests? (1 point)
3   How do helicopters plant new forests? (2 points)
4   What does the 'water bomb' do? (2 points)
5   What does *swoop* mean? (1 point)
6   Use *swoop* in a sentence. (2 points)

Total no. words: 49   Accuracy:
   No. of words correct: 90% (44)
   No. errors: 95% (47)
Reading time (wpm):   Comprehension score:

> The big jet screeches as its engines turn. It takes off with a roar and climbs swiftly into the sky.
>
> Inside the plane, the passengers hear only a muffled sound of the jet's powerful engines. The takeoff is so gentle that travelers may not even know when the plane lifts off the ground. The jets fly at from 450 to 600 miles an hour. Travelers can go from New York to Chicago in two hours. They can travel from coast to coast in five to six hours.
>
> (*My Weekly Reader*, 44, *v*, 1.)

Fifth Grade: 'Facts about Jet Planes'

Questions:

1   What are these paragraphs about? (2 points)
2   What sound does the big jet make when its engines begin to turn? (1 point)
3   How fast do jets fly? (1 point)
4   How long do jets take to go from New York to Chicago? (1 point)
5   How long do jets take to go from coast to coast? (1 point)
6   Why is it so quiet inside the jet? (2 points)
7   Give an example of a *screech* and a *muffled* sound. (2 points)

Total no. words: 87   Accuracy:
   No. words correct: 90% (78)
   No. errors: 95% (82)
Reading time (wpm):   Comprehension score:

> Kruger Park is a wild animal preserve. The fence around the park will keep the animals in and unlicensed

hunters out. The fence is one of the steps being taken to protect wild life in African countries.

Africa's wild life has been disappearing at an alarming rate. One wild-life expert says it is possible that all large animals will be gone from the continent within the next ten to twenty years.

(*My Weekly Reader*, **16**, *vi*, 1.)

Sixth Grade: 'Protection of Wild Life in Africa'

Questions:

1 What are these paragraphs about? (2 points)
2 Where is Kruger Park? (1 point)
3 Why is there a fence around the park? (2 points)
4 Why are steps being taken to protect wild life in Africa? (2 points)
5 In how many years may all large wild animals be gone from Africa? (1 point)
6 What is a wild animal preserve? (1 point)
7 What is a continent? (1 point)

Total no. words: 69   Accuracy:
    No. words correct: 90% (62)
    No. errors: 95% (66)
Reading time (wpm):   Comprehension score:

Administration of the IRI

To be of practical value to teachers, a reading inventory should be so designed that it can be administered and scored quickly and easily. Both teacher and student will find the administering of the test more convenient if each paragraph is printed on a card for the student and on a separate sheet for the teacher that contains space for recording the student's errors in oral reading and answers to the comprehension questions. Since the individual reading inventory is used as a clinical rather than as a psychometric device, the teacher may reword the questions if he thinks the student knows the answer but is puzzled by the form of the question.

The oral reading of the paragraphs may be preceded by a brief preliminary conversation to explain the purpose of the inventory and to put the student at ease. The teacher may also give a test of knowledge of spoken words, such as the Gates Oral Vocabulary Test, or a test of word recognition, such as the Wide Range Achievement Test (Jastak, 1946) to ascertain the level of paragraph difficulty at which to begin. It is better to begin testing at too low rather than at too high a level, because the student's success in reading fluently and comprehending fully the easier paragraphs gives him confidence in his ability to read the more difficult ones.

If the teacher has a double-spaced typed copy of the paragraphs to be read, he can quickly mark the errors for each student according to the following code (see also Gray, 1963):

1 Encircle all *omissions* (whole words, syllables, letter sounds, endings, etc.).
2 Insert with a caret (∧) all *insertions*.
3 Underline and write in all *mispronunciations* (writing in the mispronunciations indicates whether the child uses initial-sound clues, shape-of-word clues, or no perceptible clues at all).
4 Draw a line *through* words for which substitutions were made; write in the *substitution*. (Note whether it makes sense, indicating that the child is reading for meaning, or whether it is irrelevant to the context.)
5 Use dotted or wavy line to indicate *repetitions*.

Example

Spot was ⓐ good dog. He never ran after the boys and girls or automobiles. But Woof was ̶ saw ̶ a naughty dog. He ran after dogs boys and girls and horses and automobiles, and he barked at ⓐll of ̶ them.

The teacher may add a comprehension check after each paragraph, for example:

1 What is the story about?
2 What kind of dog was Spot?
3 How was Woof different from Spot?
4 Why was Woof a bad dog?

It is best to write each student's answers to the questions because the quality of these answers may vary widely within the limits of correctness.

As the student reads each paragraph orally, the teacher indicates his errors and jots down his responses to the questions. Usually the teacher tells the student a word on which he pauses for about five seconds or when he asks for help. When the same word recurs in the paragraph, the teacher can see how the student attacks a word when he meets it the second time. His failure to recognize it a second time is counted as another error. The teacher may aid the student's comprehension by asking what the word might mean in the sentence. Inequality of response from paragraph to paragraph is to be expected. This may be partly due to unequal interest in or degrees of familiarity with the topics. When the paragraphs become very difficult, the examiner may ask the student just to pick out the words he knows. He stops before the situation has become distressing.

If time permits, the teacher may learn more about the student's reading process by asking him about his method of reading, for example, how he got the meaning of some of the difficult words and why he had difficulty with others.

After the first oral reading the student may be asked to read the same paragraphs silently and then reread them orally. His improvement in pronunciation and comprehension is then noted. Improvement in comprehension may be due to his having the questions in mind as he rereads the paragraphs.

Asking the student to recognize and recall words that begin and end with the same sound as the stimulus word gives further understanding of his phonic ability, speaking vocabulary, and 'divergent thinking'.

The following responses were made by a ten-year-old boy (Johnny, of course!) when he was asked for: 1) words that begin with the same sound as

can king, cook
saw see, so, salt, said

and 2) words that end with the same sound, that rhyme with

can ban
keep sleep, peep
pig mig, lig

At this point the teacher said, 'What does *lig* mean?' Johnny replied, 'That gets me, too.' Teacher: 'You made it up, didn't you? We call it a nonsense syllable. It has no meaning. You have a very good ear for sounds.'

Asking a student to read a portion of a play or conversation in a story will yield further indication of his ability to read for meaning with proper phrasing and expression.

Reading aloud to the student other paragraphs beginning at or a little below his oral reading frustration level and testing his comprehension of them will show any discrepancy between his auditory comprehension and his instructional level of oral reading.

Administering a timed silent reading test composed of similar paragraphs will make possible a comparison between a child's silent and oral reading proficiency.

Instruction may be interwoven with testing in administering the individual reading inventory. If the teacher gives instruction or suggests exercises to correct difficulties as they are recognized, the student has immediate incentive to work on them.

From these procedures the teacher may select a pattern appropriate for his students. Even a recording of a student's response to one or two paragraphs has diagnostic value.

Recording of student's responses

After obtaining the student's responses on the IRI form, the teacher may record the errors and other kinds of responses to the graded paragraphs (see Checklist, page 485). The number and kinds of error usually increase as the paragraphs increase in difficulty.

To obtain a qualitative impression of the student's reading performance, the teacher may note the pattern of errors in word recognition and the quality of comprehension—whether the student answers questions briefly or at length, in his own words or those of the book; whether he reports accurately what the author says or makes up stories and inserts information that was not in the paragraphs.

From the information recorded on the reading inventory sheet, the teacher may estimate the student's reading level and capacity. The characteristics of these levels have been described by Betts (1957) as follows:

1   *Independent reading level*
Not more than one word recognition error per 100 words.
Comprehension of at least 90 per cent.
Reading well phrased, natural intonation.
Freedom from tension and anxiety.
2   *Instructional reading level*
Not more than one word recognition error per 20 words.
Comprehension of at least 75 per cent.
After silent study reads the passage in conversational tone with proper phrasing and without tension.

TABLE I. *Checklist for recording performance on oral reading paragraphs*

Name.................................. Grade.................. Date........

Paragraphs	Rating on given paragraph level						General impressions
	I	II	III	IV	V	VI	
Word attack:							
Refuses to attempt unknown words							
Omits words or parts of words							
Inserts words							
Guesses at words:							
Makes sense							
Does not make sense							
Repeats words or parts of words							
Reverses letters or words							
Spells out words							
Sounds out words laboriously							
Recognizes beginning sound							
Mispronounces the whole word							
Recognizes other sounds and tries pronunciation							
Checks pronunciation with meaning in sentence							
Uses structural parts							
Uses combination of methods							
Phrasing:							
Reads in thought units							
Poor grouping							
Word-by-word reading							
Monotone							
Ignores punctuation							
Posture:							
Good							
Book too close							
Book too far							
Finger pointing							
Speed, wpm:							
Comprehension:							
Main ideas identified							
Details							
Inference							
Vocabulary							
Comparison between oral and silent reading							
Comprehension:							
Little or no difference							
Silent reading slightly superior							
Silent reading twice as good as oral							
Little or no improvement in oral reading							
Grade levels:							
Independent							
Instructional							
Frustrational							
Capacity 75% comprehension or better							
Listening comprehension							
No better than reading							
Slightly better							
Much better							

3   *Frustration reading level*
Errors and refusals to attempt to read difficult words are numerous, as many
as 10 per cent of the running words.
Comprehension is less than half of what is read.
Tension, distractability, withdrawal from task.

4   *Probable reading capacity level*
The most difficult paragraph on which the student can comprehend at least
75 per cent when it is read aloud to him; he can pronounce and use properly
many of the words and language structures in the selection.

The percentage of accuracy and comprehension for the independent,
instructional, and frustration levels of reading is set rather arbitrarily at
different levels by various people. More important than estimates of reading level is the diagnostic information which leads directly to improvement
of reading.

On the independent level the student can do much supplementary reading for enjoyment and information. On the instructional level he can read
challenging material with some instruction and guidance from the teacher.
Subjecting students to books on their frustration level tends to perpetuate
errors and cause dislike of reading.

Interpretation

The information obtained incidentally or systematically in giving the individual reading inventory lends itself to interpretation and application.
The following are a few suggestions:

Word calling

Word callers, who read with apparent fluency but little or no comprehension, need to focus their attention on meaning rather than on pronunciation. They need exercises in reading directions to which they will respond
by action.

Word recognition

Difficulty in word recognition may stem from a hearing loss. The
examiner may check for a possible lack of auditory acuity by saying
something in a low voice when the student is not looking at him. If the
trouble stems from the student's inability to associate printed symbols
with sounds, the need for a phonic inventory is indicated. Quite frequently
any individual may be able to recognize the sounds of letters in words but

be unable to pronounce the word correctly. Some students are able to recognize only the initial sound of a word; from this they guess at the meaning. They need frequent, systematic application of word recognition skills when they meet unfamiliar words in their reading.

Critical reading and thinking

A discrepancy between the student's abilities to answer factual questions and those requiring more thought may be due to lack of practice rather than lack of ability. In the individual interview, when encouraged to think and guided in the process, many students show latent ability.

Word meaning

In recording substitutions, it is important to note what kinds of words are substituted. The student who substitutes *scurried* for *scampered* in the sentence 'The squirrel scampered' shows that he is reading for meaning, whereas the student who reads 'a bowl of soap' for 'a bowl of soup' shows lack of concern for content.

Mental ability

The individual inventory situation, if supplemented, as it usually is, by the teacher's information about the children in his class whom he already knows very well, yields clues that help the teacher interpret a student's mental ability. A student's superior mental ability may have been suppressed by his deprivation of intellectual stimulation in infancy and childhood, by anxiety, by fear, or by other environmental factors.

Attitudes and emotions

From observation of the individual's personal appearance and behavior, his friendliness or unfriendliness, his social poise or embarrassment, his enthusiasm or indifference, the teacher may gather something about his attitudes. For example, John had experienced several failures and was resentful about them. In his words, the art teacher was 'crazy'; the shop [1] teacher was 'an old guy, quite crazy, too'. In a class for slow learners, the other boys called him 'the genius' because his mother had insisted on his going into the high school academic course; she was determined that he would eventually go to college. He stopped going to church and Sunday school because he was called upon to read aloud. Hints of his subsurface hostility, which came out in the IRI, were explored further through daily observation.

1 *Editorial footnote*: shop—boys' crafts, e.g. woodwork and metalwork.

Another boy, who gave many indications of anxiety and apathy, was asked what was his favorite activity; he replied, 'Going to bed'. The fact that he was blocked on the easiest paragraph but later read a harder one fairly fluently showed that he could perform more efficiently after he realized that the situation was non-threatening.

Signs of tension such as nail biting or twisting and turning in the seat may be readily observed. It is also interesting to see how an individual responds to increased difficulty and what happens when he moves from a satisfying to an unsuccessful experience.

Interests

Students usually express their interests freely in the individual reading situation. For example, one boy spoke with enthusiasm of the wonderful time he had had on a New England farm during the summer. During the winter he spent much time watching TV.

Recommendations

Recommendations based on the individual reading inventory, plus all the other information available about the student, should be highly personal and build on assets. Among general recommendations frequently growing out of an individual inventory are the following:

1 Continued efforts in school to give the student the experience of success in reading. In every class, skillful instruction along the specific lines indicated by the diagnosis can lead to improvement.

2 Provision of suitable reading material; even 'baby books' are sometimes recommended for emotionally disturbed children who have a need to live again through the baby stage. These books have therapeutic value in addition to increasing the child's reading fluency. Older students who are eager to read better often will accept beginner books if they are convinced that this is the path to improvement.

3 Analysis and correction of underlying factors and environmental conditions that may be preventing progress. Among these are psycholinguistic deficiencies, the influences of a disadvantaged home background, and lack of intellectual stimulation.

4 Analysis of the reading tasks into sequential steps by which all may learn.

5 Referral to a counselor who can find resources for widening the individual's school activities and interests, provide supporting counseling,

and adjust the school program to meet his need. Sometimes it is desirable that the student be given a change of class or course. If the parents refuse to consent to the change, they must assume responsibility if the student continues to fail in his present course or if his reading problem becomes aggravated.

6   Work with parents when there is clear evidence that home conditions are continuing to prevent reading improvement. With adolescents whose parents have confirmed unrealistic attitudes and ambitions, it is sometimes possible to help the child change his attitude toward the home situation so that it does not continue to interfere with his progress.

7   Referral to a child guidance or mental hygiene clinic if the problem is primarily emotional.

Group reading inventories

The group reading inventory is used to obtain additional understanding of the reading proficiency of students in any class. The most important part of the inventory is the informal test already described. To this are added questions on study skills, location-of-information skills, and other skills needed in reading the particular subject. Ability to apply the ideas gained from the passage to current events or to personal problems may also be appraised in this informal group inventory.

Students mark their own papers to see for themselves their strengths and difficulties in reading. Junior high school students are especially interested in themselves as persons and like to know about their reading efficiency. When the student has corrected his inventory, he tabulates the results on the front page under each main heading. A check may indicate either skills in which the student needs instruction and practice or, if preferred, the skills he has mastered. If a student scores much below the average for his grade, he should be given an individual reading inventory.

Detailed directions for making group reading inventories for English, social studies, and science classes were worked out for teachers by Dr David Shepherd when he was serving as reading consultant at the Norwalk (Connecticut) High School. The English Group Inventory is reproduced here with his permission. Permission for reprinting parts of the social studies inventories was obtained from Harper & Row, Publishers, Incorporated (Shepherd, 1960).

TABLE 2   ENGLISH : *Group reading inventory*

Directions for making and administering a diagnostic survey test of reading skills using an English literature textbook:

1 Use between 35–40 questions.
2 Use questions designed to measure the following reading skills in the proportions shown below.

(1) Using parts of a book. Include use of (three questions in all):

    a. Table of contents ⎫
    b. Index of titles   ⎪
    c. Glossary   ⎬ If such sections are included
    d. Biographical data ⎪ in the textbook
    e. Introductory paragraph to story ⎭

(2) Vocabulary

    a. Meaning (seven to eight questions)
      1 General background of word meanings
        (*a*) select correct meanings from several dictionary meanings
        (*b*) antonyms, synonyms
      2 Contextual meanings
    b. Word recognition and attack (14–15 questions)
      1 Divide words into syllables
      2 Designate the accented syllable
      3 Note and give meaning of prefixes and suffixes
      4 Changing the part of speech of a word (i.e., noun to verb, adjective to adverb, etc.)

(3) Comprehension (11–12 questions)

    a. Noting the main idea
    b. Recalling pertinent supporting details
    c. Drawing conclusions, inferences
    d. Noting the sequence of ideas

(4) Reading rate—Have pupil note the time it takes for him to read the selection. Then figure his reading speed in words per minute. Example: Words in selection, 4,000; Time to read: 10 minutes; 4,000 ÷ 10 equals 400 words per minute. Time may be recorded by pupils noting time by clock of starting and of stopping to get total number of minutes.

(5) Skimming to locate information (2–5 questions). Use a different selection that was not used for comprehension and speed purposes.

3. Choose a reading selection of not more than three or four pages.
4 In administering the inventory:

(1) Explain to the pupils the purpose of the inventory and the reading skills the inventory is designed to measure. As the inventory is given let the pupils know the skill being measured.

(2) Read each question twice.

(3) Questions on the use of the parts of the book are asked first. Pupils will use their books.

(4) Introduce the reading selection, culling pupil background of experience on the topic and setting purpose for reading.

(5) Selection read silently. Speed noted and figured.

(6) Ask questions on vocabulary. Pupils will use books for questions measuring ability to determine meaning from context. They will not use books for other vocabulary questions. All other vocabulary questions need to be written on the blackboard or given on mimeographed sheet.

(7) Ask questions on comprehension. Pupils will not use books—books are to be closed.

(8) Skimming, new selection used. Pupils will use books to find answers to questions.

5 A pupil is considered to be deficient in any one specific skill if he answers more than one out of three questions incorrectly, or more than two incorrectly when there are more than three questions measuring a specific skill.

6 This inventory, being administered to a group, does not establish a grade level. Nonetheless, any pupil scoring above 90 per cent may be considered as reading material that is too easy for him, and any pupil scoring below 65 per cent as reading material that is too difficult for him. If the material is suitable, the scores should range between 70–90 per cent.

Form of inventory (sample)

Parts of book

1 On what page does the unit (section) entitled 'Exploring One World' begin? (shows use of table of contents)

2 What section of your book would you use to find out something about the author of a story in the book? (determines knowledge of section on biographical data)

3 In what part of the book can you find the meaning of a word that you might not know? (determines knowledge of glossary)

Introduce story: explore pupils' background of experiences on the subject of the story and set up purpose questions. Pupils read selection silently. Time for reading speed determined.

Vocabulary meaning

4 What is meant by the word *crab* as it is used in the story? (top line, second column, page 178)

Contextual meaning

5 What is meant by the word *eliminated*? (third line, second column, page 181)

R. C.'-26

Synonyms and antonyms

6 What word means the opposite of *temporary*?
7 Use another word to describe the coach when he looked *amazed*.

General knowledge of meaning

8 Select the proper meaning of the word *entice*.
   a. To lure, persuade
   b. To force
   c. To ask
   d. To caution
9 Select the proper meaning of the word *initial*.
   a. The last or end
   b. The first or beginning
   c. The middle
   d. A letter of the alphabet
10 Select the proper meaning of the word *rectify*.
   a. To do wrong.
   b. To make right
   c. To destroy
   d. A priest's home

Word recognition, syllabication

11 Divide the following words into syllables and show which syllable is accented.
12 and 13 Eliminated
14 and 15 Amazed
16 and 17 Undemocratic
18 and 19 Fraternities

Prefixes and suffixes

20 What does the prefix *un* mean as used in *undemocratic*?
21 What is meant by *pre* in the word *prescription*?

Parts of speech

22 Change the verb *astonish* to a noun.
23 Change the adjective *democratic* to a noun.
24 Change the noun *boy* to an adjective.
25 Change the adjective *slow* to an adverb.

Comprehension, main ideas

26 What is a _____ ? What happened when _____ ?
27 Such questions as indicated here that ask for
28 only the main points of the story.

Details

29 Questions to ask for specific bits of information
30 about the principal characters or ideas of the
31 material.

Drawing conclusions, inferences

32 Questions, the answers of which are not completely found in the textbook.
33 Questions beginning with 'Why,' making comparisons, predicting what
34 may happen usually measure the drawing conclusions skill. Example:
   Why did Bottle imagine he could perform such astounding athletic feats
   as setting the State high school record in jumping?

Sequence

35 (May be omitted.) Questions asking what
36 happened as a result of _____, what steps
37 did the police use to solve the mystery, etc.
38 Use a new reading selection. Questions
39 designed to have the pupil locate some
40 specific bits of information.

Directions for making a group reading inventory using the social
studies textbook are similar to those for making the English inventory
(Shepherd, 1960, pp. 20–22). The inventory includes similar questions on
location-of-information skills; specific questions on the reading of maps,
charts, and other visual aids; special vocabulary used in the social studies;
questions on the main ideas, important details, inferences, conclusions,
and generalizations appropriate to the subject.

The chart shown on page 494, with names of students to be listed along
the left-hand side and types of reading difficulties enumerated across the
top, summarizes the information for a class. When read horizontally, it
describes the individual students; when read vertically, it shows which
difficulties are common to the class. Thus the teacher learns what instruction is needed by the whole class and what special help is needed by
individuals.

For students whose comprehension score is below 50 per cent, Shepherd
recommends administering an individual inventory. Appropriate instruction should follow the administration of the inventory; this, indeed, is its
main purpose. When the inventory is repeated at the middle and at the
end of the semester, both teachers and students get a sense of accomplishment as they see improvement in reading skills.

Such a group reading inventory bridges the gap between the hurriedly

Name of class _____   Section _____   Teacher _____

Name	Use of parts of book	Vocabulary	Meaning	Contextual meanings	Synonyms and antonyms	General knowledge	Word recognition	Syllabication	Accent	Prefixes and suffixes	Part of speech	Comprehension	Main ideas	Supporting details	Drawing conclusions	Sequence of ideas	Skimming	Speed in wpm	Comments
John Jones	✓			✓	✓	✓									✓			194	(Check wherever pupil is deficient)
Robert Brown		✓	✓	✓	✓	✓	✓	✓	✓	✓	✓				✓	✓		150	

Summary Chart

made teacher test and the standardized test. It gives the teacher a concrete model for further testing-teaching-evaluating based on the text or
reference books used by his particular class.

Interest inventories

There are also numerous interest inventories of the checklist type. These
may list reading habits, types of books, characteristics of books, or actual
titles to be checked, usually under the headings of Like, Dislike, or
Indifference.

One of the earliest and most comprehensive of the interest inventories
was developed by Witty and Kopel (see Witty, 1949, pp. 302–305). It
included many items on interests and activities other than reading; it also
elicited background information and called for short answers to specific
questions. More important than the information gained from checklists
and inventories are the student's awareness and self-appraisal of his reading
pattern.

In interpreting the responses on interest inventories, the instability of
an individual's reading interests must be recognized. Reading interests
change with age, with competing interests, with changes in the peer group,

with the influence of different teachers. We would not expect reading interests reported at any one time to be permanent.

Although the interest inventory usually gives more detail about favorite kinds of reading than merely asking a student what kind of books he enjoys, it does not differentiate within broad areas of interest. For example, an individual may say that he likes adventure stories, but within this category there may be many kinds of adventure stories that he does not like.

As with other types of self-report techniques, the student may conceal his real interests in order to create a favorable impression. Since he knows that wide reading of good books is approved, he may exaggerate the number or the quality of the books he reads.

An example of the short-answer type of questionnaire that covers several areas of reading interest is given below.

TABLE 3   *My reading interests*

1 Name_____ Age_____ Grade_____

2 Check the library or libraries below that you can use. Double check those you do use.
Community library _____   School library   _____
Church library   _____   Any other library_____

3 How many books have you borrowed from friends during the last month?
_____
Give titles of some _____
_____
_____

4 How many books have you loaned to friends during the last month? _____
Give titles of some _____
_____
_____

5 Give the titles of some of the books in your home. _____
_____
_____

6 From what sources, other than those mentioned above, do you obtain books?
Check below.
1 Buy them _____   3 Rent them _____
2 Gifts   _____   4 Exchanges _____

7 What are your hobbies and collections?
_____

8 What do you intend to be? _____
Are you going to college? _____ Where?_____

9 Name the five magazines you like best. _____

10 Name the three movies you last saw. _____

11 Name the three radio or TV programs you like best. _____

12 Name the state or country farthest away that you have visited. _____

13 What sections of the newspaper do you like best? Check below.
   1 Sports _____   4 News   _____
   2 Funnies _____   5 Editorials _____
   3 Stories _____   6 Other   _____
14 Which of the following have encouraged you to read? Check below.
   1 Parents _____   6 Pals   _____
   2 Teacher _____   7 Club leader _____
   3 Librarian _____   8 Relatives   _____
   4 Hobby   _____   9 Club work   _____
   5 Friends _____   10 Other   _____

Creative-type questionnaire and essay

A unique form of questionnaire elicited some fascinating specific information about reading interests: the preferred type of book, its appeal, its style of writing (Strang, 1946, pp. 447–482). An example of this form, as filled out by a girl in the eighth grade, is reproduced below; it will give an idea of the kind of insights that may be gained from this technique.

To the students

Year in school _____*eighth*_____ Boy _____ Girl ___x___
Name (You need not sign your name unless you want to.)   *C.S.K.*
    You have, right now, the best possible information about what high school students like to read. Will you share it with us by answering as thoughtfully and fully as possible the following questions:
1 What do young persons like you most want to read about? *Adventure and mystery*

2 What kind of a book or article would you choose to read above all others? *Books about teen-age romances, etc.*

3 Suppose you were going to write a book or article that persons of your age would all want to read, what would be its title? *The Typical Teen-ager*

4 Write a paragraph or two showing how you think this book should be written to appeal most to the boys and girls in your class.

The book should be written in such a fashion that it would be both humorous and adventurous; appealing and interesting.

Life of a teen-ager, not babyish stories, story of romance, adventure, mystery and pleasure.

5 Think of the books or articles you have read this year that you just could not stand. What was it in them that made you dislike them so much?

In some books they skip from one subject to another. In mysteries they sometimes don't have any endings. Books that are mushy and foolish are also very unpopular Stories that abuse animals I don't like.

6 Think of the books or articles you have liked most this year. What was it in them that made you like them so much?

First of all they had a plot which made them interesting. I like dog stories, adventure, mystery, and almost anything in modern life that is written in typical teen-age level.

7 Which book or article that you have read during the last year interested you most keenly? Give the author, *Margaret Vail*, title *Yours Is the Earth*, magazine or publisher _____, and date _____ (if you remember it). Then write as much as you can about the book or article and why you liked it so much. (Use other side of page.)

The book is an autobiography of part of her life in France.

Margaret Vail married a French soldier. She was in Paris when her daughter was born. Then the war broke out.

It is the thrilling tale of how she escaped France and got into Spain, climbing the mountains with her daughter, then four years old.

The book had a plot. It was interesting and every page held me in suspense till the end. It was a war story, but not a gory, bloody tale.

From this type of questionnaire and from essays written on specific topics, one finds many common and many unique expressions of dislike for certain kinds of books and styles of writing:

'Hate anything like Dickens'
'Too much beating around the bush'
'Stories not true to life'
'Sob stories about teen-agers'
'Too much talk—just a bunch of people yakking'

Lack of action and suspense is frequently mentioned. Equally interesting are the reasons students express for liking a book:

'Grown-up but with words you can understand'
'Gives the feeling that you are there'

To sign or not to sign

The question of whether or not students should sign their names to these questionnaires often arises. The more personal the data, the more sensitive the individual is to the impression he is making. However, there is not the same problem with reading interest as with personality inventories. Usually students will answer questions about their reading interests thoughtfully and frankly whether they do or do not sign their names. If the information is to be used for individual guidance in reading, obviously it is necessary that the report be signed.

Using information about interests

Information about students' interests may be used by teachers, librarians, and parents in guiding the reading of individuals, in introducing books, and in capitalizing on some common interest of a group. Observation of students' interests may be used immediately in guiding their choice of books. A third-grade child chooses a book from the class library to read in his free time. If the book is one that he can read independently, the teacher approves his choice. If it is too difficult for him, the teacher may say, 'That's a good book to read later, Jimmy. Here's another book about cowboys you'd like to read right now.' If a student is enthusiastic about a book he has just read, the teacher may suggest another book that treats a similar topic, has the same appeal, or is by the same author.

If a student shows no interest in reading any book, the teacher may try to uncover some other interest or activity to which reading might contribute. For example, a boy in a social studies class (Shepherd, 1961, pp. 140–142) did not choose any of the supplementary books on the early explorers which the teacher had brought into the classroom. Most of the other students, having made their choices, had started reading. The teacher asked John about his outside interests. When the teacher learned that John was absorbed in building a boat with his father, he said, 'There's a book here I'm sure you would like. It's about the adventures of an early explorer who went around the Cape of Good Hope in a small boat.' John took the book and later made an enthusiastic report on it to the class. By tying reading in with students' outside activities, the teacher utilizes the impetus of their interests.

In addition to daily observation, interest inventories filled out by all the members of a class guide the teacher in ordering new books or in getting books for the class from the library or bookmobile. Without this information the teacher might not be aware, for example, that his young adolescent boys are most interested in certain features of war, sports, and science and in stories about real people and that the girls are interested in mysteries and stories about teen-agers like themselves. If several students mention special interests such as medicine or current problems, the teacher may make available books that contribute to these interests.

Reports of reading interests may give clues to personality patterns and sources of emotional tension. For example, an adolescent may reveal his attitude toward life, his preoccupations and anxieties, or the quality of his human relationships by such comments as the following:

> I especially like stories of people who find out what their career is going to be. Stories of people such as Florence Nightingale and *The Life and Thought of Albert Schweitzer* get you to thinking and wondering about jobs in the field of medicine. Characters who work hard and show a great deal of courage make you want to be more like them. Some books make you want to work harder and do a better job at what you're doing. . . . Books that make you happy and make you laugh are very good to read when you feel downcast or afraid. These books can cheer you up and lift your spirits and make you less afraid (Strang, 1961, p. 391).

After reading a set of these papers, the teacher becomes more aware than ever of the unique personality of each member of his class.

Questionnaires, reviews, and compositions such as have been described in this chapter, when read anonymously to a class, serve as a basis for discussion. By hearing about one student's enjoyment of certain books, others may be stimulated to broaden their reading interests. Class discussion of what makes a book interesting and worthwhile may help students to build criteria for book selection.

Last, but not least, is the value of a study of their reading interests to the students themselves. It encourages them to appraise their choices of reading materials and to challenge the assumptions that underlie their interests or lack of interests.

Concluding statement

Children are naturally interested. The more opportunities they have had to see and hear and associate with people, the wider are their interests. Children from disadvantaged homes who have not had the intellectual stimulation that more fortunate children have had often show lack of reading interests. They are the ones for whom teachers must apply, first of all, experiences that will arouse their undeveloped interests. Book clubs, discussions, role playing, and dramatization provide the social stimulation that will restore their capacity to become interested in the world which reading enables them to explore.

In general, junior and senior high school students feel strongly about the importance of having interesting reading material and interesting assignments. If the material is uninteresting, they will skim over it quickly, not caring what it says nor whether they finish reading it, getting little or nothing out of it, not noticing the important points, not remembering it, and consequently getting low marks in the subject. If they are interested they will enjoy reading, read carefully and eagerly, comprehend with less effort, note the important facts, get more out of their reading, remember it, search for more material on the same topic, and desire to learn more about related matters.

Being able to recommend the right book for the right child at the psychological moment is basic to success in teaching reading. The child's first experiences with books influence his attitude toward reading. The books recommended to an adolescent help determine whether he views reading as 'strictly for the birds' or as 'one of life's inexhaustible pleasures'.

References

BETTS, EMMETT A. (1957) *Foundations of Reading Instruction* New York: American Book Company.

JASTAK, JOSEPH (1946) *Wide Range Achievement Test* and *Manual* Wilmington, Del.

SHEPHERD, DAVID L. (1960) *Effective Reading in the Social Studies and Effective Reading in Science* New York: Harper & Row.

SHEPHERD, DAVID L. (1961) *Effective Reading in the Social Studies* New York: Harper & Row.

STRANG, RUTH (1946) 'Reading Interests, 1946', *English Journal*, 25, 447-82.

STRANG, RUTH (1961) 'Evaluation of Development in and through Reading', in *Development in and through Reading*, Sixtieth Yearbook of the National Society for the Study of Education, Chicago: The University of Chicago Press, 376–97.

WITTY, PAUL (1949) *Reading in Modern Education* Boston: Ginn and Company.

4:8 Creating questions for informal reading inventories

William J. Valmont

Teachers have been utilizing the Informal Reading Inventory (IRI) to diagnose their pupils' reading skills for a good many years. Today more individuals are creating their own inventories because of a growing awareness that the planning and production of an IRI increases its value to the user. Johnson and Kress (1965) have presented guidelines for constructing IRIs that may be followed profitably. In the past, following the teaching of Betts (1946), comprehension questions constructed for an IRI were designed to measure three areas: facts, inferences, and vocabulary. Recently, however, teachers are testing more areas of comprehension: main ideas, details, drawing conclusions, inferences, organization (sequence), cause and effect, and vocabulary.

Creating questions for the IRI is a demanding task, and the quality of the questions determines the usefulness of the instrument. The following suggestions are designed to help the novice create an IRI. They may also aid teachers or supervisors in reviewing instruments already in use.

Kinds of questions

Main idea questions

Two categories of questions may be constructed to uncover the main idea of an IRI passage: open-ended questions which do not reveal any facts, and questions that tend to aid the child in reporting the main idea. Either type may be used, but the open-ended questions appear to be more revealing of the student's ability to formulate main ideas.

VALMONT, WILLIAM J. (1972) 'Creating questions for informal reading inventories', *The Reading Teacher*, 25, 509–12.

Type 1 examples:
What would be a good title for this story?
What seems to be the main idea of the story so far?

Type 2 examples:
Why does Betty call Susan?
What does Mary want Tom and Janet to do?

Detail questions

Detail questions, which call for facts stated in the passage, generally start with *who, what, when, where.* They should be stated simply and directly. Whenever possible, detail questions should relate to and support the main idea of the passage. Insignificant questions or those that are irrelevant to the main idea are perhaps less useful.

Examples:
Who turned off the television?
What did Freddy take to the mill?

Inferences

In some IRI passages there are statements through which the author *intentionally* tries to convey an idea without directly stating it, and the reader's task is to infer a judgment or deduction which corresponds to the author's implication. It is sometimes necessary, however, to ask the student to make an inference when no implication was intended by the author. In this case the inference made is a judgment or a deduction which grows logically from the facts stated in the IRI passage.

Examples:
Why do you believe the shopkeeper was either rich or poor?
What makes you think Mr Beard was or was not a baby when his father became a citizen?

Drawing conclusions

In order to answer these questions, the pupil must draw his conclusion from two or more facts stated in the passage. Conclusions may also be drawn from inferences at times, if two separate inferences are made from two statements and a conclusion is drawn based upon the two inferences. Drawing conclusions must be distinguished from making inferences, since the two question types measure slightly different abilities. An inference, as defined here, is made from one source of information presented in the passage, but a conclusion is drawn from two or more sources of information in the passage.

Example:

Why do you or don't you think Mike would like truck drivers? (Stated: Mike liked far away places. Stated: Truck drivers talked about far away places.)

Organization questions

Two types of questions may occur here: questions dealing with the author's organization of information, and questions dealing with an important sequence of events in the passage. The first of these types is fairly uncommon because of the short passages typically used.

Type 1 example:

Into how many parts could this section of the story be divided? Why?

Type 2 example:

Name, in order, three things Mike did when the burro arrived?

Cause and effect questions

These questions are constructed so the examiner provides either the cause or the effect, and the pupil supplies the missing part.

Examples:

What will happen now that the old man found a one hundred dollar bill? (cause stated).

Why did Billy's mother make him sit in a chair? (effect stated).

Vocabulary questions

Here the examiner is looking for one of two things: Does the pupil know a definition of a word or phrase as it is used most commonly? Does the pupil know the 'special' meaning of a word or phrase in the passage being considered?

Type 1 examples:

What is a cactus?

What does 'put a damper on' mean?

Type 2 examples:
What did the word 'trips' mean in the story? (effect of drugs).
What does 'green' mean in the story? (immature).

Some guidelines

Even with the above examples to guide in the preparation of questions for an IRI, there are many pitfalls to avoid. The following hints—if examined closely—may aid in avoiding many of the common difficulties typically encountered.

1 Questions should be in the approximate order in which the information upon which they are based is presented in the passage.
2 It is generally preferable to place a main idea question first.
3 Ask the most important questions possible.
4 Check the sequence of questions to insure that a later question is not answered by an earlier one.
5 Check questions to insure that two or more questions do not call for the same response, fact, or inference.
6 A question that is so broad that any answer is acceptable is a poor question. If special questions to test divergent thinking are created, insure that reasonable, logical responses may be made.
7 A question that can be answered by someone who has not read the passage (except for some vocabulary questions) is a poor question.
8 Avoid formulating questions whose answers call for knowledge based on experience had by the pupil rather than from reading or application of information given in the story.
9 IRI questions are generally constructed to measure the student's comprehension of written matter. Therefore, insure that accompanying pictures do not aid the student in answering questions.
10 Keep your questions short and as simple as possible. Do not include irrelevant statements.
11 Generally, state questions so that they start with *who, what, when, where, how,* and *why.*
12 Do not let 'correct' grammar or syntax unnecessarily complicate the questions.
13 Avoid stating questions in a negative manner.
14 Avoid over-using questions which require pupils to reconstruct lists, such as 'List five ingredients', or 'Name four characters', or 'Tell six places',

and the like. Anxiety or memory instead of comprehension may influence the pupil's performance.

15 Avoid writing questions with multiple answers which fail to establish specifications for the response.

Poor: What happened after Susan heard the telephone?

Better: What was the first thing that happened after Susan heard the telephone?

16 Do not mistake a question that calls for the reporting of several facts or details as an organization or sequence question.

17 To learn about a pupil's grasp of the vocabulary, ask the pupil to define the word, not to recall a word from the story.

Poor: What word told you about the age of the man?

Better: What does *old* mean?

18 Avoid stating a question as if to call for an opinion when asking the pupil to relate a fact.

Poor: How do you think Skip got to the store?

Better: How did Skip get to the store?

19 If a question is asking for a judgment, phrase it as 'Why do you or don't you believe . . .'. Do not give away the information called for.

20 Avoid asking questions on which the child has a fifty-fifty chance of being correct—'yes–no' questions, or 'either–or'.

These suggestions may aid in constructing or reviewing IRI questions. It is wise to write many questions, select the best for inclusion in the IRI, try out your inventory with children, and make final revisions. Be certain that the different types of question are balanced at each level and throughout the grade level spread of the IRI. You should then have a useful diagnostic instrument if you have avoided the very common error of misclassifying questions.

References

JOHNSON, MARJORIE SEDDON and KRESS, ROY A. (1965) *Informal Reading Inventories* Newark, Delaware: International Reading Association.
BETTS, EMMETT A. (1946) *Foundations of Reading Instruction* New York: American Book Company.

4:9   Evaluation of development in and through reading

Ruth Strang

Evaluation is like Tennyson's 'flower in the crannied wall'—it reaches out in the whole universe of the reading field. It is concerned with the individual's reading development and the effect of reading on his personal development. Evaluation recognizes that improvement in any reading skill may not only affect the acquisition of subsequent skills but also the individual's self-confidence and concept of himself. Growth in reading ability may also lead to improved relationships with parents and teachers. As the child grows older he uses reading increasingly as a tool to further intellectual growth. The knowledge obtainable through reading helps him grow socially, educationally and vocationally. Evaluation, therefore, must be comprehensive and continuous; it must change somewhat with successive stages of development (Robinson, 1958).

The evaluation process begins when we state the goals of teaching reading. Some of these are fairly specific, such as learning to recognize words; others are more intangible, such as enjoyment and appreciation of literature. These goals should be stated as specific abilities, habits, attitudes, appreciations, activities, and interests that can be observed or measured in the teaching–learning situation.

To obtain evidence of these changes—which, if desirable, imply growth —we must select or devise methods and instruments. After we have obtained the evidence, the next step is to evaluate, in the light of our objectives, the adequacy, effectiveness, and worth of the teaching–learning experiences that have been offered. After this has been done, administrators, teachers, and students should apply the results of the evaluation to improve instruction in reading. Thus, evaluation helps produce growth as well as appraise it.

STRANG, RUTH (1960) 'Evaluation of development in and through reading', *N.S.S.E. Yearbook* Chicago University Press, 376–92.

Why evaluate?

Evaluation is essential to learning (Herrick, 1958). It is an incentive to students, an intrinsic part of teaching, and an aid to the administrator and the specialist in improving the program.

For students, evaluation facilitates learning and gives them a sense of direction. Psychological experiments have repeatedly shown that students learn more effectively when they know how well they are doing and what specifically they are doing wrong. Appraisal as a part of teaching helps them identify the reading processes or methods that they can use successfully.

Awareness of one's progress helps build self-confidence. Every student needs the stimulus of success. When the retarded reader sees objective evidence that he can learn to read, he begins to overcome his longstanding sense of failure. Encouraged by evidence of progress, students tend to take more initiative and responsibility for their improvement in reading. 'Nothing succeeds like observed success.'

Teachers, too, need a sense of progress and the stimulus of success. A comprehensive evaluation process, by broadening and sharpening objectives and highlighting the results that have been achieved, gives teachers an increased sense of the value of their work. On the other hand, an evaluation based on narrow tests of skills is discouraging to the teacher who is broadly concerned with attitudes, new interests, and appreciations.

Evaluation also shows the teacher where to begin. By trying to estimate students' readiness and capacities as well as by measuring their present skills and interests, the teacher can provide the learning experiences that the students need. Evaluation serves as a guide to the choice of procedures and materials.

For the administrator, evaluation may show the strengths and successful features in the program as well as indicate needs for changes in curriculum, instruction, and administrative policy. As it reveals failure in the common effort to attain objectives that have been agreed upon, the administrator asks 'why?' Do the students' inadequacies in reading stem from an unsuitable curriculum, from poorly prepared teachers, from failure to detect incompetency in the teaching of beginning reading, from lack of suitable reading materials for the wide range of reading ability that is found in most classes, or from homes or communities that are unfavorable to improvement in reading? Naturally, the administrator uses the results of evaluation in explaining the reading program to the community.

To the reading specialist, evaluation reveals strengths and weaknesses in the program. It may show that he has devoted too much time to individual cases and small groups and neglected work with and through the teachers. It may suggest strategic points in the program at which he should concentrate his efforts, such as a developmental reading course for all students or special classes for the gifted.

From the standpoint of research and contributions to the literature in the field of reading, we should have better evaluations of programs and procedures. Future writers should avoid two faults that often occur in the reports now available: *a*) a program or procedure is merely described without evidence of its effectiveness; *b*) results are presented statistically with no concrete description of the organization, methods, and materials by which they were achieved. The evaluation process will be described in this chapter, and instruments and methods for obtaining evidence will be suggested.

What is evaluated?

The nature of the evaluative process varies with the accepted concept of reading. Evaluation is a relatively simple matter if reading is conceived as merely pronouncing printed words correctly with little or no regard to their meaning. If reading is broadly defined to include thinking and feeling, the exercise of imagination and character traits, such as determination to overcome difficulties, persistence in practice, and self-confidence in attacking new tasks (Cotterall and Weise, 1959), then evaluation becomes complex, indeed. In this chapter, the description of evaluation accords with the broad view of reading that is presented in this yearbook.

Main goals

The goals to be evaluated have been stated in previous chapters, both broadly and as specific behavior that can be observed. In evaluating them, we must remember that they are not separate steps; they are interwoven in the reading process from beginning reading to maturity.

How to state objectives: with reference to students

The stated objectives for development of reading abilities and for personal development through reading should possess those characteristics that are indicated in the following paragraphs.

Be specific. General goals should be broken down into specific objectives and stated operationally as definite reading skills or behavior. For example, the objective, 'acquire skill in word recognition', should be broken down into specific behavior which can be observed or tested, such as : *a*) shows progress in associating the initial sounds of words with the appropriate letter symbols; *b*) becomes proficient in identifying sounds in words; *c*) improves in facility to give words that rhyme with the word presented; and *d*) year by year becomes more skilful in using various methods to determine the meaning of unknown words—context clues, structural analysis, syllabication, phonic analysis, and use of the dictionary. The stated objectives should also include items relating to the students' personal development; for example, is encouraged by success and evidences of progress in word-recognition skills.

Be realistic and clearly stated. Objectives should be realistic and precisely rather than vaguely stated. Similarly, we should avoid the use of words that may make the objectives ambiguous or obscure.

Accent growth. We should try to appraise the student's growth as well as his reading status. Growth is especially difficult to measure. Progress is always relative to the capacity of the student and to his opportunities for learning. As measured by gains on standardized tests, progress should be checked to determine whether it is merely a chance difference or real evidence of growth.

Show relative importance. It is also necessary to determine the relative importance of each objective at different stages in the child's development. For example, in beginning reading, acquiring a sight vocabulary and word-recognition skills are basic, dominant learnings, although thinking and feeling are also part of the pattern of objectives in the primary grades. In the intermediate grades, learning through reading in new fields becomes increasingly important. During high-school years, still deeper levels of interpretation and critical thinking occupy a central position in the pattern of objectives. Evaluation must take into consideration these changing emphases at different stages in reading development.

Recognize individual differences. Some objectives are more important and appropriate for certain students than for others. To determine this relative importance, we must have a knowledge of students' interests, abilities, and backgrounds. For example, for a retarded reader in high school, growth in basic vocabulary and word-recognition skills may be the most important evidence of progress to evaluate. For an able student who reads little, an increase of interest in worthwhile reading is most important. Some individuals who are above the test norms for their ages and grades are still achieving below their potential reading ability. On the other hand, a score that is several years below the norm may represent real achievement for a less able learner.

Show progress in patterns. Ideally, patterns of objectives paralleling the development from beginning reading to mature reading should be described. For example, a pattern of objectives at the developmental level of junior high school, applied to reading a short story, might include: *a*) show increasing interest in reading short stories; *b*) comprehend most of the words; *c*) apply word-meaning skills to unfamiliar words; *d*) are keen to pick up clues of character and plot from the descriptions of physical appearance, speech, actions, and response of others to a certain character; *e*) respond in an appropriate manner emotionally to examples of courage, cruelty, and other human qualities; *f*) communicate more effectively to others their thoughts and feelings about the story; and *g*) modify their point of view, attitude, and behavior in a desirable direction.

By setting up sequential patterns of reading development, it is possible to see more clearly how children's improvement in reading might progress simultaneously on all fronts through the school years or how a retarded reader, starting with his present pattern of reading development, might make progress.

Consider causes. If evaluation is to lead to improved practice, it is important to ascertain conditions that may be responsible for the observed growth or lack of growth. Neither teacher nor student can do much to remedy a bad situation or to improve a good one unless he knows what is causing the success or failure. These causes or conditions are complex and can best be recorded and synthesized in a reading case study for each student.

Objectives: with reference to staff responsibilities

The objectives described thus far have been stated as desirable changes in students. These are the ultimate focus of evaluation. However, an effective reading program may also be evaluated with reference to co-operation, communication, and other constructive attitudes and practices on the part of administrators, supervisors, and teachers (Zimmermann, 1958; Letton, 1958). An evaluation concerned with students' development should consider how well informed the administrator and supervisory personnel are about the reading program, how effectively they assist teachers in improving instruction in reading, and how adroitly they interpret the reading program to the public and use community resources. It would also be necessary to ascertain how well teachers were combining planning, teaching, and evaluating, and whether they were making appraisal of student progress an intrinsic part of instruction in reading.

Guides to evaluation

General procedures for evaluating may be briefly summarized as follows:

1 Evaluation should be continuous rather than periodic.
2 It should be a part of the instructional program, not apart from it.
3 It should obtain evidence on the extent to which the stated objectives have been achieved.
4 In obtaining this evidence, it should use both formal and informal methods.
5 The data collected should be used for the improvement of program and procedures.
6 Increasing emphasis should be placed on self-appraisal as the student grows older.
7 Evaluation of a reading program should be carried on by a team that includes administrators, reading consultants, other specialists, teachers, students, and parents.

Instruments and methods for obtaining evidence

In describing methods for obtaining evidence of changes in student or staff behavior, we shall relate the method or instrument to the purpose for which it may be used. In actual practice the evaluator should use a combination of methods to obtain a dynamic picture, selecting those most appropriate to each stage of reading development.

Visual and auditory factors

There are three main ways of obtaining evidence of visual efficiency: *a*) the teacher may note signs of eyestrain on the part of the pupil; *b*) students may report symptoms of eyestrain that they have noted in themselves; and *c*) visual screening tests may be used. Similarly, auditory efficiency may be checked, using an informal listening test and the audiometer.

Word knowledge

Day-by-day teaching-testing. Classroom procedures play an important role in the appraisal of vocabulary. As the teacher listens to children and asks questions about the meaning of words they read or speak, he obtains evidence about the size and growth of the students' speaking, listening, and reading vocabulary; the kind of words they have learned; and the rapidity with which they learn new words and use them in their conversation. In interviews and class discussion, the teacher may get clues as to why they made certain errors and how they remembered the correct meaning of the words taught.

Scrapbook-type class and individual dictionaries and vocabulary card files of new words made by the students provide objective evidence of growth in word knowledge and a basis for self-appraisal.

Self-appraisal. If the students analyze the kinds of words they use in their compositions, they will see for themselves how they are progressing in written vocabulary. Somewhat more formal is the method of testing the students systematically on the words they should be learning during the year. If the test requires the student to distinguish the best definition of each word from among four or five choices, each representing a certain type of error, it will be useful for diagnosis of word comprehension. If the test asks the student to write a definition of each word, it requires of him an understanding of the meaning of the word along with the ability to express its meaning clearly in writing. The student's evaluation of his performance on these tasks contributes to growth in self-appraisal.

Vocabulary tests. A still more formal appraisal may be obtained by use of standardized vocabulary tests. It is, of course, generally understood that effective instruments for all pupils from primary grades through college may be used to measure vocabulary. Simple and effective measures for the primary grades in use at the present time include the *Dolch Picture Cards* of 95 nouns and his longer test of 220 basic sight words. For Grades IV–XVI, the vocabulary section in any modern reading test will give an appraisal of word knowledge. For Grades IX–XVI, the *Inglis Vocabulary Test* is still recommended. For Grades IX–XII, the more recent *Durost-Center Word Mastery Test* is especially effective in emphasizing use of context. For Grades VII–XII, the thirty-minute *New Standard Vocabulary*

Tests published by the Educational Department of the *Reader's Digest* from 1955 to 1958 have the advantage of providing six forms.

Word recognition skills

Daily performance. Evaluation of word-recognition skills goes on simultaneously with teaching of meaningful material. For example, in the first grade the teacher may teach such material and at the same time test children's ability to identify sounds in words. Through the elementary grades he will appraise the students' progress as he gives instruction, practice, and informal tests of various word-recognition skills. In beginning reading especially, oral reading is useful in appraising word recognition and phasing. Later, it also helps develop fluency and ability to communicate the author's thought to others. Tape- or disc-recording of children's oral reading is an excellent way to make them aware of their progress. The teacher may also write dated observations of each individual's performance, compare successive scores on informal tests, and encourage students to keep charts on which the desired skills are listed and checked off as acquired.

Standardized procedures. Certain individual standardized tests of word-recognition skills are useful for both diagnosis and evaluation. For example, Durrell's 'Analysis of Reading Difficulty' includes tests of word recognition, auditory analysis of word elements, and visual memory for word forms under the more comprehensive headings of oral reading, listening comprehension, and silent reading. This is an individual test requiring thirty to ninety minutes. A teacher thoroughly familiar with such a diagnostic procedure could obtain useful information while giving classroom instruction in reading.

Comprehension

Methods for obtaining evidence about students' reading comprehension may be arranged on a continuum from the most informal to the most standardized, beginning with the daily appraisal possible in every classroom.

Appraisal while teaching. Evidence of comprehension in many fields is best gathered while one is teaching. It can then be acted upon immediately; there is no lapse of time between making an evaluation and doing something about it. For example, in teaching a class how to read a newspaper, the teacher reviewed the purposes of a newspaper, which had been brought out in the previous period: to inform, to persuade, to give opinions, to amuse. The teacher reinforced the students' somewhat tenuous impression by writing these points on the board. Next, the students applied this knowledge: In what three sections of the newspaper would you find facts? Where would you find opinions? In what part would you expect to be persuaded? Amused? Since the group had little difficulty in making this application, they were ready to go ahead with a more detailed study of how to read a news report.

Day by day the teacher should note the accuracy with which students answer factual questions and the acuteness with which they make generalizations and draw inferences from their reading. When they discuss literature or retell a story, he will note evidences of success in character analysis, of ability to see cause-and-effect relations, and of appreciation of the author's purpose and style of writing. Thus, achieving in reading becomes a continuous process of recognizing and overcoming difficulties, of diagnosis and remediation, of appraisal and improvement of instruction.

Analysis of work samples.   At all ages dated samples of the students' responses to reading may be used to show growth. For example, a student may write or make a tape-recording of his first attempt to summarize orally a section of his science book. Then he may appraise this summary according to the accuracy and number of main ideas and important details remembered, the sequence of ideas recognized, and the clarity of his statements. After instruction he may compare his summary of a similar passage with the first according to designated criteria. Similarly, any dated samples of a student's reports on reading or on the discussion of books can be used to show progress in these aspects of comprehension.

The informal group reading inventory.   This group method of appraising students' silent reading can be used in the upper elementary and high school. It employs questions on the use of the index, table of contents, and other study skills. It tests their comprehension of passages taken from the textbooks and charts the types of reading difficulties encountered by each student. To appraise growth, the teacher should repeat the inventory at intervals.

The individual reading inventory.   As one student at a time reads short passages selected from a graded series of reading books, the teacher may gain understanding of the student's attitudes and approach to reading as well as an indication of his oral and silent reading ability. The construction and use of the individual informal reading inventory has been described in detail by Betts (1957).

Teaching tests. An educational test of any kind comprises a series of situations which call forth and permit the recording of a special kind of behavior (Tyler, 1958). Teacher-made tests can cover a wide variety of reading situations and outcomes and may take many forms (Thomas, 1956).

Informal tests add more precision and continuity to the teacher's opportunistic but important observation in the classroom. For example, a procedure, *Explore Your Reading,* developed by Melnik (1960) for improving the reading of social-studies material in junior high school begins by asking students to state their aims or goals in reading a social-studies assignment. The students are then asked to read a selection from a social-studies book that is typical of the material they will be expected to read in their classes. After reading the passage they answer questions of the 'creative response' or 'open-end' type ('What did the author say?') and a number of multiple-choice questions that are designed to furnish evidence of a student's ability to get the literal meaning, to see relations, to draw inferences, to make generalizations, and to understand the meaning of key words.

As soon as the student has answered the questions, he has data before him for self-appraisal. He marks his own paper. He grades his free response on a ten-point scale, and analyzes the kinds of errors he has made in the multiple-choice questions (each choice represents a certain kind of error). Instruction immediately follows this self-appraisal, while the students are specifically motivated to learn how to get the right answers.

Later, the whole procedure is repeated with another similar selection. After the second exercise is completed and analyzed, the students are able to note the progress they have made. A third repetition of the procedure produces more marked improvement.

After completing the third exercise the students were asked to evaluate their experience by answering such a question as: How did *Explore Your Reading* help you to do better in your social studies? What part of *Explore Your Reading* did you enjoy most? In addition, the students rated each of the eleven features of the exercises as to whether it helped them 'not at all', 'a little', 'a good deal', or 'very, very much'. Of all the features, the students felt that the open-end question 'What did the author say?' had helped them most.

This testing-teaching-evaluating procedure bridges the gap between the hurriedly made teacher test and the standardized test. It relieves the teacher of some of the burden of making instructional material; at the same time it gives him a concrete model for further testing-teaching-evaluating based on the text or reference books used by his classes.

Publishers' tests.   Some publishers provide in connection with their basal reading series, tests for the use of the teacher. These tests represent an intermediate level of appraisal, more systematic than most teacher-made tests and less formal than standardized tests.

Standardized tests.   Standardized tests broaden the base of evaluation by extending it beyond the walls of one classroom; they add an authoritative emphasis to appraisal. They supplement but do not supplant the classroom evaluation. Their value depends upon the reliability and validity with which they measure appropriate objectives.

The reading objectives measured by most standardized tests are limited, as shown by Hunt (1955). In an analysis of reading tests he found that the only reading skills measured by the majority of these tests were rate of comprehension, general vocabulary, and paragraph meaning. The results of tests that measure attainment of limited objectives may be misleading. Perry (1959) found that many freshmen at Harvard and Radcliffe who scored above the 85 percentile on a standardized reading test could not give even a vague response to the question, 'What is the chapter about?'

More in accord with the broad view of reading are the Educational Testing Service's *Sequential Tests of Educational Progress* (STEP), which cover the whole age range considered in this yearbook; the *Davis Reading Test*, which is for high-school and college students; and the *Iowa Test of Basic Skills.*

An analysis of the kinds of responses made to each test item enables students to examine their errors and to determine kinds of comprehension difficulties. This use of tests as a starting point for reading instruction increases their importance in evaluation. They not only supply a central core of data but, if administered periodically, give a limited but long-range view of growth in reading. However, no test can take the place of the day-by-day teaching-evaluation-improvement process. It is wise not to spend so much time in testing that there is little time for the daily discovery and application of new evidence.

Self-appraisal.   We must recognize the inadequacy of appraisals that take into account only the product or end result of reading. From the standpoint of learning, it is of prime importance to understand the process by which knowledge is gained and attitudes are changed. Some evidence can be obtained by introspection. Difficult as it is, some students are able to write objective descriptions of their reading methods—telling how they get the main idea of a paragraph, unlock the meaning of unfamiliar words, make accurate generalizations and inferences—and can also describe conditions under which they read and comprehend best.

Each student should keep his own growth record. In his individual record folder, he would put the interpretation of test results, dated samples of his performance, and other evidences of his progress in reading. Evaluation based on this accumulated evidence should motivate him to reinforce his strengths, correct his errors, and move ahead to more mature reading achievement.

Ability to use reading

Since reading usually leads to some kind of communion with one's self or to communication, it is important to appraise students' ability to communicate ideas gained from reading. Free-response, creative-type, or open-end questions, as they are variously called, require independent thinking and develop ability to organize and express ideas in writing. Students need practice of this kind.

The extent to which students use in class discussion the ideas they have gained from reading can be appraised by the group, by the teacher, or by each student individually. The use a student makes of his reading when he writes a term paper can be appraised by comparing successive reports of a similar type. His original plays, stories, dramatizations, and illustrations based on his reading may be partly evaluated by audience reaction. His application of reading to life situations may be observed in his changed behavior.

Interests, feeling responses, and personal development

Many of the important outcomes of education are often the most difficult to measure. In the area of interests, feelings, attitudes, and personal development through reading, changes in individual students can be inferred as we observe their behavior or take at face value the statements they feel free to make to us.

From reading tests some inferences concerning personality development may be made. A gain in rate may indicate less anxiety and fear of failure in reading the material. Improvement in comprehension may result partly from self-confidence which permits a more effective use of intellectual ability. Changes in attitudes and interest in words may contribute to more rapid growth in vocabulary.

Classroom observation has the advantage of being continuous. In many reading situations teachers can sense enthusiasm, interest, absorption, enjoyment—or their opposites—outside of class or in a class discussion. They can learn to read 'the language of behavior' and become more alert to the interaction within the class group, which is a potent influence on learning. They may write dated descriptive anecdotes telling what happens when the class is allowed to browse and choose their own reading materials or when books are selected to develop certain qualities such as courage, friendliness, or responsibility. They may obtain evidence of a student's specific reading interest by noting the number of appropriate references he spontaneously makes to books and authors in reporting on a topic, in contributing to a discussion, and in conversing.

Interviews may reveal children's feeling about reading and reasons why they read or do not read. Talking with children and young people about their interests and the books they read last year helps to appraise growth as well as current reading interests and tastes.

Questionnaires have elicited from college students many responses suggesting some influence of reading on their philosophy of life, attitudes, self-concept, and adjustment to college (Weingarten, 1959). A questionnaire asking for concrete evidence of appreciation or enjoyment in reading devised as part of the Eight-Year Study (Smith and Tyler, 1942) included items indicating *a*) satisfaction in reading; *b*) desire to read more of the same kind or by the same author; *c*) desire to know more about what he reads; *d*) desire to express himself creatively in writing or in one of the other art forms with reference to the books read; *e*) identification with the persons, places, or situations about which he is reading; *f*) desire to clarify his thinking about life problems through reading; and *g*) evaluation of the thing appreciated.

Reading autobiographies, either structured or unstructured, often furnish valuable information about an individual's reading development as he views it. In the reading autobiography, students trace their reading interests and the influence that reading has had on them.

Check lists or interest inventories suggest interests to the student as well as give him the opportunity to indicate his present interests.

Incomplete sentences, such as 'Reading is ——', 'I would rather read than ——', give evidence on students' attitudes and interests.

Real problems, which encourage students' evaluation of books, can be posed: 'Which books shall we order for our class library? Which story shall we make into a radio or puppet play?'

Librarians and parents may furnish additional information about the nature and extent of children's voluntary reading.

Students' written free responses about the effect of books on themselves are of special significance. Such compositions, of course, are worthless unless the students are interested and co-operative. In a class where there is mutual respect and trust among teacher and students, much may be learned from unstructured compositions. The author has obtained many students' written responses to the following directions: 'Sometimes we wonder what reading does to people—what effect reading has on their points of view, attitudes, and behavior. Will you help us find out? This is what you can do: Think back over the books you have read. Try to remember how any of the books influenced you. Did you think differently or feel differently or act differently after you had read the book or part of the book? Just write whatever you remember about how any book changed your way of thinking or feeling or acting.'

Some of the replies from ninth-grade students were definitely discouraging:

> I have never read a book that changed me.
>
> Most books have no influence on me but *White Fang* was one book I enjoyed. It has adventure from beginning to end and makes me want to read more.
>
> In general, I hate to read books. But I do like car magazines which make me want to have a car so I can do what the guys in the book did to their cars.

The following report is representative of many of the responses received:

> Sue Barton's *Senior Nurse* changed my way of thinking very much. I used to think that nurses had to do horrible things. After reading Sue Barton's books my ideas of nursing changed completely. If I weren't so headstrong on becoming a teacher, I would like to become a nurse after reading Sue Barton's books. It seems wonderful to help ill people and new mothers.

The following statement is an unusual analysis and summary of the influence of books of different kinds on an impressionable young adolescent:

> Some books make you feel you're a different person and you are living at the period of time or the kind of place the book is based on. Some books such as *Johnny Tremain* and other stories of the United States during war time make you feel very patriotic. Other books about simple American families such as *Little Women* and *Our Town* make you feel very sentimental and more aware of your own home life. Different kinds of religious books give

you many ideas about what you really believe and start you thinking on many different trains of thought. Science fiction stories start you thinking about the future and the world to come. I especially like stories of people who find out what their career is going to be. Stories of people such as *Florence Nightingale* and *The Life and Thought of Albert Schweitzer* get you to thinking and wondering about jobs in the field of medicine. Books that show a great deal of hard work and courage make you want to be more like that. Stories of Lincoln, Jefferson, Jackson and other great American leaders influence your ideas about what makes the United States so great. Some books make you want to work harder and do a better job at what you're doing. Many books of adventure stories such as *Mrs Mike* and *Drums along the Mohawk* help to relax you and get you away from the world you live in. Books that make you happy and make you laugh are very good to read when you feel downcast or afraid. These books can cheer you up and lift your spirits and make you less afraid. Books of inspiration about simple everyday boys and girls in this country and other countries abroad make you feel that you are not different from other young people all over the world and help to promote international friendship, which is very important for World Peace.

Summary

Several main methods for obtaining evidence of development in and through reading have been briefly described:

1   Questioning-observing-appraising as an intrinsic part of teaching.
2   Recording dated observations over a period of time.
3   Analyzing students' oral and written responses to reading and other work samples.
4   Using informal teacher-made tests and questionnaires.
5   Preparing and using testing-teaching-self-appraisal exercises in each subject.
6   Administering standardized tests of intelligence and reading achievement.
7   Studying introspective evaluative reports by teachers and students.
    Which of these seven methods the evaluator will select depends upon many factors, such as the age and ability of the students and the amount of skill and time that are available for making the evaluation.

For evaluation purposes, each of these methods should be used repeatedly over a period of time. Some evidence obtained, such as day-by-day observations, can be charted to show continuous growth. Some, acquired through standardized tests, questionnaires, personal documents, and the like, may be obtained at the beginning and at the end of the year and used to show changes that have taken place in the more subtle aspects of development through reading. . . .

References

BETTS, EMMETT ALBERT (1957) *Foundations of Reading Instruction* New York: American Book Co., chapter 11, 438–87.

COTTERALL, CALVIN D. and WEISE, PHILIP (1959) 'A perceptual approach to early reading difficulties', *California Journal of Educational Research*, 10, 212–18.

HERRICK, VIRGIL E. (1958) 'Purposes and needs for an evaluation program', in Robinson, Helen M. (ed.) *Evaluation of Reading,* Proceedings of the Annual Conference on Reading held at the University of Chicago, 1958, Supplementary Educational Monographs, no. 88, Chicago: University of Chicago Press, 153–8.

HOWARD, ELIZABETH ZIMMERMAN (1958) 'Appraising strengths and weaknesses of the total reading program', in Robinson, Helen M. (ed.) *Evaluation of Reading,* Proceedings of the Annual Conference on Reading held at the University of Chicago, 1958, Supplementary Educational Monographs, no. 88, Chicago: University of Chicago Press, 169–73.

HUNT, J. T. (1955) 'Selecting a high school reading test', *High School Journal,* 39, 49–52.

LETTON, MILDRED C. (1958) 'Evaluating the effectiveness of teaching reading', in Robinson, Helen M. (ed.) *Evaluation of Reading,* Proceedings of the Annual Conference on Reading held at the University of Chicago, 1958, Supplementary Educational Monographs, no. 88, Chicago: University of Chicago Press, 76–82.

MELNIK, AMELIA (1960) 'Improvement of reading through self-appraisal', unpublished doctor's project, Teachers' College, Columbia University.

PERRY, WILLIAM G. Jr. (1959) 'Students' uses and misuses of reading skills', *Harvard Educational Review,* 29, 192–200.

ROBINSON, HELEN M. (ed.) (1958) *Evaluation of Reading,* Proceedings of the Annual Conference of Reading held at the University of Chicago, 1958, Supplementary Educational Monographs, no. 88, Chicago: University of Chicago Press.

SMITH, E. R., TYLER, R. W. and the Evaluation Staff (1942) *Appraising and Recording Student Progress* New York: Harper & Row, 251–2.

THOMAS, R. MURRAY (1956) *Judging Student Progress* New York: Longmans, Green.

TYLER, R. W. (1958) 'What is evaluation?', in Robinson, Helen M. (ed.) *Evaluation of Reading,* Proceedings of the Annual Conference on Reading held at the University of Chicago, 1958, Supplementary Educational Monographs, no. 88, Chicago: University of Chicago Press, 4–6.

WEINGARTEN, SAMUEL (1959) 'Developmental values in voluntary reading', *School Review*, 62, 222–30.

4:10   How to evaluate a reading program

Sidney J. Rauch

The purpose of evaluation is to take a comprehensive, unbiased and cooperative look at the reading program and to decide what modifications or changes, if any, should be made to improve the program. Evaluation involves value judgments. It is not a carefully controlled research study. Recommendations for improvement of the program must consider not only what should be done, but what *can* be done. Hemphill (1969) places evaluation studies within the framework of decision making rather than research. The administrator, after taking all facts from the evaluation study into consideration, then must weigh their relationship to its effect upon the community, staff, and tax structure. Hemphill (1969) lists six characteristics of school evaluations:

1   The problem is almost completely determined by the situation in which the study is conducted. Many people may be involved in its definition and, because of its complexity, the problem initially is difficult to define.

2   Precise hypotheses usually cannot be generated; rather, the task becomes one of testing generalizations from a variety of research studies, some of which are basically contradictory. There are many gaps which, in the absence of verified knowledge, must be filled by reliance on judgment and experience.

3   Value judgments are made explicit in the selection and the definition of the problem as well as in the development and implementation of the procedures of the study.

4   The study is unique to a situation and seldom can be replicated, even approximately.

5   The data to be collected are heavily influenced if not determined by feasibility. Choices, when possible, reflect value judgments of decision makers

RAUCH, SIDNEY J. (1970) 'How to evaluate a reading program', *The Reading Teacher*, 24, *iii*, 244–50.

or of those who set policy. There are often large differences between data for which the collection is feasible and data which are of most value to the decision makers.

6 Only superficial control of a multitude of variables important to interpretation of results is possible. Randomization to eliminate the systematic effects of these variables is extremely difficult or impractical to accomplish.

Four major steps are necessary in the evaluation of school reading programs. These are clarification of the roles of the evaluator, collection of data, analysis of data, and reporting of data. 'A Checklist for the Evaluation of Reading Programs' (Rauch, 1968) is used as an overall guide. The five major categories covered in this checklist are the reading program, the administrative and supervisory staff, the teaching staff, the pupils, and the parents.

Clarification of the roles of the evaluators

Since value judgments are involved, it is recommended that the evaluation be conducted by a team of two to four reading specialists from different parts of the country so that the various backgrounds and points of view can be brought to the program. This type of representative team is preferable to the selection of a number of specialists from a single university or college whose philosophy or viewpoints may be too similar.

It is strongly recommended that the team meet with administrators and teacher representatives prior to the actual evaluation to explain the purposes and procedures, and to answer any questions. It is most important that the anxieties of teachers (particularly as to classroom observations) be allayed. The evaluation concentrates on the reading program; it is not an evaluation of individual teachers. No names or ratings of teachers are to appear in the final report. The purpose of the evaluation is a constructive one, i.e. to make recommendations for improvement. It is not a criticism of individual teachers, though strengths and weaknesses of reading techniques will be listed. If the evaluation is to be successful, it must have the confidence and cooperation of all concerned. Any team approaching the program with the intent to downgrade it or pick it apart is doomed to failure. Thus, the first and probably the most important step for the evaluation team is to gain the confidence and support of the teachers. This can only be done by clarifying all objectives and procedures before the evaluation actually begins.

Collection of data

Despite the various criticisms directed at standardized tests, *test scores* still remain an important part of reading evaluation. Robinson and Rauch (1965) describe the merits of standardized tests as follows:

> Like other tools of teaching, standardized tests can be appraised in terms of both their form and their results. In their form—that is, their structure and operation—these tests have very important advantages: 1) their content is usually determined by careful design; 2) there are often parallel forms for comparison; 3) they permit many children to be treated simultaneously; and 4) they are objective in administering and scoring. In many schools, standardized tests are the first step in identifying those students who are below grade level and who are in need of further diagnosis. They are particularly useful in measuring the wide range of reading levels in a class, school or school system. They also provide standards for comparing students on a nationwide basis. Standardized tests make a valuable contribution to modern education by demonstrating rather clearly that children differ. They provide standards for making improvements in school programs in the areas of curriculum, school and classroom organization, and methods and materials of instruction.

A summary of cautions to be exercised in the use of standardized tests has been listed by Harmer (1967):

1   Test users should keep in mind that the test score is simply the result of performance on a particular day, at a particular time, and in a particular testing environment.

2   The diagnosis of reading achievement through the use of standardized tests may be fallacious unless carelessness and attitudes toward taking tests on the part of the students are controlled.

3   The grade score on a standardized reading achievement test should not be thought of as precise indication of overall reading achievement; rather, it should be thought of as a measure of reading ability on that test at a particular point in time.

4   Teachers should keep in mind that grade scores on standardized tests are derived by interpolating scores between grade levels or by extrapolating scores from one grade level to another; thus, grade scores cannot be treated as empirically obtained indications of month-to-month progress.

If these cautions are observed, and if schools begin developing their own local norms as the tests are used over a period of time, then the advantages of standardized tests will far outweigh their limitations. This point is reinforced by the American Psychological Association in its *Standards for Educational and Psychological Tests and Manuals*: 'Local norms are more important for many uses of tests than are published norms.'

In addition to the evaluation of the results of standardized reading tests, the results of individual and group IQ tests must be taken into consideration. Reading is primarily a mental process, and reading test results must be evaluated in terms of intellectual potential or capacity. For example, a different interpretation must be applied to the performance of two sixth-grade classes whose median reading score places them both in the 60th percentile on a statewide basis, but one class has a median IQ score of 106 and the other a median IQ score of 118. Obviously, the latter group is not performing up to potential and the reasons for this discrepancy must be examined.

Observation of teachers is the heart of reading evaluation. To evaluate without observing teaching performance and pupil behavior is like reviewing a book without reading it. A representative daily schedule of the evaluator follows:

9:00 a.m.— 9:30 a.m.	Observation of a first-grade teacher.
9:30 a.m.—10:00 a.m.	Conference with teacher following observation. (Class is covered by another teacher, administrator or substitute.)
10:00 a.m.—10:30 a.m.	Observation of a third-grade teacher.
10:30 a.m.—11:00 a.m.	Conference with teacher following observation.
11:00 a.m—12 noon	Conference with one or two of the following: administrator, reading specialist, librarian, school psychologist, school nurse, social worker, etc. (anyone connected with reading program).
1:00 p.m.— 1:30 p.m.	Observation of a sixth-grade teacher.
1:30 p.m.— 2:00 p.m.	Conference with teacher following observation.
2:00 p.m.— 3:00 p.m.	Evaluators confer, comparing notes on observations and results of individual conferences.

During the conference period following classroom observation, the topics covered should include: information about the class (e.g. reading range, potential, socio-economic background, interests), teacher's background and experience, her philosophy about reading instruction, and opinion about materials. It has been found most helpful to save the last five to ten minutes for the teacher's response to this type of question: 'Assuming that budget problems were secondary, what recommendations would you make to improve the reading program in this school?'

Interviews with administrative personnel give them an opportunity to express their opinions about the reading program to the evaluator. In addition, each administrator is requested to submit a brief statement in response to these three questions: 1) What are the strengths of the program? 2) What are the weaknesses of the program? and 3) What recommendations would you make to improve the program?

The author has used five *opinion surveys* as part of his evaluation of elementary reading programs. These are:

An opinion survey of parents of kindergarten children
An opinion survey of parents of children, grades 1–6
An opinion survey of kindergarten teachers
An opinion survey of teachers, grades 1–6
Grade level observation form (to be used by reading personnel)

The survey of teachers is included as an example.

An opinion survey of teachers (grades 1–6)

	strong component	good	fair	needs to be improved	unable to answer
Program in general					
Basal reading program	___	___	___	___	___
Word recognition	___	___	___	___	___
Comprehension	___	___	___	___	___
Critical reading	___	___	___	___	___
Literature program	___	___	___	___	___
Individualized reading	___	___	___	___	___
Content area reading	___	___	___	___	___
Work and study habits	___	___	___	___	___
Supplementary materials	___	___	___	___	___
Meeting needs of children					
Meeting individual needs	___	___	___	___	___
Superior reader	___	___	___	___	___
Average reader	___	___	___	___	___
Disadvantaged reader	___	___	___	___	___
Remedial reader	___	___	___	___	___
Present organizational pattern	___	___	___	___	___
Diagnostic services	___	___	___	___	___
Corrective reading program	___	___	___	___	___
Summer school program	___	___	___	___	___
Supplementary programs	___	___	___	___	___

	strong component	good	fair	needs to be improved	unable to answer
Helps to classroom teachers					
Administration	____	____	____	____	____
Consultants	____	____	____	____	____
In-service courses	____	____	____	____	____
School meetings and workshops	____	____	____	____	____
Materials	____	____	____	____	____
Atmosphere conducive to learning					
Freedom to develop own program	____	____	____	____	____
Development of children's love of reading	____	____	____	____	____
Competent reading leadership	____	____	____	____	____
Parent-teacher relationship	____	____	____	____	____

It is important that all teachers be urged to complete their 'opinion surveys' and turn them in to the evaluators. Names are not required. One reading program was harshly criticized by some members of the school board because only thirty-two out of sixty teachers had submitted their forms. The board's reaction, and rightly so, was 'How can we have confidence in these teachers if they are not concerned enough to fill out a form which will help us in our evaluation?'

In summarizing the results of the parent opinion survey, make sure that two or more parents are involved in tabulation. Unless this is done, it is always possible that some parent (who is not too happy with the program) will question the accuracy of the findings.

Analysis of data

It was previously noted that one hour at the end of each evaluation day (2:00 p.m.—3:00 p.m.) should be set aside for the evaluators to compare notes and opinions. These sessions also enable the evaluators to gather and classify data for the final report.

Each evaluator prepares his own individual report based on interviews, classroom observations, and analysis of opinion surveys. The measurement specialist on the evaluation team is responsible for the analysis of standardized test scores. The director of the study analyzes the reports of each member of the evaluation team and prepares the final report.

In evaluating classroom performance, the following 'characteristics of a good reading lesson' are used as a guide:

1 Teacher has a definite goal or purpose for lesson and that purpose is evident to students.

2   Lesson is planned, systematic, yet flexible according to dynamics of classroom situation.

3   Classroom atmosphere is a pleasant, attractive and optimistic one.

4   Attention is paid to individual differences.

5   Rapport between teachers and students is evident.

6   Teacher is diagnosing as she is teaching.

7   There is readiness for the lesson.

8   Pupils are motivated.

9   Materials are varied (basals, library books, workbooks, kits, mimeographed materials, etc.).

10   Full use is made of audio-visual aids.

✗ 11   Questions are varied to check different levels of comprehension.

12   Material is at appropriate level for students.

13   Teacher is obviously aware of such levels as 'instructional', 'independent', and 'frustration'.

14   Meaningful oral reading activities are used to check comprehension.

15   Pupils have been trained in self-direction (i.e., go from one activity to another without disturbing teacher).

16   All children are productively involved with some aspect of reading.

17   Use is made of classroom and school libraries.

18   There is application of basic reading skills to content areas.

19   Efficient record keeping is done by teacher and students.

20   Teacher has sense of perspective and humor.

21   There is evidence of review and relationship to previously learned material.

22   There are follow-up or enrichment activities.

Reporting of data

Both an oral and written report of the findings of the evaluation team are presented to the administrators' council, teacher representatives, and the school board. The school board, if it wishes, can then hold an open meeting for all parents and questions can be asked of the evaluators. Copies of the written report should be made available to all teachers. Three or four copies can be placed in the teachers' professional library or in a special section of the school library.

A representative 'Table of Contents' of the final written evaluation might follow this format:

1   Introduction (How the study was initiated)

2   Description of the school–community

Summary statement

There is a need for constant evaluation of reading programs. However, all concerned must participate. Teachers must have confidence in the evaluators, and the evaluators must recognize the many day-by-day problems faced by the average teacher. Despite the importance of standardized test results, the heart of the evaluation is classroom performance. Recommendations must be realistic. They must consider not only what should be done, but what can be done within a specific school–community environment.

In most instances, evaluation has a positive effect on the reading program. It compels administrators and teachers to take a closer look at their methods, their materials, and their children—and this close examination generally results in progress.

References

HARMER, W. R. (1967) 'The selection and use of survey reading achievement tests', in Barrett, T. C. (ed.) 'The evaluation of children's reading achievement', *Perspectives in Reading*, 8, 53–64.

HEMPHILL, J. K. (1969) 'The relationships between research and evaluation studies', in Tyler, R. W. 'Educational evaluation: new roles, new means', *The Sixty-eighth Yearbook of the National Society for the Study of Education, Part II*, 189–220.

RAUCH, S. J. (1968) 'A checklist for the evaluation of reading programs', *The Reading Teacher*, 21, 519–22.

ROBINSON, H. A. and RAUCH, S. J. (1965) *Guiding the Reading Program* Chicago: Science Research Associates.

4:11   The effective teacher of reading

Albert J. Harris

In our attempts to improve reading instruction we have had hundreds of studies of the characteristics of pupils, and scores of studies in which instructional programs and materials have been analyzed or compared, but there have been surprisingly few studies of the teacher's contribution—of the teacher characteristics that make for successful learning, or of specific forms of teacher behavior that are associated with good and poor pupil learning in the reading program.

Quite familiar to IRA members are the cooperative studies of primary-grade reading which began with twenty-seven federally assisted first-grade projects in 1964–65. Half continued through second grade, and six followed their pupils through third grade. Individual project summaries have appeared in *The Reading Teacher*, and the lengthy reports from the Coordinating Center have been published in the *Reading Research Quarterly*. These studies, taken together, form the largest-scale comparative investigation of beginning reading instruction yet made. One of the most important conclusions of the Coordinating Center's first-grade report was stated as follows:

> 9 Future research might well center on teacher and learning situation characteristics rather than method and materials. The tremendous range among classrooms within any method points out the importance of elements in the learning situation over and above the methods employed. To improve reading instruction it is necessary to train better teachers of reading rather than to expect a panacea in the form of materials. (Bond and Dykstra, 1967, p. 211.)

There are those who have discarded the notion that teacher effectiveness can be greatly improved through better teacher training and supervision.

HARRIS, ALBERT J. (1969) 'The effective teacher of reading', *The Reading Teacher*, 23, *iii*, 195–204, 238.

Their solution is to produce equipment which will teach in a way that is invulnerable to teacher incompetence or inefficiency. In other words, they want teacher-proof education.

Computer-assisted instruction, now in its infancy, promotes a close relationship between the pupil and the machine from which the teacher is totally excluded, or is obliged to play a comparatively minor role (Atkinson, 1968; Atkinson and Hansen, 1966). Closely related to this is individually prescribed instruction, in which a computer gives tests, marks them, analyzes error patterns, and determines what learning program should next be given to each pupil (Glaser, 1966; Glaser, 1968). In the early days of programmed instruction it was frequently stated that good programs would not displace the teacher, but change the teacher's role to one with more emphasis on diagnosis of learner needs, and guidance. Computer experts are now hard at work devising ways in which computers can assume these functions also. When, or if, the computer takes over as both diagnostician and instructor, human teachers may have little left to do. Thus the teacher shortage may eventually be solved by automation.

Meanwhile, for at least the next decade or two (and, I suspect, for much longer than that), nearly all children will be taught to read wholly or mainly in classrooms by human teachers. Research has shown that teachers in the same community, using the same reading materials and supposedly the same methodology with similar pupils, can come out with widely varying class results. For those who believe that we cannot afford to wait for automated education, as well as for those who believe that dehumanization is a major danger in current society, the improvement of human teaching is an urgent and important issue.

There are six main questions about the effective teacher of reading which deserve attention.

1   What criteria can we use to measure teacher effectiveness?

Studies have shown that ratings by principals, or by fellow teachers, do not correspond at all closely to the teacher's success as measured by pupil growth in reading skill. Most research workers on teacher effectiveness have decided to use the hard-boiled criterion that a superior teacher of reading is one whose pupils show above average growth on standardized reading tests. Equivalent forms are given periodically, and the statistical technique called covariance is used to remove or minimize the effects of differences among classes in intelligence and previous learning (Rosenshine, 1971). While this is a rather narrow measure of a teacher's results, it has the merit of being objectively measurable. Furthermore, it is hard to argue that a teacher whose pupils show little or no growth in reading skill is a good teacher of reading, even if her pupils adore her and the principal thinks highly of her. Growth in measured reading skill is not a complete criterion of teacher effectiveness, but it is a minimum essential.

2   *Can we really distinguish degrees of competence in teaching reading?*

Those of us who have been sure of our ability to observe a teacher for a period or two and rate his excellence as a reading teacher with some precision get no support from the research on this topic. In the cooperative first-grade studies the correlations between supervisor ratings of overall teacher effectiveness and class averages on reading tests ranged from ·10 to ·22; hardly better than zero (Bond and Dykstra, 1967, p. 206).

On the other hand, some general characteristics of good teaching are distinguishable. When the five cooperative projects with the best results were compared to the five projects with the poorest results, the high-achieving projects had much higher percentages of teachers who were given good ratings in class organization and structure, class participation, awareness of and attention to individual needs, and overall competence (Bond and Dykstra, 1967, p. 195). But within each project the supervisors were not very successful in distinguishing the superior from the inferior teachers.

One may guess that this lack of correlation between supervisor ratings of the teacher and average pupil achievement has several components. Some teachers may put on an excellent show while being observed, but slide back into easier ways when the observer leaves. The criterion, growth on standardized tests, may be too narrow. But still it seems probable that supervisors in general may have partially inaccurate conceptions of what constitutes superior teaching.

3   *What forms of motivation or class management produce superior results?*

Before discussing some of the recent research on the relation between teachers' motivational practices and reading achievement, it should be noted that all of this research involves the teacher interacting with a group of pupils. None of this research has involved completely individualized instruction and therefore the conclusions do not necessarily apply to individualized reading activities. Furthermore, periods in which pupils are working by themselves, as in silent reading, are not included. Since only part of the total reading program is covered, very high correlations with reading scores should not be expected.

Much of my information on this topic comes from a pre-publication copy of a long review of research by Professor Barak Rosenshine (1971) of Temple University, which he has graciously allowed me to use. In that paper he analyzes in detail twenty-one recent studies in which what teachers did was recorded, either by live observers sitting in the rear of the classroom or on TV tape, and later analyzed. Most of the studies used either a Flanders interaction analysis or an Observational Scale and Rating (abbreviated OScAR) of the Medley and Mitzel type. Both of these procedures have fairly elaborate classifications of kinds of verbal statements that teachers make to pupils, and the observer merely makes tally marks in the squares corresponding to the observed behaviors. Thus, use of judgment is reduced to a minimum.

The effect of teacher criticism of pupils has been found to vary with the type of criticism. Mild criticism is not related to poor achievement. On the other hand, strong criticism has significant negative relationships with achievement. To put it differently, teachers should not hesitate to tell a pupil that he made a mistake, to correct him, or to give him direction. But use of shaming, sarcasm, and other forms of strong criticism is harmful to learning.

The frequency of use of praise has not been found to be related to pupil achievement in general. However, the kind of praise used makes a difference. A study in first and third grades found that 'minimal reinforcement' through use of such comments as 'uh huh', 'right', and 'okay', was positively related to some achievement scores, while frequent use of stronger praise was not (Wallen, 1966). There are indications that praise is more effective when a reason for it is given, such as praising pupil planning or pupil interpretation of ideas. Accepting a pupil's idea and using it by restating it, applying it, comparing it to another idea, or using it in a summary tends to be a characteristic of teachers whose classes achieve well.

In the CRAFT Project (the three-year cooperative primary reading project which I directed) we found striking differences between the skills-centered and language-experience approaches in the results of positive motivation (praise) and negative motivation (criticism) (Harris and Serwer, 1966; Harris *et al.*, 1968). In the first grade language-experience classes, positive motivation tended to go with good achievement and negative motivation with poor achievement. In the first grade skills-centered classes, which used basal readers with or without supplementary phonics, none of the correlations between motivation and achievement was significant (Harris and Serwer, 1966). In the second grade, positive motivation was associated with good achievement in the language-experience classes. Negative motivation was strongly associated with poor achievement in both skills-centered methods and one of the two language experience methods (Harris *et al.*, 1968). Thus there seems to be some relationship between teaching methodology and the motivational style that works best. In all four methods, in both first and second grade, high control scores (indicating frequent verbal statements intended to control pupil behavior) were associated with poor achievement.

The picture emerges that in first and second grade, the teacher whose pupils behave themselves, without frequent reminders, tends to obtain better achievement than the teacher who has to interrupt the lesson frequently in order to restore discipline. Teachers using language-experience methodology generally obtained good results with praise and poor results with criticism. Teachers using basal readers also got poor results with frequent, strong criticism. They tended to get better results when they avoided frequent use of either strong praise or strong criticism, particularly in second grade. Apparently, a matter-of-fact concentration on reading as such was more effective for the skills-centered teachers than a more emotional style of teaching.

An interesting sidelight is the finding in one study that use of a 'warm' voice is negatively related to achievement (Spaulding, 1965). If my interpretation is correct, many children of school age resent the kind of sugary manner that seems appropriate with babies, and prefer to be treated in a more grown-up fashion.

4 *What forms of cognitive teacher behavior are related to good achievement?*

As yet there is much less information on the effectiveness of such cognitive aspects of teaching as the ability to explain new material, lecture versus discussion, and the use of different kinds of questions, than on the motivational side of teaching. It has been very difficult to develop a satisfactory coding system into which teacher statements and questions can be categorized.

One of the simplest cognitive measures is the number of verbal interchanges between teacher and pupils in a given period of time. In a typical interchange, the teacher says something or asks a question, a pupil responds, and the teacher reacts to the pupil statement. A high interchange rate suggests a lively discussion or recitation; a slow rate suggests a mono-logue or lecture. In general, high interchange rates tend to be associated with good achievement (Rosenshine, 1971). In the CRAFT Project this was stronger in first grade than in second grade; probably the greater im-portance of silent reading in second grade is the reason for this difference.

Several studies in the elementary grades have classified the kinds of questions and statements used by teachers, but none of these has yet turned up a difference that is significantly related to achievement (Rosenshine, 1971). This is a puzzling area. There are suggestions in the research that teachers who use a balanced variety of kinds of questions may get better results than those who tend to favor questions of one kind, whether that calls for facts or interpretations, a specific answer or a variety of acceptable responses. Some of the kinds of teacher statements that have been classified include highlighting the difference between concepts, pointing out salient features, providing the correct label, and relating the material to some aspect of children's lives. High-achieving teachers in the middle grades were found in one study to follow a pattern in which they usually spoke for less than half a minute, providing information or posing a situation; then asked a question; a pupil or pupils responded; and the teacher sometimes commented on the response (Soar, 1966). A lesson consisting of many such sequences apparently is more helpful than a straight lecture on the one hand, or a recitation in which question follows question with little or no explanation or clarification by the teacher. One may also see some resem-blance between such a lesson and the typical pattern of programmed in-struction which may be described as a sequence of units, each of which con-tains a small bit of information or instruction, a question, an answer, and correction.

This is, according to Rosenshine 1971, about as far as research on teacher effectiveness has gone in analyzing the cognitive structure of lessons and determining which cognitive patterns are most effective. Obviously only a beginning has been made.

5   How can the beginning teacher be helped to develop teaching skill?

In pre-service education, student teaching has for many years been regarded as a most important part of preparation for teaching. Yet much dissatis-faction has been expressed, with both the cooperating teacher in the school and the critic-teacher sent by the college coming in for a share of the criti-cism. It has been asserted that student teachers imitate the bad that they observe along with the good, and that occasional visits by a college supervisor make little impression on future teaching behavior.

A few years ago a study was made at Hunter College of the effects of recording lessons taught by student teachers on TV tape and allowing the student teacher to study and criticize her own performance in privacy (Schueler *et al.*, 1962). For each student teacher a lesson taught near the beginning of the student teaching course was compared with another lesson recorded near the end of the course. The students who had the opportunity to react to their own recorded teaching in privacy made somewhat more progress in teaching skill than the group who received conventional supervisory visits and conferences. Here the importance of feedback is once again demonstrated. Self-improvement is often difficult because one cannot observe one's own performance the way another person can. Watching and hearing one's teaching on a TV screen gives the student teacher an observer's view, and privacy removes the need for self-protective defensiveness that sometimes prevents a beginning teacher from accepting and constructively using the comments and suggestions made by a supervisor.

Another recent development in teacher training is micro-teaching. The idea of micro-teaching is to focus on very short teaching units, usually three to five minutes in duration and each focused on specified content. Students observe and discuss recorded micro-lessons. They also have opportunities to teach micro-lessons, and to take part in the critical analysis of their own and one another's performances.

At the annual convention of the American Educational Research Association in February, 1969, several papers on micro-teaching were presented. In one study, students in a first methods course each taught four micro-lessons and received feedback from the pupils taught, from the course instructor, and from listening to the recorded lesson. Students having this kind of training improved more in eighteen out of twenty-two variables than students taking the same course without the micro-teaching experience (Davis and Smoot, 1969). Another study reported successful use of micro-teaching in learning how to deal with undesirable classroom behavior (Young, 1969). In a third paper, students trained with micro-teaching were followed up in the intern year and were found to have acquired a greater number of specific teacher behaviors and teaching patterns than interns without a micro-teaching background (Young and Young, 1969). Micro-teaching seems to have much to offer as a means of improving the effectiveness of pre-service training.

A third promising development is programmed tutoring, a procedure developed by Ellson and his associates (1965, 1968) at Indiana University.

In programmed tutoring extremely specific directions are provided in printed form which tell the tutor what to do step by step. Principles of programmed instruction are followed. If a child gets a learning unit correct, he is given praise and goes on to the next unit. Each item on which an error is made is retaught until learned, using a variety of prompts which are to be used in a specified sequence. Each child is taught individually and progresses at his own rate. The teaching procedure has been successfully taught to and used by female high-school graduates with no prior training in teaching. Ellson's (1968) most recent report indicates that slow learners in the first grade who were given two 15-minute sessions of programmed tutoring a day made substantially greater progress in reading than other comparison groups.

This technique would seem to have exciting possibilities for use as a laboratory experience to accompany undergraduate courses in educational psychology or elementary school methods. Students would have vivid first-hand experience in adjusting the pace and content of instruction to an individual learner. Learning how to adjust the instructional pace to insure that one child succeeds may prove to be a highly desirable introduction to the much more difficult task of controlling the pace of group instruction and insuring learning by all members of the group.

These three new developments—self-analysis of one's own recorded teaching, micro-teaching, and programmed tutoring—provide hopeful signs that it may be possible to increase substantially the effectiveness of pre-service training in the teaching of reading.

A fourth possibility lies in the better utilization of a tool that has long been available. The Columbia-Carnegie and Harvard-Carnegie surveys showed that basal readers are used as the core of reading instruction in over 90 per cent of elementary school classrooms. The teacher's guide or manual that accompanies a basal reader embodies the best lesson plans that a team of authors has been able to devise. Careful analysis of such lesson plans, and comparison of somewhat differing plans in different series, should help to make the principles of reading instruction more concrete and meaningful to the student in a methods course. Yet many classroom teachers have reported that they never saw a teacher's guide until their principal gave them one; and some teachers say that they cannot use a guide because the school does not supply one. For the beginning teacher the guide can be an invaluable help through the many details of a reading program. For the experienced teacher, it forms a source of suggestions to be used selectively. The teacher's guide is, then, a resource for pre-service education whose possible values have not been fully exploited.

6 How can the experienced teacher keep his interest and enthusiasm high?

In a profession in which so many new entrants become dropouts from teaching within their first three years of service, maintaining the interest and improving the morale of those who do continue to teach is a most important objective.

One of the most powerful influences on teacher morale and effectiveness is the quality of administrative and supervisory leadership. In Joyce Morris's (1966, p. 328) six-year study of reading in England, the main comparison between beginning whole-word and phonic methods came out inconclusively, as there were no significant differences in reading attainment between the two beginning methods in the years corresponding to our third to sixth grades. Morris attributed major importance to the quality of teaching and particularly to the leadership provided by the 'head' or principal: 'Thus, after the attributes of their populations and material conditions had been considered, each school's success or failure in promoting good reading standards and/or progress seemed to depend primarily on the quality of its head and secondarily on that of its staff. As the "improver" schools so clearly showed, initial handicaps can be overcome if teachers are sufficiently determined never to accept defeat' (p. 72).

Support for the importance of leadership also comes from the cooperative first-grade studies. One of the conclusions of the Coordinating Center's report reads as follows:

7 Reading achievement is related to characteristics in addition to those investigated in this study. Pupils in certain school systems become better readers than pupils in other school systems when pupil characteristics are controlled statistically. Furthermore, these differences in achievement from project to project do not seem to be directly related to the class, school, teacher, and community characteristics appraised in this study. (Bond and Dykstra, 1967, p. 211.)

It does not take a great leap of the imagination to guess that quality of educational leadership was one of the major factors, if not the major factor, in the unmeasured characteristics that influenced the reading attainment in a project. As the director of one of the cooperative projects I became convinced quite early that the school principal was a key person in influencing the morale of the teachers in the project, and, indirectly, project achievement.

Within the limits of this paper it is not possible to do more than to point out the importance of the superintendent, the principal, and the reading supervisor or consultant for staff morale, and to consider two related points. One of these is the significance of involving teachers in planning and evaluative activities. Schools in which teachers are active on committees which have an important voice in the selection of reading materials and determining the reading curriculum, and in other ways play a creative professional role, tend to have much higher morale than schools in which most teachers feel like faceless cogs in an impersonal machine.

The other point is the importance of Hawthorne Effect, the well-known novelty effect that gives almost any innovation in method or material a temporary advantage, particularly in an experimental or evaluative study. It is worth considering whether a kind of permanent Hawthorne Effect could be produced by creating a school climate in which teachers are encouraged always to try to find a new and improved way. An ongoing cycle of tryout, testing, and comparison could be set up, each time trying to see if last year's results can be bettered. Not all teachers would take kindly to this ever-renewing excitement; but those who would remain and like it would almost certainly become very superior teachers.

Summary and conclusions

Unless we are willing to make the teacher merely an assistant to teaching machines, the improvement of teaching must be a major element in educational improvement. Recent research has amply demonstrated that differences among teachers are far more important than differences among methods and materials in influencing the reading achievement of children.

The main criterion used in research on teacher effectiveness is pupil gain on standardized tests. While narrow and not comprehensive, this provides an objective minimal essential. Ratings by supervisors do not correlate well enough with pupil improvement to be substituted for objective measurement.

The relationship between the motivational style of the teacher and pupil learning is not simple. Harsh criticism interferes with learning, but mild criticism and correction do not. Amount of praise is related to good achievement in some teaching methods but not in others. A matter-of-fact attitude and quiet voice seem to be more successful in many classrooms than a highly emotional or sugary manner.

Research on the cognitive structure of teaching is still struggling with complicated coding and classifying problems. Preliminary findings favor frequent verbal interchanges between teacher and pupils and the balanced use of several types of questions.

Promising new developments in pre-service teacher training include self-criticism of recorded lessons, micro-teaching, and programmed tutoring.

Finally, experienced teachers can be kept interested and even enthusiastic when they have superior leadership. One characteristic of such leadership is resourcefulness in involving teachers in responsible professional decision-making. Another is the encouragement of teachers to try out new and possibly improved ideas, and to evaluate the results. The teacher who is continually engaged in comparing the new with the old remains young in heart and mind, regardless of age.

References

ATKINSON, R. C. (1968) 'Computer-based instruction in initial reading', *Proceedings of the 1967 Invitational Conference on Testing Problems,* 55–66.

ATKINSON, R. C. and HANSEN, D. N. (1966) 'Computer-assisted instruction in initial reading: the Stanford project', *Reading Research Quarterly,* 2, 5–25.

BOND, G. L. and DYKSTRA, R. (1967) *Coordinating center for first-grade reading instruction programs* (Final Report, Cooperative Project no. X 001) Minneapolis: University of Minnesota.

DAVIS, O. L. and SMOOT, B. R. (1969) 'Effects on the verbal teaching behavior of beginning secondary teacher candidates' participation in a program of laboratory teaching', *AERA Paper Abstracts,* 112–13.

ELLSON, D. G., BARBER, L., ENGLE, T. L. and KAMPWORTH, L. (1965) 'Programed tutoring: a teaching aid and a research tool', *Reading Research Quarterly,* 1, 77–127.

ELLSON, D. G., HARRIS, P. and BARBER, L. (1968) 'A field test of programed and direct tutoring, *Reading Research Quarterly,* 3, 307–68.

GLASER, R. (1966) 'The individually prescribed instruction project', *Learning R and D Center Publications,* University of Pittsburgh.

GLASER, R. (1968) 'Adapting the elementary school curriculum to individual performance', *Proceedings of the 1967 Invitational Conference on Testing Problems,* 3–36.

HARRIS, A. J. MORRISON, C., SERWER, BLANCHE L. and GOLD, L. (1968) *A continuation of the CRAFT project: comparing reading approaches with disadvantaged urban Negro children in primary grades* (Final Report, Cooperative Research Project no. 5–0570–2–12–1) New York: Associated Educational Services.

HARRIS, A. J. and SERWER, BLANCHE L. (1966) *Comparison of reading approaches in first-grade teaching with disadvantaged children: the*

CRAFT project (Final Report, Cooperative Research Project no. 2677) New York: Division of Teacher Education, The City University of New York.

MORRIS, JOYCE M. (1966) *Standards and progress in reading* London: National Foundation for Educational Research in England and Wales.

ROSENSHINE, B. (1971) 'Teaching behavior related to pupil achievement: a review of research', in Westbury, I. and Bellak, A. A. (eds.) *Research into classroom processes* Toronto: Ontario Institute for Studies in Education, and New York: Teachers' College Press, Columbia University.

SCHUELER, H., GOLD, M. J. and MITZEL, H. E. (1962) *The use of television for improving teacher training and for improving measures of student-teaching performance* New York: Hunter College of The City University of New York.

SOAR, R. S. (1966) *An integrative approach to classroom learning* (Final Report, Public Health Service Grant no. 5-R11 MH 01096 and NIMH Grant no. 7-R11-MH02045) Philadelphia: Temple University.

SPAULDING, R. L. (1965) *Achievement, creativity, and self-concept correlates of teacher-pupil transactions in elementary schools* (Cooperative Research Project no. 1352) Hempstead, New York: Hofstra University.

WALLEN, N. E. (1966) *Relationship between teacher characteristics and student behavior—part 3* (Cooperative Research Project no. SAE OE5-10-181) Salt Lake City: University of Utah.

YOUNG, D. B. (1969) 'The effectiveness of micro-teaching and self-instructional modes in the acquisition of two teaching skills simultaneously: maintaining pupil-task orientation and lecturing', *AERA Paper Abstracts*, 114.

YOUNG, D. A. and YOUNG, D. B. (1969) 'The effectiveness of individually prescribed modules on an intern's subsequent classroom performance', *AERA Paper Abstracts*, 114-15.

Index

Bold figures indicate quoted material

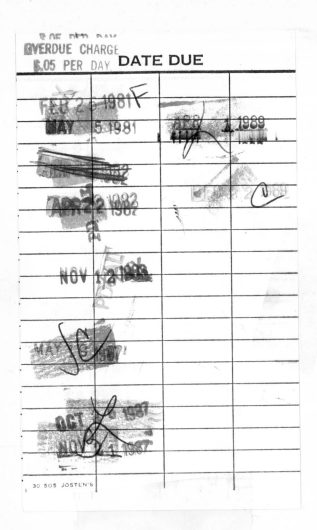

DATE DUE